D1606869

DUMBARTON OAKS COLLOQUIUM
ON THE HISTORY
OF LANDSCAPE ARCHITECTURE
XVII

John Evelyn's "Elysium Britannicum" and European Gardening

Edited by

Therese O'Malley
and
Joachim Wolschke-Bulmahn

Dumbarton Oaks Research Library and Collection
Washington, D.C.

Library of Congress Cataloging-in-Publication Data

Dumbarton Oaks Colloquium on the History of Landscape Architecture
(17th : 1993)
John Evelyn's "Elysium Britannicum" and European gardening /
Dumbarton Oaks Colloquium on the History of Landscape Architecture.
XVII; edited by Therese O'Malley and Joachim Wolschke-Bulmahn.
p. cm.
Held May 1993.
Includes bibliographical references and index.
ISBN 0-88402-240-4
1. Evelyn, John, 1620–1706. Elysium Britannicum. 2. Gardens—England—Design—History—17th century. 3. Gardens—Europe—Design—History—17th century. 4. Landscape architecture—England—History—17th century. 5. Landscape architecture—Europe—History—17th century. I. O'Malley, Therese. II. Wolschke-Bulmahn, Joachim. III. Title.
SB470.E9D85 1993
712—dc21 97—10072
CIP

Contents

Acknowledgments

Several scholars and institutions contributed considerably to the 1993 symposium "John Evelyn's 'Elysium Britannicum' and European Gardening" and to this volume, an outcome of the symposium. First, we want to thank John Ingram, University of Florida, Gainesville, who undertook the difficult and commendable enterprise of producing the transcription of John Evelyn's "Elysium Britannicum." He very generously made copies available to the participants of the symposium. John Dixon Hunt, University of Pennsylvania, was one of the initiators of the symposium and, as co-convener, helped guarantee its success. The editors are also grateful to John Harvey for contributing his essay and annotated list of plants and to Michael Charlesworth for his essay. These are important additions to this volume. The Christ Church Library at Oxford University—which at the time of the 1993 symposium was the repository of the "Elysium Britannicum"—and the trustees of the Evelyn Trust generously granted permission for the use of photographic reproductions of the manuscript for the presentations at the 1993 symposium, for the illustrations used in this volume, and for John Ingram's transcription. We want particularly to thank John Wing, librarian at Christ Church, for his support. The British Library, London, which now owns the "Elysium Britannicum," also generously approved the publication of manuscript illustrations for this volume.

Therese O'Malley
Center for Advanced Study in the Visual Arts
National Gallery of Art

Joachim Wolschke-Bulmahn
Department of Landscape Architecture
and Environmental Planning
University of Hanover

Foreword

The series Dumbarton Oaks Colloquium on the History of Landscape Architecture reflects a broad range of interests in garden history. Many facets of this history have been discussed, often with a focus on the garden design of particular nations, particular periods, or individual garden designers. The first Studies in Landscape Architecture symposium was "The Italian Garden" (1971). "John Claudius Loudon and the Early Nineteenth Century in Great Britain" (1978), "Mediaeval Gardens" (1983), and "The Dutch Garden in the Seventeenth Century" (1988) were among later subjects chosen for scholarly discourse. "The Vernacular Garden" in 1990 marked an expansion of garden historical study at Dumbarton Oaks in that it was a symposium dedicated mainly to gardens of the common people, rather than to those of the elite.

John Evelyn's "Elysium Britannicum" and European Gardening, volume seventeen in the colloquium series, is an outcome of the symposium held in May 1993 at Dumbarton Oaks. It is, on the one hand, a topic more in line with traditional interests in garden history. It refers unambiguously to elite garden culture. On the other hand, this volume represents a novel approach in our symposium series. Never before has Studies in Landscape Architecture had such a strongly focused topic, a focus not just on one individual, John Evelyn (1620–1706) (Fig. 1), but also one primarily on a single work by this individual. The "Elysium Britannicum," a work that remained unpublished, was perhaps for Evelyn's contemporaries more of an enigma than anything else and, as Michael Leslie states in his essay, "was obviously a problematic text for its author" (p. 131). That this focus is, nevertheless, justified and not too narrow is demonstrated by the contributions in this volume, which discuss the manuscript and the place of Evelyn and his work in the context of seventeenth-century European gardening. The reader of this volume should be aware that it is a tricky scholarly undertaking to focus one's research on a particular individual and that individual's work. Many biographical studies in garden history indicate how difficult it can be to make such an individual an objective topic of historical study without losing critical distance. This foreword does not discuss John Evelyn as a figure and the "Elysium Britannicum" as a manuscript; rather, it mainly serves the purpose of raising numerous questions, some of which will be answered by the contributors in their discussions of Evelyn's ideas on gardening, as reflected in the "Elysium Britannicum." Therese O'Malley provides an introduction to Evelyn and to the manuscript in question.

All page references to the "Elysium Britannicum" in this volume will refer to page numbers of the original manuscript as it was housed at Christ Church. It is now at the British Library, London. A facsimile edition, transcribed by John Ingram, will be published by the University of Pennsylvania Press in 1998 as part of a new series, Penn Studies in Landscape Architecture, edited by John Dixon Hunt.

1. Portrait of John Evelyn (photo: Dumbarton Oaks, from *Sylva,* London, 1664, frontispiece)

John Evelyn's "Elysium Britannicum" is an immensely rich document containing a great deal of information about the garden culture of the seventeenth century. Evelyn, the English virtuoso, author, garden designer, and translator of garden books, was an intriguing intellectual. The essays presented here show that both the life's work of the author and the contents of the manuscript certainly deserve analysis in the context of the international history of garden design. Some of the authors in this volume ask, What was the purpose of Evelyn's "Elysium Britannicum?" It apparently was not intended as a pragmatic garden manual offering detailed and in-depth information about horticulture, husbandry, and garden design to the contemporary reader, as did other works: John Parkinson's (1567–1650) *Paradisi in Sole Paradisus Terrestris: A Garden of all Sorts of pleasant Flowers which our English Ayre will permitt to be noursed up,* published in 1629 (Fig. 2), or Evelyn's own *Kalendarium Hortense; or, The gard'ners almanac, directing what he is to do monthly throughout the year. And what fruits and flowers are in prime,* first published as part of *Sylva; or a Discourse of Forest-Trees, and the Propagation of Timber in His Majesties Dominions* (Fig. 3) in 1664. Was the "Elysium Britannicum" intended to be a kind of literary garden cultural *Gesamtkunstwerk,* a complete work of philosophy on garden culture, through which the author wanted to discuss every facet of garden design? In his "John Evelyn as Hortulan Saint," Graham Parry suggests that the "Elysium Britannicum" "was intended to describe all the skills and knowledge that were necessary to the planting of a noble garden, but [that it] grew to be a discourse on the pleasures and virtues of gardens, and eventually became a wondering rhapsody on the religious influence of gardens on the souls of men. Beginning with mundane recommendations about the preparation and management of a garden, it moved to consider the astonishing variety of decorations and ornaments that may be introduced into a garden, and sounded a higher note when it dealt with 'Hortulan Laws and Privileges; of Hortulan Entertainments, Natural, Divine, Moral and Political, with diverse historical passages and solemnities, to show the Beauty, Wonder, Plenty, Delight and Universal Use of Gardens.'"[1]

[1] Graham Parry, "John Evelyn as Hortulan Saint," in Michael Leslie and Timothy Raylor, eds., *Culture and Cultivation in Early Modern England: Writing and the Land,* Leicester, 1992, 134.

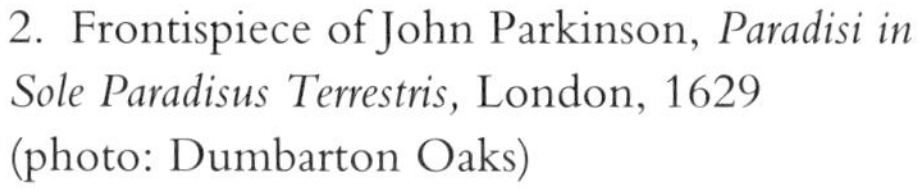

2. Frontispiece of John Parkinson, *Paradisi in Sole Paradisus Terrestris,* London, 1629 (photo: Dumbarton Oaks)

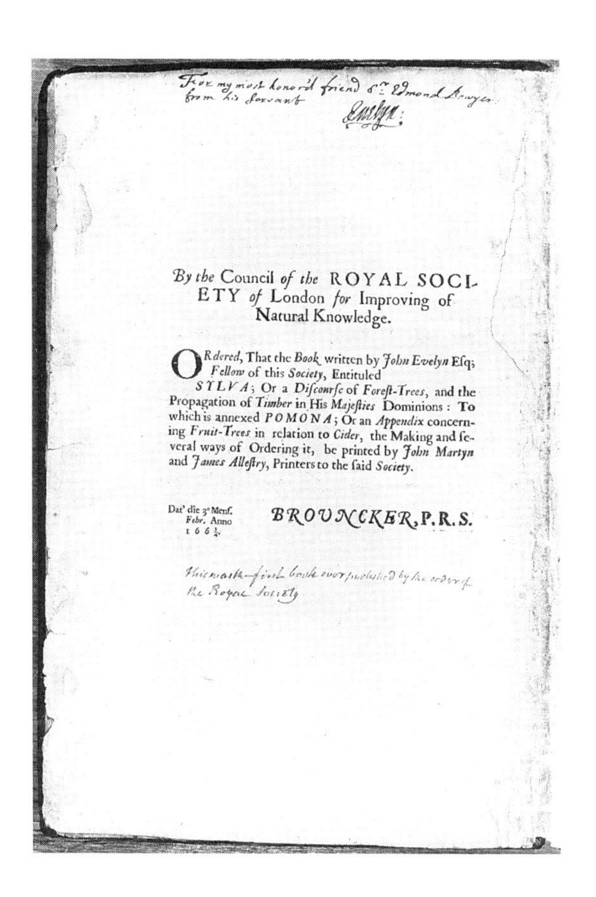

By the Council *of the* ROYAL SOCIETY *of* London *for* Improving of Natural Knowledge.

ORdered, That the *Book* written by *John Evelyn* Esq; *Fellow* of this *Society*, Entituled *SYLVA*; Or a *Discourse* of *Forest-Trees*, and the Propagation of *Timber* in His *Majesties* Dominions: To which is annexed *POMONA*; Or an *Appendix* concerning *Fruit-Trees* in relation to *Cider*, the Making and several ways of Ordering it, be printed by *John Martyn* and *James Allestry*, Printers to the said *Society*.

Dat' die 3° Mens. Febr. Anno 166½.

BROUNCKER, P.R.S.

3. John Evelyn's dedication in *Sylva,* London, 1664 (photo: Dumbarton Oaks)

Evelyn defines the task or, perhaps closer to Evelyn's thinking, the mission, of the garden designer (he used the term "Gardiner"), as follows: "To comprehend the nature of the *Earth,* and her productions: To be able to discourse of the *Elements* and to penetrate into the ~~nature~~ energie and reasons of things with judgement and assurance. In a word, What is our Gardiner to be, but an absolute Philosopher!"[2] What might Evelyn have meant by the term "Philosopher"? Apparently its denotation was different in the seventeenth century;[3] note also Richard Bradley's 1739 book, *New Improvements of Planting and Gardening; Both Philosophical and Practical,* and Evelyn's own *Terra: A Philosophical Discourse of Earth,*[4] first published in 1676. The use of "philosophical" in these contexts may have to do with a different understanding of the term "philosophy"; or it may indicate the much greater importance and intellectual significance of horticulture, husbandry, and garden design in the seventeenth century. The stress on philosophical discussion may, on the other hand, indicate Evelyn's efforts to distinguish himself from his fellow garden writers. But it may well be that, even

[2] John Evelyn, "Elysium Britannicum; or The Royal Gardens in Three Books," unpublished manuscript, British Library, London, 4 (quoted from the transcription by John Ingram, 1992).

[3] See, for example, the study of Paula Findlen, *Possessing Nature: Museums, Collecting, and Scientific Culture in Early Seventeenth-Century England,* Berkeley and Los Angeles, 1994.

[4] The full title of the 1778 edition appeared as *Terra: A Philosophical Discourse of Earth. Relating to the Culture and Improvement of it for Vegetation, and the Propagation of Plants, as it was presented to the Royal Society,* York, 1778.

when Evelyn raises specific garden tools to "philosophical" heights, he is just in line with the common practice of his time. Thus he describes an instrument to water flower beds as follows: "In summ, of all the Gardiners instruments, this ~~most~~ is the most elegant, usefull, and Philosophicall."[5]

Today, a twentieth-century scholar could be skeptical of so-called *Gesamtkunstwerke* and of authors who claim to treat in one comprehensive work every aspect of a field, a discipline, or a broad topic. Garden culture in general and the design of gardens in particular are immensely broad topics. In many cases, detailed and focused studies may be more valuable than an overly ambitious attempt that falls short. At Evelyn's time, such works had a different significance. The various sciences and the arts were not seen as separate; garden culture, for example, could be understood fully only when based on a comprehensive discussion of all related fields. But could Evelyn really have fulfilled the goal of writing an "Elysium Britannicum" for the elite among British garden experts, for the "best refined of our Nation who delight in gardens, and aspire to the perfections of the Arte"?[6] Or was the "Elysium Britannicum," in the end, similar to his "History of Trades," about which it has been stated, "It was too ambitious and diverse."?[7]

The fact that Evelyn continued working on the "Elysium Britannicum" for more than four decades indicates the enormous importance of this opus for him, such that he did not stop working on it and did not want to publish the manuscript with its shortcomings. A number of questions emerge from this reasoning: What, for example, could have motivated an English intellectual in the seventeenth century to work for such a long time on a manuscript about garden culture and design? Was it merely a personal obsession, or was the topic of overwhelming general importance in this particular period? What was the intellectual world, the cultural, social, and political milieu at that time in England in general and in Evelyn's environment in particular? Furthermore, what were the consequences of working for such a long time on one manuscript? Did it, in the end, come close to perfection? Did the many changes and additions Evelyn made over the decades improve the "Elysium Britannicum" and keep it up-to-date with the latest knowledge? And, as Evelyn claims in the chapter "Of Coronary Gardens, Flowers, & rare Plants," did those changes and additions help "to give the most perfect accomplishment we are able to the Argument"?[8] Or did these changes merely make for incoherence in the manuscript? What was the scholarly quality of the "Elysium Britannicum?" Was the botanical, garden cultural, and technical information of the "Elysium Britannicum" up-to-date or even ahead of its time, or was it only a compilation of knowledge and ideas that were widespread in the seventeenth century, with parts of it perhaps already outdated? What was the significance of this never-published work in its own time? Who knew about it, who could discuss it, contribute to it, or benefit from it? Was it unimportant in its time, except to its author and those to

[5] Evelyn, "Elysium Britannicum," 47. That the discussion and depiction of garden tools in a 16th- or 17th-century manuscript could have "more subtle meanings" than today and could be "charged with symbolic values" has been discussed by Lucia Tongiorgi Tomasi in her article, "Projects for Botanical and Other Gardens: A Sixteenth-Century Manual," *Journal of Garden History* 3 (1983), 1–34.

[6] Evelyn, "Elysium Britannicum," 10.

[7] Parry, "Hortulan Saint," 134.

[8] Evelyn, "Elysium Britannicum," 275.

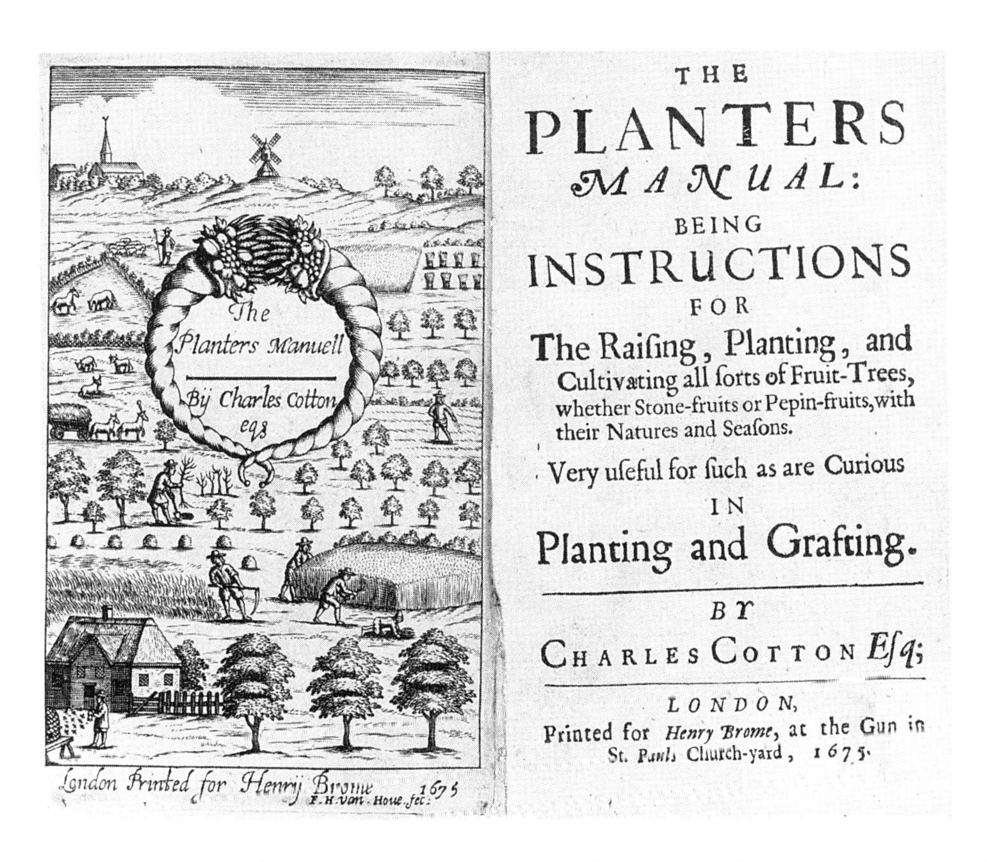

The Planters Manuell
By Charles Cotton esq

London Printed for Henry Brome 1675
F. H. Van Houe fec.

THE
PLANTERS
MANUAL:
BEING
INSTRUCTIONS
FOR
The Raiſing, Planting, and
Cultivating all ſorts of Fruit-Trees,
whether Stone-fruits or Pepin-fruits, with
their Natures and Seaſons.
Very uſeful for ſuch as are Curious
IN
Planting and Grafting.

BY
CHARLES COTTON Eſq;

LONDON,
Printed for *Henry Brome*, at the Gun in
St. *Pauls* Church-yard, 1675.

4. Title page of Charles Cotton, *The Planters Manual,* London, 1675 (photo: Dumbarton Oaks)

whom he had sent copies of chapters for their comments? Or did it have an impact on contemporary and subsequent ideas about garden culture? We might also inquire about Evelyn's actual ideas on garden design. What, for example, are the differences between his ideas and those of his contemporaries? Were Evelyn's ideas in fashion or did his particular place in society, his personal biography, contribute to ideas about gardens that contradicted those of other English authors of the time? For example, the anti-French attitude demonstrated by such contemporaries as Charles Cotton (1630–87) in his 1675 booklet *The Planters Manual* (Fig. 4) apparently was not shared by Evelyn. In this work, Cotton states that the English people "are already sufficiently *Frenchised,* and more than in the opinion of the wiser sort of men, is consistent either with the constitution, or indeed, the honour of the *English* Nation."[9] Evelyn, by contrast, often referred to French garden writers and French gardens in a positive way, and he translated Nicolas de Bonnefons' *Le jardinier françois*. Evelyn wanted to write an "Elysium *Britannicum*." How would this "Elysium Britannicum" be distinguished from an "Elysium Italicum" or an "Elysium Gallicum"? Or was it his particular intention to make Italian and French knowledge about gardening available for the future English garden? Was his "Elysium Britannicum" perhaps aimed at a supranational, or European, future of garden design, which is suggested by some of the authors in this volume?

[9] C. Cotton, *The Planters Manual: Being Instructions for the Raising, Planting, and Cultivating all sorts of Fruit-Trees, whether Stone-fruits or Pepin-fruits, with their Natures and Seasons. Very useful for such as are Curious in Planting and Grafting,* London, 1675, n.p.

Evelyn's frequent references to Greek and Latin authors on garden culture, including Theophrastus, Pliny, and Virgil, is another striking characteristic of the manuscript. This, above all, may be proof of his broad classical education, but it may also say something about his ideas on garden design. Did he write in conscious rejection or in confirmation of those ancient authors? Does his interpretation of ancient ideas about garden culture differ from those ideas that were published, for example, by Richard Bradley in his 1725 *Survey of the Ancient Husbandry and Gardening, collected from Cato, Varro, Columella, Virgil, and others the most eminent Writers among the Greeks and Romans?* Bradley describes the need for his study as follows: "It is not less surprising than unfortunate, that the Husbandry of the Ancients has not hitherto been made familiar to our *English* Gardiners and Husbandmen; since every one who has naturely consider'd the Works of Columella, Varro, Cato, Paladius, etc. must have discover'd many extraordinary Things in those Authors, for the benefiting of Estates, by Planting, Sowing, Graffing, Feeding of Cattle, and of Enriching the Ground by other Means, unpractis'd in our Days; tho' in the ancient Times, they were of great Profit to the Lords of the Soil."[10] Did Evelyn discuss the "extraordinary Things" of the ancient scholars mentioned by Bradley? Or was it simply common practice to refer to these authors, much the same as one finds Goethe quoted so frequently by German authors attempting to give their work greater erudition and authority?

What were Evelyn's actual ideas concerning garden design? Could anyone, after having read the "Elysium Britannicum," design or paint an ideal Evelyn garden? Would that have been possible? Or did Evelyn offer sometimes inconsistent and, perhaps, even contradictory ideas about garden design? Would the garden one derived from his manuscript resemble one of the garden representations done by the seventeenth-century Dutch artists Knyff and Kip? Or would it more resemble an Escher print,[11] in which everything looks very convincing and correct at first glance but which, after one studies the image more carefully, reveals that nothing really fits together, that it is full of contradictions and impossibilities? Has anyone, for example, ever examined the correctness of the information in the "Elysium Britannicum"? Perhaps Evelyn's instructions, for example, on "How to make a chaire which shall wett those that sit upon it, though no water appeare,"[12] are correct and would give unambiguous information to the craftsman who wanted to design this type of garden furniture. But can one trust his other, more complicated descriptions of how to construct fountains and other garden ornaments? Evelyn himself apparently sometimes questioned his own instructions. Take, for example, his statements in chapter twelve of the manuscript on how to construct "artificial Echo's, Musick, & Hydraulick motions."[13] Note further that, after many pages of seemingly detailed

[10] R. Bradley, *A Survey of the Ancient Husbandry and Gardening, collected from Cato, Varro, Columella, Virgil, and others the most eminent Writers among the Greeks and Romans,* London, 1725, A1.

[11] Maurits Cornelis Escher (1898–1970), Dutch graphic artist. "Escher composed works notable for their irony, often with impossible perspectives rendered with mechanical verisimilitude. He created visual riddles, playing with the pictorially logical and the visually impossible." *The Columbia Encyclopedia,* 5th ed., B. A. Chernow and G. A. Vallasi, eds., New York, 1993.

[12] Evelyn, "Elysium Britannicum," 132.3.

[13] Evelyn, "Elysium Britannicum," 167.

descriptions on "How to build another Sort of Windchest for the Animation of Birds,"[14] Evelyn ends the chapter with the explanation to the reader that he does not pursue "the subject of Hydraulique & other Automata," because, "being not fully convinced of the possibility of the Thing, we leave it to the profunder Artists, & to those who shall square the Circle having (for our owne part) promised our Gardiner, to deliver (as neere as may be) none but solid, and unsophisticated experiments."[15] Was this only the modest understatement of a seventeenth-century intellectual, or does it serve as one example of perhaps many inconsistencies in Evelyn's manuscript, which may explain why the "Elysium Britannicum" was never published and remained unfinished?

The significance of the manuscript for the study of garden history is beyond question. It is a treasure trove of information about seventeenth-century ideas of garden culture, social history, Evelyn's significance for the field of garden design, and many other related aspects of the time. It tells us about the state of knowledge in the field of garden culture in this period. To find the treasure requires some hunting, including delving into many detailed studies and critical analyses. The authors represented in this volume have done a great deal of work in that regard, and their contributions will surely stimulate future research.[16]

Therese O'Malley and I, as co-editors, have already thanked all those who have been involved in this project and who have contributed considerably to the effort to get this volume published. As director of Studies in Landscape Architecture at the time of the symposium, I thank Therese O'Malley and my predecessor, John Dixon Hunt. In 1991 they organized, in collaboration with John Ingram, a roundtable discussion at Dumbarton Oaks on Evelyn's "Elysium Britannicum," subsequently developed further the symposium topic, in collaboration with the Senior Fellows Committee of Studies in Landscape Architecture, and, as co-convenors, contributed considerably to the success of the gathering.

Joachim Wolschke-Bulmahn

[14] Evelyn, "Elysium Britannicum," 191.

[15] Evelyn, "Elysium Britannicum," 199.

[16] This research may be supported by the recent publication of various titles of John Evelyn on microfiche, among them *Terra*, *Kalendarium Hortense*, and several editions of *Sylva*. The series is John Evelyn—An English Virtuoso: Books from the Garden Library at Dumbarton Oaks, Washington, D.C., on microfiche, Inter Documentation Company, Leiden, 1995.

Introduction to John Evelyn and the "Elysium Britannicum"

THERESE O'MALLEY

I first became interested in the "Elysium Britannicum" in 1987 when preparing a paper on botanical gardens for a Dumbarton Oaks garden symposium. John Evelyn's drawing of a philosophical-medical garden (Fig. 1), which has been published several times and is perhaps the best known image in the manuscript, was then the focus of my study. I went to see it at Christ Church Library, Oxford, in 1988. As much as I was intrigued by the various sketches, I was frankly overwhelmed by the size, illegibility, and disarray of the manuscript. It is a morass of different-sized pages, covered with marginalia, interlineations, pasted-on additions, and loose sheets. Librarian John Wing came to my rescue with the information that John Ingram of the Colonial Williamsburg library was patiently transcribing the bewildering text. John has been extraordinarily generous with his work, and Dumbarton Oaks has seized the opportunity to bring the fruits of his labor to the attention of the broader scholarly world.

This paper will present an overview of John Evelyn's "Elysium Britannicum" and serve as a general introduction to the symposium volume. A literature review on Evelyn and his time reads like the bibliographical highlights of the authors represented in this volume. One need only glance at their publication lists to realize that we have gathered several of the leading experts on the subject. The contributors to the symposium and this volume approach the manuscript from diverse disciplines, including architectural history, the histories of science, agriculture, gardens, literature, and intellectual history. Such diversity reflects the complex interplay of the aesthetic, practical, and philosophical dimensions of the manuscript. We have asked these scholars to consider the manuscript now available in transcription and to discuss the interrelationship of the scientific, political, artistic, and social milieu and seventeenth-century gardening theory and practice as it is reflected in the "Elysium Britannicum."

Until now, the unpublished manuscript was available only to the hardy few who managed to tackle it in the raw, incomplete state in which it has come down to us at Christ Church, and now the British Library, London. Only about one-third of the manuscript survives. In his paper, John Ingram provides a report of the physical history of the manuscript and its provenance. We know that it was

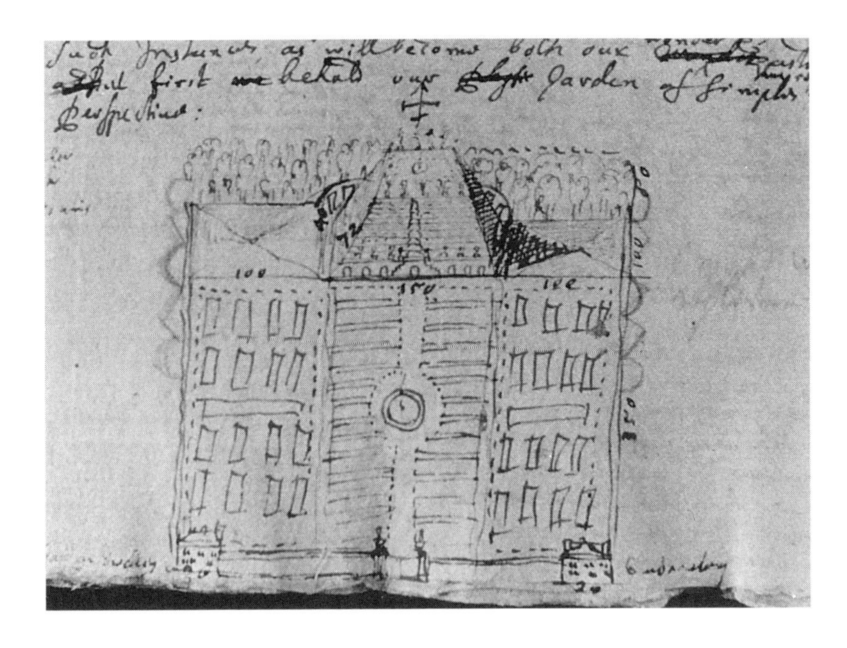

1. John Evelyn, Detail of Garden of Simples in Perspective, pen and ink drawing, ca. 1650–1700, from "Elysium Britannicum," 330. British Library, London (photo: John Ingram, reproduced with permission of the trustees of the will of Major Peter George Evelyn)

originally approximately a thousand pages long, because the manuscript includes ten pages comprising the title page and table of contents for a work Evelyn subtitled "The Plan of a Royal Garden in Three Books." In 1669 he printed an outline of the work, which he called the "Plan of a Royal Garden: describing and shewing the Amplitude and Extent of that part of Georgicks, which belongs to Horticulture."[1]

Despite the loss of nearly two-thirds of the "Elysium Britannicum" we know a great deal about its original contents. Parts of the manuscript were withdrawn by Evelyn for a separate publication in the form of a discussion of salad plants entitled *Acetaria,* published first in 1699 and again in 1706. Other material was included from previous publications, such as the *Kalendarium Hortense; or, The gard'ners almanac, directing what he is to do monthly throughout the year. And what fruits and flowers are in prime.* This first appeared in 1664 appended to his *Sylva; or a Discourse of Forest-Trees,* which also contained a section of the chapter on groves from the "Elysium Britannicum." With these components we can imagine what the complete manuscript might have been. In addition, Evelyn worked on the manuscript for more than fifty years. It was an ongoing, almost chronic, project about which there was much notice taken. In his contribution to this volume, Douglas Chambers uses material he has found in correspondences to elucidate Evelyn's intentions as well as the perception of contemporaries of this great undertaking. His study fills many of the lacunae in our understanding of the importance of the manuscript in Evelyn's life work.

In this introductory overview there are three areas of Evelyn's garden-related activities that

[1] An outline was also published in *Acetaria; a Discourse of Sallets* in 1699. Graham Parry, "John Evelyn as Hortulan Saint," in Michael Leslie and Timothy Raylor, eds., *Culture and Cultivation in Early Modern England: Writing and the Land,* Leicester, 1992, 134, n. 11; Geoffrey Keynes, *John Evelyn: A Study in Bibliophily with a Bibliography of His Writings,* 2nd ed., Oxford, 1968, 236; Sandra Raphael, "John Evelyn's Elysium Britannicum," *The Garden* 102 (November 1977), 455–61.

should briefly be mentioned in order to begin to appreciate his intense involvement in the subject and to better understand the manuscript: Evelyn's travels, his garden writings, and his garden designs. Before Evelyn wrote about hortulan subjects, he designed gardens, but before he designed gardens (with one exception), he traveled to the Continent and visited numerous Italian, French, Dutch, and German gardens. The travels are recorded in his lifelong diaries, which have become indispensable to scholars of seventeenth-century culture for their detailed descriptions of the villas and gardens he visited. As you will see, the "Elysium Britannicum" is filled with firsthand accounts of garden sites that he used for setting down principles of design.

As Keith Thomas has pointed out, Evelyn's publications are compilations of the propaganda of many earlier and contemporary landowners and other concerned writers.[2] In terms of his published writings, John Evelyn is perhaps best known for *Sylva,* which was the first book published by the Royal Society.[3] John Evelyn was one of a group of learned men who founded the Royal Society in London in 1660 in order to stimulate scientific research, discussion, and publication. *Sylva* is a compilation of practical estate management, gardening, and philosophy. It was inspired by concern for the loss of tree cover in Britain and the shortage of timber and fuel. It has been said that "no other work on arboriculture exerted greater influence on forestry in England."[4] It enjoyed great success, a fact attested to by its four editions during Evelyn's own lifetime. Michael Hunter has written that it led to the planting of millions of timber trees.[5] This is true of much of his garden writing. For this reason it is vital to understand the breadth of his sources, his network of colleagues, and range of intellectual influences, much of which our authors have addressed in this volume.

Sylva might have been his most successful publication, but Evelyn's earliest work on horticulture was his translation in 1658 of *Le jardinier françois,* a treatise first published in Paris in 1651 by Nicolas de Bonnefons. The title page describes the work as "now transplanted into English. . . . " Evelyn used copies of the original treatise plates to illustrate the English version. *The French Gardiner* was substantially different from the original French publication in its revisions and additions.[6] In the dedication Evelyn describes the content of the "Elysium Britannicum," an early prospectus that is discussed by Michael Hunter in his essay on Evelyn's intellectual activities and publications in the 1650s. Hunter, historian of the Royal Society, has concentrated on the period just before and during which the bulk of the "Elysium Britannicum" was drafted. He discusses the development of Evelyn's interests in natural philosophy, connoisseurship, and technical matters and how they played a role in the evolution of the "Elysium Britannicum."

In 1693 Evelyn published a translation from the French of *Instruction pour les Jardins Fruitiers et Potagers* by Jean de La Quintinye (1626–88), who was the director of all the gardens of Louis XIV. It was entitled *The Compleat Gard'ner . . . Made English by John Evelyn.* There is some controversy

[2] Keith Thomas, *Man and the Natural World,* New York, 1983, 198–99.

[3] Blanche Henrey, *British Botanical and Horticultural Literature before 1800,* London, 1975, 103.

[4] Henrey, *Botanical Literature,* 108. It is "the most valuable book on the subject ever appeared." Also see William Boucher, *Treatise on Forest-trees,* 1775, cited in Sandra Raphael, *An Oak Spring Sylva,* Upperville, Va., 1989, 101.

[5] Michael Hunter, *Science and Society in Restoration England,* Cambridge, 1981, 93.

[6] Sandra Raphael, *An Oak Spring Pomona,* Upperville, Va., 1990, 14–16.

about how much Evelyn had to do with the translation, but he knew La Quintinye, who had visited Sayes Court, Evelyn's family home, and had sent him directions on raising melons, which Evelyn included in the translation of 1693.[7] Over the course of forty-two intervening years between *The French Gardiner* and *The Compleat Gard'ner,* John Evelyn had come to be known as "the father of English Gardening."[8]

John Evelyn seems to have begun to design gardens at about the age of twenty-three. He wrote: "I built . . . a study, made a fishpond, an island and some other solitudes and retirements."[9] This was in the early 1640s in the garden of his brother's house at Wotton in Surrey. The garden continued to be developed with Evelyn's advice. The hillside was terraced, and on the axis of the house was a grotto with a classical portico. The courtyard had a central fountain fed by a stream that led along the terrace. It was a substantially architectural scheme, reflecting Evelyn's own interest in Italian art and architecture. He claimed that the waterworks and gardens became at that time the most famous in England.

In 1660 Evelyn bought a copy of John Parkinson's *Paradisi in Sole Paradisus Terrestris.*[10] He was inspired by the ideology of paradise and the ideal of everlasting spring and therefore sought the evergreen plants by which this state could be created on earth. These he collected in his own garden at Sayes Court in southern London, acquiring simultaneously all the newest publications of husbandry and the natural sciences to assist in the cultivation of evergreens. He also built a laboratory for experimentation. Evelyn claimed to be the first to recommend the yew for topiary, and his hedges at Sayes Court were renowned.[11]

Evelyn also created what he called a Philosophical Garden at Albury in Surrey for Henry Howard, who was a benefactor of the Royal Society, in 1667. He designed a tunnel through the hill from a raised terrace in imitation of the tunnel near Virgil's tomb, hence loading the design with literary and historical associations.[12] Douglas Chambers, in his article, "The Tomb in the Landscape, John Evelyn's Garden at Albury," explains the literary density that Evelyn introduced into the garden by utilizing a neoclassical conceit of both Arcadian timelessness and death, similar to the Arcadian tropes that preoccupied one of Evelyn's contemporaries, Poussin, whose work Evelyn admired in Rome and Paris.[13]

The drawings and descriptions of the various gardens with which Evelyn was involved are used by Mark Laird to elucidate the theory and practice of planting presented in the "Elysium Britannicum."

[7] Raphael, *Pomona,* 11–12.

[8] Stephen Switzer, *Ichonographia Rustica; or the Nobleman, Gentleman, and Gardener's Recreation,* London, 1715, 45.

[9] E. S. DeBeer, ed., *The Diary of John Evelyn,* 6 vols., Oxford, 1955, II, 81.

[10] J. Parkinson, *Paradisi in Sole Paradisus Terrestris,* London, 1629.

[11] Geoffrey Keynes, ed., *Directions for the Gardiner at Says-court,* London, 1932, 5–11.

[12] David Jacques, "John Evelyn's Time, 1640 to 1660," in *One Thousand Years of British Gardening,* London, 1979, 24, catalogue of exhibition at the Victoria and Albert Museum. Jacques also writes that Evelyn consulted on the following gardens: Cornbury, Oxfordshire, Clarendon House, the Strand for Lord Clarendon, Euston for the earl of Arlington, and Cassiobury for the earl of Essex.

[13] Douglas Chambers, "The Tomb in the Landscape, John Evelyn's Garden at Albury," *Journal of Garden History* 1 (1980), 47.

With a very close reading of the manuscript's list of plants and design principles, together with Evelyn's drawings, Laird was able to reconstruct how his gardens might have appeared.

As stated earlier, John Evelyn's interest in gardening dated from an early period in his life, the 1640s, and intensified and diversified until his death in 1706. He began to compile his massive work, the "Elysium Britannicum," in the 1650s.[14] By way of an overview, I will try to briefly describe its contents using, in order, Evelyn's drawings or "ichonismes" to guide us through a survey of the surviving manuscript. We learn from Evelyn's title page, table of contents, and introduction that the subject of the book is the pleasure garden.[15] However, all aspects of the gardener's experience are addressed, with topics ranging from the expected parterres and groves, to the construction of beehives, compost collection, music, and garden burials. Evelyn opens with the quintessential description of the garden as that "delicious place" called "Paradise," from which our forefathers had been exiled. The re-creation of Eden is immediately presented as the goal of the new gardener. Evelyn explains that, after a long time, practitioners have finally arrived at considerable perfection in this "arte of gardening." He defines a garden now as a place "of all terrestriall enjoyments the most resembling Heaven." From the beginning of the book, Evelyn asserts the dignity of gardening and pays tribute to the gardener as more universal in knowledge and accomplishments than the architect. Here he quotes Vitruvius' definition of the classical architect, a reference that serves to associate himself with that ancient treatise writer: Gardening is a "glorious name and Profession," he claims. Lord Bacon observes "that men were at the height of Building, before they were tollerable in Gardining," suggesting the degree of difficulty and refinement required to attain this art of the garden.[16] To understand Evelyn's ideas about design and theory in Restoration England, Alice Friedman was given the difficult task of connecting the fragments of architectural details, quotations, and references in the "Elysium Britannicum" to contemporary architectural theory and patronage.

The remainder of the first book is concerned with what Evelyn calls the "Mysteries of Nature," providing the gardener with "sufficient intelligence . . . to derive those advantages from this discourse, which it shall faithfully, and candidly present him withall."[17] The cosmic processes of the generation of plants, the seasons, the four elements, and the celestial influences are presented, heavily laden with references to scientific texts. For each specific subject, he advises the reader to consult Ralph Cudworth, Robert Boyle, Nehemiah Grew, and various other contemporary or recent authorities on the physical sciences.[18]

[14] Sir Geoffrey Jellicoe, Susan Jellicoe, Patrick Goode, and Michael Lancaster, eds., *Oxford Companion to Gardening,* Oxford, 1986, 180. Also Jacques, "John Evelyn's Time," 24.

[15] "Elysium Britannicum," 1–3.

[16] "Elysium Britannicum," 1–3.

[17] "Elysium Britannicum," 41.

[18] "Elysium Britannicum," 41; Ralph Cudworth, *The True Intellectual System of the Universe,* London, 1678; Robert Boyle, *Essays of the Strange Subtilty, Determinate Nature, Great Eficacy of Effluviums,* London, 1673; Nehemiah Grew, *The Anatomy of Plants,* London, 1682.

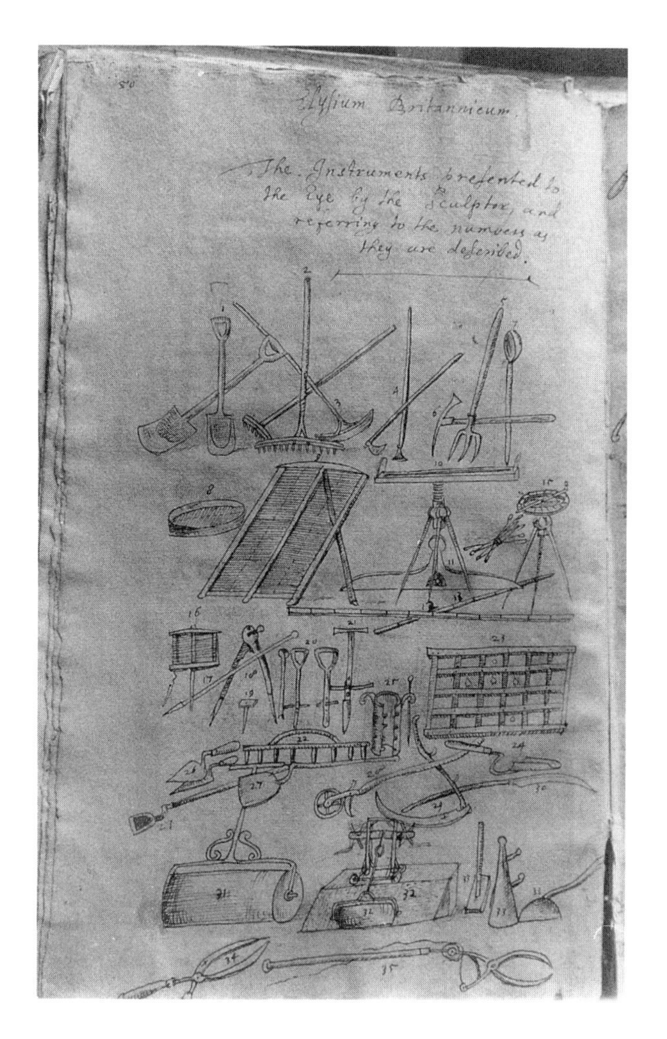

2. John Evelyn, The Instruments Presented to the Eye, pen and ink drawing, ca. 1650–1700, from "Elysium Britannicum," 50. British Library, London (photo: John Ingram, reproduced with permission of the trustees of the will of Major Peter George Evelyn)

3. John Evelyn, The Instruments Presented to the Eye, pen and ink drawing, ca. 1650–1700, from "Elysium Britannicum," 51. British Library, London (photo: John Ingram, reproduced with permission of the trustees of the will of Major Peter George Evelyn)

It is within this section of the "Elysium Britannicum" that Evelyn introduces the theme of ancient versus modern sources, with reference to classical authorities on issues of beauty and to contemporary sources for scientific questions. The theme of ancient versus modern, which recurs frequently through the manuscript, is discussed at length by Joseph Levine as a debate raging throughout the intellectual world in which Evelyn lived. Because his scientific interests were seen as modern and literary and his historical pursuits were of the ancient, Evelyn fell in the middle, and the possibility of joining the best in ancient cultures with the best in modern life was a fundamental theme in Evelyn's "Elysium Britannicum."

In book two, we advance from theory to practice, to what Evelyn calls the "artificial" as opposed to the "natural" part of his profession, beginning with the instruments belonging to a gardener and then their various uses. This is where the illustrations or "ichonismes," as he called them, begin to appear in the "Elysium Britannicum." Two pages are packed with apparatus, equip-

The firſt Booke
of Architecture, made
by Sebaſtian Serly, entreating of Geometrie.

*Tranſlated out of Italian into
Dutch, and out of Dutch
into Engliſh.*

LONDON
Printed for Robert Peake,
and are to be ſold at his ſhop neere
Holborne conduit, next to the
Sunne Tauerne.
ANNO DOM. 1611.

4. Title page, engraving, from Sebastiano Serlio, *The first Booke of Architecture made by Sebastian Serly, entreating of Geometrie,* I, 1611. Mark J. Millard Architectural Collection, © 1995 Board of Trustees, National Gallery of Art, Washington, D.C. (photo: Courtesy of the gallery)

ment, and what, according to Evelyn, was essential, "Since Gardining . . . hath, as all other Arts and Professions certaine Instruments and tooles properly belonging to it"[19] (Figs. 2 and 3). Evelyn is establishing the professional status of the gardener as parallel to that of the architect in a profession that was also represented pictorially by the tools that appeared in architectural treatises. An example is seen in Sebastiano Serlio's title page (Fig. 4) of his book entitled *The first Booke of Architecture,* owned by Evelyn.[20] The display of architect's tools, including mathematical instruments, also recalls the display of tools typically found in gardening treatises, such as those of Mascall (1572) and La Quintinye (1693) (Figs. 5 and 6).[21]

On the situation of the grounds, Evelyn declares that the ideal site for the royal garden could not be less than one thousand geometrical paces in circumference, "though some thing very princely, may be contrived in thirty akers."[22] He mentions the seat of the duke of Orleans in Luxembourg, referring to the gardens in Paris as a fine royal example at seventy acres.[23] This reference begins the numerous descriptions of real gardens that occur throughout the manuscript as illustrations for the

[19] "Elysium Britannicum," 41.

[20] *The Evelyn Library,* (Christie's) London, 1978, 151. Sebastiano Serlio, *The first Booke of Architecture . . . ,* translated from Italian into Dutch and from Dutch into English, 1611.

[21] Leonard Mascall, *The Art of Planting and Grafting,* London, 1572; Jean de la Quintinie, *The Compleat Gard'ner,* John Evelyn, trans., London, 1693.

[22] "Elysium Britannicum," 54.

[23] "Elysium Britannicum," 54.

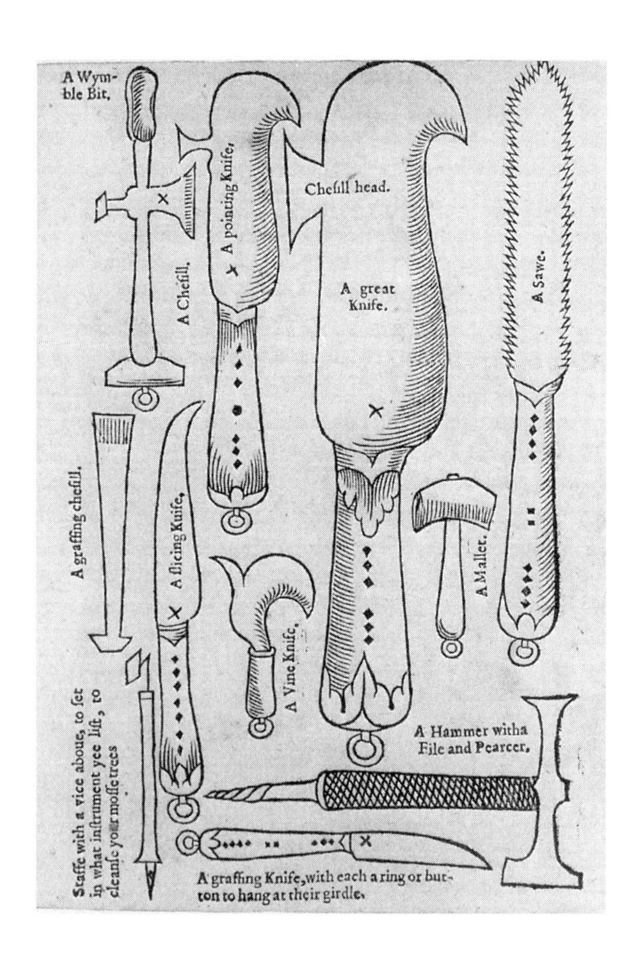

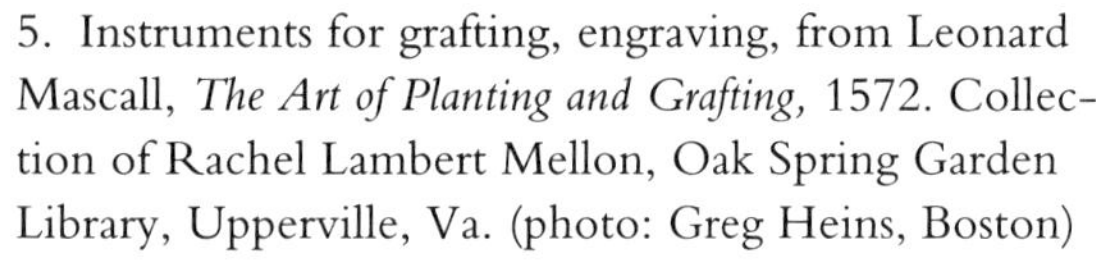

5. Instruments for grafting, engraving, from Leonard Mascall, *The Art of Planting and Grafting,* 1572. Collection of Rachel Lambert Mellon, Oak Spring Garden Library, Upperville, Va. (photo: Greg Heins, Boston)

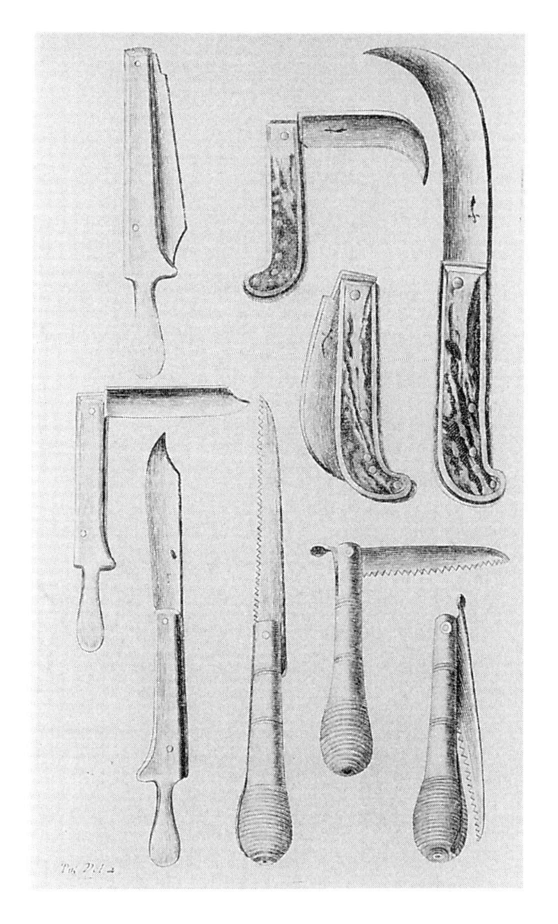

6. Pruning tools, engraving, from Jean de La Quintinie, *The Compleat Gard'ner,* 1693. Collection of Rachel Lambert Mellon, Oak Spring Garden Library, Upperville, Va. (photo: Greg Heins, Boston)

subject at hand. Although the chapter entitled "Of the most famous gardens in the world ancient and modern" does not survive, we can glean from the existing manuscript many useful references. These descriptions are not always giving praise but can serve as examples of unsuccessful gardening as well. For example, at one point Evelyn criticized the design at the Luxembourg gardens for the positioning of the central walks.[24] We also have in a letter to Thomas Browne in 1660, a list of "legendary and historical gardens, beginning with paradise and the Elysian fields and ending with modern Italy," which might have been a part of the "Elysium Britannicum."[25]

Although ancient writers are invoked as authorities for design principles throughout the manuscript, there are moments when their advice cannot serve the modern needs. For "Securing and fencing our Garden," Evelyn writes that "we shall neither consult Columella or Palladius or others of the Antients, whose hedges [or Windwalls] . . . can be no sufficient guard for our Out-Works, but a good . . . substantial Wall of two foote thicknesse, and thirteene foote in height, either of brick,

[24] "Elysium Britannicum," 79.

[25] Evelyn to Thomas Browne, January 28, 1660, in Geoffrey Keynes, ed., *The Works of Sir Thomas Browne*, 4 vols., London, 1964, IV, 275.

stone or such materialls as may neither decay nor leave any uneven & rugged surfaces."[26] For directions for setting up the support of fruit, we are referred to *The French Gardiner,* because Evelyn chooses not to include this subject in his work.[27] This type of referral is common in the "Elysium Britannicum" and leads us to numerous other authors and publications, a practice of Evelyn's that provides a rich bibliography of contemporary intellectual thought.

In the third chapter of book two, Evelyn lays out his general principles of design, emphasizing that the garden should be:

> set out, as that Art, though it contend with Nature; yet might by no meanes justle it out: There being nothing lesse taking, then an affected uniformity in greate & noble Gardens, where Variety were chiefly to be courted; . . . For seing Nature dos in the universall oeconomy of things praeceede Arte, and that Art is onely Natures ape, and dos nothing but by the power thereoff, as having first received all its principles from her Schoole. . . . At no hand therefore let our Workman enforce his plot to any particular Phantsy, but, contrive rather how to apply to it the best shape that will agree with the nature of the Place.[28]

It is here that Evelyn describes his Elysium as the most magnificent garden in the world, far exceeding those of Italy and France—not utopian but "a reall place." It has been suggested that Evelyn was describing a location known as Backbury Hill, which he considered a model for an English paradise.[29] In his essay, John Dixon Hunt explores Evelyn's ideal of the garden and of gardening art that he was seeking to define in his "Elysium Britannicum" and in various other works.

After securing and laying out the ground, Evelyn launches into instructions on the "seminary," that place where materials for planting trees, plants, and flowers—what Evelyn calls "the furniture of our Elysium"—are propagated and prepared. A sketch depicts the problems of burying gourdlike seeds point upright (Fig. 7). Evelyn then states, "Our seminary now furnished, it thrives apace. . . . Let's fall to th' work."[30]

The "work" is the design, which Evelyn says must first be done on paper. There is no part of the garden, he writes, that "requires a more exquisite hand" than this: "Knotts, Fretts, Parterrs, Compartiments, Bordures, and Embossments." Box, instructs Mr. Parkinson, is best for these purposes. The "Interstices or terrace be layed over with some splendidly colourd Sand . . . planted with low growing Flowers of various Colours which will resemble a rich & noble Tapistry."[31]

In the next section, "Of Walks, Terraces, Carpets, and Allees, Bowling greens, Beares, and Mailles," the preferred material and proportions are presented in detail. The author suggests that the

[26] "Elysium Britannicum," 54.

[27] "Elysium Britannicum," 54.

[28] "Elysium Britannicum," 55–56.

[29] "Elysium Britannicum," 56. Peter H. Goodchild, "'No phantasticall utopia, but a reall place': John Evelyn, John Beale and Backbury Hill, Herefordshire," *Garden History* 19 (Autumn 1991), 105–27. See also Parry, "John Evelyn as Hortulan Saint," 141; Michael Leslie, "The Spiritual Husbandry of John Beale," in Leslie and Raylor, *Culture and Cultivation* (as above, note 1), 162–66, where Leslie argues that this section in the "Elysium" is copied from a letter from Beale to Evelyn.

[30] "Elysium Britannicum," 74.

[31] "Elysium Britannicum," 76.

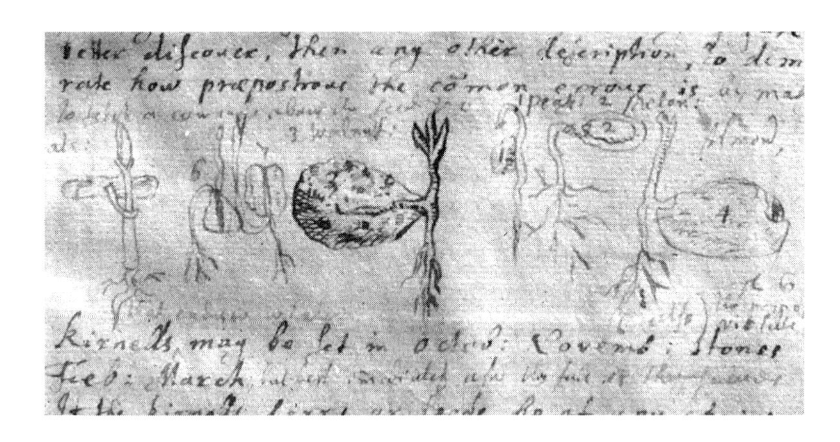

7. John Evelyn, Planting Instructions for Gourd-Like Seeds, pen and ink drawing, ca. 1650–1700, from "Elysium Britannicum," 65. British Library, London (photo: John Ingram, reproduced with permission of the trustees of the will of Major Peter George Evelyn)

most agreeable and magnificent walk is made in front of the middle point or projecture of the palace, where the door opens into the portico on a level with the area of the parterre and the walks and stretches through the whole enclosure. St. James' Park and The Tuileries are mentioned as having celebrated examples of walks.[32]

In chapter seven, Evelyn reviews the order of the book and the order of the garden plan. He describes a tripartite division of the garden plan, which did not diverge from seventeenth-century planning. It was, simply put, a progression from highly "artificial" and geometrically regular parts to increasingly less "artificial," regularly disposed parts.

Having discussed the "Parterrs, Knotts, Bordures & Compartiments which lye contiguous to the Mansion" and "Walkes, Alles and Terraces . . . we come now to the more principall parts, for such we esteeme the naturall decorations of Groves, Labyrinths, thicketts . . . which after a wonderful diversitie from the compt, polite and uniforme partes of the Walks and Parterrs, is of all other the most noble, sollume and divertissant of Garden ornaments." These areas offer "the beholder with a prospect of a noble & masculine majestie far surpassing those trifling bankes and busy knotts of our ordinary Gardens consisting of stiff and meane designes."[33] Proceeding from the mansion to the delicately and intricately designed beds, we move out, on the prescribed walks, to the larger-scale spaces planted with trees and shrubs. Evelyn then describes groves, labyrinths and mazes, cabinets, galleries, pergolae, and various configurations of trees and shrubs.[34]

The grove seems closest in Evelyn's mind to Eden and therefore sacred and spiritual in character. The section on the groves includes a plea for the reform of cemeteries, which Evelyn found unhealthy and indecent. Groves, he offered, should be where our graves may be decked with fragrant flowers, perpetual verdures, and perennial plants, "the most naturall *Hieroglyphicks* of our future Resurrection and Immoralitie; besides what they will conduce to meditateon & the taking of

[32] "Elysium Britannicum," 77, 78. Mention of St. James is on a separate sheet of paper at page 80.

[33] "Elysium Britannicum," 89–90.

[34] "Elysium Britannicum," 93–103.

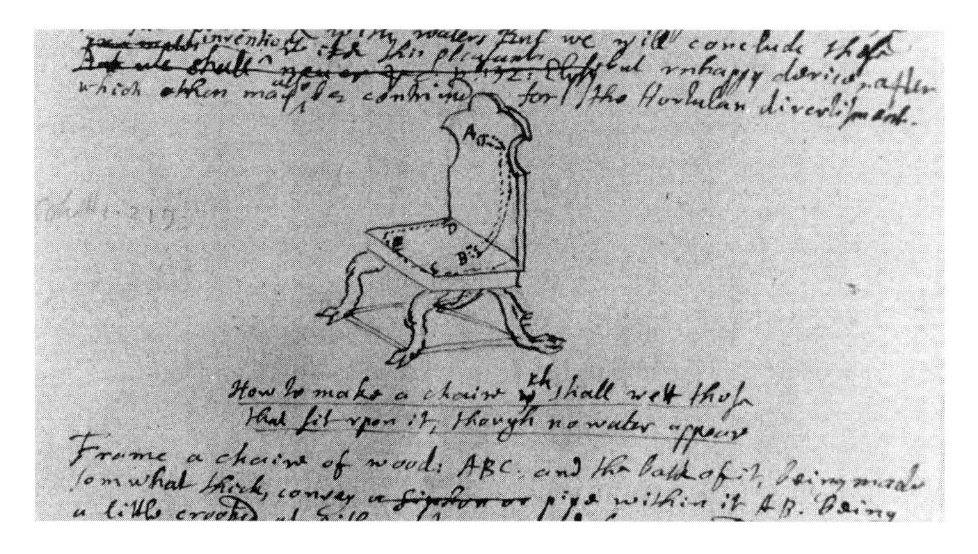

8. John Evelyn, How to make a chair which shall wett those that sit upon it, pen and ink drawing, ca. 1650–1700, from "Elysium Britannicum," 132.3. British Library, London (photo: John Ingram, reproduced with permission of the trustees of the will of Major Peter George Evelyn)

our minds from dwelling too intensely upon other more vaine objects."[35] Part of the chapter entitled "On the sacredness of Groves" was included in *Sylva.* This extensive section, eleven pages, ends simply with the statement, "Groves above all affect us most."[36]

Evelyn opens the chapter "Fountaines, Cascad's, Rivulets, Canales, Piscina's, and Water-workes" with the declaration "amongst all the embellishments, serving for use as well as ornament . . . there is none comparable to Water."[37] Having no intention "to exceede our Institution, beyond what shall be found necessary for our ingenious Gardinr," Evelyn refers to those who have written ex professo, such as Vitruvius, Kircher, and Schotti.[38] Still he explains the basic principles of gravity and various forces on which the artificial inventions for fountains depend. He then illustrates several examples of fountains and writes: "let our ingenious Gardener learne by this Modell the whole seacret of the arte."[39] The "Ichonisme" illustrates "how to make a chaire which shall wett those that sit upon it, though no water appeare" (Fig. 8).[40] This is one of several illustrations of automata in the "Elysium Britannicum." "By Cascads," Evelyn writes, "we understand all sorts of falls and praecipitations of water from Cliffs, Rocks, Stepps, & inequalities, naturall or artificiall . . . Instances

[35] "Elysium Britannicum," 108. This plea for a garden of graves presages the rural cemetery movement that did not come about until the nineteenth century. It is part of his concern for the unhealthiness of cities in general, about which he writes in his book *Fumigurium*, London, 1661.

[36] "Elysium Britannicum," 111. See Parry, "John Evelyn as Hortulan Saint," 142–43, for a discussion of the spiritual import of groves in Evelyn's *Sylva.*

[37] "Elysium Britannicum," 117.

[38] "Elysium Britannicum," 118b. Evelyn is probably referring to two books that he owned: Gaspar Schotti, *Magnia Universalis Naturae et Artis,* Wurzberg, 1658, and Athanasius Kircher, *Prodromus Coptus sive Aegyptiacus,* Rome, 1636.

[39] "Elysium Britannicum," 132.1.

[40] "Elysium Britannicum," 132.3.

whereof we have eminently in the naturall & horrid Falls of the River at Tivoli, and that of Frascati. . . . But as it is most artificiall, In the greate Cardinall's Villa at Ruelle & Vaux le Viconte."[41]

In chapter ten he begins, "Nor is there certainely anything more agreable then after the Eye has bin entertaind with the pleasure & refreshments of Verdures, the fragrant Flowers, the christall Fountaines and other delicious and sense-ravishing objects, to be unexpectedly surprised with the horror and confusion of naturall or artificiall Rock, Grotts, Caverns, Mounts, & Precipices well reppresented."[42] By now, Evelyn has moved in his garden beyond the solemne groves out to the "wilderness" area with raging waterways and craggy precipices, and here he reaches the edge of his royal plan. Next, he turns back and begins to describe the decorations and ornamentation within the parts of the garden.

In the long chapter "statues, Payntings, Columns, Dyals, Perspectives, Pots, Urns, Jarrs, Vasas and other Ornaments," Evelyn suggests "figures of those greate Heros, & Genious's that have so well deserv'd of Gardens" be represented in sculpture which offers not only ornament and

> pleasure to the eye, but to the intellect it selfe, and the furniture of the most profitable discourses, whilst we behold our Elysium inriched & (as it were) breathing with the statues of those Gallant & illustrious Persons, whose actions have filled our Histories with the most glorious instances, & whose inventions & industries have stored our Gardens with the noblest of her diversions.[43]

He then lists those worthy of eternal memory and says not to omit our Parkinson, Gerard, and Clusius, all botanists and natural historians, the heroes of the modern world.[44] Thus he expanded the Pantheon to embrace the ancient and modern heroes. Besides statues, Evelyn adds, paintings have been used in gardens and describes how to make frescoes that would ornament and through perspective arrangement extend the view beyond its walls (Fig. 9).[45] We know of many garden examples with the form of decoration with which he would have been familiar, including Villa Medici at Tivoli, a favorite garden of Evelyn.

In a section that introduces the aural dimension of design, Evelyn defines what distinguishes true garden art from all other art forms:

> It has been rightly observed that a Garden hath of all other diversions the prerogative alone of gratifing all the senses virtuously; The tinctures of its flowers . . . Redolency of the purple Violet, . . . productions of its fruite entertaine the most curious palat . . . utmost delight of the touch, . . . the tendernesse of the Grasse & flowry bankes invites every body to lye downe . . . whilst, the murmuring of the christall streames, & the warbling of the musicall birds, charm'd them to repose.[46]

[41] "Elysium Britannicum," 128.

[42] "Elysium Britannicum," 133.

[43] "Elysium Britannicum," 149.

[44] Parkinson, *Paradisi* (as above, note 9); John Gerard, *The herball; or generall historie of plantes,* London, 1577; and Carolus Clusius, *Rariorum Plantarum Historia,* Antwerp, 1601. All were owned by Evelyn. "Elysium Britannicum," 154a.

[45] "Elysium Britannicum," 159–63.

[46] "Elysium Britannicum," 167.

9. John Evelyn, example of a wall mural using perspectival grid, pen and ink drawing, ca. 1650–1700, from "Elysium Britannicum," 162. British Library, London (photo: John Ingram, reproduced with permission of the trustees of the will of Major Peter George Evelyn)

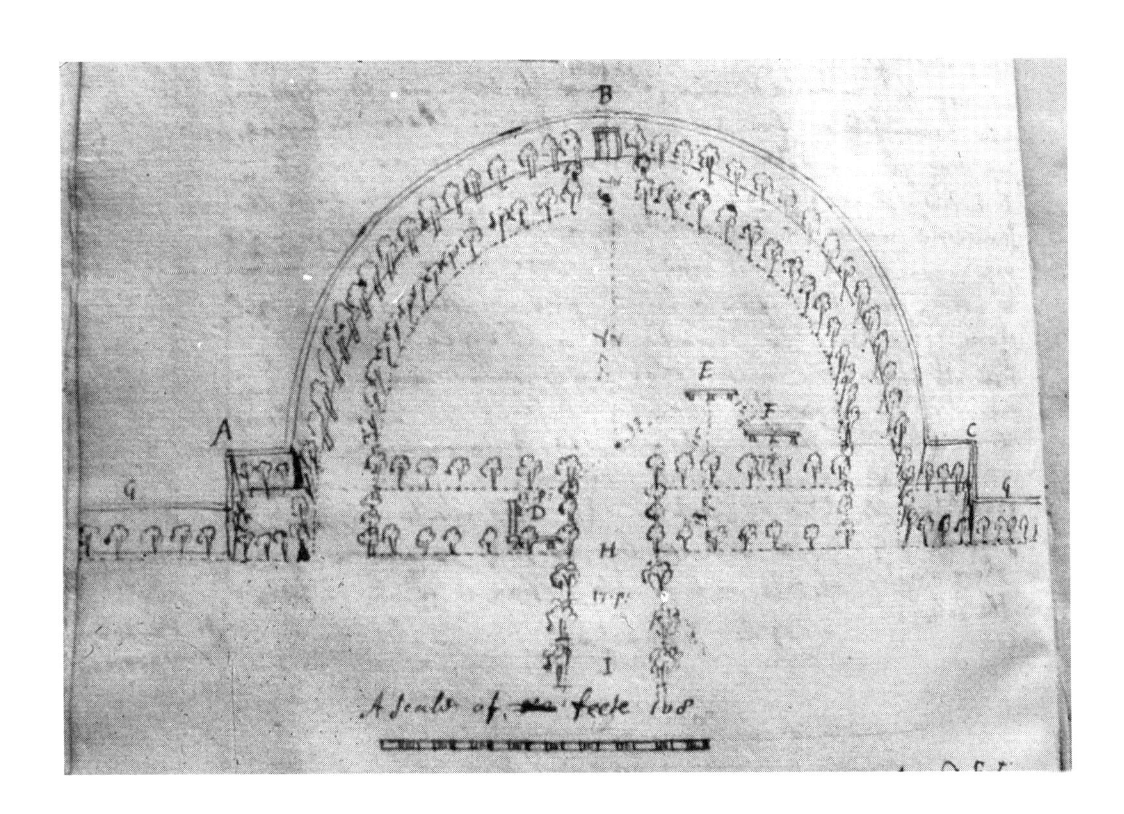

10. John Evelyn, The "artificial echo" at The Tuileries, Paris, pen and ink drawing, ca. 1650–1700, from "Elysium Britannicum," 171. British Library, London (photo: John Ingram, reproduced with permission of the trustees of the will of Major Peter George Evelyn)

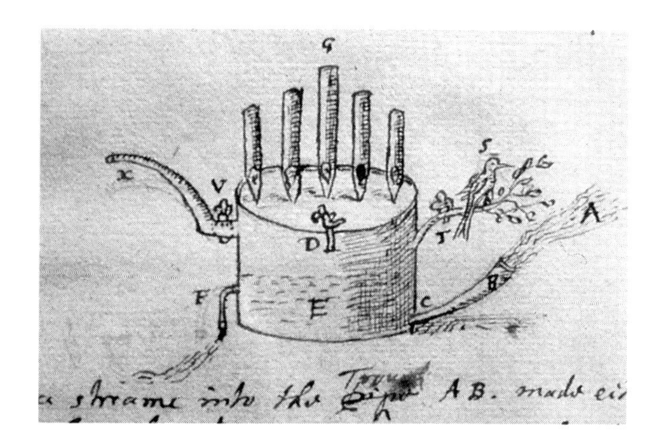

11. John Evelyn, How to build a sort of wind chest for the Animation of Birds, pen and ink drawing, ca. 1650–1700, from "Elysium Britannıcum," 191. British Library, London (photo: John Ingram, reproduced with permission of the trustees of the will of Major Peter George Evelyn)

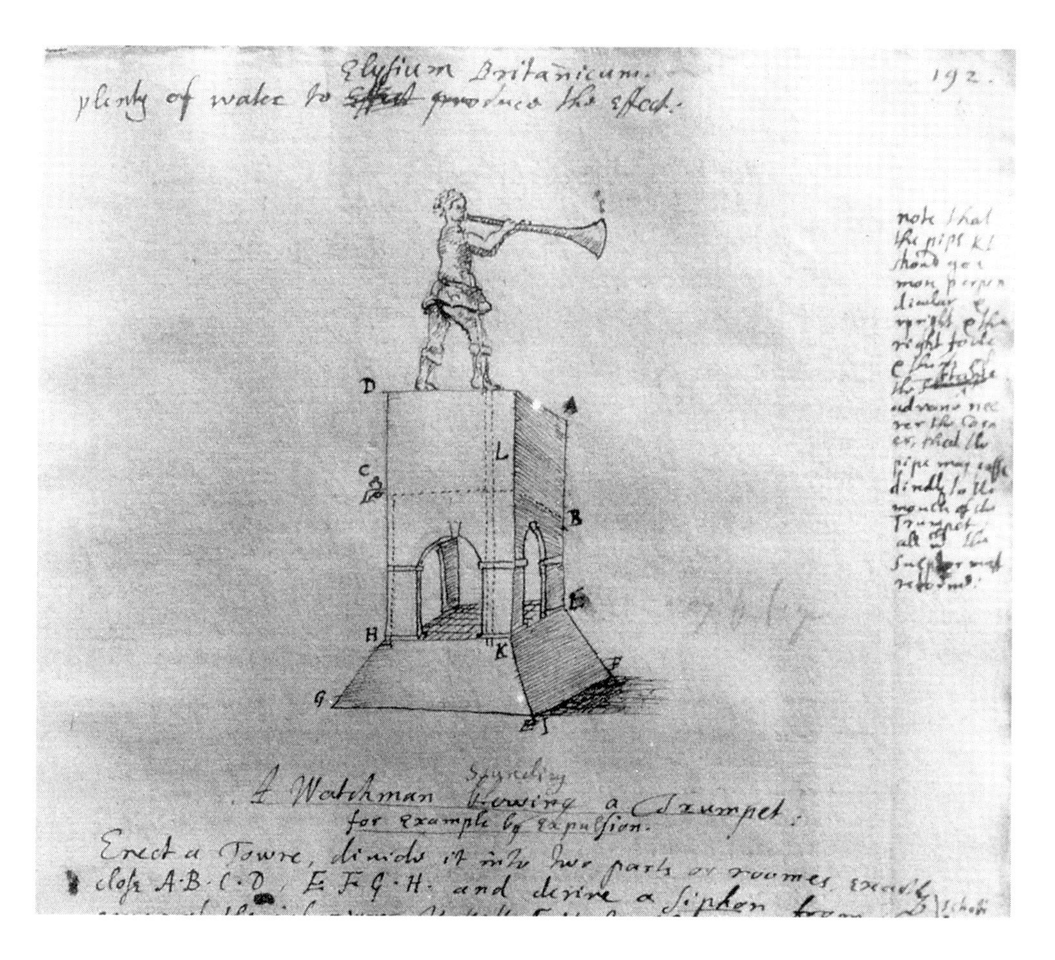

12. John Evelyn, A Watchman sounding a Trumpet for example by expulsion, pen and ink drawing, ca. 1650–1700, from "Elysium Britannicum," 192. British Library, London (photo: John Ingram, reproduced with permission of the trustees of the will of Major Peter George Evelyn)

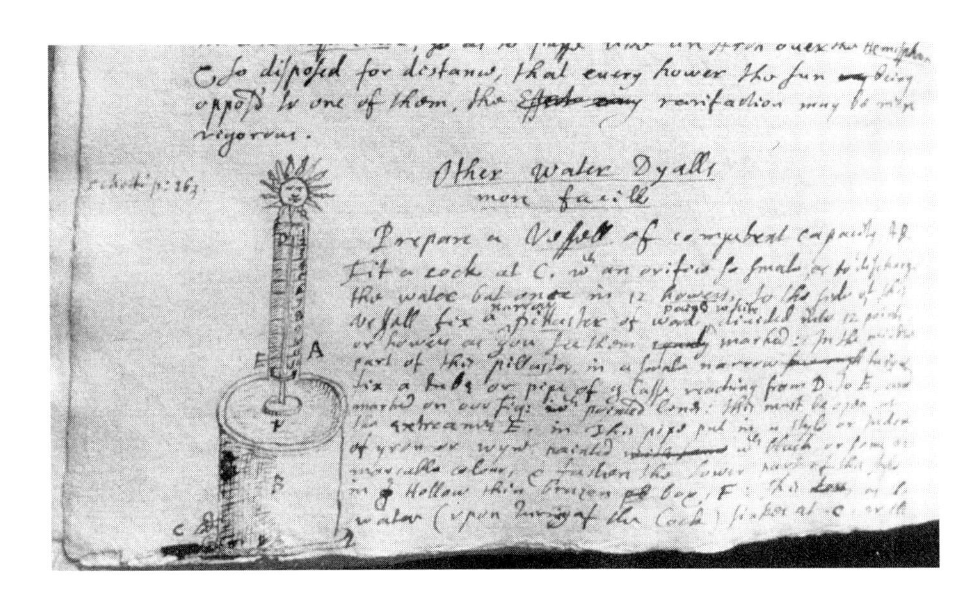

13. John Evelyn, Other Water Dyalls, pen and ink drawing, ca. 1650–1700, from "Elysium Britannicum," 193. British Library, London (photo: John Ingram, reproduced with permission of the trustees of the will of Major Peter George Evelyn)

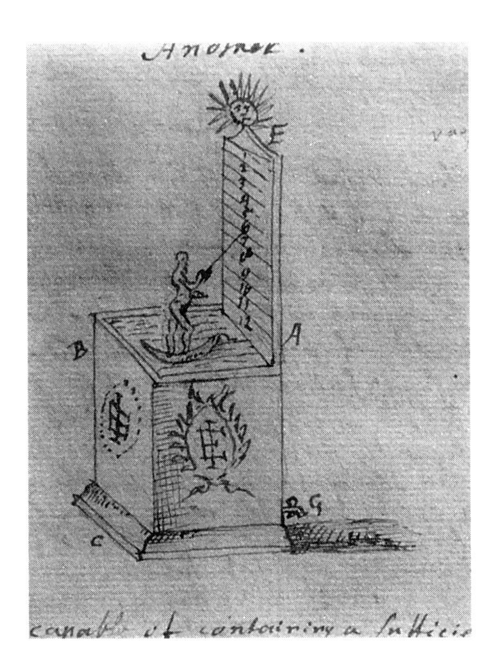

14. John Evelyn, Another Dyall, pen and ink drawing, ca. 1650–1700, from "Elysium Britannicum," 194. British Library, London (photo: John Ingram, reproduced with permission of the trustees of the will of Major Peter George Evelyn)

The stimulation of sight, smell, taste, touch, and hearing were then essential to the successful execution of garden art. When it is impossible, he wrote, to have the natural duplication by the undulating echoes of hills, rocks, and woods, then the artificial echo must be created. Now, the gardener must be the "Echotect."[47] He draws an artificial echo based on one found at The Tuileries in Paris (Fig. 10).

This discussion of echo chambers leads Evelyn to the subject of introducing music into the garden, whether alone or in consort with the voice. For music, he writes, is the most ancient of all the sciences and as Strabo tells us, philosophy and music "signified for a long time the same thing."[48] The gardener must therefore be instructed to contrive sound-producing automata, for which he must learn the principles of hydraulics and pneumatics. The subject of hydraulics leads to all sorts of instruments that could be placed in your garden, chirping birds, satyrs, and other automates, or automata. Directions and illustrations are given for many varieties, including a windchest for the animation of birds and a watchman sounding a trumpet by expulsion of water dyalls (Figs. 11, 12, 13, 14).[49]

Evelyn writes that the statue of Memnon erected at Thebes is described by Kircher in his tome on Egypt and mentioned by all the ancient writers. He suggests that a modern improvement of the ancient model would be one animated, so that the eyes and hands move and a voice could be heard to speak (Fig. 15).[50] Once again, he is refining the achievements of the ancients through modern scientific technology.

"How to contrive a Thermoscope or wheather-Glass for a Garden" is offered by Evelyn in order to "let our Gardiner know that even by this common invention, he may not onely decorate his Garden with an ingenious variety; but become very knowing in the judgement & disposition of the Aer" (Fig. 16).[51] This is one of the instruments he describes that embodies the dignified status and professionalism of the "new Gardiner-philosopher" in search of knowledge and beauty. Having declared the subject of hydraulics and automata "endless, perpetual," Evelyn admits his limited understanding beyond basic experiments. To satiate the thirst of those curious persons, he recommends several authorities for further reading.[52]

Evelyn moves from the furnishing of the garden to its inhabitants. In a chapter entitled "Of Aviaries, Apiaries, Vivaries, Insects, etc," Evelyn writes that so vital is the inclusion of "winged choristers" that he insists the aviaries be in some part of the garden where the singing of birds might "resound even to the house."[53] Evelyn continues, "Birds together with a competent number of Turtles, Quailes, Partridg & Pheasant, for the furniture of the Area . . . cages of 20 & 30 foote in length will hold birds enough to make the Welkin ring with their musique."[54] Evelyn goes on for pages on the subject of birds in the garden, remarking that he has been "more accurate & prolix

[47] "Elysium Britannicum," 168.
[48] "Elysium Britannicum," 174.
[49] "Elysium Britannicum," 174–94: for the birds, 191; for the watchman, 192.
[50] "Elysium Britannicum," 197.
[51] "Elysium Britannicum," 198.
[52] "Elysium Britannicum," 199.
[53] "Elysium Britannicum," 200, 201.
[54] "Elysium Britannicum," 202.

15. John Evelyn, The Statue of Memnon, pen and ink drawing, ca. 1650–1700, from "Elysium Britannicum," 196. British Library, London (photo: John Ingram, reproduced with permission of the trustees of the will of Major Peter George Evelyn)

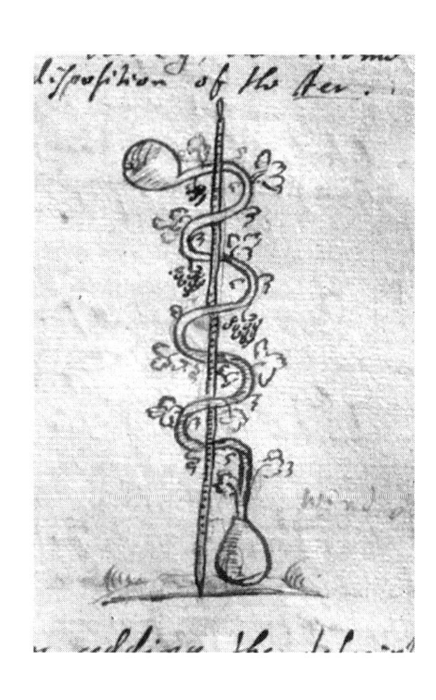

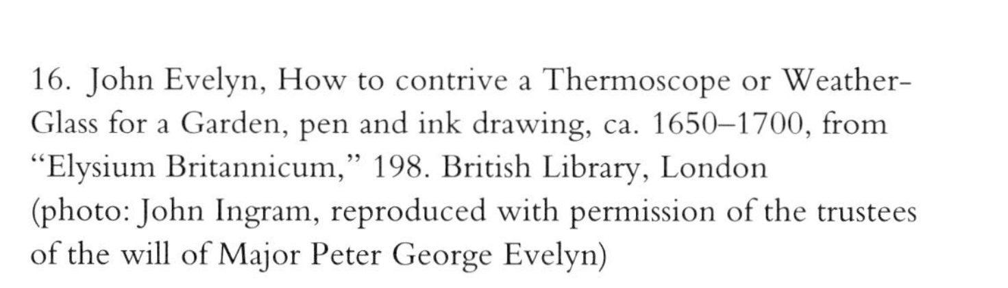

16. John Evelyn, How to contrive a Thermoscope or Weather-Glass for a Garden, pen and ink drawing, ca. 1650–1700, from "Elysium Britannicum," 198. British Library, London (photo: John Ingram, reproduced with permission of the trustees of the will of Major Peter George Evelyn)

17. John Evelyn, The Forme & Ornament of the Urne, pen and ink drawing, ca. 1650–1700, from "Elysium Britannicum," 213. British Library, London (photo: John Ingram, reproduced with permission of the trustees of the will of Major Peter George Evelyn)

because we have ever esteemed it amongst the Sweetest varieties & ornaments of our Elysium, & in which we have taken wonderfull delight."[55] He provides a sketch of a curious urn of white marble found in a Roman villa inscribed with a part of the poem "Philomela, the Nightingale" (Fig. 17). The aviary that he illustrates as an exemplar is very similar to that depicted in Giovanni Pietro Olina's 1622 ornithological treatise, which Evelyn owned (Figs. 18 and 19).[56]

"Vivaries," Evelyn wrote, "were by the Greekes calld Paradises; and are greene & shady places inclosed where wild beasts are kept . . . by diligent observations [of the wild beasts and fowl] the natures of them might be found out" because "there was almost no virtue where beasts did not exceede men." The dove teaches chastity; the stork, piety; the raven, justice.[57] Evelyn returns to the Edenic ideal of all creatures living in harmony. However, the accompanying illustration is of a subterranean warren (Fig. 20), a trap used "when the conys come forth . . . to feede they are caught at pleasure, & are reported to be altogether as sweete fatte & excellent. . . ." This design, Evelyn suggests, also will result in the most excellent compost.[58] Such a device, at first glance in seeming contradiction to Evelyn's vision of Edenic harmony, is typical of the practical and pseudoscientific basis of so much of the content of the "Elysium Britannicum."

According to Evelyn, apiaries were "an ornament that cannot be dispensed withall," and the bee itself, "of such use for contemplation and diversion," was esteemed more than any other insect:[59]

> I should fill a Volume, not a Chapter onely . . . with what may better be collected from the writings of so many considerable Authors, as have dipped their pens in hony, & treated of this sweete & profitable confection . . . the Bee is a rare Architect, forming her hexangular cell for every foote or Angle.[60]

[55] "Elysium Britannicum," 207.
[56] Giovanni Pietro Olina, *Uccelliera overo discorso della natura . . .*, Rome, 1622.
[57] "Elysium Britannicum," 216.
[58] "Elysium Britannicum," 217–18.
[59] "Elysium Britannicum," 220.
[60] "Elysium Britannicum," 221.

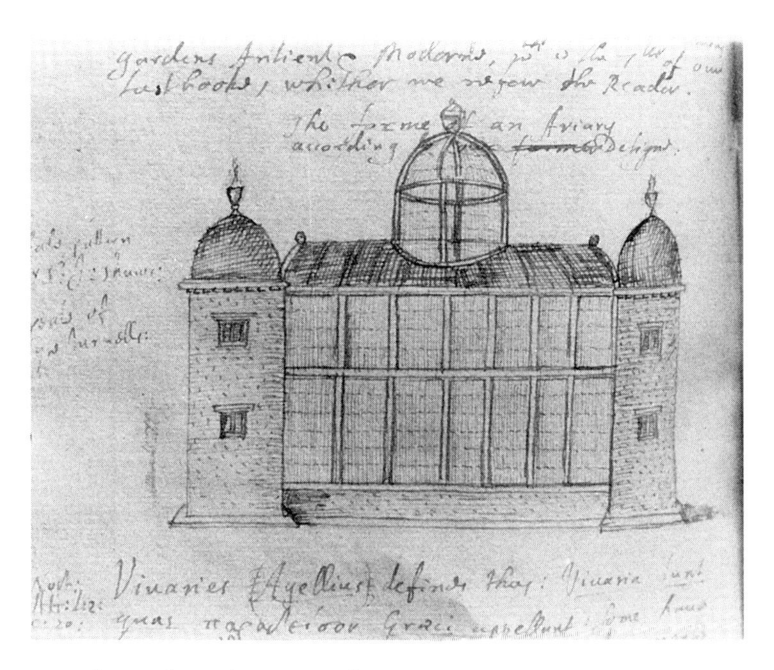

18. John Evelyn, The Forme of an Aviary, pen and ink drawing, ca. 1650–1700, from "Elysium Britannicum," 215. British Library, London (photo: John Ingram, reproduced with permission of the trustees of the will of Major Peter George Evelyn)

19. Giovanni Pietro Olina, The Aviary, engraving, from *Uccelliera overo discorso della natura . . .* , 1622, opposite p. 68 (photo: National Gallery of Art, Washington, D.C.)

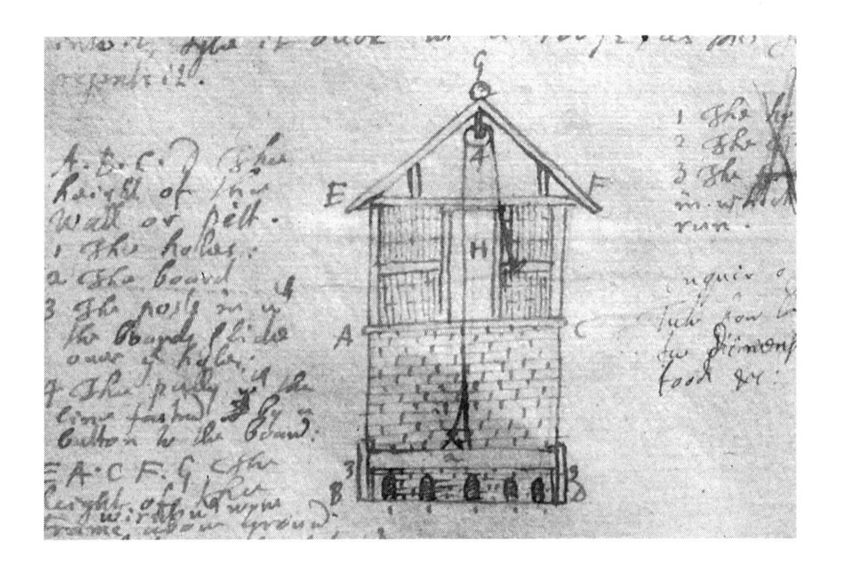

20. John Evelyn, Rabbit Warren, pen and ink drawing, ca. 1650–1700, from "Elysium Britannicum," 217. British Library, London (photo: John Ingram, reproduced with permission of the trustees of the will of Major Peter George Evelyn)

He offers observations on apian government: "They have a Citty, King, Empire, Society . . . they are the Muses birds prophetic & auspicious to Poets & eloquent men, Plato, Pindar, Virgil & St. Ambrose . . . [they are of all the creatures] the most affected to Monarchy, & the most Loyall, reading a Lecture of obedience to Rebells in every mans Garden."[61]

Evelyn proposes a design for a philosophical apiary that was transparent in order to facilitate observation and contemplation of this model society (Fig. 21). He refers the reader to Samuel Hartlib's *The Reformed Commonwealth of Bees* (1655), which was illustrated by Christopher Wren's design for a storeyed beehive. He also notes in the margin: "Jo: Loccenius: Respublica apium where in an expresse political treatise he has at large compared the regiment of Bees with that of Civil Empire."[62] It has recently been shown by Timothy Raylor that the beekeeping project was a serious economic proposition and that the discourse on beekeeping reveals a political concern informed by the perception of natural phenomena in England during Evelyn's time.[63]

Evelyn writes, "We come next to treat of the Silke-worme . . . [as the] Elysium, which as it feedes our Gardiner, with the delicious Nectar of the Bee, so it cloathes him likewise with the soft & richest spoyles of this profitable Creature."[64] The illustration shows a furnace and winder reel for silk production (Fig. 22),[65] "so that when we have then contemplated the many wonder & exellences of this Creature, it has amaz'd us, that it lay so long neglected & so little celebrated by the Antients . . . so certaine a Treasure . . . would set so many thousands on worke, augment the glory of our Nation, & tend to so publique an Emolument."[66]

[61] "Elysium Britannicum," 221.

[62] "Elysium Britannicum," 221.

[63] See Timothy Raylor, "Samuel Hartlib and the Commonwealth of Bees," 91–129, and Parry, "John Evelyn as Hortulan Saint," 130–50, both in Leslie and Raylor, *Culture and Cultivation* (as above, note 1).

[64] "Elysium Britannicum," 236.

[65] "Elysium Britannicum," 238.

[66] "Elysium Britannicum," 240–41. *The Evelyn Library,* London, 1977, 775.

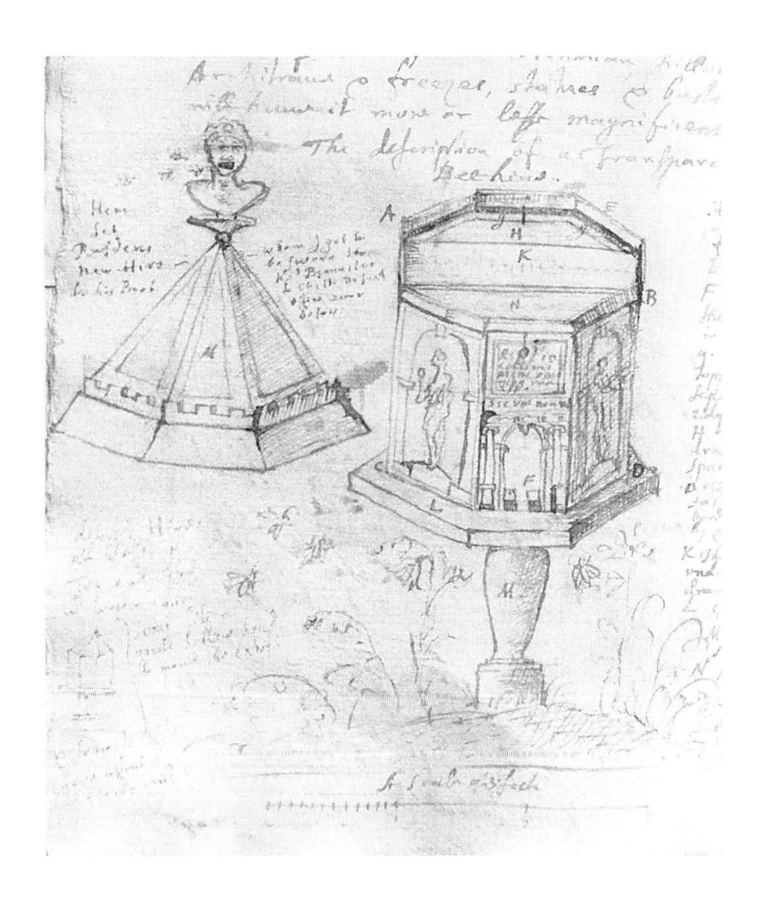

21. John Evelyn, The Description of a Transparent Bee-Hive, pen and ink drawing, ca. 1650–1700, from "Elysium Britannicum," 223. British Library, London (photo: John Ingram, reproduced with permission of the trustees of the will of Major Peter George Evelyn)

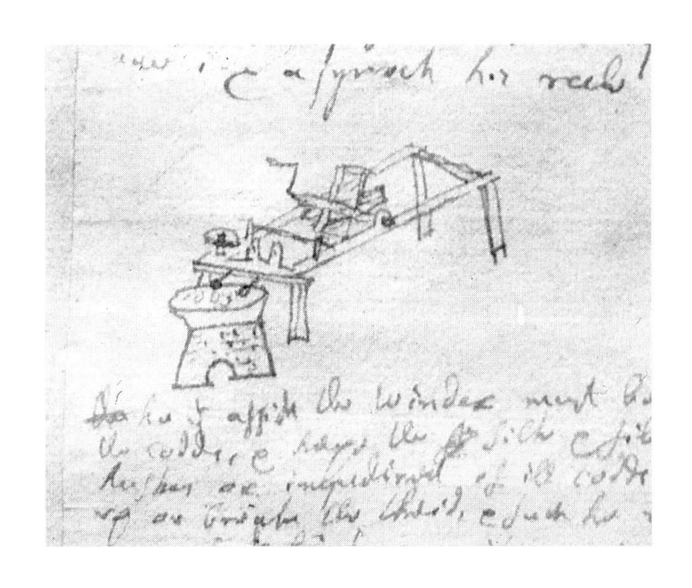

22. John Evelyn, Furnance and Silk Winder, pen and ink drawing, ca. 1650–1700, from "Elysium Britannicum," insert at p. 238. British Library, London (photo: John Ingram, reproduced with permission of the trustees of the will of Major Peter George Evelyn)

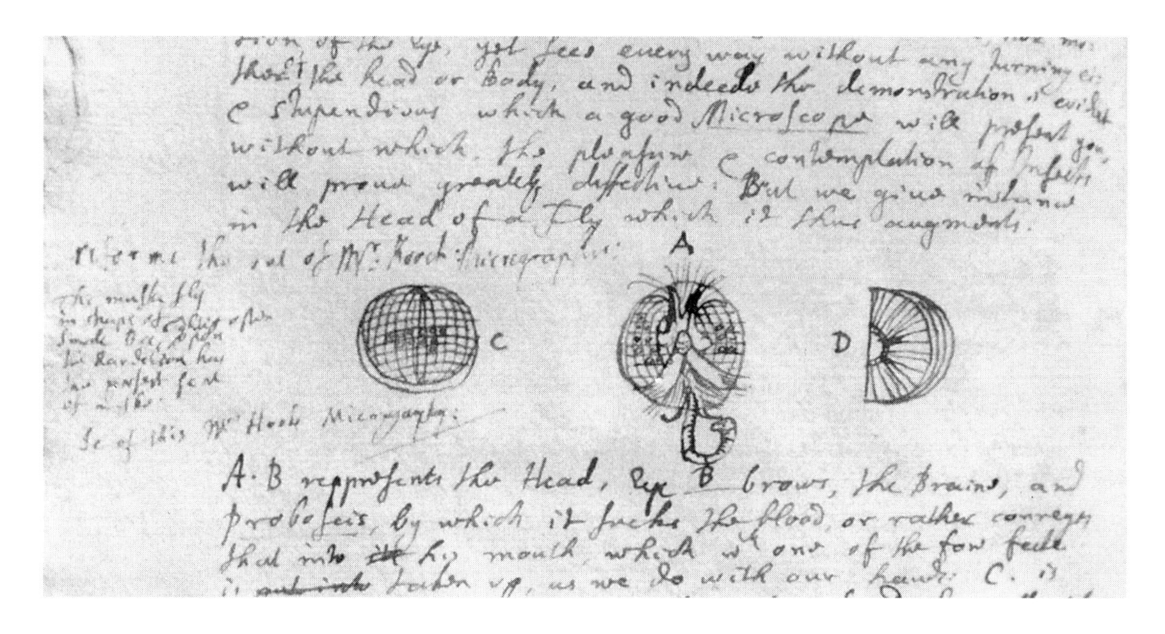

23. John Evelyn, The Head of a Fly, pen and ink drawing, ca. 1650–1700, from "Elysium Britannicum," 245. British Library, London (photo: John Ingram, reproduced with permission of the trustees of the will of Major Peter George Evelyn)

Evelyn continues on the subject: "Yet are insects infinitely worthy of our consideration . . . and have been the subject of many discourses of the greatest Philosophers." He gives an example of the fly presented through "a good Microscope . . . without which, the pleasure & contemplation of Insects will prove greatley deffective" (Fig. 23).[67] He refers to a book he owned, Robert Hooke's *Micrographia,* as the key authority that could have served as a model for Evelyn's ichonisme. In the margin he also recommends comparison with "your Jesuits dedicated to Urban VIII."[68] Here he is referring to a manuscript miscellany, of about 1625, of Francesco Stelluti's papers, specifically the earliest depiction of a subject observed through the microscope. The image is accompanied by a Latin poem complimenting Urban, the bee being the heraldic emblem of the Barberini family to which the pope belonged.

One specific discussion on insects illuminates Evelyn's mental integration of the various aspects of natural phenomena in the garden. "There is none has bin more admired for the prodigious Effects then the Tarantula" (Fig. 24). When gardeners are bitten, which is frequent in Italy, they are overtaken by symptoms that look like wild uncontrolled dancing. Just "as suddainly & strangely compos'd & dissolved, upon the hearing of certaine Musicall touches & harmonious tunes . . . yet are they more frequently pleasd with one tune above all the rest, & that goes by the name of the Turkish aire," called la Tarantella.[69] Evelyn continues for pages on the interrelationship of the insect, the dance, and the music as emblematic of the powers of certain harmonious proportions, which are the basis of musical structure in nature.[70]

[67] "Elysium Britannicum," 245.
[68] "Elysium Britannicum," 244–46.
[69] "Elysium Britannicum," 248, 250.
[70] "Elysium Britannicum," 248–50.

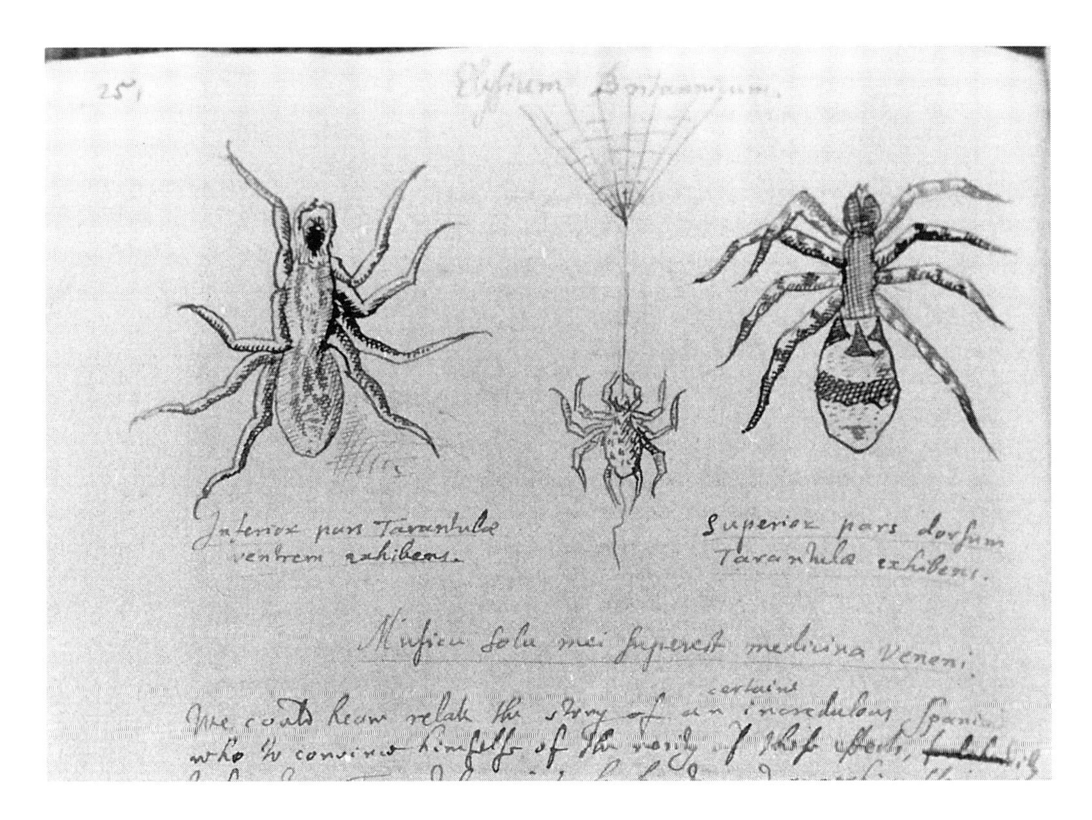

24. John Evelyn, Tarantula, pen and ink drawing, ca. 1650–1700, from "Elysium Britannicum," 251. British Library, London (photo: John Ingram, reproduced with permission of the trustees of the will of Major Peter George Evelyn)

The majority of the rest of the extant manuscript is concerned with flowers and rare plants and their propagation and management. John Harvey provides a thorough transcription of this catalogue of plants, an invaluable inventory of the species and varieties available and of interest to Evelyn and his contemporaries.

One of the final chapters of the surviving manuscript is on the philosophical-medical garden. This is "the most naturall, usefull and Philosophical" portion of our design, wrote Evelyn. Its intention is to "comprehend the principall & most useful plants, & to be as a rich & noble compendium of what the whole globe of the Earth has flourishing." Evelyn lists the many purposes for such a garden: "[It provides] opportunities for new & rare experiments . . . for enfranchising strange plants & civilizing the wild & rude . . . for the contemplation of Nature & the accomplishment of our Elysium." He describes other botanic gardens that exemplify his ideal, including Leiden, Pisa, Oxford, and Padua. The one he considers the "best furnished and Contrived" is the Jardin du Roi in Paris, "an excellent pattern for our Imitation." The mount there clearly was a model for the central feature of the philosophical-medical garden.[71]

The manuscript ends abruptly at book two, Chapter eighteen, "Of wonderfull and Stupendious Plants . . . ," which describes strange and curious species such as the Aloe, century plant, ananas,

[71] "Elysium Britannicum," 321.

banana, ficus indicus. . . . (Figs. 25 and 26). Those are not yet "denisons in our Britanique Elysium . . . yet by [the Gardiner's] industrie & curiositie be in tyme procured and ~~cultivated~~."[72] Evelyn describes these wondrous and mysterious plants in detail along with their habits and properties as well as where in Europe they have been successfully grown.

The "Elysium Britannicum" covers various aspects of the cultivation of land including horticulture, arboriculture, and apiculture and as such is representative of Evelyn's society in which land cultivation and husbandry reflected the consequences of the Reformation and the emergence of a modern nation-state. There has been recent attention given to the spread of the cultivated landscape as a key metaphor in the intersecting realms of national, religious, and individual identity and the indivisibility of political and legal state, physical environment, and social community.

Michael Leslie has co-edited *Culture and Cultivation,* a book addressing just these issues, in which he writes about the extraordinary power of the image of the cultivation of land during Evelyn's lifetime and how that image influenced more practical thinking on all forms of husbandry. Educational reform became a central concern to those people active in the organization of agriculture and horticulture in the seventeenth century, and the Royal Society was one attempt at restructuring access to knowledge. The debates in its early years were strikingly concerned with the management of lands. In his paper, Leslie addresses the implications of agricultural reform during this period as evident in the "Elysium Britannicum."

Although filled with practical utilitarian information, the "Elysium Britannicum" was integrated into the aesthetic principles of gardening and the philosophical and moral benefits of natural pursuits. But beyond gardening, Evelyn's position was ideologically complicated in such a way that demands explication in a much broader cultural context.

As has been written before, with the agricultural and horticultural writers of the early years of the Royal Society John Evelyn formed a new pantheon of hortulan saints.[73] Stephen Switzer wrote in his *Ichonographia Rustica; or the Nobleman, Gentleman, and Gardener's Recreation,* "John Evelyn esq. [was] one of the greatest writers we have had in gard'ning, as well as in several other matters . . . and to him it is owing that gardening can speak proper English."[74] So let us begin with one more apt description of our author, Evelyn:

> As he began, so he continued till his death, a great lover and observer of gard'ning; and tho 'not at his own expense, yet in his readiness to give advice he merited general thanks. In short, if he was not the greatest Master in Practice, 'tis to him is due the theoretical part of Gard'ning. But I need say so more, his own Works, which are publick, are a clearer Demonstration of the Greatness of his Genius, than any Monument I can raise to his Memory.[75]

[72] "Elysium Britannicum," 331.

[73] Parry, "John Evelyn as Hortulan Saint," 130–50.

[74] Switzer, *Ichonographia Rustica,* 59: "This ingenious and learned persons . . . was appointed for the retrieving the calamities of England, and re-animating the spirit of planting and sowing of woods in his countrymen . . . How he has acquitted himself is very well known at present, his books being almost in all hands; and, tis to be hop'd will be continued down to the farthest posterity, amongst the most ingenious and useful writings of that age."

[75] Stephen Switzer, *Ichonographia Rustica; or the Nobleman, Gentleman, and Gardener's Recreation*, London, 1718, I, 60.

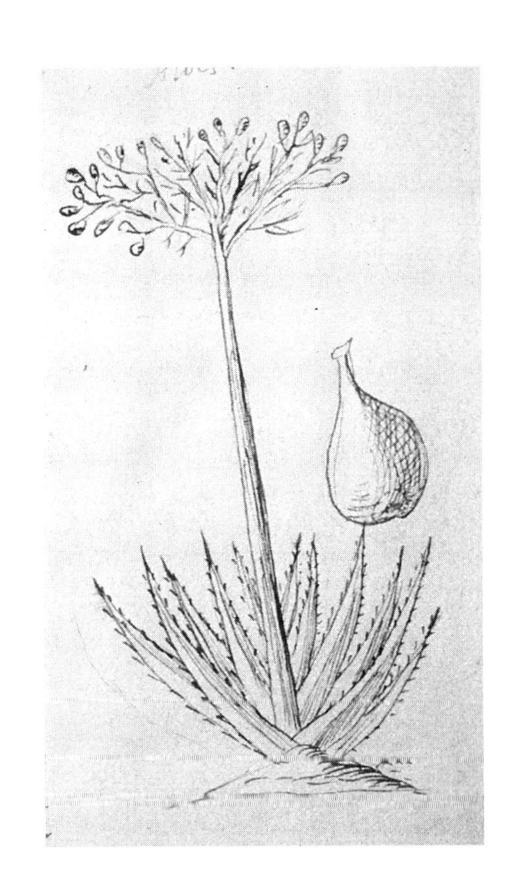

25. John Evelyn, Aloes, pen an ink drawing, ca. 1650–1700, from "Elysium Britannicum," insert at p. 333. British Library, London (photo: John Ingram, reproduced with permission of the trustees of the will of Major Peter George Evelyn)

26. John Evelyn, Plantane, pen and ink drawing, ca. 1650–1700, from "Elysium Britannicum," 337. British Library, London (photo: John Ingram, reproduced with permission of the trustees of the will of Major Peter George Evelyn)

John Evelyn's "Elysium Britannicum": Provenance, Condition, Transcription

JOHN E. INGRAM

In 1987 my colleagues from the history and landscape departments of the Colonial Williamsburg Foundation asked a favor of me. They knew that I planned to attend a three-week seminar on British librarianship, sponsored by Oxford University and the University of Oklahoma, to take place in the city of Oxford. Since I was to be at Oxford for three weeks, they asked if it would be possible for me to "take a look" at the "Elysium Britannicum," the seventeenth-century manuscript on gardening written by the English diarist John Evelyn, and totally unknown to me. Specifically, I was asked to look at the section on garden tools, a section that had earlier been transcribed by another researcher from Colonial Williamsburg, but the transcription of which seemed to leave a great deal unsaid, or at least unwritten.

The request seemed reasonable, intriguing, and, most importantly, achievable because not only was I interested in laying out my own garden in Williamsburg, but I had also devoted a great deal of time to deciphering seventeenth- and eighteenth-century handwriting, not a great deal of which I would characterize with the epithet "calligraphic." I agreed to the request, and during the latter part of May 1987 I went to the library of Christ Church, Oxford, where the "Elysium Britannicum" was housed, along with many of Evelyn's other manuscripts and correspondence, as a deposit from the Evelyn Trust. The "Elysium Britannicum" was sold in 1995 to the British Library.

I must thank the trustees of the Evelyn Trust for permission to make the transcription of the "Elysium Britannicum," and, secondly, to have the transcription published. All photographs of the manuscript are used with their kind permission. The transcription and proofreading of the text of the "Elysium Britannicum" have been supported by grants from the National Endowment for the Humanities and the American Philosophical Society. The Library and Research Division of the Colonial Williamsburg Foundation have also been generous in their support of this project as well as Dumbarton Oaks. Particularly helpful were discussions at the Dumbarton Oaks roundtable in March 1991 on the subject of the "Elysium Britannicum," by which time I had completed the initial transcription of the entire fair-copy portion of the text and a good deal of the inserted text. The library staff at Christ Church, especially John Wing, assistant librarian, have been unfailingly gracious and helpful to me, enabling my work at Oxford to be as enjoyable to me personally as it has been intellectually profitable.

Between that first eight-hour stint with Evelyn's manuscript and the ensuing five years, I spent twenty-four weeks at Christ Church preparing the transcription that was the topic for the 1993 Dumbarton Oaks Studies in Landscape Architecture symposium. In this essay, I shall present a brief overview of the manuscript's history, its length and current physical condition, and my approach to its transcription.

In my opinion, the "Elysium Britannicum" was meant to be, at the most basic level, a compendium or encyclopedia of information about gardening in all its facets, proper, first of all, for "Princes, noble-men, and greate persons," i.e., men of status or rank, and, secondarily, for persons interested in the subject but with much more modest purses.[1] Evelyn drew on the writers and writings from antiquity, from the Bible to Virgil's *Georgics,* as well as on his near contemporaries, such as John Parkinson, Walter Blith, Francis Bacon, John Rea, and many others. A brief reading of the table of contents and the initial pages of the manuscript reveals that his treatise would begin at the beginning with Adam and Eve, move from a discussion of their lost paradise to the more human labor of terrestrial gardens, starting from the ground, reaching to the four elements, and then to the results of their interactions, to the plants, grasses, and trees that would live in the garden, to artificial and natural decorations, and ending with great gardens.

The manuscript of the "Elysium Britannicum, or the Royal Gardens in Three Books" survives as a fair-copy text, that is, correct and essentially finished as written (in Evelyn's hand) and subsequently altered to accommodate changes and additions by Evelyn over at least a forty-year period.[2] The codex also contains manuscript material in other persons' hands directly inserted into the main text, e.g., a two-page set of instructions to govern bees; extracts from Pierre Morin's flower catalog of anemones and other flowers,[3] and Sir Thomas Hanmer's comments on tulips, very probably in Hanmer's own hand (Fig. 1).[4] This fair copy was likely completed in several stages, beginning in the 1650s and continuing through at least the early or mid-1660s, although it would remain ultimately unfinished, or at least, unedited. Graham Parry has suggested that it was begun around 1657.[5] Such a time frame is supported by comments in one of Evelyn's letters to Sir Thomas Browne, dated January 28, 1660. Evelyn writes: "And now to shew you how farr advanced in my worke, though rudely, yet I cannot say to have finished any thing tollerably, farther than chap: XI. lib. 2, and those which are so compleated are yet so written that I can at pleasure inserte whatsoever shall come to

[1] John Evelyn, "Elysium Britannicum; or the Royal Gardens in Three Books," manuscript, British Library, London, 4.

[2] The surviving text contains only 342 pages of an original thousand-page manuscript, which Evelyn may have considered merely a draft of main text, inasmuch as he continued to add to it in his own hand and those of other writers until his death. See below for additional details on the manuscript's composition.

[3] Pierre Morin, *Remarques necessaires pour la culture des fleurs,* Paris, 1658.

[4] A comparison of the handwriting on several insertions at pages 282, 290, and 298 of the "Elysium Britannicum" with the facsimile pages published in I. Elstob, ed., *The Garden Book of Sir Thomas Hanmer, Bart.,* London, 1933, xxxv–xxxvi, leads the present author to this conclusion.

[5] Graham Parry, "John Evelyn as Hortulan Saint," in Michael Leslie and Timothy Raylor, eds., *Culture and Cultivation in Early Modern England: Writing and the Land,* Leicester, 1992, 138.

Sr T. Hanmers paper

[illegible] p: 282

Of Tulipes.

The Tulipe is the Queene of Bulbous Flowers, surpassing all others wee know
in the richnes of colours, and variety of markings, and excellency of figure
It is only defective in odour but hath no ill sent; It is the more estimal
that it is hardy, enduring well abroad all wynter, and not quickly perishable
by spring or sommer heate.
Wee value such most as consist of most colours, and which are not confused
or brouillés (as the ffrench say) but strong and distinct, but more particularly
these things commend a Tulipe most. 1. that it bee of a good figure, not over
great, nor very small, not very sharpe pointed, nor too long leaved, for then the
flower will never open well, and the cheife beauty is when the inside is fully [2dly]
seene, the colours being stronger and livelier within, then on the outside. 2.
every leafe of the flower must bee equally markt or striped, which the ffrench
called pannacht, and the longer and bolder the pannaches are the more glorious
the flower appeares, 3.dly The more colours there are in a flower the better,
and the more unusuall and strange they are the more to bee esteemed, but it is
necessary there bee either white or yellow stripes in every good Tulipe, for
every mixture of other colours without one of them two makes up but a
dull flower, and there ought to bee good store of white or yellow yet there
may bee too much of them also. You shall seldome have more then three or
fower colours in a flower and commonly but two, and then they are of the
lowest forme, except they bee of some very good violet and white, or deepe
murrey or purple and white which are well accompted of. 3.dly The stalke
ought to bee strong and somwhat high, dwarfes are little worth. 4.^thly the
stamina or tamyns as some call them in English and ffrench too, (which are
the little shaking sprigs [heads] which stand within the flower about the seed vessell) must
bee of a rich purple colo^r, and not yellow nor pale greene as some are. 5.^thly the
must bee no part of the blew [or greenish] bottomes, within the flower remaining, but as you
will find hereafter they must bee breathed or streamed away into white or yellow pan
naches. 6.^thly The colours most in request are purples, violetts, scarletts, gridelin
shadowed and striped with white, or any odde durty rotten colo^rs as some tearme
them shadowed and markt with straw colour or stronger yellow; and these later sorts
are called about London Modes, being a la mode de ffrance, where such coloured Tulipes have of late yeares beene most prized and sought after.
It were but a vaine worke to give you the names of good Tulipes, they being soe
numerous, and soe many Catalogues of them publisht, and soe many new sorts
appearing yearly which are raised by sowing the seed both abroad and in England,
I will hasten therfore to their culture, and some observations on them not yet
common.
The ordinary Tulipes will prosper very well in a good ordinary garden soyle, but the

1. Sir Thomas Hanmer's "Of Tulipes," insertion at p. 282 of the "Elysium Britannicum"

hand to obelize, correct, improve, and adorne it."[6] This would bring the manuscript to at least page 167 of the extant volume. Again, some twenty years later, in a July 11, 1679, letter to John Beale, Evelyn writes of the "Elysium Britannicum":

> When again I consider into what an ocean I am plunged, how much I have written and collected for above these twenty years upon this fruitful and inexhaustible subject (I mean horticulture), not yet fully digested in my mind, and what insuperable pains it will require to insert the (daily increasing) particulars into what I have already in some measure prepared, and which must of necessity be done by my own hand, I am almost out of hope that I shall have strength and leisure to bring it [i.e., the "Elysium Britannicum"] to maturity.[7]

I would like to suggest that the fair-copy text of the "Elysium Britannicum" was written in several steps because of the markedly different inks used throughout the manuscript, because the character of the handwriting changes within the fair-copy text, and because of the rate and amount of changes in different sections (Figs. 2–4). It cannot be coincidence, in my opinion, that the first and last quarters of the manuscript account for approximately two-thirds of the marginalia and insertions, with the remaining text in the middle having only one-third of all such changes.

Evelyn continued his "dense overwriting" of the manuscript until close to his own death.[8] The latest dated annotation in the text is on page 161 and is for 1702, four years before his death at the age of 86: "Here consult Bernard Lamy translated into English, printed 1702; you have in your library at Wotten, Pag 122, 123" (Fig. 5).[9]

After his death in 1706, Evelyn's library and papers, including the "Elysium Britannicum," remained more or less in the Evelyn family, despite the "assistance" of individuals such as William Upcott and some of Evelyn's own descendants. William Upcott (1779–1845), sometime sublibrarian at the London Institution, was also a book collector and scholar, who with William Bray (1736–1832), a noted antiquarian, edited and published Evelyn's diary in 1818. In 1814 Upcott received an essential "free hand" to the Evelyn family papers from Lady Evelyn. "Sylva," Evelyn's[10] papers and books were apparently of special interest to Upcott. When Upcott's own library was auctioned in 1846, many of Evelyn's manuscripts and books were found in the collection, leading to Upcott's Janus-like reputation as both malefactor and benefactor of the Evelyn collection. However, as Geoffrey Keynes noted in his bibliographical study of Evelyn, one could justly claim that Upcott was indeed the real benefactor for the Evelyn collection, because the family, at least by the early nineteenth century, was perhaps somewhat "unmindful" and carefree about the importance of John Evelyn's bibliographical and manuscript legacy.[11] Whether the manuscript of the "Elysium Britannicum" was

[6] Geoffrey Keynes, ed., *The Works of Sir Thomas Browne,* London, 1931, IV, 276.

[7] Arthur Ponsonby, *John Evelyn,* London, [1933], 269.

[8] Parry, "John Evelyn as Hortulan Saint," 134.

[9] B. Lamy, *A Treatise of Perspective; or, the art of representing all manner of objects as they appear to the eye in all situations . . . ,* London, 1702.

[10] John Evelyn's nineteenth-century sobriquet, courtesy of his most popular publication that went through many editions: *Sylva; or a Discourse of Forest-Trees,* London, 1664.

[11] Geoffrey Keynes, *John Evelyn: A Study in Bibliophily with a Bibliography of His Writings,* 2nd ed., Oxford, 1968, 29.

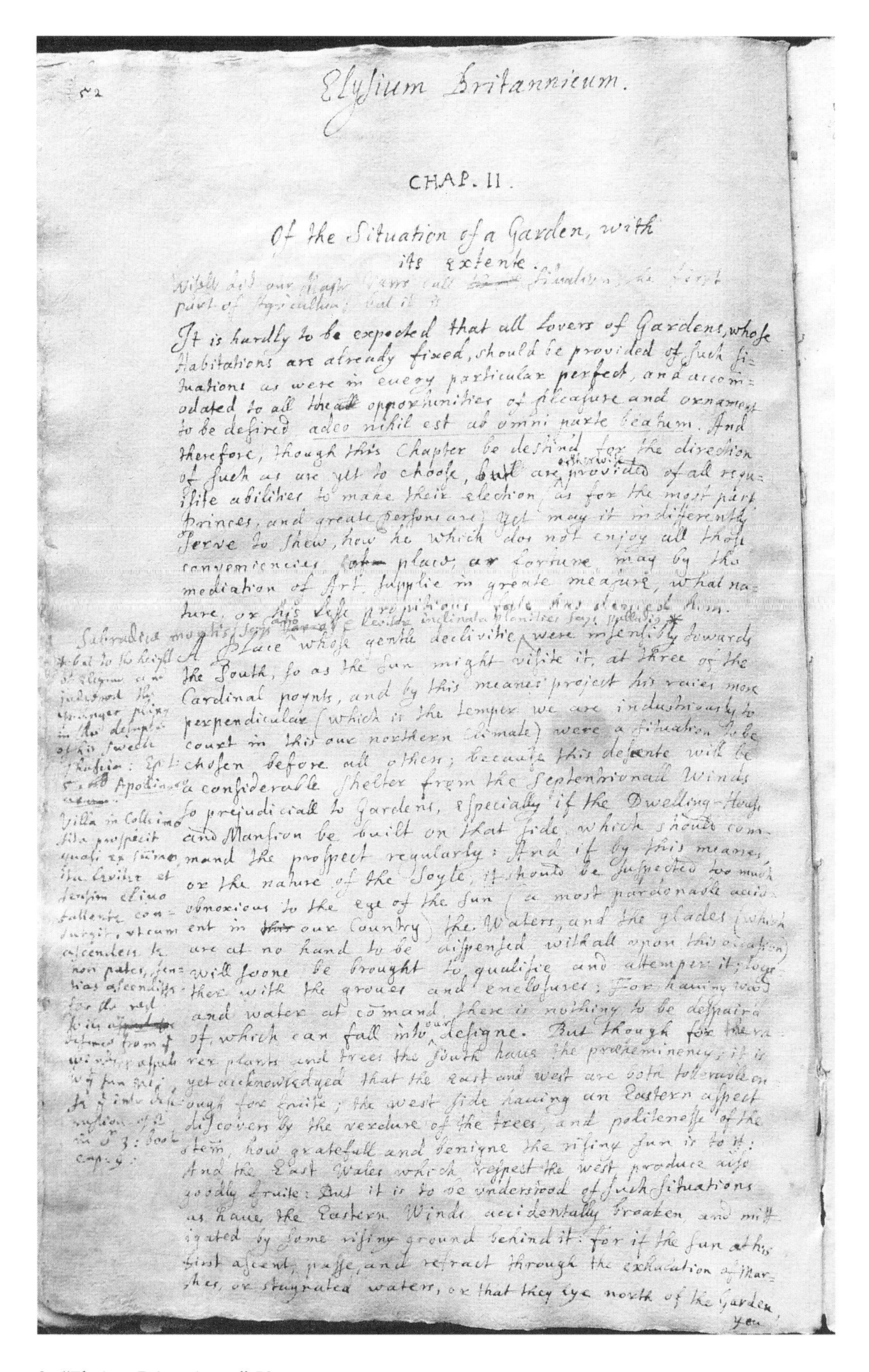
52

Elysium Britannicum.

CHAP. II.

Of the Situation of a Garden, with its extente.

It is hardly to be expected that all Lovers of Gardens, whose Habitations are already fixed, should be provided of such situations as were in every particular perfect, and accomodated to all the opportunities of pleasure and ornament to be desired adeo nihil est ab omni parte beatum. And therefore, though this Chapter be design'd for the direction of such as are yet to choose, and are otherwise provided of all requisite abilities to make their election (as for the most part Princes, and greate persons are) Yet may it indifferently serve to shew, how he which does not enjoy all those conveniencies of place, or fortune, may by the mediation of Art supplie in greate measure, what nature, or his less propitious fate has denied him.

A Place whose gentle declivitie were insensibly towards the South, so as the Sun might visite it, at three of the Cardinal poynts, and by this meanes project his raies more perpendicular (which is the temper we are industriously to court in this our northern climate) were a situation to be chosen before all others; because this descente will be a considerable shelter from the Septentrionall Winds so prejudiciall to Gardens, especially if the Dwelling-House and Mansion be built on that side, which should command the prospect regularly: And if by this meanes, or the nature of the Soyle, it should be suspected too much obnoxious to the eye of the Sun (a most pardonable accident in our Country) the Waters, and the glades (which are at no hand to be dispensed withall upon this occasion) will soone be brought to qualifie and attemper it; together with the groves and enclosures; For having wood and water at comand, there is nothing to be despaird of, which can fall into our designe. But though for the rarer plants and trees the South have the praeeminency; it is yet acknowledged that the East and West are both tollerable enough for fruite; the west side having an Eastern aspect discovers by the verdure of the trees, and politenesse of the stem, how gratefull and benigne the rising sun is to it: And the East Wales which respect the west produce also goodly fruite: But it is to be understood of such situations as have the Eastern Winds accidentally broaken, and mittigated by some rising ground behind it: for if the Sun at his first ascent, passe, and refract through the exhalation of Marshes, or stagnated waters, or that they lye north of the Garden you

2. "Elysium Britannicum," 52

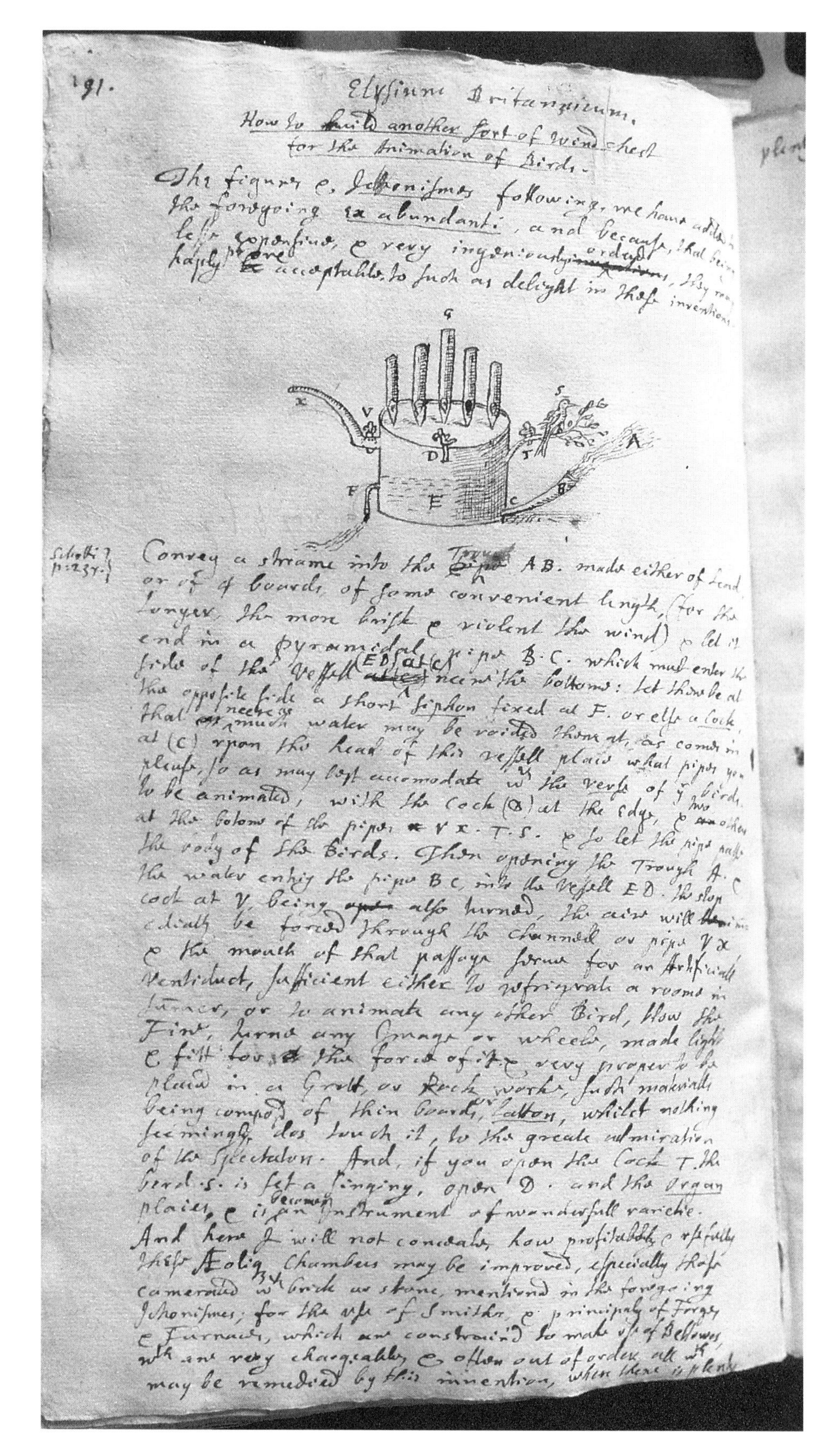

191.

Elysium Britannicum.

How to build another sort of Wind chest
for the Animation of Birds.

The figure & Schemismes following, we have added to the foregoing ex abundanti, and because, that being less expensive, & very ingeniously ordered, they may happily prove acceptable to such as delight in these inventions.

Conveigh a streame into the Trough AB. made either of lead or of 4 boards, of some convenient length, (for the longer, the more brisk & violent the wind) & let it end in a pyramidal pipe B.C. which must enter the side of the Vessell ED at C near the bottome: let there be at the opposite side a short siphon fixed at F. or else a cock, that as much water may be voided thereat, as comes in at (C) upon the head of this vessell place what pipes you please, so as may best accommodate wth the verse of ye birds to be animated, with the Cock (D) at the edge, & two others at the botome of the pipes V X. T. S. & so let the pipes passe the body of the Birds. Then opening the Trough A. the water entring the pipe BC, into the Vessell ED. the stop cock at V. being also turned, the aire will [illegible] ediatly be forced through the channell or pipe V X & the mouth of that passage serve for an Artificiall Ventiduct, sufficient either to refrigerate a roome in summer, or to animate any other Bird, blow the Fire, turne any Image or wheele, made light & fitt for the force of it, very proper to be placed in a Grott, or Rock worke, such materialls being compos'd of thin boards, or Latton, whilst nothing seemingly does touch it, to the greate admiration of the Spectators. And, if you open the Cock T. the bird S. is set a singing, open D. and the Organ plaies, & it becomes an Instrument of wonderfull rarety. And here I will not conceale, how profitably & usefully these Æolic Chambers may be improved, especially those cameraded wth brick or stone, mentioned in the foregoing Schemismes, for the use of Smiths, & principally of Forges & Furnaces, which are constrain'd to make use of Bellowes wch are very chargeable, & often out of order, all wch may be remedied by this invention, when there is plenty

3. "Elysium Britannicum," 191

Interfolia 300.

Elysium Britannicum.

Lib: 2

must be planted againe in September; but the last not be removed except for increase: the Globus & round neede neither pott, nor disturbance but for propagation: but the Tuberous would be planted about Autumne as soone as taken up: The Rootes of the Ranunculus being stamped & applied heale the plague sores. [illegible]

Salvia Sage, It will be wondered how this esculent plant came into our Coronarie Garden; but when you shall behold the imense & indicible varietie of the leaves their admirable & stupendious variegations, colour & shapes, it will haply be as much wondered why it was kept so long out: but we referr the particulars & the secrets of it to another place; in the meane tyme we know how it is propagated by slipps, in good earth moderately moistned, and its virtues are innumerable. for

Cur moriatur Homo cui Salvia ——

The Solsequium & Heliotrops are raised in warme rich grounds about the spring: 'tis an annuall plant of a stately gigantine & majesticall regard: the seedes of it are as good (though not so greate) as the Pistacia and are altogether pleasant: & it yeelds an excellent Serpentine: but the magneticall qualities we shall describe hereafter.

Thrachelium Americanum, plant in potts the earth well macerated and preserved from th' extremitie of winter: they may annualy separated and transplanted about March and the fibers buried 2 fingers deepe, watered & placed in the sun where most it thrives: the seede yeelds no varietie but its signature is for the Throate. [illegible]

Yucca, or Indian Bread delights in a strong ground, shallow planted, in the spring it may be multiplied, otherwise not to be removed or disturb'd. [illegible]

Viola tricolor is of 3. or 4 sorts, best propagated by plants but the Comon Violet being dubble, multiplie exceedingly both by seede and strings being planted early, or in the Autumne in moyst & shady grounds: ~~The purple colour, perfume wh which they tinge the aire, & the delicious & usefull Syrup advance this humble & modest plant flower, above most of the Coronarie~~. when they begin to bud for flo: cleanse them of their strings to maintaine the flo: the better, refresh them about Octob: & string them againe: The dubble do not beare seede; but take such as of dubble degenerate sow in march or Octob: Crescente Luna. but of these improvements hereafter. Whilst the magistraticall colour, perfume which they tinge the aire wth, its delicious and usefull Syrupe elevates this humble & modest flower, above most of the Coronary.

Cap: 1: lib: 3.

And here we will make an end of this voluminous and endlesse taske summarily running over, or rather naming only the lesse observable & easily governed by the rules already prescribed, which are such as follow.

4. "Elysium Britannicum," 300

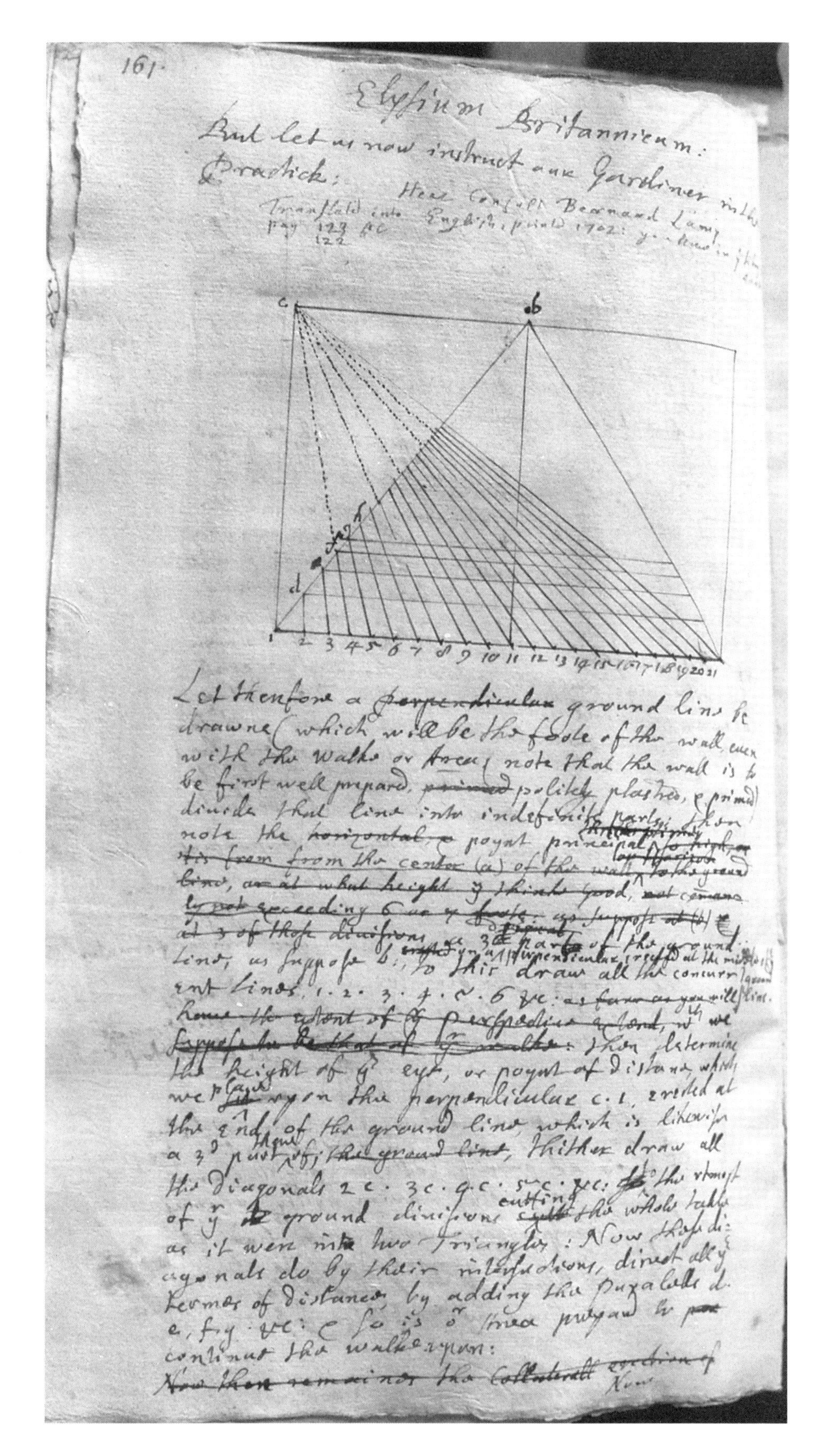
161

Elysium Britannicum:

But let us now instruct our Gardiner in the Practick:

Here Consult Bernard Lamy Translated into English, printed 1702:

pag 123 &c
122

Let therefore a ground line be drawne (which will be the foote of the wall even with the walke or Area; note that the wall is to be first well prepard, politely plastred, & primed) divide that line into indefinite parts; then note the poynt principal

part of the ground line, as suppose b; to this draw all the concurrent lines, 1. 2. 3. 4. 5. 6 &c.

Then determine the height of the eye, or poynt of distance, which we place upon the perpendicular c. 1. erected at the end of the ground line, which is likewise a 3d part of it, thither draw all the diagonals 2 c. 3 c. 4 c. 5 c. &c. the utmost of the ground divisions cutting the whole table as it were into two Triangles: Now these diagonals do by their intersections, direct all the termes of distance, by adding the parallels d. e, f, g, &c: & so is our Area prepard to continue the walke upon:

Now

5. Bernard Lamy note from 1702. Illustration of lined-through text, "Elysium Britannicum," 161

numbered among the Evelyn papers and books that were part of the Upcott auction remains unknown to me at the present time.

In due course, following the ravages of auctions and editors, as well as family attention and inattention through two centuries, the entire collection of books and papers was placed on deposit at Christ Church College in 1951 by a collateral descendant, also, and appropriately, named John Evelyn. The Christ Church Library continues to house the Evelyn collection of papers, which remains available to scholars. The books were sold at auction in 1967.

The manuscript of the "Elysium Britannicum" today contains 342 consecutively numbered pages, with one major lacuna comprising pages 25 through 36, and some misnumbered additional pages toward the end of the codex. Written principally in English, the text has numerous quotations in Latin and Greek, ranging from the classics on gardening, such as Virgil's *Georgics,* to contemporary authors, such as Abraham Cowley; there are also a few references written in Hebrew (Figs. 6 and 7). The manuscript is bound in a single small folio volume approximately 31 cm high by 20 cm wide. The binding is likely mid nineteenth century and is half-bound black morocco with paper-covered boards, the whole presenting evidence of rather heavy use.[12]

In addition to the fair-copy text of 342 pages, there are numerous inserted sections of text, ranging in length from several lines of text on a "sliver" of paper to thirteen folio-size pages of text and illustration (Fig. 8). I would estimate that the total amount of added text through insertions, marginalia, and interlineations would be equal to at least 100 pages of fair-copy text, perhaps one reason why Evelyn failed to have the text published during his lifetime, even with the support and interest of his contemporaries at the Royal Society and Oxford.

Evelyn also includes more than 80 illustrations for the work, some requiring entire pages, such as the two-page collection of garden tools. Other drawings occupy large portions of folio pages, such as the phonotactic cylinder and the music to be played on it. More frequently, however, Evelyn drew rather more modest illustrations, scaled down to fit into the margin of the main text or even the margin of an insertion (Figs. 9 and 10).

The majority of the text block remains secure, although several gatherings at the beginning of the volume have become free of their sewing. Additionally, several pages, including the printed table of contents, which is larger than the leaves of the codex, have begun to lose text through constant folding and unfolding as well as the general handling that the pages have received through the course of more than three centuries.

The table of contents is of bibliographic interest in its own right because it began its life as a broadside announcing Evelyn's grand design of the "Elysium Britannicum" and exists in several versions (Fig. 11).[13] The copy in the volume now at the British Library has had page numbers added

[12] Upcott may have been responsible for having the "Elysium" manuscript bound at the same time as another volume with similar binding, extant at Christ Church, which contains miscellaneous notes on several subjects, principally, for *Sylva.* It seems that Upcott's access to the Evelyn manuscripts, and his constant reworking of the diary and correspondence, make Upcott a logical choice for having the manuscripts bound in their similar bindings.

[13] A copy of a different and earlier broadside, located at the British Library, lists four fewer chapters and some minor word changes; there is also no annotation. The table of contents, published in *Acetaria; a Discourse of Sallets* in 1699, had 42 chapters. British Library, Add. Ms. 15950, fol. 143. This information is courtesy Dr. Helen Wallis.

celebrated in [illegible], & the etymologie is this.
Priapus signified the Solare virtue, et Hortis praeesse dicitur, propter eorum foecunditatem (sayes Isidor) [illegible]
naturaly it is the sun it selfe, as is easily deducible fro
the supposed hymns of Orpheus.

—— κὴ κόσμον
λαμπρὸν ἄγων φάος ἁγνὸν ἀφ' οὗ σε φάνητα κικλήσκω
Ἠδὲ πρίηπον ἄνακτα ——
—— per mundum
~~Emicantem ducens lucem~~, à qua te Phaneta voco
~~Atque Priapum regem~~
That round this Ball
Carriest the glorious light, whence I thee call
Phanes, and King Priapus.

For Priap is certainly the same that Horus in Egypt,
that is Sol, of which an instance out of Suidas puts
all out of question. τὸ ἄγαλμα τοῦ Πριάπου &c The
Egyptians (sayth he) calld Priapus Horus, & carved him

6. Example of Greek text, "Elysium Britannicum," 153

[illegible]

* Orchard, pomarium, an Orchard, Habuimus in Camdenianis. Sunt [illegible]
ὄρχος et ὄρχατος Homerica verba, unde tanto probabilius ad Anglos
transitus. Dubito tamen an illa vera origo. Dubitandi caussa, quod Belgae
ooft-gaerd & ooft-gaerd; ut et boomgaerd: et Germani, baum-gart:
obs-gart: (lust-garte: Paradisus:) dicunt. Unde proverbiale est, etiam [illegible]
esse verbum compositum: or-chard, vel orch-yard: (ut vine-yard et win-yard)
ut to ooft & or, sint ejusdem, ex Graeco ὀπώρα, originis: [illegible]
[illegible]

7. Example of Evelyn's etymological research with Greek and his version of Old High German or Anglo-Saxon, "Elysium Britannicum" note facing p. 1

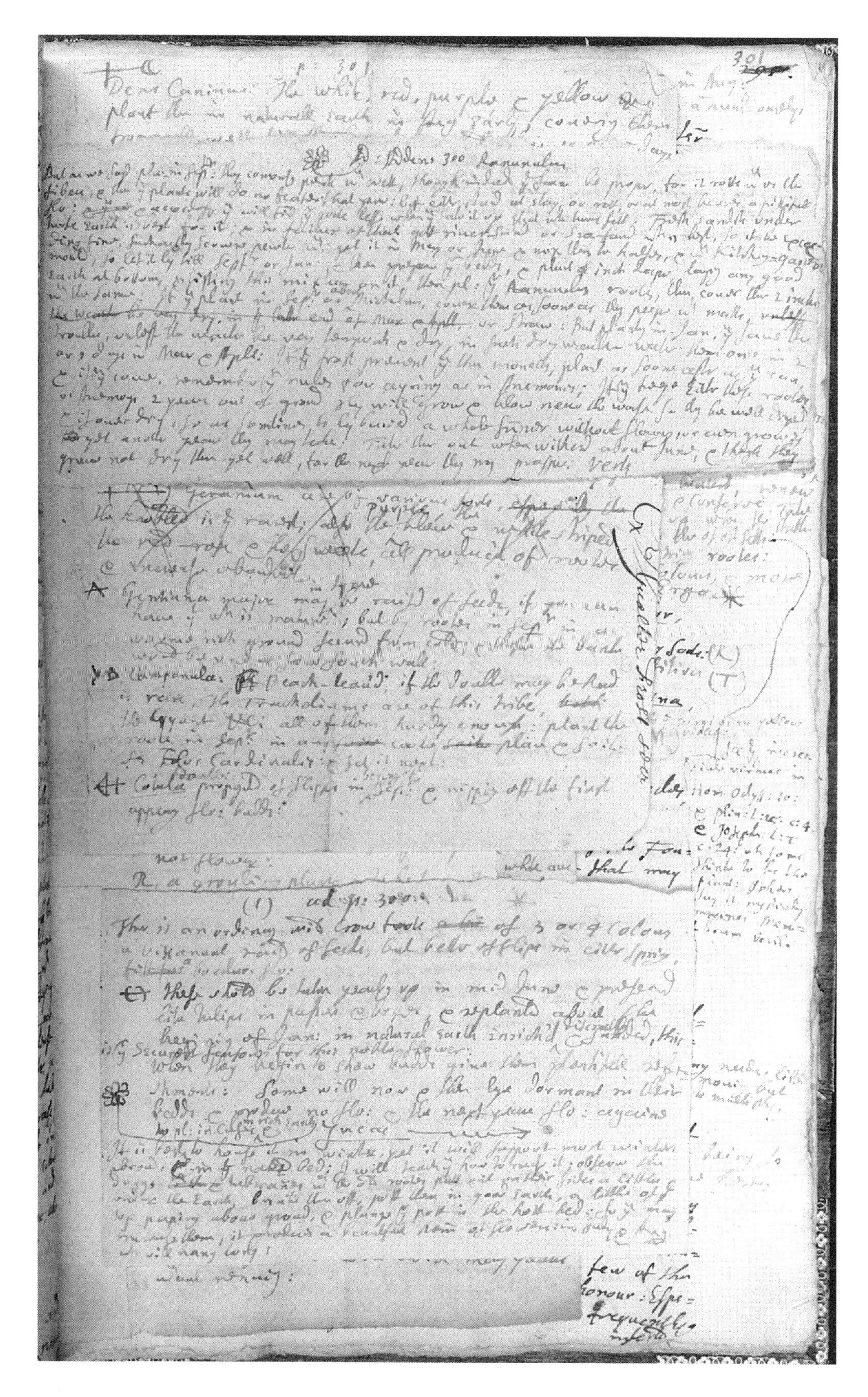

8. “Elysium Britannicum,” insertions between pp. 300 and 301

9. Margin illustration of "shover," "Elysium Britannicum," 45

10. Inserted text with illustration of "Turning Spade," "Elysium Britannicum," 44

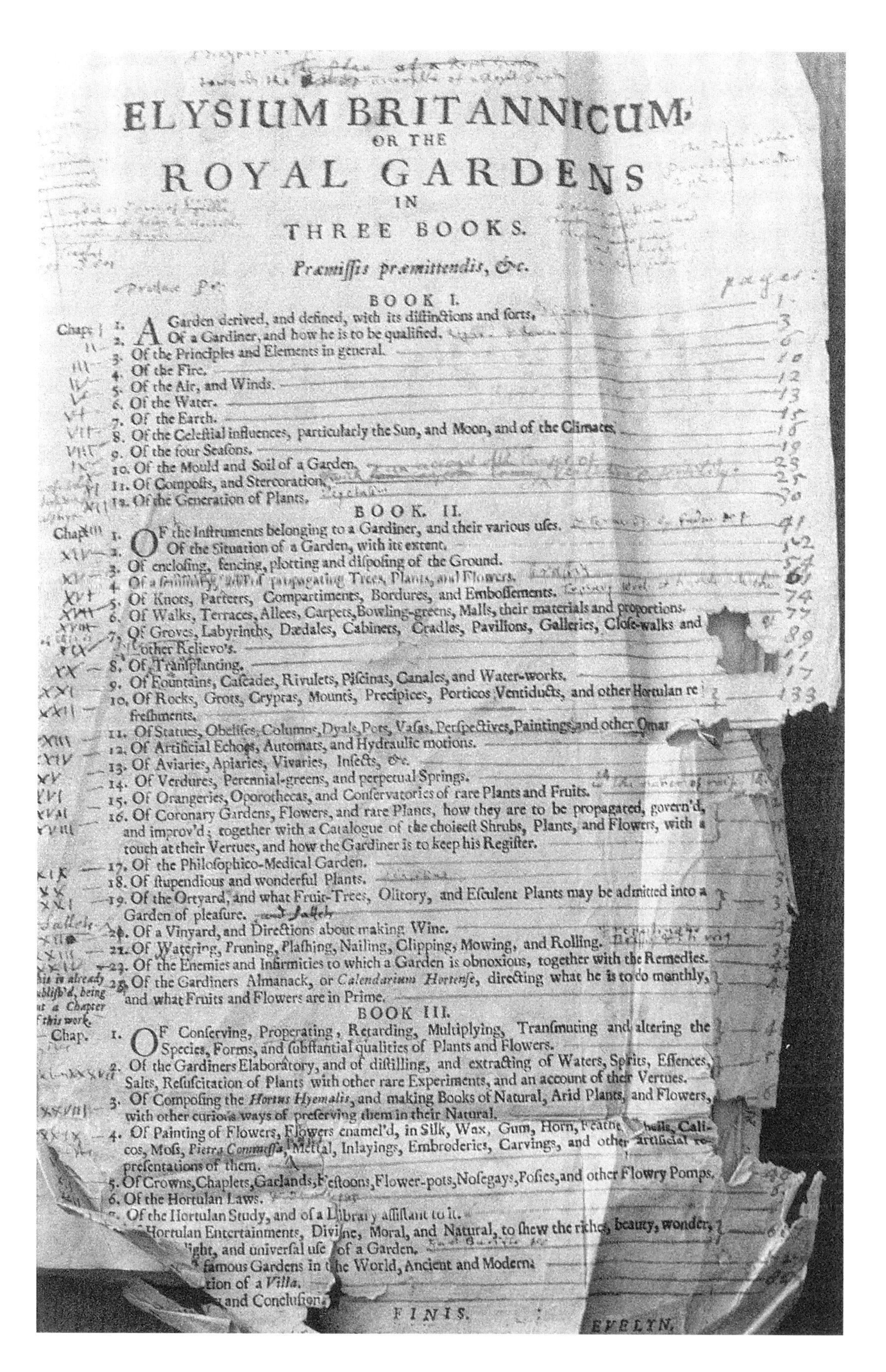

ELYSIUM BRITANNICUM, OR THE ROYAL GARDENS IN THREE BOOKS.

Præmiſſis præmittendis, &c.

BOOK I.

BOOK II.

BOOK III.

FINIS.

EVELYN.

11. Separate broadside announcing the "Elysium Britannicum," used by Evelyn as his table of contents

to the various chapters, which may indicate, although not altogether conclusively, that the original manuscript of the "Elysium Britannicum" had included at least 500 additional pages. Indeed, Evelyn noted in his preface to *Acetaria,* in an oblique reference to himself, that the manuscript had grown "to so enormous an Heap, as to fill some Thousand Pages."[14] Although the numbers on the table of contents page correspond exactly to those in the existing text, it has been suggested that the remaining page numbers, for which the text is not extant in the volume, are perhaps only estimates for the conjectured lengths of the chapters. In other words, Evelyn may never have actually finished the "Elysium Britannicum," for it is apparent from examining the actual manuscript that he had very likely completed a basic fair-copy, unedited text, which he never sent forward as a "finished" publication because of his desire to prepare the most up-to-date description of the gardener's art and science.

A preliminary review of three boxes of Evelyn's miscellaneous papers at Christ Church revealed no immediately identifiable additions to the current text, except for two inserts. There remain fifteen boxes of miscellaneous papers, which Michael Hunter has examined with some success for potential additions to the original manuscript of the "Elysium Britannicum." Because Upcott removed at least one section of the "Elysium Britannicum," other sections may also exist but have not yet been identified as belonging to the original manuscript.[15] Indeed, in a separate set of pages attached immediately after the contents page, Evelyn has set down "A Table leading to the notes in the loose Sheetes to be inserted into the Elysium Britannicum." The table lists references to 220 pages of notes to be distributed throughout the entire original text of more than 867 pages indicated in the table of contents. Thus, because of the depredations the collection has suffered at the hands of family, Upcott and Bray, and auctions, I remain convinced that we do not have the entire manuscript, and yet I retain the hope that the missing pages will be found.

My transcription of the "Elysium Britannicum" is a line-by-line literal transcription, with no wrapping around of text; that is, each transcribed line ends where the manuscript line ends. Exceptions to this rule are all interlineations, marginalia, and inserted text.[16] (See the appendix at the end of this paper for pages 52–54 of my transcription.) When the work is published, it may be more practical to include multipage additions to the text in the general text flow rather than in footnotes. In the same way, Evelyn's use of catchwords is retained as in the original.

I follow some generally accepted standards for transcription of similarly dated manuscripts.[17] For example, I silently expanded abbreviations for words such as "with," "which," "the," "that," "them," even the word "colour" in one of the inserted texts. I also eliminated all superscripts. If

[14] Paraphrased in Parry, "John Evelyn as Hortulan Saint," 146.

[15] Keynes, in his Evelyn bibliography, *Sir Thomas Browne,* 236, notes, "Portions [of the Elysium Britannicum] were probably removed by Upcott. One specimen 2½ pp. 4to, headed 'A catalogue for Tryals', was sold at Sotheby's, 3 May 1967, lot 76, inserted in a copy of the *Memoirs,* 1819, with a statement by Upcott that it had belonged to the *Elysium Britannicum.*" It is now at the William Andrews Clark Library, University of California, Los Angeles.

[16] This approach reflects most satisfactorily Evelyn's own practice, which made no attempt beyond the fair-copy text to set left and right margins.

[17] I have tried to follow the guidelines established for the Hartlib Papers edition at the University of Sheffield, specifically, their seventh amendment, September 1, 1991 (courtesy of Michael Leslie).

Evelyn had underlined a word, I underlined the word, at no time trying to introduce my own system of regularity of underlining.

Evelyn often changed his mind about phrasing and spelling in words, phrases, and sentences throughout the text, beginning with the title page and running through the last page of the surviving text. Evelyn's "system" of spelling is retained, with no conscious effort on the part of the transcriber to standardize. I have tried to recapture faithfully the text of his line-throughs and have noted his additions and replacements by means of braces { } (Fig. 5). My interpolations into the text are minimal, and I have indicated them through the use of brackets. My use of normal parentheses reflects Evelyn's use of parentheses.

In all, Evelyn's marginal notes and insertions number more than 750 entries. They range in length from simple citations of a classical author or work, such as Virgil and his *Georgics* and Lucretius' *De Rerum Natura,* to modern authors, such as Francis Bacon and Abraham Cowley. Also there are multipage additions, such as the four-page "Designe of a Physical Garden" (p. 329), a dozen or so pages on fountains and other waterworks (p. 118), and a number of multipage insertions in other hands. In some ways, Evelyn's marginalia, inserenda, and addenda are the most interesting parts of the work, for in many instances their contents represent the products of the best and the brightest of authors on these subjects for almost half a century. Because a decision still must be made regarding how the text will be published, that is, either to reproduce Evelyn's marginalia as marginalia or use a standard text format with footnotes for Evelyn's margin notes, I have used the footnote feature of the word processing software to include all marginalia and text additions on separate free or tipped-in pieces of paper, always noting the one or the other mode of addition.

For the Latin and Greek excerpts, I provide annotations in brackets, e.g., title, chapter, and line numbers where I could discover them, in order that readers may more easily consult the original texts. During this stage of the transcription I also elected to use transliteration for Greek words, not wanting to use the Greek fonts in my software; such transliterations are found enclosed within slanted lines (\\). When the transcription is published, the classical Greek alphabet should be used. Because Evelyn used a cursive style of classical Greek, I was not always able to decipher the text; however, I plan to consult with specialists in classical Greek to help with questionable transcriptions, all of which have been photographed. The astrological signs that Evelyn used to indicate the months for various planting activities and the chemical elements will also be included in the published text.

Concerning questionable readings, I used a series of three question marks to indicate words or phrases that are partially or entirely indecipherable to me, representing less than one word in a thousand. Evelyn's idiosyncratic spelling in general, and his use of several versions of proper names and plants in particular, provided innumerable opportunities to use the reference resources that were at Christ Church Library with great success. However, there remain several obscurities that can perhaps be clarified only after other researchers study the transcription. Text that had been lined or circled through and where the ink or pencil has blurred presented challenges. At such times, although originally clear, the words were more difficult to read than Evelyn's own scrawl in his marginalia and insertions. I have occasionally used a single question mark, not, however, to show that I have serious doubts in the reading but to alert the reader to the lack of absolute certainty.

Because Evelyn also used question marks in his text, albeit sparingly, there may be some confusion; however, in all cases where there could be a misinterpretation, additional notes will be given in the published text.

A particularly maddening peculiarity of Evelyn's updating of his text is his habit of adding more information to a space in the margin or on an inserted piece of paper than the space can handle. Again, his seemingly interminable, almost obsessive-compulsive additions to certain areas of the text, most notably in the section describing the plants in the coronary garden, would leave me in an extremely agitated condition at the end of a day of transcription, in which only one or two pages of text were transcribed. Equally trying on the patience of the transcriber has been Evelyn's penchant to make notes in the faintest of pencil script; this is especially true for his annotations citing sources of additional reading. I might also note that he did not restrict his marginalia to the fair-copy text but managed to add marginal notes even to his insertions!

Future scholars will now have opportunities to explore Evelyn's motives in rewriting (and eventually crossing out) most of the initial section of the first book of the manuscript where he discusses the nature of the four elements and tries to reconcile classical teaching and Baconian physics with the theories of Robert Boyle and other members of the Royal Society against the traditional background of religion. Was Evelyn more at home, perhaps, in rephrasing the architectural designs of Vitruvius and the poetic methodology of Virgil and other Latin and Greek writers than in trying to assimilate and rephrase more concrete (and more modern) aspects of landscape design, such as the use of fountains, statues, sundials, etc., to establish a specific attitude of a garden? Was Evelyn trying to incorporate so much current research on his topic within the constraints of manuscript and handset type that his project was doomed to failure as soon as it started? In sum, was Evelyn attempting more than he personally was intellectually capable of doing?

What remains to be done to bring the "Elysium Britannicum" to publication and, therefore, to scholarly access, a goal that dates to as early as January 1659, when Evelyn was being "encouraged" to finish the book by individuals such as Robert Sharrock, the two Bobarts, and John Banister?[18] When the work, with its index of personal names, subjects, places, and, hopefully, plant names, is submitted to a publisher, the transcription should be as ready as it ever will be for publication. And finally, after more than 300 years, Evelyn's hope for his "magnissimum" opus will be partially realized but with so much of its original thousand pages missing.

[18] "To Encourage the finishing of Elysium Britannicum Oxon Jan: 20. 1659," a letter now kept with the manuscript codex of the "Elysium Britannicum."

Appendix

Transcription Pages 52–54 of the "Elysium Britannicum"

[page 52]

CHAP. II.

Of the Situation of a Garden, with
its extente.

{Wisely did our Master Varro call ~~the fir~~ Situation the first part of Agriculture; but it is}
It is hardly to be expected that all lovers of Gardens, whose
Habitations are already fixed, should be provided of such Si=
tuations as were in every particular perfect, and accomm=
odated to all the ~~all~~ opportunities of Pleasure and ornament
to be desired, adeo nihil est ab omni parte beatum. And
therefore, though this Chapter be destin'd for the direction
of such as are yet to choose, but are {otherwise} provided of all requ=
isite abilities to make their election (as for the most part
Princes and greate Persons are), yet may it indifferently
Serve to shew, how he which dos not enjoy all those
conveniences, of place, or fortune, may by the
mediation of Art, supplie in greate measure, what na=
ture, or his lesse propitious fate, has denied him.
A Place whose gentle declivitie {Sub radice montis {(says ~~Varro~~ {Cato}) & leviter inclinata
planities says
Palladius}[1] were insensibly towards
the South, so as the Sun might visite it, at three of the
Cardinal poynts, and by this meanes project his raies more
perpendicular (which is the temper we are industriously to
court in this our northern Climate), were a situation to be
chosen before all others; because this descente will be
a considerable shelter from the Septentrionall Winds
so prejudiciall to Gardens, especially if the Dwelling-House

[1] Margin note: but to the height of elegiac and judgement the younger Pliny in the description of his sweete Thuscia: Ep: L: 5 [v1] Apollinaro ~~ab~~ Villa in Colle imo sita prospecit quasi ex summo ita leniter et sensim clivo fallente, consurgit, ut cum ascendere te non putes, sentias ascendisse for the rest of its ~~aspect etc~~ defence from the winds & aspects to the sun etc. Se the intir discussion of it in our 3: book cap: 9.

and Mansion be built on that side, which should com=
mand the prospect regularly: And if by this meanes
or the nature of the Soyle; it should be suspected too much
obnoxious to the eye of the Sun, (a most pardonable accid=
ent in ~~this~~ our country) the Waters, and the Glades (which
are at no hand to be dispensed withall upon this occasion)
will soone be brought to qualifie and attemper it; toge=
ther with the groves and enclosures: For having wood
and Water at command, there is nothing to be despair'd
of, which can fall into {our} designe. But though for the ra=
rer plants and trees the South have the prae-eminency, it is
yet acknowledged that the East and West are both tollerable en=
ough for fruite; the west side having an Eastern aspect
discovers by the verdure of the trees, and politenesse of the
stemm, how gratefull and benigne the rising sun is to it:
And the East Wales which respect the west produce also
goodly fruite: But it is to be understood of such Situations
as have the Eastern Winds accidentally broaken and mitt=
igated by some rising ground behind it: for if the Sun at his
first ascent, passe, and refract through the exhalation of Mar=
shes, or stagnated waters, or that they lye north of the Garden
you

[page 53]

you will soone find the inconvenience of it, both in the aire,
and in your Flowers; whereas if they be South or west, it
is nothing so considerable; because those vapours following
the course of the Sun are drawne away from your Garden
and quickly dissipated.
But, besides this, is the Situation of a Garden very consider=
able in respect of the Climate; of which we have already am=
ply discoursed; ~~likewise~~ and it wil be our Gardiners greate[2]
advantage, and no little marke of his perfection; so to order his
ground, and the accidents about it, that assisting Nature with
the addition of Arte, he bring it to such a temper as may
best qualifie it for universall productions; by which
industry, almost all the inconveniencys of our Climate may
be rectified, & places brought to a very kind, and hospita=

[2] Margin note: cap: 8: Lib: 1.

ble disposition. Of grand importance to this is the fertility
and nature of the Earth, which in the next place should
be accurately examin'd; That the mould be good, according to
the severall indications praescribd in the 10th chap: Lib:1:
Nor should we be satisfied with superficialls, but see that
the second and third beds be proportionable to the rest, aba=
ting for the severall depths: For though Flowers, and some
other Plants, wil prosper and do well enough in shallow
mould; yet trees, and the greater shrubbs require more
profunditie, that the rootes may be well fed, expatiate and
fortifie themselves.
Above all let our Gardiner be curious that the water
be excellent, in plenty. and at command; and therefore, we
thirst after a Sourse that may breake forth of some
chalky eminence, or serpenting in a channell of am=
ber colourd and smoth pibbles, it irrigate the subjacent
ground rather in a swift then slower progresse. Wee
say in aboundance to furnish the many uses both {of} necessity
and ornament; and from a spring sufficiently elevated,
for the ease both of the purse, and the body: For there
may be occasions and tymes, when it would be requisite
to inundate even some considerable part of the Garden;
and where such collines {crowne &} environ a place, so as not
to interrupt the Prospect, but at agreable distances;
There it is that we expect those temperat & salubrous
breezes, which so gently refresh both our Gardens &
our ~~bodys~~ {Spirits}; whereas, if the hills be mountainus, and the
vallys profound, the repercussion & reverberation of the Sun
chases the exhalations, renders it sulphury, pestilentiall
and impetuous.
Situations are likewise reformed, by melioration of the Earth,
by artificiall reflections, plantation of trees, erecting of
Shelters, disposing of the Levell, ~~and~~ preparation of the
mould, & by severall other artifices.
Lastly, touching the Extent and circuit of the Ground,
it is also to be modified {as able} to the designe of the person
and the Gardiners projection; for if the intent be onely to
make a parterr, compartiment, or Coronary Garden,
and his ~~intention~~ {fancy} be {narrow &} particular, a lesser {& more regular} compasse will
suffice

[page 54]

suffice;[3] But for a Royall & universall Plantation, &
to make an Elysium indeede, neither one forme, or
Situation of Ground will accommodate {the proposition} nor a smaller
[4]proportion, then a thousand Geometricall paces in
[5]circumference; {The D: of Orleans's in Luxembourg is 70 akers ~~though~~ in ~~area~~ it itselfe}
Though some thing
very princely, may
be contrived in thirty akers; allways supposing it be
exquisitely kept: For not onely dos that hold in profit
but in the pleasure and delight allso of Gardens Melior
est culta exiguitas, quam magnitudo neglecta.

CHAP. III.

Of Fencing, Enclosing, plotting and disposing the ground.

[6]The Ground, Situation and Extent determin'd, the next
to be considered is the {Munition} Securing and fencing of our Gar=
den;[7] ~~for which~~ {And yet} we {shall} neither consult Columella or Pall=
adius or others of the Antients, whose hedges {or Windwalls} though never
so artificially {erected} disposed & planted can be no sufficient
guard for our Out-Workes, but a good, strong and sub=
stantiall Wall of two foote in thicknesse, and thirteene
foote in height, either of brick, stone or such materialls as
may neither decay, nor leave any uneven & rugged surfaces,
receptacles for Snailes, and other noxious Insects.
To this purpose let the foundation be well ~~layed~~ {examined} and the mor=
tar excellently prepared.[8] The coping without and erect wi=
thin; But it shall not be necessary to insert it with
hookes, or blocks of wood for the support of Palisads, &
cancelled quarters, unlesse it be in that part onely which
shall be destin'd for fruit, in which the direction set

[3] Margin note: a tollerable ground cannot be lesse then 500 foote square for Ortchard & Flo: of which 100 to the flo: Garden:

[4] Margin note: c: 3: et:

[5] Margin note: Se: L: 3: c: 9. ~~ult~~ See ult.

[6] Margin note: mend palisads by Contrespaliers Poole hedges.

[7] Margin note: Talis humus, vel parietibus, vel sepibus hirtis claudatur, neu sit picori, neu pervia furi Col: L: 10 [27–28]

[8] Margin note: the lime made of flint (if to be had) & so beaten as not to be seene in the mortar: the joynts close layd, & with little mortar:

downe in the French Gardiner may be of use; because we
suppose it but a portion of our ~~Villa~~ {Elysium} (whereoff we do not
treate in this place expressely) and would husband our
Expenses: But in separating particular plotts, for parti=
cular Gardens within the grand Zeraglio or Enclosure,
we do by no meanes, approve of Walling, {if walls, parapetts and pedistalls} not onely
to avoyd the charge; but for that it greately detracts from
the grace and beauty of the whole, and will make them ap=
peare but like so many courts or pounds unlesse it be
for the private flower Gardens, & of choyce plants, such
as are contiguous to the flankes of the Mansion house, which
indeede should be contrived to all the advantages of Retire=
ments, & freed from all other intercourses.
Rather therefore, let such partitions be made of Contr'
Espaliers[9] and ~~palisads~~ hedges of Alaternus, Holly, {paliuras} pyrocanta,
Lawrells {cypresse, juniper}, Horne-beame, Elme, the Garden purple-flour'd Will=
ow, the peach-blosomed thorne, {white thorne, Berberies} some hedges of fruites, or the
like, which ~~will~~ in convenient tyme {will} fortifie and
become a sufficient Fence, & {gracefull} partition; especially,
where there is nothing to violate the Inclosures but

[9] Margin note: the antients calld them pergulae rectae to distinguish them from the Murales or wall Cattices for fruite so much in use in France.

John Evelyn: Between the Ancients and the Moderns

JOSEPH M. LEVINE

I

John Evelyn was not on the face of it a passionate man. Prudent in life and discreet even in the privacy of his diaries, he kept his feelings for the most part to himself. Perhaps it was the influence of an admired father whom Evelyn remembered as "exact and temperate . . . never surprised by excesse . . . of a singular Christian moderation in all his actions." Perhaps it had something to do with the temper of an age which no longer wanted to wear its heart on its sleeve. To his friends he seemed "a gentleman of a character highly respectable in every view . . . [of the] most elegant and useful accomplishments and blessed of the most amiable virtues."[1] Indeed, he seemed a man possessed of every virtue and in all his virtue self-possessed.

That was how he liked to present himself anyway, and that is pretty much how the readers of his diaries have found him, sometimes with disappointment, in the hundreds of pages which he apparently never meant to be read by strangers. And yet it is almost too consistent, too carefully contrived to be completely true. Virginia Woolf was not the only one who complained about the diary that "he never used its pages to reveal the secrets of the heart." No doubt something like that was what he intended. "His writing is opaque," she continued, "rather than transparent; we see no depths through it."[2] Yet surely behind all the restraint and respectability, the facile accomplishment and easy conviviality, the cool and careful facade, there was some strain and some cost. Evelyn's life, or what he liked to show of it, was too well fashioned to have been composed casually or accidentally.

In fact there was a passion in the man, not efflorescent but slow burning. For eighty-five years, without faltering, he kept it alight. Although Evelyn had been born to wealth and culture, to an assured income and easy connections, he was restless with activity. He could have chosen a life of ease in either court or country; instead he went to work, scribbling away unceasingly until he had filled a score of printed volumes and many more of manuscript; built, planted, and collected; con-

[1] See the autobiography prefixed to E. S. de Beer, ed., *The Diary of John Evelyn,* 6 vols., Oxford, 1955, I, 1 (hereafter *Diary*), and the anonymous obituary quoted by Sarah Marburg, *Mr. Pepys and Mr. Evelyn,* Philadelphia, 1935, 73.

[2] Virginia Woolf, "Rambling Round Evelyn," *The Common Reader,* New York, 1925, 113–23.

tributed frequently to public life; and socialized endlessly with the great and good men of his time. There is nothing more revealing of the man, I suppose, than the rules he once laid down "for spending my pretious tyme well"; the enemy was that "wasteful and ignoble sloth," which he found so often corrupting a good education.[3] Surely if there is one key to this conviction, an explanation for all this persistent and apparently endless activity, it lies in Evelyn's profound conviction that there was nothing in the world that could not be molded into something useful or artful by conscious and calculating deliberation and an effort of will—not nature, the commonwealth, the family, his gardens, or himself.

And so, necessarily, Evelyn believed passionately in education, not pedagogy in any narrow sense, but *paideia* in the exact meaning of the ancient Greeks and Romans. He believed with them completely in the shaping possibilities of culture and the human soul, and he seized upon the classical teachers as his models. He subjected himself, his family and his friends, to an unceasing self-examination and exhortation in an insistent effort to forge out of a recalcitrant human nature something useful and good. And when it was done, when eighty-five years had passed, he was perhaps entitled to that seeming complacency that has sometimes troubled posterity, even while it has admired his achievement and pored over his diaries. He had indeed fashioned his life and the life about him into art.

Yet all was not easy, not even for this very successful man, and once at least we hear a cry of pain. On January 27, 1658, Evelyn's little son Richard died, "the prettiest and dearest Child, that ever parents had, being but 5 yeares [5 months] and 3 days old . . . a prodigie for Witt and Understanding; for beauty of body a very Angel; and for endowments of mind of incredible and rare hopes." He composed the boy's epitaph in his diary and closed it simply "Here ends the joy of my life, for which I go even mourning to the grave. The Lord Jesus Christ sanctifie this and all my other Afflictions. Amen."[4] It was not the first child that Evelyn had lost, though all the rest were infants. But this was a loss, he explained to his father-in-law, "so much the more to be deplored, as our contentments were extraordinary."[5] Although he was little, Richard had been cut off early, already formed and full of promise, and it was his education that Evelyn recalled before anything else in his hour of grief, setting it down in precise and painful detail.

For once, however, it was not enough to record his anguish in the privacy of his diary; Evelyn wished to proclaim it aloud in a public monument for all to see. And he hoped, typically, that it might be put to practical use. At hand he remembered a little Greek book that he had purchased abroad, *The Right Way for Parents to bring up their Children,* by the ancient church father St. John Chrysostom. It was unknown in England and had only just been discovered in manuscript and printed in Paris. But it seemed exactly to the point, for it preached one simple and appropriate

[3] Evelyn to Lady Sunderland, August 4, 1690, in Henry B. Wheatley, ed., *The Diary and Correspondence of John Evelyn,* 4 vols., London, 1906, III, 463–65 (hereafter *Corr.*). Evelyn had rarely gotten to bed before midnight in twenty years, he wrote in 1668, and he was proud that he could "read the least print, even in a jolting coach, without other assistance." Evelyn to Beale, August 27, 1668, in Arthur Ponsonby, *John Evelyn,* London, 1933, 54–55.

[4] *Diary,* January 27, 1658, III, 206–10.

[5] Evelyn to Sir Richard Browne, February 14, 1658, *Corr.,* III, 244–45.

message: the importance of shaping a child's mind. For Chrysostom, the parent's work is like an architect with a building, an artist with a painting, or a prince with a city to govern—or, as it must have seemed to Evelyn—like a garden to be cultivated. (Eventually, Evelyn gave instructions for all of these.) Human nature is like wax, and character can be molded into virtue. There was nothing, therefore, more important than education. What could be more fitting then than to turn the little tract into English to commemorate the shaping of his own son's mind. "The golden book of St. Chrysostum," his friend Jeremy Taylor wrote gratefully on receiving a copy, "in which your epistle hath made a black enamel, has made a pretty monument for your dearest, strangest miracle of a boy . . . I paid a teare at the hearse of that sweet child."[6]

Evelyn's epistle, his introduction to the little book, was just like the memorial he was writing for his diary. He wished to show there "what may be expected from a timely education, if we will with diligence pursue it." And so he offered a brief account of Richard's education, from his learning the alphabet at three, to his construing Latin and Greek at five years of age. Beyond the rudiments of the classical languages, the little boy had learned some French, some Euclid, music and drawing, the catechism, and more—all without the least compulsion or severity. "For so insatiable were his desires of knowledge, that I well remember upon a time hearing one discourse of Terence and Plautus, and being told (upon his enquiring concerning these authors) that these books were too difficult for him, he wept for very grief, and would hardly be pacified." Just so, Evelyn remembered, had it happened to the young Thucydides. Evelyn was tempted to say more, much more, but for once his copious pen failed, and the words would not come, for "my teares mingle so fast with my ink, that I must break off here and be silent. . . . "[7]

II

The ink dried in time, and Evelyn's life went on. Fortunately, there was soon another son, several daughters, and eventually a grandson to renew his hopes, as there were also the children of friends and patrons to sustain his interest in the classical *paideia*. Again and again he proffered advice in an endless stream of letters for his own family and for the sons and nephews of others: the earl of Clarendon, the duke of Northumberland, Lord and Lady Sunderland, Samuel Pepys, and so on. Always he offered it with the conviction of one who enjoyed the company of the ancients, who knew them intimately and who appreciated their practical value in the world. For the young men of ambition who had any hopes or expectations of public life, Evelyn was confident that the first and indispensable foundation for success lay in a mastery of Latin and Greek and an imitation or emulation of the best of the ancients—coupled always with a sound religious training.

[6] Taylor to Evelyn, June 4, 1659, *Corr.*, III, 256–60. Evelyn's work is entitled *The Golden Book of St. John Chrysostum concerning the Education of Children,* London, 1659; it is reproduced in William Upcott, ed., *The Miscellaneous Writings of John Evelyn, Esq.,* London, 1825; see esp. 107–11, 115. M. L. W. Laistner, who furnishes a modern translation and some useful background, praises Evelyn's work for its "dignity and literary skill," but he sees evidence that it was translated from Latin rather than the original Greek: *Christianity and Pagan Culture in the Later Roman Empire*, Ithaca, N.Y., 1951, app., 75–84.

[7] Evelyn, Epistle Dedicatory, *Golden Book.*

In his way, Evelyn was simply repeating the wisdom of Renaissance humanism, which for two centuries now had been looking back upon classical examples for its inspiration to contemporary life. For the most part, his advice was commonplace and could easily be found in the schoolbooks, gentlemen's manuals, and the correspondence of tutors and masters, fathers and sons, throughout the early modern period.[8] It was taken for granted that the ancients had provided the skills and knowledge for most necessary things, but especially for politics and public life. Eloquence was, therefore, the capstone of the education of the gentleman in England, as it had been in ancient Rome, and the examples of the ancient orators and statesmen, historians and poets, were valued as the supreme models for imitation. Latin and Greek were the two indispensable keys to success, and the grammar school curriculum was devoted almost exclusively to them. Here was the foundation of modern *anciennete,* and Evelyn accepted it almost without question and assimilated it easily into his own life.

Evelyn was a little reticent about his own education. It is clear that he had been born to wealth and the expectation of public service. The family had made its money in gunpowder—that supreme example of modern ingenuity—and Evelyn proudly remembered his father, who had become high-sheriff of both Surrey and Sussex, holding court, surrounded by 116 liveried servants.[9] Evelyn was a younger brother and only inherited the family estate in 1699; but he was well provided for, so that, despite occasional anxieties, he never really had to work. He did not receive a particularly good early education, he says, but learned his Latin from a tutor and at the local grammar school.[10] He always regretted missing Eton, which he avoided because of its reputation for severity. When he visited Westminster School many years later, he was enormously impressed by the facility of the schoolboys there in Latin and Greek composition, "some of them not above 12 or 13 years of age."[11] Still, he managed somehow to attain that modicum of the classics that then seemed essential to a gentleman. Evelyn always took an interest in contemporary literature as in contemporary affairs generally, but he clearly preferred the company of the ancients in both literature and public life. He followed grammar school with a stint at the Middle Temple to learn some law and then went on to Balliol College, Oxford. In 1640 Evelyn returned to the Middle Temple.

The death of Evelyn's father and the civil war interrupted his work and his prospects, however, and after briefly rallying to the king, he went off prudently to visit the Continent. The idea of a Grand Tour was new but may have been encouraged by the example of his famous Surrey neighbor Thomas Howard, earl of Arundel. It was that great man, patron of the arts and indefatigable collector, who more than any other, set the fashion of visiting the principal sites of antiquity and carrying off the remains. Evelyn's travels began in the Low Countries and France and wound up in Italy. Twice he came upon Arundel, and each time he was befriended by him and shown the sights. On the second occasion, Evelyn received some travel instructions from the dying nobleman.[12] Later, he

[8] See W. Lee Ustick, "Advice to a Son," *Studies in Philology* 29 (1932), 409–41.

[9] *Diary,* I, 7–8.

[10] Evelyn to Lady Sunderland, December 22, 1688, Ponsonby, *John Evelyn,* 151–52.

[11] *Diary,* May 13, 1661, III, 287–88.

[12] Thomas Howard, *Remembrances of Things Worth Seeing in Italy Given to John Evelyn, 25 April 1646,* John M. Robinson, ed., Roxburghe Club, 1987; Mary F. S. Hervey, *The Life, Correspondence and Collections of Thomas Howard,*

was able to return the favor by preserving some of his friend's collections of Greek antiquities that had been woefully neglected, the so-called Arundel Marbles, setting them up at Oxford where they may still be seen.[13] He remembers the occasion in a note to the "Elysium Britannicum," where he especially commends the use of ancient sculpture to garden decoration and also to "learned Men and Antiquaries."[14]

Life on the Continent, which extended on and off for almost a decade, reinforced Evelyn's *anciennete* and stretched it beyond literature and history to classical art and architecture. In Rome, he had the services of a tour guide and paid homage to the great classical buildings, especially the Pantheon. He agreed with Pliny that the Laocoon was the best of all ancient and modern sculptures. At the Aldobrandini Palace he saw a Roman painting, the only one then known, and he recalls it fondly in the "Elysium Britannicum." He was enraptured by the works of Michelangelo. The Farnese Palace, he wrote, was "built after the ancient manner and in a time when Architecture was but recently recovered from barbarity." St. Peter's, he thought, was "the most stupendious and incomparable basilicam, far surpassing anything in the World and perhapps (Solomon's Temple excepted) any that was ever built."[15] While traveling, he learned to draw and to engrave.[16] Back in France, he translated a couple of works by Roland Fréart, Sieur de Chambray, who had written to expound and celebrate the architecture and painting of the ancients and which Evelyn felt the English had shamefully neglected.[17] He was entirely contemptuous of all things Gothic, even such churches as Salisbury Cathedral and York Minster, and was embarrassed by the squalor of modern London.

Already in Paris, toward the end of his stay, he was recommending travel for its educational value and offering advice.[18] "Youth is the seede-tyme in which the foundation of all things is to be layd," he wrote a few years later, urging the duke of Northumberland to send his son abroad.[19] At the Restoration he encouraged his nephew to visit Italy and to prepare himself by reading the history of Rome so that he might appreciate "what it was before and how it came to the condition you now find it—Illustrious in its very Ruines."[20] To his old companion Thomas Henshaw he wrote, remembering "the agreeable toile we tooke among the ruines and antiquitys, to admire the

---

Earl of Arundel, Cambridge, 1921, 449–55; David Howarth, *Lord Arundel and His Circle,* New Haven, 1985, 214–16; *Diary,* II, 466–67, 479.

[13] Evelyn touchingly describes the deathbed scene (April 1646) in the *Diary,* II, 479. He persuaded Henry Howard to give the marbles to Oxford, "those celebrated and famous Inscriptions Greeke and Latine, with so much cost and Industrie gathered from Greece." See under September 19, 1667, *Diary,* III, 495–96 and note.

[14] "Elysium Britannicum," transcription by John Ingram, 154.

[15] "Elysium Britannicum," 362 (Farnese Palace); *Diary,* II, 255 (St. Peter's).

[16] Some of Evelyn's sketches in Italy are reproduced in the Royal Institute of British Architects, *Catalogue of the Drawings Collection of the Royal Institute of British Architects,* London, 1972, III, 114–15.

[17] The Fréart works were *A Parallel of Antient Architecture with the Modern,* 1664, and *An Idea of the Perfection of Painting,* 1668; see Geoffrey Keynes, *John Evelyn: A Study in Bibliophily with a Bibliography of His Writings,* 2nd ed., Oxford, 1968, 165–72, 191–94.

[18] See *The State of France,* Paris, 1652, reprinted in *Miscellaneous Writings,* 39–95. In general, see George B. Parks, "John Evelyn and the Art of Travel," *Huntington Library Quarterly* 10 (1946–47), 251–76.

[19] Evelyn to Edward Thurland, November 8, 1658, *Corr.,* 249–52.

[20] Evelyn to George Evelyn, March 30, 1664, Christ Church, Oxford, letter book, no. ccxii; cf. clxxxii.

superb buildings, visite the cabinets and curiositys of the virtuosi, the sweete walkes by the bankes of the Tiber, the Via Flaminia, the gardens and villas of that glorious citty."[21] The "Elysium Britannicum" is full of references to the ancient sites and their use to modern gardeners.[22]

Evelyn's chief occupation during the interregnum was to continue educating himself and to preserve and manage his estate. Although he had come to know the king and court in exile, he was passed over for high office, perhaps gratefully, because he did not really approve of life at the Restoration court.[23] Nevertheless, he kept busy contributing to public affairs anyway. He continued to serve the king, as he had in France, with his fluent pen, and also the Anglican church to which he was unswervingly devoted; and he held a number of short-lived appointments to assist in emergencies like the plague and the fire. Some of his services were entirely voluntary, like the various schemes he devised for improving the quality of London life. Sooner or later, he got involved in almost every kind of government activity.[24] He received little enough in return, but he seems to have believed that service was the natural responsibility of a gentleman of means, particularly now that the government of England had been taken out of the hands of the rabble. Honor and happiness, he wrote to the countess of Sunderland, are not likely to be found at court, but belong rather to that "brave and generous soule, that having the advantage of Birth or Laudable Acquisition, can cultivate them to the Production of Things Beneficial to Mankind, the Government, and Eminent Station in which God has plac'd him."[25] When a little tract fell into his hands in 1665, advocating a life of retirement, he immediately dashed off a reply.

The little tract was called *A Moral Essay Preferring Solitude to Publick Employment,* and it appeared anonymously in 1665. Evelyn soon learned that its author was a very busy Scottish advocate named George Mackenzie, who was just then rising to fame in public life. Evelyn's reply was quickly composed and appeared the following year as *Publick Employment and an Active Life Prefer'd to Solitude.* The exchange is not memorable for its originality; the issue had been thoroughly and continuously explored ever since the Renaissance humanists recovered it from the pages of the classical authors.[26] Both writers were pretty much content to repeat the classical commonplaces that they

[21] Evelyn to Henshaw, March 1, 1698, in *Seven Letters of John Evelyn Written between 1665–1703,* Oxford, 1914, 17–19; Marburg, *Mr. Pepys and Mr. Evelyn,* 40–41. See also he nostalgic letter of Evelyn to his nephew's tutor, Walter Pope, March 30, 1664, *Corr.,* IV, 21–22.

[22] See especially the chapters that deal with groves, fountains, garden sculpture and decoration, and even aviaries. John Dixon Hunt treats the whole background amply in his *Garden and Grove: The Italian Renaissance Garden in the English Imagination, 1600–1750,* London, 1986, chaps. 1–2. He notices the "uncanny resemblance" of Italian Renaissance gardens to their antique originals, even though they were largely ignorant of details, until Pompeii and Herculaneum (p. 227 n. 2).

[23] See the various conversations reported by Pepys about "the vanity and vices of the Court" and the "badness of the Government, where nothing but wickedness, and wicked men and women command the King": Robert Latham and William Matthews, eds., *The Diary of Samuel Pepys,* 11 vols., Berkeley, 1970–83, VII, 29, 183, 297–98, 406; VIII, 181, 183. Nevertheless, Evelyn remembered the king fondly at his death as always "very kind to me." See the obituary he composed February 4, 1685, *Diary,* IV, 409–11.

[24] Ponsonby, *John Evelyn,* 75. Evelyn's services on various commissions are listed by E. S. de Beer, "John Evelyn (1620–1706)," *Notes and Records of the Royal Society* 15 (1960), 233.

[25] Evelyn to the countess of Sunderland, December 23, 1688, *Corr.,* III, 431–34.

[26] See Paul O. Kristeller, "The Active and the Contemplative Life in Renaissance Humanism," in Brian Vickers, ed., *Arbeit Musse Meditation: Betrachtungen zur Vita Activa und Vita Contemplativa,* Zurich, 1985, 133–52.

happily borrowed from the ancients and the moderns. But neither of them was entirely serious inasmuch as the advocate of private life (Mackenzie) was fast becoming a public figure, whereas the proponent of public life (Evelyn) was only too eager to cultivate his own garden.[27] Nevertheless, the issue was still alive in Restoration England.

The fact is that the best, perhaps the only, moral justification for the life and privileges of a gentleman lay then, as in ancient Athens and Rome, in direct participation in public life—in a life of service to the community. For the citizens of the ancient commonwealth, the obligation to service was clear and was laid out for all time in the works of the orator-statesman Cicero, the most articulate exponent of the active life in antiquity and the principal source for the advocates of the Italian Renaissance and afterward. Cicero, Evelyn reminded the countess of Sunderland on the eve of the Glorious Revolution, "reproaches a Gentleman for being solicitous about his Fish-pond, when the Commonwealth was in danger."[28] But neither England nor Scotland was a republic under Charles II, and the life of the courtier was no easy substitute for the life of the citizen. Evelyn had helped to restore the king in 1660, but he played no role in the great events of 1688–89. Retirement had always been an option in antiquity, especially under tyranny or empire, and it is no accident that Mackenzie was drawn to the Roman stoics as his principal source.[29] Curiously, both the ancients and the moderns in this argument, as so often elsewhere, drew primarily upon the classics for their inspiration.

Here Evelyn relies directly on Cicero, "one of the great book-writers of the world," and on the Greeks before him, chiefly Isocrates. It was Isocrates, after all, who had first disputed the matter with Plato and defended the political life and the arts of eloquence against the criticism of a contemplative philosophy. And it was Isocrates who had taught Cicero how to defend the ideal of the orator-statesman in *De Officiis* and *De Oratore,* those two handbooks of the *studia humanitatis* that were the best foundation for Evelyn's humanism. According to Isocrates and to Cicero, above all the commonwealth required for its success and its prosperity the active engagement of its members, and

[27] Evelyn noted, "'twere pretty, if at last it should appear, that a Publick Person has all this while contended for Solitude, as it is certain, a Private has done for Action." "To the Reader," *Publick Employment and an Active Life Prefer'd to Solitude,* in the facsimile version of both works edited by Brian Vickers, Delmar, N.Y., 1986, 135. For editions and circumstances, see Keynes, *John Evelyn,* 184–90. In an autobiographical letter to Robert Plot, Evelyn describes himself as "most of all affecting a private and studious life." He was pleased to say that he had "studiously declin'd knighthood, and other honourable employment at Court": September 14, 1667, Christ Church, letter book, fols. 37–38. Typically, some twenty-five years later, he seems to have had some second thoughts: Evelyn to Anthony Wood, May 21, 1691, *Corr.,* III, 465–67.

[28] Evelyn to the countess of Sunderland, October 12, 1688, Christ Church, letter book, fol. 104.

[29] In 1663, Mackenzie wrote an essay entitled "The Roman Stoic." See F. S. Ferguson, "A Bibliography of the Works of Sir George Mackenzie," *Edinburgh Bibliographical Society Transactions,* Edinburgh, 1938, I, 1–60; Andrew Lang, *Sir George Mackenzie,* London, 1909. One of Evelyn's opponents later pointed out that when Epicurus and his followers decided to decline all public employment, they slighted all that *paideia,* or "course of studies consisting of grammar (which in its extent included all Critical Learning, History and Chronology) and Rhetorick, and Logick, even Mathematics"; Henry Stubbe, *Legends no Histories or a Specimen of some Animadversions upon the History of the Royal Society,* London, 1670, n.p. For a time in the mid century, there was a special vogue for the Roman imperial writers Seneca and Tacitus; the classic statement remains George Williamson, *The Senecan Amble: A Study in Prose Form from Bacon to Collier,* London, 1951.

particularly the arts of communication, in a word, all that pertained to classical eloquence. "'Tis plain inhumanity,'" Cicero had said, "to flie the congress and conversation of others." It was a pity, Evelyn added many years later, that young men were so badly prepared in history and eloquence, when they were so important to success in government.[30] Public employment and the active life, Evelyn concluded, were responsible for all the best things in war and peace.

It was a polite exchange, and years later Evelyn was glad to meet Mackenzie and exchange compliments.[31] Pepys was not much impressed by his friend's performance, "though it be pretty for a bye discourse."[32] Evelyn himself apologized to another friend, the poet Abraham Cowley, who had also been advocating retreat. He admitted, "You had reason to be astonish'd at the presumption . . . that I who have so highly celebrated recesse . . . should become an advocate for the enemie." Evelyn assured him that he had not changed his mind; his own "trifling essay" was not meant seriously. On the other hand, he now urged Cowley to write a poem commemorating the activities and services of the Royal Society. The irony may not have been lost on Cowley, who promptly returned a note complimenting Evelyn's contribution to "one of the noblest controversies both modern and ancient."[33] In the middle years of the seventeenth century, there was obviously much to be said on both sides. Perhaps Evelyn's ambiguity is best reflected in his own intermittent service to the state, which in itself is a fair reflection of the condition of public life during the Restoration. It was not easy, whatever one's aspirations, to play Cicero under Charles II.

III

So Evelyn went on proferring well-meaning and platitudinous advice to the young, encouraging their classical skills and their political ambitions. And if the traditional goal of public service was not so obvious for his daughters, he did not, therefore, neglect their education. At the least they might learn how to assist and accompany their husbands.[34] Nevertheless, Evelyn's chief hope rested

[30] "The improvement of a more ornate and gracefull manner of speaking," he wrote, would assure the nation of persons "fit for any honorable imployment, to serve and speake in Parliament, and in Councils; give us good Magistrates and Justices for references at home and in the country: able ambassadors and orators abroad; in a word, qualified patriots and pillars of State, in which this age does not, I feare, abound." Evelyn to William Nicolson, November 10, 1699, *Corr.,* IV, 24; John Nichols, ed., *Letters to and from William Nicolson,* 2 vols., London, 1809, I, 141.

[31] The two had already exchanged polite letters in 1667: see *Miscellaneous Writings,* 503–4. They met in 1690: see *Diary,* V, 12.

[32] Pepys, *Diary,* May 26, 1667, VIII, 236.

[33] See the exchange between Evelyn and Cowley, March 12 and May 13, 1667, *Corr,* III, 349–52, and Cowley's essays, "Of Solitude," "Of Obscurity," and "Of Agriculture," in A. R. Waller, ed., *The English Writings of Abraham Cowley,* 2 vols., Cambridge, 1905–6, II, 316–18, 318–19, 319–20. Evelyn often proclaimed the advantages of a retired life, for example, in the *State of France* (1652) (in *Miscellaneous Writings,* 48); in a letter to Jeremy Taylor (1655) (Ponsonby, *John Evelyn,* 134–35); and in 1667 (following a spate of political activity) in a letter to Robert Plot, September 14 (Christ Church, letter book [1699], 37–38). No doubt much depended on Evelyn's personal political circumstances.

[34] "Women were not born to read authors and censure the learned," Evelyn's wife wrote to her son's tutor, "to compare lives and judge of virtues, to give rules of morality, and sacrifice to the muses." They were meant to serve the family. Mary Evelyn to Ralph Bohun (1672), in Ponsonby, *John Evelyn,* 44–45. But in her will in 1708, she recalls his lifelong concern for her education: *Corr.,* IV, 65. And Evelyn gave much attention to his daughters' education, particularly to his favorite, Mary, who learned to love the classics; he was devastated when she too died young; see *Diary,* IV, 420–31.

with his remaining son, John Evelyn, Jr. He hoped to "give him a good education," he wrote to his friend Christopher Wren, so that he could become, among other things, "a perfect Grecian," and thereby lay a permanent and solid foundation for life.[35] Young Jack's tutor, Ralph Bohun, agreed with Evelyn that "nothing can be as commendable in whatever station he is then to be able to write familiarly in Latine."[36] Eventually, the boy went on to Trinity College, Oxford, the Middle Temple, and a trip to France. While in France, he pleaded with his godfather for a longer stay, on the ground that Cicero had spent a whole year at Athens. "If my Cicero will let me stay here so long too I will endeavor to recover my time and not return empty to follow his steps to link my Greek with my Latine studyes together, and that not only in Philosophy, but also in the practice of Eloquence."[37] Evelyn made him come home.

Somehow Jack never quite measured up to his father's expectations; a natural indolence and too much drink did not help. His Greek and Latin were good enough for him to dabble at literature, but he found it very hard to make his way in the world, despite the best efforts of his father. When he died after a long illness in 1699, Evelyn's only hope for the family was left with his one grandson, then at Oxford.

Once again the old man pinned all his faith and expectations on the education of a little boy. John Evelyn III was sent to Eton where he performed prodigiously, "so that there is no dealing with him in Homer, Virgil, Horace, etc." The great classical scholar Richard Bentley assured him that his grandson was ready for the university, but Evelyn kept him on at Eton for another year to improve his Greek.[38] He meant to take no chances. Hardly a week went by without Evelyn instructing his grandson in what to read or how to compose the Latin letters that might help his prospects.[39] And indeed, all went well. By the time young Jack got to Oxford, his grandfather could boast of his proficiency in law and history, chronology and mathematics, not to mention the flute, fencing, hunting, and gardening.

[35] Evelyn to Wren, April 4, 1665, *Corr.,* III, 304–6. Evelyn recalls his "owne defects in the Greeke tongue and knowledge of its usefulnesse."

[36] See the series of undated letters from Bohun to Evelyn at the British Library, nos. 303–11. Bohun lived with the Evelyn family for five years, according to Evelyn, "well and faithfully performing his Charge"; see *Diary,* December 10, 1670, III, 566. He was rewarded much later by being given the rectory at Wotton.

[37] John Evelyn, Jr., to Sir Richard Browne, Paris, 1676, British Library, Add. MS 15948, fol. 149.

[38] Evelyn to Mrs. Evelyn, January 18, 1697, *Seven Letters of John Evelyn,* 11–14. See also *Diary,* April 23, 1696, V, 236.

[39] Some of the correspondence is summarized in W. G. Hiscock, *John Evelyn and His Family Circle,* London, 1955, 207–11. In a long letter to the young Lord Spencer, Evelyn expounded on the importance of letter writing and the use of classical models. "What should we have done without Ciceroes [letters] and the younger Plinies? to name no more because they were incomparably the best": Evelyn to Lord Spencer, January 15, 1692, Christ Church, letter book (1699), 158–59. To Pepys, he writes that young Jack "not onely keeps but greatly improves his Greek, by directly reading their historys, and now and then, among his other exercises, he turns some passages into Latine; translates select Epistles out of Cicero and Pliny, and letting them lie-by for some time . . . turnes them into Latine again, the better to judge of his improvement": Evelyn to Peyps, January 20, 1703, in J. R. Tanner, ed., *Private Correspondence and Miscellaneous Papers of Samuel Pepys,* London, 1926, 298–302. In 1665 Evelyn was appointed to a committee for refining the English language; his suggestion was to imitate the best of the ancients; see Evelyn to Peter Wyche, June 20, 1665, *Corr.,* III, 309–12; Evelyn to Pepys, October 4, 1689, in R. G. Howarth, ed., *Letters and the Second Diary of Samuel Pepys,* London, 1933, 205–10.

In truth, Jack seemed a worthy heir. When at last it was time for the old man to draw up his final testament—when Evelyn had reached the ripe old age of eighty-four in 1704—he repeated the convictions of a lifetime in a new memoir that was addressed to his now adult grandson. It was, he admitted, only a collection of "hasty notes," and they remained unpublished. As before, Evelyn meant to tie close together the education and the vocation of the aspiring young governor. Thus he hoped that Jack would gain for *his* son "by favour or purchase" some "creditable office," just as he and his father had done before him. It was important for young gentlemen "to Advance themselves . . . by dexterity of the pen, the Latine and the modern Tongues," and so enter the foreign service or even the court, and become secretaries, treasurers, clerks of council, and so on, and thus "become usefull to the publique." Evelyn believed that although nothing belonging to "humanity" should be neglected, "your maine study should be such as we have recommended to us by the most grave and wisest ancestors."[40] Evelyn's *paideia* had not changed much in a lifetime and must have seemed at least as suitable in the new century as it had been in the old. With the classics tucked safely under his belt, John Evelyn III proved a perfectly acceptable, if not a particularly distinguished, heir and country-gentleman.

IV

In dwelling on Evelyn's educational ideas, I have tried to show how the classical authors were assumed by Evelyn to furnish the principal instruction of the man of affairs for practical life. This was the basic ground for seventeenth-century *anciennete*. But I have so far left out of account John Evelyn's commitment to modernity, which was equally strong. How did it arise, and how far was it possible to reconcile it with an admiration for the ancients?[41]

Here, it seems to me, the key lies in the teaching of Francis Bacon, who cast a long shadow over the men of Evelyn's generation. Bacon's scientific credentials have long been disputed and his originality questioned, but he was a powerful exponent for a point of view that I think had particular resonance for men of Evelyn's social position, for the patrons as well as for the practitioners of the new natural science. Evelyn remembers him throughout the "Elysium Britannicum" for his views on nature and gardens. And in the instructions to his grandson, he applauds him as an example of a learned man who was yet "a person in continual employment as a Lawyer, Judge, Privy-Counseller, and in perpetual businesse."[42] But the real influence of Bacon was broader and more pervasive. He taught Evelyn's generation how to reconcile their humanist *paideia* with the new science, how to combine *anciennete* and modernity. And it was this view that Evelyn, with many of his friends, enthusiastically adopted.[43]

[40] *Memoires for my Grand-son,* Geoffrey Keynes, ed., London, 1926, 15, 42–43.

[41] For what follows I have had to tread in the footsteps of Richard Foster Jones, to whose *Ancients and Moderns,* 2nd ed., St. Louis, 1961, I am much indebted, though I have criticized it in the past; see Joseph M. Levine, "Ancients and Moderns Reconsidered," *Eighteenth Century Studies* 15 (1981), 72–89. Very helpful are the many contributions of Michael Hunter, some of them collected now in his *Establishing the New Science: The Experience of the Royal Society,* Woodbridge, 1989, and also his *Science and Society in Restoration England,* Cambridge, 1981, both with useful bibliographical essays.

[42] *Memoires for my Grand-son,* 40.

[43] Their enemies, therefore, had to deny this. According to Henry Stubbe, "The truth is the Lord Bacon is like

The trick was to keep the old idea of the usefulness of the humanities to public life and to recognize the ancient achievement in rhetoric, oratory, poetry, and history, while at the same time calling for a new natural philosophy liberated from all ancient authority. Bacon despised the scholastic teaching of the (still) medieval universities, accepting the humanist criticism of traditional philosophy that it was essentially useless to practical life. By Evelyn's day, Aristotle and the whole scholastic curriculum had come under siege from the young laymen who flooded into the colleges with other things in mind. But the peripatetic teaching remained, despite the growing displeasure of those like Evelyn who would have replaced it, and a quarrel between ancients and moderns quickly developed. Evelyn was dismayed to find in 1699 that his grandson was still being asked to read a scholastic schoolbook at Oxford.[44] What was plainly needed, he thought, was a dose of the Baconian experimental philosophy, but by then Evelyn had been a member of the Royal Society for forty years and had been friends with all the new philosophers from Hooke and Boyle to Newton and Locke.

It was Bacon's genius to see and to articulate more persuasively than anyone else how a new natural philosophy could be practical and serve the commonwealth as fruitfully as classical eloquence.[45] As the physician William Harvey complained, Bacon advocated philosophy like a lord chancellor. But this was just his contemporary appeal. Knowledge, Bacon never tired of saying, was power, and knowledge of nature meant harnessing nature for use. But knowledge of nature could only be derived from experiment and a new logic of induction, from abandoning the imperfect relations of antiquity and the sterile old logic of the schools and starting all over again. Bacon was thus an ancient in respect to the humanities and a modern with respect to science, content pretty much with the achievement of the one but determined to advance the other beyond anything yet known. He saw that the advancement of learning was dependent on cooperation and collaboration, and he tried in the *New Atlantis* to envision the means by which this might be accomplished. Elsewhere he showed exactly what needed still to be done by experiment and how to do it. It is not surprising then that many of the founders of the Royal Society, Evelyn among them, looked to him as their chief inspiration both in theory and in practice.[46] Or that natural science, which had hitherto belonged to the philosopher, should fall into the hands of the gentleman and man of affairs.[47]

---

great piles, when the Sun is not high, they cast an extraordinary shadow over the Earth, which lesseneth as the Sun grows vertical." But he could only find fault with Bacon's account of the sweating sickness in his history of Henry VIII; see Stubbe, *Legends no Histories* (as above, note 28), 28–29.

[44] The work was the *Commentarii Collegii Coimbricensis*, 1601–11; see Evelyn to John Evelyn III, August 5, 1699, Hiscock, *Family Circle,* 211; and Ralph Bohun to Evelyn, n.d., Christ Church, letter book, no. 301. Bohun recognized Aristotle as a great methodizer, but not an experimentalist, and thus incapable of making new discoveries.

[45] For what follows, see Joseph Levine, "Natural History and the New Philosophy: Bacon, Harvey, and the Two Cultures," in *Humanism and History,* Ithaca, N.Y., 1987, 123–54.

[46] Both the Mechanical Committee and the Committee for Collecting Natural Phenomena specifically invoked the *Parasceve,* 1664; see Hunter, *Establishing the New Science,* 92, 104. In 1680 Evelyn reports that he met with the Council of the Royal Society, "and [it] made an order that the next experiments to be examin'd, should be my L Verulam's, and an account to be given of them to the publique from yeare to yeare 'til we had gon through them": *Diary,* June 24, 1680, IV, 205.

[47] For the social composition of the Royal Society, see Michael Hunter, *The Royal Society and Its Fellows, 1660–*

Evelyn's interest in the new science began early and remained always practical; he was never drawn to any speculative system. His concern was for the organization of scientific activity and the accumulation of evidence. And so he read widely in the new literature of natural history and looked everywhere at the cabinets of curiosities that were then becoming fashionable. When a young man asked his advice for a trip abroad in 1657, Evelyn told him not to neglect the excellent recipes he would find, for example, at Montpelier, for perfumes, powders, and pomanders. Gentlemen who despised those things "deprive themselves of many advantages to improve their tyme." "Seeke therefore after nature," he continued, "procure to see experiments, furnish your selfe with receipts, models, and things which are rare." With such a preparation, the young man might return to England to enjoy the fruits of his experience "either by serving in some public employment (if the integrity of the Tymes invite you), or by securing your own felicity . . . in a private unenvied condition . . . of piety and knowledge."[48]

It was just before the Restoration that Evelyn concocted a scheme of his own for encouraging the new learning. Perhaps it was his friendship with Samuel Hartlib, that great Baconian promoter of all devices for the advancement of learning during the Commonwealth, that encouraged his speculation. Among other things, Hartlib had promoted a follow-up to the *New Atlantis,* which was called *Macaria* (1641), and gone on to advocate almost every kind of educational reform and technological innovation that he could discover on the Baconian assumption that knowledge could advance only by communication. By 1655 Evelyn knew that "honest and learned" person, and they corresponded busily afterward. The two men shared a particular interest in "hortulane affairs" and the bringing up of children, although they were on opposite sides of the civil war.[49] Through Hartlib, Evelyn met another kindred spirit in John Beale, also a Baconian, gardener, and advocate of the new learning. In a letter of 1662, Beale welcomes the "Elysium Britannicum" and hopes that the poets Denham and Waller will write verses for it.[50]

1700, Chalfont St. Giles, 1982. According to a contemporary (1710) source, "Most of their Members were either Men of considerable Fortune and Quality as well as Learning, or such as make their Studies their Business," 27.

[48] Evelyn to Mr. Maddox (on behalf of Dr. Needham), January 10, 1658, *Corr.,* III, 224–26; *Diary,* III, 222n. See also Evelyn to Mr. Carter, November 27, 1665, advising him on a trip to Italy: Christ Church Corr., no. 264; and Evelyn to his grandson, advising him to add natural philosophy and mathematics to his Latin and Greek: *Memoires for my Grandson,* 37.

[49] *Diary,* November 27, 1655, III, 162–63. In a very long letter of February 4, 1660, Evelyn combines the two; see Christ Church, letter book, no. clxiii. He even attributes the late troubles to a neglect of education: "I know so perfectly the capacity of Children to suck in and comprehend the most materiall instructions, that I have bin astonish't at the Experiment, and amaz'd at the great remissement of Parents." The year before, he writes from Paris to thank Hartlib for taking care of the advancement of learning and keeping him up-to-date: "I hope God bringing me back into my owne Country, to contribute to that so usefull worke": October 24, 1659, British Library, Add. MS 15948, fols. 67–68. For more on the *Macaria,* see Charles Webster, "The Authorship and Significance of *Macaria,*" *Past and Present* 56 (1972), 34–48, and for more on the Hartlib circle, see idem, *The Great Instauration: Science, Medicine and Reform, 1626–1660,* London, 1975, and George H. Turnbull, *Hartlib, Dury and Comenius,* Liverpool, 1947.

[50] Hiscock, *Family Circle,* 51–52. See also Hartlib to Evelyn, September 24, 1659, and other related correspondence in British Library, Add. MS 15948, fol. 66; for Beale, see Mayling Stubbs, "John Beale, Philosophical Gardener of Hertfordshire, I," *Annals of Science* 39 (1982), 469.

Evelyn's scheme was proposed to Robert Boyle, a congenial friend, who was already the most distinguished and influential Baconian philosopher in England. Because the times were unpropitious—it was the last troubled year of the interregnum and Evelyn was thinking of the fall of the Roman Empire to the barbarians—Evelyn thought that neither Solomon's House nor a mathematical college was likely to be realized and that a monastic retreat was more in order. The "promotion of experimental knowledge" was to be its principal end, and all of its arrangements, including provision of a laboratory, library, repository, an orchard, several gardens, and an aviary, were to be directed to that purpose. Evelyn worked it out in detail and with a relish, although how seriously, it is hard to say.[51] He even designed a building for it in an unmistakably classical style, with a broken pediment and freestanding statues, a columned chapel with scrolled pediment and cupola—thus joining the ancients to the moderns in his usual way.[52] With the Restoration and the Royal Society, it was, like some other of Evelyn's schemes, forgotten.

It was another matter with the Royal Society to which Evelyn was swiftly elected.[53] For the rest of his long life he served it faithfully, attending meetings, sitting on committees, presiding once in a while over its proceedings, and contributing occasional papers. His best service may have been to praise its efforts to the king and to the country and urge others to write in its defense.[54] Shortly after it was founded, Evelyn dedicated a little book he had translated in France to the new lord chancellor, with an introduction praising the society, which he was the first to baptize as "Royal," and for which he received its thanks. It was dedicated to Clarendon as the true successor to Francis Bacon for having helped "to set upon a Design no way beneath that of his Solomon's House."[55] The Royal Society, Evelyn declared roundly, was an assembly as accomplished as any in the history of the world.

In its very first month, the society called upon Evelyn to bring in his "Circle of Mechanical Trades," his history of engraving and etching, and his observations on trees.[56] All fell naturally within the Baconian (and Hartlibian) program for the advancement of practical knowledge, and eventually Evelyn was able to produce something of each. In 1662 he published his *Sculptura,* which he dedicated to Boyle and in which he was able to announce the new art of mezzotint.[57] In 1664, he published his most successful and ambitious book, the first to appear under the official auspices of the Royal Society and the result of much cooperation—*Sylva; or a Discourse of Forest-Trees,* to which was annexed a treatise on cider that he called *Pomona,* and *Kalendarium Hortense: or, The gard'ners alma-*

[51] Evelyn to Boyle, September 3, 1659, *Corr.,* III, 261–67.

[52] See the illustrations reproduced in Hunter, *Establishing the New Science,* 181–84, pl. 11.

[53] See *Diary,* January 2, 1661, III, 266 and note.

[54] "His Majestie was pleased to discourse with me concerning several particulars relating to our Society and the Planet Saturn, etc., as he sat at Supper in the withdrawing roome to his Bed-Chamber": *Diary,* May 14, 1661, III, 288

[55] Gabriel Naude, *Instructions for Erecting of a Library,* John Evelyn, trans. and John C. Dana, ed., Cambridge, 1903, ded. 1x–xxvi; *Diary,* III, 303–4, 306. See Keynes, *John Evelyn,* no. 30, 103–8.

[56] *Diary,* January 16, 1661, III, 268. See E. S. de Beer, "John Evelyn (1620–1706)," *Notes and Records of the Royal Society* 15 (1960), 233.

[57] Keynes, *John Evelyn,* no. 33, 116–22. *Sculptura* was presented to the society in June; see *Diary,* III, 325; and C. F. Bell, ed., *Evelyn's Sculptura: With the Unpublished Second Part,* Oxford, 1906.

nac.[58] It was this last work that inspired his friend Cowley to write *The Garden* and praise Evelyn. Later he read the society a discourse on earth and vegetation and was asked to print it.[59]

V

Next to education, gardening was the great passion in Evelyn's life. All his days he struggled to complete what was to have been his most ambitious achievement, the still unfinished and unpublished "Elysium Britannicum."[60] Through the cultivation of the soil and the cultivation of the mind, Evelyn hoped to give shape to the world, to turn life into art. But the growing quarrel between the ancients and the moderns threatened to destroy the nice harmony that Evelyn hoped to attain. Slowly, and a little reluctantly, Evelyn was forced to take sides.

In his first draft of the "Elysium Britannicum," Evelyn sketched out a long chapter on the history of gardens, which he described to his new friend Dr. Thomas Browne in 1660. Inevitably, he divided his survey into ancient and modern gardens, with the Middle Ages typically excluded. (For Evelyn and most of his contemporaries, the prejudice of Renaissance humanism was reinforced by the prejudice of English Protestantism to dismiss the Middle Ages as generally dark and barbarous.) Evelyn began with the Garden of Eden and the Elysian fields and proceeded to enumerate the most famous gardens of Greece and Rome; he then listed the most notable modern gardens in Europe, the Near East, and America, not forgetting his older brother's grounds in Surrey, "surpassing any else in England," and his own poor plot, perpetually green and not completely unworthy.[61] Jeremy Taylor was not just flattering Evelyn when he referred to Sayes Court as "Tusculanum," after Pliny's ancient villa.[62]

[58] Copies were delivered to the Royal Society February 16, 1664, and to the king, the lord treasurer, and the lord chancellor; see Keynes, *John Evelyn,* no. 40, pp. 130–40; no. 52, pp. 148–51; and no. 57, pp. 154–56. For its collaborative character, see Michael Hunter, "An Experiment in Corporate Enterprise," in *Establishing the New Science* (as above, note 40), 76.

[59] *Diary,* April 29, 1675, IV, 62–63. The work was published the following year as *A Philosophical Discourse of Earth;* see Keynes, *John Evelyn,* 206–11. Other contributions to the society by Evelyn may be followed in Thomas Birch, *The History of the Royal Society of London,* 4 vols., London, 1756–57, for which an index of proper names has been prepared in the *Notes and Records of the Royal Society* 28 (1973), 263–329. Evelyn drew on his observations abroad to make contributions to Boyle's *New Experiments and Observations Touching the History of Cold,* 1665; Hooke's *Micrographia,* 1665; and John Houghton's *Collection for the Improvement of Husbandry and Trade,* 1681; he also contributed several papers to *Philosophical Transactions;* see Keynes, *John Evelyn,* 260–62.

[60] In July 1679, Evelyn writes to Beale about what he has "written and collected for above these 20 yeares upon this fruitfull and inexaustible subject . . . not yet fully digested to my mind . . . I am almost out of hope that I shall ever have strength to bring it to maturity": *Corr.,* III, 190–92. In the preface to the *Acetaria; a Discourse of Sallets,* London, 1699, he is still writing wistfully about the enormous work, much of which has since been lost, but whose table of contents survives there. It was printed first about 1660 in a single sheet; see British Library, Add. MS 19950, fol. 143.

[61] Evelyn to Thomas Browne, January 28, 1660, in Geoffrey Keynes, ed., *The Works of Sir Thomas Browne,* 4 vols., London, 1964, IV, 274. For the date, see E. S. de Beer, "The Correspondence between Sir Thomas Browne and John Evelyn," *The Library,* 4th ser., 19 (1938–39), 103–6. The chapter was intended as book III, chapter 7 and was, according to Evelyn, "in a manner finished by itselfe." But for the rest, he supplied only brief heads for Browne, probably in the form of the broadsheet "Plan of a Royal Garden," which survives in the British Library, Add. MS 19950, fol. 143. In the "Elysium Britannicum," the essay appears to have occupied book III, chapter 9, pp. 727–866; as republished in the *Acetaria,* it has become chapter 10. It does not appear to have survived.

[62] Taylor to Evelyn, April 16, 1656, *Corr.,* III, 211–13. The garden was laid out in 1653; it was about a hundred

Evelyn does not seem to have been eager at this point to make a direct comparison between the ancients and the moderns, perhaps remembering Browne's skepticism on the matter. According to Browne, apart from the Garden of Eden, about which the world was well informed, "wee know not whether the ancient gardens doe equal those of later times, or those at present in Europe."[63] He may well have doubted it, but Evelyn's horticultural friend John Beale was prepared to side squarely with the ancients on this matter. Although he was fully convinced "that God in later dayes very amply improvd our knowledge, and hath given us the Light of many wonderfull experiments," he assured Evelyn that God's handiwork in Eden outdid anything modern and that his ancestors had continued the tradition of the first monarchy more magnificently and heroically—more divinely—"then can be paralleld by our narrowe, mimicall way."[64] Jeremy Taylor suggested that Evelyn call his great work "Paradisus" rather than "Elysium Britannicum," "seeing you intend it to the purposes of piety as well as pleasure."[65] But Evelyn held to the original title and to that combination of classical and Christian that is characteristic of his humanism—to Elysium *and* to Eden. When he was finally drawn into the controversy later in life, he preferred to divide the question; from the testimony of the "Elysium Britannicum" manuscript, it looks as though he preferred the ancients for design and ornament and the moderns for horticultural science.[66] It was the Baconian solution: *anciennete* for the arts of imitation, modernity for the arts of accumulation. Gardening, it seems, required both. Evelyn had already declared his preference for the ancients in eloquence and education and art and architecture but for the moderns in natural history and philosophy. His position in the quarrel followed naturally enough.

But I have gotten a little ahead of my story. It was in the early days of the Royal Society that the first open quarrel between the ancients and the moderns occurred in England. It is true that there had been some occasional feuding before, but it was the claims of Evelyn and his fellows that led to a great public altercation.[67] No need to rehearse the details here. Some of the members were con-

acres. Pepys admired it extravagantly; see Pepys' *Diary,* VI, 97, 253. A manuscript "Directions for the Gardiner at Sayscourt" has been edited and published by Geoffrey Keynes, Nonesuch, 1932.

[63] See the manuscript passage that seems to have been meant for Browne's *Garden of Cyrus,* in *Works of Thomas Browne,* I, 227. The *Garden of Cyrus* was first printed with the *Hydriotaphia* in 1658.

[64] Beale is quoted in Michael Leslie, "The Spiritual Husbandry of John Beale," in Michael Leslie and Timothy Raylor, eds., *Culture and Cultivation in Early Modern England: Writing and the Land,* Leicester, 1992, 164. Douglas Chambers points out that Beale, too, combined classical humanism and Christian purpose; see his "'Wild Pastorall Encounter': John Evelyn, John Beale and the Regeneration of Pastoral in the Mid-Seventeenth Century," ibid., 181. In natural science and technology, Beale was an explicit modern; see, for example, Beale to Hartlib (forwarded to Evelyn), March 16, 1660, British Library, Add. MS 15948, fols. 92–94.

[65] Taylor to Evelyn, February 10, 1660, *Corr.,* III, 275–77. There is a swift general survey of the subject in John Prest, *The Garden of Eden: The Botanic Garden and the Re-Creation of Paradise,* New Haven, 1981, with the "Elysium Britannicum" treated at 47–48.

[66] Thus, the effigies of great men (such as Alexander the Great and Julius Caesar) could serve as examples to virtue when placed in homes and gardens the way the ancients had done, when "Art became a piece of State": "Elysium Britannicum," 155.

[67] R. F. Jones describes some of the background, as well as recounting the squabble over the Royal Society, in *Ancients and Moderns.* Unfortunately, Jones did not see that the proponents of scientific modernity (such as Evelyn) could side with the ancients in other matters.

cerned at the indifference and occasional mockery of the new philosophy by the general public—perhaps even the king himself—who did not always seem to appreciate its claims. For his part, Evelyn never lost an opportunity to promote the society with Charles, as in the panegyric he addressed to the king in 1661, in which he assured him of immortality in founding an institution that would "improve practical and experimental knowledg, beyond all that has been hitherto attempted, for the Augmentation of Science, and universal good of Man-kind."[68]

More seriously, some of the humanists, such as the classical scholar Meric Casaubon and the cleric Robert South, saw the emphasis on natural science as a danger to religion and the authority of the classics.[69] Casaubon was worried particularly by what he thought was the excessively practical concern of the experimental philosophy. He tried to defend *all* the ancient learning—Aristotle *and* the literary classics—against the upstart experimentalists.[70] As a result of these criticisms, some members of the Royal Society thought it necessary to defend themselves, first through a *History,* drawn up by Thomas Sprat, and then through a series of publications by Joseph Glanvill; but these were met by further attacks and much confusion, especially from the many pamphlets of the eccentric and relentless Henry Stubbe.[71] Throughout the quarrel, the moderns were often matched explicitly against the ancients, but for the most part the quarrel was confined to the claims of natural philosophy against the Aristotelians.[72] Despite the fears of Casaubon, no one seems to have thought seriously about undermining the authority of the ancients in literature or history, and both Sprat and Glanvill preferred to use the weapons of classical rhetoric against their opponents. Neither had much direct experience with natural science, which they had to obtain secondhand.[73] Sprat was at great pains to show that the new science posed no danger to the education of the schools or "the old talkative arts." In this, as in everything else, he remained a proper Baconian.[74] He believed that the

[68] *An Apologie for the Royal Party,* 1659, and the work in which the quote appears, *A Panegyric to Charles the Second,* 1661, Geoffrey Keynes, ed., Augustan Reprint Society, no. 28 (1951), 14.

[69] South gave an oration at Oxford on July 9, 1669, since lost, which apparently "consisted of satyrical invectives against Cromwell, fanaticks, the Royal Society, and new philosophy." Evelyn thought it all "very foolish and untrue, as well as unreasonable": *Diary,* July 9, 1669, III, 531–32. South had already condemned the society in 1667: *Sermons Preached upon Several Occasions,* I, Oxford, 1823, 373–75. See Beale to Oldenburg, June 1, 1667, in A. Rupert Hall and Marie Boas Hall, eds., *The Correspondence of Henry Oldenburg,* Madison, 1966, III, 425–30 and note; Marjorie Nicolson, *Pepys' Diary and the New Science,* Charlottesville, 1965, 159.

[70] Meric Casaubon, *A Letter to Peter du Moulin,* Cambridge, 1669, facsimile in Michael Spiller, *Concerning Natural Experimental Philosophie: Meric Casaubon and the Royal Society,* The Hague, 1980, app. I. Spiller also provides some extracts from Casaubon's unpublished "On Learning," 1667, and a long introduction. But see Michael Hunter "Ancients, Moderns, Philologists, and Scientists," *Annals of Science* 39 (1982), 187–92.

[71] Even his biographer finds Stubbe's motives in entering the fray unclear; see James Jacob, *Henry Stubbe: Radical Protestantism and the Early Enlightenment,* Cambridge, 1983, chap. 5. He was certainly a more complicated and puzzling figure, and less consistently "ancient" than appears in Jones. For more on Glanvill, see Jackson I. Cope, *Joseph Glanvill, Anglican Apologist,* St. Louis, 1956.

[72] See the exchange between Stubbe and Glanvill quoted by Jones, with his comment, *Ancients and Moderns,* 338.

[73] For Sprat's facility as a writer rather than as a scientist, see *Diary,* IV, 188; and Michael Hunter, "Latitudinarianism and the 'Ideology' of the Royal Society: Thomas Sprat's *History of the Royal Society* (1667) Reconsidered," *Establishing the New Science* (as above, note 40), 49–50. Hunter also supplies an up-to-date account of the composition of the work, with some lost marginalia in Evelyn's copy and some useful references to the Evelyn-Beale correspondence about it.

[74] Thomas Sprat, *The History of the Royal Society,* Jackson I. Cope and H. W. Jones, eds., St. Louis, 1958, 35–36; and pt. 3, sect. ii, "Experiments will not injure Education," 323–27.

experimental program of the Royal Society was a practical realization of Bacon's theories, and he used Bacon's *Sylva Sylvarum* to frame the long narrative of its work.[75]

Evelyn had no trouble lining up on the side of the "moderns" against Casaubon and Stubbe. He was one of the members who first selected Sprat for the job of publicizing the society, and he encouraged the enterprise from start to finish, even coaxing Cowley to write some introductory verses for the *History,* while he (perhaps with his friend Beale) designed the frontispiece.[76] He was embarrassed to be singled out by Glanvill in *Plus Ultra* among the proponents of modern learning, but happy to applaud Glanvill's victory over his "snarling adversary."[77] He agreed with Beale on the need to protect the Royal Society and proclaim the advancement of learning, and seems to have considered publishing something on the subject himself.[78] Meanwhile he repeated the Baconian idea that the first business of the society was to gather a natural history as the foundation for higher things. Progress in knowledge lay in the accumulation of reliable information, and that is where the advantage of the moderns lay, and where Evelyn himself could hope to make a modest contribution.[79]

When Evelyn brought out a new edition of *Sylva* in 1679, he rewrote the preface for the occasion and turned it into a new defense of the Royal Society. His essay is a fulsome reiteration of the Baconian arguments for natural history against the skeptics.[80] It had been necessary, Evelyn agreed, for the members first to clear away the rubbish, and so free themselves from the tyranny of opinion; but this was not done through "an abolition of the old" so much as through the introduction of the new. Evelyn and his friends did not like to be thought of as rebels and never imagined undoing the classical *paideia* in which they had all been trained. Even as they adopted the possibilities of modernity for natural science, they remained more than ever convinced of the equally practical and coordinate value of *anciennete.*

It was this peculiar combination of activities—dabbling in science *and* imitating the classics, collecting natural curiosities *and* old coins and manuscripts—that distinguished them and labeled them as "virtuosi." This certainly was how Evelyn saw himself and how others represented him. In

[75] See H. Fisch and H. W. Jones, "Bacon's Influence on Sprat's *History of the Royal Society,*" *Modern Language Quarterly* 12 (1951), 399–406; and Paul Wood, "Thomas Sprat's *History of the Royal Society,*" *British Journal of the History of Science* 13 (1980), 1–26.

[76] See Michael Hunter, *Science and Society in Restoration England,* Cambridge, 1981, app., 194–97. Cowley's verses, "To the Royal Society," repeat the views of Evelyn and Beale.

[77] Evelyn to Glanvill, June 24, 1668, *Corr.,* III, 356–57. Glanvill had praised *Sylva* and "Elysium Britannicum," as well as Evelyn's contributions to sculpture, painting, and architecture, "and the like practical useful things with which he hath enrich't it." *Plus Ultra,* London, 1686, 73–74.

[78] Perhaps this is the long letter to Electra (Mrs. Blagge, later Lady Godolphin), in the Christ Church letter book, where he writes of the Royal Society, "our businesse is not to raise a new theorie of Philosophie, but collect plenty of Materials by new and joint Attempts for the Work." Materials must be gathered even "before the foundation is layd or any superstructure dream't of." The exchange with Beale, 1668–69, remains unpublished at Christ Church.

[79] "The Members of the Royal Society bring in occasional Specimens, not compleat Systemes, but as Materials and particulars which may in time amount to a rich and considerable Magazine," and which will lead, eventually, "to a most august and noble structure." Evelyn to Beale, July 27, 1670, Christ Church, letter book, no. cccxxix.

[80] Evelyn here echoes a letter he had written to Cowley in 1667 urging him to contribute to the cause: "In a word our Registers have outdon Pliny, Porta, and Alexis, and all experimentalists, nay, the great Verulam himselfe, and have made a noble and more faithful collection of real secrets, usefull and instructive, than has hitherto been shown." Evelyn to Cowley, March 12, 1667, *Corr.,* III, 349–51.

1657 he received the dedication to a translation of Gassendi's life of Peiresc, *The Mirrour of True Nobility,* where he was extolled for possessing, along with his French predecessor, a "sprightly curiosity [that] left nothing unreacht into, in the vast all-comprehending Dominions of Nature and Art." "The compleatly-knowing man," the translator continued, "must be Janus-fac'd, to take cognizance of Times past . . . as well as of the late-past, or present times wherein he lives." He must, if you please, be both an ancient and a modern.[81] A couple of years later, Evelyn produced his own example of the ideal type in a brief life of Signor Giacomo Favi, which he prefixed to his *Sculptura,* "as an Encouragement to the gentlemen of our Nation."[82] "This curious person," he wrote admiringly, overlooked no field of human accomplishment, all the while behaving in a "noble, disinterested and agreeable fashion and manner of conversation." Among many other things, Favi actually intended, so Evelyn had heard, "to compile, and publish a Compleat Cycle and History of Trades." He was, in a word, all that Evelyn had ever hoped for in himself.

VI

Yet not everyone was convinced. Sir William Temple was a country gentleman, like Evelyn, who had been much abroad and who had played a great role in politics until he retired to cultivate his gardens. In old age he could reflect on the frustrations of a life of action and prefer the quiet of the countryside; his essay "Upon the Gardens of Epicurus" sounds almost like a reply to Evelyn's youthful work on the active life. Evelyn visited Temple's gardens twice at least over the years and admired them extravagantly.[83] Both men loved the classical authors, but Temple had been able, even better than Evelyn, to use them in his public career and assimilate them into his life. He developed a Ciceronian style, lucid and mellifluous, that was in marked contrast to the baroque periods of Evelyn. But he deliberately denigrated natural philosophy, both new and old, insisting that the only things that were worth the attention of a gentleman were the classical humanities. He was in this respect much more an old-fashioned humanist than a newfangled virtuoso. In a little essay in 1690, he set out his thoughts on the matter and provoked the climactic episode in the quarrel between the ancients and moderns in England, the Battle of the Books.[84]

Once again some members of the Royal Society felt the slight and thought that a reply was necessary. Evelyn was now an old man and no longer so active, but he followed events closely,

[81] *The Mirrour of True Nobility and Gentility,* W. Rand, trans., London, 1657, sig. A3v-A4. See Walter E. Houghton, "The English Virtuoso in the Seventeenth Century," *Journal of the History of Ideas* 3 (1942), 51–73, 190–219. For Evelyn's predecessor, see Georges Cahen-Salvador, *Un Grand Humaniste Peiresc, 1580–1637,* Paris, 1951.

[82] It is taken, Evelyn says, from an essay on the utility of travel by Samuel Sorbière. Here I quote from the preface of the Bell edition of *Scupltura* (as above, note 56).

[83] *Diary,* August 25, 1678, and March 28, 1688, IV, 143, 576. In *Silva,* 4th ed., London, 1706, Evelyn remembers "the late elegant and accomplished Sir W. Temple" leaving his heart to be buried in his garden at his death, Ponsonby, *John Evelyn,* 319.

[84] Temple's essay of 1685 was printed in *Miscellanea, The Second Part,* 1690, and is reprinted from the 1692 edition of *Five Miscellaneous Essays,* Samuel Holt Monk, ed., Ann Arbor, 1963, 1–36. I have tried to anatomize the quarrel in my "Ancients and Moderns Reconsidered," *Eighteenth Century Studies* 15 (1981), 72–89, and to tell the whole long story in my *Battle of the Books: History and Literature in Augustan England,* Ithaca, N.Y., 1991.

particularly when it turned out that two of the main participants were friends. The society turned first to one of these, William Wotton, a brilliant young man who had recently become a member and distinguished himself by his knowledge of the ancient and modern languages, as well as the new sciences. Evelyn had met him as a child and been astonished by his precocity.[85] In 1694 Wotton replied to Temple with his *Reflections upon Ancient and Modern Learning* and immediately won Evelyn's applause. Wotton argued that the moderns had exceeded the ancients in all the fields of natural science and philosophy, although he pretty much conceded the humanities to the ancients. On receiving a copy, Evelyn was jubilant and wrote at once to Pepys, who was equally delighted.[86] Temple replied, others joined the fray, and the battle grew more acrimonious, but Evelyn stood fast with his friend and the opinions of a lifetime.

Perhaps the only new ingredient in the contest was the claim Wotton now made for modern scholarship, and this soon became the nub of the quarrel. Wotton insisted that modern philology and antiquities had given modern scholars an advantage both of method and substance unknown to previous ages.[87] With their aid, the whole past could be recovered more fully and accurately than ever before. Temple protested but supplied new fuel to the enemy by claiming as a classical author and one of the greatest of the ancient writers, the early Greek tyrant Phalaris, whose letters were still standard in the schools, although they had begun to be suspected as spurious. Wotton persuaded Richard Bentley, Evelyn's other young scholar friend, to help him out with a dissertation to prove the epistles fraudulent, and thus show by example the superiority of modern philology to anything ancient in interpreting authors and understanding the past.[88] Evelyn and his friends saw that scholarship, like natural science, was cumulative and progressive, and that the moderns, who were really ancients in point of time, as Bacon had insisted, could still stand on the shoulders of their predecessors and see farther than they.

The quarrel over Phalaris was too long and complicated to rehearse here.[89] Evelyn was not a philologist, but he did not have to be told by Wotton and Bentley how the manuscripts of classical authors could be improved by the collations and elucidations of modern critics, or how classical scholarship could generally advance the knowledge of the past. As long ago as 1666, he had advised the lord chancellor on the need to print the classics in England in correct, fully annotated editions

[85] July 6, 1679, *Diary,* IV, 172–73.

[86] See the exchange of letters, July 7 and August 10, 1694, Pepys, *Letters and the Second Diary,* R. G. Howarth, ed., London, 1933, 242–43, 247.

[87] In *Reflections upon Ancient and Modern Learning,* London, 1694, Wotton devotes the whole of chapter 27 to philology, pages 310–21.

[88] Richard Bentley, "A Dissertation upon the Epistles of Phalaris," appended to Wotton's *Reflections upon Ancient and Modern Learning,* 2nd ed., London, 1697.

[89] See Levine, *Battle,* chaps. 2–3.

[90] Evelyn to the earl of Clarendon, November 27, 1666, *Corr.,* III, 346–48. Sprat also acknowledges the useful work of the "Criticks and Philologists" who first rescued the ancients from the neglect of the Middle Ages, but cautions against remaining satisfied with the past: *History of the Royal Society,* 24–25. There is an unfinished work by Evelyn, "Of Manuscripts," in *Miscellaneous Writings* (as above, note 6), 433–48.

[91] Bentley to Evelyn, April 21, 1698, in Christopher Wordsworth, ed., *The Correspondence of Richard Bentley,* 2 vols., London, 1842, I, 167. Levine, *Battle,* 69.

like the Dutch variorums that Temple had disparaged.[90] In this matter, typically, he was ready again to throw in with the moderns and side with Bentley. And so, when the critics ganged up on the young philologist after his attack on Phalaris, Evelyn was among the few who remained steadfast.[91] Evelyn lived long enough to read Bentley's triumphant riposte (1699), although he also lived to see the resilience of the ancients, led by Swift and Pope, whose wicked satires kept their cause alive into the new century. The quarrel between imitation and accumulation, *anciennete* and modernity, would not easily be resolved.

If Evelyn was willing to stand by his modern friends, they were more than willing to reciprocate. It was just at this time, just when the battle had begun, that Bentley helped Evelyn to publish his new treatise on coins, *Numismata,* and Wotton to edit Evelyn's latest edition of *Sylva,* both of which proclaimed the superiority of modern learning. *Numismata* was subtitled *A Discourse of Medals Ancient and Modern,* and in it Evelyn usefully surveyed the field, justifying those "Vocal Monuments of Antiquity," and explaining their great use to modern historical scholarship.[92] In *Sylva* we have seen him pleading the case for the Royal Society and modern experimental science.[93] It was just about this time that he was also called upon to contribute to that wonderful epitome of modern antiquarian learning—the reissue of William Camden's *Britannia,* and he responded with some advice and some notes for the county of Surrey. Evelyn clearly knew and identified with all the latest and most active proponents of modern scholarship.[94] Once, during the Phalaris controversy, Bentley tried to organize a regular meeting in his lodgings of the most famous of the moderns: Wren, Locke, Newton, "and I hope when in Town Mr. Evelyn." It does not seem to have transpired.[95]

Under the circumstances, it is hardly surprising to find Wotton responding in his turn with a whole new chapter on gardening for the second edition of *Reflections upon Ancient and Modern Learning,* and calling on Evelyn for help. The old man was only too glad to oblige.[96] "The antients," he was now prepared to say, "had certainly nothing approaching the elegancy of the present age." What they called "gardens" were only spacious plots of ground with shady trees arranged in walks and surrounded by porticos, pillars, and other decorations. Of course, Evelyn admired these and

[92] *Numismata,* London, 1697, 2–3, 51, 64, 72. Evelyn had already instructed Pepys on the value of coins and medals to history and antiquities (with some related matters) in a letter, August 12, 1689, *Corr.,* III, 435–56. (It is dated August 26 in the copy reproduced in the *Carl Pforzheimer Library: English Literature, 1475–1700,* 3 vols., New York, 1940, III, 1216–26.) See Levine, *Battle,* 338–42.

[93] He adds a marginal note to the new edition against those "Malevolents" who had tried to divide the Royal Society from Oxford University, and welcomes their present close association. "To the Reader," *Silva,* n.p.

[94] For the "modernity" of antiquarian scholarship, see "The Antiquarian Enterprise, 1500–1800," in *Humanism and History* (as above, note 44), 73–106; and Levine, *Battle,* 327–73. For Evelyn and the *Britannia,* see ibid., 329.

[95] Bentley to Evelyn, April 21, 1698, *Correspondence of Richard Bentley,* I, 152.

[96] Among other things, Evelyn sent Wotton a copy of a poem on gardens by René Rapin without mentioning that his son had once translated it into English. The *Hortorum libri IV,* Paris, 1665, was a Virgilian imitation, or rather continuation, much in keeping with Rapin's critical stance in favor of the ancients over the moderns. Wotton especially recommends the dissertation that was appended entitled *De universa hortensis culturae disciplina,* with its historical chapters, book IV, 6–7. Wotton used it, and Evelyn included some of the poem in his second edition of *Sylva.* Another translation by James Gardiner appeared in 1706 and has been reprinted with an introduction by Irving T. McDonald, Holy Cross Press, 1932.

advocated their imitation in the "Elysium Britannicum." But his mind was now set on helping Wotton and extolling the modern achievement. The ancients, he continued, cared little for flowers and had less variety in their fruits and vegetables. "Plinie indeede enumerates a world of vulgar plants and olitories, but they fall infinitely short of our physic gardens, books and herbals, every day augmented by our sedulous botanists and brought from all over the world." Their best writers had been very industrious, but they could not stand up against the moderns, "so exceedingly of late improv'd."[97] Here Evelyn provided the usual bibliography, not forgetting to include the Royal Society's *Philosophical Transactions*.

Wotton was grateful for the letter, which he closely followed in his chapter in *Reflections,* and where, much to Evelyn's embarrassment, he found himself singled out for special praise.[98] Evelyn's *Sylva,* Wotton pointed out, furnished a complete treatment of the modern woodman's skill, and so clearly demonstrated the modern superiority over the ancients, inasmuch as the ancients had known almost nothing about the matter. Evelyn's work "out-does all that Theophrastus and Pliny have said on that Subject."[99] Nor did the ancients know much about cider, as Evelyn's *Pomona* also showed. As for gardens, it appears unlikely that Wotton got a look at the "Elysium Britannicum," though if he had, he might have found some further fuel for his argument about the superiority of the moderns in the kinds and techniques of modern gardening. But like Evelyn, he would probably have been willing to concede much to the ancients also in planning and ornament.

The Battle of the Books continued well beyond Evelyn's lifetime. Its chief merit was to clarify the issues in the old argument between the ancients and the moderns, even though it did not resolve them. It left the field divided pretty much as Evelyn had found it.[100] All during his life, he had taken an interest in the whole realm of learning, assuming that it could somehow be fit together nicely in the life of a virtuoso, and to the end he did not waver. For eighty-five years he clung to the belief that education could shape and improve the life of the gentleman, and he welcomed both the new sciences and the old humanities with the same Baconian justification that together they could bring about practical benefit for the whole community. The "Elysium Britannicum" was meant to be a compound of ancient art and planning with modern science and technology, Evelyn's tribute to the best of past and present, and his conviction that the garden, like human nature, could be molded into a shape that was both beautiful and useful. This placed him necessarily somewhere between the ancients and the moderns, closer no doubt to Wotton and Bentley, but like them still infatuated with the old Greeks and Romans and still willing to use them as the models for all public communication. The fact that he could not quite assimilate them into either his life or his prose style may say more about the times than it does about Evelyn's ambitions. "It is a common observation," Sprat remarks, "that men's studies are various, according to the different courses of life, to which they apply them-

[97] Evelyn to Wotton, October 28, 1696. *Corr.,* IV, 9–11.

[98] Evelyn to Wotton, June 26, 1697, Christ Church Corr.

[99] Wotton, *Reflections upon Ancient and Modern Learning,* 2nd ed., chap. 22, 293.

[100] To be sure, Wotton did believe in the possibility that the moderns might one day come to rival the ancients in the humanities, whereas Temple did not; and he left open some fields in which he thought they might have already done so, such as architecture. But neither he nor Bentley had any wish to denigrate the general ancient superiority here, unlike some of their more radical modern counterparts abroad.

selves; or the tempers of the places, wherein they live." It was one thing under a commonwealth, another at court.[101] In the next generation, in the mixed monarchy of the eighteenth century, it would become much easier to be a neoclassicist, and thus to welcome in different ways both the *anciennete* and the modernity we have been describing. I suppose that Evelyn, always ready to embrace every kind of human learning and always eager to admire the best of the ancients *and* the best of the moderns, would have been pleased.

[101] Sprat, *History of the Royal Society*, 19.

John Evelyn in the 1650s: A Virtuoso in Quest of a Role

MICHAEL HUNTER

In this paper I wish to get behind the image of himself that John Evelyn presented in his later years, not least in his famous diary, much of it written up in its present form in the 1680s.[1] Instead, I want to reexamine the less familiar young man who had returned from a tour of the Continent in the late 1640s, as shown in Robert Walker's rather mannered portrait of 1648, for the details of which Evelyn was himself largely responsible (Fig. 1).[2] To understand Evelyn in this formative period of his life, we have to place him in the context of the civil war and its aftermath and the intellectual ferment of that era. But it is worth doing so, because in this way we gain fresh insight

This chapter was first published in Michael Hunter, *Science and the Shape of Orthodoxy: Intellectual Change in Late Seventeenth-Century Britain,* Woodbridge, 1995.

References in the form "Evelyn MS" refer to manuscripts in the Evelyn Collection, formerly on deposit at Christ Church, Oxford, which was bought by the British Library in 1995. The numeration of the collection at its former location has been retained by the British Library pending the allocation of new numbers. "Evelyn period" refers to boxed material in the collection; "Corr." denotes letters in the bound volumes of Evelyn correspondence; "Letter book" denotes items in Evelyn's letter book, 2 vols., Evelyn MS 39; letters in the main numerical series will be cited by number, while those in the separate foreign-language sections at the beginning will be so noted. The material was consulted while it was housed at Christ Church by kind permission of the trustees of the will of Major Peter George Evelyn. I am extremely grateful to Christ Church librarian John Wing for his long-standing assistance in my work on the Evelyn Collection. Antonio Clericuzio has kindly helped with references in the Hartlib Papers.

[1] On the date of its composition, see E. S. de Beer, ed., *The Diary of John Evelyn,* 5 vols., Oxford, 1955, I, 69 f, esp. 73.

[2] For a commentary on this portrait, see Evelyn to his wife, June 27, 1648, in Evelyn Collection, box of loose Evelyn period letters. At this point he had left her for his visit to England (see below, p. 82), and he explains that its intention was to remind her of him and his malady, the "naive posture" of which it represented; he presumably refers to his melancholy as a parted lover, and it is thus that he is depicted. In his endorsement to the letter he states, "I painted afterward a Deaths head in place of this letter." At the top appears the Greek motto "Repentance is the beginning of wisdom," while on the paper in front of him is a quotation from Seneca's *Epistulae morales.* The painting was intended to accompany a treatise on marriage prepared for his wife, "Instructions Oeconomique," now Evelyn MS 143, which is finely executed in the hand of Richard Hoare (see below, pp. 84–85); see W. G. Hiscock, *John Evelyn and His Family Circle,* London, 1955, 20–21.

1. Portrait of John Evelyn by Robert Walker, 1648
(photo: National Portrait Gallery, London)

into Evelyn's intellectual personality, into the genesis of his as yet unpublished magnum opus, the "Elysium Britannicum," and into the broader milieu from which that work stemmed.

The period in question was, of course, a tempestuous one, which saw the abolition of the monarchy and its replacement by a republican regime, against the background of deeper political and religious ferment. It was also a time of extraordinary intellectual vitality, among those opposed to the regime as much as among those supportive of it. This is symbolized particularly by two groups that have received much attention from modern scholars: one, which was associated with the regime, was the circle surrounding Samuel Hartlib, whose profuse papers document an amazing range of projects for technological and intellectual innovation;[3] the other, more politically neutral, was the

[3] See, particularly, Charles Webster, *The Great Instauration: Science, Medicine and Reform, 1626–1660,* London, 1975, and the CD-ROM edition of *The Hartlib Papers: A Complete Text and Image Database*, Ann Arbor, 1995.

scientific circle that gathered at Oxford under the aegis first of John Wilkins and later of Robert Boyle. The latter constituted an intellectual powerhouse that formed the principal basis for the post-Restoration development of science associated with the Royal Society in terms of both priorities and personnel.[4]

Evelyn had links with both Hartlib and the Oxford group. He appears from 1653 onward in the notebook "Ephemerides," which Hartlib kept, and the two men corresponded later in the decade, while a well-known passage in Evelyn's diary describing a visit to Oxford in 1654 includes an account of Wilkins and his curiosities and associates.[5] Neither group, however, was an especially strong influence on Evelyn.[6] His closest contacts seem to have been with a group of royalist virtuosi in London, including his lifelong friend Thomas Henshaw, whom he had met during his travels in Italy; this was evidently one of a number of overlapping groups that made up the capital's intellectual life at the time. But in many ways, Evelyn's most significant contacts were not English but continental, particularly French. Evelyn lived in Paris from 1649 to 1652, and thereafter he kept abreast of developments there through his father-in-law, the English resident in France, Sir Richard Browne. The result was that Evelyn had close ties to writers on the arts such as Abraham Bosse and natural philosophers such as Nicaise le Fèvre, while intellectually he had links with men such as François La Mothe le Vayer, Gabriel Naudé, and Pierre Gassendi.

Indeed, as we will see, much of Evelyn's activity involved transposing French cultural ideas to England, and it might almost seem inevitable that he would make a career out of being "one of our first Virtuosi," in John Aubrey's words—the author of books on virtuoso topics and a cultural and educational consultant to the aristocracy and (after 1660) the court.[7] Certainly, his later accounts of his life—such as that in his letter to the countess of Sunderland of August 4, 1690—present his early career in this way. On the other hand, the story told there displays a great deal of retrospective rationalization and is in at least one respect demonstrably false, namely, where he attributes to the needs created by the Fire of London in 1666 his desire to translate Roland Fréart de Chambray's *Parallel of the Ancient Architecture with the Modern* into English; in fact, the *Parallel* had come out in

[4] For the fullest accounts, see R. G. Frank, *Harvey and the Oxford Physiologists: A Study of Scientific Ideas and Social Interaction,* Berkeley and Los Angeles, 1980, esp. chap. 3, and Webster, *Great Instauration,* 153–72.

[5] Evelyn, *Diary,* III, 110–11. See also below, pp. 93–94.

[6] It is possibly symptomatic that in his letter to Boyle of May 9, 1657 (see below, p. 91), he mistakenly referred to John Wilkins as "Wilkinson," which forms the basis of the elaborate hypothesis put forward in J. I. Cope, "Evelyn, Boyle and Dr Wilkinson's 'Mathematico-Chymico-Mechanical School,'" *Isis* 50 (1959), 30–32. That this is in fact "obviously a slip of the pen" has already been noted in Webster, *Great Instauration,* 175. It is perhaps worth nothing two pieces of evidence confirming this: first, that in his reply of May 23, 1657, which has recently come to light and will be included in the forthcoming Pickering Masters edition of Boyle's correspondence, Boyle presumes the reference to be Wilkins; and second, that in his commonplace book, Evelyn MS 54(2), p. 124, Evelyn was still making the same slip concerning Wilkins' name in connection with a book published in 1675.

[7] Bodleian Library, Oxford, MS Aubrey 4, fol. 120v (this passage, which is crossed through, does not appear in the modified version of the text published as *The Natural History and Antiquities of Surrey,* R. Rawlinson, ed., 5 vols., London, 1718, IV, 116–24). For Evelyn's role as a cultural consultant, see, for example, Evelyn to Thurland, November 8, 1658, in William Bray (and John Forster), eds., *The Diary and Correspondence of John Evelyn,* 4 vols., London, 1850–52, III, 106–8; Evelyn to Thomas Chiffing, 1661–62 and February 4, 1665, ibid., III, 135–36, Letter book, no. 233.

1664.[8] Even Evelyn's diary is prone to be more misleading than helpful as a guide to Evelyn's development, quite apart from its singular incompleteness as a record of his intellectual activities: the "Elysium Britannicum," for instance, makes no appearance in it at all. Fortunately, however, there is no need to rely on such retrospective accounts. They can be supplemented by an immense amount of evidence that has hitherto been little exploited—Evelyn's correspondence, his library, and his profuse manuscripts, which reveal a much more complex, and more interesting, story.[9]

What these suggest is that Evelyn's adoption of the role of full-time savant was rather at odds with his earlier expectations of his proper role in life. This has to be taken into account properly to understand his attitudes and priorities. Evelyn's upbringing—at the free school at Southover near Lewes in Sussex, where he lived in the godly household of his grandparents from the age of five onward, and then at Balliol College, Oxford, from 1637 to 1640—had led him to imbibe the commonplaces of Christian humanism, cross-fertilized with Protestantism, which had been at the heart of the educational curriculum in England for more than a century.[10] This took it for granted that it was the duty of a well-born, well-educated man such as himself to place his services at the disposal of the state; this is well illustrated by his brother George's prayer to God in 1637 "that he will blesse our studys, that hereafter we may be beneficiall to our Countrey."[11] Indeed, Evelyn was himself later to give expression to such views in his *Publick Employment and an Active Life Prefer'd to Solitude* (1667), which has been described as "a treatise which sums up much of the Humanist doctrine concerning the active life, and is perhaps the fullest and best written discussion of it in English."[12]

The problem, of course, was that it was difficult for one as committed to the royalist cause as Evelyn had become by the late 1640s to obtain public employment in republican England.[13] From 1647 to 1649, the dilemma was postponed, while Evelyn acted in a quasi-official capacity as an agent in England on behalf of Sir Richard Browne, to whom he purveyed profuse information on political and other developments as they occurred.[14] But the king's execution left the exiled royal court

[8] *Diary and Correspondence,* III, 317–19. For evidence that Evelyn began work on the *Parallel* in the 1650s, see below, pp. 88–89.

[9] For existing accounts that rely on Evelyn's later memories to a greater or lesser extent, see Margaret Denny, "The Early Program of the Royal Society of John Evelyn," *Modern Language Quarterly* 1 (1940), 481–97; Graham Parry, "John Evelyn as Hortulan Saint," in Michael Leslie and Timothy Raylor, eds., *Culture and Cultivation in Early Modern England: Writing and the Land,* Leicester, 1992, 130–50; Douglas Chambers, "John Evelyn and the Construction of the Scientific Self" (forthcoming).

[10] See Margo Todd, *Christian Humanism and the Puritan Social Order,* Cambridge, 1987, esp. chaps. 2–3.

[11] George Evelyn to Richard Evelyn, April 3, 1637, in Evelyn Collection, box of Evelyn period, loose letters, A-G.

[12] Brian Vickers, ed., *Public and Private Life in the Seventeenth Century: The MacKenzie-Evelyn Debate,* New York, 1986, xxvii.

[13] Though Evelyn spent virtually the whole period of the first civil war traveling on the Continent, suggesting a less than burning commitment to the royalist cause at that stage, from the late 1640s onward he made up for this by showing an unwavering loyalty to the monarchy as the embodiment of political stability. This is reflected in his letters to Sir Richard Browne at that stage (a selection of which is printed in *Diary and Correspondence,* III, 4–56). His royalist sentiments were later to be expressed most strongly in tracts published in 1659 and 1660: see William Upcott, ed., *The Miscellaneous Writings of John Evelyn, Esq.,* London, 1825, 169–204.

[14] For hints of a specific role on Evelyn's part, see Evelyn, *Diary,* II, 537; Evelyn to Browne, May 31, 1649, Corr.

virtually impotent, providing no further role for him. Hence, Evelyn had totally to revise his expectations, as is clear from his comments both at the time and subsequently. Writing to his son nearly thirty years later and noting how he had "allways deplor'd the condition of those Gent[lemen] (of what state or fortune soever) that take not to some calling or other," he added, "The neglect of this, or rather the calamity of the times interrupting, has ben no small affliction to me, as to my owne failing, when time was, which ought to be a document to you."[15] The same sense of disappointment appears in a letter that he wrote to his wife's uncle, William Prettyman, on December 2, 1651, when he was about to return to England: "I shall therefore bring over with me no ambitions at all to be a statesman, or meddle with the unlucky Interests of Kingdomes, but shall contentedly submitt to the losse of my education, by which I might have one day hoped to have bin considerable in my Country. A Friend, a Booke, and a Garden shall for the future, perfectly circumscribe my utmost designes."[16]

As these quotations illustrate, there was a sense in which the intellectual and cultural activities to which Evelyn now turned were something of a substitute for what he saw as his proper goal in life. Although the diary makes clear Evelyn's endless curiosity about natural and artificial phenomena, he was always left with a certain ambivalence about the value of virtuoso pursuits. This may explain a comment concerning Evelyn in a letter from John Aubrey to Oxford antiquary Anthony à Wood in 1693: "he sayes you call him a great *Virtuoso:* he had rather you had called him Coxcomb."[17] (Parenthetically, it is perhaps worth noting that this ambivalence itself went back to Evelyn's adolescence, when the penchant for drawing and painting that provides the first hint of his later inclinations was frowned on in the strongly Protestant milieu from which he came, both his father and his Oxford tutor deprecating such activities as appropriate only "as his recreation, not as his busniss."[18]) As Evelyn explained in his treatise on engraving, *Sculptura* (1662), "where we have said all that we can of *This,* or any other particular *Art,* which may recommend it to the favour, and endearment of great persons; our intention is not, that it should so far engage them in its pursuit, as to take from the nobler parts of life, for which there are more sublime and worthy objects."[19]

For the time being, however, with an anti-monarchic regime established apparently permanently in England, Evelyn had no alternative but a career as connoisseur, savant, and writer. Indeed, writing to Sir Richard Browne on June 14, 1649, shortly before his departure from England for France, he noted, "I my selfe am a little given to bookes & shall have now tyme to reduce my

---

no. 1408; and Evelyn to Browne, January 13 and November 20, 1648, in box of loose Evelyn period letters.

[15] N.D. [1679], Letter book, no. 402. Compare his earlier advice to the young traveler Benjamin Maddox to spend his days "by serving your country in some public employment (if the integrity of the times invite you)," though he did suggest "securing your own felicity" as an alternative to this. Evelyn to Maddox, January 10, 1657/58, *Diary and Correspondence,* III, 85. For evidence of Evelyn's ambivalence on this issue after 1660, see below, pp. 105–6.

[16] Letter book, no. 36.

[17] Anthony Powell, *John Aubrey and His Friends,* 2nd ed., London, 1963, 226.

[18] George Bradshaw to George Evelyn, October 25, 1637, Evelyn period loose letters A–G. Cf. Richard Evelyn to John Evelyn, 1635, Corr. no. 764.

[19] C. F. Bell, ed., *Evelyn's Sculptura: With the Unpublished Second Part,* Oxford, 1906, 143–44.

studyes into a method."[20] Over the three years that he subsequently spent in Paris, both the diary and other sources reveal him systematically devoting himself to cultural and intellectual activities. Thus, he assiduously courted artists and connoisseurs in Paris, visiting their workshops and collections of rarities, getting hints on techniques such as perspective, and picking up all sorts of technological secrets.[21] He also collected prints and other objects, commissioning a cabinet in which to store his collection (or perhaps the additions to it which he had made since commissioning an earlier cabinet in Italy in 1644).[22] In addition, he attended and made notes on various courses of chemistry, which it appears that at some later point he considered publishing.[23]

Even more important, it was now that he made a sustained attempt to build up a comprehensive library. He had, of course, purchased books earlier, not least during his travels in Italy. But analysis of the dates and places of purchase recorded in the extensive selection of books from his library sold at Christie's in London in 1977–78 reveals that a disproportionate number was bought in the years around 1650.[24] It was also now that he began to have his books bound in the distinctive style that has won him acclaim as a bibliophile.[25] More significant is the fact that he clearly set out to acquire a serious arsenal of book learning, his commitment to which is easily underrated. Thus, he bought not only virtuoso books and travel books, but also theological works by authors such as Hugo Grotius, William Chillingworth, and Richard Hooker, scientific works, canonical texts such as Bibles and the writings of Aristotle, and editions of classical and patristic authors.

No less revealing are a series of manuscript compilations that he began at this time, almost as if at this point he decided to put his affairs—and especially his intellectual affairs—on a more systematic basis. It was in Paris in 1650 that he began to enter notes on sermons in a special volume, and the fact that the letter book that he was to keep for the rest of his life is of exactly matching format suggests that it, too, was begun at this point, although the removal of its opening leaves has obscured this fact.[26] There is also a series of compendia that Evelyn made with the help of his amanuensis, Richard Hoare. One was a catalogue of his newly extended library, which, because later superseded, survives only in fragments retained because of the calligraphic virtuosity that Hoare deployed in

[20] Corr. no. 1410.

[21] Evelyn, *Diary,* II, 568; III, 10–11, 33, 35, 52; Evelyn MS 54(1), pp. 293–96; MS 65, pp. 197, 499 and passim.

[22] Hoare to Evelyn, July 1650, Corr. no. 909; Evelyn, *Diary,* III, 3. This cabinet is now in the Geffrye Museum, London. For an account of it, see Christie's, London, auction catalogue, March 31, 1977, lot 42. On the earlier cabinet, see ibid., lot 82.

[23] Evelyn, *Diary,* II, 534–55, 565; III, 49; Evelyn to Radcliffe, December 2, 1651, Letter book, no. 37; Evelyn MSS 32, 61; F. Sherwood Taylor, "The Chemical Studies of John Evelyn," *Annals of Science* 8 (1952), 285–92. See also Evelyn MS 56, a manuscript transcript of a text concerning the philosopher's stone. For references to Evelyn's subsequent chemical activity, see below, note 34, and Hiscock, *Family Circle,* 29.

[24] *The Evelyn Library,* Christie's, London, auction catalogue, 4 parts, June 22, 1977, to July 13, 1978. Evelyn's purchases were made in either Paris or London, the latter with the advice of his virtuoso contact, Jaspar Needham: see Needham to Evelyn, April 5, 1649, Evelyn MS 3.2.93; Evelyn to Needham, November 26, 1650, Letter book, no. 17.

[25] Geoffrey Keynes, *John Evelyn: A Study in Bibliophily with a Bibliography of His Writings,* 2nd ed., Oxford, 1968, esp. 23–28.

[26] Evelyn MSS 49, 39(1). This volume had earlier been intended for a different purpose and retains headings related to this; subsequently, it was supplemented by a second volume.

2 Title page to Evelyn's library catalog, 1653, written and embellished by his amanuensis, Richard Hoare.
Evelyn Collection, British Library, London, MS 185, fol. 5
(photo: Michael R. Dudley)

them (Fig. 2).[27] Evelyn also produced various manuscript digests of information. Among these are two small volumes beautifully executed by Hoare, one entitled "Vade Mecum," a compendium of knowledge from J. H. Alsted's *Encyclopaedia* and other sources, and the other a digest of medical data dedicated to Evelyn's friend Thomas Radcliffe and dated 1651: this combines general information on regimens from such sources as the writings of the reformed Galenist Daniel Sennert, with a collection of recipes.[28] More significant are two large folio volumes, which evidently superseded these. One was a recipe book for which Evelyn sought material from his family and friends. This is perhaps to be seen as an unusually elaborate version of the manuscript collections of useful data kept by many householders in early modern England, though in Evelyn's case his continental contacts gave it an abnormally cosmopolitan flavor; he and his wife were to add to it for the rest of his life.[29]

[27] Evelyn MS 185, fol. 5 (title page dated 1653, with list of contents on verso, mounted into a volume in an Evelyn binding that was otherwise blank until it was partially used for eighteenth-century accounts), MS 402 (a fragment), and further fragments in Evelyn period misc. box 11. On Hoare, see Keynes, *Bibliography,* 22–4. For later catalogues of Evelyn's library, see Evelyn MSS 19, 20, 20a, 30, and 259, and Keynes, *Bibliography,* 13–14, 298–303.

[28] Evelyn MSS 89, 91, 133: the latter comprises a disbound fragment that follows on from the last leaf in MS 89. The dismemberment of the manuscript may well have been the work of Evelyn himself, perhaps connected with the decision to begin a separate recipe collection in MS 51. It is perhaps worth noting that Evelyn's copies of both Alsted and Sennert appeared in the 1977–78 Christie's sales; the former is now British Library Eve.c.6.

[29] Evelyn MS 51. On the initial compilation of the volume, see Evelyn to Mrs. Glanvill, November 17, 1650, and June 17, 1651, Corr. nos. 1416–17.

The other was perhaps the most important of all these compendia, a commonplace book, begun, like the recipe collection, in Hoare's hand, but continued in Evelyn's. In it, extracts from his reading were entered, tabulated by key word, and sorted by subject according to the whole gamut of knowledge, human, natural, and divine.[30] This volume—which Evelyn was later to supplement with two more—is one of the most elaborate commonplace books to survive from its period; indeed, Evelyn was sufficiently proud of the method that he deployed in it to send his brother in 1658 "the frame or Idea of my Adversaria, which after many tryals & reformations, I find to be most advantagious."[31] Interestingly, it includes nuggets of information on technological and other topics that Evelyn had acquired orally; but more significant is the evidence it provides of those books that Evelyn actually read at a formative stage in his career. Two recur more frequently than any others—Hugo Grotius' *Of the Truth of the Christian Religion* and Francis Bacon's *Of the Advancement of Learning*. Beyond this, there are theological works both by contemporary authors such as Henry Hammond and patristic ones such as Minucius Felix; travel books, including J. H. von Pflaumern's *Mercurius Italicus* and Thomas Gage's account of the West Indies; works of natural philosophy, notably Johann Hevelius' *Selenography* (1647) and, perhaps more surprisingly, the Paracelsian Michael Sendivogius' *New Light of Alchymie,* of which an English edition had appeared in 1650; historical works, including Lord Herbert of Cherbury's life of Henry VIII; and virtuoso books, including Sir Henry Wotton's *Elements of Architecture.*

Evelyn's work on such projects seems to straddle his return to England in 1652. (He had already made enquiries to ensure that the notorious Engagement Oath of 1649–50 would not be a problem to one of his principles.)[32] But his homecoming seems to have stimulated new initiatives on his part, and there are two in particular that originated within a year of Evelyn's return to England and about which we hear much over the next few years. One was his work on the so-called history of trades, which was the source of much of the data on such subjects with which Evelyn furnished the Royal Society when it developed interests of this kind in the early 1660s; the other was his translation of and commentary on Lucretius' *De Rerum Natura.* I will deal with these in turn.

First, I will consider the history of trades, that project for describing technical practices advocated by Francis Bacon that attracted so much attention in mid-seventeenth-century England.[33] Evelyn's activities in this connection are documented by the report on them that appears in Samuel Hartlib's "Ephemerides" in June 1653. This is the first reference to Evelyn in that source, in which Hartlib jotted down reports of scientific and technological projects about which he heard, although

[30] Evelyn MS 54(1), initially entitled "Tomus Primus" but altered to "Tertius" when the subsequent volumes referred to in note 31 were begun.

[31] Evelyn to George Evelyn, October 15, 1658, Letter book, no. 140. He quoted Cicero's *Pro Roscio* in this connection, subsequently inserting this and other quotations in support of such adversaria in the later volumes of the series, Evelyn MSS 54(2) and 54(3), which he evidently began ca. 1660. Evelyn MS 54(4) is an index. A stray leaf from the commonplace books is to be found in British Library, Add. MS 15950, fol. 125.

[32] Evelyn to Johnson, April 17, 1650, Corr. no. 949.

[33] See Michael Hunter, *Science and Society in Restoration England,* Cambridge, 1981, repr. Aldershot, 1992, chap. 4; W. E. Houghton, "The History of Trades: Its Relation to Seventeenth-Century Thought," *Journal of the History of Ideas* 2 (1941), 33–60.

these were not always particularly accurate, especially when (as in this case) they were based on secondhand information. Hartlib noted how Evelyn had "studied and collected a great Worke of all Trades, and wants no more to it but the description of 3 Trades."[34] What Hartlib appears to have heard about must be a volume that still survives in the Evelyn Collection entitled "*Trades*. Seacrets & Receipts Mechanical. as they came casualy to hand; Alphabeticaly plac'd according to the subsequent Table."[35] The "Table" referred to, which follows the title page, was to form the basis of the well-known "Circle of *Mechanical* Trades," which Evelyn was to present to the Royal Society as a contribution to its technological program in 1661, though the prehistory of that document has hitherto been unknown.[36] This lists a comprehensive range of skills and practices, from baking to bellfounding, the bulk of them alphabetically arranged in a series of "Usefull and purely Mechaniq" techniques, which was then supplemented by a series of further occupations and skills categorized under headings of "Meane & Lesse honourable," "Servile," "Rusticall," "Femall," "Polite and More Liberall," "Curious," and "Exotick and very rare Seacrets."[37]

The source of Evelyn's rather elitist categorization is unclear. There is no mandate for it in the list of trades that Bacon had included in the "Catalogue of Particular Histories," which formed part of the *Parasceve* appended to his *New Organon*. Neither has it a precedent in the general exposition of the idea of such histories in his *Advancement of Learning*, which Evelyn had read so assiduously, and in which Bacon was rather hostile to the emphasis on "secrets, rarities, and special subtilties" that such a classification exemplified.[38] In his own list, he grouped trades according to the materials with which they worked, baker with miller, for instance, and this kind of "natural" classification is echoed in such lists of trades as those compiled by Sir William Petty or Robert Hooke.[39] Evelyn's

[34] "Ephemerides" (Sheffield University Library) 28/2/66B-67A. Cf. ibid., 28/2/71B. His source seems to have been the instrument maker Ralph Greatorex, whose links with Evelyn are otherwise documented only by a single brief reference: Evelyn, *Diary,* III, 173. Hartlib describes Evelyn as "a chymist" who "hath many furnaces a going"; Mrs. Evelyn's skills are also noted.

[35] Evelyn MS 65: the title page and table precede page 1.

[36] Evelyn, *Diary,* III, 288; Thomas Birch, *History of the Royal Society,* 4 vols., London, 1756–57, I, 10, 12; Royal Society, Classified Papers III (1) 1, printed in A. F. Sieveking, "Evelyn's 'Circle of Mechanic Trades,'" *Transactions of the Newcomen Society* 4 (1923–24), 40–47. The Royal Society version is revised and has many minor alterations and additions, especially to the last section.

[37] These titles are taken from the revised version in Classified Papers III (1) 1, the full title of which is "The History of Arts Illiberall and Mechanick, Alphabetically or according to their Antiquity, Succession, Dependence, Dignity, Necessitie &c." The categories "Polite" and "More Liberall" were originally separate but have been linked. In the version in Evelyn MS 65, the main, alphabetically arranged series of trades is untitled, and the subsequent sections are titled, respectively, "Meane & Frippery Trades," "Servil Trades," "Polite Arts & Trades," "Exotick Arts & Trades," "Trades, more Liberall," "Femal Trades & Arts," and "Occupations in & about the Country."

[38] J. Spedding, R. L. Ellis, and D. D. Heath, eds., *The Works of Francis Bacon,* 14 vols., London, 1857–74, III, 332–33; IV, 265–70. One component of Evelyn's scheme does have a Baconian precedent, the phrase "mechanical and illiberal" in connection with "the history of Arts": see ibid., IV, 257.

[39] Marquis of Lansdowne, ed., *The Petty Papers,* 2 vols., London, 1927, I, 205–7; R. Waller, ed., *The Posthumous Works of Robert Hooke,* London, 1705, 24–26. A further, similarly arranged list is to be found among Abraham Hill's papers, British Library, Sloane MS 2903, fols. 59–60. Hill also has a copy of Evelyn's list, ibid., fols. 63–65. Webster, *Great Instauration,* 425, fails to differentiate the various discrete items copied by Hill, and mistakenly presumes that all are by Petty.

arrangement may, however, reflect the extent to which his interest in describing technological practices had roots other than English ones, a possibility that has been overlooked in standard accounts of the history of trades program.[40] For in *Sculptura,* Evelyn invoked a completely different source for the history of trades, the Italian author, Giacomo Maria Favi: he gave a lengthy account of Favi's activities in collecting data on technological topics and noted how—though he died prematurely—Favi had intended "to compile, and publish a Compleat *Cycle* and *Hystory* of *Trades,*" a phrase that echoes the one used by Evelyn to describe the list that he presented to the Royal Society.[41]

The remainder of Evelyn's manuscript volume of *Trades* was divided up, with a few pages devoted to each of the crafts and techniques outlined in the initial list. But the over-optimism of Hartlib's description—quite apart from his reference to its being "divided in several volumes"[42]—is shown by the fact that much of the book is blank. Only some 44 of 605 pages have anything but a running title written on them at all. The layout of the volume shows the aspiration to a complete history of trades, however, and internal cross-references indicate that it was to have been divided into "chapters"; dates integral to the text suggest that such work on it as Evelyn did occurred between 1652 and 1656.[43]

Of the trades of which a fairly full description *is* included, most appear in the sections devoted to "Polite" and "Exotick" arts and trades, dealing with virtuoso techniques of the kind that Evelyn had learned about during his last years at Paris (some similar information had earlier been transcribed into his commonplace book, and it is possible that this may have contributed to the idea of a systematic collection of information such as he now attempted).[44] These included two items that he was to divulge to the Royal Society in 1661, namely, his description of an improved way of making marbled paper and a recipe for gilt varnish.[45] Other virtuoso skills to which lengthy sections were devoted included the mixing of colors for painting and the techniques for applying them, with specific reference to painting in miniature; enameling; mosaic work; and the use of shells for grottos. There were also sections on invisible ink and on making casts of statues, together with minor hints about various other skills and practices.[46] Here, we seem to have the germ of Evelyn's activity in related areas after 1660, including his treatise on engraving, *Sculptura.*[47] Interestingly, another project

[40] Houghton, "The History of Trades," who does, however, mention Rabelais and Vives as pioneers: 33–34; K. H. Ochs, "The Royal Society's History of Trades Programme: An Early Episode in Applied Science," *Notes and Records of the Royal Society* 39 (1985), 129–58, esp. 130–31.

[41] "An Account of *Signor Giacomo Favi,*" *Sculptura,* sigs. c4–8; see also ibid., introduction, vi-vii and viin.

[42] "Ephemerides," 28/2/71B.

[43] Evelyn MS 65, pp. 367, 448, 486. For the possibility that further material on such topics existed elsewhere than in this volume, see note 47.

[44] Evelyn MS 54(1), pp. 293–96; however, there is no direct overlap of the data recorded.

[45] For the marbled paper recipe, see Royal Society, Classified Papers, III (1) 4; for the varnish recipe, see Royal Society, Boyle Papers 26, fol. 141.

[46] Evelyn MS 65, pp. 210, 283–84, and 486f passim. One of these, a recipe for varnish, is written in a hand other than Evelyn's: ibid., p. 493.

[47] Though the published section of *Sculptura* dealing with the history of engraving has no parallel in this earlier material, the technical material included in the unpublished part—which largely comprises a translation of a book on the use of a rolling press by Abraham Bosse published in 1656—could represent work of the 1650s; see *Sculptura,* pt. 2.

that came to fruition after the Restoration, Evelyn's translation of Fréart de Chambray's *Parallel,* was also begun at this time. Evelyn's statement to this effect in the dedication to the published work is confirmed by his correspondence, although publication failed to materialize at this juncture.[48]

If the bulk of Evelyn's collection of *Trades* illustrates a hitherto unsuspected prehistory to his activity in related fields after 1600, it also contains some material of a quite different and much more down-to-earth kind that is unparalleled in his subsequent writings: a lengthy description of how to make a limekiln (Fig. 3), notes on how to calculate the price of wood, and, most remarkably, a lengthy and detailed disquisition on how to lay out the lines for a naval vessel, including instructions and calculations concerning the proportions of the hull and the correct lengths for the different masts.[49] These notes show a much closer affinity than do Evelyn's later works to the agenda for the history of trades as expounded by Bacon and exemplified by the Hartlibians. Evelyn's house at Deptford was almost adjacent to the naval shipyards, where an unprecedented program of shipbuilding was going on at this time under the auspices of the Cromwellian government.[50] Though such interest in the weaponry of the anti-monarchic regime is perhaps surprising in one so bitterly opposed to it, Evelyn was possibly intrigued by the aura of secrecy that surrounded information of this kind, which was later to be withheld from the Royal Society on the grounds of state security.[51] A further section of Evelyn's notes, that dealing with the value of timber, might be seen to prefigure his most famous book, *Sylva; or a Discourse of Forest-Trees,* published under the auspices of the Royal Society in 1664, which (as Lindsay Sharp has pointed out) owed more to precedents in the practical tradition of the interregnum than Evelyn was inclined to admit.[52] But even *Sylva* was less down to earth than these notes, and this unparalleled excursion into technological matters of direct relevance to the contemporary economy may well have been stimulated by Evelyn's contact with Hartlib and his circle at this time.[53]

Etching appears only as the heading of a blank page in Evelyn MS 65, p. 498, but for evidence that Evelyn did write on engraving at this time, see his letter to Boyle of May 9, 1657, cited below, p. 91. See also Royal Society, Boyle Papers 27, fols. 293–94, a recipe for ink for the rolling press sent by Evelyn to Boyle on April 2, 1660.

[48] *Miscellaneous Writings,* 343; Evelyn to Bosse, January 26, 1653, Letter book, Lib. II (Italian and French letters), no. 17; Browne to Evelyn, November 30, 1658, British Library, Add. MS 34702, fol. 168. See also George Evelyn to Evelyn, August 12, 1656, Corr. no. 577, and Evelyn to Browne, March 6, 1657, Corr. no. 1441. The letters suggest that Evelyn's attempts to negotiate for the plates did not succeed. In the published text he wrote that "other things intervening it was laid aside."

[49] Evelyn MS 65, pp. 247–48, 361–67, 369, 448.

[50] Bernard Capp, *Cromwell's Navy: The Fleet and the English Revolution, 1648–60,* Oxford, 1989, esp. 4–6. For references to such ships, see Evelyn, *Diary,* III, 60, 149–50.

[51] Michael Hunter, *Establishing the New Science: The Experience of the Royal Society,* Woodbridge, 1989, 30 and note 106. For the interregnum background, see Edward Hayward, *The Sizes and Lengths of Riggings for All the States Ships and Frigats,* London, 1655, reprint edition with introduction by R. C. Anderson, London, 1967; George Kendall, *The Clerk of the Surveigh Surveighed,* London, 1656.

[52] Evelyn MS 65, p. 448. See Lindsay Sharp, "Timber, Science and Economic Reform in the Seventeenth Century," *Forestry* 48 (1975), 51–86.

[53] It is perhaps worth noting here Evelyn's surviving copy of the third impression of Walter Blith's *English Improver Improved,* which he acquired in 1652, the year in which it was published. In it, the names of authors on agricultural improvement are marked in a hand that is almost certainly contemporaneous with the ownership inscription,

Lime Burner

247

To build the Kilne:

3. "Lime Burner," from Evelyn's collection of "*Trades,*" ca. 1654. Evelyn Collection, British Library, London, MS 65, p. 247 (photo: Michael R. Dudley)

Evelyn's *Trades* thus represents the high point of his commitment to useful knowledge. But his enthusiasm for such study thereafter waned, and we learn interesting details of his second thoughts about it from letters that he exchanged with Robert Boyle in 1657 and 1659. Obviously stimulated by Hartlib, Boyle must have approached Evelyn asking about the collection of technological data that Hartlib understood him to have compiled. Evelyn obliged by supplying Boyle with the information he required, but he accompanied this with a revealing apology; two years later, he again apologized for the false expectations that had evidently been aroused concerning his project, seeking to disabuse Boyle and Hartlib of any expectation they might have formed that he had prepared a methodical survey of trades in virtually publishable form.

In a well-known passage in his letter of August 9, 1659, Evelyn explains how his work on the history of trades had

> not advanced a step; finding (to my infinite grief) my great imperfections for the attempt, and the many subjections, which I cannot support, of conversing with mechanical capricious persons, and several other discouragements; so that, giving over a design of that magnitude, I am ready to acknowledge my fault, if from any expression of mine there was any room to hope for such a production, farther than by a short collection of some heads and materials, and a continual propensity of endeavouring in some particular, to encourage so noble a work, so far as I am able.[54]

In the light of what Evelyn had so far collected, I would interpret this as referring primarily to the "Usefull and purely Mechaniq" trades, to which the bulk of his volume was devoted and most of which was left blank; there is no evidence that he disliked visiting the ateliers of painters and engravers.

This is rather borne out by his comments in his earlier letter, of May 9, 1657, in which he had recorded a slightly different story. This suggests that, recognizing how his squeamishness limited his ability to execute a "general" history of trades, he had concentrated on the "virtuoso" ones that most interested him, and of certain of which he was to disseminate accounts after 1660. Evelyn noted how "I was once minded to publish (as a specimen of what might be further done in the rest) for the benefit of the ingenious" a series of treatises on artistic techniques; and it is interesting that the topics named—"Painting in Oil, in Miniature, Anealing in Glass, Enamelling, and Marble Paper"—overlap almost exactly with the topics to which he had devoted the fullest attention in his collection of *Trades,* together with "etching and engraving," the subject of *Sculptura.*[55]

---

including Hartlib and Gabriel Plattes as well as earlier authors such as Thomas Tusser, Hugh Plat, and Gervase Markham, suggesting that Evelyn was at that point unfamiliar with, but interested in, this tradition of writing; British Library, Eve. a. 97, sigs. b3v–b4 (b3 is accidentally mis-signed c3). Bacon's name is also thus marked, perhaps suggesting that Evelyn had not previously thought of him in this connection. There are also similar markings by various topics in the table of contents at the end (and pencil markings in the text).

[54] *Diary and Correspondence,* III, 115. It is disappointing to have to record that "capricious" fails to appear in the version of the letter preserved in Evelyn's Letter book, no. 154, which speaks simply of "Mechanicall persons," but the familiar text is to be preferred, as derived from that sent to Boyle.

[55] *Diary and Correspondence,* III, 92; Evelyn MS 65, pp. 486–89, 490–92, 523–24. For the likely nature of Evelyn's work on engraving in the 1650s, see above, p. 88.

Equally revealing, however, are his further remarks, for he continued:

> I have since been put off from that design, not knowing whether I should do well to gratify so barbarous an age (as I fear is approaching) with curiosities of that nature, delivered with so much integrity as I intended them; and lest by it I should disoblige some, who made those professions their living; or, at least, debase much of their esteem by prostituting them to the vulgar. Rather, I conceived that a true and ingenious discovery of these and the like arts, would, to better purpose, be compiled for the use of that Mathematico-Chymico-Mechanical School designed by our noble friend Dr Wilkinson [*sic*], where they might (not without an oath of secresy) be taught to those that either affected or desired any of them: and from thence, as from another Solomon's house, so much of them only made public, as should from time to time be judged convenient by the superintendent of that School, for the reputation of learning and benefit of the nation.[56]

Various points in this crucial passage require comment. First, there is the issue of secrecy, and the need to protect the "esteem" of trades. Evelyn's remarks to Boyle on this topic may well have been affected by his experiences in connection with the very recipes recorded in his *Trades* volume. It appears that, having collected this information, he proceeded to propagate it by divulging recipes to cognoscenti like himself. One such recipient was his friend Thomas Henshaw, who thanked Evelyn in a letter dated September 27, 1652, for giving him a "Gentil Secret" for gilding picture frames, which is evidently one of the items in Evelyn's collection.[57] Subsequently, however, Evelyn noted that his openness regarding this recipe was abused by another virtuoso who "has goten a patent for the onely making of it," and his notes reveal an attitude torn between an apparent wistfulness about the opportunity he had missed and a sense that he was above such things: "Much good may it do them," he observed.[58] In the case of another, similar recipe, it appears that he divulged it directly to craftsmen; that he was unduly open by the standards of some of his virtuoso friends is suggested by a further letter from Henshaw to Evelyn in which he passed on an "earnest request" by Mr. Paston—evidently the later F. R. S. and earl of Yarmouth—"that you would bee pleased not to make the receit of the gold vernish common, for hee having received it of mee and made experiment of it, did very much esteeme and affect it; and was passionately troubled when the plaister of Paris man at Charing crosse told him you had promised to teach it him."[59]

Such episodes illustrate an interesting ambivalence over the communication of such knowledge, from which Evelyn evidently learned. Thus, in his *Sculptura,* he referred to and included an example of the technique of mezzotinting, which he had been shown by Prince Rupert, but declined to explain exactly how it was done so as to prevent "an *Art* so curious, and (as yet) so little

[56] *Diary and Correspondence,* III, 92.

[57] Corr. no. 889.

[58] Evelyn MS 65, p. 546; Evelyn MS 52A, pp. 306, 310–11. The virtuoso in question was evidently Sir Phillip Howard; the patent to which Evelyn appears to refer was granted on March 2, 1668; see Bennet Woodcroft, *Chronological Index of Patents of Invention,* 2 vols., London, 1854, no. 158. On patents, see Christine MacLeod, *Inventing the Industrial Revolution: The English Patent System, 1660–1800,* Cambridge, 1988.

[59] Evelyn MS 52A, p. 306; Henshaw to Evelyn, January 13, 1656/57, Corr. no. 897. Cf. ibid., no. 889, which suggests that Henshaw shared similar anxieties.

vulgar" from being "prostituted at so cheap a rate, as the more naked describing of it here, would too soon have expos'd it to."[60] He also decided against including his translation of Abraham Bosse's account of the press used to print engraved plates so as not to prejudice the intended publication of the work by a practicing engraver, William Faithorne.[61] This ambivalence about the public communication of such data may help to explain why Evelyn was subsequently to transfer some of the information from his collection of *Trades* into a further compilation on such subjects that seems to have been intended exclusively for his own private use.[62]

Returning to Evelyn's letter to Boyle, equally interesting is the reason that he gave for not publishing such data—namely, the approach of a "barbarous" age. Evelyn seems to have been quite pessimistic about the time in which he lived, noting in a letter to Sir Richard Browne of December 18, 1656, how the decline of learning portended a "darke night of Ignorance & barbarity."[63] Even in 1662 in *Sculptura* he remarked of Favi's history of trades project how "this had been a Charity, and a Blessing too great for the World, because it do's not depart from its Vices, and impertinencies, and cherish such Persons, and the Virtues which should render it worthy of them."[64] Evelyn's pessimism was apparently shared by his friend, the Anglican divine, Jeremy Taylor, with whom Evelyn corresponded in the 1650s; Taylor was inclined to place a millenarian construction on this sad state of affairs, echoing the similar views of Evelyn's Surrey neighbor, the mathematician William Oughtred.[65] Evelyn, on the other hand (contrary to the suggestion of Graham Parry), seems to have remained agnostic about this: "what to say of that I know not," he wrote.[66]

Instead, he seems to have taken a more secular view as to how matters might be improved, which was to be found in the role of what might be called an aristocracy of virtue or rather *virtù*. Clearly to take the view that, because of the dismal state of the world, no such information should be disseminated at all, was self-defeating. Rather, Evelyn seems to have believed that it should be made available to selected cognoscenti, who would benefit both themselves and the skills involved by their attention to them. The agency suggested in his letter to Boyle was John Wilkins' "Mathematico-Chymico-Mechanical School"; this may have been a reference to the idea of "the erecting of a

[60] *Sculptura,* Bell ed., 147–48. The actual description of the process, with illustrations, is to be found in Evelyn MS 52A, pp. 307–8.

[61] *Sculptura,* Bell ed., 149–50. See also Evelyn to Wilkins, January 29, 1661, in Birch, *History of the Royal Society,* I, 15.

[62] Evelyn MS 52A, a compendium of technical information in a volume that in size and binding matches his recipe collection and commonplace books. Evidently, this was begun to be used for this purpose ca. 1659–60 (see the material on the first page extracted from the letters from R. J. [Richard Jones] in British Library, Add. MS 15948, 67 f. The recipes in it are inserted in numbered sequence; the recipes from Evelyn MS 65 presented to the Royal Society (pp. 308–11) were evidently both copied into it at one time (probably when they were presented). A further collection, probably begun at a similar date (though in a different binding), is Evelyn MS 44, which deals with husbandry, building, and other "country" matters; the data in this are arranged by topic and are not numbered.

[63] Corr. no. 1440. Cf. Evelyn to Taylor, [December 1655], *Diary and Correspondence,* III, 67; for the date of this letter, see E. S. de Beer, "Jeremy Taylor in 1655," *Notes and Queries* 170 (1936), 24–25. See further below, pp. 100–101.

[64] *Sculptura,* Bell ed., sig. C8v.

[65] Evelyn to Taylor, [December 1655], *Diary and Correspondence,* III, 67; Evelyn, *Diary,* III, 158.

[66] *Diary and Correspondence,* III, 67; Parry, "Evelyn as Hortulan Saint," 137. For Evelyn's later views on millenarianism, see Evelyn MS 35.

College for Experiments et Mechanicks" at Oxford which Wilkins had given £200 to promote in 1653 (though nothing came of it), or Evelyn may simply have been referring to the flourishing state of Wadham College under Wilkins' aegis. Either way, Wilkins' "Comely Aspect, and Gentleman-like Behaviour" would have been one of the factors commending his supervision to Evelyn.[67]

Evelyn's views on such matters are more fully expounded in a letter that he wrote on January 10, 1658, to Benjamin Maddox concerning the virtuoso pursuits to which he hoped Maddox would devote himself on his travels. Not only, in his view, did "gentlemen despising those vulgar things, deprive themselves of many handsom advantages to improve their time, and do service to the desiderants of philosophy; which is the only part of learning best illustrated by experiments, and, after the study of religion, certainly the most noble and virtuous." In addition, whereas such pursuits were commonly the preserve of "persons of a mean condition" whose "necessity renders them industrious," "if men of quality made it their delight also, arts could not but receive infinite advantages, because they have both means and leisure to improve and cultivate them."[68]

Evelyn seems to have believed strongly in the role of an elite, but he was disappointed by the state of the country's traditional ruling class, the landed aristocracy and gentry; as he told his brother in 1658, he wished these would pursue constructive activities "insteade of bringing into reputation those fruitlesse, vitious and empty conversations, to the prejudice of virtue, and that incomparable fruition of a mans selfe."[69] What was necessary was to imbue such natural rulers with knowledge that would break down the disparity between heredity and virtue, because he believed that "when virtue and blood are coincidents, they both add lustre and mutual excellencies."[70] Hence, much of his intellectual effort was aimed "to incite an affection in the Nobles of this nation" toward virtuoso knowledge, and to this end he was prepared "to open to them so many of the interior secrets, and most precious rules of this mysterious art, without imposture, or invidious reserve."[71]

This conviction of the need to offset the bleakness of the time by promulgating knowledge to a virtuous elite frequently recurs in Evelyn's writings in the late 1650s. For instance, in a letter to Hartlib of February 4, 1660, he praised a project for children's education that Hartlib was promoting because he saw it as a means "to obviate, and redresse those barbarous inundations, which the

[67] Walter Pope, *The Life of Seth [Ward], Lord Bishop of Salisbury,* J. B. Bamborough, ed., Oxford, 1961, 29–30. See also Barbara Shapiro, *John Wilkins, 1614–72,* Berkeley and Los Angeles, 1969, 92, 118–22, 136. A third possibility is that Evelyn might have been referring to the Oxford group of natural philosophers. See also above, note 6.

[68] *Diary and Correspondence,* III, 84. The word "handsom" is omitted from the published text and has here been instated from the manuscript version, Letter book, no. 126. Cf. Evelyn's comment to Hartlib about how "modest persons are only to be intrusted with these Secrets," Evelyn to Hartlib, February 4, 1660, Letter book, no. 163.

[69] Evelyn to George Evelyn, October 15, 1658, Letter book, no. 140; the word "of" is accidentally repeated before "virtue."

[70] Evelyn to Thurland, November 8, 1658, *Diary and Correspondence,* III, 107. Cf., for example, Evelyn to the countess of Sunderland, April 15, 1679, Letter book, no. 403. For background, see also Ruth Kelso, *The Doctrine of the English Gentleman in the Sixteenth Century,* University of Illinois Studies in Language and Literature 14, Urbana, 1929, 22–24, 29–30, and passim, and J. H. Hexter, "The Education of the Aristocracy in the Renaissance," in *Reappraisals in History,* London, 1961, 45–70, esp. 66–67.

[71] *Miscellaneous Writings,* 433.

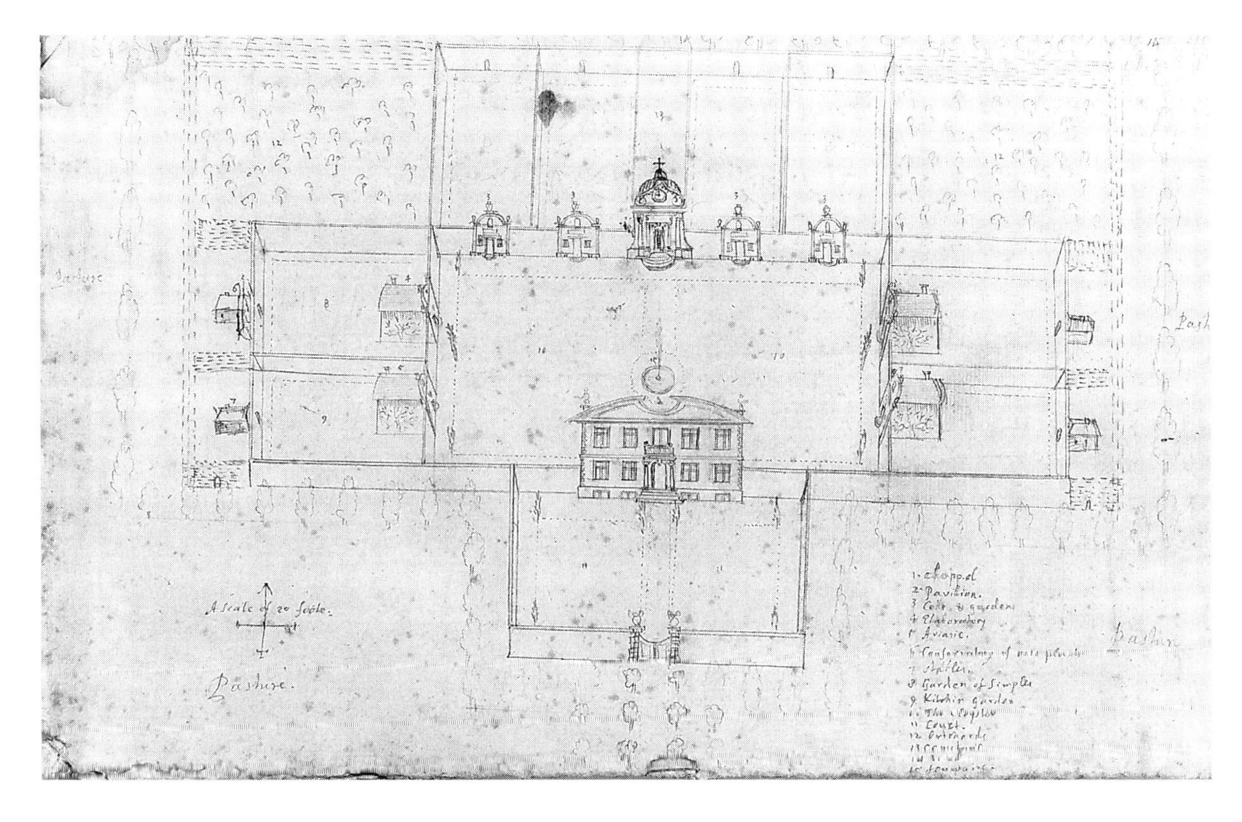

4. Evelyn's drawing illustrating his proposal for a "college," 1659. Evelyn Collection, British Library, London (photo: Michael R. Dudley)

dissolutenesse of this fatall conjunction universally menaces."[72] Such priorities also form the background to the famous plan for a "college" that Evelyn expounded in yet another letter to Boyle in these years (Fig. 4). This would have allowed a select group of gentlemen, "whose geniuses are greatly suitable, and who desire nothing more than to give a good example, preserve science, and cultivate themselves," to retire from the world in mutual seclusion, where they would provide a kind of seedbed for moral renewal.[73] It reinforces my point about the social dimension to Evelyn's view of how this reformation was to be effected that he assured Hartlib that the reason why such "Monastical Societies" were needed in addition to the existing universities was the latter's irremediable "Pedantry, for want of that addresse & refinement of a more generous Conversation."[74] Interestingly, it appears to have been above all the Royal Society that Evelyn saw as exemplifying his ideals, to judge from the extent to which he divulged to that body information he otherwise witheld from publication, including the accounts of marbled paper, varnishing, and mezzotinting that have already been referred to.[75]

[72] Letter book, no. 163. It is ironic that among the symptoms of the state of affairs that Evelyn deprecated were the "late Rebellions," from which Hartlib had benefited so much.

[73] Evelyn to Boyle, September 3, 1659, *Diary and Correspondence,* III, 116–20. The illustrations of his scheme that Evelyn refers to in his postscript survive in the Evelyn Collection and were first reproduced with a commentary in Hunter, *New Science,* 181–84.

[74] Letter book, no. 163.

[75] See above, pp. 88, 91. It is worth noting that Evelyn endorsed his own copy of his varnish recipe (i.e., the item now in Royal Society, Boyle Papers 26, fol. 141): "Given into our Society by J. Evelyn the 29 Jan: 1661. and thence to the whole nation" (Evelyn MS 52A, p. 311).

By the end of the 1650s, Evelyn was at work on the "Elysium Britannicum," and, as we will see, the set of ideas that I have expounded is much in evidence in the rationale of that book. First, however, let us retrace our steps to 1652–53, and to the second component of Evelyn's intellectual program at that point to which I have already referred, his translation of Lucretius' *De Rerum Natura,* on book one of which he was clearly at work as early as 1653.[76] This section of the translation appeared in print in 1656 (Fig. 5), and extant correspondence suggests that it was well received, despite the fact that the proof correcting, which Evelyn had deputed, was inadequately executed.[77] Indeed, one accolade that Evelyn received as a result of this publication was the dedication to him of the English translation of Pierre Gassendi's *Life of Peiresc* (1657) by Dr. William Rand, who attributed to Evelyn "the Principalitie of learned Curiositie in England."[78]

Evelyn also prepared a translation of and notes on the remaining books of Lucretius' poem. More than half of the translating appears to have been done before book one was published, and it was completed and the commentary prepared in 1656–57, when Evelyn seems to have hoped to bring out an edition of the remaining books in conjunction with a revised version of his translation of the first.[79] In the end, however, he decided against publication, and the manuscripts of both the text of and commentary on books three through six (though not, for some reason, book two) survive among the Evelyn manuscripts.[80] The published and unpublished translations are both workmanlike, and the notes comprise a lengthy series of comments and animadversions that display a considerable degree of learning in both ancient and contemporary sources. On the other hand, the notes are undeniably scrappy, particularly those to books three through six, which are often accompanied by a "q.," signaling the need for further research. Evidently this reflects the fact that, at some point during his work on it, Evelyn decided to abandon the undertaking, leaving the manuscript unfinished "in the dust of my study, where 'tis like to be for ever buried," as he explained to the cleric Meric Casaubon a decade and a half later.[81]

Evelyn's *Lucretius* presents us with a puzzle. Why did the project appeal to him in the first place, and why did he abandon it? First, on the question of its appeal, I think we have to return to

[76] It is clear that the royalist diplomat and poet Sir Richard Fanshawe saw Evelyn's translation of book one in that year; see Fanshawe to Evelyn, December 27, 1653, British Library, Add. MS 28104, fol. 6; John Evelyn, *An Essay on the First Book of T. Lucretius Carus: De Rerum Natura,* London, 1656 (hereinafter *Lucretius*), 6–9. See also Fanshawe to Evelyn, October 7, 1653, Letter book, no. 66.

[77] Evelyn, *Diary,* III, 173; *Diary and Correspondence,* III, 76–77, 95: Wilkins to Evelyn, August 16, 1656; Taylor to Evelyn, September 15, 1656; Snatt to Evelyn, May 25, 1657.

[78] Rand to Evelyn, March 13, 1657, Corr. no. 1122; W. Rand, trans., *The Mirrour of True Nobility and Gentility,* London, 1657, sigs. A3–6. Interestingly, Evelyn initially believed that Rand had singled him out for this accolade "upon the report (it seemes) of our collection and Cimelium of raritys": Evelyn to Browne, March 6, 1657, Corr. no. 1441. Correspondence with Rand himself, however, clarified the matter: Corr. nos. 1122–23.

[79] See Evelyn to Browne, October 18, 1656, Corr. no. 1438; Evelyn to Rand, April 9, 1657, Letter book, no. 109; and, for example, Taylor to Evelyn, September 15, 1656, *Diary and Correspondence,* III, 77. See also below, note 80.

[80] Evelyn MSS 33 (the commentary), 34 and 34a. MS 34a is the draft for the latter part of book six, dated at the end September 11, 1657; MS 34, which is a fair copy, gives out in the course of book six, with some overlap with MS 34a. Various sections in Evelyn MS 33 bear dates in 1657: pp. 39, 71–72, 113.

[81] Evelyn to Casaubon, July 15, 1674 [*sic*], *Diary and Correspondence,* III, 247.

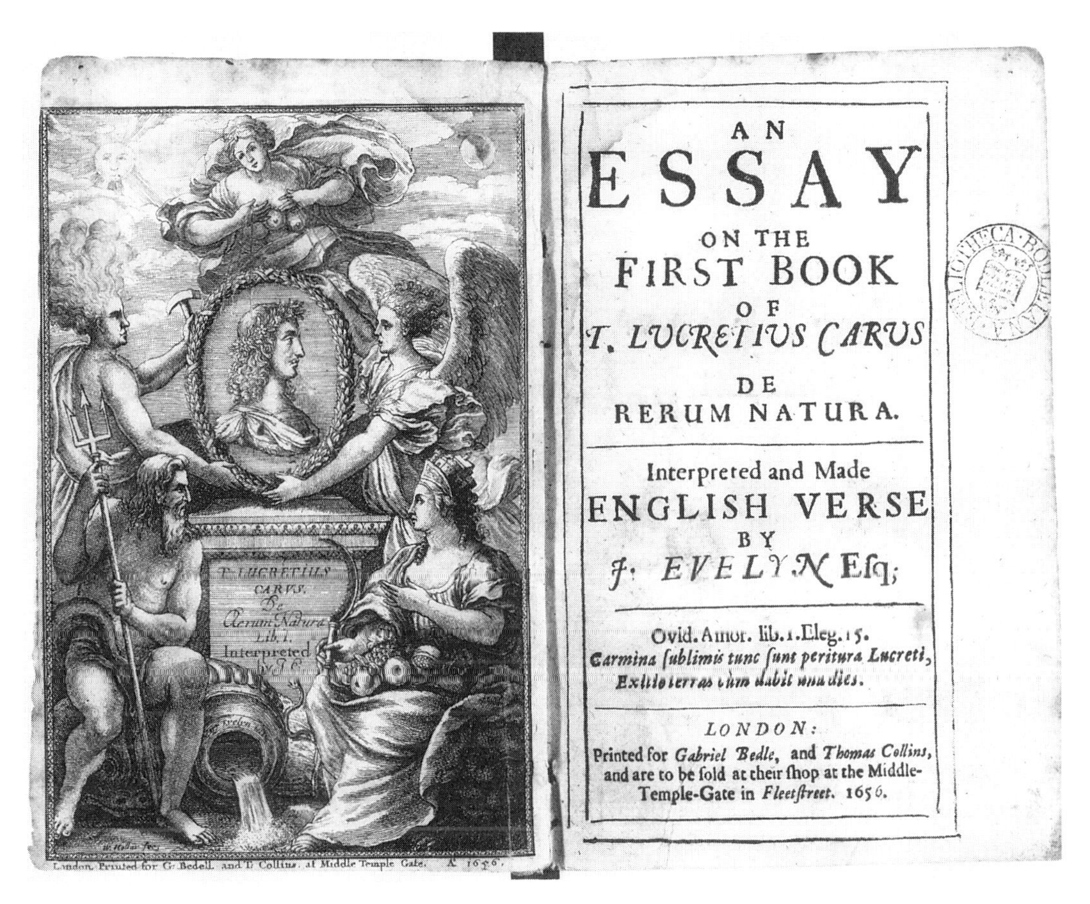
AN

ESSAY

ON THE

FIRST BOOK

OF

T. LUCRETIUS CARUS

DE

RERUM NATURA.

Interpreted and Made

ENGLISH VERSE

BY

J. EVELYN Eſq;

Ovid. Amor. lib. 1. Eleg. 15.

Carmina ſublimis tunc ſunt peritura Lucreti,
Exitio terras cum dabit una dies.

LONDON:

Printed for *Gabriel Bedle,* and *Thomas Collins,* and are to be ſold at their ſhop at the Middle-Temple-Gate in *Fleetſtreet.* 1656.

5. Title page and frontispiece of Evelyn's translation of book one of Lucretius' *De Rerum Natura,* 1656. Bodleian Library, Oxford, Art. 8° L 17 BS (photo: courtesy the library)

the issue of how it was appropriate for an intellectual to employ his time. In dealing with Evelyn's commitment to "practical" virtuoso activities, we have rather lost sight of that parallel commitment to erudition that is in evidence in his library and commonplace book: the man who had devoted so much time to reading and absorbing ancient and modern learning and collecting obiter dicta might reasonably feel that he had skills of composition and exegesis that were rather wasted in purveying information on practical skills, even of so refined a variety as gilding picture frames.[82] Evelyn had exemplified the kind of self-conscious prose that resulted from the cultivation of such materials in the introductory sections to his two earliest books, both of which comprise a patchwork of allusions to and quotations from classical authors.[83] In addition, Evelyn clearly fancied himself as a poetaster and translator, and it was for Lucretius' excellence as a writer that he most frequently expressed enthusiasm in his commentary: "A most elegant description," Evelyn wrote at one point, and "the verses are worthy to be written in Gould." Of Lucretius' description of the origins of human society

[82] It is worth noting that the descriptions in his volume on *Trades* are entirely devoid of literary self-consciousness.

[83] See his translation of La Mothe le Vayer's *Of Liberty and Servitude,* 1649, and his *The State of France,* 1652: *Miscellaneous Writings,* 5–6, 41–52.

in book five he expostulates, "hee proceeds by so natural & incomparable a description of the Innocent age, as were worthy the learning by heart."[84]

Evelyn's choice of Lucretius can be seen as a further example of his role in purveying contemporary French culture to an English audience. By this time he had already translated into English a freethinking treatise by the French *érudit* François La Mothe le Vayer, *Of Liberty and Servitude.*[85] Evelyn's interest in Lucretius must have been aroused by knowledge of the great Epicurean project that the scholar Pierre Gassendi had by this time virtually completed. Indeed, Evelyn was not unique in taking an interest in such ideas and seeking to divulge them in English, inasmuch as his Oxford contemporary Walter Charleton similarly sought to divulge Epicurean ideas to his countrymen by publishing a kind of English summary of Gassendi's *Animadversions on the Ten Books of Diogenes Laertius* in his *Physiologia Epicuro-Gassendo-Charltoniana* (1654).[86] In addition, Evelyn must have been aware of the first French translation of *De Rerum Natura* by Michel de Marolles, published in 1650, because the frontispiece to the published section of Evelyn's translation (Fig. 5) is obviously derived from that of Marolles.[87]

It remains, however, slightly surprising that Evelyn was attracted to Lucretius, for, despite his appeal to men such as Gassendi and Charleton, Lucretius was a figure who had long been frowned on in orthodox circles. To understand this, I think we have to recall the turmoil that English royalist thought was in at this time, the defeat and humiliation of the civil war seeming to challenge the very basis of old certainties. The most obvious symptom of this was the extent to which Evelyn's contacts succumbed to the attractions of Roman Catholicism; Evelyn retained copies of more than one impassioned letter that he wrote to such figures urging the counterattractions of Anglicanism, though acknowledging the extent to which he, too, had felt the seductive charm of the Roman church.[88] Equally symptomatic was the range of new ideas canvassed in the circles in which Evelyn moved, including those of Thomas Hobbes; thus, Evelyn's cousin Samuel Tuke's enthusiasm for Hobbes was such that "I may assume the stile of his disciple," a sentiment with which he assured Evelyn that his friends agreed.[89] As for Evelyn himself, one of the more surprising components of the earliest phase in his commonplace book are his extensive notes on the works of Machiavelli, whose political

[84] Evelyn MS 33, fols. 21, 100 ("natural" replaces "sweete," deleted), 106. Compare his praise of the later books of the poem in a letter to Sir Richard Browne of October 18, 1656, as "full of incomparable and most usefull variety": Corr. no. 1438. On Evelyn's literary pretensions, see, for example, Waller to Evelyn, August 3 and 22, 1646, Corr. nos. 1341, 1343; Evelyn to Waller, December 20, 1649, Letter book, no. 6; Evelyn MS 41—Evelyn's play "Thersander," which could date from the 1650s—and Evelyn MS 124, a verse commonplace book entitled "Otium Evelyni."

[85] *Miscellaneous Writings,* 5–40.

[86] For a recent account, see Howard Jones, *The Epicurean Tradition,* London, 1989, chap. 7–8; on Gassendi's project, see especially Lynn Joy, *Gassendi the Atomist: Advocate of History in an Age of Science,* Cambridge, 1987.

[87] See C. A. Gordon, *A Bibliography of Lucretius,* London, 1962, 151, 154–55 and pl. 16, which reproduces Marolles' plate. Evelyn's frontispiece, designed by Mrs. Evelyn and engraved by Hollar, closely echoes that of Marolles in comprising a medallion containing the poet's portrait surrounded by the four elements and surmounted by Venus.

[88] See Evelyn to Keightley, Annunc. B. V. 1651, Letter book, no. 23; see also Evelyn to Cosin, January 1, 1652, Letter book, no. 38 (and *Diary and Correspondence,* III, 58f). Compare Hugh Trevor-Roper, "The Great Tew Circle" in his *Catholics, Anglicans and Puritans,* London, 1987, esp. 183–84, 200–201.

[89] Tuke to Evelyn, October 25, 1650, Corr. no. 1277.

realism he clearly found fascinating, despite his later view of Machiavelli as "shewing what men may do, not what they ought."[90]

Hence, initially, Evelyn perhaps thought that he could handle Lucretius by doing justice to his worthwhile ideas while using his commentary to "provide against all the ill consequences" of Lucretius' more questionable opinions.[91] But in the course of working on the text, he evidently discovered that his instincts led him to a less radical position than that of the French *esprits forts* whom he had initially emulated. There is something distinctly unsatisfactory about Evelyn's *Lucretius,* particularly the commentary; indeed, it is revealing that he had second thoughts even about the publication of his notes on book one, though the publisher explains that he ignored these so as to make the book of a viable bulk.[92] In my view, Evelyn's notes reveal a fundamental uncertainty as to where he stood in relation to Lucretius' most influential ideas and a growing disapproval of some of their corollaries.

In particular, I have been unable to find in Evelyn's commentary any of the sense of excitement about the simplicity and clarity of Lucretius' atomistic view of nature displayed by Gassendi and Charleton.[93] Evelyn had read these authors—indeed, his notes on Charleton's *Physiologia* occupy more pages in his commonplace book than those on any other single work—and he dutifully cites them about the plausibility of the atomist hypothesis.[94] But it is quite unclear how far he was convinced by it, and particularly how far he saw it as excluding other views of nature. Rather, my reading of Evelyn's notes on Lucretius suggests that his entire instinct was to *synthesize;* in contrast to men such as Gassendi and Charleton, who used Epicureanism as a vehicle for attacking Aristotle and his ideas, Evelyn seems to have wanted to form a synthesis between the two. He is constantly to be found collating Aristotle with Lucretius, noting how far the ideas of the two were in conflict, and sometimes preferring peripatetic views to Epicurean ones.[95]

His dilemma is further illustrated by other evidence, not least book one of "Elysium Britannicum" (written a year or two later, as we shall see). This suggests that Evelyn had a worldview that could hardly be further from a clear, atomistic exposition of things. Indeed, as he explained in the "Elysium Britannicum," though he would have liked "to reconcile whatsoever we may have spoken to the well restored doctrine of *Epicurus,*" he admitted that his notions—from which "we neither do, nor intend to receede"—seemed "to interferre upon a superficial view."[96] As book one of "Elysium Britannicum" reveals, Evelyn was a syncretic philosopher. Indeed, of the authors abstracted in his commonplace book, he arguably owed more to the Paracelsian Michael Sendivogius than he did to

[90] Evelyn MS 54(1), pp. 332 f; Evelyn to Rand, April 9, 1657, Letter book, no. 109. Cf. Packer to Evelyn, February 19, 1649, Corr. no. 1066. Evelyn also met Hobbes, and he owned a copy of Herbert of Cherbury's *De Veritate: Diary,* III, 41, 58, 163.

[91] Evelyn to Taylor, April 27, 1657, *Diary and Correspondence,* III, 73.

[92] *Lucretius,* 80.

[93] Or compare William Rand, who wrote to Evelyn, "What greater Argument can be required of an Universal Intellect, then to be delighted with the Speculation of Infinite Space, & infinite matter, variously figured & marshaled into an infinite Systemes of Worlds": Corr. no. 1122.

[94] Evelyn MS 54(1), pp. 253–71; *Lucretius,* 172–73, and 97f passim; Evelyn MS 33, front flyleaf and passim.

[95] See, for example, Evelyn MS 33, fols. 11, 52–53, 67, 127, and passim.

[96] "Elysium Britannicum," Evelyn MS 45, p. 9.

the Epicurean Charleton, and his worldview was as eclectic as any of those that research has brought to light in the mid-seventeenth century.[97] In this section, he attempts a synthesis of Aristotelianism with Paracelsianism, accepting the four elements and the four qualities, but explaining them in terms of the Paracelsian three principles, and subordinating the whole to a neo-Platonic universal spirit or spirit of the world. With such ideas Lucretian atomism made a rather uncomfortable match.

What made matters worse from Evelyn's point of view was Lucretius' notorious heterodoxy. That this was proving problematic even before he published his translation of the first book is clear from his correspondence with Jeremy Taylor at that point.[98] Moreover, if initially Evelyn thought that he could offset such dangerous corollaries through his notes, his anxieties about them evidently grew as the work progressed, perhaps in connection with his increasing sense of the degeneracy of the times. Thus, in a passage in his commentary evidently written in 1657, he expressed concern about the likely appeal of questionable views like those of Lucretius "in this Catalysis of piety amongst us, and Hydra of Errors."[99] One problem was the section at the end of book four in which Lucretius discussed sexual procreation, which Evelyn simply omitted from both his translation and his commentary, explaining to Sir Richard Browne how although "what I scruple at in the fourth booke, is by the poet physicaly intended; but as this age is now deprav'd I had much rather all the poems in the world should perish, then that any thing of mine should contribute & minister to vice."[100]

More serious was the issue of the soul's mortality, which, as Evelyn himself was aware, was integral to Lucretius' work, the first three books of the poem effectively reaching a climax with the assertion of this toward the end of the third.[101] Initially, Evelyn seems to have edged toward a mortalist position, perhaps encouraged by William Rand, who proved in his correspondence with Evelyn to be a well-informed and enthusiastic advocate of mortalism.[102] In 1657, Evelyn appears to have echoed such views himself in a letter to Jeremy Taylor; Taylor, in replying, not only pointed out that the position was heretical but also adduced some cogent arguments against it which seem to have stimulated severe self-searching on this issue on Evelyn's part.[103]

[97] See, for example, Michael Hunter, *John Aubrey and the Realm of Learning,* London, 1975, chap. 2; B. J. T. Dobbs, "Studies in the Natural Philosophy of Sir Kenelm Digby," *Ambix* 18 (1971), 1–25; 20 (1973), 143–63; 21 (1974), 1–28. Dobbs' findings indicate how Evelyn's ideas were probably formed, not only by his reading, but also by the chemistry classes by Nicaise le Fèvre that both he and Digby attended. See above, note 23.

[98] Evelyn to Taylor, April 27, 1656, *Diary and Correspondence,* III, 72–74.

[99] Evelyn MS 33, fol. 4 ("and declension of" has been deleted after "Catalysis"). It is perhaps worth noting in this connection Evelyn's concern about the heightened activity of the Anabaptists at this time; *Diary,* III, 202; Evelyn to Taylor, October 9, 1656, Letter book, no. 99; Evelyn to Browne, December 18, 1656, Corr. no. 1440.

[100] Evelyn to Browne, October 18, 1656, Corr. no. 1438; an overlapping but not identical version of the same letter appears in the Letter book, no. 106, dated February 12, 1656/57. See also Taylor to Evelyn, September 15, 1656, *Diary and Correspondence,* III, 77.

[101] Evelyn MS 33, fol. 40.

[102] Rand to Evelyn, March 13 and May 10, 1657, Corr. nos. 1122–23.

[103] Taylor to Evelyn, August 29, 1657, *Diary and Correspondence,* III, 98–100. For the claim that the interlocutor "Lucretius," who adopts a mortalist position in Walter Charleton's *The Immortality of the Human Soul,* 1657, is Evelyn, see Lindsay Sharp, "Walter Charleton's Early Life, 1620–59, and Relationship to Natural Philosophy in Mid-Seventeenth Century England," *Annals of Science* 30 (1973), 311–40, on 335–36. However, I think it unwise to draw conclusions about Evelyn's views on this basis.

It is, therefore, symptomatic that, having completed his commentary on Lucretius, Evelyn reverted to this issue on the blank leaves at the end of the volume he had used,[104] and it seems probable that his anxieties on this score ultimately led him to suppress the work. The immortality of the soul was of concern to him precisely because he linked the denial of this doctrine with the debauchery that he saw as characteristic of his age—that proclivity toward vice that was the reason for his advocacy of the pursuit of virtue.[105] Indeed, it is almost certainly not coincidental that it was in 1657—just at the time when his Lucretius project reached its climax—that Evelyn undertook a further work, *The History of Religion,* "Collected for the *Settling* and *Establishment* of my own *Choice*"; moreover, it is significant that he apologized in this for being especially prolix on the issue of the soul's immortality and its implications.[106]

Hence in 1657–58 Evelyn quietly abandoned his *Lucretius* and is to be found taking up other, safer tasks, relating yet again to his role as a purveyor of French culture in England. One was a translation of the *Golden Book* of St. John Chrysostom, the manuscript of which, discovered in the Cardinal's Library in Paris, had been published in 1656; Evelyn evidently found solace in this text when his beloved son Richard died early in 1658.[107] A second was a translation of a work by another French intellectual, Gabriel Naudé, of his *Instructions concerning Erecting of a Library,* which, though published only in 1661, was evidently largely executed at this stage, with the encouragement of Bodley's librarian, Thomas Barlow, and Oxford don Peter Pett.[108] Perhaps most significant was the translation that Evelyn now executed of Nicolas de Bonnefons' *The French Gardiner,* in which he seems to have been encouraged by his old virtuoso contact Thomas Henshaw.[109] When it was done, Henshaw thanked Evelyn for his kindness "that you would at my intreating, deprive your self of that high satisfaction you take in studies of a higher and nobler nature, to bestow so many houres uppon a Translation," praising "the great paynes you have taken in so knotty a peece, to make england emulous of the pleasure and profit france receives in its gardens, and to give part to this little world of the delights you and I particularly take in this divertisement of gardening."[110]

[104] Evelyn MS 33, fols. 153v–155. In addition, further leaves that evidently had notes on them have been torn out at this point.

[105] Evelyn MS 33, fols. 34–35. See above, p. 93.

[106] John Evelyn, *The History of Religion,* R. M. Evanson, ed., 2 vols., London, 1850, I, xiv, xxvii. The manuscript of this work is Evelyn MS 37; the current recension is later, but there seems no reason to doubt that the work was begun in 1657, as stated on the title page.

[107] *Miscellaneous Writings,* 112 and 103–40 passim; Keynes, *Bibliography,* 55–58.

[108] See Keynes, *Bibliography,* 103–8. For its initial composition in 1658, see Evelyn to Pett, April 5 and October 16, 1658, Letter book, nos. 133, 141, and the letter to Barlow printed on the last leaf of the published work. The further letter to Barlow of June 10, 1661, in *Diary and Correspondence,* III, 132–33 shows that publication was delayed partly because the manuscript was mislaid; it now survives at Queen's College, Oxford, MS 231 (with dedicatory epistle to Barlow dated October 5, 1658).

[109] Nicolas de Bonnefons, *The French Gardiner,* John Evelyn, trans., London, 1658. See Henshaw to Evelyn, January 11, 1657[?/58], Corr. no. 896, and Evelyn's dedicatory epistle, *Miscellaneous Writings,* 97–98; see also Henshaw to Evelyn, January 13, 1657[?/58], Corr. 897.

[110] Henshaw to Evelyn, February 28, 1658/59, Corr. no. 898. The translation is usually accepted as exclusively the work of Evelyn (e.g., in Keynes, *Bibliography,* 46–47). But the letters of Henshaw cited in note 109 suggest that one section of it may in fact have been translated by Dr. Needham, another member of Evelyn's and Henshaw's virtuoso

It was in the preface to *The French Gardiner* that Evelyn made the first public announcement of the "Elysium Britannicum," in words that Henshaw echoed in this same letter, dated February 28, 1659; he there told Evelyn how his statement "hath raised a longing in many Curious persons who doe already question mee when it will come out." Evidently it was at this point that Evelyn actually embarked on this work, and it seems likely that it was the translation of *The French Gardiner* that formed the direct stimulus to it. But, as Evelyn implied in his announcement, in which he stated that he had "long since had inclinations and a design of communicating some other things of this nature from my own experience; and especially, concerning the ornaments of gardens, &c.,"[111] the intended work drew on a theme in his virtuoso activities that had been present throughout the period dealt with in this paper. Evelyn had made alterations to the family garden at Wotton as early as 1643, and he embarked on major improvements to the garden at Sayes Court on his return to England in 1652, planting thousands of trees and plants in emulation of Pierre Morin's celebrated garden in Paris.[112] Indeed, it is even possible that Evelyn had begun to write on gardening at that point, though no manuscript material of this date survives, presumably because it would in any case have been subsumed into the "Elysium Britannicum."[113] Hence, Evelyn was well equipped for work on this major treatise, much of the text of which dates from 1659 and 1660.

The enthusiasm with which Evelyn embraced the "Elysium Britannicum" at this point reflects the extent to which it encapsulated the themes that have been surveyed in this paper. First, it combined Evelyn's wish to disseminate useful information and his literary aspirations. Much of the text gave practical advice on everything that a garden required from seedbeds and orangeries to echoes and wind organs, often illustrated by reports on practices or gadgets that Evelyn had seen on his travels or tried at home; indeed, in a sense the work subsumed Evelyn's earlier study of the history of trades.[114] Yet it was presented in a highly literary way, with elaborately constructed sentences, quotations from the classical poets, and the like. It was also highly erudite, constantly adducing apposite stories from antiquity or more recent times to illustrate points, and thus utilizing Evelyn's

---

circle, who had earlier advised Evelyn on book purchases (see above, note 24) and supplied Evelyn with the copy of Gassendi's epitaph that Evelyn included in *Lucretius,* [186–88] (see Needham to Evelyn, January 13, 1655[?/56], Corr. no. 1026). However, it is difficult to reconcile what is said in the letters with the component parts of the published work.

[111] *Miscellaneous Writings,* 97–98. He went on to summarize the "Elysium Britannicum's" intended content, but added how "some other things unexpectedly intervened, which as yet hinder the birth and maturity of that embryo."

[112] Evelyn, *Diary,* II, 81. Cf. ibid., III, 60–61. The work at Sayes Court was assiduously discussed in his correspondence with Sir Richard Browne between 1652 and 1656; for a summary account, see Hiscock, *Family Circle,* 28f.

[113] See Evelyn to Maddox, [March/April 1657], Letter book, no. 108, in which he refers to his "longsinc-begun designe of propagating Garden Plants." In his letter to Lady Sunderland of August 4, 1690 (*Diary and Correspondence,* III, 317), Evelyn states that he had compiled his *Kalendarium Hortense* forty years earlier and that it had been published thirty years earlier; the latter tallies with its actual publication as part of *Sylva* in 1664, and it is possible that the *Kalendarium* preceded "Elysium Britannicum" and was simply grafted into it. (See the printed contents list of the "Elysium Britannicum.") However, on the dangers of accepting the evidence of such retrospective accounts, see above, pp. 81–82. It is unclear on what grounds Hiscock (*Family Circle,* 32) dates the start of "Elysium Britannicum" to "1653 or so." There is some material on gardening in Evelyn MS 54(1), pp. 293ff; for the section on using shells for grottos in MS 65, p. 499, see above, p. 88.

[114] Cf. Evelyn to Boyle, August 9, 1659, *Diary and Correspondence,* III, 115.

wide reading in ancient and modern authors, which is documented in his commonplace book. In this, the work differed from earlier English books on horticulture, usually written by men who were themselves gardeners. It is equally revealing to compare it with the comparable work of Robert Sharrock, a member of the Oxford group of natural philosophers who, like Evelyn, sought to bridge the gap between head and hand in his *History of the Propagation & Improvement of Vegetables by the Concurrence of Art and Nature* (1660). For Sharrock deliberately eschewed "Rhetorical Tropes" and extraneous citations, keeping his "directions so plain, as if appointed for the instruction of some Artists rude and untaught Apprentice."[115]

On the other hand, the method that Evelyn used was to recur in his later writings, most notably *Sylva,* on which, since it was published, contemporaries commented. As the bluestocking Margaret Cavendish, duchess of Newcastle, revealingly remarked, "though it is large through number and variety, yet you have enclosed it with elegancy and eloquence, all which proves you more proper to be the head than a member of the Royal Society."[116] Others had reservations, seeing these literary pretensions as distancing the work from its proper audience. Indeed, the former Hartlibian John Pell commented on the work, "I wish that some body, without any Embellishments & Flourishes, would give us the *plaine precepts* for planting & ordering of woods, hedge-rowes, Orchards & Gardens."[117] But the Yorkshire doctor, Nathaniel Johnston, who similarly recognized as a potential "failing" the fact that "the countryman must go learn Latin and the poets to understand our author," perceptively recognized that this was not the point; for he saw that, in writing "scholar and gentleman like of this subject . . . his design was to make gentlemen in love with the study, and that will effect the whole of his intendment." Indeed, as I have argued elsewhere, in some ways this helps to explain the work's undoubted success.[118]

This was linked to a further characteristic of "Elysium Britannicum"—that it was unashamedly elitist. As Evelyn himself put it, he was not addressing himself "to *Cabbage-planters;* but to the best refined of our Nation who delight in Gardens, and aspire to the perfections of the Arte."[119] Here, as later in *Sylva,* he took it for granted that "there is nothing more becoming and worthy of a *Gentleman*" than horticultural and related pursuits, urging them to learn about such matters for themselves rather than defer to "their ignorant *Hinds* and *Servants,* who are (generally speaking) more fit to Learn then to Instruct."[120] Dealing as he was with the most refined parts of horticulture, he had "no designe to nauseate the world, with repetitions of those trite and vulgar observations, which hitherto have composed the greater part of bookes extant on this subject."[121] In addition, his format made it appropriate for him to divulge knowledge without fear of being accused of disseminating it to

[115] Sharrock, *History of Vegetables,* Oxford, 1660, 2–3 and passim.

[116] Duchess of Newcastle to Evelyn, February 1670, *Diary and Correspondence,* III, 226.

[117] Pell to Haak, March 30, 1667, Bodleian Library, MS Aubrey 13, fol. 93v.

[118] Hunter, *Science and Society,* 93, 100–101. For Johnston's views, see Johnston to Slingsby, January 20, 1666, *Sixth Report of the Royal Commission on Historical Manuscripts,* London, 1877, appendix, 337a.

[119] "Elysium Britannicum," 10.

[120] *Sylva; or a Discourse of Forest-Trees,* London, 1664, sig. B2.

[121] Evelyn to Le Franc, July 5, 1659, Letter book, no. 152.

unworthy recipients (though, even here, he was aware that it was undesirable to "prostitute, more then dos become me to reveale").[122] More importantly, "Elysium Britannicum" linked his technological and more intellectual ambitions in the extent to which it dwelt on the *philosophy* of gardens, on the "seacret & powerfull influence" that the gardener could achieve through his art, and on "how the aire and genious of Gardens operat upon humane spirits towards virtue and sanctitie"—thus alluding to his wider goals in the late 1650s.[123]

Lastly, one thing that was new about the "Elysium Britannicum" was that Evelyn seems now to have learnt the message of the Hartlibians (and later of the Royal Society) of the value of cooperation. In his earlier activities surveyed in this paper he had essentially been a "loner," collecting and recording virtuoso recipes and divulging them to a few friends. As stressed at the outset, he had hitherto not had particularly close links with either the Hartlib circle or the Oxford group. For the "Elysium Britannicum," however, he both requested information from a wide range of correspondents and sent them sections for their advice. As he explained to one of these, "I have blotted many sheetes of paper upon the particulars mentiond; which before I transcribe for the Printer, both for the dignitie of the subject, and my owne reputation, I should be glad might be adorned, with such aides & subsidiaries, as either my friends, or other worthy persons (conversant in Gardens) will contribute to it."[124] Indeed, it is worth emphasizing what others have illustrated elsewhere—that it was this project that first stimulated Evelyn to correspond with Hartlib, and through him with John Beale, who shared many of the same interests and priorities as Evelyn;[125] he also solicited contact with Sir Thomas Browne in this connection, and he exploited his existing contact with Boyle to gain material for the work.[126] In a sense, the "Elysium Britannicum" thus provided a model of what Evelyn was able to achieve with *Sylva,* when even more disparate information came together under the supervision of his "exquisite pen."[127]

Hence, in a way, the "Elysium Britannicum" looked forward to Evelyn's activities under the auspices of the Royal Society over the next few years, and it is to these that we must briefly turn. Evelyn was genuinely enthusiastic about the work of that body from his election to it early in 1661 onward: yet it is ironic that his participation in it had the effect of diverting his attention from the "Elysium Britannicum" at a critical stage in its development toward projects that related more directly to the tastes of his peers. It was in 1661 that the society's enthusiasm for the history of trades

[122] Ibid.

[123] "Elysium Britannicum," 155; Evelyn to Browne, January 28, 1660, in Geoffrey Keynes, ed., *The Works of Sir Thomas Browne,* London, 1964, IV, 275.

[124] Evelyn to Le Franc, July 5, 1659, Letter book, no. 152.

[125] See Parry, "John Evelyn as Hortulan Saint," in Leslie and Raylor, *Culture and Cultivation* (as above, note 9), esp. 138–41; Michael Leslie, "The Spiritual Husbandry of John Beale," ibid., 151–72; and Douglas Chambers, "'Wild Pastorall Encounter': John Evelyn, John Beale and the Renegotiation of Pastoral in the Mid-Seventeenth Century," ibid., 173–94. Mayling Stubbs, "John Beale: Philosophical Gardener of Herefordshire, Part 1," *Annals of Science* 39 (1982), 486 note 121; Evelyn to Hartlib, August 8, 1659, Letter book, no. 153.

[126] Evelyn to Browne, January 28, 1660, Keynes, *Works of Browne,* IV, 273–79; Evelyn to Boyle, August 9, 1659, *Diary and Correspondence,* III, 114–15.

[127] See Hunter, *Science and Society,* 93. On the making of *Sylva,* see also Sharp, "Timber, Science and Economic Reform," 63–64.

encouraged Evelyn to resuscitate the material from his earlier work on related subjects and to prepare his *Sculptura* as a more learned contribution to the same enterprise. When writing to John Wilkins on the society's behalf on January 29, 1661, promising *Sculptura* and sending other data, he requested that "knowing upon what other subject I was engaged before I had the honour to be elected one of this august Society, I may obtain its indulgence, not to expect other things from me 'till it be accomplished"—a direct allusion to the "Elysium Britannicum."[128] But in fact he was to be persuaded in 1662 to undertake what materialized as *Sylva,* which, though related to the "Elysium Britannicum" and deploying the skills exemplified there, clearly delayed his progress on that work.

Moreover, although in the same letter to Wilkins he requested the society to "take all occasions which may contribute to my design," and although the society made various encouraging noises about the "Elysium Britannicum" in its public and private pronouncements,[129] this undertaking remained somewhat peripheral to the society's research in its early years, which was otherwise focused. On the one hand, it concentrated on more directly utilitarian projects, as in the work of the Mechanical Committee of 1664, which, significantly, utilized many of the same texts on hydraulics and the like as Evelyn in "Elysium Britannicum," but directed its efforts not toward waterworks for gardens but toward improving the water supply to London.[130] On the other hand, it encouraged basic botanical research, like that of Nehemiah Grew, who, though praising Evelyn and Beale for their contribution to the knowledge of plants through "the ordering of them with respect to their *Alimental* and *Mechanick* Uses," made clear that this was incidental to his own priority, which was "an inquiry into the Nature of *Vegetation.*"[131] Moreover, as Evelyn himself noted, research like that of Grew had the side effect of necessitating a total rewriting of book one of the "Elysium Britannicum."[132]

Equally significant is the extent to which the Restoration itself, that event to which Evelyn had so long aspired, inevitably distracted him from the scale of intellectual activity in which he had indulged in the interregnum. For Evelyn was now presented with an acute dilemma in terms of choosing between the life of the leisured savant, which he had enjoyed in the 1650s, and the public commitments that he had always felt a man in his position should properly fulfill. Initially, he avoided such positions. In August 1660 he was offered a military commission, but, replying that his skill in tactics reached "no further than the disciplining of a few Flowers in my Garden, and ranging the

[128] *Diary and Correspondence,* III, 131. This text is taken from the copy in the Letter book, no. 173, dated February 17, 1660/61. However, the correct date is clearly that given in the slightly different version of this letter in Birch, *History of the Royal Society,* I, 13–15. For other aspects of Evelyn's role in the society in its formative years, see Hunter, *New Science,* 16–17, 41–42, 52.

[129] See, for example, Joseph Glanvill, *Plus Ultra,* London, 1668, 73–74; *Philosophical Transactions* 4 (1669), 1073; Birch, *History of the Royal Society,* IV, 289.

[130] Hunter, *New Science,* chap. 3, esp. 115–18, cf. "Elysium Britannicum," 117f. This chapter also deals with the work of the Georgical Committee, which concentrated on agriculture and on kitchen gardens.

[131] N. Grew, *The Anatomy of Plants,* London, 1682, 1, 3. Grew's interests also extended to practical matters, but these were directly related to economic improvement; see Sharp, "Timber, Science and Economic Reform," 71–73.

[132] "Elysium Britannicum," 6; Evelyn's endorsement to the chapter heading at this point indicates his intention to carry out a full-scale revision that he never actually executed.

[133] Evelyn to Spencer, August 28, 1660, Letter book, no. 168.

Bookes in my studye," he expressed the hope that the king might find him a more suitable post.[133] Indeed, at this point, he seems to have hoped to have his cake and eat it, explaining in a letter of September 2, 1660, to the clerk of the signet, Sir Philip Warwick, how he hoped an opportunity might arise that would allow him to execute some public duty "without taking up so much tyme from the nobler parts of life." His experience in the 1650s had evidently raised his estimate of what he could achieve without sacrificing the "infinite felicitie in a private and even life."[134]

But increasingly the call of duty triumphed, and in 1664 Evelyn accepted the post of commissioner for sick and wounded mariners and prisoners of war during the Second Dutch War, which his correspondence shows that he found a grueling and disillusioning experience.[135] Subsequently, he found a task that might have provided the ideal combination of intellectual skills and public service, a project for writing a history of the Dutch wars, which he undertook in 1669. In the end, the work was abandoned due to the difficulty of reconciling Evelyn's historiographical goals with the political priorities of the statesmen who had commissioned the work in the first place; only the preface was ever published, as *Navigation and Commerce, Their Original and Progress* (1674). Nevertheless, it was clearly very time consuming.[136] Later still, under James II, Evelyn attained high government office as commissioner for the privy seal. Each time, he discovered the extent to which "secular affairs" were "the burial of all philosophical speculations and improvements";[137] each time, such duties removed him further from the task that he had begun in the halcyon days of 1659.

Hence, though Evelyn long continued to collect material for the "Elysium Britannicum" and to express the optimism that he would one day complete it,[138] it gradually slipped from his grasp. It remains a monument to the moment at which it was conceived—to the conjunction in the late 1650s that I have sketched here, of literary aspiration in the pursuit of humanist virtue, against the background of the technological concerns of the period.

[134] Letter book, no. 171. Note also the ambivalence about the message of his *Active Life* which he expressed in a letter to Abraham Cowley of March 12, 1667: *Diary and Correspondence,* III, 194.

[135] *Diary and Correspondence,* III, 148f passim, esp. 171–75; Letter book, nos. 222f passim, esp. 258–63.

[136] See esp. *Diary,* III, 523n, and the sources there cited; *Miscellaneous Writings,* 625–86. For manuscript material relating to this work, see Evelyn MSS 134, 545.

[137] Evelyn to Beale, July 11, 1679, *Diary and Correspondence,* II, 393.

[138] See Douglas Chambers, "'Elysium Britannicum not printed neere ready &c': The 'Elysium Britannicum' in the Correspondence of John Evelyn," this volume, pp. 107–30.

"Elysium Britannicum not printed neere ready &c": The "Elysium Britannicum" in the Correspondence of John Evelyn

DOUGLAS CHAMBERS

The "Elysium Britannicum" is not simply the most important unpublished document in English garden history, it is one of the central documents of late European humanism. Written by a founder of the Royal Society, who published in more than twenty different fields, it represents the world of Peter Burmann's *Sylloges Epistolarum*[1]—the intellectual community of Europe into which Milton had introduced himself only six years before Evelyn followed in his Continental footsteps.

I am not referring here simply to the French intellectuals whose acquaintance Evelyn made during his interregnum exile, chiefly at the home of his future father-in-law, Sir Richard Browne. I am talking also about the origins of the "Elysium Britannicum" in the horticultural and botanical advice of such men as the German scholar Henry Oldenburg, who was the first secretary of the Royal Society and tutor to the nephew of another of Evelyn's close friends, Robert Boyle. From the contributions of many such scholars, Continental and English, Evelyn was to construct the "Elysium." Similarly, from works as diverse (and now obscure) as Giovanni Bumaldi's *Historia Botanicorum* (1657), Benedictus Curtius' *Hortorum Libri Triginta* (1560), and his own (first) translation (in 1656) of Lucretius' *De Rerum Natura,* he was to bring into the mainstream of English (and even European) thought the horticultural and philosophical material of recent and antique scholarship.

The "Elysium" is the nexus of this scholarly enterprise, along with the whole Hartlibean project for the reform of English society, beginning with its agriculture and horticulture: the shift from a deracinated pastoral to an animating georgic.[2] It is also at the center of the debate about ancients and moderns, composed as it was during the very period when the foundations of modern

[1] *Sylloges Epistolarum a viris illustribus scriptorum tomi quinque,* Leiden, 1727.

[2] See my "'Wild Pastorall Encounter': John Evelyn, John Beale and the Renegotiation of Pastoral in the Mid-Seventeenth Century," in *Culture and Cultivation in Early Modern England: Writing and the Land,* Michael Leslie and Timothy Raylor, eds., Leicester, 1992, 177, 182–83.

taxonomy were being laid and the structure of science, as we still (largely) have it, were being put in place.

On the one hand, theoretical and speculative in the manner of Evelyn's friend Sir Thomas Browne, on the other empirical and skeptical, the "Elysium" represents a debate about the nature of science and knowledge (especially in book one) that is central to Western thought. Evelyn's notes on Lucretius[3] indicate his awareness of chaos theory as much as his attention to the craft of gardening indicates his belief in a knowledge that is not confined to the traditional limits of academic discourse.[4] The "Elysium," then, is a sort of microcosm, both of the great *magna instauratio* of the Royal Society and of scientific, specifically, agricultural and horticultural, thought in western Europe in the late seventeenth century. To see it as preoccupied with subjects that are marginal to the history of intellectual thought is to misread totally the centrality of cultivation to culture—what one of Evelyn's early correspondents called "making agriculture and gardening parts of liberal knowledge."[5] To read the "Elysium" in this way is to misunderstand the whole foundation of the landscape revolution that was its progeny. Its continuous presence in Evelyn's correspondence over a period of nearly fifty years is testimony to its significance throughout the era in which modern scientific and philosophical discourse took shape.

There are two basic problems in pursuing the "Elysium" in Evelyn's correspondence. The first is that, potentially, there is a vast amount of Evelyn correspondence that no one has seen. The majority of the correspondence is in the two letter books that are at British Library along with the several other collections of letters there. But there are many lacunae in Evelyn's correspondence, many letters to him for which no reply is present in the letter books, for example. And, in any case, we would naturally expect letters *from* Evelyn to be with the papers of his respective correspondents. However, almost none of the letters in those collections has ever been published. The second problem is a nominalist one: That the "Elysium" is not mentioned by name in these letters does not mean that the vast subject matter that it addresses does not arise in a great deal of the correspondence; it does. Among the subjects that reappear in the correspondence are Evelyn's own garden, Continental gardens, greenhouses, exotic plants (primarily from America and the Caribbean), the philosophical contexts of the "Elysium," and the garden problems and experiments about which his friends wrote to him. Much of this falls under that part of the "Elysium" that is now missing—the latter part of book two and the whole of book three. What I am suggesting is that a digest of this body of

[3] These were with the Evelyn papers in the library of Christ Church College, Oxford. In 1995 the Evelyn archives were purchased by the British Library.

[4] For the relation between Evelyn's practical and philosophical interests during his early career, see Michael Hunter, "John Evelyn in the 1650s: A Virtuoso in Quest of a Role," this volume, 79–106.

[5] William Nicholson, March 25, 1701, in William Bray, ed., *The Diary and Correspondence of John Evelyn,* 4 vols., London, 1859, III, 720. Because all the letters referred to here are contained in volume three, citations hereafter will be by *Correspondence* and page number only. Wherever a letter is published, I have used the version in the 1859 Bray edition, unless it is defective or corrupt. None of the many editions of the letters is complete, and there is considerable variance among them both as to the letters included and regarding spelling. The published letters are also occasionally misdated, and they seem sometimes to be based on versions that I have not traced. In transcribing the manuscript letters from Evelyn's two-volume letter book, I have expanded common contractions. The letters there are numbered in three series. As most of the letters cited here are from the third series, no series number is cited unless the letter is from series one or two.

correspondence might serve as an appendix to the work, suggesting the way in which Evelyn's thoughts were developing over the more than half-century during which he was working on the "Elysium."

The title of this essay "Elysium Britannicum not printed neere ready &c," is taken from Evelyn's letter to Dr. Robert Plot, written on March 18, 1683. Plot was acting as an agent for Anthony à Wood, then beginning to compile his *Athenae Oxoniensis,* and Evelyn was, not for the first time, considering his long publishing career. He was, of course, to live for nearly another quarter of a century, during which time he published part of the "Elysium" (presumably II.17) as *Acetaria; a Discourse of Sallets* and added to another part he had already published, the *Kalendarium Hortense,* the results of his further experimentation with a heated greenhouse. Presumably, he also included in the two "advertisements," with his translation of Jean de La Quintinye (1693), material that was derived from the "Elysium."

On August 4, 1690, looking back over a long life of writing, Evelyn wrote to the countess of Sunderland, apologizing for the "innocent diversion" of publishing his *Kalendarium Hortense* and noting that it was "almost forty years since I first writ it, when horticulture was not much advanced in England." What he writes in that letter, about the composition of his *Sylva; or a Discourse of Forest-Trees* might equally be said of his great horticultural enterprise, the "Elysium," of which *Sylva* was both a part and an outgrowth.

> When many years ago I came from rambling abroad, observed a little there, and a great deal more since I came home than gave me much satisfaction, and (as events have proved) scarce worth one's pursuit, I cast about how I should employ the time which hangs on most young men's hands, to the best advantage; and when books and severer studies grew tedious, and other impertinence would be pressing, by what innocent diversions I might sometime relieve myself without compliance to recreation I took no felicity in, because they did not contribute to any improvement of the mind.[6]

In fact, Evelyn rarely refers to the "Elysium" by name in his correspondence. Most commonly, he uses some such phrase as "my Hortulan Work,"[7] especially when writing to friends for comments on his first proposal.[8] And equally, as late as 1701, William Nicholson (later bishop of Carlisle),

[6] *Correspondence,* 317. Like many of Evelyn's works, this letter "recycles" almost verbatim material from a letter to Lady Clarendon of June 16, 1690 (Letter book, 626). In a letter to Richard Bentley seven years later, January 20, 1697 (Letter book, 783), Evelyn refers to being "foolishly fond of these and other rustications [probably *Sylva* and *Architectura,* but also other material for the "Elysium"], which had been my sweet diversions during the days of destruction and devastation both of woods and buildings whilst the rebellion lasted so long in this nation" (*Correspondence,* 365).

[7] Letter to the earl of Sandwich, August 21, 1668 (Letter book, 305). Writing to Lady Puckering on January 12, 1660, he refers to "the designe which I here make bold to enclose" as a hoped for gratification for her "wonted passion for the Hortulan entertainements" (Letter book, 160). A year later, on July 9, 1661, he writes to Jeremy Taylor in Ireland, "I am still upon my Hortulan designe" (Letter book, 176).

[8] A letter of May 8, 1659, to Samuel Hartlib reveals Evelyn at work on material that both Hartlib and John Beale were also addressing (Letter book, 153). On February 1, 1660, Evelyn wrote to Beale enclosing what he had already written (presumably of "Elysium") and giving him full power to correct and add to it (Letter book, 152). See also my "'Wild Pastorall Encounter,'" 177, 182–83.

writing to Evelyn (on March 25, 1701) to thank him for his *Acetaria,* refers to "your royal plan; the several chapters whereof I shall much long to see published."[9]

The separate publication of *Acetaria* had long been considered. Twenty years before its appearance, in the midst of his distraction with the Dutch wars, Evelyn had written to John Beale (on July 11, 1679) about *Acetaria* and its relation to the "Elysium" as a whole:

> 'Tis very true that I have sometime thought of publishing a Treatise of *Acetaria* which (tho but one of the Chapters of *Elysium Brit*) would make a competent Volume unaccompanied with other accessories, according to my manner. But whilst I as often think of performing my so long-since promis'd (more universal) hortulan work, I know not how to take that Chapter out, & single it for the presse without some blemish to the rest.[10]

Often, however, one is left to infer the "Elysium's" presence from the material referred to in correspondence. A letter to Lady Clarendon, one of Evelyn's regular garden correspondents from the 1670s and 1680s, is typical. On February 21, 1679, he wrote to her of "the sweete and innocent Recesse of Groves & Gardens" and spoke of them as:

> above all earthly contentments, for the Assistance they afford me in Contemplating the Worke of God, & of nature in her highest Splendor & Varieties. You have seene Madame, [he continues] the Contente of another Discourse [obviously "Elysium"] upon this subject as it comprehends the intire *Mysterie.*

Presenting Lady Clarendon with what was probably the third (1679) edition of *Sylva,* with the first appearance of *Pomona*—largely the work of another correspondent, John Beale[11]—Evelyn goes on to say:

> Judge then by this Volume, the paines I have taken, and the Amplitude of the Work; when I assure your Ladyship: the Book I now present you, containes not above 3 or 4 Chapters of that laborious, and (I hope) useful piece tho this (as happily of more immediate concerne and benefit to the publique) I have thought fit to send abroad before it (*tanquam explorator*) to discover by its Entertainement in the world, whether it might be worth my while to gratifie, or trouble it with any more.[12]

This letter, then, reveals three important things about the development of the "Elysium": first, that the plan of the work, initially published in 1658 and disclosed most famously to Sir Thomas Browne in 1660 (Ep. III.161), was still being shown to friends two decades later;[13] second, that Evelyn saw

[9] *Correspondence,* 384.

[10] Letter book, 406.

[11] A letter of November 25, 1675, to Beale about the publication of a book in which Evelyn thanks him for having "furnisht to this discourse all that is in it the most refin'd & useful" suggests that Beale also contributed extensively to Evelyn's *Terra: A Philosophical Discourse of Earth,* published in that year. In *Terra,* Evelyn notes Beale's supplying "the choicest Documents upon *this* and many other curious subjects" (*Silva,* London, 4th ed., 1729, 15).

[12] Letter book, 392.

[13] A letter of October 16, 1668, to Thomas Lloyd of Whitminster, Gloucestershire, refers to "a very comprehensive design of mine concerning the improvment of the Hortulan subject [that] has engaged me for some time, upon a

the publication of *Sylva, Pomona,* and *Kalendarium Hortense* (and, possibly, even *Terra: A Philosophical Discourse of Earth*) both as parts of that larger work and as essays in its reception; and, third, that Evelyn was still, at the end of the 1670s, soliciting advice and help with the "Elysium" itself, specifically, in this case with book two, chapter sixteen. I might add that the subsequent gradual expansion of *Sylva,* until the fourth edition, is an analogy of the way in which the "Elysium" continued to grow. Both are Protean, not Procrustean, enterprises.

Evelyn's letter is not just a presentation formality. He goes on to ask for Lady Clarendon's "choice Observations about the parterr, and the Coronary Garden," a subject in which he was better versed than he affects. This is revealed in a letter to Lord Arlington, Sir Henry Bennet, seven years earlier about what Evelyn calls "tulipomania." Recognizing that Arlington is not one of the "*Florist Virtuosi*" but wants only "to furnish some beds for the lustre of your Parterrs," Evelyn looks over what seems to be an extensive catalogue of tulips in the hands of Serjeant Stephens and recommends that for five or six pounds Arlington "may annualy maintaine and furnish your ground with sufficient both for delight & credit."[14]

Naturally, though, Evelyn cannot leave it at that, and he goes on to recommend the catalogue of flowers that appears in "Elysium" II.16—anemonies, ranunculi, polyanthus, auriculas, and carnations—everything Arlington will desire "to render yr Garden a little Paradise." Perhaps Evelyn was right to do so, for he had already remarked (on March 29, 1665), about Arlington's town house—Goring House, on the site of Buckingham Palace—that it was "capable of being made a pretty Villa";[15] Dryden was to celebrate it, in a still little known Latin poem, for its flowers:

> Here in the midst there is a wondrous bed,
> Where serried rarities the eye surprize,
> Revealing nature's secrets that lay hid:
> And dazzle with their gifts the viewer's eyes.[16]

Arlington was one of Evelyn's more interesting gardening correspondents and, within a year, Evelyn was advising him on the relandscaping of his country estate, Euston, in Suffolk. In town, Evelyn was prepared to recommend a gardener, "one well experienced in the Culture of Fruit Trees, and Esculents, which are rare qualities in that profession among whom there are so many pretenders." He also recommended that Arlington plant an avenue of horse chestnuts that, says Evelyn, "are to be had of a prety stature in the Nurseries; It is a florid Tree, and will exceedingly become their stations."[17]

What this letter reveals is the exchange of garden information at the center of which the "Elysium" was a sort of work-in-progress. The correspondence also reveals Evelyn's sense of the

---

Work exceedingly beyond my forces." Evelyn proposes "to importune you [Lloyd] with my impertinences" in the same manner as he was later to ask help of Lady Clarendon (Letter book, 310).

[14] Letter book, 331.

[15] E. S. de Beer, ed., *The Diary of John Evelyn,* Oxford, 1955, III, 404, hereafter referred to as *Diary.*

[16] The poem appears in Dryden's *Sylvae* but is not included in modern editions of his works. The translation is mine.

[17] Letter book, 331.

"Elysium" as a multi-authored project, a model, perhaps, for its current edition.[18] He both drew on the resources of his correspondents for the work and used it as a resource for garden advice and for other works that he cannibalized from it. Over time, the "Elysium" also became a kind of hortulan manifesto for the Royal Society, effectively the project of the Georgical Committee, whose members had been instrumental in the society's foundation. The "Elysium" also became more democratic. Like Evelyn's sense of his garden subject, its *ingentia rura* was not confined by the pale of royal and princely gardens, but included ordinary gardens and nurserymen. From the correspondence, there is no doubt about the impact of the "Elysium" on contemporary gardening.

In a March 6, 1679, follow-up to his previously cited February 1679 letter to Lady Clarendon, Evelyn refers to "the profoundest Mysteries of Nature, which I pronounce to be the offspring of the Parterr," and goes on to praise Lady Clarendon in Virgilian philosophical terms, "not as a *Weeder,* or inferior *Labourer* but as an *Intelligence* who has no superior save the *Cause of Causes.*"[19] A decade later he was to write to her (on October 12, 1688) in the midst of the 1688 crisis, to thank her for an offer of garden roots. Chastising himself for not being able, at such a time, to "forbeare this innocent diversion," he quotes Cicero "for you reade his worke [he says to her] and understand him too."[20]

Throughout the nearly half-century during which the "Elysium" project continued to grow, Evelyn also continued to add to *Sylva* the increasingly philosophical material that forms what ultimately became its fourth book, "Dendrologia." Much of this material still malingers in his manuscript notes to *Sylva,* although I have noted the very interesting correspondence between Evelyn and his father-in-law, Sir Richard Browne,[21] correspondence that antedates the supposed origins of the landscape garden by more than half a century. This is also, in part, the material of "Elysium" II.6, material to which Evelyn refers in a letter of December 3, 1686, to Lord Danby who, as lord treasurer, was responsible for the preservation of royal woods and forests. Antique and philosophical in its referents, it discusses the world of revived Augustanism that Evelyn, Abraham Cowley, and Edmund Waller had hoped for from the Stuart court and that survived as an ideal for the Tory Scriblerians of the next generation:

> yet had *Augustus* and other mighty princes, their *Malles Additus* and would sometimes heare poemes recited, and *Scipio* would converse with *Lelius,* & sometimes with *Lucilius* too: *Cicero, Hortensius* & the purpl'd Senators in the midst of Buisinesse & State Affairs, went often to their *Tusculans* and Wimbledons to irrigate and refresh the *Platanus* with whose very hands they sign'd the Fate of Empires, and controll'd the World.[22]

[18] Writing to Evelyn as late as February 7, 1701, the Rev. Joshua Walker offered not only his own papers but those of a neighbor about "setting willows" and "planting and fencing quick-set hedges." Although these seem to be meant for *Sylva* and *Pomona,* they might as easily serve for the "Elysium."

[19] Letter book, 399. On June 2, 1702, Richard Richardson wrote to Evelyn to request permission to print a Latin translation of the *Kalendarium Hortense* with the second edition of his long garden poem *De Cultu Hortorum.* Flattering Evelyn by placing him before La Quintinye and Rea, he justifies his enterprise as "after the example of Columella and our master Virgil" (*Correspondence,* 386).

[20] Letter book, 592.

[21] See my *Planters of the English Landscape Garden,* New Haven, 1993, chap. 3.

[22] Letter book, 553.

This is also the classic philosophical appeal of Evelyn's letter to Beale on July 17, 1670, in which he attacks Henry Stubbe, who had in turn been attacking the Royal Society as a nest of papists.[23] Evelyn's answer is to assert the Royal Society's inductive lineage from Bacon by noting "that Experimental Philosophie [which] was the onely Philosophie 'til the Gothic Inundation." What he suggests is the practice of the Royal Society was, in fact, his own practice in the "Elysium":

> The Members of the R: *Society* bring in Occasional *Specimens* not Compleate *Systemes;* but as Materials and particulars which may in time amount to a rich and considerable Magazine, capable of furnishing a most august & noble Structure: But therefore they do not fill their Papers with praescriptions out of *Miraldus, Alexis* of Peimont, *Kirchner,* and the Montebanques, to render their Histories compleate.[24]

One could find a worse description of the "Elysium" than "a rich and considerable Magazine, capable of furnishing a most august and noble Structure." That description invokes Evelyn's continuous assembly of materials for the work over a period of nearly fifty years, while at the same time suggesting the work's model as a vast cabinet of philosophical and horticultural curiosities.[25]

What struck Evelyn as particularly outrageous was that Stubbe was apparently in league with "our *Alma Mater* men," the Oxford scholars around Dr. John Wilkins, in attempting to appropriate the work of the Royal Society for his own ends. More specifically, he deplored their attempt to appropriate the Tradescant tradition by having "beg'd the Relique [collection] of old Tradescant, to furnish a Repository [Museum]."[26] Eight years later, Evelyn's diary triumphantly records (on July 23, 1678),[27] that this collection of curiosities had been acquired by Elias Ashmole, who had "given them to the University of Oxford, and erected a lecture on them, over the laboratory, in imitation of the Royal Society." Once again, one is reminded of the structure of the "Elysium" itself, in which the last book proposes a "Gardiners Elaboratory" and a "Hortulan Study" and library.[28]

Two years earlier (on July 1, 1676), Evelyn wrote to Margaret Blagge, later the famous Mrs. Godolphin, whose pious biography he was to write after her death two years later. At that point he

[23] Letter book, 329. In a letter of June 24, 1668, to the Cambridge Platonist Joseph Glanvill, Evelyn refers to Stubbe as a "snarling adversary" and the opponents of the Royal Society as "moon-dogs" (*Correspondence,* 204). In the July 17 letter to Beale, he describes Stubbe as a "Universall Intellect [who] has pick'd up by Reading and Meditation, and the Coffee-houses (to say nothing of his Bermudas and Jamaicas peregrinations. . . ."

[24] Letter book, 329.

[25] William Schupbach remarks that the cabinet of curiosities merits deeper study because it "is no longer readily intelligible even to many scholars, especially among English-speakers, whose modern language is in other respects so rich but is demeaned by a narrow and historically perverse definition of the word 'science'" : "Some Cabinets of Curiosities in European Academic Institutions," *The Origins of Museums: The Cabinet of Curiosities in Sixteenth- and Seventeenth-Century Europe,* Oliver Impey and Arthur MacGregor, eds., Oxford, 1985, 169.

[26] Letter book, 329. John Dixon Hunt notes that the association of garden with museum was common in many of the gardens that Evelyn saw in Italy: "'*Curiosities* to adorn *Cabinets* and *Gardens,*'" *The Origins of Museums* (as above, note 25), 196.

[27] *Diary,* IV, 139.

[28] Arthur MacGregor notes that Ashmole's laboratory and lecture hall "claimed more scientific interest than the museum itself" ("The Cabinet of Curiosities in Seventeenth-Century Britain," in *Origins of Museums* [as above, note 25], 152). In "'*Curiosities* to adorn *Cabinets* and *Gardens*'" (p. 199), John Dixon Hunt also notes the scientific purposes attached to Sayes Court.

had known her for seven years, and this letter constitutes one of his long pedagogical exercises in his relationship with her. Plainly stung by the performance of Thomas Shadwell's *The Virtuoso,* he reproves her acceptance of Shadwell's, and the court's, mockery of the Royal Society:

> I have learnd more profitable, and usefull things, from some hours Conversation in that Meeting, than ever I have don from the quintessence and sublimest Raptures of those empty Casks, whose noise you do so admire at Court when they have been declaiming against it. If I should affirme, that all the Books of Science, my Education in the University, and Abroad,[29] together with some practical Observations which I had collected during a life (not much resign'd to sloth) have not furnish'd me with so many solid, and excellent Notices, or due also to Actions practical, and of real Use, and no ignoble Speculation, as has the bare Register of the discourses, and Experiments, which inrich their vast Collection; I should confesse a general Truth without any reproch to the spending of my Time, before its constitution.[30]

Once again, it is the analogy with the "Elysium" that is so striking. What was this "Collection of the most solid and noble Materials, for the building up of a more certain, & usefull Institution and Fabrique of Philosophie," if not the larger structure in which the "Elysium" would take its philosophico-horticultural place? The word "collection," moreover, reveals the indebtedness of both enterprises to the cabinets of curiosities that Evelyn had admired in Florence and Rome, had himself built up, and had offered advice about to Thomas Chiffinch (February 7, 1664), who, as page of the back-stayres to Charles II, was responsible for the royal collections.[31]

Evelyn's proposed catalogue for this royal collection includes, among its fifteen heads, "Curiosities & Rarities of all sorts, not reducible to the former heads." This *omnium gatherum* would, presumably, cover the kinds of botanical curiosities that were in the Tradescant collection, for instance, the *Hortus Hyemalis,* which Evelyn refers to in "Elysium" III.3 as "Books of Natural, Arid Plants, and Flowers." Not satisfied with this, however, Evelyn goes on to assert that there should also be the following:

> in another Register the names and portraitures of all the exotic and rare Beasts, and fowles which have at any time been presented to his Matie: and which are daily sent into his Paradise at St. James's Parke, and this Booke I would inititule *VIVARIUM REGIUM.* Because they are truely Royal curiosities, and in some respects to be preferrd before those dead and inanimat rarities of art and nature; They are instructive diversions, and such as have render'd Kings and Princes famous to posterity amongst Writers and Learned men for their universal and greate genius's, as we find recorded in the holy stories of Solomon and in that of the lives of Alexander and Cyrus, and is usefull to Philosophy; and to many profitable Speculations.[32]

Actually, Solomon is not mentioned in Evelyn's apology for the *vivarium* in "Elysium" (p. 216), but Alexander is, and (more importantly) Evelyn (perhaps recollecting Jeremy Taylor's early

[29] In a letter to Sir George Radcliffe from Paris on December 2, 1651, Evelyn refers to attending a "Course of Chymisterie" there with Sir Kenelm Digby (Letter book, 37).

[30] Letter book, 381.

[31] Letter book, 233; for "Fabrique of Philosophie," see Letter book, 382.

[32] Ibid. See also "Elysium," 219.

argument that his work be called the *Paradisus Britannicum*)[33] traces the garden to Adam (II.13, p. 216). The Adamic enterprise of renaming the world is just what Evelyn invokes in requesting Cowley (on March 12, 1667) to write an ode for Thomas Sprat's *History of the Royal Society,* but, as he does so, he outlines, in effect, the matter of book one of the "Elysium":

> The Heavens, the Seas, the Whole Globe of Earth (from the variously adorned surface, to the most hidden Treasuries in her bowels) all Gods visible workes, are your Subject; as *their* [the Royal Society's] buisiness to unlock the abstrusest things, and to transforme the whole face and entrailes of Nature into all accomodations of Art etc. . . . In a Word, our Registers have outdon Pliny [the Elder] and Porta and Alexis and all the Experimentalists, nay the greate and illustrious Verulame himselfe, and has [*sic*] made a nobler, and more faithfull Collection of real Seacrets Usefull and Instructive, than the World has ben able to shew us these 5000 Yeares.[34]

It is this spirit of experimental scientific inquiry that Evelyn invokes in his letter to the president of the Royal Society, Dr. John Wilkins, on February 17, 1661. He refers to his argument that the growth of a tree is greater on the side facing the sun as his "trifling observations concerning the Anatomy of Trees, and their vegetative motion." This, too, is a matter that he touches on in "Elysium" I.12, a chapter that is, unfortunately, defective. It is also of a piece with Evelyn's interest in a Christianized Lucretian atomism and his identification of himself with his pioneer translation and apology for the *De Rerum Natura.*[35]

Nowhere, however, is the emplacement of the "Elysium" within the larger work of the Royal Society more evident than in Evelyn's correspondence with William Wotton thirty years later. Writing to Evelyn about *Acetaria* (on March 25, 1701), William Nicholson refers to "Wotton's making agriculture and gardening parts of liberal knowledge."[36] Five years earlier (October 28, 1696), Evelyn had written to Wotton, recommending chapters six and seven of René Rapin's *Hortorum Libri IV* as a source of information about "the gardening and husbandry of the ancients," presumably a source he himself had used for "Elysium" III.9. (Certainly much of the material treated in "Elysium" II is also invoked in the letter.) In an unashamedly modernist apology, Evelyn asserts

[33] Letter of February 10, 1660 (*Correspondence,* 128). In his notes for "Elysium" in British Library, Add. MS 15950, fol. 169a, Evelyn refers to John Selden as his authority that the ancients called Britain "Elysium." This subject is treated at length in Selden's preface to *Historiae Anglicanae Scriptores,* London, 1652; here Selden traces this belief to Servius's commentary on the fifth book of the *Aeneid,* to Sallust and to Homer, xxx, sig. [d3v].

[34] Letter book, 185. This letter is also printed in *Correspondence,* 294, but that version omits the first paragraph quoted here and the wording of the second paragraph is different.

[35] Quote is from Letter book, 173. Only one book of Evelyn's translation was ever published. I have treated Evelyn's identification of himself with Lucretius in a paper given at the Hartlib Conference, "Peace Unification and Prosperity," in 1992 and forthcoming in a collection of articles on the Restoration. Evelyn especially admired Claude Fabri de Peiresc of Aix, the French apologist for Lucretius and another owner of a vast cabinet of curiosities. Walter Charleton wrote of Evelyn as the English Peiresc, and Evelyn himself, in a letter to Benjamin Maddox on January 19, 1658, imagined Peiresc's genius not only still filling his native town, but infusing the curiosity of Maddox's mind (Letter book, 126). On the other hand, Descartes was opposed to such cabinets. See also Schupbach, "Cabinets of Curiosities in European Academic Institutions," 173, 177.

[36] *Correspondence,* 384. This was an old Hartlibean project that, says Nicholson, was objected to by Richard Baker, the historian whose work was completed by Milton's nephew, Edward Phillips. Evelyn employed Phillips as a tutor for his son.

that antiquity "had nothing approaching the elegancy of the present age":

> What they call their gardens were only spacious plots of ground planted with plants and other shady trees in walks, and built about with porticos, xystia, and noble ranges of pillars, adorned with statues, fountains, piscariae, aviaries, etc. But for the flowery parterr, beds of tulip, carnations, auricula, tuberose, jonquills, ranunculas, and other of our rare coronarics, we hear nothing of; nor that they had such store and variety of exotics, orangeries, myrtle, and other curious greens; nor do I believe they had their orchards in such perfection, nor by far our furniture for the kitchen. Pliny indeed enumerates a world of vulgar plants and olitories, but they fall infinitely short of our physic gardens, books, and herbals, every day augmented by our sedulous botanists, and brought to us from all the quarters of the world. And as for their husbandry and more rural skill, of which the same author has written so many books in his *Natural History,* especially lib. 17, 18 etc, you will soon be judge what it was. . . . when you have read over Cato, Varro, Columella, Palladio, with the Greek Geoponics, I do not think you will have cause to prefer them before the modern agriculture, so exceedingly of late improved, for which you may consult and compare our old Tusser, Markham, and *Maison Rustic,* Hartlib, Walter Blith, the *Philosophical Transactions,* and other books which you know better than myself.[37]

Evelyn's reverence for antiquity, in other words, did not put him on the side of the ancients. The Arundel Marbles, those antique stone inscriptions collected by Thomas Howard, were his concern throughout a great deal of his life. Clearly, he thought of them as part of the garden furniture of antiquity,[38] but they were also important as being associated with the genius of the present age. Writing to Obadiah Walker about them, he hoped to persuade Lord Henry Howard to have "his Statues, Bass'relievos etc" engraved "which might contribute farther to the Use of Learned-men as well as to the glory of his Name and Country."[39] Whether in medals or in histories, his concern is as much with the contemporary as with the antique, as if he were already writing the program for the Temple of the Elysian Fields at Stowe, which, in a sense, he was.[40]

At what might seem a more mundane level, the "Elysium" was also the occasion of plant and

[37] *Correspondence,* 363–64. Bray's edition of this letter footnotes other material from the Evelyn archive, including the dates of sylvicultural planting at Sayes Court from 1656 to 1670.

[38] He refers to them as such in "Elysium," II.11, 154/358. Compare Evelyn's interest in the "rare Basse-relievos and statues" of the Villa Medici and the "statues inscriptions, [and] ancient marbles" at the Villa Montalto in Rome (*Diary,* II, 240, 288). John Dixon Hunt notes the precedents for this in the Vatican Belvedere and the Cesi collections, and that in 1651 Christopher Arnold stated that there were "certain gardens on the Thames, where there are rare Greek and Roman inscriptions, stones, marbles; the reading of which is actually like viewing Greece and Italy at once within the bounds of Great Britain." The Arundel Marbles were originally placed around the outside of the Sheldonian Theatre in Oxford ("'*Curiosities* to adorn *Cabinets* and *Gardens,*'" 200–201).

[39] Letter book, 309.

[40] See his letter about Lancelot Andrewes hanging up the portrait of his schoolmaster, Mulcaster (Letter book, 113), his list for Lord Clarendon of the pictures of the learned that should be collected (Letter book, 287), and his letter to Samuel Pepys (August 12, 1689) about the place of "the Boyles, the Gales, and the Newtons" among the medals of antiquity (*Correspondence,* 295). In *Numismata,* London, 1697, 282, Evelyn proposes having medals struck to honor great collectors, including John Tradescant and the Lucretian, Walter Charleton.

seed exchange. But this was part of the replanting of Europe, a process that radically changed the vegetation of the continent and the very concept of nature. In a letter of August 21, 1668, to Dr. Stokes, one of the royal chaplains (probably David Stokes, at Vienna), Evelyn anticipates Stokes' voyage to the Holy Land—a journey Evelyn himself had hoped to make when he was in Italy.[41] Evelyn asks for "Seedes, and kernels of Plants and Flowers . . . with other natural Curiosities."[42] Two years later (on December 13, 1670), he is writing to Sir Thomas Hanmer (the "Prince of Florists," as he calls him), not only to thank him for his instructions in planting but to apologize that, as "a Cabbage planter," he has "wholly addicted [himself] to the propagation of Foresters and rusticities of that nature." He has, he says, "miserably neglected my little Flower garden," and he begs one of the tulips, named after Sir Thomas, in order to redress "a little Parterr neere my House."[43] Readers of the "Elysium" should be aware that Evelyn was indebted to Hanmer for more than the odd tulip; the whole of the chapter on coronary gardens (II.16) is laced with floral appendices gleaned from Hanmer's writings.[44]

Certainly, Evelyn's intentions to have a flower garden were of long standing. In a letter to his friend Benjamin Maddox in 1657, he refers to his "longsinc-begun disigne of propagating Garden Plants; especialy Ever-greenes which have much thriven with me."[45] Maddox was off on a Grand Tour that was to include Montpelier.[46] There is no evidence as to whether he ever sent Evelyn Phyllareas, Alaternus, and Ilices as requested, but Evelyn certainly went ahead with Sayes Court. Refusing an army commission, in a letter of August 25, 1660, to Col. Spencer (probably Lord Charles Spencer), he refers to his inability to go "further then the disciplining of a few Flowers in my Garden."[47] And he was to refer to himself as a "country gardener" in a letter (of September 9, 1665) congratulating Lord Clarendon's son on his marriage.[48]

The Virgilian and Horatian theme of retirement is also one that Evelyn frequently returns to in *Sylva,* his diary, and his correspondence. In the last, it was the subject of a debate with Sir George Mackenzie that resulted from Evelyn's *Publick Employment and an Active Life Prefer'd to Solitude* in 1667. This seems a paradoxical work to come from Evelyn's hand, so frequently did he return in his correspondence to the pleasures of withdrawal and retirement.

Retirement animates his first proposal of the Royal Society to Boyle, and it is reflected soon after the society's inception in Evelyn's withdrawal from the Restoration court. Writing to his cousin Samuel Tuke (on April 8, 1661) about a place where "those who do virtuously, are condemn'd

[41] Letter to John Crafford, June 21, 1645: Letter book, 1.

[42] Letter book, 306.

[43] Letter book, 332.

[44] In his manuscript notes for "Elysium Britannicum" (British Library, Add. MS 15950, fol. 164), Evelyn lists gardens to consider, including one "in Wales by Sir T Hanmer."

[45] Letter book, 108.

[46] It also included print collecting, though whether of gardens is unclear (Ep. III.137).

[47] Letter book, 168.

[48] Letter book, 251. A letter of November 22, 1673, to Lady Yarbery suggests that Evelyn had by then become a source for plant supply (Letter book, 357). Another to Cowley on March 20, 1663, refers to supplying him with flowers (Letter book, 199).

to perpetuall oblivion," Evelyn chooses to "make choyce of my solitude beyond it, which, I assure you is now so sweete, and so silent" that it lacks only Tuke's return for its perfection.[49]

Whether writing to Lord Arlington[50] about political brawls or to Cowley, urging him to write a poem about the Royal Society, the language of Evelyn's apology for horticultural retirement and solitude is classical and philosophical, the language that also animates the last book of *Sylva* and chapters six and seven of "Elysium," book two. More than a quarter of a century later, Evelyn writes to the countess of Sunderland (on December 22, 1688) in terms that would have suited Horace or Pliny the Younger:

> I have preferred the recess of near thirty years . . . [and] have found nothing solid, nothing stable, and worth all this hurry, disquiet, and expense of time, but the pursuit of moderate things for this life . . . piety, sincerity, justice, temperance, and all that series and chain of moral virtue, recommended to us, as well by the wiser heathen as by God Himself, and the very dictates of nature, are the only means of obtaining that tranquil and happy state a prudent man would choose.[51]

These are also the ideals of humanist retirement, from the world of Johann von Nassau Siegen to Marvell's patron, Lord Fairfax, or Pope's Twickenham.

It seems highly likely that the lost "Elysium" chapter (III.10), "The Description of a Villa," would have returned to this Augustan ideal, as *Sylva* takes it up extensively in the fourth edition.[52] This ideal is exactly what Evelyn's correspondent James Quine claimed for himself (and, by implication, for Evelyn) when Evelyn was seventy-five (January 9, 1695). Quine speaks of having "cultivated poverty, and found it a greater treasure than riches, and which, if Suetonius may be credited, was with a happy retirement, the biggest ambition of Augustus, and a fortune he preferred to that of the Roman Empire."[53]

Throughout the darkest days of the civil war and interregnum half a century earlier, the life of the country "villa"—as Evelyn called it long before the *OED* condescends to recognize the word "in English use" in 1711—represented everything that was the antithesis not just to faction and disturbance but also to what he calls the "places of common resort about London."[54] There, indecency is the mode, a mode he deplores in *A Character of England* as early as 1651. In contradistinction to this is Evelyn's recollection of Lord Arundel's Albury, "that sweet *Villa*"[55] or Lady Newton at

[49] Letter book, 174.

[50] October 7, 1661: Letter book, 187.

[51] *Correspondence,* 291.

[52] Evelyn continued to revise and expand *Sylva,* using material from "Elysium," II.7, 103–11. On January 17, 1670 (*Correspondence,* 221), he wrote to Meric Casaubon enquiring whether his father, Isaac, ever published a work on staves. It is not clear whether the "treatise which I am adorning" that he refers to is *Sylva* (just published in its second edition) or "Elysium." Whichever, it seems that Meric was not able to discover anything in his father's papers (*Correspondence,* 224–25), and there is no evidence of it in "Elysium."

[53] *Correspondence,* 344.

[54] Letter "To my Cousen: S," presumably Samuel Tuke, July 13, 1655 (Letter book, 72). In "Elysium" II.6, Evelyn specifically excludes walks in public town parks and gardens from his consideration "because they commonly end in drink and idle associations" (p. 88).

Charleton, "the fayre Genius in the Grove or in the Garden, whose ornament and Intelligence you once were."[56]

What Evelyn admired in an English garden is nowhere better illustrated than in his panegyric to his old friend Jaspar Needham on June 15, 1653. Needham had been visiting Wotton, Evelyn's ancestral home, where the gardens were partly of his designing, and to which he returned at the end of his life. His picture of it is classical, philosophical, humanist, sylvan, and exotic all at the same time. It is only his fondness for his wife, says Evelyn, that keeps him from being

> amongst so many persons of honour, and illustrious Ladys, as make it now the Court of Wotton, and the evening circle there the onely scene of ingenious divertissement, from where some Boccatian witt might furnish a better decameron; Imagine yet, how my thoughts waite on you into the grounds, and about the fountaines; how they assent in your preferring of that Tulip, or this Anemonie; that I breath the same ayre, commend the same prospect, philosophize in the same Peristyle, upon that artificial Iris which the sunn reflects from the watry girandola below it, or the beauties of those faire Nymphes who admire it
>
> *Quid loquor inclusus inter Laquearia Sylvas!*
> *Vernula quae raris carmine ludis avis.*[57]

And it is just those "laquearia sylvas" (the golden-ceilinged woods) that William Wotton praises half a century later (January 22, 1702). Writing to Evelyn to deplore their loss, he describes them as "those charming groves that made Wotton so delicious a seat . . . the greatest ornament of the finest county in England."[58]

Retirement is also central to the long Pindaric that Evelyn wrote in reply to Cowley's famous poem in that mode, a poem contained in his essay on gardens (1664) addressed to Evelyn.[59] Probably it was this essay that John Beale referred to when he wrote of Cowley in 1668: "What he hath bestowd for Mr. Evelyns Elysium, may to good purpose get abroade as a Prodrome [forerunner] to recommend that Auguste worke."[60] If so, Beale's remark suggests how much wider the project was seen as being than the text of the "Elysium" itself.

Evelyn's (still unpublished) essay in this new Pindaric form, first sent in a letter to Cowley on August 24, 1666, reappears in the correspondence nearly a quarter of a century later dated June 16, 1690, in a slightly different form. Here are the last three stanzas, addressed now to Lady Clarendon, not to Cowley:

[55] August 8, 1646: Letter book, 3.

[56] March 12, 1655: Letter book, 83.

[57] Letter book, 64.

[58] *Correspondence,* 385.

[59] J. R. Lumby, ed., *Cowley's Prose Works,* Cambridge, 1891, 121–30. Cowley's essay-poem was itself a reply to Evelyn's dedication of the *Kalendarium Hortense* to him.

[60] Letter of July 13, 1668 (British Library, Add. MS 4294, fol. 35v). The letter is signed "Anonymous" but is clearly from Beale.

5.

My other skill in *Plants* and *Herbs* Impart,
Thou, thine owne *Garden* Art,
And *Gard'nesse* too, and dost produce
The fragrants't *Flowers* for sent, and sweetest *Fruits* for *Juice*
Where every *Grotte,* and every Shade,
Is of a *Tree* of *Knowledge* made,
Which men may *Touch,* and *Tast* without offence,
Secur'd by Thyne Exemplar Innocence:
Gardens our *Poets* do Inspire:
Thalia is the Garden *Muse:* [comedy]
To *Gardens* Lovers oft retire:
Ah, who would not the *Garden* choose,
Where the first *Friendships* of the World were knit,
And where (if any still on Earth remaine) 'tis yet!

6.

Under the *Chertsean Platane,* free
From *Noisie Worldes,* ambitious Care
And empty Shew,
I'd rather *sup* upon a *Leafe,* I sweare
Alone with Thee,
Than *Feast* 'mongst all th'*Apician* crue,
Who surfeit on our *healthful Toile,*
And a whole *Garden* at a Collation Spoile;
Without one Graine of *Sense,* or *Wit*
(That *Salt of Life,* as well as *Health*)
Tho they had all the World can boast of, Cheese and Wealth:

7.

Earths Heaven! If in lesse
Than *Heaven* itselfe, be ought of Happinesse,
'Tis *here,* 'Tis here (my Friend) where Vertues move
The Senses; which unguarded, Traytors prove;
And Natures Gifts betray, and we *polute*
The sweetest *Flowers, poyson* the *wholesoms't Fruit:*
A *Garden* is a Consecrated place,
Where the first *Covenant of Grace*
Was with our *parents made,* 'Til sinn did chace
Them thence; And there it is, unhappy men

May hope to gaine that Blissful state agen:
When like my *Cowley* they do wisely choose
Aegypt, for *Canaan,* to loose:
Who then the *Sweets* of *life* sets out to seeke
Let him his *Argo* steere to this safe *Creeke.*
He *Colchas,* nor the rugged Seas
Needs tempt, here, here's *Hesperides.*[61]

This idyllic, almost Jonsonian, portrait of rural and horticultural life is a paradigm of the "Hortulan Entertainements" Evelyn lists for "Elysium" III.8. But the "*Chertsean Platane,*" a reference to Clarendon's estate of Swallowfield, which first appears in the 1690 version of the poem, suggests the importance of exotics in the late seventeenth-century garden.[62] Primarily, these exotics came from the English plantations in America and the Caribbean. In 1681 Evelyn wrote to Sir Christopher Wren, sending him papers that were "the project of a most Industrious man (in order to a *Natural Historie* of our *American* plantations)." Evelyn's request was that Wren "direct and assist him, with what he seems to desire from us; and consider what Rarities and Exotics we should request him to send us for the *Repositorie* [of the Royal Society], and to propagate in this *Climate.*"[63]

Through a remote cousin, Daniel Parke,[64] who had returned from Virginia to England and renewed acquaintance with the family, Evelyn was contacted by John Walker in Virginia. On December 26, 1693, Walker promised Evelyn "a draft of our dryed plants and flowers that you may see in part what we have,"[65] material for his projected *Hortus Hyemalis* in "Elysium" III.3.

Evelyn's reply on May 12, 1694, in turn expresses his thanks for "The Catalogue of Plants you set downe, [which] are many of the[m] Rare with us; but thro' this your generous Communication, we may hope to be further enrich'd."[66] And, indeed, Evelyn wrote to Parke himself on the same day to thank him for his "intended Favour in contributing to my Hortulum Inclinations," probably the "Elysium" or the collections that Evelyn was making in conjunction with it.[67] Some of these are, presumably, the plants that turn up in II.16 of the "Elysium": Virginia daffodils, Virginia yellow violets, the red Jasmin of Canada (*Campsis radicans* [Trumpet Vine]), and the American Jasmin, as well as the *Rubus americanus* (*Rubus odoratus* [Virginia Raspberry]).[68]

[61] Letter book, 276.

[62] The Royal Horticultural Society's *Dictionary of Gardening* does not record the London Plane before 1700, though plainly it was already cultivated among connoisseurs.

[63] Letter book, 433. It seems likely that this author was William London (see below, note 75), who is addressed in the following letter in the copybook. Evelyn writes of him as one not "altogether fitted for the Writing of an Historie . . . yet methinks the Method of what he designes is tollerable enough."

[64] Parke, who had a checkered career, was finally made "governor of Her Majesty's Charibee Islands in the West Indies" as a reward for bringing the news of the Battle of Blenheim to Queen Anne in 1704.

[65] Incoming letters, 1338.

[66] Letter book, 701.

[67] Letter book, 702. For a discussion of Parke's botanical connections with Evelyn, see Ruth Bourne, "John Evelyn, the Diarist, and His Cousin Daniel Parke II," *Virginia Magazine* 78 (1970), 27–28.

[68] Pages 298–304.

As early as 1661, Evelyn was writing to the earl of Peterborough, Henry Mordaunt, asking that he make collections of plants while he was at Tangier.[69] It was with Peterborough's more famous successor, however, that Evelyn wished to be "a Brother of the Spade" and share a "part of your Hortulan Treasure."[70] In return for many favors of plants, Evelyn offers him "some *Akorns* of the *Ilix,* and *Corktree,* lately sent me from *Ligorne.*"[71] This Lord Peterborough, who was later Pope's friend, came to be a great gardener and a collector of botanical rarities,[72] the sort of thing that filled the pages of the *Transactions* of the Royal Society in the latter part of the seventeenth century. His wife was a friend of Lady Littleton who, in 1661, went to Jamaica. In 1684 Evelyn wrote to one Peter Fountain in Jamaica in search of its rarities, "Roots, Seeds, Kernels, etc," reminding him "how acceptable they use to be among such Lovers of the parterr."[73]

Not all of these rarities were for the parterre. Writing to William Wotton on April 13, 1697, Evelyn remarks on a cedar that would have been of interest to him in the composition of the section on evergreens in "Elysium" II.9: "A roote of this *exotic* [he writes], was bestowed on me by the late (unhappy) Earle of *Essex,*" Arthur Capel, also the creator of Cassiobury, the first garden to be made entirely with trees. It "is not the *Conifera,*" he continues, "but beares a round berry four times as big as the *Juniperus,* which is also to be reckoned in the Classe of Cedars."[74]

On September 27, 1681, Evelyn wrote to William London[75] in Barbados, asking about "an *Orange* of the most prodigious size" and inquiring about sugar, cinnamon, cloves, indigo, and nutmeg. Evelyn had himself had some foreign and exotic flower seeds that he had "sowed and set, but with very little success" during the previous spring. There is, he says, "no trust in our mercenary seedsmen of London for anything."[76]

The alternative was direct import by botanical gentlemen such as London, men prepared to smuggle in rarities jealously guarded by the Dutch. Referring to botanical curiosities, Evelyn says,

[69] Letter book, 177.

[70] Letter book, 563. In *Terra,* Evelyn refers to the garden at Parson's Green that belonged to Mordaunt's father, John. Viscount Mordaunt's "Knowledge in all *hortulan* Elegancies [he says] requires honourable Mention" (*Silva,* 37).

[71] Another letter of the late 1680s from Robert Ball at Leghorn (January 30, 1688) speaks of sending Evelyn "a pretty big box of acorns of the cork tree"—said by the Royal Horticultural Society's *Dictionary* not to have been introduced until 1699—and promises to send grafted olive slips in the next post (*Correspondence,* 286). A subsequent letter from Henry Capel (October 19, 1688) seems to suggest that Evelyn has passed some of these acorns on to him (*Correspondence,* 287).

[72] Maynard Mack, *Alexander Pope: A Life,* New York, 1988, 373.

[73] Letter book, 486.

[74] Letter book, 787. This is in the context of the publication of the third edition of *Sylva,* but it touches on material also germane to the "Elysium." I have not been able to identify the juniper.

[75] A letter from the earl of Clarendon to Evelyn on August 7, 1686, refers to the general exodus of planters from Ireland to "the plantations" because of the troubles caused by Lord Tyrconnel (Richard Talbot), an old enemy of Clarendon. See also *Diary,* IV, 622, 630–31. Clarendon also refers to London's going to Swallowfield, Clarendon's estate near Reading, of which there is a lengthy account in the diary entry for October 22, 1685. See also *Diary,* IV, 481, for an account of Swallowfield. It seems London was to give "directions" for its gardens (*Correspondence,* 671). This, however, seems likely to have been George London of the Brompton Nursery, to whom Evelyn refers in his letter to Daniel Parke in May 1694 (Letter book, 701). George London had, it seems, "an ingenious Servant of his, in Virginia, not unknown to you [Parke] by this time." See also note 64.

[76] *Correspondence,* 258.

"You will greately oblige that Assembly of *Virtuosi* [the Royal Society] in communicating any productions of the places you travel thro."[77] London proposed publishing a natural history of Barbados, to which Evelyn commented, "I do not see that your design is anywhere defective."[78] He was, however, concerned that London get a good illustrator and that the plates be as well done as those of the recently published *Hortus Malabaricus*.[79]

Publication was very much in Evelyn's mind at this time, but his interest in the literature of garden flowers was of even longer-standing. Writing to Monsieur Le France on July 8, 1659, he speaks of the time spent, since publishing his translation of Nicolas de Bonnefon's *Le jardinier françois* the previous year, as taken up with considering what "might concerne the Ornamental part of Gardens." He has, he says, at his friends' urging,

> blotted many sheetes of paper upon the particulars mention'd; which before I transcribe for the Printer both for the dignitie of the Subject, and my owne reputation, I should be glad might be adorned with such aides and subsidiaries, as either my friends, or other worthy persons (conversant in Gardens) will contribute to it.[80]

Even before writing to Sir Thomas Browne about his ideas, he speaks of writing to a Mr. Lovering, also of Norwich, to "receive some instructions about the ordering [i.e., laying out] of the choycest plants, and of whatsoever is rare in the Coronarie garden."[81] In a letter to Robert Boyle of November 23, 1664, he refers to John Rea's

> very usefull booke concerning the culture of flowers but it dos in nothing touch my long-since attempted designe on that entire subject, with all its ornaments and circumstances: . . . God onely knows when my opportunities will permit me to bring it to maturity.[82]

Throughout his correspondence, Evelyn was also naturally concerned with the designs of gardens themselves, sometimes his own designs, sometimes those of others. Writing to the earl of Bristol on February 3, 1661, for example, he refers to Bristol's estate, Wimbledon, "the plot [plan] of which Garden I have excogitated [i.e., drawn up], I hope to yr. liking."[83] And more than two decades before he translated La Quintinye, he wrote to him (on April 20, 1669) asking that he show Evelyn's brother-in-law round the "Jardins, Batiments, Cabinets, Peintures et autres Curiosities dans Paris, et aux environs."[84]

Evelyn's connection with La Quintinye was through their mutual friend Henry Oldenburg, to whom John Beale communicated his observations on light and motion early in the same year.

[77] *Correspondence,* 258.

[78] *Correspondence,* 257.

[79] Letter book, 434. Because of Bray's faulty transcription I have used the letter book version of the letter here. The *Hortus Malabaricus* is also referred to in "Elysium."

[80] Letter book, 152.

[81] Letter book, 152.

[82] Letter book, 225. Rea's book, *Flora,* was published in 1665. It has three parts: "Flora," "Ceres," and "Pomona."

[83] Letter book, 191; cf. above, p. 112.

[84] Letter book, II, 20.

Evelyn's comments on these observations, in a published letter to Beale[85] dealing with perspective, were consonant with his treatment of perspective in "Elysium" II.11 and II.5.[86] Similarly, it seems likely that the illustrated letter (of October 21, 1664) to Beale about how to build an ice-house would have been germane to the first two lost chapters of book three.

Presumably, the first of Evelyn's two published letters "upon the Hortulan subject," addressed to the earl of Sandwich in Spain in 1667, was soliciting "some short descriptions of the most famous gardens and villas of Spain" with a view to their inclusion in "Elysium" III.10. In that letter, certainly, he refers to "the Catalogue which I here presume to send to your Excellency and the pains I have already taken to render it no trifling or unuseful speculation,"[87] presumably the outline of the "Elysium" and his subsequent work on it.

The second letter (of August 21, 1668)[88] includes material on vegetables and fruit that would have gone into "Elysium" II.19 and did appear in part in *Pomona* and *Acetaria*. This letter also deals with the usefulness of cork in conservatories, a first exploration of material that was not to appear until the 1691 edition of the *Kalendarium Hortense*. That material—Evelyn's later development of the heated greenhouse and the correspondence with the antiquary Sir Dudley Cullum in the early 1690s—is a significant chapter in the relation of Evelyn's correspondence to the development of ideas in the "Elysium," in this case, material dealt with in II.15.[89]

Evelyn corresponded with Sir Richard Southwell, sometime president of the Royal Society, about the use of yews for making close walks for the winter, a subject germane to "Elysium" II.6.[90] Southwell was also interested in promoting cider production, the stuff of classic self-sufficiency. This was a subject presumably to be dealt with in "Elysium Britannicum" II.19, as it was in *Pomona* and in Evelyn's correspondence with John Beale and Moses Cook, the gardener at Cassiobury who became one of the founders of the Brompton Nursery. Writing from Kingsweston in Somerset on January 8, 1685, Southwell gives an account of "one Rogers a learned Quaker," who has invented an improved cider mill for which he buys even the wild apples and pears of the forest and is capable of making 1000 hogsheads of cider a year. Some of this he exports to Ireland and the West Indies, some he converts into brandy.[91]

Evelyn's early correspondence with Henry Oldenburg, the future secretary of the Royal Society, was far more interesting. His contact was through Robert Boyle's nephew, who would later create Ranelagh Gardens, whose tutor in Paris at the time was Oldenburg. Early in 1659, Evelyn's "Elysium" proposals were circulated among Hartlib and a number of other scholars, and, in a letter to Evelyn on September 24, 1659, Hartlib enclosed a long "Extract of a Letter" from a scholar on

[85] August 27, 1668: *Correspondence,* 207–10.

[86] Cf. Evelyn's letter to Monsieur Rose of July 19, 1669, commending his book of architecture and "les Lecons Geometrales et Perspective" (Letter book, II, 22).

[87] December 13, 1667: *Correspondence,* 201.

[88] *Correspondence,* 205–6.

[89] See my "John Evelyn and the Invention of the Heated Greenhouse," *Garden History* 20 (1992), 201–6.

[90] See my " 'Wild Pastorall Encounter' " (as above, note 2).

[91] British Library, Add. MS 15858, fols. 167v–68.

the Continent to whom he had also sent a summary of the "Elysium." This "extract" was, in fact, a reading list of all the modern authors on gardens and botany that Evelyn ought to consult in composing his works, a list, probably compiled by Oldenburg, that amounted to a bibliography of botany and garden history.[92]

Throughout this period, Evelyn was searching for a copy of Benedictus Curtius' *Hortorum Libri Triginta,* a (still untranslated) work that was plainly influential both in his history of ancient gardens and in Sir Thomas Browne's *The Garden of Cyrus.* It is cited in the extant manuscript of "Elysium" (II.4, p. 66) and must surely have been the ground for Evelyn's intended history "Of the most famous Gardens in the World, ancient and modern," book three, chapter nine, in his proposal. Evelyn's own sense of those "most famous gardens" was, of course, partly the result of his trip to France and Italy in 1644.[93] In Tom Stoppard's play *Arcadia,* Hannah, the scholar of garden history, rebukes Bernard, the literary scholar, for imagining that Capability Brown's landscapes are "the real England":

> You can stop being silly now, Bernard. English landscape was invented by gardeners imitating foreign painters who were evoking classical authors. The whole thing was brought home in the luggage from the grand tour.[94]

Throughout his life Evelyn continued to advise travelers to the Continent what to see there. "You are inquisitive of me to know how I would advise you to employ your intended Travells in Italy," he writes to Francis Carter on November 27, 1665:

> I would recommend to your notice whatsoever you think may hereafter be of use and for Ornament in your owne Country at your returne. In particular for the propagation of Gardning and Agriculture, be it in governing Flowers, Fruits, Plants etc. Learne by some faithfull and ocular Process how they extract their Essences of Oranges, Jassmine, Hyacinths, Violets and other esteemed perfumes . . . Conserving dry Fruites, as they do them at Genoa; Refreshing Beveriges etc: Also to make Cements, artificial marbles, stone, pasts; the red floores of Venice. . . . Keepe Registers of things of Art for the decoration of houses, studies, etc Designe the plotts and Landskips of delicious places, Fountaines, Vasas, Aviaries, Country houses and Villas; noble pieces of Architecture. Visit ther Mechanics and Manufactures; Collect all Curious Bookes upon any of these Subjects: In summ, looke into every thing in Citty and Country.[95]

This letter is virtually a recipe for the composition of the "Elysium" itself, or for Books two and three, at any rate. It is also a sort of record of what Evelyn himself had looked for when he was

[92] British Library, Add. MS 15948, fols. 71–73. See also A. Rupert Hall and Marie Boas Hall, eds., *The Correspondence of Henry Oldenburg,* Madison, 1966, XIII, 385–87. One of the items, Bumaldi's *Bibliotheca Botanica,* itself contains an extensive bibliography of botanical works that deal with garden history.

[93] A letter to Robert Boyle on September 13, 1661, thanking him for the loan of "*Schotti,*" seems to suggest (as de Beer claims) that Evelyn's account of his Continental trip was written up retrospectively out of Schottus' guide to Rome (Letter book, 184).

[94] *Arcadia,* London, 1993, 25–26.

[95] Letter book, 264.

abroad twenty years earlier. Looking back from his seventy-eighth year, on March 1, 1698, he wrote to his old friend Thomas Henshaw, whom he had met at Pisa on his Italian trip and with whom he had spent the rest of that journey.[96] Henshaw was something of a virtuoso; Evelyn mentions his having "two rare pieces of Steenwyck's perspective" in his diary entry for January 1, 1649,[97] and it was this aspect of him that Evelyn remembered in 1698:

> I frequently call to mind the many bright and happy moments we have passed together at Rome and other places, in viewing and contemplating the entertainments of travellers who do not go abroad to count steeples, but to improve themselves. I wish I could say of myself so as you did; but whenever I think of the agreeable toil we took among the ruins and antiquities, to admire the superb buildings, visit the cabinets and curiosities of the virtuosi, the sweet walks by the banks of the Tiber, the Via Flaminia, the gardens and villas of that glorious city, I call back the time, and, methinks growing young again, the opera we saw at Venice comes into my fancy, and I am ready to sing, *Gioconda Gioretri, memoria sola tu, con ramento m'il fu, spesso spesso vien a rapir mi, e qual che si sia ancor ringiovenir mi.* You remember, Sir, the rest, and we are both near the conclusion, *hai che non torni, non torni piu—mo—ri—bondo.*[98]

Throughout much of the previous decade, Evelyn had been in correspondence with Robert Berkeley of Spetchley in Worcestershire, a man first introduced to him on November 13, 1683, and noted (in the diary) as being "very Curious in Gardning."[99] Berkeley provides the most interesting instance of the "Elysium" project as a center of horticultural information exchange. Apparently, Evelyn sent him, shortly after their first meeting, a collection of papers that had to do with Boyle's experiment with the air pump. These papers led Berkeley (in a letter of April 14, 1684) to speculate "whether, or no, it may give such a Vacuum, as to preserve fruits, and flowers, in their Natural," a subject plainly of interest to the author of "Elysium" III.2.[100]

Berkeley also had a conservatory with lemons and oranges and a wide range of evergreens in his garden, which, like Evelyn's, had suffered badly from the severe winter. It seems that he had also already been to Sayes Court, for he writes of the greens (shrubs) in Evelyn's wilderness, "where they are so agreeable."[101] Clearly, the next winter was no better, and a letter from Evelyn of January 12,

[96] For an account of Evelyn's Continental travels with Henshaw and his artistic interests, see Antony Griffiths, "The Etchings of John Evelyn," *Art and Patronage in the Caroline Courts,* David Howarth, ed., Cambridge, 1993, 51–67. For an interesting account of what depictions of antiquity Evelyn might have seen on his 1644 trip, see section one of the catalogue *The Paper Museum of Cassiano del Pozzo,* Milan, 1993.

[97] *Diary,* II, 546. In a letter of February 28, 1659, Henshaw (thanking Evelyn for dedicating his translation of *The French Gardiner* to him) was the first of Evelyn's correspondents to mention the "Elysium": "I call to minde you have half made a promise to gratifie the world with a peece concerning the Ornaments of Gardens which hath raised a longing in many Curious persons who doe already question mee when it will come out" (Incoming Letters, 898).

[98] *Correspondence,* 376.

[99] *Diary,* IV, 345. Berkeley was the nephew of Evelyn's friend John Packer, who was clerk of the privy seal. He was also the cousin of Ralph Bohun, who was tutor to Evelyn's son.

[100] British Library, Add. MS 15857, fol. 42.

[101] British Library, Add. MS 15857, fol. 20; *Correspondence,* 273. Several times in the diary and at least once in the notes for "Elysium" (British Library, Add. MS 15950, fol. 164), Evelyn refers to the Carew's estate, Beddington in Surrey, that was famous for its orange trees, planted in the 1590s and not protected by a conservatory.

1685, tells of his having been "forc'd quite to alter my poore Garden" on this account and that "'tis a late day with me to begin new Paradises." Not surprisingly Evelyn, who was already interested in improving conservatories, speaks strongly of an account of Dutch greenhouses where "at small changes in the fabric secures their Curosities without stove or fire during the severest season."[102]

A year later, on January 4, 1686, Berkeley was worried that Evelyn's new position as one of the commissioners of the privy seal might not "hinder or divert you from finishing your grand design."[103] Clearly, the "Elysium" was still very much a work in progress. In the late spring of 1686, Berkeley went to the Netherlands, and on July 16, Evelyn sent him a list of the most famous gardens there.[104] These included the garden of Hans Willem Bentinck (Zorgvliet), the gardens of Lord Beverning, Gaspar Fagels, Daniel Desmarets, Madam de Flines (i.e., Agnes Block, Magdalena Poulle, Lady of Gunterstein), Pieter de Wolff, and the Leiden "*Hortus Botanicus,*" as well as the duke of Arenberg's garden, Enghien.

This list seems to have been meant as part of the "Elysium," for Evelyn describes it as "from among my confusd papers, and Notes, in order to a designe I once was so vaine to shew you the plans of." "I perswade myself," Evelyn continues,

> you will make your Remarks on thire Horticulture none of the least of your darlings [doings?] and communicate the fruits of it to your Friends: Gardens are there so universaly affected (the narrownesse of the Country, and frugality of the Inhabitans [sic] denying them most other diversion) that their Veneration of *Flora,* and the parterre is extraordinary; and tho the French at present may boast of their vast designee [*sic*], their *Versailles* and portentous workes; yet Gardens can no where be so spruce, and accurately kept.[105]

Berkeley was not slow to take Evelyn's advice. A letter from him at The Hague, dated August 16, 1686, provides an account of the gardens at Ten Bos, as well as at Mr. Bentinck's, whose garden Evelyn had recommended. What attracted Berkeley was not Bentinck's large plantations and wilderness, which he thought inferior to Evelyn's, but

> the Conservatory which indeed is Grand, built semi-circular with a fair Ro[o]me well painted in the middle, where the Court is often entertaind, in prospect of the most beautiful Greens that I have seen, both in the Garden belonging to it, which has three descents to an oval Fountain; or in the Hous where the Greens stand in the winter, two Rows on each side, with a fine walk of 12 ft between them; these two wings are about 60 yds distant from each other when you enter the garden where there's nothing more worthy observation; in the hous are two large stoves on each side, and vents atop, to keep them in what temperature of heat the Season may require, there is moreover an Engine to remove the Cases of what might soever, into their places with little trouble, the dores being made large at each end for that design.

[102] Letter book, 490.

[103] *Correspondence,* 280.

[104] Letter book, 538. A presumably earlier note about Enghien in the manuscript notes for "Elysium" (British Library, Add. MS 15950, fol. 150) reads: "Duke of Anscots garden in Flanders enquire its description: tis said to be the finest in Europ." I am indebted to Erik de Jong for the identification of the gardens.

[105] Letter book, 538.

> Besides these, I don't remember one thing worth communicating to you, except their double Espaliers, which I presume, only the less [?] good are, bearing fruit on each side, the posts being large for that purpose, and to allow such ample ro[o]me between, that the fruit ripens exceeding well, and the trees not prejudice each other.[106]

Berkeley was disappointed at being unable to get any prints of Bentinck's garden (as doubtless Evelyn had advised him), but he did have what appeared to be a model of it "in pastboard,"[107] certainly something far beyond any of the instruments that Evelyn thought of as belonging to a gardener.

In his earlier list of recommendations, Evelyn had also suggested that Berkeley go to the duke of Arenberg's garden in Flanders, "which is for extent, fountains, Terrace, parterrs, Grotts, Statues, Plants and all the Hortulan Amoenities, beyond all description."[108] Here again was a garden, Enghien, that sounded like an advertisement for the "Elysium," and Berkeley, in a letter of March 18, 1687, announced his intention to go there. "If I find any draughts of the garden exact," he writes, "I shall send you one; here are some prints of it."[109] Clearly, Evelyn was incredulous of the scale of Enghien; he never went there, nor does it appear in his correspondence. He wrote back to Berkeley on November 11, 1687: "If it answer the designe, it is indeede a Magnificence far surpassing any thing of that nature in *Italy,* or, I believe, any where else." But he also commented on the expense of having "to maintaine such a Paradise in the trim it appears to be on Paper," and said that that is probably why Virgil recommended praising a large estate but cultivating a small one.[110]

After his return to England, Berkeley continued to write to Evelyn, although the correspondence ceases with Berkeley's death in 1693. Evelyn continued to be for him the horticultural genius for "discovering to us several Secrets in the Mistery of that Art, which before we were altogether Ignorant of." Berkeley singles out, for special mention, Evelyn's cultivation of cedars as an aspect of his making a "Variety of Nature in a perpetual Spring."[111] Most telling, however, is Berkeley's cultivation of "Indian Plants," thanks to Evelyn's invention of an "Ingenious Stove" for the greenhouse.

Here then are the philosophical, the sylvicultural, and the horticultural joined together, as they are in the "Elysium." Berkeley continued both to take from Evelyn (chiefly in being introduced to La Quintinye's work) and to suggest in return authors for Evelyn's consideration: Morin, Le Gendre, and Laurent.[112] Honored by Evelyn in the *Kalendarium Hortense,* Berkeley continued to expect the

[106] British Library, Add. MS 15857, fol. 46. *Correspondence,* 283, gives a version of this letter, but it is inaccurate.

[107] British Library, Add. MS 15857, fol. 49.

[108] Letter book, 538. Ten years earlier, in 1676, William of Orange had been there. An account of his visit and of the architect Nicodeme Tessin (in 1687) is given in Erik De Jong's "A propos des beaux jardins du duc d'Arenberg," *Extrait des Annales du Cercle Archéologique d'enghien* 26 (1990), 1–12.

[109] British Library, Add. MS 15857, fol. 49. The reference above to prints and a pasteboard model is also from this letter.

[110] Letter book, 575.

[111] British Library, Add. MS 15857, fol. 56. Like many of Evelyn's letters, this seems to exist in more than one state. The version printed by Bray omits the section dealing with Berkeley's conservatory.

[112] Pierre Morin was a Parisian botanist; see the note in *Diary* II, 132. Le Gendre is probably Jean Baptiste Le Gendre, who wrote about Gassendi, a collector and philosopher to whom Evelyn was compared. I have been unable to identify Laurent.

great work, of which it was only a part. Evelyn's works, he states "comprehend the universal art of gardening; and were they printed, as they are wished by all who have the knowledge of them, would be the most celebrated in the world, and remain as a rule to govern us in future ages."[113]

From the beginning, Evelyn's *Sylva* was seen as a central work in the reshaping of the English consciousness of landscape. Practical in its inception, it nonetheless developed, in a manner not unlike the "Elysium," into a philosophical apology for the planting of trees. Like *Acetaria, Pomona, Terra,* and the *Kalendarium Hortense,* moreover, *Sylva* derives from the "Elysium Britannicum" and represents the greater instauration of learning, of which work it was, in turn, a part.

Berkeley's phrase "the universal art of gardening" invokes the project for recreating Eden, which animated the creation not only of Renaissance botanic gardens but also the remaking of a landscape no longer seen merely as fallen. Thomas Burnet's *Sacred Theory of the Earth* (1681) is, in that sense, only a Restoration theological apology for this project of restoring Paradise, economically, politically, socially, agriculturally, and horticulturally. Berkeley's confidence "in future ages" is Baconian; it looks to the re-instauration of the world in terms of the reestablishment of the knowledge of the first gardener, Adam

In this enterprise the "Elysium" is the great encyclopedia of the physical earth, of its soil, climate, plants, and design. It is the lost book of Adam's knowledge retrieved from the texts of antiquity, as well as from the observations of modern science and of practicing gardeners. It is empirical not Cartesian, inductive not deductive, paratactic not hypotactic, a cabinet of knowledge not a scheme to contain it. To men like Berkeley, what Evelyn had done and was doing in "Elysium" was the enactment of the Horatian *utile dulci.* What Evelyn writes to Cowley about the Royal Society in 1667 is as true a definition of the "Elysium": It is a "nobler, and more faithfull Collection of real Seacrets Usefull and Instructive, than the World has been able to shew us these 5000 years," that is, since the Fall.[114] How could it be otherwise to a man placed, as Joseph Levine, in this volume, describes him, between a reverence for antiquity and a conviction of the importance of the Baconian enterprise? "The wisest heads prove at last almost all Scepticks, and stand like *Janus* in the field of knowledge," Sir Thomas Browne wrote,[115] meaning by that that they could, as Milton puts it in *Areopagitica,* see that truth "may have more shapes than one." It may address the particulars of a parterre's creation within a reflection on the notion of how Creation itself came about, just as Browne does in *Urne-Buriall* and *The Garden of Cyrus.*

As modern readers we approach garden history through Pope and his contemporaries. We read Evelyn in the context of the tradition that *he* created, not recognizing the revolutionary aspects of what he was doing at the time. Complicitous in this is the way in which the "Elysium" was the victim of its own success. By creating an audience that understood and enacted its precepts, it was overwhelmed in its own teleology. It was, and is, also a victim of its transgressional genre. Neither simply a philosophical treatise nor a gardening manual, it defies the generic categorizations that are the shibboleths of modern criticism.

[113] October 16, 1693: *Correspondence,* 338.

[114] Letter book, 285.

[115] *Religio Medici, The Works of Sir Thomas Browne,* Geoffrey Keynes, ed., London, 1964, I, 83.

Throughout the half century of the "Elysium's" composition, Evelyn's correspondence is testimony to the enormous cultural impact of the concerns represented in his great work. Robert Berkeley was not alone in thinking that the whole of this publishing enterprise would be "the most Celebrated of any in the world."[116] Nor was he wrong. Without the cultural hotbed prepared by Evelyn's various horticultural works and the widespread dissemination of his ideas through correspondence, Addison, Pope, and Switzer could not have written as they did. Sixty years before Addison, Evelyn proposed the incorporation of garden in landscape, and he did so with the Virgilian texts that Pope and Switzer were also to invoke. Out of the "Elysium" came the landscape garden that Pevsner claimed as the distinctively English art. The "Elysium" is the *fons et origo* of the garden history that we study today. Three hundred years later, it is time to show it to the world.

[116] Letter to Evelyn, October 26, 1693 (British Library, Add. MS 15857, fol. 34).

"Bringing Ingenuity into Fashion": The "Elysium Britannicum" and the Reformation of Husbandry

MICHAEL LESLIE

Most discussions of the "Elysium Britannicum" focus on the matter of gardening, and rightly so, stressing Evelyn's aesthetic interests, his plantsmanship, his botanical knowledge, and his awareness of the history of landscape art, for instance. There is plenty of evidence in the "Elysium Britannicum" to support these emphases, which so clearly coincide with Evelyn's interests, as evidenced in other works, notably those published after the Restoration. This essay will approach Evelyn's great work from a different standpoint, however. I shall not question the appropriateness of the gardenist context, but rather explore why this context is so appropriate, both to us and to Evelyn. I shall do this in part by outlining some of the alternatives available to Evelyn, which are present in limited and ultimately denied form in the "Elysium Britannicum."

The "Elysium Britannicum," never completed and never published, was obviously a problematic text for its author. The remarkably expressive manuscript—worked, reworked, supplemented, and curtailed—speaks eloquently of Evelyn's ambition and frustration and is witness to the difficulty he had in defining the work's purpose and audience. In particular, the initial chapters of the "Elysium Britannicum," the part of the work on which this paper will concentrate, suggest in Evelyn's repeated attempts to give the work an appropriate opening that he was constantly unsure of its genre. And this uncertainty became the only constancy, as he discovered both his mind and his topic metamorphosing over the years.

This uncertainty was surely justified. When seeking to situate the "Elysium Britannicum" in its appropriate context, an obvious starting place is a comparison with the works from which its author borrowed—not plagiarism, but in the honorable tradition of incorporating good ideas from other texts. Evelyn's principal sources seem to lie among the earlier and contemporary works not on "gardening," as the term is now commonly understood, but on husbandry and the reformation of agriculture, particularly those produced in and around the circle of the polymath and intelligence broker Samuel Hartlib (ca. 1600–1662), whose group of investigators had turned increasingly to this study in the decade immediately preceding Evelyn's work on the "Elysium Britannicum."[1] Evelyn's dependence on these and on unpublished correspondence between members of the Hartlib circle might seem to suggest that his manuscript should be viewed, at least initially, as belonging to the same large genre; that conclusion would seem to be supported by Evelyn's involvement with the Hartlib circle in the 1650s, which is documented in both his own "Diary" and by Hartlib in his logbook, the "Ephemerides," and elsewhere. But was Evelyn really a member of the Hartlib circle? And, more specifically, in view of its dependence on that group's previous productions in the genre, is the "Elysium Britannicum" to be read as another work within the tradition of English husbandry writing or the Hartlibean genre of the reformation of various trades and activities? My answer to both these questions is "No"—Evelyn was not at the heart of the Hartlib circle, and the "Elysium Britannicum" is not really a work in the reformed husbandry genre. I hope the process of justifying these conclusions will shed light on Evelyn and his place in cultural history: Evelyn and his manuscript are related to the Hartlib circle and their husbandry writings, but they stand at a tangent to them, and the precise angle of intersection is evidence of an area of conflict in the evolution of seventeenth-century English thought, particularly aesthetics. It also constitutes one of the problems never resolved by the "Elysium Britannicum," contributing to Evelyn's failure to complete the work.

The fact that the "Elysium Britannicum" is continually seeking to modify its relationship with a pre-existing genre makes this a particularly revealing topic. Evelyn's own emphasis, at the beginning of the "Elysium Britannicum," on his view that the true mark of the gardener is not his physical labor but "his abilitie to discourse of it,"[2] makes essential an analysis of the manuscript as a self-conscious—perhaps overly self-conscious—work. An examination of the issues raised is of broader significance than either the study of Evelyn or of the Hartlib circle: the reform of husbandry and agriculture was a central concern throughout the seventeenth century; Hartlib and Evelyn occupied central positions in the development of, respectively, Interregnum science and the early Royal Society; Evelyn also played a key role in the development of English aesthetics. The diverse fates of these two men and their works constitute a valuable indicator of larger changes in early modern intellectual culture.

From one perspective, the fact that we are able to see Evelyn's unpublished work as being first and foremost concerned with aesthetic gardening is itself problematic, not least because the boundaries of husbandry, horticulture, and pleasure gardening in the seventeenth century were not where we, in the late twentieth century, think they are. Our untroubled assimilation of the "Elysium Britannicum" to the bibliography of aesthetic gardening is evidence of an ability to read over and ignore the close connections with husbandry in this and other texts. How did we learn to do this?

[1] For Hartlib, see George Turnbull, *Hartlib, Dury, and Comenius: Gleanings from Hartlib's Papers,* Liverpool, 1947. The best overall accounts of the activities of the Hartlib circle are that by Charles Webster, *The Great Instauration: Science, Medicine and Reform, 1626–1660,* London, 1975, and a volume of essays edited by Mark Greengrass, Michael Leslie, and Timothy Raylor, *Samuel Hartlib and Universal Reformation: Studies in Intellectual Communication,* Cambridge, 1994. For the Hartlib circle and the seventeenth-century reformation of husbandry, see Michael Leslie and Timothy Raylor, eds., *Culture and Cultivation in Early Modern England: Writing and the Land,* Leicester, 1992.

[2] Quotations from the "Elysium Britannicum" are taken from John Ingram's transcription and are referenced to the page numbers of the manuscript. The quotation above is from page 3.

Despite its continued reference to utility as well as beauty, the "Elysium Britannicum" and its author play key roles in creating their own context and in our acceptance of that context as dominant. For the late-twentieth-century reader, the word "garden" immediately conjures up the image of the pleasure or aesthetic garden, so much so that we require to be taught the linguistic interconnectedness of such terms as "garden," "yard," "orchard," and "town."[3] But, as T. C. Barnard has trenchantly pointed out in the context of "Gardening, Diet and 'Improvement' in Later Seventeenth-Century Ireland," the limits of this concept of the garden, inherited from the intervening centuries, are sometimes misapplied to the gardening of earlier periods; previous chroniclers "have described only the most prodigious achievements, seemingly of a leisured and self-indulgent group of landowners." Even if the kitchen garden is allowed, that may not be sufficiently expansive. As Barnard asserts, "In the seventeenth century the literature of horticultural improvement often merged into that of agricultural improvement. In the mind, as in practice, the boundaries between the kitchen garden, the orchard, and the fields beyond were difficult to maintain."[4] For many, including those most closely connected with the Hartlib circle of universal reformers, godly increase was itself a thing of beauty, perhaps the greatest beauty of the garden; Barnard's comment on reforming landowners of contemporary Ireland, themselves deeply influenced by the Hartlibean project, can be taken more widely: "Any attempt to separate the motives of profit, pleasure, duty and display in the most ambitious gardening schemes . . . is not only difficult but fundamentally misconceived."[5]

But in Evelyn's manuscript we see the difficult process whereby these motives became separable, and why, by 1720, it would no longer be misconceived to separate them. At a crucial historical moment, in the early days of 1660, just as the apparently triumphant Hartlibean enterprise began to totter, Evelyn wrote to Sir Thomas Browne, "Our drift is a noble, princely and universall Elysium, capable of all the amoenities that can naturally be introduced into Gardens of Pleasure, and such as may stand in competition with all the august designs and stories of this nature, either of antient or moderne times."[6] And Evelyn's emphasis on his manuscript's place in the bibliography of gardens of pleasure, despite its more practical sections, is accepted by modern historians. Aptly, though thinking to make a different point, Roy Strong concludes his remarks on Evelyn, and his book *The Renaissance Garden in England,* by concurring that "a new chapter in the history of gardening in England is about to begin." Strong's book is characteristic in its assumptions concerning "the Renaissance garden," concentrating entirely on "places of pleasure" without a sense of the selectivity and suppression that entails.[7]

[3] See A. van Erp-Houtepen, "The Etymological Origin of the Garden," *Journal of Garden History* 6 (1986), 227–31.

[4] T. C. Barnard, "Gardening, Diet and 'Improvement' in Later Seventeenth-Century Ireland," *Journal of Garden History* 10 (1990), 71–72.

[5] Barnard, "Gardening, Diet and 'Improvement,'" 77. For further explorations of the connections between the reformers clustered around Samuel Hartlib and the "improvement" of Ireland, see T. C. Barnard, "The Hartlib Circle and the Cult and Culture of Improvement in Ireland," 281–97, and Patricia Coughlan, "Natural History and Historical Nature: The Project for a Natural History of Ireland," 298–317, both in *Samuel Hartlib and Universal Reformation* (as above, note 1).

[6] Evelyn to Sir Thomas Browne, January 28, 1659/60, in Geoffrey Keynes, ed., *The Works of Sir Thomas Browne,* 4 vols., Chicago, 1964, IV, 275.

[7] Roy Strong, *The Renaissance Garden in England,* London, 1979, 221 and 222.

The peculiarity of this concentration on pleasure gardening in the late 1650s can be indicated by seeking the antecedents of the "Elysium Britannicum's" among previous works on aesthetic gardening in English. Some years ago, John Dixon Hunt edited a collection of texts called *The English Landscape Garden.*[8] One of the most interesting features of the list of texts it contains is the paucity of material worthy of inclusion from barely 100 years before the great period of the English landscape garden. Even among those deemed worthy, it is difficult to identify more than one or two that are principally focused on the aesthetic, rather than the practical.

Perhaps the outstanding aesthetic work is Sir Henry Wotton's *Elements of Architecture* (1624), the influence and importance of which are entirely belied by its length. And yet, whatever its influence, Wotton's book is brief on the aesthetics of landscape art and is suggestive, rather than comprehensive or prescriptive. It partakes too of the author's exoticism: Wotton had spent much of his life representing his monarch and government in Venice, and his discussions of art, architecture, and gardening are stories from afar rather than indications of what was about to happen in England.[9] Indeed, the inclusion of such texts as Gervase Markham's *The English Husbandman* (1613) suggests an altogether different rhetoric, suggesting that the development of the literature of gardening in this period came about as a result, in part, of intersections with other literatures, some with long histories but short futures.

I am not suggesting that the *English Landscape Garden* series was wrong to include either Wotton or Markham, or both, but it is instructive that most of the early works in the series are marginal to the grand tradition of which the later texts are monuments. Perhaps the first text that looks entirely at home in the series after Wotton is *The Compleat Gard'ner* (1693), the translation of Jean de La Quintinye, possibly by Evelyn. This also is significant: In order to form the intellectual context for the aesthetic gardening of the later period, England had to incorporate French and Italian texts, simply because equivalent ways of thinking about the garden did not exist in English culture. Iain Pears, an historian of the English art market, has made a similar point in relation to the history of English works on painting:

> With most of the seventeenth century books on art in English being practical manuals on painting and drawing, only a few made much of an attempt to communicate an idea of the history and stylistic evolution of painting as it was then conceived. Nearly all of these were translations or heavily dependent on foreign models, such as Evelyn's translation of Fréart de Chambray in 1668, Aglionby's *Dialogues* or the 1699 translation of Monier's *History of Painting.*[10]

Evelyn's activity as a translator, not just of words but of whole ranges of ideas, was again prominent. Pears uses this point to make a highly important assertion concerning the development of art and

[8] John Dixon Hunt, ed., *The English Landscape Garden: Examples of the Important Literature of the English Landscape Garden Movement Together with Some Earlier Garden Books,* 29 vols., 1982.

[9] Although this is not a point he is making, it is instructive to examine Luigi Salerno's discussion of the origins of Wotton's aesthetic theories and his citation of the examples on which Wotton draws. See Salerno's "Seventeenth-Century English Literature on Painting," *Journal of the Warburg and Courtauld Institutes* 14 (1951), 234–58, esp. 241.

[10] Iain Pears, *The Discovery of Painting: The Growth of Interest in the Arts in England, 1680–1768,* New Haven, 1988, 199–200.

aesthetics in England. It is seductively easy to see the burgeoning of private collections of paintings and sculpture in the early seventeenth century as the beginning of the connoisseurship for which England became famous in the eighteenth century and to suppose that, with the unfortunate hiatus of the Civil Wars and Interregnum, the rise of an English appreciation of the visual arts is relatively constant and unbroken. The same confidence is implicit in much of the writing of the history of landscape art in England: Italian and French renaissance styles of gardening discovered in English gardens or plans of the late sixteenth and early seventeenth centuries seem obvious steps on the pathway that leads to the English landscape garden of the eighteenth century. But as Pears remarks, such confidence is misleading and is based on time's foreshortening and a failure to recognize the profound changes in English culture that occurred in the 1670s and 1680s:

> The history of interest in the arts in England was fractured so that it cannot be seen as a progressive development beginning with the court of Charles I. The early collectors such as Arundel and Buckingham should instead be seen as having acted in a vacuum, their procurement of works of art being a personal business conducted not only independently of the rest of society but even partly at odds with it. The pattern of collecting in the eighteenth century was very distinct from the form established in the 1620s and 1630s and had its origins in largely different roots. What had been an eccentricity became an accepted and widely-spread activity and the great collections, far from existing in isolation, depended both economically and socially for their very existence on the fact that they were now merely the pinnacle of a general interest. The grand assembly of works of art, in other words, changed from being an assertion of independence into being one of conformity to the standards of the period."[11]

One of the greatest achievements of the Restoration was, perhaps, its ability to convince itself and later ages that the new culture surrounding the restored monarchy was, in fact, the good old culture that prevailed before the Civil Wars. As Evelyn put it in *Numismata,* the "happy time . . . had been much in Queen *Elizabeths;* all the Reign of K. *James* the *First;* and till our unnatural Divisions broke out, for almost a full *Century* of Years of a *Golden Age.*"[12] Forty years earlier, Evelyn had declared to Sir Thomas Browne that the "Elysium Britannicum" was part of a project by which "to redeem the tyme that has bin lost."[13]

There is no way of determining the accuracy of Pears' assertion of a seventeenth-century England in which the period of the Civil Wars is to be seen less as an interruption than as only the most heightened manifestation of its essential discontinuity. But while he may be wrong in so rigorously denying "progressive development," there is no question but that Evelyn and his contemporaries would have recognized and sympathized with his description of a fractured intellectual culture, full of competing and opposing forces. During the seventeenth century, those certain of the ultimate success of their political, religious, social, or cultural views were, in fact, sure only of disappointment—Royalists and Republicans; Catholics, Laudians, and Calvinists; Baconians and

[11] Ibid., 106.

[12] *Numismata: A Discourse of Medals,* 1697, 110.

[13] Evelyn to Sir Thomas Browne, January 28, 1659/60, in *The Works of Sir Thomas Browne,* IV, 275.

millenarians; lovers of European art—all had their periods of ascendancy and despair, after which confidence of predestined triumph must have been hard to sustain.

The decision to compose the "Elysium Britannicum" was taken at a point when Evelyn must have felt particularly disheartened; few in the late 1650s predicted the quick return of the monarchy, in which he was emotionally, politically, and aesthetically invested. His treatise was conceived in a world in which its author had to struggle hard not to feel himself an exile, and preparing it for that world involved acts of suppression and reorientation that are evident in the manuscript. Evelyn was too cautious to declare his troubles openly,[14] but his fellow gardener John Beale gives a sense of the niceties of self-censorship necessary for either of them to prosper in circles such as those around Hartlib. Like all within that group, Evelyn and Beale had to correspond by means of open letters through Hartlib's house in Axe Yard, and after Hartlib's death, Beale confesses to having found this system of communication irksome:

> And thus wee may be in all respects more open than formerly, through our old friends hand, who did allwayes (& with some iealousy & impatience) confine mee to open packets; & I was bound to obey his lawes, as for many other respects, soe chiefly for some shelter, which hee by friendly relations gave mee, when I was obnoxious to the rules and rulers of those dayes. For though by remoovales, & secrete assistances of compassionate friends I lay then under coverte, yet I was also under three Sequestrations, & had sharpe & wachfull eyes upon mee. And this unknowne to Mr Hartlib.[15]

Needs must: Beale's nice play on words—he is "confine[d] . . . to open packets"—should warn us against taking much at face value if freedom's price was caution and dissimulation.

Despite these difficulties, we must acknowledge that Evelyn occupies a crucial position in the history of the development of English ideas concerning the landscape. At the beginning of the seventeenth century, there were few English documents beside Wotton's text that addressed the question of the aesthetic garden: Bacon's essay "Of Gardens," sections of Spenser's *The Faerie Queene* (1590–96), and Sidney's *Arcadia* (1590), and a few other short poems in print or manuscript.[16] And these are the very contributions to which Evelyn alludes in the "Elysium Britannicum"—Bacon on a variety of occasions, but Spenser and Sidney in one significant passage to which I shall return. John Beale was himself somewhat puzzled by Evelyn's failure to use Wotton, whom Beale claimed as a patron:

> I must aske whether you thought of the name of Sr H. Wotton, That if you mist him here you may remember him in your Elysium. For he was the first that brought Sculpture, picture & those noble Artes from beyond the Alpes into our English Courte. We contented our selves

[14] The Pauline diction (Eph. 5:7) indicates another essential context. Characteristically, Evelyn implies, but does not openly express, his judgment on the Interregnum by omitting the phrase that follows: "for the days are evil."

[15] Beale to Evelyn, August 30, 1662, in William Upcott, ed., *The Miscellaneous Writings of John Evelyn,* London, 1825, item 28.

[16] The range and paucity of verse materials can be easily surveyed in two recent anthologies: Alastair Fowler, ed., *The Country House Poem: A Cabinet of Seventeenth-Century Estate Poems and Related Items,* Edinburgh, 1994, and John Dixon Hunt, ed., *The Oxford Book of Garden Verse,* Oxford, 1993.

> with Mittens & some French adventures before, but had not the taste of the Italian perfection. . . . Sr H. W. was at the request of the greate D. of Buck. my Tutor, & after was my deare friend and patron, as you may find in his Reliquiae in 3 livres. In the 2d edition, I see his Architecture, where he hath a touch of Gardens picture sculpt.[17]

Beale's description of the *Elements of Architecture* is revealing: he calls it not a work of English aesthetics, but "a taste of Italian perfection"; not a comprehensive account, but "a touch of Gardens." By the end of the century, all that had changed, and an extensive English literature of gardening had begun to be formed. It is equally important that, at the beginning of the seventeenth century a dominant genre was the husbandry or horticultural manual (of which Markham's is an example); but by the end of the century, though works of this kind continued to be published, the genre had lost its preeminence, and the literature of aesthetic gardening had begun to take its place. The crucial period in the history of both genres was from the 1640s to the 1660s, when the cultural, political, and social conditions in which they existed were in the process of rapid and fundamental change. This, again, is the period of the origins of the "Elysium Britannicum."

The discourse of husbandry itself occupied an extremely interesting and prominent position in this period. Few works were as eagerly awaited as those in this field; few were received with such seriousness by public bodies. Ralph Austen's work on the growing of fruit trees was distributed to members of Parliament,[18] and the discussion of husbandry was a recurring topic in the House of Commons throughout the middle years of the century.[19] After the Restoration, the matter of the effective development of the landscape continued to be high on the intellectual agenda, forming one of the key topics of the Royal Society, its interest embodied in the Georgical Committee, in which Evelyn had such a prominent role.

Although interest remained high throughout the century, the history of the literature of husbandry is far from uneventful and is influenced by the ferment of religious, political, and social ideas; how could it not be when one of the notorious events of the Interregnum was the attempt of Winstanley and the Diggers to take over St. George's Hill in Surrey for the purposes of husbandry? The conversion of land from unprofitable uses to those of godly productivity was not restricted to common land or wildernesses: in the late 1650s, the great royal estates of the abolished monarchy were being parceled up into small holdings, including Theobalds Place and both the Great and Little Parks at Windsor. Theobalds Place was described by a contemporary with a significant choice of vocabulary as having become "a little commonwealth."[20]

[17] Beale to Evelyn, August 30, 1662, *Miscellaneous Writings of John Evelyn,* item 28. Evelyn displays his knowledge of Wotton's *Elements of Architecture* elsewhere and at exactly this time; see also Evelyn's *Sculptura; or the History, and Art of Chalcography and Engraving in Copper,* 1662, 24.

[18] See the discussions in his letters to Hartlib, particularly the interestingly late proposal, made after the Restoration, to resuscitate their attempt to persuade lawmakers to take a more active interest: Austen to Hartlib, May 3, 1661, Hartlib Papers, University of Sheffield, 41/1/139. I am grateful to the librarian and the directors of the Hartlib Papers Project for permission to quote from their edition of the Hartlib Papers.

[19] See Joan Thirsk, ed., *The Agrarian History of England and Wales,* vol. 5, 1640–1750, part 2: *Agrarian Change,* Cambridge, 1985, chap. 16.

[20] See Thirsk, *Agrarian History of England,* 323.

It might be thought that Evelyn's great work on gardening stands at a sufficient distance from these events and contexts for us to be able to ignore them. But at just the time when the former royal estates were under such threat, there is an implicit declaration of political allegiance in the subtitle to the "Elysium Britannicum": "the plan of a royal garden." Although Evelyn himself remains resolutely silent on the subject, his grafting into native gardening of the traditions of France and Italy is also significant in the context of the previous sixty years of aesthetic history; the association of foreign aesthetic traditions with the unreformed and potentially absolutist monarchy and the vices of Roman Catholicism had not faded from memory. Similarly, the use of Sidney and Spenser suggests, firstly, Evelyn's cautiously repressed political and religious preferences and, secondly, the connected and no less important role he played in a fundamental movement in English aesthetics away from the acknowledgment of the political and moral contexts of art. After his incorporation and adaptation of John Beale's description of an imaginary paradisial garden on Backbury Hill in Herefordshire, Evelyn crowns the account of Beale's "phantasticall utopia" with citations from the *Arcadia* and, crucially, *The Faerie Queene*.[21] What is significant here is Evelyn's refusal to acknowledge the deeper resonances both Spenser and Sidney gave their literary gardens, resonances which—if acknowledged—would have made impossible simple comparison with Beale's Backbury Hill paradise.[22] Was this simply a lapse in sensibility, surely one of which Beale himself would never have been guilty? I doubt it; rather, it seems crucial to Evelyn that such considerations should, so far as possible, be permitted to wither through neglect. It is often the case that what is significant in the "Elysium Britannicum" is silence. As Sherlock Holmes observed, pay due attention to the dog that does not bark in the night.

As his assertive title indicates, Evelyn was well aware that he was engaged in making the cultural history of the nation. The importance of this activity was recognized by contemporaries, as for instance in the revival of controversy over Inigo Jones's theories about Stonehenge, debate about which reached new heights in the 1650s, and in Denham's *Coopers Hill* (1642) or Marvell's *Upon Appleton House* (ca. 1651). These poems in particular demonstrate that there was nothing secret about the politics of landscape, but Evelyn prefers to let sleeping dogs lie, in the understandable hope that, after so much disturbance in the previous twenty years, they might never bark again. Evelyn was in the forefront of a movement that has remained strong to the present day, a determination that, in English culture, aesthetics and politics should be separated.

From all that we know of Evelyn, it is hardly surprising that he was at the leading edge of a movement to emphasize a depoliticized aesthetic, but what is extraordinary is the fact that the "Elysium Britannicum" is immersed in and emerges from the work of a group that held fundamentally different views and whose members were working to such fundamentally different ends. For Hartlib and his closest colleagues, study and the reformation of all activities were inevitably religious

[21] See Peter Goodchild, "'No phantasticall utopia but a reall place': John Evelyn, John Beale and Backbury Hill, Herefordshire," *Garden History* 19 (1991), 105–27, and Michael Leslie, "The Spiritual Husbandry of John Beale" in *Culture and Cultivation in Early Modern England* (as above, note 1), 165.

[22] On the political and moral interpretation of actual and literary gardens in the English Renaissance, see Michael Leslie, "Sidney, Spenser, and the Renaissance Garden," *English Literary Renaissance* 22 (1992), 3–36.

and political; Evelyn, conversely, recognized that his purpose was to construct and escape into a mental universe free of these disagreeable connections, "cultivating the *Sciences,* and advancing useful knowledge, emancipated from the strong contentions, and little fruit of the former; Envy, and imposture of the latter Ages."[23]

The difference between Evelyn and the more closely connected members of the Hartlib circle is pronounced and can be gauged by their different publication histories. Throughout the Interregnum, the dominant force in the reformation of husbandry had been Hartlib, not because he was the author in his own right of significant works on agriculture or horticulture, but because of his authority in the means of communicating ideas within those fields, as in so many others. Hartlib engaged in two principal activities that established his preeminence, and both were connected with publishing. First, his correspondence activities led to the creation of multiauthor volumes composed of practical advice for husbandmen. In a series of volumes, he drew together the advice on husbandry that he received from around the known world, notably in his somewhat oddly named *Legacy* (after which one correspondent congratulated him on not yet being dead, despite the title),[24] and in his work on apiary, *The Reformed Commonwealth of Bees* (1655). These volumes were miscellanies but were far from randomly composed. Hartlib distributed for informed commentary any contributions he received, returned criticisms to the original authors, and printed the whole debate for the judgment of his audience. Hartlib's second contribution is closer to the style of the modern publisher: when he found a potential author, he encouraged him, suggested the specific topic to be addressed, supplied reference works, teased out the manuscript, edited and copy edited it, organized the printer and publisher (sometimes even obtaining the paper), determined the print run and the price, and distributed copies. Perhaps the best documented example of this extraordinary activity is the case of Ralph Austen's *A Treatise of Fruit-Trees* and *The Spirituall Use of an Orchard,* published as a single volume in 1653, the documentation being in the form of 148 pages of letters from Austen among the Hartlib Papers at the University of Sheffield.[25]

Such was Hartlib's industry that immediately before the Restoration his reputation in this regard could not have stood higher. Shortly after 1660, when the poet Abraham Cowley communicated his design for a college of husbandry to John Evelyn, he said that the obvious candidate to preside over such an institution was someone "so industrious and publick-spirited as I conceive Mr. Hartlib to be." Cowley's praise can stand for that of many, but it is significant that the sentence continues, "if the Gentleman be yet alive."[26] By 1660 Hartlib—who would, indeed, be dead in two years—was falling out of sight. The closeness of his connection with the Cromwellian regime made him persona non grata at the Restoration: never a member of the Royal Society, penniless, and largely friendless. And with him fell a whole range of husbandry and horticultural authors, whose

[23] *Sculptura,* A3r.

[24] William Spenser to Hartlib, June 5, 1651, Hartlib Papers, 46/7/15: "I received your last this weeke, and your Legacie of husbandry about a fortnight since (though doe not yett suppose you dead) but rather your owne executour distributing your good things in your life tyme, whilst others are like swine good for nothing vntill dead."

[25] Hartlib Papers, 41/1 and 41/2.

[26] Abraham Cowley, *Essays, Plays, and Sundry Verses,* A. R. Waller, ed., Cambridge, 1906, 405.

works suddenly ceased to be reprinted. None of Hartlib's own works was reprinted after 1660, despite their importance in the preceding decade. Sir Richard Weston's influential *Discours of Husbandrie used in Brabant and Flanders* was never again heard of (despite his royalism and Catholicism and despite the fact that his publication by Hartlib in 1650 was purely accidental); he was, perhaps, too tarred with the Hartlibean brush. Cressy Dymock, another highly influential writer of the Interregnum, lived on but was never elected to the Royal Society and was spirited away to the North West by Brereton in 1661.[27] Perhaps most oddly of all, Walter Blith's *The English Improver, or a New Survey of Husbandry,* printed in 1649, 1652, and 1653—and clearly remaining a key text thereafter, being mined for information in popular husbandry works after 1660—was never printed again. Despite their being acknowledged as seminal in the development of agriculture, most of the key husbandry works of the Hartlib circle were never republished.

It was not that these works were simply becoming outmoded; there was no prejudice against older works on husbandry. Gervase Markham, whose star had waned in the 1640s and 1650s, returned to the booksellers' shelves as though nothing had happened, and some of Hartlib's authors did get republished, Ralph Austen being one. But they did so with certain changes, notably, in Austen's case, the removal of anything that smacked of a religious enthusiasm no longer welcome, the censorship in this case effected by none other than Robert Boyle.[28] We perhaps get the clearest sense of what was going on from private correspondence. In a letter to Evelyn after the Restoration, John Beale proposes the republication of some of the key works of the Reformation, but he suggests that in a volume such as the Geneva Bible, some of the marginal glosses should be suppressed.[29] By contrast with authors either ignored or controlled, Evelyn went from strength to strength: *Sylva* (1664), *Acetaria* (1699), *Pomona* (1664). And Evelyn moved to the heart of matters to do with husbandry, sitting on the Royal Society's Georgical Committee and acting as receiver of its correspondence.

Joan Thirsk remarks ironically that Evelyn's *Sylva* threatened to become the equivalent of one of Hartlib's miscellany publications, so welcoming did it become to the contributions of others. But the irony goes deeper than Thirsk realized, for Evelyn's position as Hartlib's heir in georgical matters only becomes most apparent in this connection. In this field, Evelyn was in many respects a post-Restoration equivalent of Hartlib; as Douglas Chambers writes elsewhere in this volume, Evelyn took over Hartlib's role as a universal information exchange in the matter of husbandry and agriculture. Like Hartlib, his name lent a text authority that it otherwise might not command, even when he was not the sole contributor. But he was not an exact equivalent, because it was more than the names, more even than the structures of knowledge and scientific communication, that had changed. The change went to the heart of what Evelyn represented.

The reformation of husbandry was obviously one of the key areas of scientific investigation in the middle years of the century. Because the overall development of the literature on husbandry has been so well treated by, among others, G. E. Fussell, Joan Thirsk, and Charles Webster, I shall not

[27] Thirsk, *Agrarian History of England,* 562.

[28] See Leslie, "The Spiritual Husbandry of John Beale," 157.

[29] British Library, Evelyn MSS, letter 27, Beale to Evelyn, undated.

rehearse the story.[30] Suffice it to say that the important groundwork carried out by the sixteenth-century husbandry writers had proved a solid foundation for more systematic investigations of the means to reform agriculture both before and during the Civil Wars. The spread of printing had facilitated the dissemination of new agricultural practices, and there is considerable evidence of a real impact on farming and horticulture as country gentlemen took to experimenting with new crops, new livestock techniques, new fertilizers, drainage and irrigation, ploughing, and sowing. Despite the harsh harvest failures of the late 1640s, there does seem to have been a gradual, measurable increase in productivity, and given the well-documented lag in the effect of husbandry literature on farming practice, the greater achievements of the late seventeenth and eighteenth centuries are credibly attributed to the pioneering work of the period of Evelyn and Hartlib.

What those more closely connected with the history of the natural sciences and technology often do not emphasize, however, is the underpinning of the reformation of husbandry in religion and politics. All who have read the debates on the Merton thesis about the relationship between religion and scientific development in this period will recognize my need for caution at this point; but although a blanket assertion of connections between reformed husbandry and reformed religion will not survive challenge, we can, nonetheless, draw attention to the frequency with which keen interest in agricultural reform went hand in hand with militant Protestantism, even if—as in the case of Hartlib and his closest collaborators—that militancy was irenicist and not confrontational. A sense of the divine purposes to be served by rendering the earth more fertile, more productive, and more beautiful pervades much of the immensely practical writing on husbandry throughout the Interregnum. Like many other figurative religious usages in the period, usages that easily crossed the threshold from the figurative, this outlook was based largely on the words of St. Paul, 1 Corinthians 3:6–9:

> I have planted, Apollos watered; but God gave the increase.
>
> So then neither is he that planteth any thing, neither he that watereth; but God that giveth the increase.
>
> Now he that planteth and he that watereth are one: and every man shall receive his own reward according to his labour.
>
> For we are labourers together with God: ye are God's husbandry, ye are God's building.

God the great husbandman joins the better-remembered Divine Architect; man becomes both the plant and the emulating planter—with all that that diction suggests about the idealistic colonialism of the period—man collaborating with his God to produce what Paul calls "increase," which could be translated into Hartlib-speak as "lucriferousness."

Hartlib published *The Reformed Husband-man* in 1651, but the next year he published *The Reformed Spiritual Husbandman,* a text attributed in library catalogues to John Dury. The title expresses clearly the aim of the volume, complementing the practical matter of the earlier book and providing its essential context, just as Ralph Austen was to do the following year in the companion works *A Treatise of Fruit-Trees* and *The Spirituall Use of an Orchard.* In an unprinted letter to Hartlib

[30] In addition to the works of Thirsk and Webster already mentioned, still valuable is G. E. Fussell's *The Old English Farming Books from Fitzherbert to Tull, 1523 to 1730,* London, 1947.

that accompanied the text of the preface to *The Reformed Spiritual Husbandman*, Dury makes it clear that the intellectual force behind the book was Hartlib's. Dury writes that his letter to the "Intelligent Reader" expresses "*your* notion of husbandrie in a spiritual sense."[31] But even when Hartlib is producing the most practical of his handbooks, the sense that "Husbandry" is in some sense spiritual and "Universal"—not a casual use of the word, I think—is bound to creep in. Indeed, it is in the prefatory material to *The Reformed Husband-man,* rather than that to *The Reformed Spiritual Husbandman*, that one finds the quintessential statement of the interpenetrative motives of the reformed husbandry movement:

> The *Matter* thereof concerns *Husbandry,* which is the most harmless, the most necessary, and the safest, & of all others the most profitable *Industry* unto *Humane Society*; wherein the *Providence*, the *Power*, the *Wisdom* and the *Goodness* of *God*, appeares unto man more eminently then in any other way of *Industry* whatsoever.[32]

Hartlib and his collaborators resisted the separation of practical farming and horticultural reform from the godly task of fulfilling the divine purposes of salvation—the salvation of the individual, no doubt, but in a manner more pronounced, the salvation of the godly commonwealth. So part of the religious duty of the true Christian was not only to reform the land but also to feed the needy and create employment for the poor. It is one of the starker ironies of the period that Gabriel Plattes, who in *Macaria* (1641) had written perhaps the most influential text of this sort to emanate from the Hartlib circle, himself died of starvation in the streets of London.

The "Elysium Britannicum," as I have said, clearly emanates from this context. It draws heavily on the work of the non-gardenist husbandry writers, particularly those of the Hartlib circle. A cursory reading of the manuscript reveals how much Evelyn simply borrowed from their work, which is sometimes indicated in the text. Peter Goodchild and I have both written on Evelyn's incorporation, with slight alterations, of letters sent to him through Hartlib by John Beale. Timothy Raylor has suggested the extent to which Evelyn's remarks on beekeeping and beehives are dependent on Hartlib's *Reformed Commonwealth of Bees*; and throughout the "Elysium Britannicum" there are obvious borrowings from such works as Hartlib's *Legacy* (1655), *Cornu-Copia* (1652?), and *The Reformed Husband-man*, as well as from the other principal husbandry authors among Hartlib's contacts.[33] Indeed, one of the first tasks in producing a commentary on the "Elysium Britannicum" would be to identify just what proportion of it is, in effect, copied directly from such sources, and then to interpret Evelyn's dependence.

Although at times Evelyn is explicit in his religiosity, it would be false to suggest that his version of the divine context for the "Elysium Britannicum" is really similar to that which Hartlib gave his works. Hartlib himself may not have been a millenarian, but his circle is obviously colored

[31] Hartlib Papers, 4/2/11 (emphasis mine).

[32] *The Reformed Husband-man,* 1651, fol. A2v.

[33] See Goodchild, "'No phantasticall utopia'"; Leslie, "The Spiritual Husbandry of John Beale"; and Raylor, "Samuel Hartlib and the Commonwealth of Bees," in *Culture and Cultivation in Early Modern England* (as above, note 1), 91–129, esp. 92 and 97.

by an enthusiasm for the expected earthly perfection of the rule of the saints and for man's active role in promoting the conditions in which that rule could commence. Evelyn's statement in the "Elysium Britannicum," that "God Almighty was the first Gardiner we have Scripture said," encompasses none of the active, intervening quality of the Hartlibean conception of the divine role in gardening. Evelyn goes on to quote from the bald statements of Genesis, rather than to address the vigor of St. Paul's metaphorical usage. Nonetheless, the dependency on the works of members of the Hartlib circle does indicate a real and significant connection, though it is complex and shifting. Evelyn began composing his treatise at a point when the possible audiences for such a work were fragmented and changing, and his attempts to obtain support show a hesitancy born of determination to gather behind him as many influential people as possible. The same is true of his correspondence with Hartlib and Robert Boyle, two rather dissimilar contacts who, nonetheless, shared interests in the field that Evelyn was working in. One suspects that both Hartlib and Boyle knew Evelyn's strengths and weaknesses rather well, and it is clear that they were communicating about the value and potential of his work (as was, indeed, normal for members of the Hartlib circle).

The context into which the "Elysium Britannicum" needs to be fitted is, indeed, one that stimulated both Boyle and Hartlib and which derived from the suggestions of Francis Bacon. The publications of the Hartlib circle were designed to promote good practice in all fields, but it was recognized that, for these isolated and somewhat ad hoc improvements to be truly successful, what was needed was a larger and more systematic "History of Trades," as had been advocated by Bacon and which came eventually to be one of the prime objectives of the early Royal Society. In his pioneering article on this subject, Walter E. Houghton, Jr., documents Evelyn's involvement in the various attempts to fulfill and develop Francis Bacon's ambition to create such a universal history of trades.[34] Houghton also notes from the printed sources that Evelyn had embarked on a history of the trade of gardening and thought that the sections Evelyn eventually completed were published in *Sylva* (p. 54). Houghton was obviously working only from the printed sources and appears not to have known the manuscript of the "Elysium Britannicum." We can correct this by now saying that the manuscript sections of the history of the trade of gardening that Evelyn submitted to Hartlib, and which both Hartlib and Evelyn appear to have asked Boyle to comment on, was the "Elysium Britannicum." This is confirmed in the letter from which Houghton quoted, sent by Evelyn to Boyle on August 9, 1659, mentioning "our common & good friend Mr. Hartlib." Evelyn protests that the struggle of composing a History of Trades has proved too much for him, and he has not progressed in the work; nonetheless,

> a specimen whereof I have transmitted to Mr. Hartlib, concerning the ornaments of gardens, which I have requested him to communicate to you, as one from whom I hope to receive my best & most considerable furniture; which favour, I do again & again humbly supplicate; & especially, touching the first chapter of the third book, the eleventh & twelth of the first; & indeed, on every particular of the whole.[35]

[34] "The History of Trades: Its Relation to Seventeenth-Century Thought as Seen in Bacon, Petty, Evelyn, and Boyle," *Journal of the History of Ideas* 2 (1941), 33–60.

[35] William Bray, ed., *The Diary and Correspondence of John Evelyn,* London, 1879, III, 260–61.

It is clear from this description that the "Elysium Britannicum" is the specimen work abstracted for consideration as a section from that greater History of Trades.[36]

The placing of the "Elysium Britannicum" within this activity, and perhaps all the texts of reformed husbandry need to be placed in some relation to it, makes it possible to look at the manuscript in a new way, emancipating us—if only temporarily—from seeing it proleptically as a work of horticultural or gardenist theory. This emancipation enables us to look at the text's motives and to perceive the extent to which it succeeds, and the extent to which it fails to meet the objectives of the genre, and indeed avoids those objectives as they had been modified in the mid century.

Evelyn swam into the pool dominated by Hartlib precisely in the context of the History of Trades, as a potentially useful participant in a carefully defined and well-recognized area of activity. Evelyn appeared entirely willing to assume this role, hanging out various flags to establish his Baconian credentials. Like everyone else, he cites Bacon with frequency, and his selection of topic is precisely in the area that Bacon himself had recommended. When detailing the kind of thing that the great History of Trades should address, Bacon begins his list of topics to do with the natural world with that of agriculture, but as he subdivides his topic, Bacon's next heading is the history of gardens. So Evelyn's choice of subject might well seem entirely correct, even if it is characteristic of the man to select the diminutive, rather than the larger, field.

However, it is revealing that in the "Elysium Britannicum" the move from agriculture to gardens is not presented as a subdivision but as a refinement: "since *Gardining* is one of the noblest and most refined parts of *Agriculture*," "the first and noblest part of *Agriculture*."[37] His inversion of Baconian hierarchy raises the question of whether Evelyn's involvement in the History of Trades movement was ever more than superficial or even, at some level, camouflage. Though he hits all the right notes, it is clear from the outset that his heart is not in the project, as normally defined; indeed, within a few years of first meeting Hartlib, agreeing on this project with Robert Boyle, and seeming to embark on his chosen task with gusto, Evelyn began to withdraw, leaving the "Elysium Britannicum" in manuscript form, even though that manuscript continued to evolve. In the years after its first composition, Evelyn sought to incorporate a bias to turn his text further away from the idea of a work of potential benefit to a wide readership, instead defining his text more and more closely as pertaining to an exceptionally limited audience: "the *Gentlemen* of our Nation (for whose sakes we have diverted other studies with this Worke)"; "we intend this Booke chiefly for the divertissement of Princes, noble-men and great persons."[38] Despite the seeming correctness of the subject, therefore, conformity to the underlying principles of Baconian study is constantly undermined from within.

Evelyn's motives for abandoning the History of Trades approach to the writing of natural history is a subject of some debate. The most common view is that elucidated by Michael Hunter and others and expressed clearly and with a certain regrettable smugness by Evelyn himself in a letter

[36] Compare with Graham Parry's rather different reading in "John Evelyn as Hortulan Saint," in *Culture and Cultivation in Early Modern England* (as above, note 1), 130–50, esp. 134.

[37] "Elysium Britannicum," 41 and 1.

[38] "Elysium Britannicum," 5 and 3.

to Robert Boyle. Evelyn explains that he simply did not like the necessity of mixing with rude mechanicals, that he could not support "the many subjections . . . of conversing with mechanical capricious persons."[39] As Michael Hunter notes, Evelyn separated out for the Royal Society those trades he considered "Usefull and Purely Mechanic" from those "Polite and more Liberal." The terms in which Evelyn admits his distaste show a close familiarity with the classic passage in *Parasceve,* in which Bacon defines the purpose of the History of Trades:

> Among the parts of history which I have mentioned, the history of Arts is of most use, because it exhibits things in motion, and leads more directly to practice. . . . Upon this history therefore, mechanical and illiberal as it may seem, (all fineness and daintiness set aside) the greatest diligence must be bestowed.[40]

Evelyn seems deliberately to remodel himself linguistically as incapable of the Baconian immersion in the world of the illiberal. (His is a very interesting use of that word, which is used without the class consciousness and with radically different intent by writers, such as Hartlib, to promote freedom of information.) The echoes of *Parasceve* seem designed to stress Evelyn's unwillingness to set aside fineness and daintiness.

We must always be sensitive to Evelyn's linguistic subtlety: his understatements, tropes of modesty, the tones and timbres of his writing that convey biases without stating them explicitly. The obvious smugness of this is somewhat suspicious, and Evelyn's diction—talking of subjection—raises another possibility, no doubt related, which is confirmed in his letters to William Wotton late in life, concerning his connections with Boyle. Evelyn writes:

> Myself then intent on collections of notes in order to an History of Trades and other mechanical furniture, which he [Boyle] earnestly encouraged me to proceed with: . . . The design and apparatus on several other subjects and extravagances growing beyond my forces, was left imperfect upon the restoration of the banished King, when everyone expected a new world, and had other things in view than what the melancholy days of his eclipse suggested to pass away anxious thoughts, by those innocent employments I have mentioned.[41]

The point is that Evelyn's interest in the increase of knowledge was decidedly different from that of Hartlib or most of his circle. Hartlib's activities were invariably directed toward the public good: in the prefatical letter "To his worthy and much Honoured friend," which opens the *Legacy* (1655), Hartlib writes particularly of the virtues of "Open-hartedness," a quality essential to the "Commonwealth of Learning." Evelyn—though his reserve concealed this adequately—was largely indifferent to the Hartlibean project of the betterment of mankind. Instead, scientific activities fulfilled roles in his life, oriented much more to the creation of personal happiness: in the case of the History of Trades, involvement was a diversion from things Evelyn found uncongenial in the political circumstances of the time.[42] In *The Compleat Husband-man,* published in 1659, the same year that Evelyn is

[39] Michael Hunter, *Science and Society in Restoration England,* Cambridge, 1981, 99.

[40] *Parasceve* in J. Spedding, R. L. Ellis, and D. D. Heath, eds., *The Works of Francis Bacon,* London, 1858, IV, 257.

[41] *Diary and Correspondence,* 724.

[42] Evelyn's consciousness of his use of study as "diversion" existed much earlier, however. In *Sculptura,* the same

turning away from the History of Trades, Hartlib again states the importance of his public motive in his Letter to the Reader:

> If it please God to blesse these Motions, and that accordingly the *Nationall Husbandry* of this *Common-wealth* be improved, we may hope through Gods blessing to see better days, and to be able to beare *necessary* and *Publique burdens* with more ease to ourselves, and benefit to *Humane Society* then hitherto we could attain unto. Which more and more to advance, in reference to *Publique* and *Universal Interest*, as subordinate to *Higher things*, and which, though lesse visible and sensible, are more permanent, and to truly *Rationall* and *Spirituall Husbandmen* as perceptible, shall be the uncessant prayers and endeavours of *Thy faithfull Servant* Samuel Hartlib.[43]

One cannot miss the constant emphasis on the general interest of man in Hartlib's list of activities—*"Publique Trust,"* *"Publique Concernment,"* *"Publique and General Welfare"*—nor the extremely explicit end in view, the betterment of mankind in general. Equally, the sense that this practical reformation of husbandry is inseparably linked to the perception and facilitation of "*Higher things*" cannot be missed. There is an acute difference in cultural intent in the way in which Hartlib defines the nation as a community and Evelyn's formulation: Britannicum—external, mythic, removed from the mass of the English. As ever, Evelyn uses language to impose a distance between himself and the community of his fellows, particularly those illiberal and mechanical. Only occasionally in the original drafts of the "Elysium Britannicum" is Evelyn prepared to consider the wider interest of the community, as when he says that through possessing "some tincture in Medicine" the gardener may become "one of the most usefull members of Humane Society"[44]—a rare use of the Hartlibean formulation at the end of that phrase. And talking of the usefulness of silkworms, he notes that a silk industry might create employment. But this sentiment is clearly taken over directly from his source in Hartlib's *Reformed Commonwealth of Bees*. His explanation of what the gardener does in studying the medicinal uses of plants also seeks to shrink the involvement apparently embraced, placing the emphasis on the penetration and contemplation of the secrets of nature for their own sake, or for the sake of his own sensibility, rather than for use in the benefit of society.

At the same time as he was considering his involvement in the History of Trades, Evelyn was also proposing the establishment of a for the study of, inter alia, husbandry, and in that he was not alone. But his version was fundamentally different in motive from that of other proposers. Whereas Hartlib and others, including Evelyn's own protégé Cowley, envisaged an establishment dedicated to the dissemination of improved practice for the public good, thoroughly engaged with the worlds of industry and trade, Evelyn's purpose was inward-looking, and his ideal was the secluded and incommunicative monastery. Indeed, his scheme for a monastical community was interesting, not least in that it was so unlike the version of Solomon's house that Hartlib and others had envisaged in

---

conjunction of class restrictiveness and a turning away from other, uncongenial, perhaps noxious, activities occurs in the "Epistle Dedicatory" to Robert Boyle: "you are pleased to judge it useful for the encouragement of the Gentlemen of our Nation, who sometimes please themselves with these innocent diversions" (fol. 2v).

[43] *The Compleat Husbandman,* 1659, fol. 33r.

[44] "Elysium Britannicum," 4.

the 1650s. For them, the college was to be very much an integral part of an increasingly practical educational system and society. Evelyn almost relishes the apparent collapse of the changes of the original conception of the college and devises a version of his own that has a much more reserved and limited application. His was to be for gentlemen, for those "who desire nothing more than to give a good example, preserve science, & cultivate themselves."[45]

Again, Evelyn's diction is telling: the objective of self-cultivation indicates how closely his gardening concerns fitted with his greater view of the purposes of knowledge. At just the point when Evelyn was toying with his ideal monastic community, Hartlib sent him word of a German community then established; however, Hartlib's was a utopian, or in this context, macarian, first step to the re-establishment of the ideal ordering of wider society, just as the related schemes for plantations in Bermuda, the Americas, and Ireland had been. It is characteristic of both Evelyn and Beale that the imaginary paradise of Backbury Hill, a place for solitary study and meditation, can be described as a "utopia," a term which, from its first use, had denoted a society. Their diversion resembles that commented on wittily in Marvell's contemporary poem, "The Garden": "Two paradises 'twere in one / To live in paradise alone."

As I suggested at the beginning of this paper, so much of Evelyn's initial effort seems to have gone into the first book of the "Elysium Britannicum" that we must concentrate our attention there. It is obvious that this section gave him extraordinary difficulty, as he made repeated attempts to construct an appropriate opening for his work, an opening that would orient it to his satisfaction and construct a suitable audience. One of the most poignant lines in John Ingram's transcription is that which reads, "My purpose was quite to alter the philosophical part of this first booke."[46] And as an index of his dissatisfaction with his work's opening, many of the initial pages are crossed out—an eloquent statement that passages on which he had lavished so much attention, to which he had given such literary elegance, could seem within a few years so inadequate as to require complete excision.

What was it that Evelyn was finding so difficult? Elsewhere in this volume, Michael Hunter draws our attention to the startling contradiction between Evelyn's early interest in Lucretius and resurgent modern atomism and his poetically worded Platonic theology of gardens in book one. As is suggested by his remarks about being willing to see the destruction of all books, rather than to compromise his integrity, Evelyn was making a deliberate decision to suppress the newer theories of the organization of matter, theories of which he had an intimate knowledge, so that he could continue to permit his text to affirm the ordered harmony of previous systems. However, those parts of the work concerned with the practice of gardening are clearly dependent on an entirely different approach to, and conception of, the natural world, which bear little, if any, relation to the extravagances of the initial chapters. The contrast is rendered all the more obvious to us, and surely was to Evelyn, by awareness of his sources in the husbandry writings of the Hartlib circle, the ideological origins of which were so different. Evelyn incorporated the results but resisted the ideology of what one might call muscular Baconism, but the strains of doing so are manifest in what is written into and what is written out of the manuscript.

[45] Evelyn to Boyle, September 3, 1659, in *Diary and Correspondence of John Evelyn,* 590.

[46] "Elysium Britannicum," 6.

This point flows immediately into the subject addressed by Joseph Levine in this volume—Evelyn's stance in relation to ancient and modern learning. Again, there were few contemporaries who could claim greater knowledge of either realm, but the text of the "Elysium Britannicum" does not manage the combination with ease. Rather, the text once more is the result of a series of choices, some of which are contradictory. Evelyn's diction is constantly betraying the tension between his enthusiasm, on the one hand, for the Baconian project of the reform of education and, on the other, his essential conservatism, arising from a wish to ignore the deeply distressing results of his own century's innovations, results both political and concerning the structures of knowledge. So for all his apparent espousal of the new educational theories of the Hartlib circle, which through Jan Amos Comenius and others was offering a radical departure from earlier humanist educational practice, Evelyn's manuscript is notable for its implicit endorsement of the educational concerns of the previous century. Again and again in the early chapters of the "Elysium Britannicum," one is aware of Evelyn leaping back through time to the heroic period of the first generations of humanists, in effect pretending that the intervening questioning of their achievements and their ideology had not occurred. The pervasiveness of classical authors in the opening sections of the "Elysium Britannicum" is not window dressing; rather, it is a declaration of Evelyn's continued preference for systems of knowledge that depend on traditional authority and not on the democracy of experimental science that existed temporarily in the Interregnum. The same point should be made about Evelyn's selection of a Latinate diction at certain points of the "Elysium Britannicum." It is true that sometimes Evelyn must say, in Latinate words, what hitherto has only been said in Latin, but this is not the whole story. The selection of a particular range of diction is a conscious declaration of allegiance and also an affirmation of separateness from the popular.

In this awareness of the limitations of his preferred ideology and his reluctance nonetheless to modify it, we can see one of the principal reasons for his close affinity with John Beale, the writer on cider and gardens whom Hartlib brought into contact with Evelyn and who suppressed his own planned works on gardens in order to contribute instead to the "Elysium Britannicum." Beale too was unwilling in the 1650s and 1660s to choose between versions of reality derived from the sixteenth-century's speculative philosophy and the brave new world of Baconian and later science. And, like Evelyn, one of Beale's strategies for dealing with the conflict was to resist the placing of his considered thoughts before a public that would demand a reconciliation of the fundamentally opposed sides of his thought. Both Beale and Evelyn were late entrants to the Hartlib circle, but because of the increasing importance for Hartlib of the matter of husbandry in the 1650s, they became quite central to his activities as the decade wore on. However, although their interests in gardening and husbandry mesh with Hartlib's own, these two men were, at some deep level that occasionally rises to the surface, opposed to Hartlib's wider concern with the dissemination of ideas and the widest possible distribution of knowledge. Evelyn's caution about revealing the secrets of particular trades, lest their promiscuous availability destroy their delightful aura of the arcane, matches Beale's chronic dislike of the contamination of print, which so frustrated some of his colleagues in the Hartlib circle. Through the avoidance of widespread publication, by remaining in manuscript and delaying the ultimate test of presenting a final, definitive version to the printer, both men achieved their aim of postponing the day of judgment, when others might draw attention to the contradictions within their works.

For Hartlib, such challenges were the glorious advantage of the technology of printing: the books that bear his name make no attempt to conceal the processes of discussion, argument, and rejection that we all know are part of the evolution of knowledge. But such an embracing of vigorous debate was anathema to Evelyn and Beale, who preferred to try to keep in the suspension of incompletion those of their texts that were both essential to them and, they knew, most open to the challenges of rigorous logic. Though prepared to publish studies of more limited scope, neither Evelyn nor Beale seemed willing to submit their greater schemes to the potentially withering scrutiny that printing would permit. With time, Evelyn himself would recognize the impossibility of composing a satisfactory, grand, overarching theory to validate his disparate enthusiasms, hence the failure to act on his intention to rewrite comprehensively the first book. Promiscuous dissemination would also destroy the small-scale collegiality of the knowledgeable, so comforting and so controllable. In this we may see a counterpart to the indecision of Evelyn as to whether he should relinquish his private studies and enjoyments for thorough engagement and employment in the public sphere.

I return at this point to an earlier comment: that the "Elysium Britannicum" is a conscious intervention in the formation of the cultural history and identity of England, a point also made, splendidly, by Douglas Chambers (in this volume) when he suggests that the "Elysium Britannicum" was building toward a kind of "Temple of British Worthies" for its time. Evelyn's text is not overtly political, but implicit within the choices it makes is a vision of the nation; the title makes this explicit. A question often asked is, In what way is the garden style promoted in the "Elysium Britannicum" particular to England? I would answer this by stating that what makes Evelyn's text so forceful is its election not to attempt to distinguish an English garden style from that in which he delighted throughout France and Italy. In other words, as in the description of the imaginary paradise on top of Backbury Hill, which Evelyn transcribes from Beale's letters, the emphasis is not on the affirmation of a radically idiosyncratic national style but of the ability of the English landscape to be so modeled that it can be assimilated into the European tradition.

At the outset, I posed the question of why the "Elysium Britannicum" looks so normal to our eyes. I think it is because although the text has only limited direct effect through partial manuscript circulation, it is nonetheless crucial evidence for the shift in attitudes toward culture that have persisted almost to the present day. Evelyn came to maturity during a period in which many of the certainties, forms, and structures of the earlier Renaissance were undergoing fierce scrutiny and in which alternatives were being canvassed and explored; the challenge in England to monarchy can stand for them all. Through Samuel Hartlib, Evelyn had access to much of this radical questioning and utopian planning of alternative societies, to which the management of the land in all its forms was essential. But he put his whole weight behind a restoration much wider than simply that of the monarchy, and one should not underestimate his own success and that of like-minded writers. His appeal over the heads of his own generation to the educational ideals of the earlier humanists foreshadowed the dominance of the humanities in eighteenth-century education. His dislike of the democracy of print and his desire to use the quest for knowledge for the cultivation of an elite were fulfilled in the Royal Society's increasing isolation. His redefinition of the English garden, orienting it away from Baconian associations with agriculture and husbandry and toward the aesthetic, has been so successful that we hardly notice it. Similarly, his construction of the Europe into which he wished England's gardens to be integrated is now so normal that few are aware of its radical partiality. Despite his knowledge of Alstead and other Germanic thinkers, despite the Hartlib circle's close ties with northern and central Europe, Evelyn essentially defined the Continent as France and Italy, the heartland of the aristocratic Grand Tour and of connoisseurship.

None of this was easy for Evelyn; it was both conservative and also, in the context of the 1650s, radical. He was composing the "Elysium Britannicum" during a period in which new ideas were being aggressively promoted, old ideas questioned, and some decisively discarded. Those new ideas were not safely theoretical but impinged on every aspect of life. Like many others, Evelyn was torn between excitement at the possibilities of the new and fear of the chaos and personal disadvantage that could come in the wake of the collapse of the old. The manuscript of the "Elysium Britannicum" is a site of extraordinary contradictions: between the public and the private, between the corporatist and the intensely individualist, between the rational and the mystical. Evelyn's successive attempts to get that first book right—attempts that must have driven John Ingram almost to distraction—constitute one of the most moving documents from the period of the struggle of a mind schooled in one intellectual culture to come to terms with the emergence of a new one, and to channel that new culture in directions congenial. The fact that the manuscript is so complex to edit is an index of the intensity of the struggle, and that is what gives John Ingram's representation of all that is there on the page its extraordinary value.

The final recorded contacts between Hartlib and Evelyn poignantly indicate their changed relationship at the Restoration. By this time, Hartlib was extremely ill, racked by the stone even to the point of having to abandon his life's work of correspondence; he writes to Evelyn, "In my next I have some extraordinarie matter to impart only into your bosome as that, by which you will see what a singular and reall value I put upon your noble Friendship in which observances as long as the Lord affords mee any—lucida Intervalla—I shal remaine ever Dearest Sir your most willing faithful Servant. Sam. Hartlib."[47] Many of his correspondents write to his address, uncertain as to whether he is still alive. In any event, with the return of Charles II, Hartlib's influence over the course of events in any sphere became negligible, and his surviving papers from the period make melancholy reading. Despite his care in covering, to some extent, the degree to which he had been associated with the Cromwellian regime, it was impossible to conceal it sufficiently. It is a dreary irony that Hartlib tells Evelyn that hopes for his rehabilitation rest with his ne'er-do-well son, young Sam, who appears to have had some clandestine role in the return of the monarchy. But, as Hartlib told Evelyn, that role could not be made public in the immediate aftermath and, therefore, the Hartlib family could not be adequately recompensed.[48]

Hartlib had long exhausted his private means in the support of worthy causes and had been existing on subventions from like-minded patrons and from Parliament. Indeed, one of the final acts

[47] British Library, Evelyn MSS, letter 866, Hartlib to Evelyn, dated by Evelyn, April 14, 1660.

[48] British Library, Evelyn MSS, letter 868, Hartlib to Evelyn, November 26, 1660.

of Parliament before the return of the monarchy was to consider and recommend state funding for him: "It was ordered by the last Councel of State that brought in his Majesty that my Case should bee presented to the Parliament which Lord Annesly hath promised to doe assoone as privat businesses shall bee admitted in their next session."[49] Alas, the resolution was ignored, and Hartlib was reduced to begging from his friends. He was clearly successful in approaching Evelyn for loans, but in the following letter of November 26, 1660, he admits that his long delay in writing had been, in part, due to his embarrassment at the impossibility of his returning the £5 Evelyn had lent him:

> Most Honoured Sir
>
> I have not presented to you my wonted Paper respects by reason chiefly of my engagement for that noble and faithful kindnesse of the Loane, which I thought should have beene discharged before this time. But I have more cause then ever to try your patience for some times longer by reason of the continuance of my multiplied and most urgent necessities that doe oppresse mee to this very houre. Sir I acquainted you heretofore what Votes had passed concerning Pensions and debts under the former Powers. Since it hath beene Resolved that no Motion is to bee made concerning Mony-matters till the Debts of the Army and Navy bee first satisfied. Both those votes fall most heavily upon your tormented Servant, so that hee hath nothing to expect of all his Arreares nor of his yearly Pension setled upon him by the first Parliament consisting of Lords and Comons.[50]

Evelyn refers to his help at this time in his late letter to William Wotton: "I had very many letters from him, and often relieved him."[51] Hartlib was largely abandoned by his wealthy and influential friends after 1660, and his less well positioned friends often had to look to their own safety or showed their true colors in response to Hartlib's sadness. Another late mention of Hartlib in Evelyn's papers comes in the correspondence he had initiated between Evelyn and John Beale, though clearly the relationship between Hartlib and Beale had become strained with the change in political circumstances. Hartlib writes to Evelyn, "I am very sorry that our Correspondency with the Worthy Man is much interrupted as to the present Field and Garden Imploiments and Delights. For though stil wee write weekly one to an other yet they are on unpleasant, if not ugly arguments sometimes."[52] Beale, who had navigated his way reasonably ably through the treacherous waters of the Restoration, continued to correspond with Evelyn until his death. Among other things he tells Evelyn of his collection of medical recipes collected from Hartlib's correspondence, particularly with reference to Hartlib's own terminal illness, from the stone: "And I thinke you knowe that Hartlib gave me notice of all his freaks of medicines once twice & sometimes thrice a weeke for more than 7 yeares." In a cryptic postscript, he explains why there is no grave for Hartlib:

> Sr you remember that Hartl[?] gave his body for an anatomy. And then was seene all the effects of his medicines upon his stone, bladder &c.[53]

[49] British Library, Evelyn MSS, letter 867, Hartlib to Evelyn, dated by Evelyn, October 14, 1660.

[50] British Library, MSS, letter 868, Hartlib to Evelyn, November 26, 1660.

[51] *Diary and Correspondence,* 724, Evelyn to William Wotton, September 12, 1703.

[52] British Library, Evelyn MSS, letter 868, Hartlib to Evelyn, November 26, 1660.

[53] British Library, Evelyn MSS, letter 42, Beale to Evelyn, July 30, 1664.

For the results to have been visible during dissection, the effects of these attempts at treatment must have been truly terrible. (This is, by the way, an extremely early example of someone giving his own body for an anatomy; most bodies used were those of criminals.)

Hartlib and Evelyn formed an interesting duo throughout their lives and, indeed, after their deaths. Evelyn belonged to a different world in a number of ways, and an index of that is contained in their very different posthumous histories. Of Hartlib very little remains to capture the popular imagination: we know exceptionally little about him as an individual, and his persona is almost entirely professional. There are few personal letters; there is no portrait. Perhaps most strikingly, the closest he comes to a diary is his "Ephemerides," kept for virtually thirty years. But this contains almost nothing of a personal character, being more akin to a logbook of information crossing his desk. Even when he does appear, it is often under a pseudonym, Albureth. Evelyn, by contrast, is one of the best known of individuals from the period: letters, diaries, elements of autobiography, portraits, and published works substantially by him, all abound. There is no tomb for Hartlib, and no body; everything was absorbed into the enterprise of knowledge.

Evelyn harkened back to the very different intellectual context from which Hartlib and his colleagues sought to release their culture, but he also lived to play a considerable role in the creation of the new culture of the Restoration, which in part modeled itself intellectually on a selective version of the England of Elizabeth and her immediate successor. In this context, the self-effacing activities of a Hartlib were no longer the ideal, nor were his priorities those which established the characteristics for acceptable publications.

Of all Evelyn's works, the "Elysium Britannicum" is that which most clearly mirrors the conflicts of those troubled times. Begun in one intellectual milieu and attempting to satisfy its criteria, the incomplete volume runs aground on a sandbar between two cultures, unable to resolve the contradictions it embodies. In other works, Evelyn was to demonstrate how ingenuity was to be brought into fashion, but the very unfinished state of the "Elysium Britannicum" is testimony to the fact that this was not to be the way in which it was to be achieved.

John Evelyn and English Architecture

ALICE T. FRIEDMAN

Despite his many published works, John Evelyn is a difficult man to get to know, and harder still to understand. As shown in a portrait by Robert Walker, painted in 1648 after his return from his Grand Tour of the Continent (Fig. 1), Evelyn appears as the melancholic gentleman scholar, his dark, wavy hair flowing down to his shoulders, head in hand, the long elegant fingers of his right hand resting on a skull, with the motto, in Greek, above him—"Second thoughts are the beginning of philosophy."[1] This portrait hardly fits the image we have of Evelyn in his later life, bristling with efficiency and energy, a tireless commissioner for every conceivable cause and problem: overseeing the Royal Mint, caring for sick and wounded soldiers, rebuilding the streets of London, and redesigning Old St. Paul's. Is this Evelyn the advisor to kings and statesmen, Evelyn the committee member and notetaker, the man whom David Howarth rather uncharitably called the "great minute-taker of Restoration culture?"[2] And there are still other Evelyns to account for: What of the member of the Royal Society, full of curiosity about science and new technology? What of the inveterate collector of natural and scientific curiosities, the man for whom no visit was complete without a viewing (and a full assessment) of the treasuries, museums, and cabinets of his hosts? What of the improver of landscapes, the arbiter of taste in the arts and architecture, so full of what John Summerson aptly called "Royal Society hauteur"?[3] In 1648, few of these many facets of John Evelyn are even suggested. Here, we see the thoughtful, spiritual side of the man, the commissioner and committee-man were yet to appear.

Something of this same ambiguity, and ambivalence, can be found in Evelyn's complex and elusive views on architectural theory and practice. Architectural subjects are treated frequently in Evelyn's writings: descriptions of buildings in Italy and England abound in Evelyn's diary and letters,

[1] The portrait is discussed by G. Keynes in *John Evelyn: A Study in Bibliophily with a Bibliography of His Writings*, Oxford, 1968, 5, and by D. Chambers in "The Tomb in the Landscape: John Evelyn's Garden at Albury," *Journal of Garden History* 1, 1 (1981), 37–54.

[2] D. Howarth, *Lord Arundel and His Circle*, New Haven, 1975, 26.

[3] J. Summerson, "The Mind of Wren," *Heavenly Mansions*, New York, 1983, 62–63.

1. Robert Walker, portrait of John Evelyn, 1648 (photo: National Portrait Gallery, London)

while a number of works, notably the *Fumifugium* (1661) and the preface to his translation of Fréart de Chambray's *Parallel of the Antient Architecture with the Modern* (1664 and 1707), are devoted to matters of planning and design. Evelyn enjoyed close friendships with the most prominent classicist architects of his day: Christopher Wren, Hugh May, and Roger Pratt. Yet despite his outspoken public enthusiasm for the revival of ancient architecture and its systematic discipline, and his equally vehement denunciations both of English craftsmen and of the Gothic style, Evelyn's private views—as indicated by his informal comments about medieval English churches and manor houses, for example, or by his love for his rambling country house at Wotton (Fig. 2)—suggest a more complex oscillation between points of view and modes of discourse. Like a number of his contemporaries in England, particularly men associated with the Royal Society, such as Wren and John Aubrey, Evelyn attempted to accommodate both his commitment to scientific improvement—associated with the systematic measurement, geometry, and symmetry of classicizing architecture and urban design—and his deep emotional ties to English tradition and history, expressed through antiquarian research and literary nostalgia. Thus, a work such as the "Elysium Britannicum" presents a mixture of disparate points of view, seemingly in contradiction to its author's own public stand on architectural propriety.

It is evident from even a quick glance at the extant parts of the manuscript of the "Elysium Britannicum" that it does not really deal with architecture at all. One searches in vain for sketches of facades or elevations or for plans showing the layout of either buildings or gardens; true, there are a few sketches of structures in the garden—an aviary (p. 215), an artificial echo (p. 169), a rabbit hutch (p. 217), and an elaborate beehive (p. 223)—as well as a number of perspective diagrams, but there is nothing substantial that might help us understand what the author thought about built form or, more important, about the quality of the spaces that the buildings enclose. It is not that Evelyn never

2. John Aubrey, view of John Evelyn's family home at Wotton, Surrey, detail. Bodleian Library, Oxford, MS Aubrey 4, fol. 95r (photo: reproduced courtesy the library)

touches on architectural issues in the "Elysium"—for he does, indeed, cite passages from architectural treatises by Vitruvius, Palladio, and Henry Wotton, among others, and he addresses questions having to do with the relationship between house and garden—but it is clear that he has far more passion for texts and for literary images, for descriptions of buildings in Spenser and Sidney, for example, and for citations of theoretical treatises, than for the buildings themselves.[4] Ultimately, the "Elysium" appears to be far more concerned with the *things* in the garden, particularly mechanical devices and automata, than it is with architecture or even landscape architecture. Even allowing for the loss of proposed sections of the treatise on the villa, which would no doubt have focused more fully on architectural design, the manuscript's failure to set forth a systematic overview of formal relationships, and its evident preoccupation with visual and mechanical "events," rather than with aesthetic principles, suggests that the lessons of the Italian Renaissance in matters of design had far less meaning for the author than he would elsewhere have us believe. Here we find the characteristic

[4] The citations from Vitruvius do not emphasize matters of design but instead focus on the most widely cited texts: the education of the architect (p. 3), acoustics (p. 143), the "Egyptian Room" (p. 143, with a reference to Wotton's commentary in the *Elements of Architecture*, 1624), mechanical devices (p. 118b), topiary (p. 96), and sunken walkways in the garden (p. 86). The references to Spenser's "Bower of Bliss," as described in *The Faerie Queene*, 1590, and to Kalender's house in Sidney's *Arcadia*, 1590—both well-known passages—occur on page 58. On Sidney and history, see A. F. Kinney, "Sir Philip Sidney and the Uses of History," in H. Dubrow and R. Strier, eds., *The Historical Renaissance: New Essays on Tudor and Stuart Literature and Culture,* Chicago, 1988, 293–314.

approach of the antiquarian and virtuoso, intent on the study of natural and artistic objects, not on the concerns of the architect or theorist.

The habits of mind revealed in the "Elysium" were established early in Evelyn's career. Very few sketches by Evelyn survive, but drawings made in Italy in the 1640s and now in the collection of the Royal Institute of British Architects reveal a great deal about Evelyn's early attempts to understand built form. As in the "Elysium Britannicum," Evelyn seems most interested in details rather than in whole buildings, and in how specific things work rather than exclusively, or even predominantly, in how they look. In his studies of a spiral staircase, in sketches showing the construction of a dome and its coffering, and in his drawing of the facade of a timber-framed shop, Evelyn reveals his interest in building construction and materials; the specifics of dome construction were of particular concern to him because of their unfamiliarity in England. Although these drawings are rather crude, they do reveal some knowledge of the conventions of architectural draftsmanship, making use of elevations, sections, perspectives, and profiles. Another page of drawings shows an iron railing and the profiles of various types of baluster, as well as the facade of the domed and temple-fronted church of San Andrea on Via Flaminia in Rome, built by Vignola for Julius III in 1550–54. Here Evelyn again focuses on details and especially on domed structures. This interest would reappear in later years, when, in assessing the various designs submitted for the rebuilding of Old St. Paul's after the Great Fire of 1666, Evelyn was to remark that the dome, or "noble cupola," as he called it, was "a form of building not yet known in England but of wonderful grace."[5]

Evelyn's reactions to works of Italian and French architecture, as recorded in his diary during this period, reveal a similar quality. Much of what he says about particular monuments comes from the guidebooks that he carried with him and read carefully. When he does make original observations, he tends to focus on the gardens, on details of specific buildings or places, on curiosities of construction or ornament or, more likely, on the specific objects in the collections that he saw. When he visited the Chateau Richelieu, built by Lemercier in the 1630s, for example, he compared the old chateau to the new one, praising the "modern design" of the new part and noting that the old castle had "too great a mixture of the Gotic [*sic*]";[6] he also remarked on a little chapel with a dome in the garden that he calls "an handsome order of Architecture."[7] However, he was most interested in the gardens themselves, with their terraces and cascades, galleries and grottos, and, as he does throughout the diary, he uses his brief discussion of the chateau as a lead-in to a more extended description of the landscape nearby.

In Rome in 1644, he visited the Capitoline Hill, the design of which was one of Michelangelo's crowning achievements. Here Evelyn takes no notice whatsoever of the giant order of pilasters that tie the three buildings together, nor of their facade design, nor of the spatial harmony of the piazza created by the juxtaposition of the three buildings. Instead, Evelyn focuses on the Senatorial Palace

[5] E. S. de Beer, ed., *The Diary of John Evelyn,* 6 vols., Oxford, 1955, III, 388 (hereafter Evelyn, *Diary*). The drawings are in the collection of the Royal Institute of British Architects; they are reproduced in *Catalogue of the Drawings Collection of the Royal Institute of British Architects,* London, 1972, III, 113 (fig. 83).

[6] Evelyn, *Diary,* II, 111.

[7] Evelyn, *Diary,* II, 112.

at the far end of the piazza, the one building on the site that retained some of its original medieval form. He notes that it has a "handsome Towre . . . battlements . . . a stately double payre of staires and a stately *posario,*" a word apparently coined by Evelyn to refer to the arched platform that formed the terrace at the top of the stairs.[8] By far the majority of his account of the Capitoline is given to descriptions of the collections of antiquities and curiosities housed on the site.

The young traveler of the mid-1640s was, like all Englishmen of the period, quite unprepared for what he saw on the Continent. Three major factors conspired to overwhelm him as he tried to make sense of Paris and Rome and to respond to the splendors of Renaissance architecture; it is these three things that hold the key to understanding Evelyn's mature approach to architecture. The first and foremost factor was the vast difference between these new places and the world he knew in England. Although architectural historians, and Evelyn himself, focused attention on the clarity of monumental classicizing works by such innovative and atypical architects as Inigo Jones and Christopher Wren, London in this period was a visually chaotic place and, as Evelyn himself reminds us in the *Fumifugium,* it was a city of timber that had evolved haphazardly over time. Jones' works were unique in their time and, more importantly, appealed to only a small coterie of patrons associated with the royal court.[9] Evelyn and his contemporaries had never seen anything even remotely similar to the houses, churches, and gardens (much less the antiquities) that they encountered in Italy; perhaps more than other travelers, the English turned to guidebooks, handbooks, treatises, and works of art theory to make sense of what they saw.[10]

This emphasis on books was particularly appropriate, because the literary and intellectual Renaissance, as opposed to the artistic one, had flourished for decades in England.[11] Evelyn, like many of his kinsmen, had an appreciation for antiquity that came from reading Virgil, Cicero, and Livy; moreover, he understood the structures of Latin grammar and thus could appreciate the system of rules that gave rise to classical architecture. Respect for the system was completely separate from the experience of built form, however.

The wide gulf that separated the appreciation for classical culture from the experience of built form is clear when we look at the case of the fourteenth earl and countess of Arundel. The earl (Thomas Howard) was the foremost collector both of antiquities and of Renaissance painting of his time, a tireless and voracious connoisseur whose agents scoured the Continent in search of new acquisitions, which were duly shipped back to England and installed at Arundel House in London.[12]

[8] Evelyn, *Diary,* II, 220.

[9] On Jones, see J. Harris, S. Orgel, and R. Strong, *The King's Arcadia: Inigo Jones and the Culture of the Stuart Court,* London, 1973, and J. Summerson, *Inigo Jones,* New York, 1966.

[10] For the use of books by English travelers, see C. Anderson, "Inigo Jones and the Language of Architectural Classicism in England, 1580–1640," Ph.D. diss., Massachusetts Institute of Technology, 1993. On his arrival in Rome in November 1644, Evelyn sought out a number of long-time residents for, he says, "I resolv'd . . . to spend no moment idly here." From these he "receiv'd instructions, how to behave our selves in Towne, what directions, Masters and bookes to take in search and view of the Antiquities, churches, Collections etc." (Evelyn, *Diary,* II, 213–14).

[11] For the intellectual history of the Jacobean and Caroline courts, see R. M. Smuts, *Court Culture and the Origins of the Royalist Tradition in Early Stuart England,* Philadelphia, 1987.

[12] For Arundel's activities as a collector, see Howarth, *Arundel* (as in above, note 2).

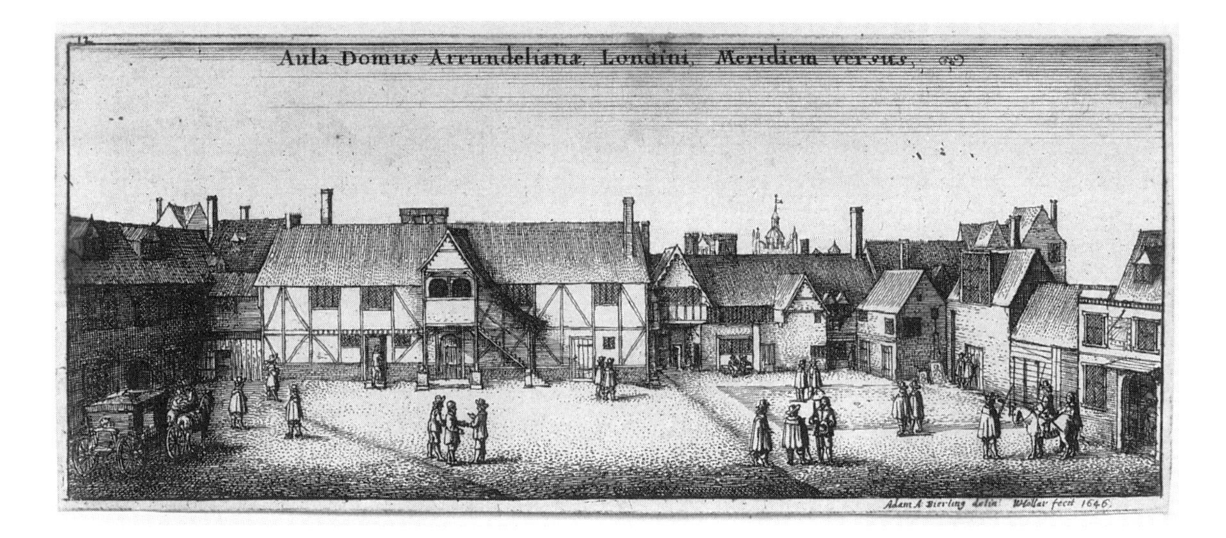

3. Wenceslas Hollar, Arundel House, London, 1646 (photo: Museum of Fine Arts, Boston)

Arundel was also the patron of Inigo Jones, the man whom Jones accompanied on his first visit to Italy in 1612. He was thus a legend in his own time, viewed by many as the father of Renaissance culture in England. Daniel Mytens' 1618 portraits of Arundel and his wife, a granddaughter of the great Tudor builder Bess of Hardwick, show them set against the background of their collections and some of the architecture they favored. The earl gestures toward a row of life-sized antique statues that recedes down a long hallway, terminating in an arch-framed vista of the Thames; the countess is placed before a long gallery covered with pictures of various kinds, and the gallery ends with a vista of a garden.

Given this portrait, it is startling to encounter Hollar's view of Arundel House, dated just a few years later (Fig. 3). We expect arches and pediments and columns, not rambling half-timber structures. Although the long gallery shown in the portraits might have been carved out of existing buildings, there is nothing here of the integration of symmetry and geometry that we associate with the Renaissance. It was this sort of cityscape that Evelyn knew well, a place in which buildings such as Jones' Banqueting House of 1619, with its light-colored stone facade of repeated geometric modules, stood out as curiosities.

The second factor that contributed to Evelyn's confusion was his awareness of the very foreignness of the architectural forms that he saw on the Continent. He knew he was impressed by the works of architecture that he visited, but also he knew that both the style and the planning of these works were alien to English culture. Protestant England tended to associate Renaissance classicism with papal Rome and with Catholicism; moreover, the customary use of English houses and gardens discouraged axial planning, because etiquette required a circuitous route for visitors before reaching the master of the house.[13] For Evelyn, then, as for other Englishmen, there was little opportunity for

[13] This topic is treated by M. Girouard, *Life in the English Country House: A Social and Architectural History,* London, 1978, chaps. 1–4.

imagining how one might re-create this aesthetic experience on his own native soil; there was no clear course of action for bringing back his newfound knowledge in the way in which designers always ultimately hoped to bring home the fruits of their travel experience. This same contradiction had, of course, confronted Inigo Jones some twenty-five years earlier.

The third and final factor was that Evelyn was traveling as an exile from his homeland. The civil war and the political and social upheavals that preceded it had far-reaching implications that were both cultural and psychological. From the mid-1630s until the Restoration in 1660, men and women of Evelyn's class lived in fear of the growing rebellion, anxiously protecting their estates and townhouses from seizure by opposing factions or from the casual theft and damage that resulted from the breakdown of social structures.[14] Some feared for their lives, and all—whether Royalists or Parliamentarians—feared for their property and for the way of life that they knew. Thus Evelyn and others of his generation were preoccupied with events beyond their control, frightened and anxious for the future. Many, such as Evelyn, developed deep spiritual and religious convictions and a nostalgic, utopian yearning for the world that had existed before the conflict, particularly for the world of the English countryside. The popularity of the so-called country house poems of writers such as Jonson, Carew, and Herrick reveals the widespread yearning for continuity, tradition, and the stability of the past inspired by the increasing awareness of new developments on the Continent and by the upheavals of the English civil war.[15]

Taken together, these three factors account not only for Evelyn's unfamiliarity with Renaissance architecture as a young man setting out to discover the Continent but also for his lack of intuitive response to its fundamental principles of design, in particular the idea of a spatial sequence and the extended composition involving various effects of mass and space. Moreover, the emotional distance that Evelyn and other English travelers felt from this architecture tended to cause them to intellectualize their interest in it, to read books, to systematize, and to see both antiquity and the Renaissance as a storehouse of significant rules and monumental achievements but not of spiritual poetry or artistic experience.

For Evelyn, then, the experience of meeting the earl of Arundel in Padua in 1645 and 1646 must surely have been a special pleasure and a unique opportunity to learn about a subject with which few Englishmen were familiar. Arundel the patron, the hero of the English court, the dedicated servant of the crown, was now an old man living out his days in exile. In June 1645 on their first afternoon together in Italy (the two had actually met once before in Holland), they visited the garden of Alvise Cornaro in Padua, where, Evelyn records, they saw the casino, "a room covered with a noble Cupola built purposely for Musique."[16] He also notes the use of earthenware jars in the

[14] See, for an example, the case of Lady Anne Clifford, countess of Pembroke. She reports in her diary that she took up residence at Baynard's Castle, her husband's London house, for six years during the 1640s, because it was "then a houseful of riches and was ye more secured by my lying there" (in D. J. H. Clifford, ed., *The Diaries of Lady Anne Clifford,* Stroud, 1990, 95).

[15] See W. A. McClung, *The Country House in English Renaissance Poetry,* Berkeley, 1977, and Smuts, *Court Culture,* esp. 96 ff.

[16] Evelyn, *Diary,* 466.

walls as an acoustical device.[17] At their second meeting, in April of the following year, Evelyn records that Arundel gave him a list of monuments to see in Vicenza, Verona, and Milan.[18] His description of the aged earl, sitting in bed, reduced to tears by the many private and public humiliations that he had endured over the previous six years, is one of the gems of the diary:

> It was Easter Monday that I was invited to breakfast at the Earle of Arundels; I took my leave of him in bed, where I left that greate and exellent Man in teares upon some private discourse of crosses that had befaln his Illustrious family, particularly the undutifullnesse of his *Grandson Philips* turning Dominican frier, the unkindness of his *countesse,* in *Holland,* the miserie of his countrie, now embroiled in a Civil War, etc., after which he caused his gentlemen to give me directions all written in his own hand, what curiosities I should enquire after in my journey.[19]

This experience, no doubt, left Evelyn, a staunch Royalist and an exile himself, in some conflict about his reactions to the monuments that Arundel urged on him, including the work of Palladio at the villa Rotunda. His comments on it and other buildings from Arundel's list are often very close to the earl's own notes to him, and they have a wooden and automatic quality that betrays his lack of genuine feeling for the work. This coolness stands in sharp contrast to his enthusiasm for the cultural values that these works of architecture represented in a general sense and for the great patron who had recommended them to him.

Back at home, Evelyn recorded his reactions to the many places that he visited throughout the 1650s. Again, it is striking that it is the gardens and the specific details of buildings that capture his attention. In July 1654, he visited Wilton House, the country seat rebuilt by the earl of Pembroke in the 1630s to the designs of Inigo Jones, together with his assistant John Webb and the garden designer Isaac de Caus. Here we would expect that Evelyn's love of Renaissance classicism would translate into an appreciation for the new style of the house, or at least of the garden front (which he refers to as "the modern part towards the garden").[20] Instead he focuses on what he calls the Dining Room, which we know as the Double Cube Room, remarking on its decoration, rather than on its design, on the magnificent chimney pieces "after the French manner" elsewhere in the house, and on a "paire of artificial winding-stayres."[21] Here he notes that the garden was "heretofore esteem'd the noblest in all England,"[22] but his reaction to it is lukewarm, and his attention is directed elsewhere: "After all," he says, "that which to me renders the seate delightfull, is its being so neere the downes and noble plaines about the country and contiguous to it."[23] Ultimately it is the countryside, rather than either the house or its gardens, that moves Evelyn most deeply here.

His visit to York the following month yielded another revealing entry in his diary. Of the many sites in the town, he says, the

[17] Evelyn, *Diary,* II, 466.

[18] Evelyn, *Diary,* II, 479. See J. M. Robinson, ed., *Remembrances of Things Worth Seeing in Italy: Given to John Evelyn by Thomas Howard, 14th Earl of Arundel . . . with an Extract from John Evelyn's Diary,* London, 1987.

[19] Evelyn, *Diary,* II, 479.

[20] Evelyn, *Diary,* III, 113.

[21] Evelyn, *Diary,* III, 114.

[22] Evelyn, *Diary,* III, 114.

[23] Evelyn, *Diary,* III, 114.

> most remarkable and worthy seeing is St. Peter's Cathedrall, which alone of all the greate Churches in *England* has best ben preserv'd from the furie of the sacrilegious, by Composition with the Rebells, when they tooke the Citty, during the many incursions of *Scotch* and others: it is a most intire, magnificent piece of Gotic [*sic*] Architecture.[24]

Here he takes note of the choir screen and its carving, and then turns his attention to a velvet and silver Bible and Book of Common Prayer in the cathedral, two things, he says, which are "a greate rarity in these days."[25] Like his friend and colleague John Aubrey, Evelyn reveals himself in these years to be first and foremost an antiquarian, an ardent preservationist of objects, buildings, and traditions in the face of war and neglect, and a collector of curiosities.[26]

These are the impressions we must keep in mind as we enter into conversation with another side of Evelyn—that of Evelyn the translator of Fréart de Chambray's *Parallel,* the reader of Renaissance treatises and proponent of rules, the self-righteous classicist who deplores Gothic architecture. For, after the Restoration, Evelyn began to live a very different sort of life from the one he had known on the Continent and as a private citizen on his country estate. From 1660 on, we meet Evelyn the commissioner and member of the Royal Society, a man whose attention is devoted to bureaucracy, to politics, and to the improvement of England in every way: economic, agricultural, scientific, medical, and architectural.

Evelyn's efforts to reform English architecture primarily took the form of theoretical writings, notably, the preface to his translation of Fréart de Chambray, entitled "Account of Architects and Architecture," which appeared first in 1664 and was updated and expanded with a new dedication to Sir Christopher Wren for the 1707 edition. Nevertheless, two examples of his own architectural designs survive: a project for a residential college, with cell-like living quarters for the students and a neoclassical main building (Figs. 4 and 5), described in a letter to Robert Boyle of September 3, 1659, and a plan for the rebuilding of London (Fig. 6), submitted in September 1666 after the Great Fire.[27]

The college project is notable for a number of reasons. Its overall style and compositional themes were derived from the work of Roger Pratt, a prominent court architect with whom Evelyn had lived for a time in Rome (1644–45): not only is the main building graced with a fashionable split pediment and characterized by simple geometries and symmetry in the treatment of its facade but also the overall layout of the project is axial and very obviously controlled by principles of design that are typical of Renaissance planning not found in the "Elysium Britannicum." Moreover, the

[24] Evelyn, *Diary,* III, 128.

[25] Evelyn, *Diary,* III, 129.

[26] For Aubrey's antiquarian research, see M. Hunter, *John Aubrey and the Realm of Learning,* New York, 1975, esp. chap. 3.

[27] The college design, among Evelyn's papers at the British Library, London (Evelyn period, Box XI), was published by M. Hunter in *Establishing the New Science: The Experience of the Early Royal Society,* Woodbridge, 1989, 181–84; the text of the letter to Boyle appears in William Bray, ed., *Memoirs of John Evelyn . . . and a Selection of His Familiar Letters,* 5 vols., London, 1827, III, 116–20. The plan of London was one of a series of three engraved by Vertue for the Society of Antiquaries in 1748; these were reprinted in the *Journal of the Royal Society of British Architects* 27, 3rd ser. (1919–20), 467–70. Evelyn's project was republished with commentary by W. Maitland, *History and Survey of London,* London, 1756, I, 447–50, and by E. S. de Beer, ed., *London Revived: Consideration for Its Rebuilding in 1666,* Oxford, 1938 (see Keynes, *Bibliography,* 167 n. 3). Evelyn mentions the project in his diary (see Evelyn, *Diary,* III, 465).

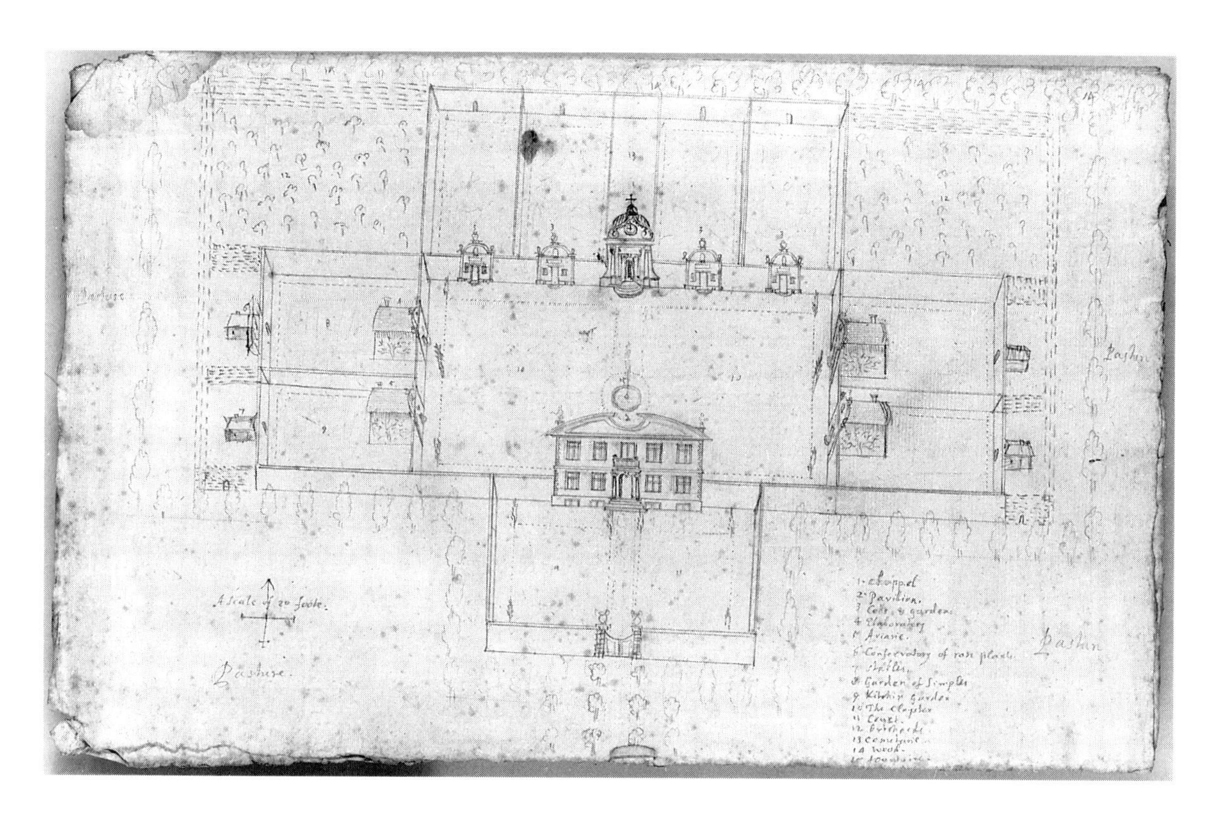

4. John Evelyn, design for a college, 1659, bird's-eye view. British Library, London, Evelyn period, box XI (photo: Michael R. Dudley)

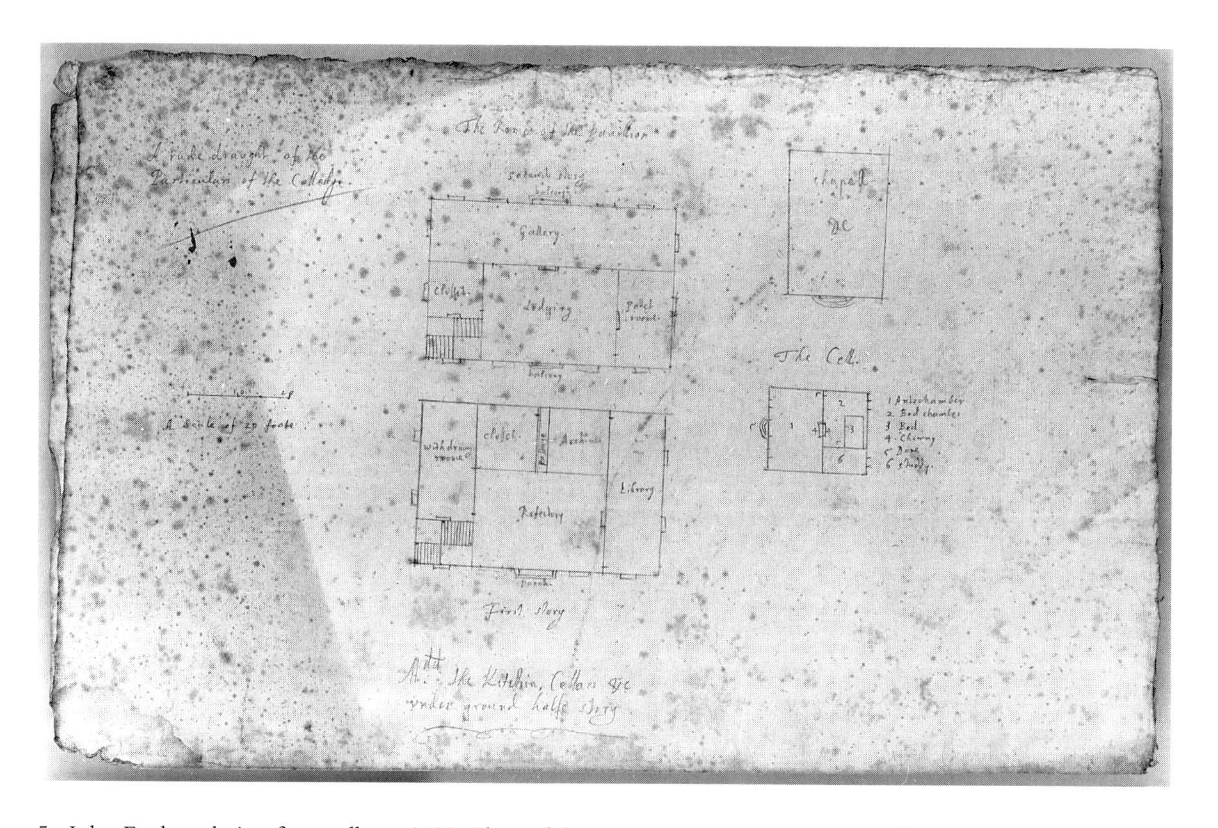

5. John Evelyn, design for a college, 1659. Plans of the principal floors in the main building and of the chapel. British Library, London (photo: Michael R. Dudley)

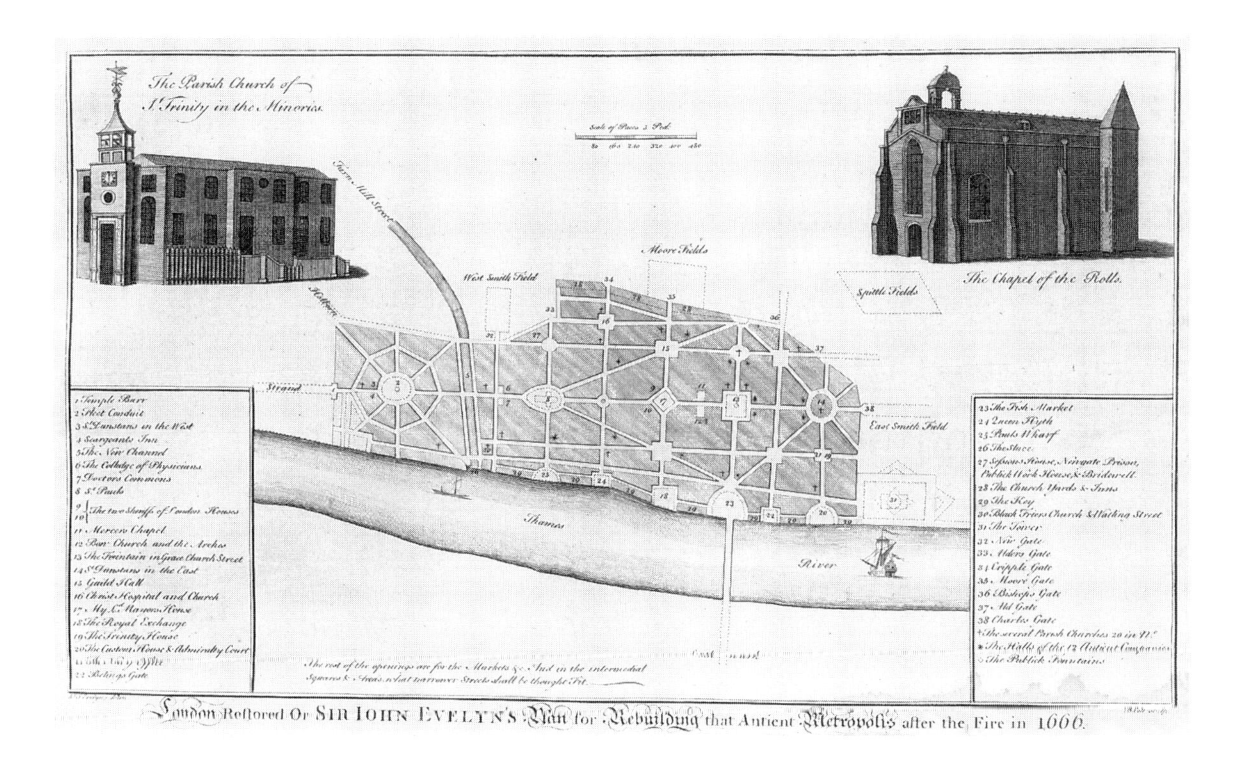

6. John Evelyn, plan for the rebuilding of London in 1666, from W. Maitland, *History and Survey of London,* 1756, 447 (photo: by permission of the Houghton Library, Harvard University)

plan of the main house conforms, in a general sense, with Pratt's "double pile" type, described in his notebooks and known to Evelyn from the example of Coleshill of ca. 1650.[28] These features indicate that in most matters of design, particularly for official purposes, Evelyn was, like his friends Pratt and Hugh May, a committed classicist; the special status of the Elysium as a utopian country retreat is perhaps revealed in its lack of such features.[29]

Evelyn expressed his appreciation for another well-known house designed by Pratt, Clarendon House in London, in a letter to Viscount Cornbury on January 20, 1666:

> Let me speak ingenuously: I went with prejudice, and a critical spirit, incident to those who fancy they know anything in art. I acknowledge to your Lordship that I have never seen a nobler pile: my old friend and fellow traveller . . . has perfectly acquitted himself. It is, without hyperbole, the best contrived, the most useful, graceful, and magnificent house in England. As I said my Lord, here is state and use, solidity and beauty most symmetrically combined to-

[28] For Pratt, see J. Summerson, *Architecture in Britain, 1530–1830,* Harmondsworth, 1970, 149–53, and R. Gunther, *The Architecture of Sir Roger Pratt . . . from His Notebooks,* Oxford, 1928. Contemporary country-house architecture is treated extensively in O. Hill and J. Cornforth, *English Country Houses: Caroline, 1625–85,* London, 1966.

[29] A reference to May's encouragement of Evelyn in his translation of Fréart de Chambray appears in the dedicatory letter to Sir John Denham in *A Parallel of the Antient Architecture with the Modern, written in French by Roland Fréart, sieur de Chambray, made English . . . by John Evelyn,* 1701, n.p. (first published 1664). See also E. Harris, *British Architectural Books and Writers, 1556–1785,* Cambridge, 1990, 196–201. Evelyn refers to May's help with the plates in a letter to Lady Sunderland on August 4, 1690 (Bray, *Memoir . . . Letters,* III, 464).

> gether; seriously, there is nothing abroad that pleases me better; nothing at home approaches it . . . I pronounce it the first palace in England.[30]

Pronouncements such as this one are typical of Evelyn's publicly expressed views on architecture, dating from the 1660s to the end of his life. His preference for "state and use, solidity and beauty most symmetrically combined together" is certainly evident in the plan that he proposed for the rebuilding of London. Organized as a series of avenues forming a network of connections between variously shaped piazzas, the plan (like Wren's of the same year) attempts to impose a system of roadways on the fabric of the city, isolating monuments in an effort to achieve both formal order and urban grandeur in the manner of the Baroque gardens of Le Nôtre. Here again we have evidence of Evelyn's ability to grasp the principles of design, albeit in a rudimentary way, which underlie the classicist architecture he favored; such an overview is notably lacking from the "Elysium Britannicum."

Evelyn's translation of the *Parallel of the Antient Architecture with the Modern* was an outgrowth of his work as a reformer, part of an effort to provide English architects and craftsmen with models and rules. His original contributions to *Parallel* consist of two dedicatory letters and the "Account of Architects and Architecture." The 1664 version of the "Account" merely provided definitions for specialized architectural vocabulary and included none of the extended discussion of Evelyn's guiding principles and prejudices that appeared in the 1707 version or in the dedicatory letters. Whereas Fréart's text and illustrations attempt to compare various theoretical treatments of the orders with existing Roman works, Evelyn appears not much interested in doing that. His remarks, particularly in the earlier edition, say little of geometry or proportion. For Evelyn, the real crux of the matter lay in the effects of symmetry on physical welfare and mental acuity. The dedication to Sir John Denham, the surveyor of the kings works, presents his position clearly:

> You well know that all the mischiefs and absurdities in our modern structures proceed chiefly from our busie and Gotic [*sic*] trifilings in the Compositions of the Five Orders . . . its is from the *asymmetrie* of our Buildings, want of decorum and proportion in our *Houses* that the irregularity of our *humours* and *affections* may shrewdly be discerned.[31]

Evelyn's role as a proponent of the healthful advantages of classicism is further revealed by his remarks about the city of London:

> But neither here must I forget what is alone due to you *Sir* for the reformation in the *streets,* as by your introducing that incomparable form of paving to an incredible advantage to the *Publick,* when that which is begun in Holborn shall become universal, for the saving of wheels and carriages, the cure of noysom gutters, the deobstruction of Encounters, the dispatch of Business, the cleanness of the way, the beauty of the object, and the preserving of both the mother and the babe, so many of the fair sex and their offspring having perished by mischances (as I am credibly informed) from the ruggedness of the unequal street.[32]

[30] Bray, *Memoir . . . Letters,* III, 177–78.

[31] "Epistle to Sir John Denham," *Parallel,* 1707, n.p.

[32] "Epistle to Sir John Denham," *Parallel,* 1707, n.p.

Evelyn blames English architects and craftsmen for the lack of improvement in English architecture, citing both their ignorance and stubbornness, and he calls for the establishment of an academy of design:

> Great pity I say it is, that amongst the Professors of Humanity (as they call it) there should not be some lectures and schools, endowd and furnished with Books, Instruments, Plots, Types and Models of the most excellent Fabricks both in Civil and Military Architecture. . . . Our vulgar workmen, who for want of some more solid directions, faithful and easy rules in this nature, fill as well whole cities as private dwellings with rubbish and a thousand infirmities, with the most shameful incongruities and inconveniences in all they take in hand, and all this for their want of canons to proceed by and humility to learn, their being hardly a nation under heaven more conceited of their understandings and abilities, and more impatient of Direction than our ordinary mechanics.[33]

Here is Evelyn the improver, the writer of treatises on everything from forests to London smoke, from the history of all the mechanical arts to the "Elysium Britannicum" itself. From a treatise such as Fréart's, Evelyn and his readers learned a great deal about the correct form of the orders and the reasons for deploring the lack of good taste in modern architecture. In the expanded version of the "Account of Architects and Architecture," dedicated to Wren in a letter dated February 21, 1697, Evelyn makes an attempt at architectural history, yielding his strongest anti-Gothic statement on record. It was "the Goths, Vandals and other barbarous nations" who introduced

> a certain fantastical and licentious manner of building, which we have since call'd Modern (or Gothic rather) congestions of heavy, dark, melancholy and monkish piles, without any just proportion, use or beauty, compar'd with the truly Antient.[34]

It was they who began to "debauch noble and useful art":

> For proof of this (without travelling far abroad) I dare report myself to any man of judgement, and that has the least taste of order or magnificence; If after he had look'd a while upon King Henry the VII's chapel at Westminster, gaz'd on its sharp angles, jetties, narrow lights, lame statues, lace and other cutwork and crinkle crankle; and shall then turn his eyes on the Banqueting-House built at White-Hall by Inego [*sic*] Jones after the Antient manner; at on what his majesty's present surveyor Sir Christopher Wren has lately advanced at St. Paul's; and consider what a glorious object the designed cupola, portico, colonads [*sic*] and other (yet unfinished) parts will then present. . . . I say, let him well consider and compare them which of the two Manners strikes the Understanding as well as the Eye with the more majesty and solemn greatness, tho in so much planer and simple dress."[35]

Here Evelyn aligns himself squarely behind Wren and the Royal Society in matters of architecture

[33] *Parallel,* 1707, 5.

[34] *Parallel,* 1707, 9.

[35] *Parallel,* 1707, 10–11. His new historical approach can be compared to Aubrey's "Chronologica Architectonia" of 1669, a much more detailed study of English architecture. See M. Hunter, *John Aubrey and the Realm of Learning,* London, 1975, 157–58.

and improvement. The critique of Gothic had a long history in English architectural criticism, beginning with Henry Wotton's statement that Gothic buildings

> both for naturall imbecility of the sharpe angle itself, and likewise for their very uncomelinesse, ought to be exiled from judicious eyes, and left to their inventors, the Goth or Lombards, amongst other relics of that barbarous age.[36]

Evelyn was a careful reader of Wotton, but clearly such pronouncements represent only one side of Wotton's—or Evelyn's—response to the English architectural heritage. Wren, himself, drew significant lessons from English precedents, even as he, like Evelyn, deplored Gothic and spoke out in favor of the new classicism. He is a complex figure in the history of architecture, one whose classicism was tempered both by his Englishness and by an approach to design that combined bookishness, a love of details, and a focus on the public good.

Wren's fame derives from his work at St. Paul's in London after the Great Fire of 1666 and from the rebuilding of the city churches in the 1670s and 1680s.[37] Much less is known about Wren the scientist, inventor, and member of the Royal Society, but it is precisely this aspect of the architect's career that ties him closely to Evelyn and provides us with yet another point of access into the complexities of Evelyn's approach. Wren's design for a beehive (published in Samuel Hartlib's *The Reformed Commonwealth of Bees,* 1655), for example, was undertaken in the same spirit of inquiry and improvement that inspired his mechanical designs or his drawing of a brain, published in a treatise on the anatomy of the brain by Thomas Willis in 1664; these are reminiscent of the inventions and devices in the "Elysium." Similarly, like Evelyn, Wren drew on the illustrations in books and on the descriptions of ancient buildings in treatises such as those of Palladio or Vitruvius when he was drawing up his designs. For example, for the Sheldonian Theatre in Oxford, built between 1664 and 1669, Wren based his design on that of a Roman theater, as described by Vitruvius and illustrated in numerous editions of his text. The combination of a semicircular seating area and a squared-off stage is taken directly from the description and represents a form of theater design not in fashion in England at that time.[38]

Similarly, Wren's distinctive steeple designs for his city churches derive from a conflation of Gothic precedents, Dutch examples (notably, De Keyser's Zuyder Kerk at Amsterdam), Jones' project for the rebuilding of St. Paul's, and models taken from Serlio and Vitruvius.[39] It is possible to understand Wren's designs as a response to two sets of contradictory conditions also experienced by Evelyn: first, a desire to update traditional English Gothic forms by turning to models in the classical style; and second, the need to base these new forms as much as possible on respected textual sources. Yet we must also pause here to emphasize a key difference: while the two men seem to have shared certain habits of mind and interests, it is nonetheless significant that Wren turned his attention to

[36] H. Wotton, *The Elements of Architecture,* London, 1624, 51.

[37] For Wren, see K. Downes, *Sir Christopher Wren,* London, 1982, and idem, *The Architecture of Wren,* 2nd ed., Over Wallop, 1989. See also Summerson, *Architecture,* chap. 12.

[38] Summerson, *Architecture,* 198–99.

[39] Summerson, *Architecture,* chap. 13, and Downes, *Architecture of Wren,* 55 ff.

architectural design in a way that Evelyn never did. Evelyn, in turn, pursued the idea of improvement through garden design and horticulture with an enthusiasm for science and technology that Wren seems to have left behind in his later career.

However, it is helpful to see much of Wren's design work as a response to the complex social and cultural factors that also affected Evelyn's attitudes toward architecture. Without the intuitive sophistication that might develop from firsthand experience of Renaissance and Baroque architecture—Wren had been to Europe only once, and that was for a trip to Paris for one year in 1665—and determined to anglicize the classical forms that he discovered in books, Wren's designs often have the quality of pastiche—from the Gothic spire of the so-called Warrant Design for St. Paul's of 1675 to the final form of the dome and towers that appear in the building as constructed. Working in the City of London, Wren could not afford to ignore the Gothic style of the buildings that stood around him any more than Evelyn could fail to see the glories of York when he visited the cathedral there. Thus, at St. Paul's we see the survival of the Gothic style in the classicized spires that form the towers on the facade, just as we see the bookishness of the scholar that resulted in the imposition of a temple front between them (borrowed from Claude Perrault's East Front at the Louvre, which Wren saw on his visit to Paris) and the engineering spirit that motivated the crowning of the whole with an enormous dome, that wonder of architectural design unknown in England, which Evelyn himself had called "a form of wondeful grace."[40]

Returning, once again, to the illustrations in the "Elysium Britannicum," we can recognize that their form and content suggest a far less sophisticated student of architecture than Evelyn had become by the end of his life. In place of the type of overall plan showing the site or the relationship between house and garden that we might expect at the beginning of such a treatise, we find a diagram of gardening tools laid out as they would be in a cabinet of curiosities. In place of columns, profiles, or sections, we discover diagrams of automata (Fig. 7), waterworks, and minute sketches of garden insects. As noted earlier, Evelyn makes a number of references to works of architectural theory, citing texts of Vitruvius, Palladio, and Wotton's *Elements of Architecture,* but the texts that he chooses have little to do with design. He cites Vitruvius on the education of an architect, topiary, sunken walkways, and on the use of jars for acoustical devices in theaters, but none of these texts is of the type that would be of interest, primarily, to a designer. On the contrary, they confirm an interest in details and devices that we noted earlier.

Evelyn makes a point of talking about the relationship between house and garden, even citing Palladio on the need to place gardens to the south of the house (a bit of advice for which he hardly needed the authority of a great Renaissance theorist).[41] Furthermore, he notes that the principal rooms should be situated to provide the best views of the parterres in the garden, not only to provide diversion to the ladies but also to provide encouragement, as he says, to the owner while the rest of the Elysium remains unfinished.[42] Thus Evelyn addresses the interdependence of architecture and

[40] Evelyn, *Diary,* III, 388.

[41] John Evelyn, "Elysium Britannicum"; or The Royal Garden in Three Books," British Library, 52.

[42] "Elysium Britannicum," 52.

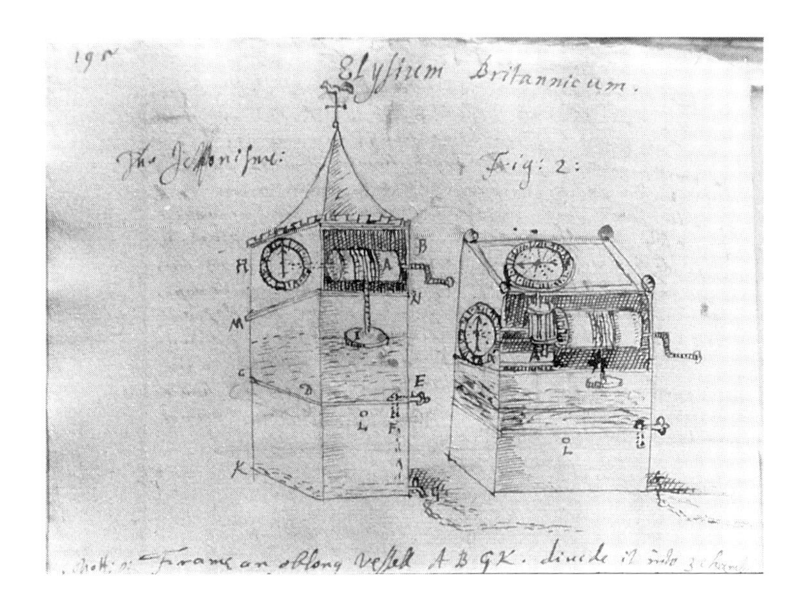

7. John Evelyn, hydraulic automoton clock, from the "Elysium Britannicum," 195. British Library, London (photo: John Ingram, reproduced with permission of the trustees of the will of Major Peter George Evelyn)

landscape in a sensitive way; yet the sort of insistence on a particular style of design that one might expect from the translator of Fréart is strangely absent.

As for a possible explanation for the absence of any identifiable site plan or overall layout in Evelyn's treatise, one passage in particular stands out—the text in which Evelyn tells the reader that his garden "is no phantasticall Utopia but a reall place."[43] The site, he says, is

> among the severall eminences upon which Antient Britanns, the Silures, or at least the Romans did extremely affect to plant themselvs for safty and delight, a place called . . . Backbury, belonging to a worthy person.[44]

He describes the qualities of the landscape and then moves on to discuss another place nearby:

> a furlong distant from this sweet and naturall garden [is] the vale of Misery . . . [with] woods, and other vast objects of rocks, caves, mountaines, and stupendious solitudes fitting to dispose the beholder to pious ecstacies, silent and profound contemplation.[45]

Evelyn's choice of this ancient Romano-British site, a choice that Michael Leslie has suggested was first proposed to Evelyn by his friend John Beale, was his way of confronting the contradiction between Englishness and Roman antiquity that had bothered him since his first travels on the Continent.[46] Embedded in the English countryside, and filled with the memories of primeval occupation, it is a site of originary importance, comparable to that of Rome itself. As such, it is both historically important and spiritually meaningful. Moreover, Evelyn tells the reader that the site is

[43] "Elysium Britannicum," 55.

[44] "Elysium Britannicum," 56. See P. Goodchild, "'No phantasticall utopia but a reall place': John Evelyn, John Beale and Backbury Hill, Herefordshire," *Garden History* 19 (1991), 105–27.

[45] "Elysium Britannicum," 57.

[46] See M. Leslie, "The Spiritual Husbandry of John Beale," in M. Leslie and T. Raylor, eds., *Culture and Cultivation in Early Modern England: Writing and the Land,* Leicester, 1992, 163.

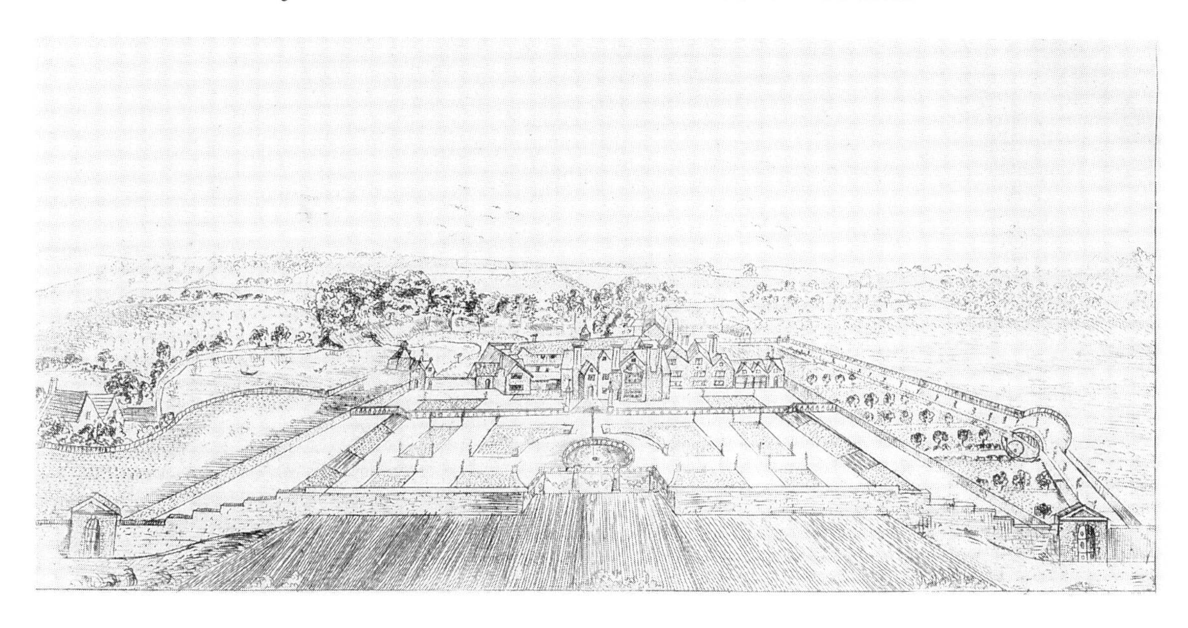

8. John Evelyn, view of Wotton from the top of the terraces, 1653 (photo: British Museum, London)

adjacent to an inspirational place of natural wildness and beauty in which piety and contemplation are inspired.[47] For Evelyn, a landscape such as this fulfilled his desire for a place beyond the grasp of the painful events of the real world, a place comparable to the one suggested by Beale in a letter written to Samuel Hartlib in 1659:

> O for a Paradyse in which wee might retreate from the noyse of Trumpet and Drum, though it were but such as God had indeated in our Spirits.[48]

Whereas the perfect symmetry of Evelyn's college design was something he could propose in the abstract, as a model of rational clarity, his Elysium was to be a "real place" embedded in the English countryside. For Evelyn, such a place of refuge and spiritual retreat, a place "fitting to dispose the behoulder to pious ecstacies" as he says in the "Elysium," would have to share much more with the spirit of the countryside.[49] Ultimately, one suspects, because the Elysium was to be an *English* paradise, it would have to look English and share in English tradition—like Wotton or Sayes Court.

Ultimately it is this sense of yearning for an English pastoral that shapes the "Elysium Britannicum" and creates a conflict so profound that it becomes impossible for the author to conceptualize the work in its totality. As Graham Parry has written, "The 'Elysium Britannicum' was essentially a garden of the mind: practical aspects of it find their way into print, but perhaps the whole was a private, even secret, possession of its designer."[50]

[47] "Elysium Britannicum," 57.

[48] British Library, Add. MS 15948, fol. 82, as cited in Leslie, "Spiritual Husbandry," 153.

[49] "Elysium Britannicum," 57.

[50] G. Parry, "John Evelyn as Hortulan Saint," in *Culture and Cultivation in Early Modern England* (as above, note 46), 130–50, esp. 146.

It is possible to understand Evelyn's lack of insistence on the Renaissance style in his garden as part of a very English and Anglican unwillingness to give up the pleasures of the rambling manor houses that he and those in his circle had grown up in in favor of palaces of stone. A similar motive seems to have guided one of Evelyn's contemporaries, Lady Anne Clifford, who, by choosing to live in her Westmoreland and Yorkshire castles, rather than at her husband's house at Wilton (or, instead, building her own new house), rejected fashionable styles in favor of a nostalgic return to the past.[51] There are other examples that suggest a pattern. We know, for example, that the duke and duchess of Chandos, builders of the baroque country house called Canons in the early seventeenth century, ultimately chose to live in an Elizabethan manor in Berkshire, rather than enjoy the stateliness of their stately home.[52] Both the informality and the Englishness of the house made it appealing to them.

Evelyn probably felt the same way. While he sat on his commissions and advocated that the king in his wisdom build enormous symmetrical buildings of brick and stone at Greenwich and Chelsea, at Wotton he chose to sketch the gardens from the hillside, looking back on the old manor house (Fig. 8).[53] Evelyn the rationalist might feel most at home in the city with its formal institutions and official boardrooms, but Evelyn the poet, the traveler, and the spiritual seeker found lasting inspiration in the countryside.[54] It is this that ultimately enables us to understand Evelyn as a product of his time and place; as a man for whom the new learning suggested the possibility of many rewards of experiment and rationality but for whom the ravages of civil war inspired both a love of the English countryside and a deeply felt desire to lose oneself in its "pious ecstacies."

[51] See G. Williamson, *Lady Anne Clifford, Countess of Dorset, Pembroke and Montgomery, 1590–1676,* Kendal, 1922.

[52] See J. Johnson, *Excellent Cassandra: The Life and Times of the Duchess of Chandos,* Gloucester, 1981, 119–20.

[53] J. D. Hunt, *Garden and Grove: The Italian Renaissance Garden in the English Imagination, 1600–1750,* Princeton, 1986, 145–52.

[54] There is something similar in the contrast between Aubrey's anti-Gothic pronouncements and his antiquarian research. His drawings of medieval architecture suggest an interest and sensitivity entirely obscured by his comments condemning Gothic barbarism. Like Evelyn, he viewed architectural classicism as a vehicle for improvement (Hunter, *John Aubrey,* 217–18).

Parterre, Grove, and Flower Garden: European Horticulture and Planting Design in John Evelyn's Time

MARK LAIRD

In memory of Donna Salzer

Chapter five, book two of John Evelyn's "Elysium Britannicum" ends with an instruction: "Place here the ~~fig~~ {draughts} of the Parterrs." Similarly chapter seven, book two concludes with a reminder: "Here inserte the Plotts of Groves & {other} Relievos."[1] Because all of these illustrations are missing from the manuscript, however, the challenge of reading Evelyn's text is to translate his verbal account into visual form. At first sight, the survival of a single plan for a parterre in the Drawings Collection of the British Architectural Library in London seems to offer an answer (Fig. 1), for it contains an inscription by William Upcott: "Sketched by John Evelyn of Wotton for his 'Elysium Britannicum'—not printed."[2]

Yet, closer examination of this sketch reveals the complexities behind the matching of text to image. Firstly, there is reason to doubt the validity of the inscription, because the words around the

I would like to thank John Harvey for his willingness to identify the plants mentioned by John Evelyn in connection with planting in the parterre, grove, and flower garden. He has, over many months, provided further invaluable comments on my text and offered useful suggestions on sources. I am also grateful to the following people who have helped in various ways to improve the final text: C. Allan Brown, Douglas Chambers, Michel Conan, Peter Goodchild, Michael Hunter, John E. Ingram, Erik de Jong, John Dixon Hunt, Susan Taylor Leduc, Prudence Leith-Ross, Nicholas Purcell, Ada Segre, Ruth Stungo, Sally Wages, Robert Williams, and Jan Woudstra. Finally, I would like to thank John Wing, librarian at Christ Church, Oxford, for his kind help in providing access to the manuscripts.

[1] See here the manuscript kept at the British Library, London: John Evelyn, "Elysium Britannicum; or The Royal Garden in Three Books," chap. 5, p. 77, and chap. 7, p. 111. I have used John E. Ingram's transcription of October 1992 for all quotations in this essay.

[2] This plan was first published in J. Brown, *The Art and Architecture of English Gardens,* London and New York, 1989, 39. The execution of the 1653 plan seems problematic. Michael Hunter had originally suggested to me that it was in the hand of Evelyn's amenuensis, Richard Hoare, who did bits of calligraphy for him ca. 1650. However, in a letter of October 18, 1993, Hunter elaborated on the handwriting of the key: "This does *not* look like Hoare's hand, but it is certainly not Evelyn's either: i.e., it could be the hand of another professional scribe (and the drawing could be by a professional draughtsman)."

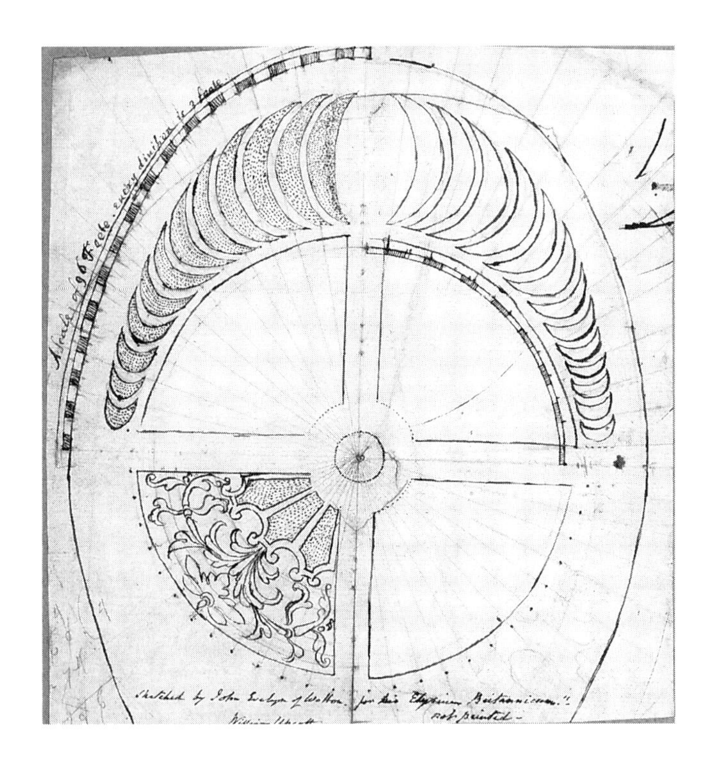

1. Sketch plan of a parterre, attributed to John Evelyn by William Upcott but of uncertain draftsmanship (photo: British Architectural Library/ RIBA. Drawings Collection, London)

edge of the sketch are not in Evelyn's hand and because Upcott's caption has no authority in itself. Secondly, as the design resembles the parterre at Sayes Court in the well-known plan of 1653 (Fig. 2; see also Fig. 7), there is a good chance that the sketch could be a proposal for Evelyn's own garden, begun on January 17, 1653, rather than a figure for the manuscript as such.[3] Thirdly, even if some version of this Sayes Court parterre was meant to be one of the "draughts" for chapter five, there is still a need to explain the choice of figure. For it is apparent that the "oval Square" parterre at Sayes Court was influenced by Pierre Morin's oval garden in Paris, which Evelyn visited in 1644 and 1651 (see here Fig. 8).[4] Yet, Morin's layout was more of a florist's flower garden than a conventional parterre or knot, and Evelyn seems to acknowledge this in writing to his father-in-law, Sir Richard Browne: "If God prosper us, [my Morine Garden] will farr exceede that both for designe & other accommodations?"[5]

Thus, to reconstruct an image of what Evelyn understood by the terms "parterre," "grove," and "flower garden" requires more than merely a search for the missing figures and "plotts." Two complementary tasks of interpretation are needed: the first entails tracing the origins of Evelyn's ideas, both in the gardens and in the gardening and horticultural literature of contemporary Europe;

[3] See E. S. de Beer, ed., *The Diary of John Evelyn,* 6 vols., Oxford, 1955, III, 80.

[4] See here M. F. Warner, "The Morins," *National Horticultural Magazine,* July 1954, 168–76; and G. Parry, "John Evelyn as Hortulan Saint," M. Leslie and T. Raylor, eds., *Culture and Cultivation in Early Modern England: Writing and the Land,* Leicester, 1992, 130. Evelyn's letter to Richard Browne is quoted from P. Leith-Ross, "A Seventeenth-Century Paris Garden," *Garden History* 21, 2 (Winter 1993), 153. It was David Sturdy who first discovered the plan of Pierre Morin's garden in the British Library, and he drew it to the attention of Prudence Leith-Ross, Lady Hartopp. I am indebted to her and John Harvey for the reference. For Evelyn's visits to Morin in Paris, see de Beer, *Diary,* I, 85–87; II, 132–33; and III, 33; and Leith-Ross, "A Seventeenth-Century Paris Garden," 150–57.

[5] The letter is dated May 2, 1653, and is kept at Christ Church, Oxford.

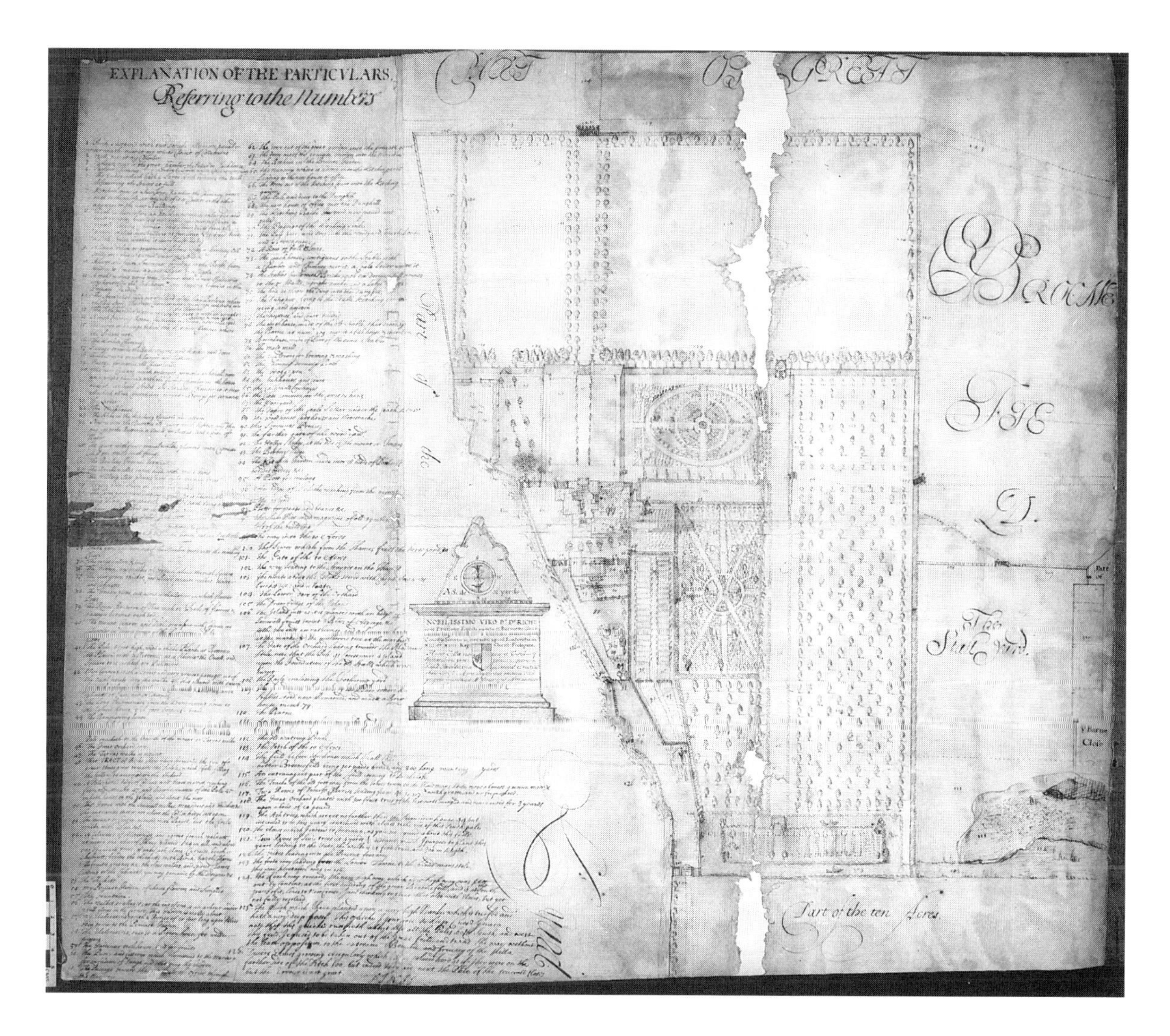

2. Plan of John Evelyn's garden at Sayes Court, 1653. Both handwriting and draftsmanship uncertain (photo: Christ Church, Oxford; reproduced by permission of the trustees of the will of Major Peter George Evelyn)

the second involves relating those ideas to the forms of the layout at Sayes Court. For it is the Sayes Court plan of 1653 that appears to offer the best visual correlation to the text of the "Elysium Britannicum" at its conception in the late 1650s and early 1660s.

Before we can begin the task of reconstruction, a few distinctions are necessary. Evelyn writes: "Those who are most pleased with distinctions have constituted fowre, or five sortes of Gardens. As the *Parterre knot* and *Trayle-worke* for one: The *Coronarie* or Flower-Garden for a second: The *Medicinal,* or Garden of Simples for a Third: The Ortchard, {Olitory} and Garden of {Fruite &} *Esculent* plants for a Fowerth and Fift."[6] Evelyn qualifies these further by associating the orchard with the fruit grower, the "olitory" or kitchen garden with the cook, the medicinal or physic garden with the

[6] "Elysium Britannicum," 2–3. It is notable that Olivier de Serres in his *Le Théâtre d'agriculture et mesnage des champs,* Paris, 1600, 501, distinguishes four types of garden: le potager, le bouquetier, le medicinal, and le fruitier. But Evelyn's four or five distinctions were clearly derived from another text, Jacques Boyceau's *Traité du jardinage selon les raisons de la nature et de l'art,* Paris, 1638, 81–82. The close parallels between the two texts suggest that Evelyn was familiar with Boyceau's publication.

botanist, and the "coronary" or flower garden with the florist.[7] It is reasonable to assume, of course, that the first category of "parterre" garden is used here as a shorthand for the entire ornamental garden as it extended outward from the house and parterre to the allées and groves.

Within the scope of "Gardens of Pleasure," fit "chiefly for the divertissement of Princes, noble-men and greate persons,"[8] come the first three types of garden: the parterre garden (with groves), the flower garden, and the medicinal garden. The "Elysium Britannicum" is thus concerned essentially with the ornamental pleasure garden, as opposed to the productive garden. Indeed, the chapters envisaged (but now missing) on the orchard and kitchen garden were conceived only in relation to the "Garden of Pleasure," for, as Evelyn points out, they had been covered in their own right in his translation of Nicolas de Bonnefons's *Le jardinier françois* (*The French Gardiner*) (1658).[9]

If the horticulture of vegetables and fruit lies beyond the scope of this essay, the same is true of the medicinal garden, John Evelyn's "Philosophico-Medicall Garden" of chapter seventeen, book two. It is certainly significant that Evelyn regards it as "an ornamentall . . . addition {to} . . . these our Royal Gardens."[10] But as a physic garden, it demands discussion in relation to taxonomy, the history of medicine, and the history of botanical gardens. Likewise, chapter fifteen, book two, "Of Orangeries, {*Oporothecas*} and Conservatories of rare Plants & Fruites," takes us beyond the domain of horticulture and ornamental planting design into the realm of plant collecting and botany.[11]

Let us begin the task of reconstruction with the parterre. First, we need to interpret terms, thereby establishing some sources for Evelyn's usage; then we can try to relate those terms to the

[7] Evelyn elaborates further on florists and flowers, "Elysium Britannicum," 3: "such as make profession of selling and making gaine by their beauties." The commercial aspects of the florist trade, and the "anthomania" of the tulip craze, however interesting in relation to the "coronary" garden, lie beyond the discussion in this essay. It is important to add that the "florist" of the period was not necessarily engaged in commerce; indeed, the term often refers to the avid collector and grower of rare and select varieties of tulip, auricula, anemone, carnations, ranunculus, etc. Sometimes, such amateur florists profited from exchange of rare plants, but as we read in George London and Henry Wise's *The Retir'd Gard'ner,* London, 1706, 246, "A Florist, who ought to be curious himself, ought in like manner to satisfie any ones Curiosity, who desires to see his Garden, provided he has any Assurance that the Persons he admits will not gather his Flowers." This openness cost Pierre Morin dearly on one occasion, as John Evelyn relates, when a rival florist gathered seed surreptitiously on glue stuck to his cloak. See here de Beer, *Diary,* I, 86–87, and "Elysium Britannicum," 292, margin note. For further discussion of florists, see R. Duthie, *Florists' Flowers and Societies,* Shire Garden History Series, Aylesbury, 1988.

[8] "Elysium Britannicum," 3.

[9] Ibid., 3.

[10] Ibid., 321.

[11] "Elysium Britannicum," 262. See here D. Chambers, "John Evelyn and the Invention of the Heated Greenhouse," *Garden History* 20, 2 (Autumn 1992), 201–6. In practice there proves to be much overlap between the plants of the conservatory and those of the grove and flower garden; in this sense the concerns of chapter 15 are germane to the discussion and are examined later in this essay. One phrase used by Evelyn in this chapter should also be noted. He refers to the flower pots being arranged on "benches & shelves *Theatricaly* placed in degrees one above another": "Elysium Britannicum," 272. This idea of "theatrical" disposition, also expressed in the form of the "auricula theater," was eventually to enter into the vocabulary of ornamental planting in the pleasure grounds of the 18th century. See, for example, R. North's catalog frontispiece of 1759 and N. Swinden, *The Beauties of Flora Display'd,* 1778, i, where he describes graduation in a flower bed: "The lowest plants being placed in front, and rising gradually in height from the edge upwards, will form the appearance of plants placed in a Greenhouse, or seats in a Theatre."

layout at Sayes Court. The heading of chapter five, book two, "Of knotts, {Fretts} Parterrs, Compartiments, Bordures, and Embossements," reflects the period in which new ideas from France were changing the vocabulary of planting. The knot was giving way to the parterre; germander, thyme, and hyssop were being replaced by box. Yet, at no point in the text is Evelyn explicit about the distinction between the knot and the parterre. Indeed, the two terms sometimes seem interchangeable. Evelyn writes, for example:

> We have seene the ordinary *Frith,* and *dubble Daisie* do exceedingly well in this kind of ornament. When your parterr is thus planted, and the heads of the box clipped into exact . . . {forme}, if the *Interstices* or *terrace* be layed over with some . . . {splendidly} colourd Sand, it will make {a} very glorious {effect}: Or there may some of these spaces be a little embossed with mould, planted with low growing Flowers of various Colours which will resemble a rich & . . . noble Tapistry.[12]

Here Evelyn is applying the term "parterre" to old-fashioned knots: the "closed" knot—a pattern of interlocking herbs (e.g., thrift and double daisy), infilled with flowers—and the "open" knot—infilled with "colourd Sand."

The interlineation "Fretts" is equally elusive. As it occurs in John Rea's *Flora* (1665), it may have been added at this time.[13] It evokes the fretwork of the architect or cabinetmaker and seems to relate to the earlier forms of the knot. Evelyn could also have been influenced by the passage of Francis Bacon's *Sylva* (1626): "We see in Garden-knots, and the Frets of Houses, and all equall and well answering Figures how they please."[14] Here, the connection between gardening and architecture is tangible, but a precise image of the "frett" remains fuzzy. Only through reconstructing Rea's flower garden can we picture the fret more clearly as a geometric configuration of flower beds that interlock like a knot.[15] Although it seems likely then that Evelyn had Rea's *Flora* in mind, it should not go unnoticed that he has unwittingly slipped from focus on the parterre to focus on the flower garden—the subject of chapter sixteen of the "Elysium Britannicum."

The term "compartiments" looks back to the time of Charles Estienne and Jean Liébault's *L'Agriculture et maison rustique* (1564), though Evelyn would have encountered the same word in more recent works by Jacques Boyceau and Claude Mollet. Liébault had referred to the "compartiment" as a single square in the form of a knot.[16] It is noteworthy, for example, that his "bordure avec son compartiment du millieu" (Fig. 3) from *L'Agriculture* was reproduced in the 1608

[12] "Elysium Britannicum," 76. It is interesting to note that the phrase "noble Tapistry" may be derived from J. Parkinson's *Paradisi in Sole Paradisus Terrestris,* 1629, 14: "a piece of tapestry of many glorious colours."

[13] See here P. Goodchild, "John Rea's Gardens of Delight: Introduction and the Construction of the Flower Garden," *Garden History* 9, 2 (Autumn 1981), 99–109, and R. Duthie, "The Planting Plans of Some Seventeenth-Century Flower Gardens," *Garden History* 18, 2 (Autumn 1990), 77–102, esp. 78–81.

[14] F. Bacon, *Sylva,* 1626, § 111, quoted in the *Oxford English Dictionary,* 2nd ed., Oxford, 1989. The *OED* also gives the reference to Evelyn's *Architect,* 1664, 138: "Roofs . . . Emboss'd with Fretts of wonderful relievo."

[15] See again Goodchild, "John Rea's Gardens of Delight," 109.

[16] See K. Woodbridge, *Princely Gardens,* London and New York, 1986, 98. It should be noted that Charles Estienne's *Praedium rusticum* was first published in 1554 and only translated from Latin into French by his son-in-law, Jean Liébault, in 1564. Other editions followed from the 1570s onward, with additional material by Liébault.

3. "A border with his feuerall proportion in the midst" (Bordure avec son compartiment du millieu), from Charles Estienne and Jean Liébault, *L'Agriculture et maison rustique,* 1564, Richard Surflet, trans., London, 1600 (photo: Dumbarton Oaks)

4. Design for a *compartiment* by Claude Mollet, from Olivier de Serres, *Théâtre d'agriculture et mesnage des champs,* 1600 (photo: Dumbarton Oaks)

edition of Thomas Hill's *The Gardener's Labyrinth,* replacing the original diagram of "a proper knot." In Olivier de Serres's *Le Théâtre d'agriculture et mesnage des champs* (1600), the term "parterre" begins to be used along with "compartimens" (Fig. 4), and, in time, what Boyceau and the Mollets called "compartimens en broderie" or "parterre en broderie" was to evolve into what is now known as "parterre de broderie."[17] Thus, by the time Evelyn was first writing the "Elysium Britannicum" in the 1650s, the concept of the knot or "compartiment" was slowly going out of fashion, and the term "parterre" was in the ascendant.

It was Etienne du Pérac who gave Claude Mollet the idea of the *parterre*—the unified design in box, as opposed to smaller interlocking patterns in various herbs.[18] This was at Anet, after his return from Italy in 1582. As Mollet recalled in his *Théâtre des plans et jardinages:*

> At the time I began to make the first *compartimens en broderie,* box was still rarely used, because very few people of rank wished to have box planted in their gardens, so that I planted my *compartimens en broderie* with several kinds of garden plant which gave a variety of green. But such plants cannot last long in this French climate, because of the extremes of heat and cold that we have. It was the great labour and expense of remaking and replanting the compartments every three years which led me to experiment with the box plant. . . . [19]

After Anet came the parterres of Saint-Germain-en-Laye and Fontainebleau. This was around 1595, but as Sten Karling pointed out some years ago, from the evidence of Claude Mollet's illustrations in de Serres' *Théâtre,* there were hardly any *broderie* elements in the parterres of the 1590s. Not until Alexandre Francini's views of Fontainebleau and Saint-Germain-en-Laye in 1614 do embroidery-like scroll forms appear for the first time. And within several decades—as Boyceau's *Traité* of 1638 indicates—broderie had become a fully developed art form.

According to Evelyn's account, the use of box was promoted in England by John Parkinson after "a greate dispute amongst Gardiners."[20] Parkinson was, of course, writing in his *Paradisus Terrestris* (1629). Yet, Gervase Markham had already anticipated the recommendation to use box in his *The English Husbandman* (1613).[21] This did not mean, however, that box broderie automatically replaced

[17] See here Boyceau, *Traité;* C. Mollet, *Théâtre des plans et jardinages,* Paris, 1652 (published posthumously); and A. Mollet, *Le Jardin de plaisir,* Paris, 1651.

[18] See here Woodbridge, *Princely Gardens,* 110, and a fuller discussion in S. Karling, "The Importance of André Mollet and His Family in the Development of the French Formal Garden," in E. B. MacDougall and F. H. Hazlehurst, eds., *The French Formal Garden,* Washington, D.C., 1974, 3–25.

[19] As quoted in Woodbridge, *Princely Gardens,* 108. The original manuscript for the *Théâtre* seems to have been finished about 1615. The fact that Evelyn mentions myrtle being used in Italy instead of box may suggest that this is what Du Pérac saw on his visit there. See Mollet, *Théâtre des plans et jardinages,* 199–203.

[20] "Elysium Britannicum," 75. The perennial objection to box was of its "ill sent," the "naughtie smell" as Gervase Markham put it. Evelyn claimed that this could be avoided by keeping the box short, but this did not stop critics like John Worlidge from objecting to the scent and its effect on the soil. Evelyn comments that the roots "emaciate the ground," and that it had become "almost banished . . . out of our Gardens {in England} as an ornament altogether out of fashion" (pp. 75–76). Compare here Stephen Blake, *The Compleat Gardeners Practice,* London, 1664, 76: "almost out of fashion, for the roots of it drieth and impoverisheth the earth." I am indebted to Jan Woudstra for this reference.

[21] G. Markham, *The English Husbandman,* London, 1613, 120. Whether he means the "dwarfe box" (*Buxus semperivirens* L. "Suffruticosa") recognized by Parkinson is uncertain, as he suggests that the box be kept 18 inches wide

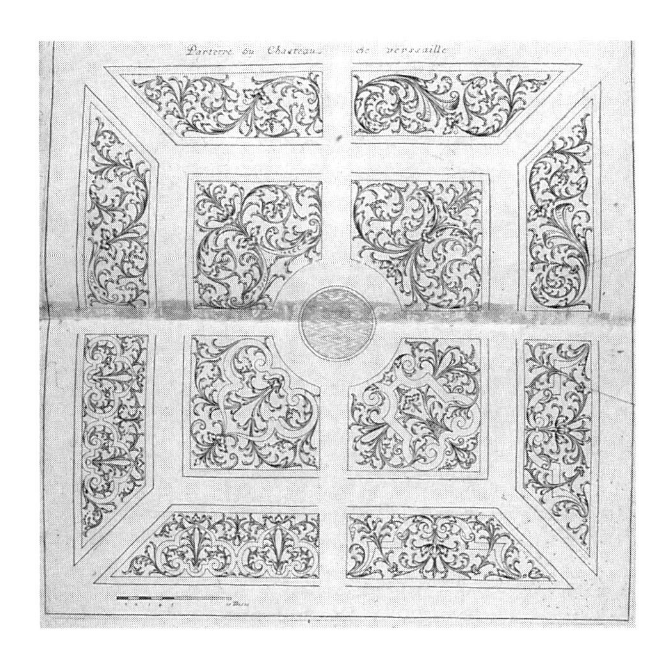

5. Design for the *parterre de broderie* at Versailles, from Jacques Boyceau, *Traité du jardinage,* 1638 (photo: Dumbarton Oaks)

knots of interlocking herbs. As in France, that process was gradual. Nevertheless, the fact that Evelyn used various terms to describe box broderie—"embrodery," "moresco," "*Grotesco,*" "*Foliage,*" etc.—implies some recognition in England of the parterre's gaining ascendancy over knotwork. The terms also suggest familiarity with the planting style of Boyceau and André Mollet as it developed in the 1630s and 1640s, and its origins in embroidery, grotesque ornamentation, and the decorative use of organic forms (Fig. 5). Boyceau writes, for example:

> Les Parterres sont les embellissemens bas des Iardins, qui ont grande grace, specialement quand ils sont veus de lieu eslevé: ils sont faits de bordures de plusieurs arbrisseaux & sous-arbrisseaux de couleurs diverses, façonnez de manieres differentes, de compartimens, feuillages, passements, moresques, arabesques, grotesques, guillochis, rosettes, gloires, targes, escussons d'armes, chiffres, & devises.[22]

The link with embroidery is suggested in Boyceau's use of the word "passement," which means a braiding of gold, silver, or lace; the same word was used in English during the period to mean "gold or silver lace, gimp or braid of silk, or other material, for decorative trimming."[23] And Boyceau's

at the bottom, compared to the 2 inches recommended by Evelyn. This could confirm Claude Mollet's observation that the ordinary box was favored initially for its hardiness. I am indebted to Jan Woudstra for the reference in Markham.

[22] Boyceau, *Traité,* 73. Compare also Evelyn's phrase in "Elysium Britannicum," 74, "The flattest Embelishments of Gardens are . . . *Parterrs,*" with Boyceau's "Les Parterres sont les embellissemens bas des Iardins." See, here, M. Conan's "Postface" to André Mollet's *Le Jardin de plaisir,* Paris, new edition, 1981, for a discussion of the evolution of that style. See also Karling, "André Mollet and His Family," for further discussion of the role played by the Mollet family in the development of the *parterre de broderie.*

[23] *Oxford English Dictionary,* 2nd ed.

reference to escutcheons, ciphers, and devices—alluding to the earlier emblematic style of Claude Mollet (see again Fig. 4)—is reflected in Evelyn's "*Impresses, Mottos, Dialls, Escutchions, Cyphers* and innumerable other devices. . . . "[24]

Such emblems could still have been seen in the England of the 1650s and 1660s. Indeed, David Loggan's illustration of the garden at New College, Oxford, in *Oxonia Illustrata* (1675), shows coats of arms and dials in the four quarters. Moreover, "open" and "closed" knots of old-fashioned design were also being made in smaller gardens at this time, as the designs of the Reverend Walter Stonehouse (1631–40) and the plates of Stephen Blake's *The Compleat Gardeners Practice* (1664) indicate.[25] Yet, the elaborate *parterres de broderie* at Wilton show that the André Mollet style had reached the grandest gardens of England by the 1630s (see here Fig. 18).[26]

These diverse planting forms—from knot to parterre—are thus mirrored in the "Elysium Britannicum" and in the diverse and rather elusive vocabulary that Evelyn uses. As we have seen, some of the terms—"compartiment," for example—are French words adopted wholesale from French texts, but without necessarily remaining synonymous in meaning or fixed in usage. Just as in French, "compartimens" covered the transition from the knot to the parterre, so in English, the word "compartiments" had its own evolutionary passage. In the "Elysium Britannicum," for example, Evelyn's definition of a "compartiment" seems to resemble a border: "{narrow &} thinner *knotts* running along the sides of Allies in which *flowers, Cypresse, shrubbs,* etc. may be planted at pleasure."[27] By the time Philip Miller was writing in his *Gardeners Dictionary* in 1731, that association with beds and borders had becomed strengthened in a vague formulation: "*Compartiments* are Beds, Plats, Borders, and Walks, laid out according to the Form of the Ground."[28]

In contrast to "compartiment" and "parterre," Evelyn also uses words of English origin or of uncertain provenance. "Trayle-worke," for example, defies easy definition, despite the description: "another kind of intermixture cutt out upon the Turfe or Carpet."[29] It could just possibly have been the *compartiment de gazon,* as illustrated by André Mollet in *Le Jardin de plaisir* (1651) (Fig. 6).[30] For at

[24] "Elysium Britannicum," 75.

[25] See. R. Strong, *The Renaissance Garden in England,* London, 1979, 40; and M. Hadfield, *The History of British Gardening,* London, 1979, 103.

[26] See again Strong, *The Renaissance Garden,* 147–61; and also T. Mowl, "New Science, Old Order: The Gardens of the Great Rebellion," *Journal of Garden History* 13, 1–2 (January–June 1993), 16–17.

[27] "Elysium Britannicum," 76.

[28] P. Miller, *The Gardeners Dictionary,* London, 1731, s.v. "compartiments."

[29] "Elysium Britannicum," 76.

[30] See here W. Hansmann, "Parterres: Entwicklung, Typen, Elemente," in D. Hennebo, ed., *Gartendenkmalpflege,* Stuttgart, 1985, 151–53. Hansmann rightly distinguishes the *compartiment de gazon* from the "cutwork" of the later *parterre à l'angloise.* The narrow, mazelike bands of lawn that are framed by flower borders seem to evoke the "trayle work" of Evelyn. Another variant is the *parterre de pelouse* at Versailles, illustrated by Jacques Boyceau in his *Traité du jardinage.* I am grateful to Sally Wages for drawing my attention to this. Michel Conan has pointed out to me, however, that "pelouse" did not always mean a grass surface; it could indicate a carpetlike surface composed of any plant. This is clear in Boyceau's statement that follows his account of parterres as containing escutcheons, cyphers, and devices: "Ou bien par planches, se recontrans sur des formes parfaites, ou semblables, dans lesquelles on employe des plantes rares, fleurs, & herbages plantez en ordre, ou faisant des pelouses épaisses, d'une ou plusieurs couleurs, en forme de tapis de pied" (*Traité,* 73).

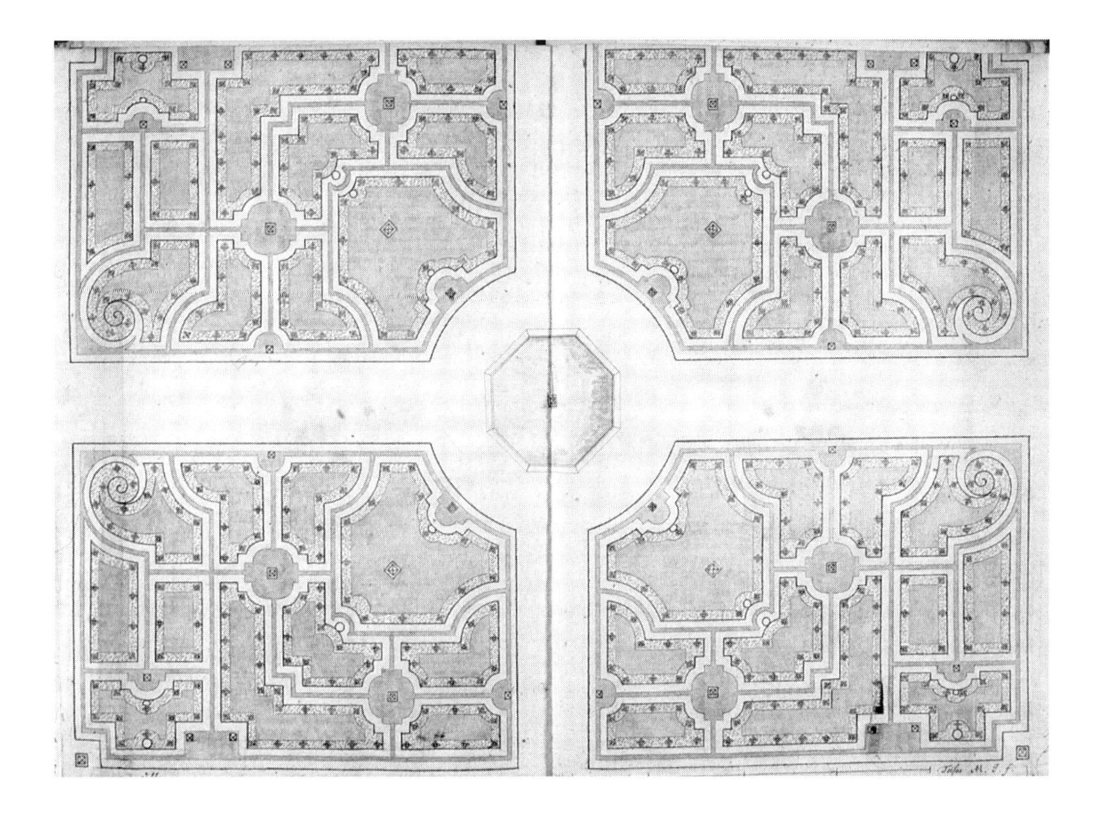

6. Design for a *compartiment de gazon,* from André Mollet, *Le Jardin de plaisir,* 1651 (photo: Dumbarton Oaks)

the Luxembourg, as one example, Evelyn noted the knots in "trayle or grass Worke."[31] But this remains a problematic term in the manuscript.

Likewise, "embossments" finds no French equivalent and is probably an English term, suggesting raised beds that resembled "fretwork." They may have been circular beds; for Evelyn refers in the same breath to "the *Bordure,* or Circle . . . for Cammomile."[32] Certainly, the fact that Evelyn associates the term "embossements" with the idea of an earth camber does not appear to distinguish it from his "bordure," which was also gently raised to the center: "These we name *Embossements,* which like to *Bordures,* are made with a gracefull swelling and *Relievo.*"[33] This "swelling" was later called the "ass's back" or "carp's back."[34] But the border itself was in flux in regard to meaning and is thus hard to pin down. In the "Elysium Britannicum," for example, Liébault's elaborate framing "bordure" of knotwork or "carreaux rompus" (see Fig. 3) has been converted into the simple flower "border," despite Evelyn's retention of the French spelling: "*Bordures* are the most simple of ornaments, & are commonly for edges, and under the outmost wales [walls]."[35]

[31] See de Beer, *Diary,* II, 130.

[32] "Elysium Britannicum," 76.

[33] Ibid., 76.

[34] The "dos-d'âne" or "dos de carpe." See London and Wise in *The Retir'd Gard'ner,* 242; they indicate that a 6-inch rising to the center is sufficient.

[35] "Elysium Britannicum," 76.

Evelyn goes on to elaborate how borders are sometimes edged with inorganic materials such as timber, stone, tile, and brick, or with the "*Partrig-Ey'd* or *Spanish Pinke*"[36] (almost certainly *Dianthus plumarius* L. var. *annulatus,* although probably more than one species or variety of matted pink was used). Thomas Hanmer's *Garden Book* (1659) and John Rea's *Flora* confirm the traditional use of "boarded" beds—beds that were raised by edging boards a few inches above the walks.[37] But Evelyn then admits that boards were better suited to the flower garden: "Let such *Embossements* as enter into the *Parterr* be bordurd with the same verdure of the knotts."[38] And by "verdure" he meant either box or one of the herbs. Thus, it transpires that, whether in relation to "fretts" or "embossements," Evelyn was straying once again, almost unheeded, out of the parterre proper into the domain of the flower garden.

To visualize what Evelyn describes in this chapter, therefore, we should move away from the slippery ground of words to the slightly firmer terrain of text and image. Here we must return to the Royal Institute of British Architects (RIBA) parterre sketch (Fig. 1), to Sayes Court (Fig. 7), and to Richard Symonds's plan of Pierre Morin's garden in Paris, drawn in 1649 (Fig. 8). On his first visit to Morin in April 1644, Evelyn recorded that the garden was "an Exact *Ovall* planted with very talle Cypresse, cut very Even, & with *Nices* [niches] of the same for heads & statues, besides the Parterrs, of the richest *Tulips, Anemonies, Ranunculus, Crocus's, Polyants,* that could any where be seene."[39]

On Symonds's plan of 1649 some of these elements are apparent: at *B*, for example, is the "lofty hedge of Cipresse trees" that contained "9 Arches of Stone wherein is a statue {in each} 3 foot above ground" (marked *A*); *C*, meanwhile, denotes the "beds compassed with box where in the middle grow all sorts of rare Tulips, poples, flowers, herbes rare all";[40] and *E* marks the cypresses—"cutt close & of this fashion. almost 4 foot high"—around the fountain *D*; at *F* are 4 tall cypresses—"that spread about 4 foot above ground & grow loose & neate without cutting"; *G* are "boxes wherein grow Oringes, mirtle, philaria; and all choice greenes"; *H* indicates "greene walkes all the yeare long of Alaternus, which lynes the wall round"; and *I* seems to be "od places wherein loosely grow, all Green trees rudely like a wood."[41]

[36] Ibid., 77.

[37] See I. Elstob, ed., *The Garden Book of Sir Thomas Hanmer, Bart.,* London, 1933, transcribed by Ivy Elstob, with an introduction by E. S. Rohde; Goodchild, "John Rea's Gardens," passim; and Duthie, "Planting Plans," 83, in which she corrects some errors in the Elstob edition. For further details of inorganic edgings, see "Elysium Britannicum," 76, margin notes, and also 277.

[38] "Elysium Britannicum," 76–77. Peter Goodchild has pointed out to me that the reason John Rea used boards rather than box as edging in his flower garden was to protect his choice flowers from competition with the box plants. This would explain why Evelyn suggests "boarded" beds for the flower garden but box for the borders of the parterre.

[39] See here de Beer, *Diary*, I, 86. This account in *De Vita Propria* differs a little from the description in the diary (II, 132–33): "His Garden is of an exact Oval figure planted with Cypresse, cutt flat & set as even as a Wall could have form'd it: The Tulips, Anemonies, Ranunculus's, Crocus's &c being of the most exquisite; were held for the rarest in the World, which constantly drew all the Virtuosi of that kind to his house during the season; even Persons of the most illustrious quality." See also "Elysium Britannicum," margin note on 296: "all the allys of . . . Morins Garden planted or edged with *Cyclamen* the large lying flat make a rare grotesco: planted before the bordur at the edge of the ally: cf. Dr: Needham:"

[40] John Harvey has suggested that "poples" could mean *Agrostemma githago* specifically or simply annuals of bright colors in general.

[41] British Library, Harl. MS 1278, fol. 82.

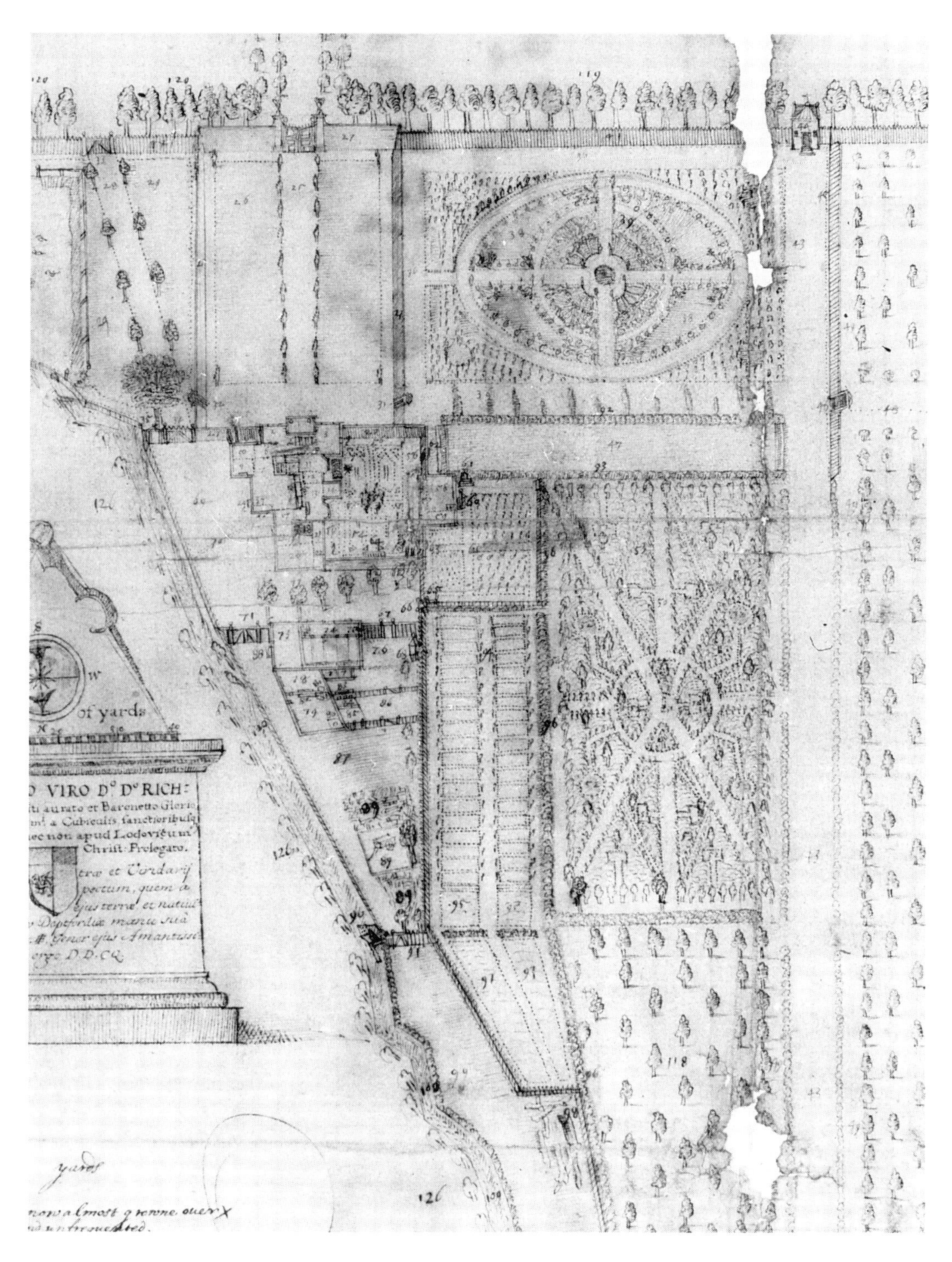

7. Detail of the plan of John Evelyn's garden at Sayes Court, 1653 (photo: Christ Church, Oxford; reproduced by permission of the trustees of the will of Major Peter George Evelyn)

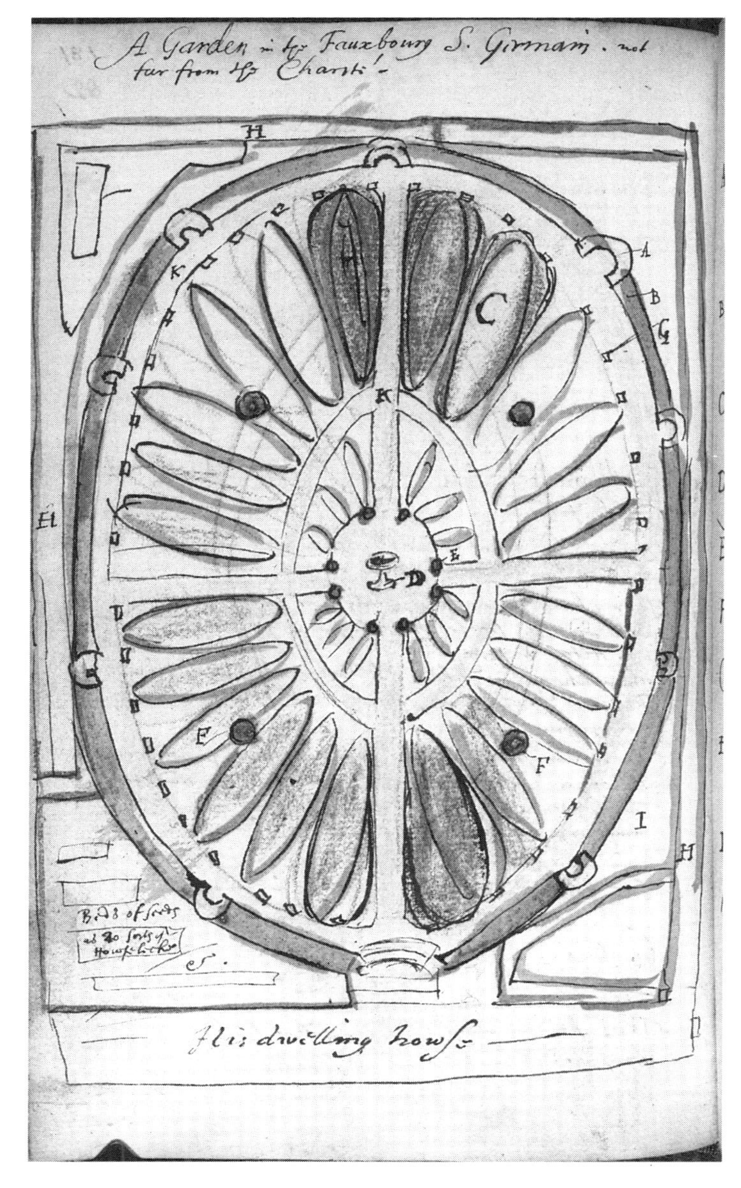

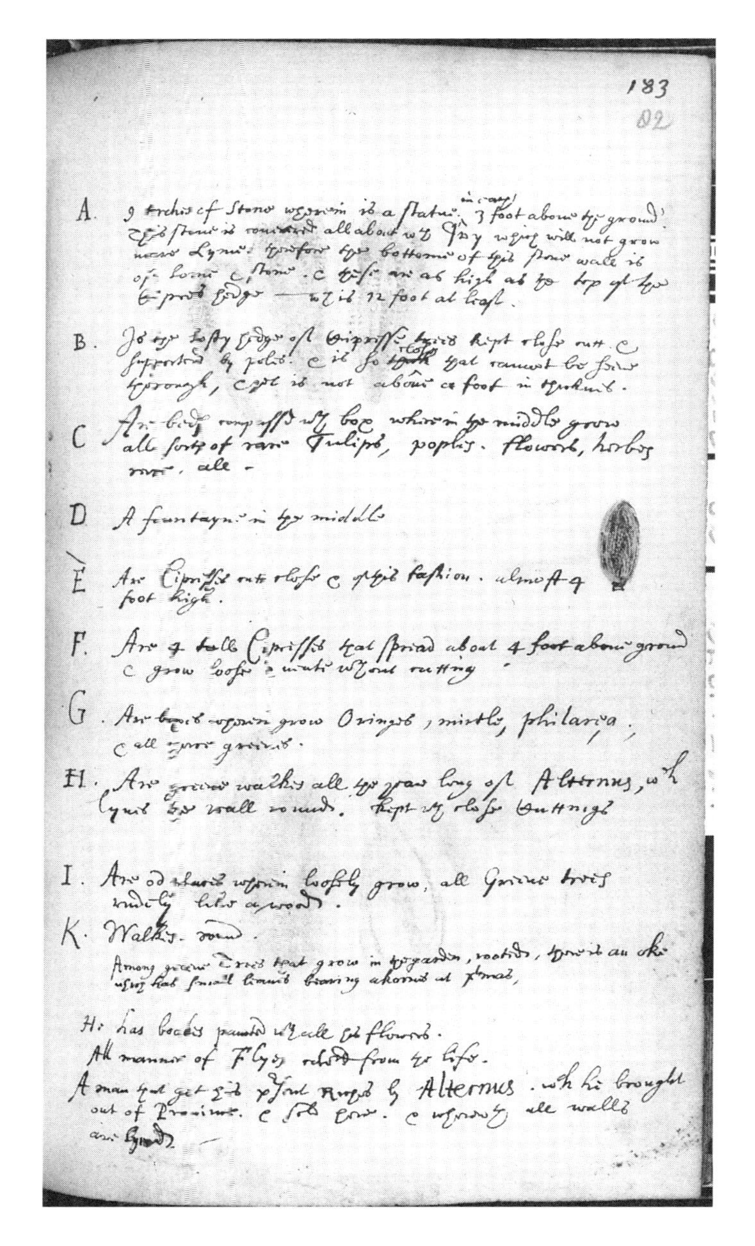

8. Richard Symonds's sketch plan with key of Pierre Morin's garden in Paris, 1649. British Library, Harl. MS 1278, fols. 81v and 82 (photo: By permission of the British Library)

A comparison of the Sayes Court parterre with the Morin garden points to the repeated use of eight cypress trees at the center of the composition, this time around the "mount" and "dial." Cypresses also occur at every junction of parterre, grass plat, and path. Yet, the design suggests how a complex hierarchy of elements had replaced Morin's oval beds. The progression from broderie to grass parterre to bosquet, normally expressed in terms of a linear declension from the house, is here compressed into a single form—the "oval Square," as Evelyn called it. It is a remarkable composition, viewed from the terrace, rather than directly from the house itself.

At the center lies the "Round Parterre of Box with 12 Beds of flowers & passages betwixt each bed."[42] The RIBA plan helps to clarify the shape of those beds and the configuration of the broderie. Further sketches in the British Library confirm (with slight differences) the form of the broderie and increase the chances that the Sayes Court parterre (or a variant of it) was intended as one or two illustrations in the "Elysium Britannicum" (Figs. 9 and 10).[43] My perspective reconstruction offers a conjectural interpretation of how these elements fitted together (Fig. 11).

Beyond the parterre at Sayes Court were the "Grasse plotts sett about with a Border, in which flower plotts." Then, as an oblong frame around the circle within the oval, Evelyn shows two different settings: on the one side, "evergreen thicket, for Birds private walkes, shades—and Cabinetts"; and on the other, "Two Cantons with a Strait and very private passage out of the oval neich into the walke 43." Evelyn adds some detail on the planting of the latter: "This planted with dwarfe fruit. Raspberris Strawberries, Currants & Cherries, and 2 Cabinetts of Ivie, and Aliternes."[44]

In September 1644, the same year that Evelyn visited Pierre Morin's garden, an excursion was made to Cardinal Richelieu's garden of Richelieu, to the south of Tours. In his diary, Evelyn recorded, "The Gardens without are very large & the Parterrs of incomparable imbrodry, set with frequent statues both brasse, & Marble: The Groves, Meadows & several excellent Walkes are a real Paradise."[45] It is not clear whether the "incomparable imbrodry" referred to the parterre adjacent to the château or to the Grand Parterre de la Demi-Lune beyond the canal. The latter is depicted by Adam Perelle and shows the *parterre de broderie,* the crescent-shaped hedge of *phillyrea*—cut into niches for statues—and the flanking pavilions or *grottes* (Fig. 12).[46] Certainly, what is striking are

[42] "Explanation of the Particulars," key to the 1653 plan.

[43] I am grateful to John Ingram for drawing my attention to these. Michael Hunter, in his letter to me of October 18, 1993, commented: "The caption (and the pentacle/'XVII' endorsements) are *definitely* in Evelyn's hand, and the numbers also look to me like Evelyn's." This may mean that the drawings are also by him, but that remains to be established. The caption certainly implies the connection with Sayes Court: "See in yr notes of Husbandry for the true draught of th Garden at Says Court befor the [? ?] was made"; and the endorsements—the pentacle is the symbol used here for the "Elysium Britannicum" and the "XVII" (= chapter 5, book II, "Of Knots, Parterrs"), the chapter number—indicate the intention of inclusion in the "Elysium Britannicum." I am grateful to Douglas Chambers for checking this information at the British Library.

[44] "Explanation of the Particulars." In the interpretation of planting within the flower borders, I have relied on information from slightly later sources published previously in M. Laird and J. H. Harvey, "'A Cloth of Tissue of Divers Colours': The English Flower Border, 1660–1735," *Garden History* 21, 2 (Winter 1993), 158–205. However, the principle of creating a "carpet" of flowers or an "enamelled" effect through intermixing single flowers in repeated patterns was, I believe, already established in the 1650s. See, for example, Mollet, *Théâtre,* 189–90.

[45] De Beer, *Diary,* II, 151.

[46] See here Woodbridge, *Princely Gardens,* 143–47.

9. Sketch for a parterre, certainly endorsed and possibly drawn by John Evelyn. British Library, Add. MS 15950, fol. 173 (photo: By permission of the British Library)

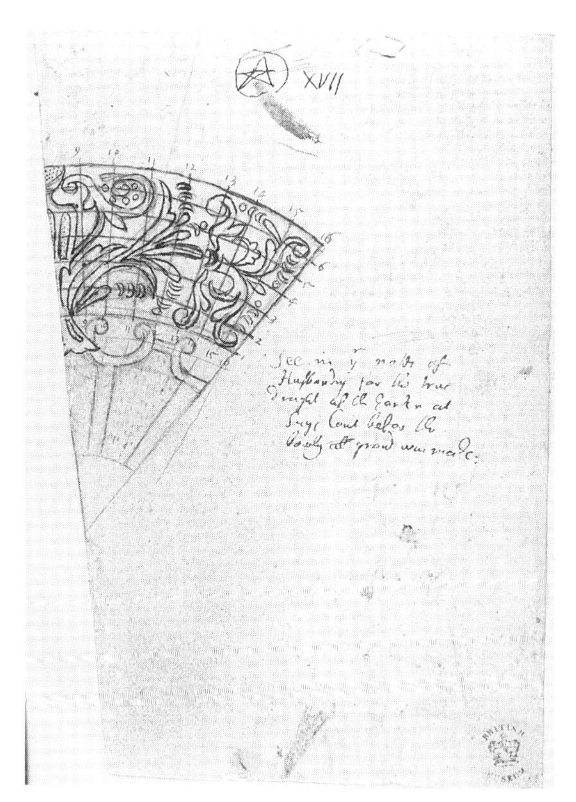

10. Sketch detail for one-quarter of a parterre, certainly endorsed and possibly drawn by John Evelyn. British Library, Add. MS 15950, fol. 174 (photo: By permission of the British Library)

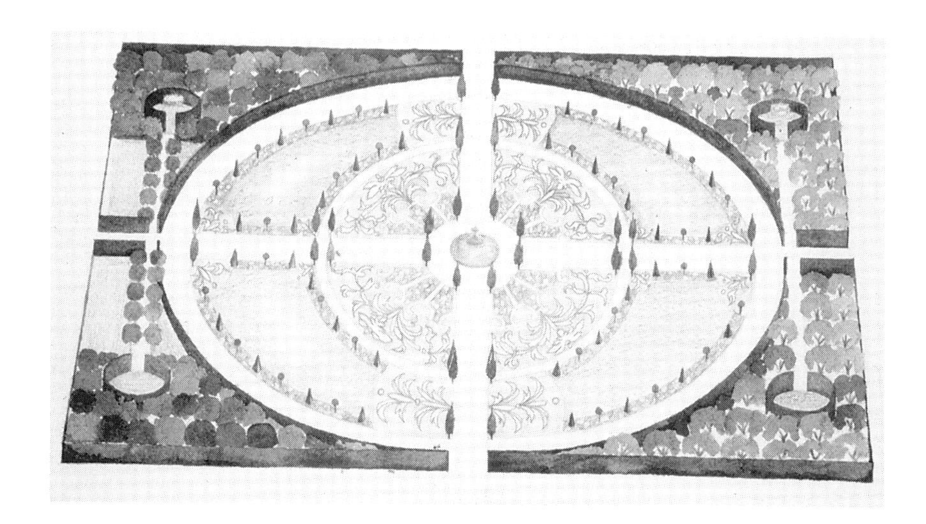

11. Conjectural reconstruction as bird's-eye perspective of the parterre at Sayes Court, based on the plan of 1653 and drawings in the British Architectural Library and the British Library. Painting by Mark Laird

12. Engraving by Adam Perelle of the Grand Parterre de la Demi-Lune at Château de Richelieu, from *Veues des belles maisons de France,* Paris, ca. 1650 (photo: Dumbarton Oaks)

certain affinities between Evelyn's circular parterre and that at Richelieu. The form of broderie, the relationship of a circle (respectively oval) to a square or rectangle, and the use of cypress trees as sentinels are some common elements.

For all the apparent inspiration of Morin and possible inspiration of Richelieu, however, the parterre at Sayes Court eludes facile comparison. Above all, the integration of the twelve flower beds into the four quarters of broderie seems an idiosyncratic and novel feature. Could it be that Evelyn drew inspiration directly from the plate in Olivier de Serres's *Théâtre* (Fig. 4), or, more likely, from plates in Boyceau's *Traité* and Claude Mollet's *Théâtre,* in which flower beds are shown incorporated into the center of the *parterres de broderie* (Figs. 13–15)?

At Richelieu, in contrast, the flower beds are to the sides of the parterre in conventional oblong and circular patterns. In both the RIBA plan and the sketch in the British Library (Fig. 9), Evelyn is seen experimenting with alternative crescent-shaped beds to the outside of the four quarters; there are twelve (or thirteen) per quarter. Could these forty-eight (or fifty-two) beds have been influenced by the Bed of the Seasons at the Hortus Palatinus, in which the flowers were distributed in seventy-two compartments according to the seasons?[47] Or were they merely a version of Morin's

[47] The reference to Salomon de Caus and Heidelberg on page 271 of "Elysium Britannicum" implies some knowledge of the *Hortus Palatinus.* See here R. Zimmermann, "The Hortus Palatinus of Salomon de Caus," in M. Mosser and G. Teyssot, eds., *The History of Garden Design,* London, 1991, 157–59, and R. Zimmermann, "German and Austrian Renaissance Gardens," in J. D. Hunt, ed., *Garden History: Issues, Approaches, Methods,* Dumbarton Oaks Colloquium on the History of Landscape Architecture 13, Washington, D.C., 1992, 100: "Each of the large quarters is dedicated to

13 and 14. Two designs for parterres with broderie and flower beds, from Jacques Boyceau, *Traité du jardinage,* 1638 (photo: Dumbarton Oaks)

15. Design for a parterre with broderie, grass, and flower beds, designed by Jacques Mollet for Claude Mollet's *Théâtre des plans et jardinages,* 1652 (photo: Dumbarton Oaks)

oval flower beds, or Boyceau's curved "planches"? Or, indeed, could the crescent forms in the parterres at the château de Fromont have been known to him through Israël Silvestre's engraving (Fig. 16)? In a letter of January 28, 1659/60, to Sir Thomas Browne, Evelyn refers to his chapter on the history of the garden, which "is in a manner finished by itselfe." He then listed the legendary, ancient, and modern gardens that he had in mind for the chapter, and amongst those of France was the name "Froment."[48] This would have been chapter nine, book three of "Elysium Britannicum," now sadly missing.

These unresolved questions remain to be explored. But chapter five of the "Elysium Britannicum" and the "oval Square" of Sayes Court both imply that the parterre of the 1650s to 1660s did not conform to rigid categories, as later codified by A.-J. Dezallier d'Argenville, e.g., *parterre de broderie* or *parterre à l'angloise*. In France and England there seems to have been room for imaginative fusions of broderie and beds, often with lawn too: in Boyceau's *Traité* and Mollet's *Théâtre,* for example, and in Evelyn's mix of broderie, beds, and grass plat with borders.[49] Le Nôtre was to work with the three elements at Issy, and the same *mélange* found expression in J.-F. Blondel's design of 1738 for a *parterre de broderie melé de gazon entouré de platebandes de fleurs.*[50] Thus, Evelyn's vision of parterre has resonance beyond his time. Indeed, for all his apparent attachment to old-fashioned "knotts" and "compartiments" in the text of the "Elysium Britannicum," Evelyn was clearly committed to the progressive form of the parterre, which is evident in his actual design for Sayes Court. And it is implied by the two figures that, almost certainly, would have been incorporated into chapter five, book two to provide the "draughts" for that text.

While in France Evelyn also observed various types of grove, allée, and other "Relievos"—those areas that formed the "relief" to the flatness and openness of the parterre.[51] Evelyn considered them the "more principall parts" of a garden, offering diversity after the "compt, polite and uniforme" parterres and walks.[52] At Rueil he saw a grove of "Perennial Greenes;" at Saint-Germain-en-Laye, Blois, and Tours he saw the pall-mall allées; and at the Tuileries he saw a "Labyrinth of Cypresse."[53]

---

one of the four seasons, and each of the individual beds is dedicated to a different month. In fact, the flowers are planted in such a way that those blooming in a certain month are together in the appropriate bed. Accordingly, the 'round field' not only creates the illusion of eternal spring, but also organizes the world of flowers according to a rational principle, namely, the period in which they bloom." Given Evelyn's preoccupation with the *Ver Perpetuum*—discussed later in this essay in the context of the grove and flower garden—it is conceivable that he had some such idea in mind.

[48] Adams, *The French Garden,* 76. The date should be 1659/60, not 1657, as given by Adams. See here the letter from Evelyn to Sir Thomas Browne, January 28, 1659/60, in G. Keynes, ed., *The Works of Sir Thomas Browne,* Chicago, 1964, IV, 273–78, in which "Froment" is listed. For further information on Fromont, see *Bulletin de la Société historique et archéologique de Corbeil, d'Estampes et du Hurepoix* 10 (1904), 37–38. I am grateful to Susan Taylor Leduc for this reference.

[49] For an example of the typical English plat with flower borders, see Robert Thacker's painting of the parterres to the east front of Longleat House, reproduced in Laird and Harvey, "'A Cloth of Tissue of Divers Colours,'" fig. 15. Plate 17 of André Mollet's *Le Jardin de plaisir* provides a further example of broderie, grass, and flower borders combined in one composition.

[50] See Hansmann, "Parterres," 154–55, and the example of Schwetzingen described in H. W. Wertz, "Wiederherstellung und Unterhaltung von Parterreanlagen," in *Gartendenkmalpflege* (as above, note 30), 174–204.

[51] See here Boyceau, *Traité,* 74, the chapter entitled "Du Relief."

[52] "Elysium Britannicum," 90.

[53] See de Beer, *Diary,* II, 106, 108–9, 111, and 142. Discussion of pall-mall allées, beares, carpets, and bowling

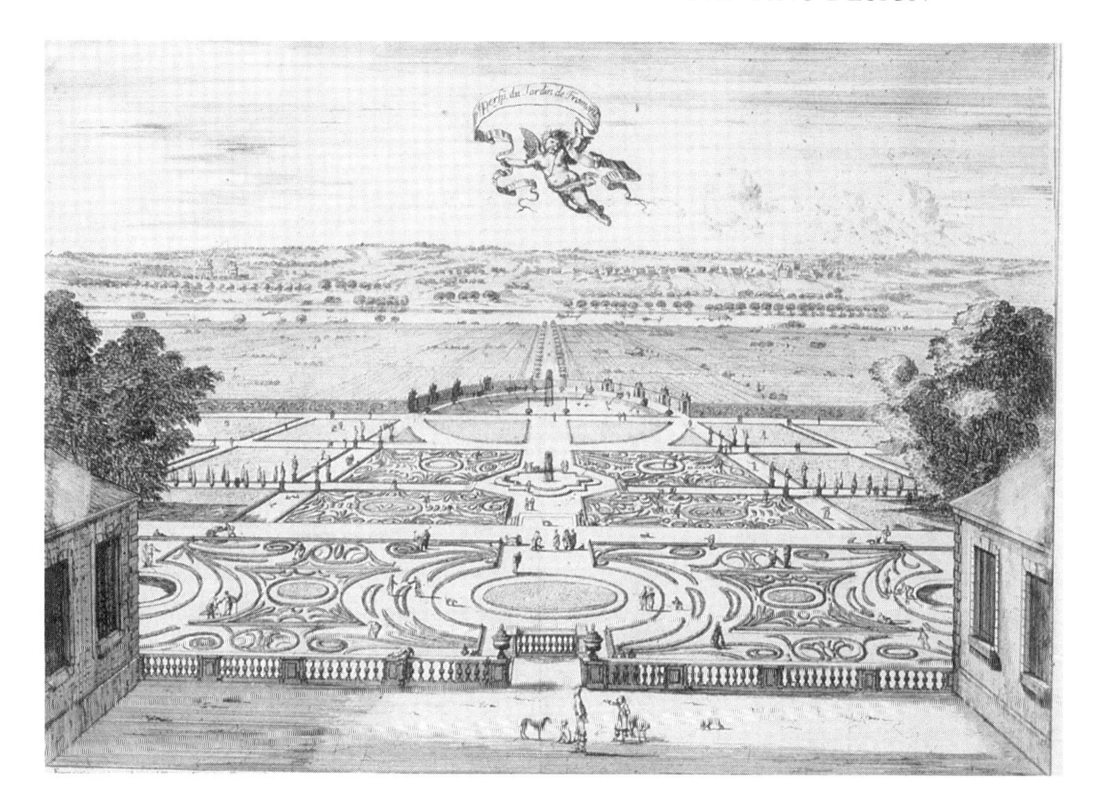

16. Etching and engraving by Israël Silvestre and Stefano della Bella of the garden at the château de Fromont, ca. 1649 (photo: Dumbarton Oaks)

17. View of the grounds of the Villa Borghese, Rome, from G. B. Falda, *Il Giardini di Roma,* 1683 (photo: Dumbarton Oaks)

But it was in Italy, above all, that he encountered groves that had a pervasive influence on the "Elysium Britannicum." At the Villa Borghese, for example, he commended the groves of "Cypresse and Lawrell, Pine, Myrtil, Olive &c. . . . " (Fig. 17).[54] Such evergreen plantations found their way into chapter seven, book one, "Of Groves, Labyrinths, Daedales, Cabinets, Cradles, Pavilions, Galleries, Close-Walkes and other Relievo's," and also into chapter fourteen, book two, "Of Verdures, Perennial-greenes, and perpetuall Springs." He describes how through evergreens "an English Gar den, even in the midst of Winter, shall appeare little inferiour to the Italian, where the Seasons are more . . . benigne, and the gardens almost perpetually florid."[55]

We have come now to a second major type of ornamental planting feature discussed in the "Elysium Britannicum"—the grove. The distinction, if substantial, between grove, wilderness, and thicket is never precisely articulated (nor, indeed, is that between labyrinth, daedales, and maze).[56] Evelyn appears to have relied on English usage here, even though equivalent French terms existed for the "grove" or "wilderness": Boyceau had talked of "Les Corps relevez" and "bosquets" in his *Traité;* in Claude Mollet's *Théâtre* and André Mollet's *Le Jardin de plaisir* "bosquet" is used. Yet, Evelyn's detailed terminology came directly from French sources; cabinets, cradles, pavilions, galleries, etc., were translations of "cabinets," "berceaux," "pavillons," and "galleries," etc.[57]

These various architectural features or arbors within the grove were constructed from either "quarters, or poles"; the two types are apparent in the engraving of Wilton (Fig. 18).[58] "Quarters" are timber that has been squared for an arbor, whereas "poles" are untreated wood. Or, as Evelyn expresses it himself on page 94: "If you frame the worke of quarters, let the timber be of Oake, . . . cleft of 6 inch Square which is best for lasting. This for the punchions [upright supporting posts]: Fower Inches broad & 2 inch thick for the thwart pieces . . . For this worke poles of ground Ash and

greens—the focus of chapter 6, book II—is not pursued further in this essay, although they involve interesting aspects of planting design.

[54] Ibid., 252. Mirka Beneš has demonstrated that these groves of evergreens were planted in the "major revision" of the layout, beginning in 1624–25 and described by Jacopo Manilli in 1650. The laurels in the four compartments closest to the villa were the smallest and most densely planted. Beyond them were compartments of taller firs, succeeded by the outer compartments of the tallest umbrella pines (*Pinus pinea*). This "tree garden" replaced the compartments of fruit and nut trees planted from about 1610 to 1614. See M. Beneš, "The Social Significance of Transforming the Landscape at the Villa Borghese in Rome, 1606–1630: Transpositions of Territory, Trees, and Agriculture in the First City Park in Baroque Rome," in A. Petruccioli, ed., *Theory and Design of Gardens during the Time of the Great Muslim Empires, Muquarnas Supplement,* vol. 7, Studies in Islamic Art and Architecture, Leiden, 1996. I am greatly indebted to Mirka Beneš for allowing me to consult her manuscript before publication.

[55] Ibid., 259.

[56] The "thicket" could indicate a grove that is underplanted, as opposed to an "open" grove of trees without underplanting—a distinction that is clear in later horticultural literature. On the other hand, "thicket" also seems to be associated with underplanting itself, as in "for the under-{under} woods, . . . thicketts & *Vepreta* of Groves": "Elysium Britannicum," 95. "Vepreta" are brakes of brambles in classical usage. Evelyn also uses the term "Coppse" for underplanting on one occasion: ibid., 95.

[57] See, for example, the discussion of "Les Corps relevez" in Boyceau, *Traité,* 74; for the construction of "berceaux," see Mollet, *Théâtre,* 115–16.

[58] For the planting of such arbors, see "Elysium Britannicum," 95, and 103, where "*Virginian Ivy,* with divers sorts of *Gourds & Calibasses*" are recommended for "temporary" cabinets, etc.

18. Bird's-eye perspective of the gardens at Wilton, from Isaac de Caus, *Wilton Garden,* 1647 (photo: Dumbarton Oaks)

Chessnutt are the best: The stakes would be 5· or 6· inches about the collaterall 3. the breadth and the height of the walkes." Ancient as well as contemporary models seem to have inspired Evelyn. He speaks of the cabinet in Verona, "canopied with Ivy at excessive heights" and of the hornbeam arbor at Hampton Court.[59] He also refers to the idea of an opening at the center of the grove—"a large and goodly *Circus* ressembling some *Amphitheatre.*"[60] Here Pliny's account seems close at hand.[61]

John Beale's influence was clearly pronounced in the use of classical terms such as "Viridaria," "Vireta," "Vepreta," "Cypresseta," "Myrteta," "Daphnonas,"[62] and in the advocacy of extensive

[59] "Elysium Britannicum," 95. See also de Beer, *Diary,* III, 324, where he refers to the "Cradle Walk of hornbeame" at Hampton Court.

[60] "Elysium Britannicum," 95, and margin note.

[61] See here the Loeb Classical Library edition, *The Letters of Pliny,* Cambridge and London, 1972, I, 348–51. The section of the letter in book V, vi, 31–36, describes the hippodrome with its planting of planes, ivy, box, cypress, and roses. This account was to continue to influence the planting of amphitheaters until into the 19th century, as the hippodrome at Charlottenhof, Sanssouci, in Germany illustrates.

[62] See here, for example, the letter from Beale to Evelyn, September 30, 1659, quoted by P. H. Goodchild, "'No phantasticall utopia, but a reall place': John Evelyn, John Beale and Backbury Hill, Herefordshire," *Garden History* 19 (Autumn 1991), 118–19. "Daphnonas" is a term used in Martial to denote a stand of laurels: "Daphnonas, platanonas et aerios pityonas" (laurel-groves, plane-groves and airy pine-groves). *Epigrams,* XII, 50.

gardening and groves "already planted by Nature."[63] Francis Bacon's voice is heard in the account of flowers perfuming the walks[64] and seems to be joined with Beale's as Evelyn reaches the conclusion: "For thus the {naturall} Groves, parterrs, Viridaria . . . {hills} . . . Mounts . . . fields, {Walkes} [&] statues, Grotts, Fountaines, streames {large} & frequent enclosures would reppresent the beholder {with} a prospect of a noble & masculine majestie far surpassing those trifling bankes and busy knotts of our ordinary Gardens."[65] On the other hand, Evelyn does not dismiss entirely the attractions of "artificial" topiary: "we do not alltogether decrie the moderat use of this worke, especially in Pyramids, Globes, Embossements, Battlements, Nieches, Skreenes & Triumphall Arches."[66] Thus, as in the parterre, Evelyn presents a spectrum of traditional and progressive ideas on planting through use of a heterogeneous vocabulary.

To visualize how Evelyn's complex terminology was expressed in actual design, we should return to the Sayes Court plan of 1653 (Fig. 7). To the north of the parterre, and separated from it by the terrace walk or mount, lies the "Grove with the severall walkes, meanders and Thickets &c." The rectangle, some 40 yards by 80 yards, is contained to the south by a barbery hedge, and to the east (and possibly the north) by a lilac hedge. To the west lies a codlin hedge, for he notes: "The entrances into it, are where the Codlin hedge does open." The central circle is a mount, "planted with Bayes, but the Circle Walke with Laurel." This implies an evergreen area, in which laurel lined the walks, with the interior being filled with bays. In this circle are two of the fourteen "Cabinetts of Aliternies." The others are disposed symmetrically around the rest of the grove. We can visualize these as small spaces; but whether they were hedged around or trellised over with the evergreen *Rhamnus alaternus* is unclear.[67]

Evelyn also notes how a "great French walnutt" [*Juglans regia*] is placed at every one of these fourteen cabinets. They, and an additional ten trees, show up on the plan as larger features—twenty-four in all. In this sense, Evelyn seems to have loosely followed the example of Claude and André Mollet. In *Le Jardin de plaisir,* André Mollet illustrated a plan of a bosquet with trees in several

[63] "Elysium Britannicum," 90, where Evelyn makes the point that natural groves are "preferrable to all artificiall additions."

[64] "Elysium Britannicum," 90–91. Evelyn's phrase in the marginal note on 91—"for the breath of flo: is sweeter in the aire then in the hand"—comes directly from Bacon's essay "Of Gardens," 1625: "the *Breath* of Flowers, is farre Sweeter in the Aire, (where it comes and Goes, like the warbling of Musick) then in the hand" (as quoted in "Francis Bacon (1561–1626)," in J. D. Hunt and P. Willis, ed., *The Genius of the Place: The English Landscape Garden, 1620–1820,* Cambridge, MA, and London, 1988, 52).

[65] "Elysium Britannicum," 91. For the links between Beale and Bacon, see Goodchild, " 'No phantasticall utopia,' " passim, and Leslie and Raylor, *Culture and Cultivation* (as above, note 4), appendix 3, 226–31. The same reference to Bacon's observation, "that the breath of flowers is far sweeter in the ayre, than in the hand" occurs, for example, as point nine of Beale's "The Argument." Point eight alludes to "The advancement of the Lord Bacons ayme at Ver perpetuum," which is also pursued by Evelyn in chapter 14, "Of Verdures, Perennial-greenes, and perpetuall Springs" (see p. 261). It appears that Evelyn is using the terms "Vireta" and "Viradaria" simply to denote evergreen plantations.

[66] "Elysium Britannicum," 97.

[67] "Explanation of the Particulars." There are various statements on cabinets in the "Elysium Britannicum": "By *Cabinetts* we signifie Arbours & Summer houses {~~whereoff some are open ???~~} if they be covered" (p. 93); "Cabinets may be also Cupola'd above, open or close in the center to let in a gloomy light, or they may be canopied with Ivy at excessive heights" (p. 95).

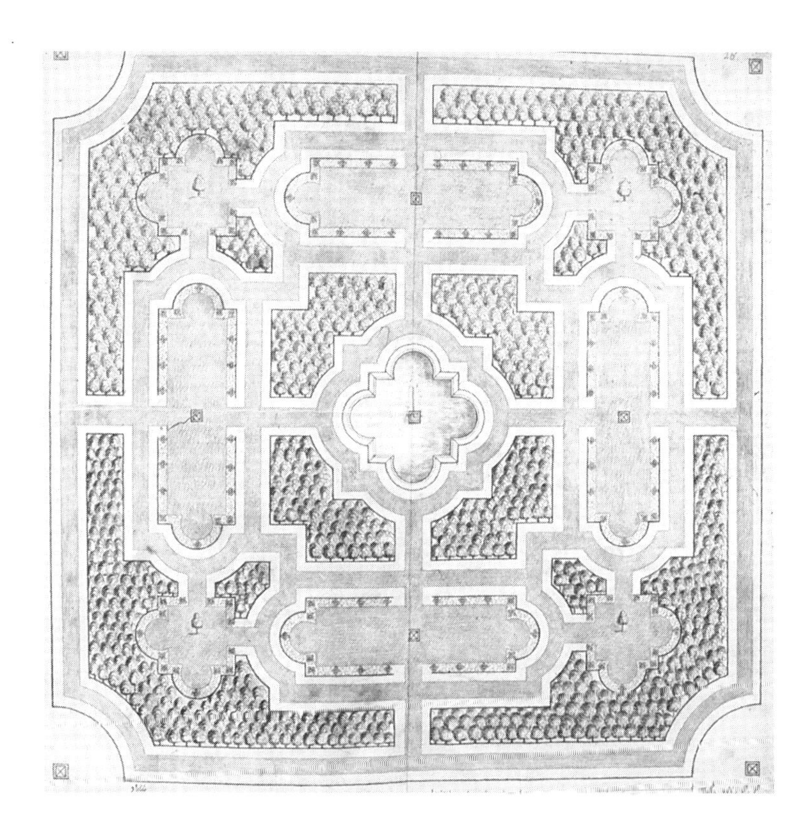

19. Design for a bosquet, from André Mollet, *Le Jardin de plaisir,* 1651, fol. 26. It is described as having "une plate-bande de gazon au milieu, comme aussi dans les salles, ou cabinets, lesquels sont bordés d'un espace de trois pieds de large pour mettre des fleurs, comme il est décrit sur les dessin" (photo: Dumbarton Oaks)

cabinets. He wrote of "les cabinets communicant l'un à l'autre, et les statues et arbres posés par ordre et correspondance, . . ."[68] In another plan, trees are located at the centers of cabinets embellished with flower borders (Fig. 19). Claude Mollet had described one such type of cabinet in his *Théâtre.*

> Aussi si vous desirez faire planter quelques Cabinets, c'est du moins que vous leur puissiez donner que quatre toises & demie, ou cinq toises en quarré, & laisser croistre la Palissade à hauteur de vingt pieds; & faut planter un Arbre qui soit beau & bien droíct, soit Telleau, ou Orme femelle, iustement au milieu pour donner de l'ombre: mais il le faut tailler par les branches lors qu'il en sera besoin, pour empescher qu'elles ne s'estendent sur vos Pallissades."[69]

However, as the largest of Evelyn's cabinets measured only five yards across (as opposed to five "toises," i.e., around ten yards), it is unlikely that the hedges were allowed to grow up to the twenty feet recommended by Mollet. It also seems unlikely from the evidence of the Sayes Court plan, that Evelyn intended his French walnuts to stand at the centers of the cabinets; rather, they are disposed to the sides within the thicket. To judge from the plan, the four circular cabinets seem to have

[68] Mollet, *Le Jardin de plaisir,* 35.

[69] Mollet, *Théâtre,* 114. Compare here "Elysium Britannicum," 95: "{I have seene them coverd by one tree, as Elme, Lime, etc: by half cutting the branch & bending them down in forme of an umbrilla, . . ."

contained a central area of lawn, whereas the remaining rectilinear ones were in sand or gravel. They may have contained sculptural ornaments, but this is not specified. It certainly seems probable that Evelyn avoided the extremes of artifice found in the French bosquet: the fountains, sculpture, and topiary.[70]

Evelyn refers to planting "above 500 standard trees, of oake, ash, elme Ceruise [*Sorbus domestica*], beech-chesnutt,"[71] some of which appeared to line the perimeter of the grove, but they no doubt filled the quarters too. From Evelyn's remarks in the "Elysium Britannicum" it might be inferred that the interior trees were planted in a random manner; he recommended "the confused & irregular planting of them far before the ranging of them in lines."[72] But the tight geometry of the grove might equally have led to disposing them in rows. The underplanting, here described as "thicketts," is composed of "Birch, hazel, Thorne, wild fruites, greenes &c." He concludes, "the close walkes, and spiders Clawes Leading to the Cabinets, you may perceive by the designe &c."[73] It is reasonable to assume that these "close walks" were in the form of arbors or "berceaux." But in comparison to the French prototypes, they may have been quite simple, made of poles, rather than quartered timber. The urge to naturalness implied in the adoption of Beale's ideas—albeit in the context of extensive gardening—may have counterbalanced the architectural influences of the Continental bosquet. My perspective reconstruction helps to illustrate how the grove might have looked as a whole (Fig. 20).

It is not clear from the key that hedges lined all the walks, but it is reasonable to infer this from contemporary practice. We are also left without specification for the height of those hedges. The proportions of the walks in the grove are much smaller than their Continental prototypes; even the main walks are only about ten feet wide, compared to the twenty or thirty feet width of some French allées.[74] On the principle of the hedges being "two thirds of the breadth of the Allees,"[75] it is reasonable to assume that those at Sayes Court were not above six or seven feet. Some Italian hedges in the *bosco* appear to have been lower than the French, and Evelyn may have had them in mind as models.[76]

[70] See Boyceau, *Traité,* 74. In the "Elysium Britannicum," 94, Evelyn does, however, mention "*Niches,* in the verdure it selfe, for statues, Seates, Fountaines, Tables of Marble."

[71] "Explanation of the Particulars."

[72] "Elysium Britannicum," 92.

[73] "Explanation of the Particulars."

[74] It is interesting to note once again Evelyn's close reliance on Boyceau's *Traité.* Compare, for example, "Elysium Britannicum," "For Cover'd Walkes do make the Allee seeme broader to the Eye than the open and free" (p. 78), with *Traité,* "Mais nous reconnoissons que le couvert . . . fait sembler l'espace plus grand, que quand l'air & la veue sont libres" (p. 72); "the . . . altitude of the Palisade or pole hedges containing two thirds of the breadth of the Allees" (p. 78), with "la hauteur de la pallissade doit estre mesuree, luy donnant les deux tiers de la largeur de l'Allée" (p. 72); and "Thus, the middle Walke of the Thuilleries which is planted with stately Elmes is 30 foote {in} breadth and of far more beauty than the two collaterall of Platanus, which is onely 20· though {it be} 600 foote long" (pp. 78–79), with "ainsi qu'il se voit aux Tuilleries l'Allée d'Ormes, qui a trente pieds de large, beaucoup plus belle que les deux de Platanes qui sont es costez, qui en ont seulement vingt, sur trois cens toises de longeur" (p. 72).

[75] "Elysium Britannicum," 78.

[76] G. B. Falda's view of the Villa Borghese in the 1680s (Fig. 17) suggests that the hedges around the fir and pine compartments were still maintained at a height not much above eye level. On the other hand, Evelyn commented on the

20. Conjectural reconstruction as bird's-eye perspective of the grove at Sayes Court, based on the plan of 1653. Painting by Mark Laird

In the "Elysium Britannicum," Evelyn clearly prefers evergreen to deciduous hedgework: "For *Palisade-hedges,* and *Contr'Espaliers Cabinets, Close-walkes, Mazes* etc there is none to be compared to the *Alaternus's* of severall sorts which we first brough[t] into use and reputation for these workes in England."[77] He also commends the holly that he used on the terrace at Sayes Court for a hedge with topiary: "The *Agrifolium* exceedes all . . . {the perenniall} greenes whatsoever for hedges

hedges of myrtle at the Quirinal that were over a man's height (*Diary,* 287). On the question of low hedges and the tendency toward higher hedges in Italian gardens of the seventeenth century, see C. Lazzaro, *The Italian Renaissance Garden,* New Haven and London, 1990, 33 and 275–76.

[77] "Elysium Britannicum," 101. For further discussion of hedges or palisades, see ibid., 54, where Evelyn advocates hedges in preference to walls as a means of enclosure: "Rather therefore, let such partitions be made of Contr' Espaliers and ~~palisads~~ hedges of Alaternus, Holly, {paliuras} pyrocanta, Lawrells {cypresse, juniper}, Horne-beame, Elme, the Garden purple-flour'd Willow, the peach-blosomed thorne, {white thorne, Berberies} some hedges of fruites . . . "; see also p. 78 margin note, where the distinction between "palisade" and "contr'espalier" is defined. His "palisade" is what is usually termed an espalier today: "that which covers the Walle {or serves in stead}," whereas the "contr'espalier" is a "pole-hedg" standing by itself. However, "palisade" is often used in the period for a free-standing hedge. See, for example, John Rea's *Flora: seu, De Florum Cultura,* London, 1665, 6: "*Pallisado's* (or, as we usually call them, *Pole-hedges*) are much in fashion in *France,* and there set with dwarf Fruit-trees; such are troublesome to keep in order, and subject to strong Winds, fit onely for spacious Gardens."

of Service."[78] Other evergreens used for hedging seem to have included cypress, laurel, pyracantha, juniper, yew, and box—an interesting selection by the standards of today. John Rea, like Evelyn, favored evergreen hedges of pyracantha, phillyrea, and alaternus, etc., over deciduous ones.

Although it is apparent that some evergreen trees and shrubs were kept apart in the Sayes Court grove (i.e., the mount), "intermixing" is implied in the underplanting.[79] By contrast, in the "Elysium Britannicum," Evelyn emphasizes: "This also we thinke fit to caution, that he at no hand admitt of any plant which sheads its leafe, to be mixed with his pereniall verdures; because it would be a very greate deformation to the rest, make a gapp, and looke like a patch ill sorted in a new and fresh garment."[80]

Other evidence of Sayes Court adds to this ambiguity. First, there is a reference in a letter of January 28, 1659/60, to Sir Thomas Browne. In a list of important English gardens, Evelyn adds, "my owne poore Garden may for its kind, perpetually greene, not be unworthy mentioning."[81] Then there is a letter of 1684 from Robert Berkeley, cited by Douglas Chambers in this volume, in which he speaks of the greens in Evelyn's wilderness, "where they are so agreeable."[82] Yet, the mount and hedges aside, they are not clearly identifiable in the 1653 plan. The explanation for this, and the resolution to the apparent ambivalence toward the principles of "intermixture" and "segregation," is to be found in Evelyn's lists of plants in chapters seven and fourteen.

The first list on pages 99 and 100 of chapter seven ("Of Groves . . .") contains evergreens itemized in four sections: trees, shrubs, shrubs and herbs, and herbs. It is preceded by a short separate list of deciduous trees and shrubs. The insertion on page 260 of chapter fourteen ("Of Verdures, Perennial-greenes, and perpetuall Springs") duplicates these lists of evergreens but includes many additional species. John Harvey's identifications in "The Plants in John Evelyn's 'Elysium Britannicum' " (this volume) allows us to interpret what Evelyn had in mind for his distinct "evergreen grove."

First of all, many of the evergreen trees or shrubs listed were tender exotics. They required hothouse or greenhouse treatment over winter or, in a few cases, an environment protected from cold winds and frost. The trees and shrubs that must have been overwintered indoors in boxes or large pots included *Capparis spinosa* (caper), *Ceratonia siliqua* (carob), *Cinnamomum zeylanicum* (cinnamon), *Citrus aurantifolia* (lime), *C. aurantium* (Seville orange), *C. medica* (citron), *Dracaena draco* (dragon

[78] "Elysium Britannicum," 101.

[79] Evelyn appears to have liked the effect of evergreen underplanting to a deciduous wood: "For thus have we sometymes beheld a very tall wood of . . . {goodly} Trees {whose leaves had forsaken them} having in the middest of winter an under wood or Coppse of perenniall Greenes, no lesse divertissant to the eye in that cold {& naked} season then coole fresh & usefull in the heate of Summer" ("Elysium Britannicum," 95).

[80] "Elysium Britannicum," 102.

[81] Keynes, *The Works of Sir Thomas Browne,* IV, 278. This assessment of his own garden as "perpetually greene" may, of course, be attributed simply to the presence of so many alaternus hedges. See here Leith-Ross, "A Seventeenth-Century Paris Garden," 156, quoting an Evelyn letter of October 1656: "Of Alaternus I have thousands: and yet desire more seede: for I intend to plant all ye grove with them, & other Greenes, which is neere an acher of Ground."

[82] See D. Chambers, " 'Elysium Britannicum not printed neere ready &c': The 'Elysium Britannicum' in the Correspondence of John Evelyn," this volume, 126.

tree), *Guiacum officinale* (lignum vitae), *Nerium oleander* (oleander), *Olea europaea* (olive), *Opuntia ficus-indica* (prickly pear or barbary fig), *Passiflora incarnata* (passion flower), *Persea gratissima* (avocado), *Phoenix dactylifera* (date palm), *Santalum album* (sandalwood), and *Tamarindus indica* (tamarind). In addition, Evelyn listed some smaller "evergreen" shrubs and herbaceous plants that were clearly in need of winter protection in pots, such as *Adiantum capillus-veneris* (maidenhair fern), *Globularia alypum* (herb terrible), and *Origanum marjorana* (marjoram).

Those that were borderline hardy, but may well have been kept in cases or pots, included *Cneorum tricoccon, Convolvulus cneorum, Cupressus sempervirens* (cypress tree), *Myrtus communis* and vars. (myrtle), *Pistacia terebinthus, P. vera,* and *Sassafras albidum.* All these plants that were kept in boxes or pots must have been brought out into the cabinets of the wilderness each spring. As Evelyn wrote in his handbook "Directions for the Gardener at Says-Court" (1687), "Never expose your *Oranges, Limons,* & like tender Trees, whatever season flatter; 'til the Mulbery puts-forth its leafe, then bring them boldly out of the Greene-house; but for a fortnight, let them stand in the shade of an hedge; where the sun may glimer onely upon them."[83] In summer—set against the alaternus hedges—the rows and ranks of potted herbs, boxed oleanders and oranges, lemons and limes, carob and cinnamon, date palms and "dragon trees" must have created the sense of a miniature Eden, perennially fruitful and green.[84]

Of course, in winter, these evergreens were not performing their function as "verdure" in the grove itself; they were away in the hothouse or greenhouse (Fig. 21). Evelyn seems to have been aware of this, noting:

> Now then let us but imagine the beauty, . . . verdure, {& variety} which all these must needes produce; the hardy at all tymes, the tender and more choyce in their seasons, . . . sometymes in the *Conservatory,* other whiles under the portico's & peristyles . . . in both which they may be transported in their cases, & orderly ranged so as to forme most delicious groves, even in the very middest of the Winter.[85]

It also seems likely that Evelyn shared a misguided belief, then widely held, that even the evergreen plants from the tropics might eventually be acclimatized to the English winter. He highlighted a group of seven species from warmer climates with an asterisk, commenting that they might be "a stranger with us, but prompting to experiments"; these were the gum arabic, cinnamon, the dragon tree, avocado, sandalwood, sassafras, and tamarind.[86]

The second qualification is that not all these tender exotics were in fact evergreen; *Jasminum grandiflorum* and *Melia azedarach* are deciduous. Some of the plants that are borderline hardy also lose

[83] See MS 136 (Christ Church, Oxford), fol. 27, now at the British Library, London. The manuscript was edited by G. Keynes for the Nonesuch Press in 1932.

[84] It should be noted that my bird's-eye reconstruction of the grove at Sayes Court portrays the appearance of the planting in spring, i.e., before the tender exotics have been placed out in the cabinets. For a wider discussion of the perpetual spring and the evocation of Eden, see J. Prest, *The Garden of Eden: The Botanic Garden and the Re-Creation of Paradise,* New Haven, 1981, reprint 1988, chap. 6.

[85] "Elysium Britannicum," 261.

[86] Ibid., insertion on p. 261. Only the sassafras from North America proved half-hardy.

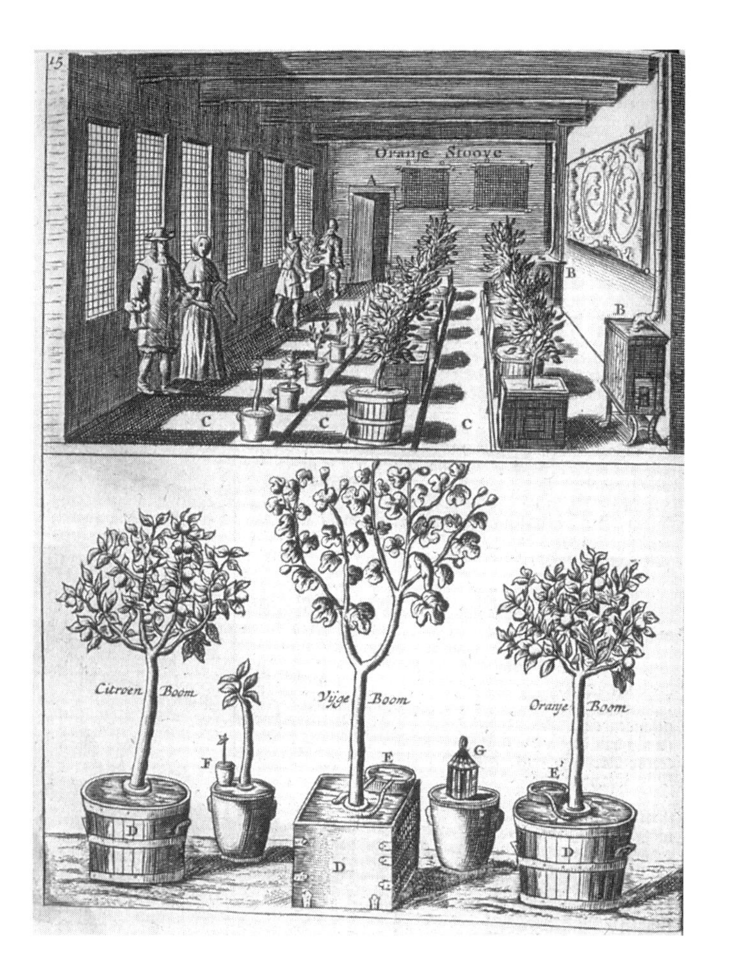

21. Tender trees and shrubs arranged in ranks in the orangery for winter protection (*top*), and detail of citrus fruit, fig, and other plants in cases, tubs, and pots (*bottom*), from Jan van der Groen's *Den Nederlandtsen Hovenier,* Amsterdam, 1683, pl. 15 (photo: Dumbarton Oaks)

their leaves—the sassafras, for example. And the maidenhair fern is undecided, needing a sheltered home to remain evergreen. In attempting to assemble the greatest variety of plants that might create his "perpetuall Spring," Evelyn was thus stretching the limits of the category "evergreen." That he was conscious of this is apparent from his deletions in the list of "evergreens" drawn up for the insertions in "Elysium Britannicum." He has, for example, struck through "Larix. the Larch tree. 1365 Looseth his leaves X."; and against the turpentine tree (*Pistacia terebinthus*), he noted his doubts over the plant remaining evergreen.[87]

This tension between the ideal and the real is even more apparent in the hardy plants that were listed under "evergreens." A good number of these trees and shrubs were in fact deciduous, even if there were reasons for Evelyn to suspect they might retain their leaves. These included *Artemisia abrotanum, A. absinthium, Daphne gnidium, D. mezereum, Dorycnium suffruticosum, Prunus cerasifera,* and *Rubus fruticosus.*[88] In the case of the herbaceous plants, Evelyn perceived that there was a blur between his two categories, when he wrote:

[87] See here MS 38 (Christ Church, Oxford), fols. 219–21, now at the British Library, London, which relate to Evelyn's insertions of evergreen plants. See also John Harvey's introduction to the lists I.A and I.B in "The Plants in John Evelyn's 'Elysium Britannicum,'" this volume, 221–26. It is noteworthy that, whereas the larch is deleted in MS 38, it still appears as an "evergreen" in the insertion in the "Elysium Britannicum," 260.

[88] *Artemisia abrotanum* is an example of a plant that is deciduous to semievergreen. *Coriaria myrtifolia* was regarded by Loudon as still an "evergreen" in 1829, but today is listed under deciduous plants. The full list is itemized with the other plants that Evelyn called "deciduous" in Harvey, "Plants," list I.B.

> Now though all these are greene in Winter; yet may we not acurately speaking, name them all to be perennial {& vivaces?} because some of them shead their Seedes (especially the Herbes) and to renew themselves; Others produce succkers; and some are {annual &} to be sowne yearely, Some bisannual, & others every three yeares.[89]

In other words, Evelyn had observed how many herbaceous plants—even some annuals and biennials, by seeding—would retain or produce new green leaves and shoots throughout the winter period, despite the fact that they were not evergreen in the sense of woody plants like ivy. These provided a semblance of a green carpet on the floor of the grove, even in December or March. Some were, indeed, what we would now call "ground cover"—periwinkles (*Vinca major* and *V. minor*), for example, or the spurge laurel (*Daphne laureola*)—but others would only have covered the ground with green rather intermittently. In addition, Evelyn included a selection of plants that flower in the late winter: hellebore, primrose, winter aconite, crocus, daisy, and hepatica. Although these and the early-flowering shrub *Daphne mezereum* are in no sense true evergreens, they relate to the concept of *Ver Perpetuum,* as described by Francis Bacon—a continuum of flowering throughout the year.[90]

In assembling the greatest variety of partially evergreen herbaceous plants, Evelyn also stretched the limits of what might have been practical for underplanting in the grove. He included some plants that are suited to maritime conditions or rock gardens. Samphire (*Crithmum maritimum*), for example, is indigenous to coastal areas and is difficult to cultivate because of its saline requirements. Likewise, the cotton weed (*Otanthus maritimus*) grows best on rocks near the sea. The houseleek and pennywort (*Umbilicus rupestris*) cling to stones, walls, and roofs. Moreover, Evelyn also included many herbs, salad plants, and vegetables, only some of which would have grown well under trees and shrubs. Here, we might note the wild leek (*Allium ampeloprasum*), wild celery (*Apium graveolens*), and beets (*Beta vulgaris*), brassicas (*Brassica rapa*), and rocket salad or Italian cress (*Eruca sativa*). Especially interesting is scurvy grass (*Cochlearia officinalis*), which was a popular salad vegetable in the mid-seventeenth century. Its place in the grove is, however, questionable.[91]

To what extent Evelyn actually used such plants in his own grove at Sayes Court remains a matter for speculation: the parasitic mistletoe (*Viscum album*), for example, or the stream-loving watercress (*Rorippa nasturcium-aquaticum*); the tricky alpine rhododendrons (*R. ferrugineum* and *R. hirsutum*), or the rock-loving sedums. But it does seem reasonable to assume that his concept of a partially evergreen "ground cover" was exploited in some way. These "Herbae Semper virentes," together with the alaternus hedges and his collection of tender evergreens, may account for the

[89] "Elysium Britannicum," insertion on p. 260.

[90] See Bacon, "Of Gardens," as quoted in "Francis Bacon (1561–1626)" (as above, note 64), 51–52.

[91] Evelyn seems to have appreciated the difficulty of cultivating Samphire, which he also called "an excellent Salad" (p. 137). In chapter ten, book two, within the section on plants suitable for rocks and grottoes, he writes, "*Sampier* seedes frequently sprinkled in the chinkes of your rockworke, where there is mosse, mortar or Earth will take hold" (p. 137). It clearly had a place within the "habitats" of the mount in Evelyn's Philosophico-Medicall Garden ("*Crithmum* in the wall") (p. 327) and in the rugged terrain of a wilder grove ("a natural cliff & precipice . . . with now and then a . . . rift . . . for . . . Sampier {& Caper}") (pp. 141–42). But whether rockwork was located in formal groves such as the one at Sayes Court seems more doubtful.

claim that his "owne poore Garden . . . perpetually greene" could be included in the list of important English gardens. Whether, of course, this verdant floor was seen from over the hedges or from within the woodland is a matter for further conjecture. It may imply that the hedges were lower than six to seven feet, indeed, around four feet or beneath eye level.

In the concept at least of segregated planting, in the use of alaternus hedges, and in the configuration of the grove as a whole, Evelyn may have had some influence on later planting design. Philip Miller and James Meader continued to advocate segregation until the late eighteenth century.[92] And the diagonal, orthogonal, and circular structure of the path system at Sayes Court was to recur in various forms at Sir William Temple's Moor Park, at the duke of Lauderdale's Ham House, and at Sandywell in Gloucestershire in the early eighteenth century.[93] The idea of the "Ver Perpetuum," building on Francis Bacon's account, also had a lasting influence in the creation of evergreen shrubberies and winter gardens.[94] However, the use of tender exotics wheeled out of the greenhouse for display each summer was to be largely abandoned, along with topiary, in the shift from the formal wilderness to the informal shrubbery.[95] Nevertheless, the attempt to evoke the "perpetually florid" effects seen in Italy—through the greenhouse and conservatory—was an imaginative vision, suggestive of the future in landscape gardening.[96] Working on the mind by association, "it would even strike and surprise the Winter Spectator, who might imagine himselfe . . . transported into some new or inchanted Country."[97] Above all, Evelyn's use of alaternus for hedgework was innovative, analogous to the introduction of classical, French, and Italian words into the language of gardening; it was an act of translation.[98]

[92] See here M. Laird, "Ornamental Planting and Horticulture in English Pleasure Grounds, 1700–1830," in Hunt, *Garden History* (as above, note 47), 266.

[93] See J. D. Hunt and E. de Jong, eds., "The Anglo-Dutch Garden in the Age of William and Mary," *Journal of Garden History* 8, 2–3 (1988), 245–47, 255–58, 264–65.

[94] See M. Laird, "Approaches to Planting in the Late Eighteenth Century: Some Imperfect Ideas on the Origins of the American Garden," *Journal of Garden History* 11, 3 (1991), n. 44, 172.

[95] There is some evidence that tender exotics in tubs and pots were still being used in shrubberies of the late 18th and early 19th centuries. See here J. Harris, *The Artist and the Country House,* London, 1979, fig. 363a, a view of the "orange tree garden" at Wanstead House, Essex, attributed to Charles Cotton the Elder, ca. the 1760s, and fig. 393, a view of Lord Northwick's villa, Harrow Manor House, Middlesex, ca. 1820 by John Glover. Sinking the tubs in the ground was also an alternative to arranging them on grass. One finds, for example, "Large Orange Trees sunk into Brick'd Pits" mentioned on a proposal plan ascribed to Placido Columbani for what became the Elysian Garden at Audley End. See Michael Sutherill, *The Gardens of Audley End,* London, 1995, 32. This appears to date from the 1780s. Columbani also refers to "Clumps of Myrtles, Geraniums, Cistus's, & other low exotick plants, the pots plung'd in Earth, & Intermix'd with Sweet Flowers." In this sense, the tradition lived on—the artificiality of tubs being replaced by the apparent naturalness of "plunged" exotics. I am grateful to Peter Goodchild for raising this issue.

[96] The Elysian Garden at Audley End confirms the survival of this tradition, while Painshill Park demonstrates the use of planting features in the landscape garden that transported the visitor to other times or places; for example, Charles Hamilton's evergreen "amphitheatre" at Painshill was surely meant to evoke a "perpetually florid" Italy.

[97] "Elysium Britannicum," 259–60.

[98] According to Prudence Leith-Ross, the vogue for alaternus as a hedging plant was attributable initially to Pierre Morin, who made his fortune out of it, by calling it "Filaria" (Phillyrea). See here Leith-Ross, "A Seventeenth-Century Paris Garden," 155–56. I am grateful to John Harvey for alerting me to this point. Like some of Evelyn's linguistic introductions, the alaternus hedge did not survive much beyond his period. John James, translating from the French,

Whereas John Beale helped to provide Evelyn with precedent in antiquity for extensive gardening, Sir Thomas Browne offered an account of ancient practices in the use of flowers, especially "flowry Crowns and Garlands." He sent Evelyn a letter from Norwich that was later published in 1684 under the title "Of Garlands and Coronary or Garland-Plants."[99] This was consulted for chapter sixteen, book two of the "Elysium Britannicum," "Of Coronary Gardens, Flowers, and rare Plants . . ."

In analyzing this third feature of Evelyn's ornamental planting, we are confronted with a difficulty in defining his use of the term "coronary"—a difficulty compounded by the absence of chapter five, book three, "Of Crowns, Chaplets, Garlands, Festoons, Flower-pots, Nosegays, Posies, and other Flowry Pomps." There is very little in the extant text that relates to the "convivial, festival, sacrificial, nuptial, honorary, funebrial" customs of antiquity that Browne describes, or of the "Gestatory," "Portatory," "Suspensory," or "Depository" forms of garland that Evelyn's correspondent associated with the "Ancients."[100] Here we might compare the "Elysium Britannicum" with a near-contemporary work to highlight what is missing in Evelyn's account. In his *A Display of Heraldrie* (1610), for example, J. Gwillim writes:

> *Coronarie Herbes* are such as in respect of their odiferous smell have beene of long time, and yet are used for decking and trimming of the body, or adorning of houses, or other pleasurable use for *eie* or *sent:* as also in respect of their beautifull *shape* and *colours,* were most commonly bestowed in making of Crowns and Garlands; of which uses they received their name of *Coronarie.* Amongst which, we may reckon the *Rose* before expressed, to be one of the chiefest, as also *Violets* of all sorts, *Clove-Gillofers, Sweet Majoram, Rosemarie, White Daffodil, Spikenard, Rose Campion, Daisie,* &c. But of all other, the *Flower de Lice* is of most esteeme, having beene from the first *Bearing,* the *Charge* of a *Regall Escocheon,* originally borne by the *French Kings.*[101]

Likewise Sir Thomas Browne, having described the coronary traditions of the ancient world, was

could still recommend it in *The Theory and Practice of Gardening*, 1712; but when Philip Miller was writing his *Gardeners Dictionary* a few years later, he stressed that *Rhamnus alaternus* was not good for making hedges; it was labor-intensive and required clipping three times a year.

[99] See here G. Keynes, ed., *The Miscellaneous Writings of Sir Thomas Browne,* London, 1946, 57–61. According to John Harvey, Browne's catalogue of coronary plants was compiled ca. 1657–58 (personal communication, 1993).

[100] See here Keynes, *Writings of Sir Thomas Browne,* 57–58. It should be stated, however, that Browne also used the example of the ancients to provide a contrast with the modern gardener, who had a wider choice of newly introduced flowers at hand: "The Catalogue of Coronary Plants is not large in Theophrastus, Pliny, Pollux, or Athenaeus: but we may find a good enlargement in the accounts of Modern Botanists" (p. 59). Thus, his plant list contains mostly exotics. Ada Segre has commented to me on the fact that the names of the American exotics, Browne's allusion to the "Inhabitants of Nova Hispania," and his account of feather crowns made by "American Nations" are derived from works such as Hernandez's *Thesaurus Mexicanum,* 1651, and Mannucci's *Trattato del Fiore e del Frutto,* 1605. For the use of garlands and floral crowns in antiquity, see W. F. Jashemski, *The Gardens of Pompeii,* New Rochelle, N.Y., 1979, 267–75. See also J. Harvey, "Coronary Flowers and Their 'Arabick' Background," in G. A. Russell, ed., *The 'Arabick' Interest of the Natural Philosophers in Seventeenth-Century England,* Leiden, 1994.

[101] J. Gwillim, *A Display of Heraldrie,* London, 1610, III x, 114. Spikenard, now identified as the Himalayan *Nardostachys grandiflora,* may have meant the lavender or other similar plants with fragrant inflorescences on spikes. I am grateful to Ada Segre for this insight.

more precise in his definition of the modern floral crown, which was also dedicated to Gwillim's pleasures of "*eie* and *sent*":

> but our florid and purely ornamental Garlands, delightfull unto sight and smell, not framed according to mystical and symbolical considerations, are of more free election, and so may be made to excell those of the Ancients; we having China, India, and a new world to supply us, beside the great distinction of Flowers unknown unto Antiquity, and the varieties thereof arising from Art and Nature.[102]

It is true that Evelyn includes a section on gathering flowers "for Nosegays, for shew, for the House etc.,"[103] and makes a passing allusion to garlands: "For then the statues of our most renound & illustrious Gardiners [Gardens?] are celebrated with Elogies, Garlands and Festoones."[104] But there is no explicit categorization of "coronary" plants—whether according to scent, color, shape, etc., or according to the rituals of love, marriage, domestic or community festivals, or to the customs surrounding birth, death, and so on—a categorization that would help distinguish them from other flowers in the flower garden.[105] Sir Thomas Browne, in contrast, compared antique "convivial Garlands . . . preventing drunkenness" or "solemn festival Garlands" to modern garlands, which were composed for "Beauty and good Odour" alone, and which consisted of new exotics, rather than old "coronary" flowers such as the rose, lily, and violet, favored by the Romans.[106] Thus, despite Evelyn's chapter heading, the text is essentially concerned with the *growing* of choice flowers in the private garden to one side of the palace or residence. Evelyn called the area a "*Serraglio* . . . at one of the Flankes of the Mantion."[107]

As with Evelyn's account of the parterre and grove, there is an initial problem in visualizing what he describes as the structure and ornamentation of his ideal flower garden: "But for the forme . . . & disposition of the Beds, they may be either mixed with parterrs, . . . Traile-worke . . . Compartiments (& Grasse plotts), or be so marshald by themselves as to be brought to an agreable

[102] Keynes, *Writings of Sir Thomas Browne,* 58.

[103] "Elysium Britannicum," 317.

[104] Ibid., 318.

[105] See here "The Coronary Flower Garden," chapter 4 of Ada Segre's Ph.D. thesis, "Horticultural Traditions and the Emergence of the Flower Garden (*ca.* 1550–1660)," University of York, 1995. She argues that scent, color, longevity (when dried), etc., were factors in the choice of coronary flowers. I am greatly indebted to her for the opportunity to consult this chapter before the completion of the thesis. For a wider discussion of the social history of garlands and floral crowns, see J. Goody, *The Culture of Flowers,* Cambridge, 1993, especially 66–70, 75–80, 157–61, 167–69, and 202–5.

[106] Keynes, *Writings of Sir Thomas Browne,* 57–58. The distinction between antique and modern practices is, however, vague in Browne. For a discussion of which flowers were favored by the Romans, see Jashemski, *The Gardens of Pompeii,* 271.

[107] "Elysium Britannicum," 275. The sense of private enclosure implied by the term "seraglio" suggests the *giardino segreto* of Italian Renaissance gardens, the private space adjacent to the villa, which was inaccessible to the casual visitor and which was often used for growing rare and valuable plants. See here E. B. MacDougall, *Fountains, Statues, and Flowers: Studies in Italian Gardens of the Sixteenth and Seventeenth Centuries,* Washington, D.C., 1994, 221. It is interesting to note how Evelyn saw the Coronary Garden as a place moderate enough in size for the owner to care for himself: "it . . . dos argue that there be a mediocrity in the extent . . . as the Master himselfe may take the greatest pleasure to cultivat with his owne hands, be he Prince or Subject" ("Elysium Britannicum," 276).

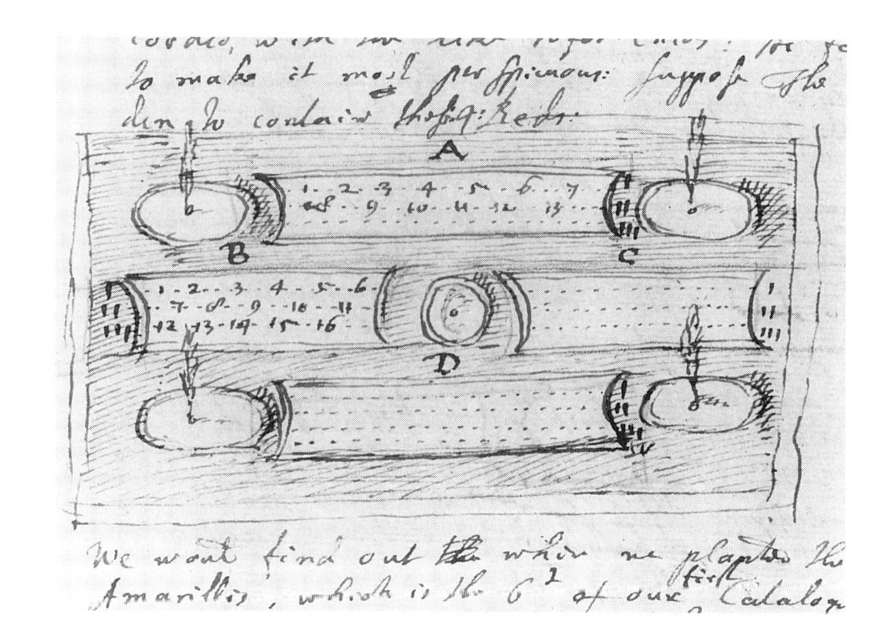

22. Design for a Coronary Garden, "Elysium Britannicum," 317 (photo: Christ Church, Oxford; reproduced by permission of the trustees of the will of Major Peter George Evelyn)

worke."[108] On this occasion, however, an illustration is provided that shows a simple arrangement of beds interspersed with what appear to be cypresses, and perhaps a pool and fountain at the center (Fig. 22). The flower beds seem, therefore, closer to what he describes as "marshald by themselves," and he confirms elsewhere, "(To speake our owne sense) we do least of all affect the planting of Flo: in the Compartiments {or in the knotts}."[109] Likewise, the "Private Garden of choice flowers, and Simples" at Sayes Court appears to contain geometric flower beds without broderie or "traile-worke." At the center is a fountain, and at one end is the "Beehive," perhaps indicative of the garden's role as a store of honey-providing herbs and flowers.[110]

There follows then a long and interesting account of how the flowers might be grown in the "bordures": first, the idea that the borders around the walls be reserved for taller flowers—"graduately ranged" down to the low flowers in the center borders; second, the idea of those interior borders being $3\frac{1}{2}$ to 4 feet wide, so that they can be easily tended; third, the idea that the earth should be raised to the center by about 8 inches to create "Embrodered Cushions for thence *Pulvini*";[111] and

[108] "Elysium Britannicum," 276. Among the plants that are singled out for broderie or knotwork, the following should be mentioned: *Bellis perennis,* which Evelyn commends for "lower embroderie," as well as for edging (p. 293), and *Primula vulgaris* vars., "which become a parterr the best of any being planted thick, because they couch low, and may be wrought in rare imbroderies the colours well sorted" (p. 299).

[109] Ibid., 276. Evelyn also seems to like the idea of grass plats with flower borders and a little broderie: "Carpet, Environed with bordures . . . then a branch of the Parter for the greater variety" (p. 277). This sounds like the arrangement he used in his parterre at Sayes Court. He mentions an illustration at the end of the chapter, but this appears to be missing.

[110] "Explanation of the Particulars." See here Segre, "Coronary Flower Garden," for a discussion of the coronary flower garden and bees.

[111] "Pulvini," as John Harvey pointed out to me, is the Latin for cushions or pillows; "Pulvinus" was still used in texts such as Stephanus' *Hortus* (1539) to denote "beds." See also Prest, *The Garden of Eden,* 1, for the use of the term *pulvillus.*

fourth, the idea that they should be edged with pinks, thrift, or box or, alternatively, with two- to three-inch high white boards, brick, or klinker.[112]

Evelyn then elaborates on the first idea of a graduated disposition of flowers, the tallest around the walls, the shortest in the central beds:

> Now as the environing bordures serve for the taler flo: so these beds for the more humble & lower: The *Coronary Garden* admitting the *Verticulate, Umbeliferat, Corymbiferat, Capitate, Campaniforme, papiforme,* some *Gigantine,* some of the Ordinary stature, Even to the dwarfish {groveling} & abortive.[113]

At this point he wisely crosses out "Fungus and Mosses" and clarifies the graduation: lilies, crown imperials, and Turk's cap lilies next to the walls; then tulips, irises, narcissus, carnations, and larkspur in the adjacent borders; and primroses, crocus, anemonies, ranunculus, auriculas, hepaticas, gentians, and hyacinths in the central beds.[114] The purpose was to intersperse the flowers in such a way "that the Beds appeare furnished at all Seasons," an idea that invokes *Ver Perpetuum* once again.[115]

The all-inclusiveness of Evelyn's Coronary Garden—from spring and summer bulbs and rhizomes to herbaceous summer annuals and perennials, from tender exotics in pots to hardy roses and clipped evergreens, from aquatic plants to climbing plants, from fruit trees to the occasional esculent plant—suggests, indeed, the fusion of several traditions. There was the coronary floral tradition that had been revived by the sixteenth century from antiquity; the florists' tradition of exotics that was gaining ground in the seventeenth century with the influx of new bulbs; and a separate physic garden tradition—the medicinal plants of the Philosophico-Medicall Garden.[116] Evelyn might concede that the florists' bulbs are "commonly the most rare of the *Coronary Garden,*"[117] but his flower garden was open to all comers. Thus to the traditional coronary flowers mentioned by Gwillim—the carnation, the rose, the Madonna lily, the sweet violet, the iris, the daisy, sweet marjoram, lavender, and the various amaranths, etc.—were added Morin's and Hanmer's bulbs: the tulip, the fritillaries, and the hyacinths.[118] And to all these Evelyn appended a group of plants more suited to the physic garden such as British native orchids—even just possibly "Fungus and Mosses."

[112] "Elysium Britannicum," 277. More unusual flowers for edging included *Bellis perennis* (daisy) (p. 293) and *Cyclamen* (p. 296), used to edge all the walks in Pierre Morin's garden.

[113] "Elysium Britannicum," 277. This version of graduation could be derived from Claude Mollet's *Théâtre,* in which he describes how tall flowers should be planted around the edges of the beds, with the shorter flowers inside the bed either in embroidery patterns or in other designs. This idea was derived in turn from earlier French authors, such as de Serres.

[114] The three tiers of the graduation are elaborated in "Elysium Britannicum," 278. To visualize the tripartite division of flower beds, see Goodchild's reconstruction of John Rea's flower garden in "John Rea's Gardens of Delight," 107.

[115] "Elysium Britannicum," 277.

[116] See here, again, Segre, "Coronary Flower Garden." She classifies Evelyn's flower garden as "mixed," because in combining traditional coronary plants with the newer bulbous plants, his practice differed from the separation of "coronary" and "exotic" beds in Italian gardens of the 16th and 17th centuries.

[117] "Elysium Britannicum," 280.

[118] See Segre, "Coronary Flower Garden," for a discussion of how new exotics were incorporated into the traditional coronary garden through her "theory of the reference groups."

The inclusion of the terms "Verticulate" or "Corymbiferat," for example, indicates an interesting preoccupation with dividing plants into families on a natural basis. (John Ray had used "umbelliferous" in a modern sense by 1662, and "corymbiferous" was used within a few years after; "Capitate" seems to be what we call composite today—daisies, thistles, etc.)[119] Evelyn was thus thinking of his flower garden as not merely decorative, not merely for cut flowers or choice flowers; indeed, his ordering system suggests an overlap with the order beds of a physic garden. That this overlap, however, sometimes stretched the ornamental and practical functions of the Coronary Garden is apparent from Evelyn's occasional remarks, especially those on the aquatic plants, which had to be squeezed into "some corner . . . in some place that may not disorder the Garden," or which, like *Menyanthes trifoliata,* were perhaps better suited to the "Marshes" of the Philosophico-Medicall Garden.[120]

The ordering of the flower garden according to "Recension & enroulement"[121] is developed further in Evelyn's description of the illustration. Each bed is given a letter—A, B, C, D, etc.—and divided into rows that are enumerated in Roman cyphers I, II, III, IV, etc. Within each row, the individual plants are labeled according to the "barbarous" figures 1, 2, 3, 4, etc., inscribed or "stamped" on "*Tallys* or *Tesserae*"—the five-inch-high lead labels that we still see in some botanic gardens today (Fig. 23).[122] This allowed the owner and gardener to record each and every plant with location and other information in a book or catalogue, such as the one Evelyn saw in the Netherlands in Leyden on August 28, 1641.[123] The "curious" collector of flowers could marshal his regiments.

When Evelyn writes of the owner and gardener as a "Monarch & Generall of all this multitude" taking "accoumpt of his severall subjects & Souldiers,"[124] we are inevitably reminded of Andrew Marvell's "Upon Appleton House" of the early 1650s, especially of these lines: "See how the Flow'rs, as at *Parade,* / Under their *Colours* stand displaid: / Each *Regiment* in order grows, / That of the Tulip Pinke and Rose."[125] Thus, the disposition of flowers in rigid rows or regiments was not peculiar to the physic garden of medicinal plants. It was commonplace for the period. Indeed, Evelyn reminds us that the "*French* have invented a Frame of Wood . . . contrived like a *lattice,* every square of competent dimension, this they presse edgewise upon the Bed, & where the impression

[119] Personal communication, John Harvey, January 21, 1993. See here R. Dodonæus, *Stirpium Historiæ Pemptades Sex,* Antwerp, 1583, 295, for the classification "De Umbelliferis Herbis," which was used to distinguish this group of plants from other families. Ray was thus following an earlier precedent. I am grateful to Ada Segre for this insight.

[120] "Elysium Britannicum," 301. See also *Datura stamonium* (thorn apple), which Evelyn suggested planting in "some wast[e] corner for variety, not much ornament" (insertion on p. 301), and *Scorpiurus sulcatus* (caterpillars), "a grovling plant . . . & only for curiosity not the flowers" (insertion on p. 301).

[121] Ibid., 316.

[122] Ibid. See also A. Huxley, *An Illustrated History of Gardening,* London, 1983, 125–26: "The French appear to have been using tallies in the eighteenth century, if not earlier. These were, in fact, great wooden sticks, in which Roman numerals were cut with a knife, read upward from the base." Evelyn makes a point of noting that his tallies were in lead.

[123] De Beer, *Diary,* II, 52–53: "I went also to visite their Garden of Simples, which was indeede well stor'd with exotic Plants, if the Catalogue presented to me by the Gardiner be a faithfull register."

[124] "Elysium Britannicum," 316.

[125] Quoted from Hunt and Willis, "Andrew Marvell (1621–78)," *The Genius of the Place* (as above, note 64), 72.

23. Illustration of tools, including "A box of Lab?ells, or Tallies . . . to prick in next the stalke of the choycest flowers & plants" (no. 65) and "A Register or booke wherein are the names of all the flowers and plants in the Garden" (no. 66), "Elysium Britannicum," 51 (photo: Christ Church, Oxford; reproduced by permission of the trustees of the will of Major Peter George Evelyn)

remaines, there make the holes" (Fig. 24).[126] The interval for disposing bulbs in a grid of this kind was around three to four inches—not closer than the "span of 4 fingers" as Evelyn remarked.[127]

This did not mean, of course, that bulbs or other flowers were always disposed singly; we are told expressly of the gladiolus that "you may cluster halfe a dozen together for the better shew."[128] Moreover, in some cases flowers such as the "*Tuberous,* etc." were better planted "with the *dibber,* & without more trouble then marking their Spaces with the Compasse."[129] In other cases, flowers were plunged in pots. And in a few cases, flowers such as the *Ranunculus* required beds or pots of their own; they were "unsociale" plants.[130] But often enough flowers were mixed together, as Sir Thomas Hanmer recorded in his garden at Bettisfield in 1660.[131]

[126] "Elysium Britannicum," 280. As Ada Segre pointed out to me, this account seems to come from G. B. Ferrari, *Flora sive Florum Cultura,* Rome, 1633, 233–34. Ferrari referred to the "Gallicam cratem."

[127] "Elysium Britannicum," 280; and Laird and Harvey, "'A Cloth of Tissue of Divers Colours,'" 158–59.

[128] "Elysium Britannicum," insertion on p. 296.

[129] Ibid., 281.

[130] Ibid., 300. The Spanish narcissus and the tulip were likewise "*inimica inter se*" (p. 280).

[131] See Duthie, "Planting Plans," (as above, note 13), 83–87; Elstob, *Garden Book of Sir Thomas Hanmer* (as above, note 37).

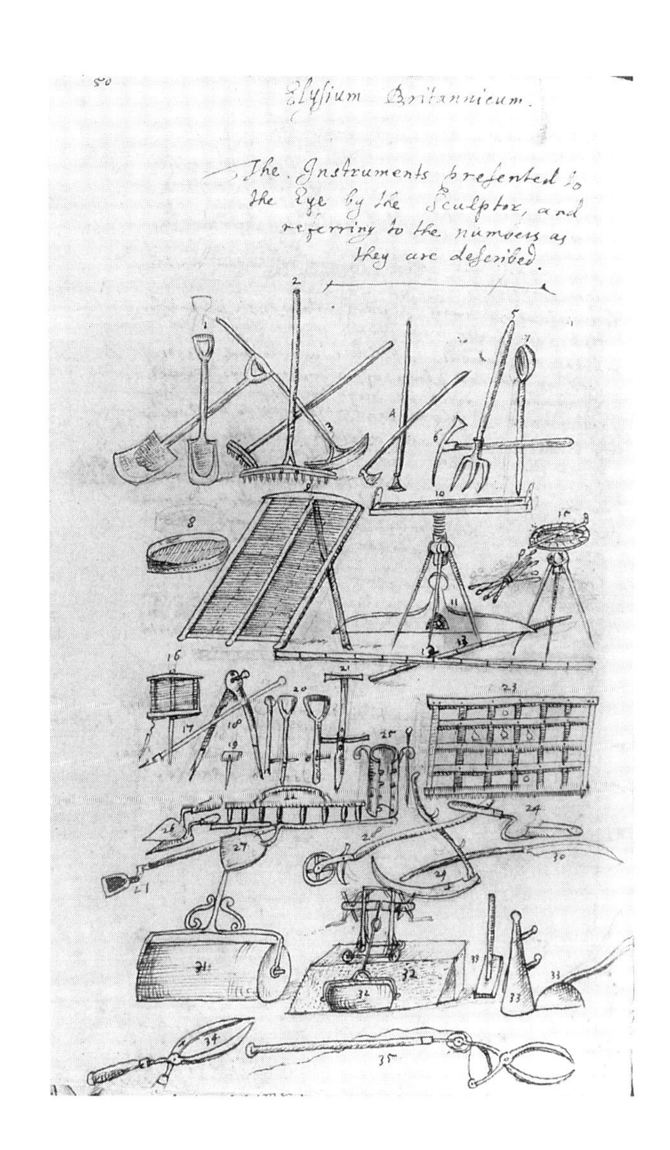

24. Illustration of tools, including "A Planting Lattice . . . of 6 foote in length, 3 in breadth, each square at competent distance for *bulbous rootes* . . . " (no. 23), "Elysium Britannicum," 50 (photo: Christ Church, Oxford, reproduced by permission of the trustees of the will of Major Peter George Evelyn)

It was Thomas Hanmer who provided Evelyn with detailed notes on individual flowers. Evelyn writes in the manuscript, for example, "{Here review & insert Sr T: Hanmers paper: of Tulip}";[132] it was likewise for the other flowers of the florist, such as anemonies and auriculas. Hanmer recorded a number of beds at Bettisfield in sufficient detail to allow for visual reconstruction. Bettisfield was, of course, in no way a traditional coronary garden, being more of a florist's garden. Yet, Hanmer's system of ordering flowers doubtless corresponded to what Evelyn had in mind in the "Elysium Britannicum." The first and fourth beds were essentially for tulips, whereas the third bed represents an interesting mixed arrangement, as my perspective illustrates (Fig. 25).

Whether the flowers were meant to read clearly as individuals, or would merge together, is uncertain. Evelyn writes that the beds should be "so richly furnished, as that nothing of Earth appeare naked & which were not perpetually covered with their Enamell."[133] Such was clearly the

[132] "Elysium Britannicum," 282.

[133] Ibid., 276. The spacings given by Evelyn are fairly dense, often a few inches apart, e.g., some irises "2 fingers deepe & span distant" (p. 297). For the illustration, I have assumed an average spacing around six inches, though the narcissi would then have been from up to nine inches to one foot apart. This assumption is based on the premise that the

25. Conjectural reconstruction as perspective of Sir Thomas Hanmer's planting record of flower beds in the Great Garden at Bettisfield, 1660. The left view represents the appearance of the third "boarded bed" in March to April, and the right view the appearance of the same bed in May to June. Painting by Mark Laird

intended effect at Pierrepont House, Nottingham, as depicted in the anonymous painting of ca. 1705 (Fig. 26). But illustrations of the period suggest that wide spacing was also common, especially in the Low Countries (Fig. 27).[134] The density of spacing depended, to a large extent, on whether the individual flower was more important than the overall effect of the planting pattern. For florists such as John Rea the value of the individual flower was paramount.[135]

Within the regimented disposition and a broadly symmetrical organization of Hanmer's third bed, there is a degree of variation that is hard to analyze; it does not follow any logical pattern. The outer three rows on each side correspond in all but the miscellaneous fritillary in row two. The inner rows are roughly balanced but not symmetrical. The degree of symmetry and the effect of "enamell" also depended on the season and the horticultural practices. If Hanmer had wished to force and

---

bed would have been around four feet wide (i.e., Evelyn's maximum width, and an average width in Europe, as John Harvey pointed out to me in a letter of October 30, 1993, since at least the time of Ibn Baṣṣāl in Andalusia ca. 1080). Within this, Hanmer's maximum eight rows would take up forty-two inches, leaving three inches spare at the margins. The length works out to about six feet on this basis. Evelyn uses various terms to describe the effect of the flower borders and beds. A "rich & . . . noble Tapistry" (p. 76) has already been noted. But there were others, such as "the most glorious enamell, wherewith *Nature* is used to diaper and embroider our Gardens with flowers and fruits" (pp. 20–22). Among these, the term "enamell," which occurs in Milton, *Paradise Lost,* book 4, 149, has an enduring history that goes back into medieval literature. See here Prest, *The Garden of Eden,* 66, who quotes S. du Bartas, *His Divine Weekes and Workes,* J. Sylvester, trans., 1605: "With flowrie Ver's innameld tapistrie"; A. Marvell, *Bermudas:* "gave us this eternal Spring, / Which here enamells every thing." See also London and Wise, *The Retir'd Gard'ner,* 234: "the Enamel of the Flowers"; and Dezallier d'Argenville in *La Théorie et la pratique du jardinage,* Paris, 1722, 258: "le mélange émaillé de toutes sortes de couleurs."

[134] See, for example, the well-known illustration in Crispin de Passe, *Hortus Floridus,* 1614, or the painting by Frans Decker, "De tuin van het Proveniershuis in Haarlem," 1707, a detail of which is reproduced on the cover of E. de Jong, *Natuur en Kunst: Nederlandse tuin-en landschapsarchitectuur, 1650–1740,* Amsterdam, 1993.

[135] See here MacDougall, *Fountains, Statues, and Flowers,* 238, for evidence that Italian gardeners of the 17th century were advised to leave ample space around the individual plant to allow for air and light.

26. Painting of the flower garden at Pierrepont House, Nottingham, ca. 1705, artist unknown. Yale Center for British Art, Paul Mellon Collection (photo: courtesy of John Dixon Hunt)

27. Painting of Gerard van der Rijp in his town garden, showing flower beds with sparse planting, ca. 1700, artist unknown. Kerkaraad van de Verenigde Doopsgezinde Gemeente (photo: courtesy of Erik de Jong)

retard bloom so that all the bulbs flowered at the same time, then it is conceivable that a perfect climax could have been achieved over several weeks in the spring.[136] Yet, there is no indication in his writings that he followed this practice. His entry on tulips, for example, which is included in the "Elysium Britannicum," states, "The early or Precoces Tulipes begin to flower in the end of March, and the rest about the middle of Aprill, and are all past by the end of May."[137] Moreover, the resources at Bettisfield may have allowed only for autumn planting, not for "bedding out," and so the bulbs would have followed their normal succession. Thus, Hanmer's third bed might have looked spick-and-span in March or April, when the narcissi were in flower; but by May to June, only the fritillary, iris, and *Scilla peruviana* would have been in bloom. The symmetry of the four tall *Fritillaria persica*[138] would have been offset by the asymmetry of the irises and the one *Fritillaria pyrenaica,* and by the fact that the narcissi were no longer flowering. In the context of the garden as a whole, however, Hanmer's third bed might have been balanced by what was in bloom in other beds in May or June.

Such variation within order may have been as instinctive as variable spelling at the time. Or it may have resulted from the fact that gardeners were often moving plants around each season, as Keith Goodway has demonstrated for Beaufort House, Chelsea, in the 1690s.[139] Tom Wright has suggested that the exceptionally cold seasons of the period from 1670 to 1700 may have contributed to the practice of rearranging the planting every year.[140] Yet, there must always have been alteration attributable to experimentation with new and rare flowers. Hanmer records, for example, that one of the three "Iris dell'Abbaye" had died, and the following season he might not have been able or might not have wanted to replace it in kind. Evelyn also points out that soil needs regular renewal "every 3d or 4th yeare," and that this is better done "yeare by yeare successively, now one bed, now another, to avoyd disturbing the whole garden at once, & discomposing the order"; and in the case of Anemones, Evelyn writes, "Every two {or 3} yeares you may do well to take them out of the . . . beds . . . & truly in out climat to prevent the snows & cold thawes a caution not amisse."[141] This might have led to further variations from bed to bed, from year to year.

[136] Elstob, *Garden Book of Sir Thomas Hanmer,* xxii. See MacDougall, *Fountains, Statues, and Flowers,* 233, for evidence of forcing and retarding bloom in Italian gardens of the 17th century.

[137] "Elysium Britannicum," 282.2.

[138] *Fritillaria persica* seems to be of variable height. According to a range of sources from Philip Miller to the R.H.S. *Dictionary of Gardening,* it may achieve three feet but is often much lower in stature, around fifteen to eighteen inches. I have assumed in my illustration the possibility of a maximum height. To help visualization, I have also shown an extended flowering period, even though it would often be over by May.

[139] See here Duthie, "Planting Plans," 88–102, and the *Planting of Gardens, 1660–1705,* a collection of papers prepared for a research seminar at Chelsea Physic Garden, October 26, 1992, edited and distributed by Lorna McRobie, English Heritage, 1993. Goodway's paper is entitled "Seasonal and Annual Changes in Planting," 49–50.

[140] Tom Wright, "The British Climate and Weather during this Epoch," 55–60, in *Planting of Gardens, 1660–1705* (as above, note 139), which includes interesting extracts from Evelyn's diary from 1684 to 1706.

[141] "Elysium Britannicum," 279 and 291. In reference to Anemones, Evelyn adds: "Gardners will, I believe, not soone forget the yeare 1662" (p. 291). The indication of the date after which Evelyn must have written this passage, is noteworthy. See here also Rea, *Flora,* 9: "And every year, as your stocks increaseth, you may dispose them according to your own fancy, or alter the places of any Roots that lose their Fibres, at your pleasure; but such Flowers, whose Roots retain them are considerately to be placed at first, where they may stand divers years without removing."

28. Flower garden illustrated in Joseph Furttenbach, *Architectura privata,* 1641 (photo: Dumbarton Oaks)

When we look at illustrations of the period, it is worth remembering that the artist presented an ideal portrait of the planting; the flowering seasons are often compressed so as to render a composite picture, akin to still lifes or representations of fireworks in the period. This compression may have been realized in practice through forcing and retarding bloom but would have required enormous expenditure of labor.[142] Nevertheless, whether ideal or real, artists' representations allow us to recognize certain ordering principles, including that of seeming randomness in the midst of strict geometry. Two illustrations from Germany offer good examples.[143] The first is in Joseph Furttenbach's *Architectura privata* (1641) (Fig. 28). The hierarchical structure of the planting is unlike the graduation mentioned by Evelyn. It is closer to the composition of a vase of flowers in a still life. An extra-large specimen of a crown imperial, for example, dominates the center of the composition; four smaller ones accentuate the axes of the cross-shaped middle bed. Lilies also provide similar accents at the corners of the surrounding beds, or as counterpoint to the predominant rows of tulips. Yet, they are not always symmetrically disposed, and the enormous variety in colors and types of tulip would also

[142] See MacDougall, *Fountains, Statues, and Flowers,* 236–37, where it is suggested that each individual flower might have received its own "pocket" of soil when "bedded out." See also "Elysium Britannicum," 278, where Evelyn mentions that there are "some so curious about this particular alone, as to prescribe a peculiar soil for every plant."

[143] These are discussed in Hansmann, "Parterres," 162–64.

militate against a uniform impression. Furthermore, the smaller narcissus, hyacinths, anemonies, etc., that are interplanted between tulips and lilies would break up the otherwise rhythmic structure of the planting.

The anonymous painting of a flower garden on the outskirts of Hamburg in the first half of the seventeenth century provides an image in color.[144] Here the ordering principle appears to be unwavering symmetry to the right of the central axis, with modified symmetry to the left. Some of the beds are mixed, but most are devoted to single types of flower such as tulips. Plants in pots play an important visual role; they help balance the regularity of the design. There is little sense of an overall graduation, as Evelyn proposed. Yet, it is clear from other examples, whether in Italy or the Low Countries, that no one organizing system was followed in Europe as a whole.[145]

John Harvey's identification of the plants listed by Evelyn in the chapter on the Coronary Garden[146] allows us to visualize his own organizing system for shrubs as well as flowers. It is clear, for instance, that tender plants in pots and boxes would have played a role in his flower garden, just as they had done in the grove. These included the acacia (*Acacia farnesiana*), jasmines (*Jasminum humile* and *J. sambac*), the lignum vitae (? *Guiacum officinale*), the sensitive plant (*Mimosa sensitiva*), oleander (*Nerium oleander*), and passion flower (*Passiflora incarnata*), among many others.

Some of these would have been plunged into warm borders or placed in glass frames. The instructions for the humble and sensitive plant (*Mimosa pudica* and *M. sensitiva*), for example, are "plunging the pott in the Earth, & keeping it covered with a Glasse . . . when the Sun shines not out."[147] The *Pelargonium triste* from the Cape of Good Hope, first sent to the Tradescants from René Morin in 1631, was likewise best preserved in winter by "setting the pott under a south wall, & covering it with mosse, & a bell glass, or better in the Conservatory."[148] But the pomegranate, prickly pear, and passion flower we may imagine arranged on paths and along walls in summer like the rows of containers in the Hamburg painting. They might have been combined with a few hardy plants grown in pots for decorative effect—cyclamens, cistus, ranunculus, or peonies. "The Male [*Paeonia mascula*] is more choyce, & therefore by Somer set in a pott or . . . case,"[149] comments Evelyn.

In the case of the passion flower, Evelyn specifies that it should be trained up a stake, "for it will else grovell."[150] This was true of a number of climbing plants: *Phaseolus coccineus* (the scarlet bean), for example, or the everlasting pea (*Lathyrus latifolius*), or *Pharbitis hederacea* (morning glory),

[144] Ibid., fig. 31, p. 145.

[145] See, for example, the planting plans discussed by G. Masson, "Italian Flower Collector's Gardens in Seventeenth-Century Italy," in D. R. Coffin, ed., *The Italian Garden,* Washington, D.C., 1972; see also MacDougall, *Fountains, Statues, and Flowers,* 221–347, esp. 233; Segre, "Coronary Flower Garden," for a detailed study of the Cisterna flower garden.

[146] John Harvey, "The Plants in John Evelyn's 'Elysium Britannicum,'" pp. 221–68.

[147] "Elysium Britannicum," insertion on p. 301.

[148] Ibid., insertion on p. 296. See also the list in "Directions," for "Coronarie Flowers" (p. 24), and for rarer exotic flowers, including those to be raised in the hot beds (p. 26). Here we find the "Bellvedere" and oranges and lemons mentioned along with some other plants listed in chapter 16 of "Elysium Britannicum" and on page 32, for trees and shrubs that Evelyn considered "rare" and probably suitable, therefore, for the Coronary Garden.

[149] Ibid., insertion on p. 299.

[150] Ibid., 304.

for which Evelyn recommends "a stake or threid to climb by."[151] Other tall flowers, such as the hollyhock, were, of course, staked for practical reasons, especially to guard against wind, but the training of these climbing plants on poles was also an aesthetic question. Combined with topiary and standard shrubs, they provided a vertical accent, as did carnations supported on sticks or rods. We may imagine them disposed in rhythmic intervals along the beds of the Coronary Garden (see Fig. 27). Clipped evergreens, as well as shrubs trained into obelisks and balls, appear to have provided terminal accents at the corners or ends of the bed (see Fig. 26). Evelyn speaks of the honeysuckle, shaped like a cypress or a globe, "being planted at the head . . . {or} corners of *Coronary* beds, & sustaind by a stake at moderate hight."[152] As a mopheaded standard, the honeysuckle would branch at around three feet, thus forming a miniature tree of about five feet. As an obelisk, the flowers would be carried from the ground upwards.[153] For the corners of larger compartments, *Cercis siliquastrum* (Judas tree) is proposed;[154] a white double-flowered cherry, *Prunus cerasus flore pleno,* appears, along with the double-flowered peach, *Prunus persica plena,* as suitable for wall fruits.[155]

Flowering shrubs trainable into miniature trees included various roses, when "shaped into a comely forme,"[156] and *Spartium junceum* (Spanish broom), which "makes a pretty heading, & also dos well for shew in standard."[157] Evergreens used as topiary included cypress, alaternus, bays, laurels, arbutus, etc., and the phillyrea, which Evelyn calls the "most proper to forme into knobbs & boules."[158] Citrus fruit and clipped myrtles in cases were also, according to Evelyn, "placed in your Walkes & at the head of Beds & Compartements."[159] But many climbing plants and "tonsile" shrubs were used to form hedges or to clothe walls: *Arbutus unedo, Campsis radicans, Pyracantha coccinea, Jasminum officinale, Rhamnus alaternus,* etc.[160]

Having itemized the various woody plants that belong in the Coronary Garden and described their uses, Evelyn reminds the reader:

> onely the Flowers are the chiefe; & the . . . Trees, Shrubbs Spires, boales & pyramids, of the taller plants, but the lesser Ornaments; of which if there seeme to have bin too many introduced in this Chapter, the Choice & admission is in the breast of our Gardiner, he may make what collation he pleases; but some he ought of necessitie to make best but for the . . . fortifing of Nose-Gays, Garlands, & other flowry ornaments which without some verdure will be . . . defective.[161]

[151] Ibid., insertion on p. 301.

[152] Ibid., 307.

[153] Ibid. In an insertion, Evelyn comments on how the French trained the suckers of the honeysuckle into the main stem, but he seems to prefer a single stem with the suckers removed entirely. Other plants used at the "heads of bordures" included *Daphne mezereum, Viburnum tinus,* and *Syringa vulgaris* (p. 278).

[154] Ibid., 302–3, insertion.

[155] Ibid., 306, insertion.

[156] Ibid., 307.

[157] Ibid., 304.

[158] Ibid., 307.

[159] Ibid., 306; see also 278, where Evelyn mentions *Solanum pseudocapsicum* and *Nerium oleander.*

[160] Ibid., 302–7.

[161] Ibid., 307.

In other words, there was no one prescription for Evelyn's Coronary Garden; its composition was as various as the flowers themselves, "producing ten thousand varieties, & glorious beauties perfuming the aire, & ravishing all the senses."[162] Indeed, it had lost its specific "coronary" purpose, and the flowers signified more than their original association with garland-making or nosegay-arranging. They were there for beauty and for curiosity, and they were at once symbolic, medicinal, esculent, and even cosmetic: the roots of the asphodel "makes the haire to come curled,"[163] and the *Fritillaria meleagris,* by its chequered "signature," was there "to take away spotts & freckles."[164]

The approach to color composition was no doubt equally various. Evelyn refers to the one example of Sir Henry Fanshaw at Ware Park. He is, of course, alluding to the account in Henry Wotton's *The Elements of Architecture* (1624), in which Fanshaw "did so precisely examine the *tinctures,* and *seasons* of his *flowres,* that in their *setting,* the *inwardest* of those which were to come up at the same time, should be alwayes a little *darker* then the *outmost,* and to serve them for a kinde of gentle *shadow,* like a piece not of *Nature,* but of *Arte.*"[165]

We can only attempt to imagine such effects; they remain open questions, as with much else in the history of planting design in Evelyn's time. They cannot be reconstructed in the mind, and they cannot be replicated in the living form. Almost none of the vast array of tulips that Evelyn and his contemporaries described so lovingly exists today: the "Paltots," the "Morillion," the "Achates," the "Marquetine."[166] We can only look at a still life of the period (Fig. 29) and listen to Evelyn's voice:

> Whith what delight & satisfaction dos our Gardiner {then} behold some {of these} moddest {&} flowery {Nymphs} mantled in their greene scarfes, others halfe dressed (in the . . . smocks of lawne) or indeede hardly borne! You would take some to be clad in white sattin {or so much figured snow} pinked plaited, chambletted & embroiderd & chammare'd with gold; some have the resemblance of a soft mother of pearle, or a tender Emra{u}ld; some like golden bells, silver, & of {flexible} Saphire, others . . . present you with inammeled capps, pretty paniers, & boxes lined with crimson damaske. . . . {with} vasetts of chrystall {achates} & rubies {of a gemmy luster} Their colours are . . . purpurine, celestiall: incarnadine, blushing Aurora, & virgine-white so innocent, so faire {& smiling upon you} sparkleling lively, orient, flaming & radiant: They peepe . . . {out of} their buds as out of so many Eyes {mealting & trickling into tears of joy} & turne themselves into a hundred thousand formes & protean changes.[167]

Only through these words and images can the flower garden of three hundred years ago come alive

[162] Ibid., 275.

[163] Ibid., 293.

[164] Ibid., 297.

[165] Ibid., 277. This passage is quoted from "Henry Wotton (1568–1639)," in Hunt and Willis, *The Genius of the Place* (as above, note 64), 49.

[166] See here Duthie, *Florists' Flowers and Societies,* 70, where she states that "Konings-Kroon" is today's "Keizerkroon" and that "Duke van Thol" tulips "are still on the market and closely resemble the species *T. schrenkii.*" I am grateful to Prudence Leith-Ross for this reference.

[167] "Elysium Britannicum," 319.

29. Vase of flowers, by Roelandt Savery, 1624. Collection of the Centraal Museum, Utrecht (photo: courtesy of Erik de Jong)

for us as it did for Evelyn every spring after the "last cruell Winter"—"a kind of Resurrection from the dead."[168]

Evelyn died on February 27, 1706, and was buried at Wotton, where he had lived since 1694.[169] By 1706 much had changed in the world of gardening. The French sites that Evelyn had visited in the 1640s and 1650s had been eclipsed by André Le Nôtre's work at Vaux-le-Vicomte and Versailles. The *parterre de broderie, parterre de pièces coupées pour des fleurs* and *parterre à l'angloise* had supplanted the knot, the fret, and "trayle-work." Het Loo and Hampton Court had both been redesigned by the 1690s, and the earl of Essex had planted the forest garden of Cassiobury in the 1670s.

Evelyn's involvement in woodland or "extensive gardening," as exemplified by Cassiobury, is all too evident: through the exchanges with John Beale, through the publication of *Sylva* in 1664, and through the expansion of this work in subsequent editions to the end of his life.[170] In contrast,

[168] For Evelyn's association with millenarianism, see Parry, "John Evelyn as Hortulan Saint," 137–38. See further "Elysium Britannicum," 275.

[169] See de Beer, *Diary*, V, 179.

[170] See here D. Chambers, "'Wild Pastorall Encounter': John Evelyn, John Beale and the Renegotiation of Pastoral in the Mid-Seventeenth Century," in Leslie and Raylor, *Culture and Cultivation* (as above, note 4), 173–94, esp. 183. See also D. Chambers, *The Planters of the English Landscape Garden: Botany, Trees and the Georgics,* London and New Haven, 1993; M. Leslie, "The Spiritual Husbandry of John Beale," in Leslie and Raylor, *Culture and Cultivation,* 151–72; and Goodchild, "'No phantasticall utopia,'" 105–27.

no such clear progression in hortulan thinking is discernible in those revised chapters of the "Elysium Britannicum" devoted to parterre, grove, and flower garden. The insertion of lists of evergreens suggests, it is true, that Evelyn's revisions were keeping pace with new plant introductions,[171] and a cursory reference to Vaux-le-Vicomte in one interlineation indicates a tentative acknowledgment of Le Nôtre's work.[172] Furthermore, as Douglas Chambers has made abundantly clear in his essay in this volume, Evelyn's continued engagement in new developments in garden design shines through the pages of his correspondence, if not through the pages of the manuscript itself, for example, in the exchanges with Robert Berkeley over Zorgvliet and Enghien in 1686/87.[173] Yet, despite all this and for whatever reason, it must be affirmed that the main text of the "Elysium Britannicum" (as it has come down to us today) remains rooted in the horticulture and planting design of the 1650s and 1660s.

The formative influences on Evelyn's concept of ornamental planting were various and complex. Firstly, there were the gardens seen on his visits to France and Italy—Pierre Morin's garden in Paris, for example, and sites like Richelieu and the Villa Borghese; in addition, there were other European gardens, known through publications as much as direct experience, which offered a subsidiary source of ideas—Salomon de Caus's *Hortus Palatinus,* for example.[174] Secondly, there were the antique and modern texts, from Pliny to Francis Bacon. Among these, Boyceau's *Traité* published in 1638 was undoubtedly a primary source of ideas on the parterre and grove. Thirdly, with regard to the flower garden, there were the works of botanists and florists, most of them homegrown horticultural writers. It is surely significant that these modern authorities were active in the early to mid-seventeenth century and not later: There was John Gerard, for example, who died in 1612—Evelyn used Johnson's revised edition of Gerard's *Herball,* published in 1633—and G. B. Ferrari, whose *Flora* appeared in 1633 and 1638. (Evelyn's own copy is in the British Library in London.)[175] There was John Parkinson, who died in 1650; John Rea, who produced his *Flora* in 1665;[176] Sir Thomas Hanmer, who was active at Bettisfield from 1646 to 1678; and Pierre Morin, who published his catalog in 1651.

[171] This is implied by the date of introduction of some of the plants listed and confirmed in the correspondence. See here Harvey's, "Plants in John Evelyn's 'Elysium Britannicum,' " where he suggests a date ca. 1685 for the later insertions; see also, for example, the correspondence cited by Chambers, " 'Elysium Britannicum not printed,' " 121: Evelyn with John Walker and Daniel Parke in the 1690s.

[172] "Elysium Britannicum," 128.

[173] See Chambers, " 'Elysium Britannicum not printed,' " 127. There are a few indications of very late insertions—for example, "{Here consult Bernard Lamg? Translated into English, printed 1702: you have in your library at Wotton. Pag 123 etc.}" (p. 161)—but these are rare and do not relate to planting as such.

[174] See the "Elysium Britannicum," 166, insertion. There is an interesting list of "Names of such Workemen as have excelled in their calcographicall descripiptions [*sic*] . . . both of Gardens & their Ornaments." This confirms familiarity with the Mollets' work on broderie. The reference to "that large Cutt of the Heidelburg gardn," which is deleted (perhaps because of the incorrect authorship—Issac, instead of Salomon de Caus), implies some knowledge of *Hortus Palatinus,* which is further strengthened by the reference to Salomon de Caus and Heidelberg on p. 271.

[175] John Harvey has established that Evelyn used Johnson's revised edition of the *Herball* from the code Evelyn used in MS 38 at Christ Church.

[176] See here the reference in Chambers, " 'Elysium Britannicum not printed,' " 123, to the letter to Robert Boyle of November 23, 1664, in which he mentions John Rea's "very usefull booke." See also "Elysium Britannicum," 293, margin note, in which Sir Thomas Hanmer's comments allude to 1667, thus suggesting when this material was incorporated into the manuscript.

If Evelyn's concept of parterre, grove, and flower garden developed beyond those formative years, as we might expect, then clues could be found through a detailed study of his correspondence, and through locating other parts of the manuscript, especially the missing "figures," "draughts," and "plotts." Further research into the evolution of planting at Sayes Court could also throw light on his mature ideas on planting design and on the way he absorbed new ideas from Europe. The conjectural reconstruction of the parterre and grove from the 1653 plan certainly reveals a designer of considerable flair and ingenuity, adjusting the models seen on the Continent and at home to the small scale of his site. Adjustment was inevitable. Sayes Court was after all more of a gentry than a princely garden; its purpose and its proportions were other than the grand Continental prototypes. In this sense, it must be admitted that Sayes Court provides only a limited visual counterpart to the verbal constructs of the "Elysium Britannicum"—"The Plan of a Royal Garden."[177] It remains a valuable counterpart nonetheless.

The functions and forms of a graciously representative garden such as Richelieu had little relationship to the personal spaces of Sayes Court: Evelyn's "Elaboratorie with a Portico of 20 foot long upon Pillars open towards the Private Garden,"[178] for example. Moreover, although French influences may have been dominant in shaping details of the parterre and grove in 1653, the translation of French into English did not extend to the structure of the garden as a whole. What strikes the eye immediately in the overall layout is the additive, compartmentalized, and seemingly random ordering of the parts that reflects little of French Baroque hierarchies. There may have been an axial approach to the house, but the overall alignments are askew, like the wings of the house itself. In this sense, the Sayes Court layout of 1653 retained something essentially English in its composition, something alien to the French way of ordering space.

Evelyn was later to write to Berkeley of the Dutch "Veneration of *Flora,* and the parterre," and went on to extol the gardens of the Netherlands: "tho the French at present may boast of their vast designee [*sic*], their *Versailles* and portentous workes; yet Gardens can no where be so spruce, and accurately kept."[179] In this letter of 1686, Evelyn seems to eschew the grandiose effects of royal gardening that he had ostensibly celebrated in those earlier years. But what does this tell us about the development of his ideas and his gardening at Sayes Court after 1653?

Acquaintance, vicarious or direct, with Continental and English designs in the 1670s, 1680s, and 1690s would certainly have affected his own planting at Sayes Court. In 1678, for example, he visited the gardens of Ham House and Cassiobury. In 1680 he returned to Cassiobury and recorded details of the earl of Essex's woodland garden. In 1685 he was at Swallowfield and in 1688 at Althorp and Hampton Court. Yet, all we know of the later layout at Sayes Court is from two plans from about 1690–1700 (Figs. 30 and 31). These seem to suggest an elimination of the parterre, an enlargement of the grove, and a new (perhaps even Baroque) axiality.

[177] It should be noted that although Evelyn intended the "Elysium Britannicum" to be "chiefly for the divertissement of Princes, noble-men and greate persons," he does qualify this: it "may (we hope) be of exceeding use also, and emolument for persons of all Conditions whatsoever, who are either Masters of, or delight in Gardens" (p. 3).

[178] "Explanation of the Particulars."

[179] See Chambers "'Elysium Britannicum not printed,'" and his reference to letter book, 538, on p. 127.

30. "A colored plan of the manor of Sayes Court, in the parish of Deptford, the property of John Evelyn, Esq., as surveyed by Joel Gascoyne in 1692." British Library, King George III's Topographical Collection, K. Top. XVIII. 17. 2 (photo: By permission of the British Library)

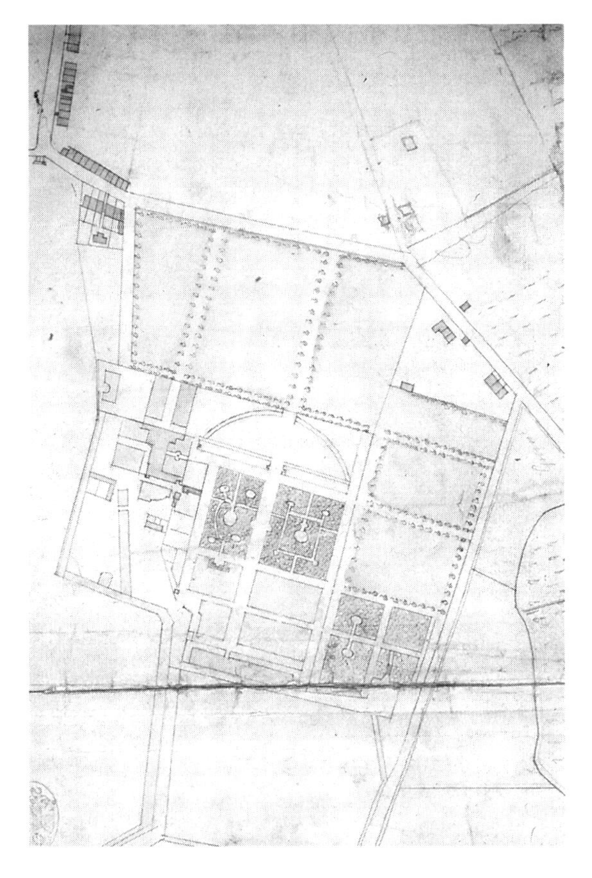

31. "A colored plan of the manor of Sayes Court, in the parish of Deptford with the dock-yard; drawn apparently about 1700 [by John Grove?]." British Library, King George III's Topographical Collection, K. Top. XVIII. 17. 3 (photo: By permission of the British Library)

In a letter of December 13, 1670, to Sir Thomas Hanmer, it is surely significant that he speaks of being "wholly addicted to the propagation of Foresters & rusticities of that nature" and of having "miserably neglected my little Flower garden."[180] This may imply that the garden at Sayes Court was already changing in the direction of the extensive groves that appear in the later plans. However, until further research is possible, only tentative conclusions should be drawn on what these changes signify. Evelyn's increasing preoccupation with extensive woodland gardening was just one impulse that may have affected the layout at Sayes Court. The plain lawns and enlarged groves were, after all, entirely in keeping with a widespread stylistic shift in English garden design after 1660: an impulse to simplicity, exemplified in the eight unadorned grass plots at Ham House. But the pronounced axiality of the later layout—a more coherent organization around a central axis—could also indicate

[180] Ibid., reference to letter book, 332, on p. 117. There could have been religious or royalist/republican influences at work in Evelyn's shift from flowers to "rusticities" in the years after the Restoration. See here Goody, *The Culture of Flowers,* 202–5.

that Baroque influences, whether from the Continent or from less "portentous" layouts within England, were reflected in these alterations. On the other hand, it is equally conceivable that the neglect of his "little flower garden," in favor of "rusticities," simply betokened pressures of upkeep or shortages of time and resources.

It must be admitted that beyond the evidence of these plans, we are reliant on mere fragments: the handbook "Directions for the Gardiner at Says-court" (1687) and some miscellaneous remarks in his diary and other writings. There is, for example, one entry in his diary of 1684 as to how evergreens, including cypress, were damaged by the severe frosts of that winter,[181] and there is the reference in a letter of January 12, 1685, to being "forc'd quite to alter my poore Garden" through those frosts.[182]

Thus, while the manuscript "Elysium Britannicum" appears locked in the horticulture of the mid-seventeenth century, Evelyn's gardening at Sayes Court progressed over nearly five decades: from the garden plan of 1653 to the end of the century, when another form of damage was inflicted on one particular evergreen. In 1698, while staying at Sayes Court, Peter the Great was pushed back and forth through the holly hedge in a wheelbarrow. As Evelyn later recalled:

> Is there under *Heaven* a more glorious and refreshing Object of the kind, than an impregnable *Hedge* of about *four hundred foot* in *length, nine* Foot *high,* and *five* in *diameter;* which I can shew in my now ruin'd *Gardens* at *Say's-Court* (thanks to the *Czar* of *Moscovy*) at any time of the Year, glitt'ring with its arm'd and varnish'd *Leaves?* The taller *Standards* at orderly distances, blushing with their natural *Coral:* It mocks at the rudest assaults of the *Weather, Beasts,* or *Hedge breakers.*[183]

Between these two dates lies a changing world, in which inveterate ways and inchoate ideas came together for the first time. It is hard to situate John Evelyn's protean vision of gardening in that changing world. On the one hand he may be viewed as the traditionalist, perpetuating the forms and systems of early- to mid-seventeenth-century garden design, for example, in his attachment to the vocabulary of "knotts," "fretts," and "embossements," or in his patchwork structuring of the garden at Sayes Court in 1653. On the other hand, he may be viewed as an innovator: in his introduction of alaternus for hedging; in his promotion of the word "parterre"; in his design for the highly original "oval Square" at Sayes Court; or in his advocacy of extensive landscaping after the inspiration of John Beale. Only through further intensive study of the "Elysium Britannicum" and other writings, through meticulous analysis of the documentation for Sayes Court, and through complementary case studies will it be possible to assess John Evelyn's decisive contribution to European horticulture and planting design during the second half of the seventeenth century.

[181] De Beer, *Diary,* 365.

[182] Chambers, "'Elysium Britannicum not printed,'" 127.

[183] J. Evelyn, *Silva; or a Discourse of Forest-Trees,* 4th ed., London, 1706, 182.

The Plants in John Evelyn's "Elysium Britannicum"

JOHN H. HARVEY

Great Britain, and more especially England, is unusually fortunate in the recording of garden plants and their dates of introduction. In a few instances, this goes back even to the fourteenth century, but it is William Turner's *The Names of Herbes* (1548) that first provides general coverage. The notable *Herball* of John Gerard (1597), as well as the *Paradisus Terrestris* (1629) and *Theatrum Botanicum* (1640) of John Parkinson, with various subsidiary sources, carry the story into the lifetime of John Evelyn. While most of the available lists are derived from inventories of what was grown in individual gardens, for example, those of the Tradescants in 1634 and 1656, or that of Sir Thomas Hanmer (1659, but not published until 1933), Evelyn drew upon literature, nursery catalogues, and voluminous correspondence with the gardeners of his time. In his "Elysium Britannicum," he was playing the role of master gardener, attempting to include everything worth growing. In particular, as we shall see, he concentrated attention on evergreens, which could form a grove of interest at all seasons, and on plants that were of purely aesthetic interest, then called coronary flowers. The content of his manuscript refers to the period between 1660 and 1685, comprising an original collection dating from before publication of his *Sylva* and *Kalendarium Hortense* (1664), and it includes additions that he made over the next twenty years. It seems, from what survives, that Evelyn made little or no effort to bring his work up to date during the last two decades of his life.

Evelyn's alternative titles, "The Plan of a Royal Garden" or "The Royal Gardens," may be significant here. The year 1660 witnessed the Restoration of Charles II, after nearly a generation of civil war and revolution. A new age of monarchical enthusiasm had dawned, and it is likely more than a coincidence that the death of the king in 1685, ushering in another period of political uncertainty, came at the end of Evelyn's serial annotations to his text. However true this may be, the categories of plants that he named in the course of twenty-five years, when grouped together, form a virtually complete horticultural conspectus, valid for southeastern England and the London area.

I wish to express my warm thanks to Mark Laird for the suggestion that I attempt this identification and for much subsequent help, to the late Richard Gorer whose expert botanical assistance has been essential, and to Dumbarton Oaks, which provided a copy of the transcription of "Elysium Britannicum" by John E. Ingram.

Thus, in listing his trees, shrubs, and flowers, we can re-create the garden flora of the reign of Charles II. After three centuries of neglect, this royal garden once more shines forth, thanks to the labors of John Ingram in transcribing meticulously all that remains.

Evelyn's listing is sharply divided into the two categories: one mainly of bulbs and herbaceous plants for the ornamental pleasure or coronary garden, the other of trees, shrubs, and underplants for the grove. There is little overlap between the two classes. It seems that the aim of the grove was to use the greatest possible variety of different evergreens, including large numbers of tender species that would have to be housed for the winter in a greenhouse or conservatory. A relatively short selection of deciduous trees[1] is prefaced to divide lists of evergreens into four sections: trees, shrubs, shrubs and herbs, and herbs.[2] A later insertion duplicates these lists but includes many additional species.[3] All identified species are included in the present lists.

The flowers begin with the tulip in variety and other bulbs,[4] continuing with herbaceous plants; again, there are later insertions.[5] Evelyn apparently based his original list on information from Sir Thomas Hanmer, baronet, of Bettisfield, Flintshire, in north Wales,[6] but then added to this tremendously as time went on. The period over which these additions were made may be roughly estimated from known dates of introduction of some species, but it is not intended here to attempt such dating in detail. What can be said is that the earliest draft lists go back approximately to the time of the Restoration in 1660;[7] a probable *terminus ante quem* is set by the mention of only one "Nasturtium indicum," as the arrival in 1686 of *Tropaeolum majus* could not have escaped Evelyn's notice.[8] Few other dates of introduction are so firmly recorded, but the inclusion of Prince's feather (*Amaranthus hypochondriacus*) of 1684,[9] and of several plants first noted in 1683—*Centaurea sempervirens, Juniperus phoenicea*, and *Quercus coccifera*—would appear to confirm a date of ca. 1685 for the later insertions.[10]

[1] "Elysium Britannicum," 98. The basis for this identification of Evelyn's plants is the transcription by John E. Ingram, 1992.

[2] "Elysium Britannicum," 99–100; at 307a, "our *Coronary Gardens* where onely the Flowers are the chiefe" are contrasted with the "Groves, Walks & thicketts." See also J. Harvey, "Coronary Flowers and Their 'Arabick' Background," in G. A. Russell, ed., *The 'Arabick' Interest of the Natural Philosophers in Seventeenth-Century England,* Leiden, 1994, 297–303.

[3] "Elysium Britannicum," 260.

[4] Ibid., 282.

[5] Ibid., at 282–301.

[6] See, e.g., ibid., 282–82.1: "(Here review & insert Sr T: Hanmers paper: of Tulip)"; "Sr: T: Hanmers paper." See I. Elstob, ed., *The Garden Book of Sir Thomas Hanmer, Bart.,* London, 1933, 18–26. The version printed was compiled by Hanmer in 1659. Two variant manuscripts of Hanmer's book are in the National Library of Wales, Aberystwyth: MS Bettisfield 1667 and MS 21753 B, both in Hanmer's hand. I am grateful to Peter Hayden for information on these manuscripts. Evelyn was obtaining further details from Hanmer in 1668; extracts from Hanmer's letter to Evelyn of May 1, 1668, are in *Garden History* 21 (1993), 117.

[7] "Elysium Britannicum," 326, refers to "the *Hortus Regius Blesensis* belonging to the late D(uke) of Orleans," who died on February 2, 1660. Page 337 refers to the Royal Society, founded under that name in 1661.

[8] C. Linnaeus, *Species Plantarum,* Stockholm, 1753, 345, states that the plant was brought to Europe in 1684; the introduction to Britain in 1686 is recorded in W. Aiton, *Hortus Kewensis,* London, 1789.

[9] S. Morris, "Legacy of a Bishop (Part 2)," *Garden History* 21 (1993), 20.

[10] Aiton, *Hortus Kewensis.*

No attempt is made here to identify the plants listed in chapter seventeen, "Of the Philosophico-Medicall Garden,"[11] though many of them had already appeared in the two ornamental categories. What is of considerable interest in this latter list is that Evelyn specifies the treatment required to display the tender plants, by setting them out in pots or in "cases." Such treatment would have been essential for a considerable number of the plants included in his grove and coronary garden. The cases were evidently boxes for carrying, of the kind extensively used for citrus fruits, and involved longer or shorter periods of overwintering, in an orangery or greenhouse.

Identification is simplified by Evelyn's classifications, into evergreen or deciduous; trees, shrubs, or herbs; and by his mentions of annual or biennial ("bisannual") duration. The Latin names used are occasionally specified as derived from one of several printed authorities. He used, among other books, Besler's *Hortus Eystettensis* (1613),[12] Caspar Bauhin's *Pinax* (1623),[13] Parkinson's *Paradisus* (1629),[14] and *Theatrum* (1640)[15] and, especially, Thomas Johnson's revised edition of Gerard's *Herball* (1633).[16] Some of Evelyn's lists of plants, parallel to those in "Elysium Britannicum,"[17] give page references to the 1633 Gerard. These are included here within parentheses, along with Latin and English synonyms derived from these papers.[18]

The grove seems to have been an attempt to recreate "eternal spring" by the use of evergreens of all types. Not only did Evelyn include evergreens in the strict sense, but also he remarks on the use of wild plants and annuals or biennials that could provide partial ground cover, even in winter, showing his dependence, inevitable in the English climate, upon any and every scrap of greenery that might show during the chilly months, or at least during some part of them.[19] In a few instances, the same botanical species appears as part of the grove and also as a coronary flower but, in the latter case, only as a double form.[20] Doubles are, indeed, often specified, being evidence of a noteworthy fashion of the time.

The coronary plants include annuals, biennials, and perennials, with bulbs and the occasional flowering shrub, but this is essentially a collection of what we would now describe as plants for beds and herbaceous borders throughout the year. Apart from a few isolated references, the names are in two alphabetical series, the first incorporating matter sent by Sir Thomas Hanmer[21] and also that

[11] "Elysium Britannicum," 321–30.

[12] B. Besler, *Hortus Eystettensis,* Altdorf, 1613; facsimile from 1713 edition, Grünwald b. München, 1964; see also G. G. Aymonin, ed., *The Besler Florilegium,* New York, 1989, with the plates in full color.

[13] C. Bauhin, *Pinax theatri botanici,* Basel, 1623.

[14] J. Parkinson, *Paradisi in Sole Paradisus Terrestris,* London, 1629; facsimile, *A Garden of Pleasant Flowers,* New York, 1976.

[15] J. Parkinson, *Theatrum botanicum,* London, 1640.

[16] J. Gerard, *The herball; or generall historie of plantes,* enlarged and amended by T. Johnson, London, 1633; facsimile, *The Herbal,* New York, 1975.

[17] Notably in Evelyn MS 38, British Library, London. I owe thanks to Mark Laird for references to this and other Evelyn papers.

[18] References to page numbers of Gerard (1633) are here noted in the lists with the initial G. and placed in parentheses.

[19] "Elysium Britannicum," 260, insertion.

[20] Compare *Chrysanthemum parthenium* in I.A and II.

[21] "Elysium Britannicum," 282–300.

from the printed catalogue of Pierre Morin of Paris.[22] The second alphabet was a lengthy supplement of plants regarded by Evelyn as "the lesse observable."[23] Some additional plants have been incorporated in the present list from Evelyn's *Directions for the Gardiner at Says-court* (1687);[24] these are distinguished by his names being placed within roman brackets. Plants found elsewhere than in the main lists (see above, notes 1–5) are indicated by the page number in parentheses.

In the lists that follow—I.A The Grove, I.B Deciduous trees and shrubs, II. Coronary plants—the modern scientific binomial is placed on the upper line, with Evelyn's Latin and English names below. His use of I and J, U and V, is preserved, but variant spellings of names are not noted. The nomenclature is, as far as possible, that of the *Dictionary of Gardening* of the Royal Horticultural Society,[25] but authorities have been added. Where generic names have been changed more recently, cross-references are given. When a question mark appears before a name, this indicates uncertainty even as to the genus; a query before the specific name implies insufficient evidence for precise identification but certainty as to the genus.

Prefixed to the Latin binomials are the letters E for evergreen and T for tender. Owing to the wide climatic variations in Britain, the latter indication may include plants that require hothouse treatment at one extreme or that may survive in the open with some protection at the other. All other entries are regarded as hardy in the London region and within much of Britain. The precise degree of protection contemplated by Evelyn remains an area for conjecture. Evelyn marked with an asterisk a group of seven species in his "Trees for the Taller Shades and maine of the Grove,"[26] namely, *Acacia arabica, Cinnamomum zeylanicum, Dracaena draco, Persea gratissima, Santalum album, Sassafras albidum,* and *Tamarindus indica,* on which he commented that each of these was "a stranger with us, but prompting to experiments."[27] It seems that he was inclined toward the view, then widely held, that even plants from the tropics might gradually be acclimatized. It remains doubtful whether he was ever able to grow such trees.

Apart from these, Evelyn listed a few plants now hard to understand, notably the China rose "or Ferrarius his rose of a rare beauty . . . yet strangers with us, but have ben perfected in Italy."[28] Are we to suppose that *Rosa chinensis* had already reached Europe before 1633, the date of publication at Rome of G. B. Ferrari's *De florum cultura?* It seems certain that it was not in Britain until after the middle of the eighteenth century. The "Indian" species of Evelyn's "Narcissus" and "Hyacinthus" remain obscure, though from Hanmer's more detailed descriptions,[29] and the entries in Parkinson's *Paradisus,*[30] it seems certain that they included at least *Brunsvigia gigantea* (Fig. 1), *Haemanthus coccineus,*

[22] P. Morin, *Catalogues de quelques plantes a fleurs,* Paris, 1651, with later editions in 1655 and 1658.

[23] "Elysium Britannicum," 301–2, with many insertions.

[24] G. Keynes, ed., *Directions for the Gardiner at Says-court,* London, 1932.

[25] F. J. Chittenden, ed., *Dictionary of Gardening,* 2nd ed., P. M. Synge, ed., London, 1956, corrected 1965; with *Supplement,* London, 1969.

[26] "Elysium Britannicum," 260, insertion.

[27] Ibid., 261, insertion; cf. 260, insertion.

[28] Ibid., 307, insertion.

[29] Elstob, *The Garden Book,* 26–37.

[30] Parkinson, *Paradisus,* 67–108, 111–34.

1. *Brunsvigia multiflora (gigantea)* (photo: from *Curtis's Botanical Magazine* 39 [1814], pl. 1619)

Hippeastrum equestre, Polianthes tuberosa, Sprekelia formosissima, and *Zephyranthes atamasco.* The group of British native orchids is also of interest, though in this Evelyn was following Parkinson.[31]

Each scientific name is followed by an indication of the type of plant: A, B, C1, P, S, T, indicating, respectively, annual, biennial, climber, perennial (bulb or herb), shrub, or tree. The colors of flowers are intended as generalizations, but some attempt has been made to distinguish the various shades of red and to discriminate between truly blue flowers and those so described in old authorities (but which were really mauve, purple, or violet). Seasons of flowering (in Britain) are mostly from Loudon's *Encyclopaedia of Plants,* which consistently provides overall seasons and not merely a single month.[32] The dates of introduction *to Britain* are those given by Aiton in *Hortus Kewensis,*[33] but some have been corrected by recent research; plants native to Britain are marked ———. Dates within parentheses are those of the earliest definite mention; for example, (1597) shows that the plant was stated to be in British gardens at the publication of Gerard's *Herball.*[34] Dates not within parentheses are believed to be those of the first introduction. Recent research has carried many dates back beyond the "1548" of Turner's *The Names of Herbes*[35] to several manuscript herbals compiled between ca. 1370 and 1390,[36] or as far as the basic list of Aelfric the Grammarian of A.D. 995. A few

[31] Ibid., 192–93.

[32] J. C. Loudon, *Encyclopaedia of Plants,* London, 1829.

[33] See above, note 10, and 2nd ed., W. T. Aiton, ed., London, 1810–13.

[34] J. Gerard, *The herball,* London, 1597.

[35] W. Turner, *The Names of Herbes,* London, 1548; facsimile, W. T. Stearn, ed., The Ray Society 145, London, 1965.

[36] Especially the Latin original of the "Agnus Castus" herbal, British Library, London, Sloane MS 2948, dated close to 1370; a herbal translated into English by John Lelamour in 1373, Sloane MS 5; and the herbals by Henry Daniel, OP (*Ordinis Predicatorum* = Order of Preachers = Black Friars), of ca. 1375–90, British Library, Arundel MS 42 and Add. MS 27329 (see J. Harvey, "Henry Daniel, a Scientific Gardener of the Fourteenth Century," *Garden History* 15 [1987], 81–93; and J. Harvey, *Mediaeval Gardens,* London, 1981; revised ed., 1990).

dates, mostly attributed by Aiton,[37] are later than Evelyn's death in 1706, but are now regarded as incorrect and are here placed within quotation marks.

The normal heights of the plants, given in inches and feet, are taken from standard reference books, but, in some instances, these differ greatly. In dealing with the grove, the heights are those likely to have been reached in the garden conditions of Evelyn's time.

For colored illustrations of most of Evelyn's plants it is now convenient to consult *The Besler Florilegium* of 1613,[38] here marked E. (Eichstatt), with plate number. For later introductions, references are given to the *Botanical Magazine*—thus, BM 7.227 up to volume fourteen (1800), the last edited by William Curtis, whose policy it was to publish traditional garden plants; later references are to plate numbers, as BM t.1740. References—M—are also given to the first five volumes (1825–34) of Benjamin Maund, *The Botanic Garden*. For roses, references are given to the numbered forms of Parkinson from his *Paradisus Terrestris* (e.g., P.8), and also to the colored plates of Mary Lawrance, *A Collection of Roses from Nature* (1796–99) (e.g., Lawr. t.22).[39] Most of the plants in these illustrations are likely to have remained substantially unaltered since the time of Evelyn. Where the same species is listed under both the grove (I) and coronary flowers (II), the full references are given only in section II.

The lists are here presented in alphabetical order of scientific binomials, but it has to be said that after some three centuries, "identification" is a relative rather than an absolute term, and is an interpretation rather than an equation. What is offered is a Linnean aggregate, probably covering a range of forms and even of varieties and subspecies, though some of these variants existed in Evelyn's time. A few plants have probably become extinct and are noted as such here. For the purpose of understanding the intentions of horticultural designers of the Restoration period in England, those identifications linked to colored illustrations, for the most part, should provide historians with an adequate clue. Where actual re-creation of gardens of the period is to be attempted, it will be necessary to seek modern forms that agree in appearance with the illustrations.

Identification has been largely based on the thorough investigation of the literature by William Aiton and his botanical advisors before the publication of *Hortus Kewensis* in 1789 and has been greatly assisted by the recent work of Prudence Leith-Ross, *The John Tradescants,* London, 1984. There has been independent correlation of early and modern names, carried out with the generous help of the late Richard Gorer, for the essential illustrated works: Besler, 1613; Parkinson, 1629; and Gerard/Johnson, 1633. Most of Evelyn's names are thus clearly intelligible and amount to more than 500 trees, shrubs, herbs, and bulbs available in his time to English foresters and gardeners.

[37] Aiton, *Hortus Kewensis* (as above, notes 10 and 33).

[38] See the editions, as above, note 12.

[39] Parkinson, *Paradisus,* 412–20.

The Lists of Plants in "Elysium Britannicum"

I.A The Grove: Evergreen trees, shrubs and herbs, with green underplants

E		ABIES alba Miller T. Abies or Firr (The firre tree. G.1363) E.4.iii		1603 90 ft
E	T	ACACIA arabica Willd. T. Acaceia Virg. Ægypt.		(1656) 12 ft
E		ACHILLEA ageratum L. P. Yellow Ageratum E.211.i	August–October	(1570) 1½ ft
E		? ACHILLEA alpina L. P. White Balsamita flo: alb:	July–November	"1731" 6 in
E		ACHILLEA millefolium L. P. White/Pink Millefolium E.136.ii, iii	June–October	——— 2 ft
		Achillea—See also II		
	T	ADIANTUM capillus-veneris L. Fern Capillus veneris (Maidenhaire. G. 1143)		——— 9 in
E	T	AEONIUM arboreum (L.) Webb & Berth. S. Yellow Sedum arborescens (majus); Tree-housleeke E.352.i	January–March	1633 3 ft
E	T	AGAVE americana L. S. Aloe folio mucronato; Prickly sea house leek E.356; BM t.3654		1633 25 ft
		ALCHEMILLA vulgaris L. (xanthochlora) P. Yellowish-green Alchimilla E.103.ii	June–August	——— 1 ft
		ALLIUM ampeloprasum L. (porrum) P. Whitish Porrum E.202.i; BM t.1385		? 3–6 ft
		ALLIUM senescens L. P. Rose Allium montan: fol: Narciss: majus B. Pin. BM t.1150	June–July	(1596) 2 ft
		Allium—See also II		
E		ANASTATICA hierochuntica L. A. White (Rosa hierocontea major; Heath rose of Jerico G.1386) E.354.ii, iii; BM t.4400	July	(1597) 6 in
		Anchusa—See PENTAGLOTTIS		
		ANGELICA lucida L. B. Pale yellow Angelica lucida Cornuti Canadensis (bisan.)	July–August	(1640) 2 ft
		ANTENNARIA dioica (L.) Gaertner P. Pink/White Pilosella min: E.65.ii, iii; M 3.247	May–July	——— 3 in
E		ANTHEMIS (Chamaemelum) nobilis L. flore pleno P. White Chamaemelum (Cammomille G.754) E.276.iii; See also II	July–September	——— 1 ft
E		ANTHEMIS tinctoria L. P. Yellow Buphthalmum Offi:	July–August	——— 1½ ft

E T	ANTHYLLIS barba-jovis L. S. Pale yellow Barba Jovis, silver bush BM t.1927	March	1629 8 ft
E	ANTIRRHINUM majus L. Antirrhinum; See in II		
E	APIUM graveolens L. B. Greenish-white Apium	June–August	———— 2–4 ft
E	ARBUTUS unedo L. S. White Arbutus (Strawberry tree G.1496. Cane apple) See also II BM t.2319; M 4.361	September–December	———— 40 ft
E	ARCTOSTAPHYLOS alpina (L.) Sprengel S. Greenish-white Vaccinia nigr: Panon:	April–June	———— 6 in
	ARISARUM vulgare Targ.-Tozz. P. Livid purple Arisarum BM t.6023	April–June	(1596) 1 ft
E T	ARISTOLOCHIA rotunda L. P. Dark purple Aristolochia E.194.i	March–October	(1596) 2 ft
E	ARMERIA maritima (Miller) Willd. P. Pink-lilac Caryophyllus marinus (Thrift); See also II	May–August	———— 1 ft
	Armoracia—see COCHLEARIA		
	ARUM maculatum L. P. Pale green, spotted Arum E.33.i	May–July	———— 1 ft
E	ASARUM europaeum L. P. Dull brown Asarum E.102.ii	May	———— 9 in
E	ASPHODELINE lutea (L.) Reichenb. P. Yellow Asphodellus Luteus BM t.773; M 3.246 See also ASPHODELUS in II	May–June	(1596) 3 ft
	ASPLENIUM ruta-muraria L. Fern Herbae Capillares See also ADIANTUM capillus-veneris		———— 4 in
	ASPLENIUM trichomanes L. Fern Herbae Capillares See above and ADIANTUM		———— 6 in
	Asplenium—See also CETERACH, PHYLLITIS		
E	ASTRAGALUS tragacantha L. S. Pale yellow Tragacantha, Goats thorn (G.1328)	May–July	1629 1½–3 ft
E	ATRIPLEX halimus L. S. Greenish	July–August	1632 5 ft
	——— (Halimione) portulacoides L. S. Green Halymus, Portulaca marina, sea purslan (or shrubby sengreene G.523) E.342.ii	July–August	———— 2 ft
E	BARBAREA vulgaris R.Br. P. Yellow Barbarea	May–August	———— 1½ ft
E	BELLIS perennis L. Bellis; Daisie; See also II		
E	BETA vulgaris L. B. Green Beta	August	(1200) 1 ft
	Betonica—See STACHYS officinalis		

E		BRASSICA rapa L. B. Yellow Rapum	April	——— 2 ft
E		BRYUM murale L., etc. Muscus; Mosse; See also II		——— 1 in
E		BUPLEURUM fruticosum L. S. Yellow Seseli Æthiopicum frutex (Shrub sesili or hartwort of Æthiopia. G.1421)	July–September	(1596) 5–10 ft
E		BUXUS sempervirens L. T./S. Buxus; Box; See also II		
		CALAMINTHA ascendens Jordan P. Violet Calamintha E.232.ii	July–August	——— 2 ft
E		CALLUNA vulgaris (L.) Hull S. Purplish-pink [Fuzz] E.252.i	July–October	——— 2 ft
E	T	ERICA arborea L. S. White	March–May	(1658) 5-10 ft
E		——— ciliaris L. S. Bright pink BM 14.484	July–November	——— 1 ft
E		——— cinerea L. S. Purple M 5.434	June–September	——— 1–2 ft
E		——— mediterranea L. (erigena) S. Pink BM 14.471; M 1.74	March–May	(1648) 4 ft
E		——— tetralix L. S. Pale pink	June–August	——— 1 ft
E		——— vagans L. S. Purplish-pink Erica omnis generis; Heath	July–November	——— 3 ft
		CARDAMINE pratensis L. P. Cardamine; Ladys smocks; See also II		
		CARDARIA (Lepidium) draba (L.) Desv. P. White Draba repens	May–June	(1596) 1 ft
E	T	CARTHAMUS arborescens L. S. Yellow Carthamus Perennis BM t.3302	August	"1731" 6 ft
		Carthamus—See also II		
E		CEDRUS libani A. Rich. T. Cedrus Conifera Libani; (The Cedar tree of Libanus, G.1352)		1638 70–100 ft
E	T	CENTAUREA sempervirens L. P. Red, yellow Jacea Lusitan: semp: vir: "Babylon"	July–August	(1683) 2 ft
		Centaurea—See also II		
		Centranthus—See KENTRANTHUS		
E	T	CERATONIA siliqua L. T. (Fig. 2) Red & yellow Carube sive siliqua dulcis (Ceratia; The Carob tree or St. Johns bread. G.1429)	September–October	(1570) 15 ft
E		CETERACH officinarum DC. (Asplenium ceterach) Fern Asplenium or Ceterach		——— 9 in
		Chamaemelum—see ANTHEMIS		

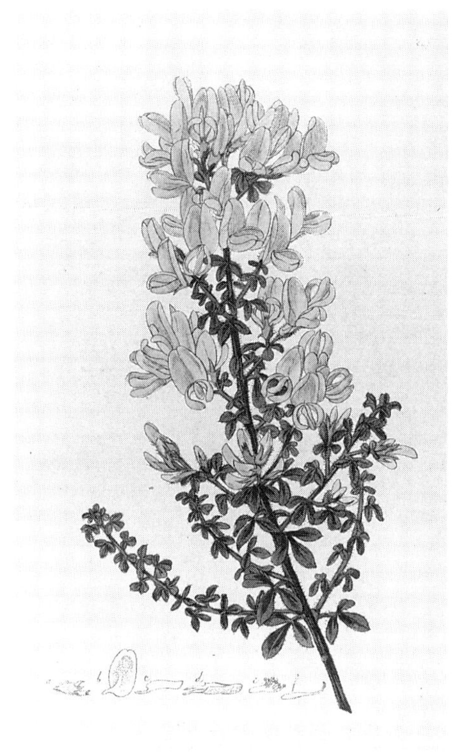

2. *Ceratonia siliqua*
(photo: from *The Botanist's Repository* 9 [1816], pl. 567)

3. *Cytisus canariensis*
(photo: from *Botanical Register* 3 [1817], pl. 217)

E		CHAMAEROPS humilis L. T. Chamaerriphus, Little wild date tree (G.1519) BM t.2152		"1731" 8 ft
E		CHEIRANTHUS (Erysimum) cheiri L. B./P. Viola Lutea; Keyri; See also II		
		CHELIDONIUM majus L. P. Yellow Chelidonium majus (Great Celandine. G.1069)	April–October	——— 2 ft
E		CHRYSANTHEMUM (Tanacetum) parthenium (L.) Bernh. P. White Matricaria; See also in II E.210.i	July–August	——— 3 ft
E	T	CINNAMOMUM zeylanicum Blume T. Green & yellow Canella; "We have seene a smale Cinnamon tree" BM t.2028	June–September	"1763" 20 ft
E		CISTUS albidus L. incanus S. Pale rosy-lilac (Cistus; Holly rose. G.1275)	June–July	(1596) 4 ft
E		CISTUS ladanifer L. S. White, crimson blotch Ladanum: (Ledon or Ladanum. G.1285) BM 4.112	June	(1629) 4 ft
		Cistus–See also in II		
E	T	CITRUS aurantifolia Swingle T. White Lyma	May–July	(1648) 10 ft
E	T	CITRUS aurantium L. T. White E.140.i, iii	May–July	(1595) 15 ft
E	T	——— sinensis (L.) Osbeck T. White Orange (Malus Arantia; Orange tree. G.1463)	May–July	(1595) 15 ft

E	T	CITRUS limonia Osbeck (limon) T. White Limon (Malus Limonia; Limon tree. G.1462)	May–July	(1648) 15 ft
E	T	CITRUS medica L. S. White (Malus Citronia; Malus Medica vel Citria; Citron tree) E.140.ii	May–July	(1648) 8 ft
E		? CLEMATIS cirrhosa L. S.Cl. Cream Clematis BM t.1070	January–March	(1596) 10 ft
E	T	CNEORUM tricoccon L. S. Yellow Chamaelea tricoccos, sive oleago vel oleustellus; Widow wail (or Spurge flax. G.1402)	June	(1596) 1–2 ft
		COCHLEARIA officinalis L. (Armoracia cochlearia) A./B. White Cochlearia	April–May	——— 1 ft
E	T	CONVOLVULUS cneorum L. S. Pale pink (Cneorum album oleae folio; White rock rose. G.1597) BM 13.459	May–September	(1640) 1-3 ft
		Convolvulus—See also in II		
		CRATAEGUS monogyna Jacq. T. White Spina acuta	June	——— 15 ft
		CRITHMUM maritimum L. P. White Crithmum marinum; Sampier; See also in II	July–September	——— 1 ft
		CROCUS sativus L. P. Lilac-violet Crocus E.191.iv	September–October	ca. 1340 6 in
		Crocus—See also in II		
E	T	CUPRESSUS sempervirens L. T. Cupressus; Cypresse; See also in II.		ca. 1375 150 ft
		Cymbalaria—See LINARIA cymbalaria		
		CYNOGLOSSUM officinale L. B. Dark purple Cynoglossum E.243.ii	June–July	——— 1–3 ft
E	T	? CYTISUS (Genista) canariensis (L.) Steud. S. (Fig. 3) Bright yellow Cytisus semper virens; evergreene shrub Trefoile; Genista	May–July	1659 6 ft
		Cytisus—See also in II		
E		DAPHNE cneorum L. S. Pale pink Cneorum Mathioli; white rockrose BM 9.313; M 3.256	May–June	(1629) 1 ft
E		DAPHNE laureola L. S. Yellowish-green Laureola (Spurge Laurel. G.1404)	February–March	——— 2–5 ft
		DAUCUS carota L. lucida B. White Daucus lucida	July–August	‘1807’ 2 ft
E		DIANTHUS barbatus L. Armeria; See also in II		
E		DIANTHUS caryophyllus L. Caryophullus (Gilloflowers of all sorts) See also in II.		
		DORONICUM pardalianches L. P. Yellow Doronicum Roman: E.19.i	May	——— 3 ft
E	T	DRACAENA draco L. T. White Draco BM t.4571		(1640) 10 ft

E		EQUISETUM hyemale L. P. Equisetum [Dutch Rush]		———— 1½ ft
		ERANTHIS hyemalis (L.) Salisb. P. Aconitum hyemale; (Winter Wolfe bane); See also II		
		Erica—See under CALLUNA		
		ERUCA sativa Miller A. Whitish Eruca	July	(1573) 1½ ft
E	T	EUPHORBIA officinarum L. S. Euphorbium		(1597) 6 ft
E		EUPHORBIA spp. Tithymalus et Esula		
		FOENICULUM vulgare Miller P. Yellow Foeniculum	July–August	———— 6 ft
E		FRAGARIA vesca L., etc. Fragrariae; Strawberries; See also II		
		Galeobdolon—See LAMIUM galeobdolon		
		Genista—See CYTISUS, SPARTIUM, and see also II		
		GENTIANA acaulis L. P. Gentianella verna; See also II		
E	T	GLOBULARIA alypum L. S. Pale blue Alipum montis Ceti; herb terrible (G.506)	August–September	1633 2 ft
E		GNAPHALIUM ? uliginosum L. A. Yellow (Gnaphalium siue Chamaexylum; Cudweede)	August	———— 1 ft
E	T	? GUIACUM officinale L. Lignum vita [or Arbor Thyrea]; See also II		
		Halimione—See ATRIPLEX		
E		HEDERA helix L. S.Cl. Yellowish-green Hedera; Ivy (G.858)	October–November	———— 40 ft
E		HELIANTHEMUM nummularium (L.) Miller (chamaecistus) Yellow Helianthemum E.282.ii; See also I.B	June–August	———— 6 in–1 ft
		HELLEBORUS niger L. P. Heleborus maj: See also II		
		HEPATICA triloba Choix (nobilis) P. Hepatica nobilis; See also II		
E	T	? HYPERICUM aegyptiacum L. S. Yellow Hipericum Alexand: BM t.6481	June	"1787" 2 ft
E	T	HYPERICUM coris L. S. Golden-yellow Coris BM 5.178, t.6563	May–September	(1640) 1 ft
E		HYSSOPUS officinalis L. S. Bluish-purple, &c Hissopus (Hyssope. G.579) E.283.ii-iv; BM t.2299; M 5.466	June	ca. 1200 1–2 ft
E		ILEX aquifolium L. S./T. Agrifolium; Holly; See also II		———— 30–80 ft
E	T	JASMINUM humile L. S. (Jasminum luteum Indicum; Yellow Jasmine. G.893); See also II		
		Jasminum—See also in I.B and II		

E		JUNCUS ? acutus L. P.		————
		Juncus		6 ft
E		JUNIPERUS communis L. S.		————
		Juniper minor (The Juniper tree. G.1372); See also II		15 ft
E		JUNIPERUS oxycedrus L. S./T.		"1739"
		Oxycedrus Phaenicea; crimson prickly cedar (Cedar Juniper, a shrub. G.1374)		15 ft
E		JUNIPERUS phoenicea L. S.		(1683)
		Juniper major		15 ft
E		JUNIPERUS sabina L. S.		(1200)
		Sabina or Cedrus Baccata; Savine (tree. G.1376)		4 ft
E		———— ———— tamariscifolia S.		1562
		[Spanish Juniper]		4 ft
		? KENTRANTHUS (Centranthus) ruber (L.) DC. P. Red/Pink/White	May–July	————
		Valeriana E.151.i		1½ ft
		Keyri—See CHEIRANTHUS cheiri in II		
		LAMIUM galeobdolon (L.) L. variegatum (Galeobdolon luteum) P. Yellow	May	————
		Lamium Luteum variega:		1½ ft
		Lamium—See also in II		
E		? LATHYRUS aphaca L. A. Yellow	June–July	————
		"Aphurea" (? Aphaca)		3 ft
		Lathyrus—See also in II		
E		LAURUS nobilis L. T.		(995)
		Laurus dommestica; Bay; common bays (G.1407) E.6.ii		20–30 ft
E		LAVANDULA spica L. (angustifolia) S. Pale grey-blue	July–September	(1265)
		Lavandula, sive stoechas E.310.ii,iii, 347.ii,iii		4 ft
	T	———— stoechas L. S. Purple	June	1568
		(Lauander of seuerall sorts. G.583); See also in II		3 ft
E		LAVATERA arborea L. B. Purple	July–October	————
		Malva arborescens (bisannual) E.221		6 ft
E	T	? LAVATERA maritima Gouan S. Pale pink & purple	May	(1597)
		Althea Cret. semp. Vir:		4 ft
E	T	? LAVATERA micans L. S. Purple	June–July	"1796"
		Malva hisp: Semp: vir: arboresc: rosea		3 ft
E		LEPIDIUM graminifolium L. P. White	June–September	(1683)
		Iberis Cardamantica		2 ft
		Lepidium—See also CARDARIA		
		LEVISTICUM officinale Koch P. Pale yellow	June	(995)
		Lygusticum		6 ft
E		LIGUSTRUM vulgare L. S.		
		Ligustrum; Privet; See also II		
E		LILIUM candidum L.		
		Lillium; See also in II		
E		LINARIA cymbalaria (L.), Miller (Cymbalaria muralis) P. Pale violet	May–November	(1617)
		Cymbalaria Italica E.220.ii; M 4.300		3 in

		LINARIA vulgaris Miller P. Linaria sylvest: See also II		
		LOBELIA cardinalis L. P. Trachelium Americanum; See also II		
		MARRUBIUM peregrinum L. P. White Marrubium odorat: E.224.iii, 231.ii	July–September	(1596) 1–3 ft
		MATTHIOLA incana (L.) R.Br. B. Leucoium; See also II		
E		MEDICAGO arborea L. S. Yellow Cytisus Maranthae sive cornutus; (horned shrub Trefoile. G.1305) [Cytisus lunatus] E.12.ii	May–November	(1596) 8 ft
		Medicago—See also II		
		MENTHA pulegium L. P. Pulegium (Penny royall); See also II		
E		? MYOSOTON (Stellaria) aquaticum (L.) Moench P. White Alsine	July	——— 1 ft
E	T	MYRTUS communis L. S.		
E	T	——— ——— flore pleno		
E	T	——— ——— ssp. tarentina Myrtills of severall sorts (The Myrtle tree. G.1411); See also II		
		Nasturtium—See RORIPPA		
E	T	NERIUM oleander L. S. Laurus Rosea, Nerium or Oleander (Laurus alexandrina. Rose Bay. G.1406); See also II		
		OENANTHE pimpinelloides L. P. White Oenanthe apij fol:	June–August	——— 2 ft
E	T	OLEA europaea L. T. Olea (Oliva; The Olive tree. G.1392)		(1570) 15–20 ft
		ONONIS spinosa L. (procurrens) S. Pink Anonis sive Resta Bovis (Ground furze. G.1322) E.263.iii	May–August	——— 1–2 ft
		ONOPORDON arabicum L. (nervosum) B. Purple Acanthium Lusitan:	July	"1686" 8 ft
		ONOPORDON illyricum L. B. Purple Acanthium illyricum	July–August	(1648) 6 ft
E	T	OPUNTIA ficus-indica (L.) Miller S. Opuntia, sive Ficus Indica (O. major, Indian Figg tree. G.1512)		
E	T	OPUNTIA vulgaris Miller (humifusa) S. Opuntia minor		
		Opuntia—See also II		
E	T	ORIGANUM creticum L. P. White Origanum Hisp. et Creticum; Majoram rotundo folio (Marjorum)	July–August	(1596) 1 ft
		ORIGANUM dictamnus L. P. Dictamus; Dittany of Crete; See also II		
E	T	ORIGANUM majorana L. Majoram; See also II		

		ORIGANUM ? onites L. P./S. Whitish Amaracus (Marjoran siue Sampsuchus) E.322.ii	July–November	"1759" 1 ft
		? ORIGANUM syriacum L. B. Marum syrianum; See also TEUCRIUM marum, and II		
		Origanum—See also II		
E		OTANTHUS maritimus (L.) Hoffm. & Link S. Yellow Gnaphalium maritimum	July–September	——— 9 in
		OXALIS acetosella L. P. White, veined purple Wood Sorrell (p. 95) E.94.ii	April–May	——— 3 in
E	T	PASSIFLORA incarnata L. S.Cl. Marecoh (Granadile or Passion Flower); See also ? CLEMATIS virginiana in I.B and II		
E		PENTAGLOTTIS (Anchusa) sempervirens (L.) Tausch. P. Blue Borago Semper virens (Neuer dyinge borage. G.797) E.242.i	May–June	——— 2 ft
E	T	PERSEA gratissima Gaertner (americana) (Fig. 4) T. Persea arbor BM t.4580		"1739" 25 ft

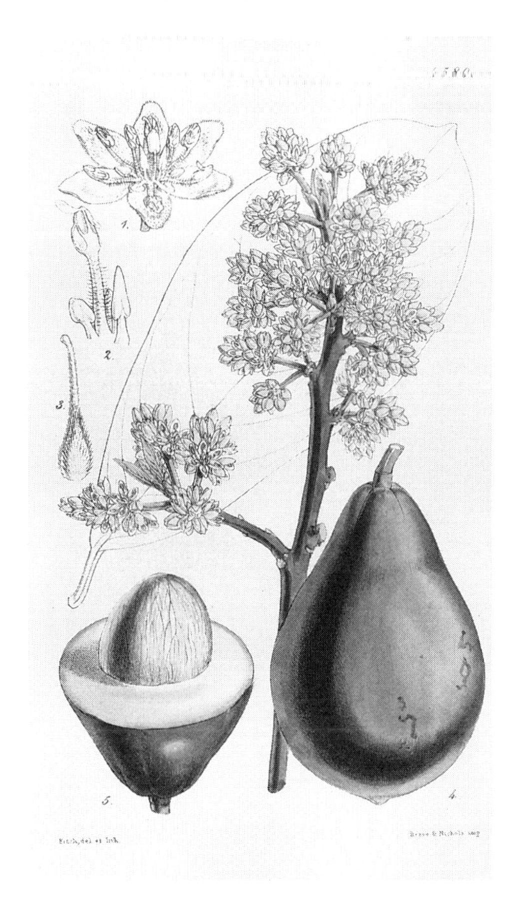

4. *Persea gratissima*
(photo: from *Curtis's Botanical Magazine* 77 [1851], pl. 4580)

E	T	PERSEA indica (L.) Sprengel T. Laurus Indica (American Laurel); See also II		
E		PHILLYREA angustifolia L. S.; See also II		
E		——— latifolia L. S./T. Phillyrea; Phylerea (Diuersi generis; Mock Priuet. G.1395)		(1597) 15 ft

E		? PHLOMIS herba-venti L. S. Purplish-violet Stachia Monspeliensium BM t.2449; M 5.464	July–September	(1596) 2 ft
E	T	PHOENIX dactylifera L. T. Dactylus (Palma; Dates)		(1597) 30–100 ft
E		PHYLLITIS (Asplenium) scolopendrium (L.) Newman Fern Lingua Cervina		——— 1½ ft
E		PICEA abies Karsten (excelsa) T. Picea; The Pitch Tree. (G.1353)		ca. 1300 90 ft
E		PINUS pinaster Aiton T. Pinaster or Pseudo-pinus		(1596) 60 ft
E		PINUS pinea L. T.		ca. 1500 40–60 ft
E		——— sylvestris L. T. Pinus; Pine (The Pine tree. G.1355)		——— 80 ft
E	T	PISTACIA lentiscus L. T. Lentiscus (The Masticke tree. G.1432) BM t.1967		1632 20 ft
		Pistacia—See also in I.B		
		PLANTAGO psyllium L. A. Green Psyllium (Plin. Fleawort. G.587)	July–August	(1562) 6 in
E		POLYGALA chamaebuxus L. S. Yellow, tipped purple Buxus arbor auratus; apicibus auratus Chamae-buxus E.105.iii; BM 9.316; M 1.24	May–June	(1658) 6 in
		POTENTILLA alba L. P. White E.114.iv	February–August	——— 6 in
		——— argentea L. P. Sulphur yellow Pentaphylla	May–August	——— 1 ft
		Poterium—See SANGUISORBA		
		PRIMULA auricula L. P. Auricula ursi; See also II		
		Primula Veris—See PRIMULA vulgaris in II		
		PRUNELLA vulgaris L. P. Purple Prunella E.135.ii	June–September	——— 6 in–1 ft
E		PRUNUS laurocerasus L. S. Laurus Laura Cerusus; Cherry bay, Common Lawrell (G.1603); See also II		
E		PRUNUS lusitanica L. T. White Laurus Caesarea	June	(1648) 20 ft
		Prunus—See also II		
E	T	PSORALEA bituminosa L. P./S. Pale blue Trifolium bituminosum E.272.i, ii	April–September	(1570) 4 ft
E		PYRACANTHA coccinea Roem. S. Pyracantha; Evergreen thorne; See also II		(1629) 15 ft
E		PYROLA rotundifolia L. P. White Pyrola E.214.i	June–August	——— 6 in
E		QUERCUS coccifera L. T. Ilex coccigera sive Kermes (The scarlet Oake. G.1342)		(1683) 15 ft

E	QUERCUS ilex L. T. Ilex Arbor or Evergreen Oak; See also II		1580 60 ft
E	QUERCUS suber L. T. Suber latifol:; The Corke (tree)		(1677) 40–60 ft
E	——— ——— ? var. angustifolia Phelodrys (Note: "Phellodrys" was also applied to Q. ilex var. fagifolia)		
E	RHAMNUS alaternus L. S. Alaternus (Fruitless priuet. G.1398)		(1629) 20 ft
E	——— ——— folijs variegatis (ex albo & viridi)		
E	——— ——— (ex luteo & viridi)		
E	——— ——— "Glaber" S. Celastrus, the staff-tree; Theophrast: Clus; See also II		(1629) 10 ft
E	RHODODENDRON ferrugineum L. S. Deep rose Chamaerrhodendros Alpigena; Dwarfe Rose Bay of the Alps (G.1407)	June	"1752" 4 ft
E	RHODODENDRON hirsutum L. S. Rose-pink Balsamum BM t.1853; M 1.63	June	(1629) 1½ ft
E	RORIPPA nasturcium-aquaticum (L.) Hayek (Nasturtium officinale) P. White Nasturcium (aquaticum; Watercresses. G.257)	May–July	——— water
E	ROSA sempervirens L. S.Cl. White Rose Semp: virens; Rose	June–August	(1629) 20 ft
	Rosa—See also I.B and II.		
E	ROSMARINUS officinalis L. S. Pale violet Rosmarinus; Rosemarie (G.1292) E.284.iii ——— ——— latifolia ——— ——— angustifolia; See also II.	May	1340 6 ft
E	RUMEX sanguineus L. P. Green Lapathus sanguineum	June–July	——— 3 ft
E	RUSCUS aculeatus L. S. Greenish Ruscus sive Bruscus; Myrtus agria siue syluestris; knee holly, knee herme (Kneeholme or butchers broome. G.907) E.2.i	March–April	——— 3½ ft
E	RUSCUS hypoglossum L. S. Yellow Laurus Alexandrina sive hyppoglossum; hors tongue. E.128.i	April–May	(1596) 1½ ft
E	RUTA graveolens L. S. Yellow Ruta (Hearbe grace)	June–September	(995) 3 ft
	SALVIA aethiopis L. B./P. White Aethiopis E.240	May–June	(1570) 1 ft
	SALVIA officinalis L. P. Salvia		
	Salvia—See also II		
E	SANGUISORBA minor Scop. (Poterium sanguisorba) P. Green Pimpinella (Pimpinell, Burnet. G.1044)	May–August	——— 1½ ft
	SANICULA europaea L. P. White Sanicula E.103.iii	June–July	——— 1 ft
E T	SANTALUM album L. T. Santalum BM t.3235		"1804" 15 ft

E	SANTOLINA chamaecyparissus L. S. Yellow [Lavender-Cotton] (p. 77) E.311.iii	July	(1373) 2 ft
E	SATUREIA montana L. S. Pale purple Satyreja sempiterna radice (Winter savory. G.575) E.286.iii	June–July	(995) 1½ ft
	SECURIGERA securidaca (L.) Degen & Dörfler (coronilla) A. Yellow Hedisarum	July–August	(1562) 1½ ft
E	SEDUM acre L., etc. P. Yellow Sedum diversi generis (omnis Generis) E.298.iii; See also II	June–August	———— 3 in
E	SEDUM cepaea L. A. White Cepaea Paucij (Brooklime. G.621; annually sows itself)	June–July	1633 1 ft
E	SEDUM telephium L. P. Red-purple Telephium	July–September	———— 2 ft
	Sedum—See also in II		
E	SEMPERVIVUM tectorum L. P. Pale pink Semper vivum majus (Greate housleeke. G.511) E.298.i (Note: Elsewhere named Sedum semp: vir:; the plant was probably in England before A.D. 800)	June–September	(————) 1 ft
E T	SENECIO cineraria DC. (Cineraria maritima) S. Yellow Jacobaea marina (Sea raggweede. G.280) E.212.ii; M 5.454	June–October	(1633) 2 ft
	SENECIO jacobaea L. P. Yellow Jacobea	July–August	———— 2 ft
	SISON amomum L. A. White Sison	July–August	———— 3 ft
	SIUM latifolium L. P. White Sion	July–August	———— 3 ft
	? SOPHORA alopecuroides L. P. Yellow Sophorea seu Aegypt. vitiosa	July	"1731" 4 ft
	SPARTIUM junceum L. S. Yellow Genista Hispan: (Spartum Hispanum); Spanish broome E.137.ii; BM 3.85; See also II	June–September	(1548) 10 ft
	Stachia Monspeliensium—See ? PHLOMIS herba-venti		
	STACHYS officinalis (L.) Trevisan (Betonica officinalis) P. Red-purple Betonica	June–August	———— 1 ft
	Stellaria—See MYOSOTON		
E	SUAEDA fruticosa Forsk (vera) S. Vermicularis frutex major or Stone-crop; See also II		———— 2 ft
E T	TAMARINDUS indica L. T. Tamarindus BM t.4563		(1633) 60 ft
	TANACETUM vulgare L. P. Yellow Tanacetum E.208.ii,iii	July–September	———— 2–3 ft
	Tanacetum—See also in II		
E	TAXUS baccata L. T. Taxus; Yuf (Yew tree. G.1370)		———— 60 ft

E	TEUCRIUM chamaedrys L. (x lucidrys) P. Rose Chamaedrus sive Teucrium (majus; Germander. G.657) E.125.iii	July–September	ca. 1200 1½ ft
E	TEUCRIUM fruticans L. (latifolium) S. Lavender blue Teucrium arboresc: BM 7.245	June–September	1633 5 ft
E T	? TEUCRIUM marum L. S. Reddish-purple Marum syrianum; See also ORIGANUM syriacum	July–September	(1640) 1 ft
E T	TEUCRIUM polium L. S. White, etc. Polium montanum	June–August	(1562) 1 ft
E	THUJA occidentalis L. T. Arbor Vitae; sive Thuyae; See also II		(1596) 30 ft
E	THYMELAEA tartonraira (L.) All. S. White Tarton raire (Guttwort. G.507) M 2.110	May–July	(1640) 3 ft
E T	THYMUS cephalotos L. S. Purple-violet Tragoriganum	July–August	"1759" 9 in
E	THYMUS serpyllum L. agg. S. Purplish Serpillum (Wild time. G.570); See also II	June–August	——— 3 in
E	THYMUS vulgaris L., etc. S. (Thymum-Diuersi generis); Time (G.573) ——— ——— latifolius Thymum myrtifol; (tyme); See also II		
E	ULEX europaeus L. S. Golden-yellow Scorpius sive genista Spinosa; Fuzzes (Furzes)	April–May	——— 4 ft
E	UMBILICUS rupestris (Salisb.) Dandy P. Greenish-white, dotted Cotyledon	June–July	——— 6 in
	URTICA pilulifera L. A. Green Urtica Romana E.230.i	June–August	(———) 1½ ft
	Valeriana—See KENTRANTHUS		
	VERBASCUM ? nigrum L. P. Yellow Verbascum virid: Luteum. purpur: E.265.iii (Note: Evelyn elsewhere refers to a "Verbascum viride purp. annual," which might be V. chaixii Vill., introduced "1821")	May–August	——— 2 ft
	Verbascum—See also in II		
E	? VERONICA fruticans Jacq. S. Blue Veronica	June–August	——— 6 in
	Veronica—See also in II		
E	VIBURNUM tinus L. S. White Laurus Tinus; wild bay (tree. G.1409) BM 2.38; See also II	September–March	(1560) 10–15 ft
E	VINCA major L. P. Purple Clematis Daphnoides (major) E.129.i	August	(———) Creeping
E	——— minor L. P. Blue/Violet/White C. D. (minor) E.7.ii–v Clematis Daphnoides perevincia (siue Vinca pervinca, Peruincle. G.894); See also II.	August	——— Creeping

Viola Matronalis—See HESPERIS matronalis in I.B and II

E	VISCUM album L. S. (parasite) Viscum; Miseltoe (G.1350)		———— (2 ft)
E	YUCCA gloriosa L. S. Creamy-white Yucca (of which Bread Casaue is made. G.1543); See also II BM t.1260; M 3.286	July–September	ca. 1550 4 ft

I.B Deciduous trees and shrubs

(Note: Other deciduous plants were included by Evelyn in his list of evergreen species for the Grove; See I.A above.)

ACER campestre L. T. Maple		———— 25 ft
ACER pseudoplatanus L. T. Sicomor, Sycamor, Sycomore		ca. 1550 100 ft
AESCULUS hippocastanum L. T. Castanea Equina; Horse Chessnutt; See also II		
ALNUS glutinosa (L.) Gaertner T. Alder		———— 25 ft
ARTEMISIA abrotanum L. S. Dull yellow E.164.iii	August–October	(995) 4 ft
———— arborescens L. S. Yellowish Abrotonum femina; Southernwood. G.1106)	June–July	(1640) 10 ft
ARTEMISIA absinthium L. P. Yellow Absynthium E.287.i	July–September	———— 3 ft
BERBERIS vulgaris L. S. Yellow Barbery E.9.iii; M 5.383	April	———— 8 ft
BETULA pendula Roth. T.		———— 40 ft
————pubescens Ehrh. T. Birch		———— 40 ft

5. *Capparis spinosa*
(photo: from *Curtis's Botanical Magazine* 9 [1795], pl. 291)

T	CAPPARIS spinosa L. S. White (Fig. 5) Capparis BM 9.291	June	(1596) 3 ft
	CARPINUS betulus L. T. Hornebeame		——— 40 ft
	CASTANEA sativa Miller T. Chesse-nutt		——— 50 ft
	Chamaenerion—See under SALIX purpurea		
	? CLEMATIS virginiana L. S.Cl. Green [Clematis verginiana]; See also PASSIFLORA incarnata in I.A and II	June–August	"1767" 15 ft
	COLUTEA arborescens L. S. Colutea Vesicaria; Bastard Sena; See also II		
	CORNUS mas L. T. Yellow Cornelia (p. 55) E.367.iii	February–April	(1596) 15 ft
	CORNUS sanguinea L. S. White [Dog-wood]	June–July	——— 8 ft
	CORYLUS avellana L. S. Haisell		——— 15 ft
	CORYLUS maxima Miller S. Filbert [Filberd]		? 15 ft
	CRATAEGUS monogyna Jacq. T. White (Spina acuta)	June	——— 15 ft
	——— oxyacantha L. T. White Haw, Thorne [White-thorne]	June	——— 15 ft
	CUCURBITA maxima Duch. ex Lam. A.Cl. Yellow Calibasses E.346.iii	June–August	(1570) 15 ft
	CYDONIA oblonga Miller T. White Quince (p. 55)	May–June	(1200) 20 ft
	CYTISUS (Sarothamnus) scoparius (L.) Link S. Yellow Genista s. Spartum; (Broome. G.1311) E.11.iii	May–June	——— 8 ft
	Cytisus—See also II		
	DAPHNE gnidium L. S. White Thymelaea (Spurge flax or Mountaine Widow waile. G.1403) M 1.72	July–September	(1597) 4 ft
	DAPHNE mezereum L. S. Chamaelea Germanica, sive Mezereon (Spurge flax or dwarf bay. G.1402); See also II		
	Diospyros—See under PRUNUS cerasifera		
	DORYCNIUM suffruticosum Vill. (Lotus pentaphyllus) S. Pinkish-White Dorycnium Monspeliensium (Venemous trefoile of Montpelier. G.1309) E.11.i	June–September	(1640) 3 ft
	Epilobium—See under SALIX purpurea		
	EUONYMUS europaeus L. S. [Spindle tree]		——— 15 ft
	FAGUS sylvatica L. T. Beech		——— 90 ft

	FRAXINUS excelsior L. T. Ash		———— 80 ft
	? HELIANTHEMUM (Lechea) canadense (L.) Michx. S. White Chamaecistus tetraphyll: American: See also I.A	July–August	"1780" 3 ft
	HESPERIS matronalis L. P. Viola matronalis; See also II		
T	JASMINUM grandiflorum L. S.Cl. White Span: Jessamine E.147.i	June–October	(1629) 15 ft
	JASMINUM officinale L. S.Cl. White Jassmine, Jessamine, Gessamine E.275.i; BM 1.31	June–September	(1548) 30 ft
	Jasminum—See also II		
	JUGLANS nigra L. T. [Virginian Wallnutt]		(1629) 30 ft
	JUGLANS regia L. T. Wall-nutt		(995) 100 ft
	LAGENARIA vulgaris Ser. (siceraria), etc. A.Cl. White Gourd, Calibass	August	(1597) 10 ft
	LARIX decidua Miller T. Larix or Larch [Larinx]; See also in II		(1618) 90 ft
	Lechea—see HELIANTHEMUM		
	LIRIODENDRON tulipifera L. T. [Tulip-tree or Virgin Maple] BM 8.275		(1638) 60 ft
	LONICERA periclymenum L. S.Cl. [Caprifol: Honisuckle vulgar]; Wood-bynd; See also II		
(E)	LONICERA sempervirens L. S.Cl. Scarlet [Caprifolium Americanum] BM 20.781	May–August	(1656) 15 ft
	Lotus—see DORYCNIUM		
	MALUS sylvestris Miller flore pleno T. White Crab; apple (p. 55, 92) E.5.i	April–May	———— 30 ft
T	MELIA azedarach L. T. Lilac [Bead-tree] E.136.i; BM t.1066	June	(1656) 30 ft
	MORUS alba L. T. [White-Mulberie]		1596 30 ft
	MORUS nigra L. T. Mulbery		ca. 1150 30 ft
	Myricaria—See TAMARIX		
	PALIURUS spina-christi Miller S./T. Paliurus; See also II		(1597) 15 ft
	PARTHENOCISSUS quinquefolia (L.) Planch. S.Cl. Hedera Virginian; Helix, Virginian Ivy; See also II		(1629) 25 ft
	PHILADELPHUS coronarius L. S. White Syrinx or pipe-tree, White E.2.ii,iii; BM 11.391; See also II	June	(1596) 10 ft
T	PISTACIA terebinthus L. T. Terebinthus (Turpentine tree. G.1433)		1634 20 ft

T	PISTACIA vera L. T. Pistachiam nutts, Pistacios (p. 68) E.6.i		(1570) 15 ft
	PLATANUS occidentalis L. T. [Plane, Occidental] ——— orientalis L. T. Platanus [P., Oriental, or Zinar]		1638 70 ft ca. 1350 50 ft
	POPULUS alba L. T. Abeal or white Poplar		(———) 100 ft
	POPULUS nigra L. T. Poplar		——— 100 ft
	POPULUS tremula L. T. Asp(en)		——— 60 ft
	PRUNUS avium (L.) L. T. White Chery-black [Black-cherry]; See also II	April–May	——— 50 ft
	? PRUNUS cerasifera Ehrh. S. White Prunus Ægypt: E.142.ii; BM t.5934 (Note: possibly not a true plum, but a fruit such as DIOSPYROS lotus L. T. Yellow & green E.13.i	March–April June–July	(1629) 30 ft (1596) 20 ft
	PRUNUS cerasus L. T. White Chery (p. 55) (E.4.i); See also II	April–May	——— 20 ft
	PRUNUS padus L. T. White Bird cherry [Birds-cherry] E.4.ii	April–May	——— 50 ft
	PRUNUS persica (L.) Batsch T. Pale rose Peach (p. 55)	April–May	ca. 1200 15 ft
	PRUNUS spinosa L. S./T. White Sloe [Black-thorne]	March–April	——— 10 ft
	Prunus—See also II		
	PUNICA granatum L. S. Scarlet Malus Punica, Balaustia; Pomegrand, Pome-granade, Granatt E.141.i, 142.i, 143.ii; BM t.1832; See also II	June–September	ca.1350 20 ft
	QUERCUS petraea (Mattuschka) Liebl. T. ——— robur L. T. Oake		——— ——— 100 ft
	Quercus–See also II		
	RHAMNUS catharticus L. S. [Rhamnus-Buck-horne]		——— 15 ft
	ROBINIA pseudoacacia L. T. White Acatia	June	ca. 1625 70 ft
	ROSA eglanteria Miller (rubiginosa) S.Cl. Pink Sweete Brier E.99.i, iv; See also II	May–June	——— 5–7 ft
	ROSA moschata Herrm. S.Cl. White Musc rose (p. 91)	July–October	(1590) 12 ft
	ROSA spp. S. Roses, all sorts; See also I.A and II		

	RUBUS fruticosus L. agg. S.Cl. Pink Rubus	June–September	———— 10 ft
	Rubus—See also in II		
	SALIX alba L., etc. T. Willow		———— 80 ft
	SALIX caprea L. T. Sallow (p. 92)		———— 25 ft
	SALIX fragilis L., etc. T. Withy (p. 92)		———— 90 ft
	SALIX purpurea L. S. The Garden purple-flour'd Willow (p. 54)		———— 10 ft
	(Note: Evelyn's English name is ambiguous and might mean ? EPILOBIUM (Chamaenerion) angustifolium L. P. Purple E.156.i	July–August	———— 4 ft
	SALIX viminalis L. S. Osier (p. 92)		———— 20 ft
	Sarothamnus—See CYTISUS scoparius		
T	SASSAFRAS albidum Nees T. Sassafras; See also II		(1633) 50 ft
	SMILAX aspera L. S.Cl. Pale green Smilum aspera [Sarsaparilla or Smilax aspera]	August–September	1632 8 ft
	SORBUS aucuparia L. T. White Witch Haisell or Quic-beam [Quick-beame or Whichen]	May–June	———— 60 ft
	SORBUS domestica L. T. White Service	May	ca. 1530 40 ft
	SYRINGA vulgaris L. S./T. Lilac/White Syrinx or pipe-tree, Blue E.1.ii,iii; BM 6.183	May	ca. 1580 20 ft
	Syringa—See also II		
	TAMARIX gallica L. S.		1558
	MYRICARIA germanica (L.) Desv. S. Tamaris; Tamarisks; See also II		1582 6 ft
	TILIA x europaea L. T. Lime		———— 100 ft
	ULMUS procera Salisb. T. Elme		———— 100 ft
	VACCINIUM myrtillus L. S. Hurtles (p. 95)		———— 1½ ft
	VIBURNUM opulus L. S. White Guelder Rose E.10.i	June	———— 10 ft
T	VITEX agnus-castus L. S. White & blue [Agnus Castus] BM. n.s. 400	September	(1570) 6 ft
	VITIS vinifera L. S.Cl. Vines		ca. 280 30 ft

II. Flowering plants for the Coronary Garden

	Plant	Flowering	Date / Height
E T	ACACIA farnesiana (L.) Willd. T. Yellow Acacia Indica "flowers twise a yeare."	June–August	(1656) 20 ft
	? ACHILLEA ptarmica L. flore pleno P. White "Phalmia" (? Ptarmica) E.288.iii "the double white encreased of the stemm rootes."	July–November	(————) 1 ft
	Achillea—See also I.A		
	ACONITUM lycoctonum L. P. Yellow Aconitum Luteum Ponticum E.159.ii; BM t.1119, t.2570	July–August	(1596) 3 ft
	ACONITUM napellus L. P. Dark blue Aconitum Napellus E.160.ii; BM t.8152; M. 3.210	May–July	(1596) 4 ft
	ADONIS aestivalis L. A. Red [Flos Adonis] E.214.ii	June–July	1629 1½ ft
	AESCULUS hippocastanum L. T. White Castanea Equina; Horse Chessnut; See also I.B	May	ca. 1616 50 ft
	Agrostemma—see LYCHNIS coronaria		
	Alcea—See ALTHAEA		
	ALLIUM moly L. P. Yellow Moly E.79.ii; BM 14.499	June	1604 1 ft
	ALLIUM multibulbosum Jacq. (magicum, nigrum) P. green & white Mioly, Indian BM t.1148	May–June	(1596) 2 ft
	ALLIUM ? roseum L. P. Pale purple Moly Montpeliense BM t.978	June	(1629) 1 ft
	Allium—See also I.A		
	? ALOPECURUS pratensis L. P. [Foxtaile]		———— 2 ft
	ALTHAEA (Alcea) rosea (L.) Cav. B./P. (Various) Hollihocks, Holyhoc E.222, 223; BM t.892, t.1916, t.3198	July–September	ca. 1275 6–8 ft
	AMARANTHUS caudatus L. A. Red Amaranthus, greate purple E.338.i	August	(1596) 3 ft
	AMARANTHUS gangeticus L. tricolor A. Red, yellow Amaranthus of 3 colors E.337	June–September	(1548) 2 ft
	AMARANTHUS hypochondriacus L. A. Deep crimson Princes feather, a sort of Amaranth	July–September	1684 2–5 ft
	AMARANTHUS spp. Flower-Gentle; See also CELOSIA		
	Amberboa—See CENTAUREA moschata		
	ANACYCLUS valentinus L. (radiatus) A. Yellow Chrysanthemum Valentinum Clusij (p. 68)	June–July	(1656) 1 ft
T	ANAGALLIS linifolia L. monelli P. Blue Anagallis (p. 68) BM 9.319, t.3380; M 5.399	May–September	(1648) 1 ft
	ANARRHINUM bellidifolium (L.) Desf. B. Purple Linaria; Toad flax, Sweete purple BM t.2056	June–August	(1629) 1½ ft

E	ANCHUSA officinalis L. P. Purple Buglosse E.243.i	June–October	——— 2 ft
	ANEMONE coronaria L. P. (Various) Plush Anemone E.31.i, 32.i; BM t.841	April–May	(1596) 6 in
	——— hortensis L. P. (Various) Starr Anemone E.31.ii,iii, 32.ii,iii	April–May	(1597) 9 in
	——— pavonina Lam. P. (Various) Anemone BM 4.123	April–May	? 1 ft
E	ANTHEMIS (Chamaemelum) nobilis L. flore pleno P. White Camaemelum; Cammomile, double (Cammomille. G.754) E.276.iii; See also I.A	July–September	——— 1 ft
	ANTHERICUM liliago L. P. White Phalangium non ramosum BM t.914, t.1635; M 4.290	May–June	(1596) 1 ft
	ANTHERICUM ramosum L. P. White Phalangium, White Italian E.109.ii; BM t.1055	May–June	(1570) 2 ft
	Antholyza—See CHASMANTHE		
E	ANTIRRHINUM majus L. B./P. Red/White/Yellow Antirrhinum; Snap-dragon E.157.i,ii, 158; M 3.279; See also in I.A	February–April	ca. 1500 2–3 ft
	AQUILEGIA canadensis L. B./P. Yellow & red Columbine—the Virginian BM 7.246; M 4.322	May–July	1632 2 ft
	AQUILEGIA vulgaris L. B./P. (Various) Columbine E.170–173	May–July	——— 2 ft
E	ARBUTUS unedo L. S. White Arbutus; (Strawberry tree. G.1496. Cane apple) BM t.2319; M 4.361; See also I.A	September–December	——— 40 ft
	ARGEMONE mexicana L. A. Yellow Papaver, golden-yellow E.288.i; BM 7.243; M 1.85	July–August	1592 2 ft
E	ARMERIA maritima (Miller) Willd. P. Pink-lilac Thrift, Frith (p. 76) (Armeria, Caryophyllus marinus); See also I.A	May–August	—— 1 ft
	ARTEMISIA abrotanum L. S. Dull yellow Abrotanum viridi flore amplo; Southernwood E.164.iii	August–October	(995) 4 ft
	ASPHODELINE lutea (L.) Reichenb. P. Yellow Asphodellus Luteus; Asphodel, yellow BM t.773; M 3.246; See also I.A	May–June	(1596) 3 ft
	ASPHODELUS albus Miller (form) P. (White) Asphodelus, flesh colored	May–June	(1596) 2–3½ ft
	ASPHODELUS fistulosus L. P. White Asphodelus minor BM t.984	June–September	(1596) 1½ ft
	ASPHODELUS microcarpus Salzm. & Viv. (aestivus, cerasiferus, ramosus) P. Pinkish-white Asphodelus, large white-striped E.132.i; BM t.799; M 3.251	May	(1551) 2–3 ft
	Asphodelus—See also HEMEROCALLIS, SIMETHIS		
	ASTER amellus L. P. Purple Aster Atticus; the Italian or blew Marigold E.215.ii,iii; M 2.188	August–September	(1596) 2 ft
	ASTER (Crinitaria) linosyris (L.) Less. P. Yellow Helichrysum "Goldy locks" E.162.i; M 4.358	September–October	(1596) 2 ft
	Aster—See also ERIGERON		

	BELLIS perennis L. cvs. P. White/Crimson	March–August	————
	Bellis; Daisie E.112.i–iii, 294.ii,iii; BM 7.228; See also I.A		3 in
	BORAGO officinalis L. A. Blue/White	June-September	————
	Borrage E.107.iv,v		3 ft
	BRASSICA oleracea L. bullata sabauda variegata B. Yellow	April–June	————
	Caulis crispatus variatus		2 ft
	BRIZA media L. P.		————
	Gramina tremula		1½ ft
T	BRUNSVIGIA gigantea Heist. (multiflora, orientalis) (Fig. 1) P. Red	June–August	"1752"
			1 ft
	Narcissus, Sphericall BM t.1619		
E	BRYUM murale L., etc.		————
	Muscus; Mosse; See also I.A		1 in
	BULBOCODIUM vernum L. P. Purple	February–March	(1629)
	(Colchicum, vernal, spring-flowering) E.33.iii, 50.iii; BM 5.153		3 in
E	BUXUS sempervirens L. T.		————
	Buxus; Box (The Boxe tree. G.1410) E.1.i		30 ft
	———— ———— suffruticosa		ca. 1600
	(Box), Dutch dwarfe		1 ft
	———— ————		
	edg'd with gold, the Auratus		
	———— ———— ————		
	dwarfe gilded; See also in I.A		
	CALENDULA officinalis L. plena A. Orange	June–September	(995)
	Crysanthemum, double Marygold E.206.ii, (207.iii); BM t.3204		3 ft
	CALTHA palustris L. P. Yellow	April–May	————
	Caltha palustris E.113.i, 364.ii		1 ft
	CAMPANULA medium L. B. (Various)	June–September	(1597)
	Viola Mariana (bearing bells) E.151.ii,iii, 152.i, 153.i		4 ft
	CAMPANULA persicifolia L. flore pleno P. Blue/White	July	(1596)
	Campanula, the double peach-leav'd E.156.ii,iii; BM 11.397		3 ft
	CAMPANULA trachelium L. P. Violet	June–August	————
	Campanula Trachelium, Gyant E.154.ii,iii		4 ft
	CAMPSIS radicans (L.) Seem. S.Cl. Orange-red	July–August	(1640)
	Red Indian Jasmine of Canada "which must have a propp or smale Palisade" ("yet another Indian Jassmine of a crimson & noble Colour, which grows very tall being supported & very well indures the winter") BM 14.485; M 2.123		20 ft
	CANNA indica L. P. Red/Red & yellow	January–December	(1570)
	Canna Indica E.332, 333; BM 13.454		2 ft
	CAPSICUM annuum L. A. White	June–July	(1548)
	Piper ind: (p. 68) [Capsicum indicum] E.324–331		1 ft
	CARDAMINE pratensis L. P. Pale purple	April–May	————
	Cardamine; Ladys smocks E.17.iii,iv; See also I.A		1 ft
	CAREX spp.		————
	Sedge (p. 137)		6 in-3 ft
	CARTHAMUS tinctorius L. A. Orange	June–July	(1551)
	Cyanus; bastard Saffron E.276.i; M 2.162		3 ft
	Carthamus—See also I.A		

	CATANANCHE caerulea L. P. Blue Sesamoides coronopus (p. 68) E.207.ii; BM 9.293; M 1.15	July–October	(1596) 3 ft
	CELOSIA cristata L. (argentea cristata) A. Red, etc. Amaranthus; Flower-Gentle, lesser purple E.339,i,ii; See also AMARANTHUS	June–September	(1570) 9 in-1 ft
	CENTAUREA cyanus L. A. Blue/Pink/Purple/White Cyanus; Blew bottles, blew bells, Corne flo: E.115.i-vii	June–August	——— 3 ft
	CENTAUREA (Amberboa) moschata L. A. Purple Cyanus; Sweete Sultan	July–October	(1629) 2–3 ft
	——— ——— alba Snow-white		
	——— ——— flava (C. suaveolens) A. Yellow (Sweet Sultan, yellow) M. 1.95		(1683) 2 ft
	CENTAUREA polyacantha Willd. P. Reddish-purple Parkinson's Jacea marina Baetica	July	(1629) 6 in
	CENTAUREA ? pullata L. A. Purple Cyanus, Spanish (Parkinson's Cyanus Baeticus supinus)	June–August	"1759" 2 ft
	Centaurea—See also I.A		
	CEPHALARIA alpina (L.) Schrader P. Cream Scabious Montan: (p. 69) E.257.i	June–July	(1570) 3 ft
	CERCIS siliquastrum L. T. Purple/White Arbor Iudae [A. Judae] E.3.i; BM t. 1138	May–June	(1596) 20 ft
T	? CHASMANTHE (Antholyza) aethiopica (L.) N. E. Br. P. Orange	May–June	"1759" 3 ft
	Indea flag BM t.561		
	CHEIRANTHUS (Erysimum) cheiri L. B./P. Yellow, etc. E.168. ii, iii, 169,ii, iii Leucoium, Viola lutea or (Keyri); Wall-flo: (G.456) (Keris: double white, greate single, double yellow, double red, simplex majus, greate double, pale yellow)	April–July	ca. 1275 2-3 ft
	——— ——— maximus B./P. Yellow Leucoium, greate yellow E.169.i (? extinct)	April–July	? 3–4 ft
	Cheiranthus—See also I.A		
	CHRYSANTHEMUM coronarium L. A. Yellow Crysanthemum; Candy corne Marigold E.209.ii,iii; M 2.143	July–September	(1629) 1–3 ft
	CHRYSANTHEMUM (Tanacetum) parthenium (L.) Bernh. flore pleno P. White Parthenium, (Matricaria) E.210.ii; See also I.A	July–August	——— 3 ft
	CHRYSANTHEMUM segetum L. A. Yellow Corne Marigold	June–August	——— 1½ ft
E	CISTUS albidus L., etc. S. Pale purple Cistus mas; or holly rose (G.1275)	June–July	(1596) 2 ft
E	CISTUS ladanifer L. (? x cyprius) S. White Cistus (Ladanum), Ledon BM 4.112	June–July	(1629) 4 ft
	Cistus—See also I.A		
	CLEMATIS viticella L. S.Cl. Purple/Red Clematis, or Virgins bower, Lady-bower E.300.ii,iii, 303.ii,iii; BM t.565	June–September	(1569) 20 ft

	COLCHICUM agrippinum Baker P. Lilac chequered white Colchicum, the Agrippina BM t.1028	September–October	? 3 in
	COLCHICUM autumnale L. P. Purple/White Colchicum E.350.i-iv, 353.ii,iii ———— ——— flore pleno (double) E.351.ii ———— ——— striatum (striped) E.352.ii	September–October	——— 3 in
	COLCHICUM byzantinum Ker-Gawler P. Purple Colchicum, darke purple E.351.v; BM t.1122	August-October	(1629) 3 in
	COLCHICUM variegatum L. P. Purple chequered Colchicum, the variegated sorts; the freckled of Chio E.349.iv,v; 351.i; BM t.6090	August–October	(1629) 3 in
	COLUTEA arborescens L. S. Bright yellow Colutea (Senna) E.12.i; BM 3.81; See also I.B	June–September	(1548) 12 ft
	Consolida—see DELPHINIUM		
	CONVALLARIA majalis L. P. White Lilium Convallium E.92.ii ——— rosea of a redish hue E.92.iii	May–June	——— 8 in
	CONVOLVULUS tricolor L. A. Blue, white & yellow Convoluulus BM 1.27	July–August	(1629) Trailing
	Convolvulus—See also PHARBITIS, and in I.A		
E	CORIARIA myrtifolia L. S. Green Rhus Myrtifolia; [Rhus, Myrtil]	May–August	(1629) 6 ft
	CORONILLA (Hippocrepis) emerus L. S. Red & yellow Colutea Scorpoides; Bastard Sena BM 13.445	April–June	(1596) 3 ft
	CORTUSA matthioli L. P. Rosy-purple Beares eard Sanicle or Cortusa Mathioli BM t.987; M 4.296	April–June	(1596) 6 in
	CORYDALIS cava (L.) Schweigger & Koerte P. Purple Radix cava BM 7.232; M 3.262 ———— ——— albiflora White Radix cava, white BM t.2340	February–April	(1596) 6 in
	CREPIS rubra L. rosea A. Pink Chondrilla incarnat: (p. 68) E.256.i	June–July	1632 6 in-1½ ft
	Crinitaria—See ASTER linosyris		
	CRITHMUM maritimum L. P. White (Crithmum marinum); Sampier (p. 137); See also I.A	July–September	——— 1 ft
	CROCUS aureus Sibth. & Sm. (flavus flavus) P. Yellow Crocus; yellow, large yellow E.362.ii; BM 2.45, t.1111, t.2655, t.2685, t.2986	February–March	(1597) 3 in
	CROCUS biflorus Miller P. White Crocus, large white BM t.845, t.3868	February–March	(1629) 3 in
	CROCUS byzantinus Ker-Gawler (iridiflorus) P. Purple & lilac Crocus, purple striped BM t.6141	September–October	(1629) 3 in
	CROCUS sativus L. P. Lilac-violet Saffron, ordinary E.191.iv	September–October	ca. 1340 6 in
	CROCUS susianus Ker-Gawler (angustifolius) P. Yellow	February–March	(1597)

	Crocus, yellow striped E.362.iii; BM t.652; M 2.121		3 in
	CROCUS vernus All. P. Purple/Striped	February–April	?
	Crocus, purple; Vernal Safron E.35.iii, 47.iv, 191.iii		6 in
	———— ——— albiflorus		
	Crocus, white E.35.ii		
	Crocus—See also I.A		
E	CUPRESSUS sempervirens L. T.		ca. 1375
	Cupressus (foemina); Cypresse (G.1367) E.137.i		150 ft
E	——— ——— horizontalis T.		?
	(Cupressus; The Cypresse tree) mas; See also I.A		20 ft
	CYCLAMEN coum Miller (vernum) P. Carmine/White	January–April	(1596)
	BM 1.4, n.s. t.29; M 3.229		2 in
	——— repandum Sibth. & Sm. P. Carmine	April–May	(1629)
	Cyclamen, Spring, Vernal		3 in
	CYCLAMEN europaeum L. (purpurascens) P. Pale red	August	?
	Cyclamen, Summer E.347.i, 348.ii,iii		3 in
	CYCLAMEN ? libanoticum Hildebr. P. Rosy red	Spring	1633
	Cyclamen, Levanties		4 in
	CYCLAMEN neapolitanum Ten. (hederaefolium) P. Rose/White	July–November	(1596)
	Cyclamen, Autumnal, purple E.348.i; BM t.1001		6 in
	———— ——— album		
	white; Ivy leavd Angustifol:		
T	CYCLAMEN persicum Miller var. P. Red/White	February–April	(1629)
	Cyclamen Antiochenum; double BM 2.44		3 in
	CYPRIPEDIUM calceolus L. P. Maroon & yellow	May–July	———
	Calceolus Mariae E.122.i		1 ft
	CYTISUS sessilifolius L. S. Yellow	May–June	(1629)
	Cytisus secundus Clusij; Trefoile BM 8.255		6 ft
	Cytisus—See also I.A, I.B		
E	DAPHNE cneorum L. S. Pale pink	May–June	(1629)
	Cneorum Mathioli; white rockrose BM 9.313; M 3.256		1 ft
E	DAPHNE laureola L. S. Yellowish-green	February–March	———
	Laureola (Spurge Laurel. G.1404)		2–5 ft
	DAPHNE mezereum L. S. Pink-red	February–March	———
	Chamaelea Germanica, sive Mezereon (Spurge flax or dwarf bay. G.1402) E.367.ii		5 ft
	Daphne—See also I.A, I.B		
	DATURA stramonium L. A. White	July–September	———
	Stramonium, Pomum Spinosum; Thorne Apple E.343.i		3 ft
	DELPHINIUM ajacis L. & cvs. ("Consolida ambigua") A. (Various)	June–July	(1573)
	E.175.ii,iii		3 ft
	——— consolida L. & cvs. ("Consolida regalis ssp. regalis") A./B. (Various)	July–September	(1596)
	Consolida regalis; Delphinium or Larks spurr, Larks-heele E.175.i, 176, 177, 178; M 5.432		2 ft
	DIANTHUS barbatus L. B.(P.) (Various)	June–July	(1573)
	Armeria; Sweete Williams E.253.i–iii; BM 6.207		1½ ft
	———— ——— (Spotted form)		

	Armeria; Pride of Lond(on) ———— ———— (Deep crimson form)		
	Armeria; Velvet; See also I.A		
	DIANTHUS carthusianorum L. flore pleno P. Red Armeria; double John E.318.i; BM t.2039	July–August	(1573) 1½ ft
	DIANTHUS caryophyllus L. cvs. B./P. Crimson, &c E.308, 309.i,iii, 310.i, 311.i, 312.i, 313, 314.i,iii, 315.i; BM 2.39, t.1622, t.2744; M 2.137, 3.287	June–August	ca. 1475 2 ft
	———— plumarius L. cvs. P. White & purple E.309.ii, 315.ii,iii, 316.ii,iii, 318; M 3.253 Caryophyllus, (Dios anthos; Carnations, Gilliflowers, Gilloflowers of all sorts. G.588)	June–August	(1629) 6 in
	DIANTHUS deltoides L. P. Flesh Caryophyllus; ordinary Pinke M 2.142	June–October	———— 9 in
	DIANTHUS plumarius L. flore. pleno P. White & purple Pinke, double Pinke E.309.ii, 315.ii,iii, 316.ii,iii; M 3.253	June–August	(1629) 6 in
	DIANTHUS plumarius L. annulatus P. Partrig-Ey'd or Spanish Pinke	June–August	(1629) 6 in
	DIANTHUS sylvestris Wulfen (virgineus) P. Pink Caryophyllus; Birds eye or French pinke; "will matt prettily for bordures" E.181.ii,iii, 316.i, 318.ii,iii; BM t.1740	June–July	"1732" 1 ft
	DICTAMNUS albus L. (fraxinella) P. Purplish-red/White Fraxinella E.130.i; BM t.8961; M 4.307	May–July	(1596) 1½–3 ft
	DIGITALIS ambigua Murray (grandiflora) P. Pale yellow Digitalis, greate yellow E.149.iii	July–August	(1629) 3 ft
	DIGITALIS dubia Rodr. (minor) P. Purple Digitalis, lesser BM t.2160; M 4.299	June–July	"1789" 9 in
	DIGITALIS ferruginea L. P. Brown Digitalis Ferruginea BM t.1828	July–August	(1597) 4 ft
	DIGITALIS lutea L. P. Pale yellow Digitalis, small pale yellow M 1.94	July–August	(1596) 2 ft
E T	DIGITALIS ? obscura L. P. Orange Digitalis, Orange tawny BM t.2157	July–August	"1778" 1 ft
	DIGITALIS purpurea L. alba B. White Digitalis, Greate White E.150.i	June–September	———— 5 ft
	DIPCADI serotinum (L.) Medicus P. Brownish Hyacinths; Serotine Iacynth E.48.i, 93.i; BM t.859	June–August	(1629) 9 in
	ECHINOPS ritro L. (bannaticus) P. Blue Carduus minor BM t.932	July–September	(1570) 3 ft
	ECHINOPS sphaerocephalus L. P. Light blue Carduus globus Major E.280.i	July–August	(1596) 5 ft
	ELAEAGNUS angustifolia L. S./T. Yellow Oleaster, or Wild Olive	June	1632 20 ft
	ENDYMION (Hyacinthoides) hispanicus (Miller) Chouard P. Pale blue Hyacinths, Spanish BM 4.128	May–June	(1633) 1 ft
	ENDYMION (Hyacinthoides) non-scriptus (L.) Garcke P. Blue	March–June	————

Hyacinths, Belgic E.40.i-v, 44.ii,iii, 49.ii		9 in
ERANTHIS hyemalis (L.) Salisb. P. Yellow Aconitum hyemale; Winter-Wolfe bane E.365.ii; BM 1.3; See also I.A	January–March	(1596) 4 in
ERIGERON annuus (L.) Pers. A./B. Whitish Aster; Starr-wort annual, Star-flower	July–September	1633 1 ft
? ERODIUM cicutarium (L.) L'Hér. A. Purple E.22.i	April–September	———— 9 in
? ———— moschatum (L.) L'Hér. A. Purple Geranium, sweete E.24.i	May–July	———— 1 ft
ERYNGIUM planum L. P. Light blue Eringium planum (p. 69) E.283.i	July–September	(1596) 3 ft
Erysimum—See CHEIRANTHUS		
ERYTHRONIUM americanum Ker-Gawler P. Yellow Dens Caninus, yellow BM t.1113; M 2.178	April–May	1633 6 in
ERYTHRONIUM dens-canis L. P. Purplish-rose Dens caninus (purple) BM 1.5; M 2.181	March	(1596) 6 in
———— ———— albiflorum White white E.15.ii	March	
———— ———— rubrum Red red E.15.iii; M 2.181	March	
FRAGARIA vesca L. P. White Fragrariae; Strawberries (p. 91) E.116.ii,iii; (BM 2.63); See also in I.A	April–May	———— 6 in
FRITILLARIA hispanica Boiss. & Reut. (lusitanica; messanensis hispanica) P. Brown-purple Fritillaria, Spanish E.58.ii; BM t.9659	June	"1825" 1 ft
FRITILLARIA imperialis L. P. Yellow/Bronze Crowne Imperial E.80–82; BM 6.194, t.1215	March–April	1590 3–4 ft
FRITILLARIA latifolia Willd. P. (Various) Fritillaria, yellow; (Greenish) BM t.853, t.1207, t.1538	April–May	1604 1 ft
FRITILLARIA lusitanica Wikstr. P. Brown-purple Fritillaria, Portugal	June	"1825" 6 in
FRITILLARIA meleagris L. P. Purple, chequered Fritillaria; Dodoneus' Flos Meleagris E.56.i, 57.i.ii; M 2.183	March–May	? 1 ft
———— ———— alba Fritillaria, early white E.57.iii		
FRITILLARIA ? nigra Miller P. Yellow & purple Fritillaria, lesser darke & yellow BM 18.664; See also F. pyrenaica	May	(1596) 1 ft
FRITILLARIA persica L. P. Brown-purple Lilium Persicum E.83.i; BM t.962, t. 1537	April–May	(1596) 1–3 ft
FRITILLARIA pyrenaica L. P. Dark purple Fritillaria, Black E.58.i; BM t.952; See also F. nigra	May–June	1605 1½ ft
FRITILLARIA ? tubiformis Gren. & Godr. P. Purplish, chequered yellow Fritillaria, red & Sabell	May	? 1 ft
GAGEA lutea (L.) Ker-Gawler (sylvatica) P. Yellow Ornithogallum, yellow E.39.i	April–June	———— 9 in

	Plant	Flowering	Introduced / Height
	GALANTHUS nivalis L. P. White Leucoium Bulbosum, lesse Snow flowers E.361.iii	January–March	? 6–8 in
E T	GELSEMIUM sempervirens (L.) Aiton f. S.Cl. Deep yellow [Jasminum Americanum flo: luteo]; BM t.7851 Another Indian or American Jassmine	May–June	(1640) 20 ft
T	GENISTA (Lygos, Retama) monosperma (L.) Lam. S. White Genista, the white BM t.683	June–July	"1690" 10 ft
	GENTIANA acaulis L. P. Blue Gentianella verna BM 2.52; M 1.51; See also I.A	March–May	(1596) 4 in
	GENTIANA lutea L. P. Yellow Gentiana major	June–July	(1596) 4–6 ft
	GENTIANA pneumonanthe L. P. Blue Gentiana Pneumonanthe E.248.ii; BM t.1101	August–September	———— 6 in–1 ft
	GERANIUM macrorrhizum L. P. Purple Geranium; or Cranes bill, purple E.30.ii; BM t.2420	May–June	1576 1½ ft
	GERANIUM ? palustre L. P. Purple E.23.ii	June–August	"1732" 2 ft
	———— ? sanguineum L. P. Blood-red Geranium, red-rose E.30.i	June–September	———— 9 in
	GERANIUM pratense L. P. Blue Geranium; or Cranes bill, bleau E.22.ii	May–July	———— 1–3 ft
	———— ———— albiflorum White E.22.iii		
	GERANIUM tuberosum L. P. Pink Geranium, knobbed E.30.iii	May–August	(1596) 1 ft
	GLADIOLUS communis L. P. Bright rose Gladiolus, bright red E.201.iv, 203.iii; BM 3.86	June–July	(1596) 2 ft
	———— ———— flore albo white E.203.ii		
	———— ———— ssp. byzantinus Bizantine BM t.874		
E T	? GUIACUM officinale L. S. Blue Lignum vitae [or Arbor Thyrea]; See also I.A	July–September	"1694" 40 ft
	Gynandriris—See IRIS sisyrinchium		
	Habenaria—See PLATANTHERA		
T	HAEMANTHUS coccineus L. P. Red Narcissus, Indian BM t.1075	August–October	1629 1 ft
	HEDYSARUM coronarium L. A./B. Scarlet Hedysarum Clypiatum; or French Honysuckle E.295.i	June–July	(1596) 4 ft
	HELIANTHUS annuus L. A. Yellow Crysanthemum, Solsequia or Heliotrops; Sunflower gigantic . . . annual E.204	June–October	(1596) 6 ft
	HELLEBORUS atrorubens Waldst. & Kit. (orientalis abchasicus) ———— purpurascens Waldst. & Kit. P. Purple & green Heleborus albus atro rubens BM t.3170, t.4581	March–April	"1817" 1½ ft
	HELLEBORUS niger L. P. White Heleborus (maj:), white "bearing its flo: in winter" E.361.i; BM 1.8; M 1.8; See also I.A	January–February	ca. 1300 1 ft

	Plant	Flowering	Introduced / Height
	HELLEBORUS viridis L. P. Green Heleborus, true Black E.362.i	March–April	——— 2 ft
	HEMEROCALLIS flava (L.) L. (lilioasphodelus) P. Yellow Asphodelus; Lily kind, yellow E.130.iii; BM 1.19	June	(1570) 2 ft
	HEMEROCALLIS fulva (L.) L. P. Fulvous Asphodelus; Lily kind, day lilly E.133.i; BM 2.64	June–August	(1576) 4 ft
	HEPATICA triloba Choix (nobilis) P. Blue/Red/White Epaticas, Hepatica, (H. nobilis); doubles E.34.i,ii, 35.iv,v; BM 1.10; M 4.323; See also I.A	February–April	1573 4 in
	HERMODACTYLUS tuberosus (L.) Miller P. Green, purple-brown Hermodactyles E.83.ii; BM 15.531	March–April	(1597) 1 ft
	HESPERIS matronalis L. P. Purple/White Hesperis, (Viola Matronalis); Dames Violet & Queene Gillyflo: E.119.ii,iii; M 1.39, 70; See also I.B	May–August	ca. 1275 3 ft
	? HESPERIS tristis L. B. Livid BM t.730	April–June	(1629) 1 ft
	? MATTHIOLA fruticulosa (L.) Maire P. Livid BM t.729 Leucoium Melancholeum	May–July	(1629) 1½ ft
	HIBISCUS syriacus L. S. (Various) Althaea frutex E.144.i, 145; BM 3.83; M 1.77	August–October	(1596) 8 ft
T	? HIPPEASTRUM equestre (L.f.) Herb. P. Scarlet Narcissus; Indian "from the Barbadoes" BM 9.305, t.2315	July–October	1655 2 ft
	Hippocrepis—See CORONILLA emerus		
	Hyacinthoides—See ENDYMION		
	HYACINTHUS orientalis L. P. Blue/Purple/White Hyacinths, Iacinth, Oriental; Zumbul E.36, 37.i-iii, 38.ii,iii, 39.ii,iii, 46.ii,iii, 47.i,iii; BM t.937; M 4.367 ——— ——— semiplenus Hyacinths, Double; White & Double blue E.46.i,iv,v, 47.ii	March–April	(1596) 1 ft
	IBERIS umbellata L. A. Purple/White Thlaspi Creticum; or Candy Tufts E.236.ii,iii; BM 3.106	June–August	(1596) 6 in-1 ft
E	ILEX aquifolium L. S./T. White Agrifolium; Holly (G.1338) ——— ——— var. Variegated with gold yellow; gilded white; See also in I.A	May–June	——— 30–80 ft
	IMPATIENS balsamina L. A. Red/Yellow Balsamina Foemina; The Balsom Apple, Annual E.323.i-iii; BM t.1256	July–October	(1596) 3 ft
	Ipomoea—See PHARBITIS purpurea		
	IRIS alata Poir. (planifolia) P. Blue Iris; greate Bulbosa of Clusius BM t.6352	June	"1801" 6 in
	IRIS chamaeiris Bertol. (lutescens) P. Blue/Purple/White/Yellow E.117.iii,iv, 118.ii,iii; BM t.6110	April–May	(1596) 3–9 in
	——— pumila L. P. Purple/Yellowish E.117.i,ii, 118.i,iv; BM 1.9, t.1209, t.1261; M 3.263 Iris, Chamaeiris's	April–May	(1596) 4–5 in

		IRIS crocea Jacq. (aurea) P. Golden-yellow Iris, the Tripoly golden	June	(1629) 4 ft
		IRIS florentina L. (germanica "Florentina") P. White Iris Alba versicolor E.120.ii; BM t.671	May–June	(1200) 2 ft
		IRIS germanica L. P. Lavender-blue & purple Iris, the purple E.121.i; BM t.670	May–June	(995) 3 ft
		IRIS pallida Lam. P. Light blue Iris, Dalmatic E.120.iii; BM t.685; M. 4.303	May–June	(1596) 3 ft
		IRIS persica L. P. Blue & yellow Iris, Persian BM 1.1	March	(1629) 6 in
		IRIS sambucina L. P. Mauve, straw & light blue Iris, Camerarius E.123.i; BM 6.187; M. 5.471	June	1658 2 ft
		IRIS (Gynandriris) sisyrinchium L. P. Blue Sisyrinchium; The Spanish nut, a kinde of Iris E.190.i; BM t.1407, t.6096	May–June	(1597) 6 in
		IRIS susiana L. P. Speckled on whitish Iris, Chalcedonians E.120.i; BM 3.91; M. 1.30	March–April	(1573) 2 ft
		IRIS xiphioides Ehrh. (latifolia) P. (Various) Iris bulbosa, white purple striped E.198.i, 199.i, 200.i, 201.i; BM t.687	June–July	(1571) 2 ft
		IRIS xiphium L. P. Blue, white, yellow Iris angustifolia bulbosa persico flo: E.197.iii, 199.ii,iii; BM t.686 Iris; greate yellow bulbosa E.185.ii, 191.i, 197.ii, 200.ii,iii, 202.ii,iii	May–June	(1596) 2 ft
		——— ——— lusitanica P. Yellow Iris; Yellow Spanish BM t.679	April	"1796" 2 ft
	T	JASMINUM grandiflorum L. S.Cl. White Jassmin, Spanish or Catalonian E.147.i; See also I.B	June–October	(1629) 15 ft
E	T	JASMINUM humile L. S. Bright yellow Indian (Jasmine) flauum or yellow E.275.ii; See also I.A	June–July	1634 4 ft
		JASMINUM officinale L. S.Cl. White Jasminum; Jassmine, the white flo: E.275.i; BM 1.31	June–September	(1548) 30 ft
E	T	JASMINUM sambac Aiton S. White Arabian (Jasmine) BM t.1785	January–December	1665 6 ft
		Jasminum—See also I.B		
E		JUNIPERUS communis L. S. Juniper minor (The Juniper tree. G.1372); See also I.A		——— 15 ft
		KNAUTIA arvensis (L.) Coulter flore albo P. White Scabiosa; English white (E.257.iii)	July–October	——— 2 ft
		KOCHIA scoparia Schrader A. Green Linaria; Broome Toad flax, Belvederes (p. 68) BM t.8808	June–September	(1629) 3 ft
		LABURNUM alpinum (Miller) Bercht. & Presl T. Yellow Laburnum; or Beane trefoile E.8.ii; BM 5.176	June	(1596) 15 ft
		LABURNUM anagyroides Medicus T. Yellow Laburnum; or Beane trefoile (greate) E.8.i	May–June	ca. 1560 20 ft
		? LAMIUM orvala L. P. Dark purple Dragons-Claw "of Seede sowd in Aprill & transpl: . . . they flo: from May 3 or 4 moneths . . . they are for bough potts etc." BM 5.172	May–July	(1596) 2 ft
		Lamium—See also I.A		

		LARIX decidua Miller T. Larix; or Larch [Larinx]; See also I.B		(1618) 90 ft
		LATHYRUS latifolius L. P. Pink Lathyrus; ever lasting pease E.299.ii	July–September	——— 6 ft
		LATHYRUS vernus (L.) Bernh. P. Purple Lathyrus, Orbus Venctus E.20.ii; BM t.521; M 1.28	March–April	(1629) 1 ft
		Lathyrus—See also in I.A		
E		LAVANDULA spica L. (angustifolia) S. Lilac E.310.iii, 347.iii	July–September	(1265) 2 ft
E	T	——— ——— alba S. White E.310.ii, 347.ii		
E		——— ——— latifolia (L.) Vill. S. Lilac	July–September	
E	T	——— stoechas L. S. Lilac Lavendula & Stoechas; Lauander of seuerall sorts (G.583); See also I.A	May–July	1562 1½ ft
E	T	LAVANDULA dentata L. S. Lilac (Fig. 6) Lavendula (of 4 sorts) BM 12.400 (t.401)	June–September	(1597) 3 ft

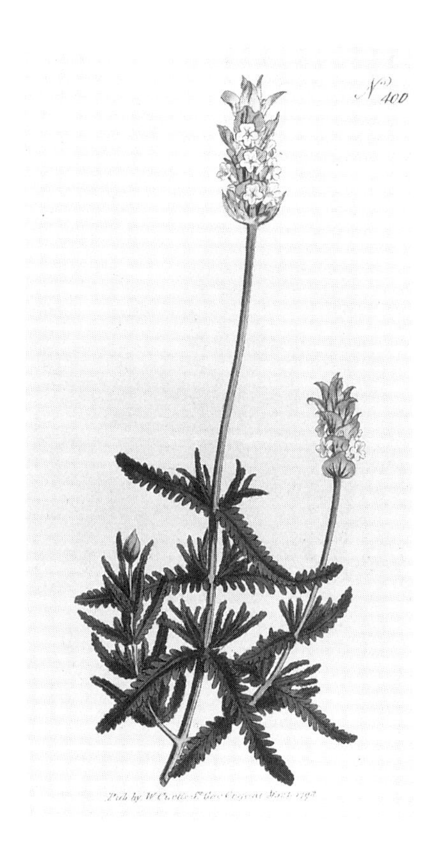

6. *Lavandula dentata*
(photo: from *Curtis's Botanical Magazine* 12 [1798], pl. 400)

		Lavatera—See I.A		
		Legousia—See SPECULARIA		
		LEUCOJUM aestivum L. P. White Leucoium Bulbosum; latter; Bulbous Violets E.66.iii, 76.ii; M 2.186	April–May	——— 1½ ft
		LEUCOJUM vernum L. P. White Leucoium Bulbosum; early; Bulbous Violets E.361.iv,v; BM 1.46	January–March	(1596) 9 in

E	LIGUSTRUM vulgare L. S. White	June–July	———
	Ligustus; Privet E.13.ii; See also I.A		10 ft
	LILIUM bulbiferum L. P. Reddish-orange	June–July	(1596)
	Lilium; red E.86.i,ii; BM 1.36, t.1018; M 1.31		3 ft
	——— ——— flore pleno		
	red double E.84.i		
	——— ——— croceum P. Orange-yellow	June–July	(1596)
	yellow E.85.i,ii, 87.i		3 ft
	LILIUM canadense L. P. Yellow or pale red, spotted	July	(1629)
	Martagon; Indian or Americane BM t.800, t.858; M 2.112		4 ft
E	LILIUM candidum L. P. White	June–July	(995)
	Lilium; white E.88.i,iii; BM 8.278		2–4 ft
	——— ——— cernuum P. White	July	
	Byzantine E.89.i,iii		
	——— ——— plenum		
	double white; See also I.A		
	LILIUM carniolicum Koch P. Orange-red	May–June	(1629)
	Martagon Panonicum		2–3 ft
	LILIUM chalcedonicum L. P. Scarlet	July–August	(1596)
	Martagon Byzantinium E.88.ii, 186.i,ii, 191.ii; BM 1.30, M 4.292		4 ft
	LILIUM martagon L. P. Purple	June–July	(1596)
	Martagon; spotted E.187.i, ii; BM t.893, t.1634; M 4.332		2–4 ft
	——— ——— album P. White	June–July	
	white E.188.iii; M 5.426		
	——— ——— sanguineo-purpureum		
	Imperiall E.181.i, 182		
	Turke-caps, Turks-cap		
	LILIUM pomponium L. P. Red	May–June	(1629)
	Martagon; Pomponian E.189.i; BM t.971; M 5.444		3 ft
	LINARIA chalepensis (L.) Miller A. White	June–July	1680
	Linaria; white		1 ft
	LINARIA purpurea (L.) Miller P. Bluish-purple	July–September	(1648)
	Linaria; purple E.343.iii; BM 3.99; M 1.34		1–3 ft
	LINARIA triphylla (L.) Miller A. Yellow & purple	June–September	(1596)
	Linaria; Valentia BM 9.324		1 ft
	LINARIA vulgaris Miller P. Pale yellow	May–October	———
	Linaria sylvest:; yellow E.162.iii		2 ft
	Linaria—See also ANARRHINUM; See also I.A		
	LOBELIA cardinalis L. P. Scarlet	May–September	(1629)
	T(h)rachelium Americanum, Companula, Flos Cardinalis; or the Cardinals flower BM 9.320; See also I.A		2–3 ft
	LONICERA periclymenum L. S.Cl. Cream & purple	June–August	———
	[Caprifol: Honisuckle vulgar], Periclymenas, Periclymenum; Wood-bynd E.129.iii		20 ft
	——— ——— serotina	August–September	
	Caprifol: serotinum flo: rubro; See also I.B		
	LUNARIA annua L. B. Pale purple	May–June	(1570)
	Viola (Lunaris) E.21.ii		4 ft
	——— ——— albiflora		
	white		

LUPINUS albus L. A. White Lupines [white] E.297.i,ii	July–August	ca. 1300 3 ft
LUPINUS hirsutus L. A. Blue Lupines, blew greate "is best"	July–August	(1629) 2 ft
LUPINUS luteus L. A. Yellow Lupines [yellow] E.296.iii; BM 4.140	July–August	(1596) 2 ft
LUPINUS varius L. A. Blue Lupines [little blue] E.296.ii	July–August	(1596) 3 ft
LYCHNIS chalcedonica L. rubra plena P. Red Lychnis Constantinop:, Chalcedonica, dubble; None-such E.254.i; BM 8.257; M 1.87 ——— ——— alba plena double white E.254.iii ——— ——— carnea blush single E.254.ii	June–July	(1596) 2 ft
LYCHNIS (Agrostemma) coronaria (L.) Desr. P. Purplish-carmine Rose-Campion E.251–2; BM 1.24	June–September	(1596) 1–2½ ft
Lychnis—See also VISCARIA		
LYCOPERSICON esculentum Miller A./P. Green Pom(m)um amoris E.319.i, 320	July–September	(1596) 3 ft
Lygos—See GENISTA monosperma		
MATRICARIA (Tripleurospermum) maritima L. plenissima A. White Cotula; double	June–October	——— 1 ft
Matthiola fruticulosa—See under HESPERIS tristis		
MATTHIOLA incana (L.) R.Br. B. Purple/Red/White Leucoium; or Stock Gilloflower (G.458), Dubble-stock E.165, 166, 167, 168.i, 179.i; See also I.A	May–November	ca. 1260 1–2 ft
——— ——— graeca flore pleno A. White Leucoium; double white Keris	May–November	? 2 ft
MEDICAGO intertexta (L.) Miller A. Yellow Medica Spinosa [Hedg-hogs &c]	June–August	(1629) 1 ft
MEDICAGO scutellata (L.) Miller A. Yellow Medica cochleata	June–August	1562 1 ft
Medicago—See also I.A		
MELAMPYRUM pratense L. A. White/Pale yellow Parietaria lutea (p. 91) E.285.ii	July–August	——— 3 ft
MELANDRIUM (Silene) album (Miller) Garcke (latifolium) flore pleno A. White Lychnis; ordinary Campion E.250.ii	May–June	——— 2 ft
MELANDRIUM (Silene) dioicum (L.) Coss. & Germ. (rubrum) flore pleno A. Red Lychnis Hortensis; or Batchelors Buttons E.250.i	May–June	——— 2 ft
MENTHA pulegium L. P. Purple Pulegium, the tufted sort E.163.ii; See also I.A	August–September	——— 3 in
MENTHA spicata L. P. Purplish Mint	July–August	——— 2 ft
Mentha—See also I.A		

		MENYANTHES trifoliata L. P. White Trifolium palustre E.109.iii	May–July	——— 1 ft
	T	MIMOSA pudica L. P. Rose-purple Planta Sensitiva; The Humble plant (p. 68)	April–September	1638 1 ft
	T	MIMOSA sensitiva L. B. Purple Planta Sensitiva; The Sensitive or Mimous plant (p. 68)	April–September	(1648) 3 ft
		MIRABILIS jalapa L. P. Red, etc. Mirabile peruvianum; single & doub: E.334.i, 335; BM 11.371; M 1.16	June–September	(1596) 2 ft
		MUSCARI botryoides (L.) Miller P. Blue Hyacinths Botrodydes inodorus; Grape flowers E.34.v; BM 5.157	April–May	(1596) 6 in
		MUSCARI comosum (L.) Miller P. Blue Hyacinths Comosus, (ramosus elegantior) E.49.i; BM 4.133; M 3.222, 3.250	April–May	(1596) 6 in
		MUSCARI moschatum Willd. (muscarimi) P. (Various) Hyacinths, Muscari E.42.ii,iii, 45.i,ii; BM t.734	April–May	(1596) 3 in
		Myricaria—See TAMARIX		
E	T	MYRTUS communis L. S. White Myrtus; Myrtil (G.1411); 9 or 10 sorts E.146.i,ii; See also I.A	July–August	(1562) 6–10 ft
		NARCISSUS bulbocodium L. P. Yellow Narcissus; large Junquille E.53.v; BM 3.88	March–April	(1629) 3 in
		NARCISSUS hispanicus Gouan P. Yellow Narcissus; crowned, greate Spanish yellow E.50.i; BM 2.51, t.1301	March–April	(1629) 1 ft
		NARCISSUS x incomparabilis Miller P. Yellow Narcissus; Nonparell E.55.i,ii; BM 4.121	April–May	(1629) 1 ft
		NARCISSUS jonquilla L. P. Yellow Narcissus, Juncifolia or Junquilia E.52.iii, 53.i,iii, 56.ii; BM 1.15; M 3.225	April–May	(1596) 1 ft
		NARCISSUS minor L. P. Yellow Narcissus; smale E.54.iv; BM 1.6	March–April	(1629) 6 in
		NARCISSUS x odorus L. P. Yellow Narcissus Angustifolius aureus BM t.934	April–May	(1629) 1 ft
		NARCISSUS pseudonarcissus L. cv. 'N. plenissimus' P. Yellow Narcissus Pseudo Narcissus; Tradescant's, Daffodiles E.52.ii, 54.i-iii, 55.iii, 56.iii; BM n.s. 216	March–April	——— 1 ft
		NARCISSUS serotinus L. P. Pale yellow Narcissus, Autumnale	August–October	(1629) 6 in
		NARCISSUS tazetta L. P. White [Narcissus of Constantinople] E.61.i-iii, 63.ii,iii, 64.i-iii; BM t.925; M 3.244	March–April	"1632" 1 ft
	T	NERINE sarniensis (L.) Herb. P. Pale salmon Narcissus of Japan; Japonius lilly BM 9.294	September–October	(1659) 1 ft
E	T	NERIUM oleander L. S. Red/White Laurus Rosea, Nerium, Laurus alexandrina or Oleander Laur., (Rose Bay. G.1406) E.138.i, 139; See also I.A	June–October	(1596) 8–15 ft
		NIGELLA damascena L. flore pleno A. Light blue Nigella of Damascus; double flo: annuall E.174.iii; BM 1.22	June–September	(1570) 2 ft

	Plant	Flowering	Date / Height
	NIGELLA hispanica L. A. Bright blue Nigella; Spanish E.174.i; BM t.1265	June–September	(1629) 2 ft
	NUPHAR lutea (L.) Sm. P. Yellow Nymphaea lutea E.111.iii	June–July	——— Floating
	NYMPHAEA alba L. P. White Nymphaea alba E.111.i,ii	June–July	——— Floating
	OCIMUM basilicum L. A. White Basil E.138.ii,iii, 234.ii, 235.i,ii, 306.ii,iii	July–August	ca. 1350 1 ft
	OENOTHERA biennis L. B. Yellow Primula; Primerose tree	June–September	(1629) 4 ft
	OPHRYS apifera Hudson P. Purple Orchis Satyrium; Bee	June–July	——— 9 in
	OPHRYS insectifera L. P. Purple Orchis Satyrium; Fly	May–June	——— 9 in
E T	OPUNTIA ficus-indica (L.) Miller S. Bright yellow Opuntia, sive Ficus Indica; the large sort (O. major, Indian Figg tree. G.1512) E.359.i, 360	June–July	(1629) 10 ft
E T	——— vulgaris Miller (humifusa) S. Golden-yellow Opuntia minor BM t.2393, t.3911; See also I.A	July–August	(1596) 2 ft
	ORCHIS mascula (L.) L. P. Purple Orchis	April–May	——— 1 ft
	ORIGANUM dictamnus L. P. Pink Dictamus; Dittany of Crete BM 9.298; See also I.A	June–August	(1551) 1 ft
	ORIGANUM ? heracleoticum L. (x applei, vulgare hirtum) P. White Dittany of Crete, white	June–November	(1640) 1 ft
T	ORIGANUM majorana L. A./B. Pink Marjoram, Sweete; Marjoram Gentle E.147.ii; See also I.A	June–July	ca. 1200 1 ft
	ORIGANUM onites L. var. P. Pink Maiorana Aurea; gilded E.322.ii	July–November	(1597) 1 ft
T	ORIGANUM syriacum L. B. Pink Marum Syriacum, 'a rare plant'; See also TEUCRIUM marum and I.A	June–July	"1823" 1 ft
T	ORNITHOGALUM arabicum L. P. White Ornithogallum; Arabic E.91.i; BM t.728, (t.3179)	March–April	(1629) 1½ ft
	ORNITHOGALUM comosum L. P. Greenish-white Ornithogallum; Hungarian E.93.iii	Jun-Aug	(1596) 6 in
	ORNITHOGALUM ? latifolium L. P. White & green Ornithogallum; greate white BM t.876	June	1629 2 ft
	ORNITHOGALUM narbonense L. (pyramidale) P. White & green Ornithogalla: Perigrinum Spicatum E.93.ii; BM t.2510	July	(1656) 2½ ft
	ORNITHOGALUM nutans L. P. White & green Ornithogallum; Neapolitan E.44.1; BM 8.269	April–May	(1634) 1½ ft
T	ORNITHOGALUM ? hispidum Horn. P. White (or)	June	"1824" 6 in
T	——— ? thyrsoides Jacq. P. White Ornithogallum; Aethiopic BM t.1164 (One of these was probably introduced to Britain ca. 1605)	June–July	"1757" 1½ ft

	ORNITHOGALUM umbellatum L. P. White Ornithogallum; or Starre of Bethlehem E.38.i, 43.iii	April–June	ca.1560 1 ft
	PAEONIA mascula (L.) Miller P. Red Paeony, Male E.103.i, 104.i, 105.i, 106.i	May–June	——— 4 ft
	PAEONIA officinalis L. P. Red Paeony, Female E.100.i, 101.i, 108.i	May–June	(995) 3 ft
	PAEONIA peregrina Miller P. Dark purple Paeony, Constantinople E.102.i, 107.i; BM t.8742	May–June	(1629) 2 ft
T	PALIURUS spina-christi Miller S. Pale green Paliurus; Christs thorne E.353.i; BM t.1893, t.2535; See also I.B	June–July	(1597) 15 ft
	PANCRATIUM illyricum L. P. White E.65.i; BM t.718; M 2.159	May–June	1615 1½ ft
T	——— maritimum L. P. White Narcissus; Sea daffodill	May–July	1597 2 ft
	PAPAVER somniferum L. A. Pink/Purple/Red/White Papaver; Popy E.290.i, 291, 292.ii,iii, 293 vars:- dubble; dubble particoloured; red striped; scarlet, etc.	July–August	ca. 900 2–4 ft
	PARADISEA liliastrum (L.) Bertol. P. White Phalangium; or Spider wort of Savoy, white Lily Asphodelus E.92.i; BM 9.318; M 1.88	May–June	(1629) 1½ ft
	PARTHENOCISSUS quinquefolia (L.) Planch. Cl. Hedera, Virginian; Virginian Ivy; See also I.B		(1629) 25 ft
E T	PASSIFLORA incarnata L. S.Cl. Pink Marecoh; Granadile or Passion Flower BM t.3697; See also I.A and ? CLEMATIS virginiana in I.B	July–August	(1629) 30 ft
T	PELARGONIUM triste (L.) Aiton P. Brownish-yellow Geranium; or Cranes bill, Nocte olens (BM t.1641)	May–October	1631 1 ft
	PERIPLOCA graeca L. Cl. Brown Periploca Verginiana; or Virginian silke BM t.2289; M 5.410	July–August	(1597) 10 ft
E T	PERSEA indica (L.) Sprengel T. Laurus Indica (American Laural); See also I.A		1665 20 ft
	? PHALARIS arundinacea L. picta P. Gramen Dactyles, striated		——— 4 ft
	PHARBITIS (Ipomoea) hederacea (L.) Choix A. Blue Convoluulus; greate blew E.301.iii; BM 6.188	July–September	(1597) 10 ft
	PHASEOLUS coccineus L. (multiflorus) A. Scarlet Scarlet kidney beane [Scarlet-beans]	July–September	1633 12 ft
	PHILADELPHUS coronarius L. dianthiflorus (plenus) S. White Syringa; White dubble flo: Pipe-tree E.2.ii; See also I.B	May–June	(1596) 8 ft
E	PHILLYREA angustifolia L. S. Phillyrea; See also I.A		(1597) 10 ft
	PLATANTHERA (Habenaria) bifolia (L.) Rich. P. White Orchis Satyrium; Gnatt E.196.iv	May–June	——— 1 ft
	PLATANTHERA (Habenaria) chlorantha (Custer) Rchb. P. White Orchis Satyrium; Butterflies E.114.i	May–July	——— 1½ ft
T	POLIANTHES tuberosa L. P. White Hyacinths, Indian; White tuberous Iacynth BM t.1817	August–September	(1629) 3 ft

	PRIMULA auricula L. P. Red/White/Yellow	April–May	(1596)
	Auricula, -lus E.16.i-iii; BM t.6837; M 3.203, 4.345; See also I.A		3–6 in
	PRIMULA elatior (L.) Hill P. Yellow	March–May	———
	Primula; Oxlip		1 ft
	PRIMULA farinosa L. P. Lilac/White	June–July	———
	Primula; Birds Eyes E.112.iv,v; M 1.96		3 in
	PRIMULA x variabilis Goupil (x polyantha) (Various)		ca. 1650
	Primula, etc. [Polyanthus]		6 in
	PRIMULA veris L. P. Yellow	May–June	———
	Primula; Cowslip E.19.iv, 128.ii, 364.v		6 in
	PRIMULA vulgaris Hudson P. Pale yellow	March–May	———
	Primula veris E.15.v		3 in
	——— ——— plena		
	dubble E.19.iii; BM 7.229; M 1.60		
	——— ——— ssp. sibthorpii P. Red		(1640)
	Primula; red primrose E.15.v; BM 7.229		3 in
	& purple that flo: twise a yeare		
	scarlet, double red M 1.60		
	Orange coloured Red		
	PRUNUS avium L. flore pleno ("Plena") White	April–May	———
	The Meris(z)iere or double blossom'd Chery; See also I.B		60 ft
	PRUNUS cerasus L. flore pleno ("Rhexii") White	May	?
	Cerasus alb: multiflora; white dubble flo: Chery E.4.i		20 ft
E	PRUNUS laurocerasus L. S. White	April–May	1611
	Laurocerasus; Common Lawrell, Cherry Bay (G.1603); See also I.A		15 ft
	PRUNUS persica (L.) Batsch plena T. Blush	April–May	ca.1200
	Peach bearing the dubble flo:		15 ft
	Prunus—See also I.A, I.B		
	PULMONARIA officinalis L. P. Pink-blue	May	ca. 1525
	Primula; Jerusalem Cowslip or Pulmonaria E.15.iv		1 ft
	PULSATILLA vulgaris Miller P. Violet	April–May	———
	Pulsatella (p. 69) E.366.ii,iii; M 3.198		6 in
	PUNICA granatum L. flore pleno S. Scarlet	June–September	ca. 1350
	Malus punica; Balaustia, duble-flo:; Pomegranade E.142.i, 143.i; See also I.B		20 ft
E	PYRACANTHA coccinea Roem. S. White	May	(1629)
	Pyracanth(a); (Euergreene Thorne. G.1603); See also I.A		15 ft
E	QUERCUS ilex L. T.		1580
	Ilex glandifera; (seu yren scarlet Oake. The euergreene Oake. G.1344); See also I.A		60 ft
	Quercus—See also I.B		
	RAMONDA myconi (L.) Schultz (pyrenaica) P. Purple	May	(1629)
	Burrage leavd Auricule BM 7.236; M 1.83		3 in
	RANUNCULUS acris L. flore pleno B./P. Yellow	June–July	———
	Ranunculus; an ordinary wild crow foote . . . a bisannual E.28.iii; BM 6.215		2 ft
	RANUNCULUS asiaticus L. P. (Various)	May–June	(1596)
	Ranunculus; Byzantine or Asiatic E.29.i-v; BM t.9380; M 3.271		9 in

	RANUNCULUS bulbosus L. flore pleno P. Yellow Ranunculus; Tuberosus E.26.iii, 28.i	May–June	——— 6 in
	RANUNCULUS spp. & cvs. Ranunculus; "etc."		
E	RHAMNUS alaternus L. "Glaber" S. Yellow-green Celastrus (Theophrast: Clus: The staff tree. G.1600); See also I.A	April	(1629) 10 ft
	Rhamnus—See also I.B		
	RHUS typhina L. (hirta) T. Rhus; or Indian Sumach [Virginian sumach]		(1629) 25 ft
	RICINUS communis L. A. Green Ricinus, seu Palma Christi E.248.i, 249.i; BM t.2209	July–August	(1548) 6 ft
	ROSA x alba L. S. White White Rose P.1; E.96.ii; Lawr t.37 ——— ——— "Alba Maxima" dubble white E.94.i, 96.i; Lawr t.25 ——— ——— "Great Maiden's Blush" The Blush Rose P.2; E.97.ii; Lawr. t.32 — — ——— var. S. Vergin rose without thornes P.14	June–July	(900) 6 ft (1597) (1550)
	ROSA canina L. flore pleno S. Pink Canina, double	June–July	——— 8 ft
	ROSA x centifolia L. (R. gallica centifolia) S. Centifolia P.5; E.95.i, 96.iv; Lawr t.22, t.40, t.44; M 5.465 ——— ——— provincialis (R. provincialis) Province P.6; E.95.iii; Lawr t.1, t.8	June–August	ca. 1580 5 ft
	ROSA ? chinensis Jacq. (indica) S. Blush China, or Ferrarius his rose of a rare beauty "They are yet strangers with us, but have ben perfected in Italy" (This introduction presumably extinct) Lawr t.26; M 2.185, 5.445	January–December	? 20 ft
	ROSA cinnamomea L. (majalis) S. Lilac-pink [Cinamon Rose] P.15; E.98.ii ——— ——— flore pleno double	May–June	(1600) 6 ft
	ROSA x damascena Miller S. Pink Common Damaske P.4; Lawr t.5, t.38 ——— ——— x bifera (x d. semperflorens) Monethly or Italian (flo: pleno) ——— ——— "Versicolor" (variegata) Yorke & Lancaster P.8; Lawr t.10	June–July	ca. 1520 3 ft
	ROSA eglanteria L. (rubiginosa) S.Cl. Pink Wild Eglantine P.22 ——— ——— Cynorrhodon or Eglantine P.23; E.99.i,iv; Lawr t.65 ——— ——— inodora Inodura	May–June	——— 7 ft
	ROSA foetida Herr. (lutea) S. Yellow Single yellow P.16; E.98.i; BM 11.363 ——— ——— "Bicolor" (R. punicea) S. Red & yellow Austrian BM t.1077	June June	ca. 1585 5 ft ca. 1590 5 ft
	ROSA x francofurtana Gmelin (turbinata) S. Pink Frankford stock P.11; E.97.i; Lawr t.63, t.69	June–August	(1629)

	Plant	Flowering	Date / Height
	ROSA gallica L. S. Red	June–July	(900)
	Red Rose P.3; E.97.iii; Lawr t.16		3 ft
	———— ———— "Versicolor"		(1659)
	Rosa mundi (striped red) E.95.ii; Lawr t.13		
	———— ———— var.		
	Bataua, Batavian Rose Lawr t.11		
	———— ———— "Marmorea"		
	Marble Rose (probably extinct)		
	———— ———— vellutinaeflora		
	Velvet Rose P. 13		
	ROSA hemisphaerica Herrm. (sulphurea) S. Yellow	July	1586
	Dubble Yellow (Rose) P.17; E.95.iv		10 ft
	ROSA moschata Herrm. S.Cl. White	July–October	ca. 1515
	Muske rose P.18; Lawr t.53, t.64		12 ft
	ROSA pimpinellifolia L. (spinosissima) foliis variegatis S. White	June–July	————
	Variegata; Variegated-leaved Rose		2 ft
E	ROSA sempervirens L. S. White	June–August	1629
	Rosa Semp: virens P.24		20 ft
	ROSA villosa L. S. Carmine-pink	June–July	————
	The Apple rose		8 ft
	ROSA spp. vars. S.		
	———— ———— Christall P.9		
	———— ———— Ponfraict		
	———— ———— Red dwarfe double P.10		
	———— ———— The Spanish Muske P.20		
	See also I.A and I.B		
E	ROSMARINUS officinalis L. S. Pale purple	January–April	ca. 1340
	Rosemary E.284.iii		4 ft
	———— ———— latifolius		
	Latifolia		
T	———— ———— foliis-aureis ("Aureus")		
	Rosemarium Aureum; Golden		
T	———— ———— foliis-argentiis		
	Silverd		
	———— ———— flore pleno		
	double flowered (? extinct); See also I.A		
	RUBUS odoratus L. S. Red	June–July	(1656)
	Rubus odoractus, Indicus or Americanus BM 9.323		7 ft
	Rubus—See also I.B		
E	SALVIA officinalis L. P. Purple	June–July	(995)
	Salvia; Sage E.238.i,ii		2 ft
	———— ———— var.		
	musky		
	———— ———— variegata ("Icterina")		
	variegat		
	Salvia—See also I.A		
	SAMBUCUS nigra L. T. White	May–July	————
	Sambucus; or Elder rose		15 ft
	SAPONARIA officinalis L. flore pleno P. Pink	July–October	————
	Saponaria flo: dupl. (E.261.i)		2 ft
T	SASSAFRAS albidum Nees T.		(1633)
	Sassafras; See also I.B		50 ft

	SAXIFRAGA x geum L. (hirsuta) P. Pale pink Sanicula guttata major E.128.iii	May–July	——— 1 ft
	SCABIOSA atropurpurea L. A./B. Dark crimson Scabiosa; Scabius, Red Indian E.259.i,ii; BM 7.247; M 2.119	July–September	(1629) 3–4 ft
	SCABIOSA sylvatica L. P. Purple Scabiosa, Red Austrian	July	(1633) 3 ft
	Scabiosa—See also CEPHALARIA, KNAUTIA		
E T	SCHINUS molle L. S. Green Lentiscus Peruviana BM t.3339	July–August	(1597) 12 ft
	SCILLA bifolia L. alba P. (Blue)/White Hyacinths, Stellatus flo: albo E.37.iv; BM t.746; M 2.125, 176	February–April	——— 3 in
	SCILLA peruviana L. P. Lilac-reddish Hyacinths, Iacynth of Peru E.41.i; BM t.749	May	1607 1 ft
	SCILLA verna Hudson P. Pale blue Ornithogallum; Spanish E.33.iv	April–May	——— 3 in
	SCORPIURUS sulcatus L. A. Yellow Scorpoides; Caterpillars	June–July	(1596) 2 ft
E	SEDUM acre L. P. Yellow E.298.iii	June	——— 3 in
E	——— album L. P. White	June–July	——— 3 in
E	——— reflexum L. P. Yellow Sedum; Trickmadame; See also I.A	June–July	——— 1 ft
	SILENE armeria L. A. Carmine/White Muscipula; for Summer and Autumne flo: [Lobels Catchfly] E.155.ii,iii	May–September	——— 1½ ft
	SILENE muscipula L. A. Red Muscipula	July–August	(1596) 1½ ft
	Silene—See also MELANDRIUM, VISCARIA		
	SIMETHIS planifolia (L.) Gren. & Godron (mattiazzii) P. Purple & whitish Asphodelus minimus	June-July	——— 1 ft
	SOLANUM aethiopicum L. A. White Pomum Aethiopicum (p. 68) E.322.i	July–September	(1597) 1½ ft
	SOLANUM dulcamara L. variegatum Cl. Purple shrub Solanum with variegated leaves E.180.ii,iii; M 2.109	June–July	——— 4–6 ft
E T	SOLANUM pseudocapsicum L. S. White Amomum Plinij E.148.i	June–September	(1596) 4 ft
	SOLDANELLA alpina L. P. Purple Soldanella BM 2.49; M 4.317	April	(1629) 3 in
	SPARTIUM junceum L. S. Yellow Genista Hispan: Spartum Hispanum; Spanish broome E.137.ii; BM 3.85; See also I.A	June–September	(1548) 10 ft
	SPECULARIA (Legousia) pentagonia (L.) Druce E.109.i		"1686" 1 ft
	——— speculum (L.) A.DC. A. Purple/White Speculum Veneris [Venus looking-glasse] BM 3.102; M 2.147	May–August	(1596) 1 ft

		SPIRAEA hypericifolia L. S. White Hypericum frutex	April–May	1633 6 ft
		SPIRAEA salicifolia L. S. Pink/White Spiraea Frutex; S. Theophrasti or Mock Willow	June–August	(1586) 5 ft
	T	? SPREKELIA formosissima (L.) Herb. P. Crimson Narcissus; Long necked Indian BM 2.47	May–August	(1629) 1 ft
		STAPHYLEA pinnata L. S. White Nux Vesicaria; Bladder nut E.7.i	May–June	(1596) 15 ft
		STERNBERGIA lutea (L.) Sprengel P. Yellow Colchicum; Autumnall, yellow E.349.i; BM 9.290	August–September	1596 6 in
E		SUAEDA fruticosa Forsk. (vera) S. Vermicularis frutex; See also I.A		———— 2 ft
		SYRINGA x persica L. "Laciniata" S. Lilac Persian (Jasmine) BM 14.486	May	1634 8 ft
		SYRINGA vulgaris L. S. Lilac/Purple/White Syringa; blew Pipe-tree E.1.ii,iii; BM 6.183	May	(1597) 8 ft
		Syringa—See also I.B		
		TAGETES erecta L. A. Yellow Floss Affricanus, "maximus multiplex"; Affricane E.305.i, 306.i	June–September	(1596) 3 ft
		TAGETES patula L. A. Yellow & orange Floss Affricanus; lesser French, French Marigold E.305.ii,iii, 307; BM 5.150, t.3830; M 1.56	July–October	(1573) 2 ft
E		TAMARIX gallica L. S. Flesh	May–October	?1558 12 ft
E		MYRICARIA germanica (L.) Desv. S. Pink Tamariscus siue Myrica, Tamarix. (The Tamarisk tree. G.1378); See also I.B	June–September	1582 8 ft
		Tanacetum—See CHRYSANTHEMUM parthenium; See also in I.A		
E	T	? TEUCRIUM marum L. S. Reddish-purple Marum Syriacum; See also ORIGANUM syriacum and I.A	July–September	(1640) 1 ft
		THALICTRUM aquilegifolium L. P. Light yellow Thalictrum Hispan: album Alpina; white Spanish Tufts E.25.i,ii; BM t.1818, t.2025	May–July	(1629) 3 ft
E		THUJA occidentalis L. T. Arbor vitae sive Thugae (Thuia or Tuya. Tree of life. G.1369); See also I.A		(1596) 30 ft
E		THYMUS x citriodorus Schreber S. Purple Limon Tyme E.345.ii	June–August	? 3 in
E		THYMUS serpyllum L. agg. S. Purple Serpillum; Time (G.570)	June–August	———— 3 in
E		———————— moschatus Muske		
		———— ———— ? Tufted		
E		———— ———— variegatus Gilded; See also I.A		
		THYMUS vulgaris L. S. Pale purple Thymus (Serpillum); Time E.345.iii	June–August	ca. 1200 8 in

	Plant	Flowering	Introduced / Height
	Thymus—See also I.A		
	TRADESCANTIA virginiana L. P. Blue Phalangium; Virginian BM 3.105	May–October	(1629) 1½ ft
	TRIGONELLA radiata (L.) Boiss. A. Yellow Medica cochleata; (lunata)	June–July	(1629) 6 in
	Tripleurospermum—see MATRICARIA		
	TROLLIUS europaeus L. P. Yellow Ranunculus Globus; Globe-flo: E.26.ii; M 3.209	May–June	———— 2 ft
	TROPAEOLUM minus L. A. Yellow Nasturtium indicum E.294.i; BM 3.98	June–October	(1596) 6 in
	TULIPA gesneriana L. P. (Various) Tulips E.67–75, 76.i, 77, 78.i, 79.i; BM t.1135; M 3.245	April–May	1577 1–2 ft
	VERBASCUM blattaria L. B. Yellow Blattaria; Moth Mullen, annuals E.265.i,ii	July–August	———— 4 ft
	VERBASCUM lychnitis L. A./B. Cream Blattaria; white E.266.iii	June–August	———— 3 ft
	VERBASCUM phoeniceum L. P. Purple Blattaria; purple BM t.885, M 1.45	May–August	(1596) 2–3 ft
	VERBASCUM thapsus L. A./B. Yellow Blattaria; greate Yellow E.266.ii	July–August	———— 6 ft
	VERBASCUM sp. P. Pale yellow Blattaria; sweete yellow (? extinct)		(1629) 3 ft
	Verbascum—See also I.A		
	VERONICA ? longifolia L. P. Blue [Veronica] E.89.ii	August	"1731" 2 ft
	Veronica—See also I.A		
	VIBURNUM opulus L. S. White Guelder Rose E.10.i	June	———— 10 ft
E	VIBURNUM tinus L. S. White Laurus tinus; Laurus tine; wild bay (tree. G.1409) 3 sorts BM 2.38	September–March	(1560) 10–15 ft
E T	———— ———— lucidum (shining)		(1596)
E T	———— ———— strictum (upright); See also I.A		(1596)
E	VINCA major L. P. Purple Clematis Daphnoides (major) E.129.i	August	(————) Creeping
E	———— minor L. P. Blue/Violet/White C. D. (minor) E.7.ii-v Clematis Daphnoides perevincia (siue Vinca pervinca; Peruincle. G.894); See also I.A	August	———— Creeping
	VIOLA odorata L. flore pleno P. Purple Viola; Common dubble (Violet. G.849) E.18.i-v	March–May	———— 6 in
	VIOLA ? pubescens Aiton P. Yellow the Virginian yellow violet	May–July	"1772" 1 ft
	VIOLA tricolor L. A./P. Purple & yellow Viola tricolor (or Herba Trinitatis; Paunsies. G.853) E.48.ii, 289.ii, 364.iv; M 5.421	April–September	———— 6 in-1 ft

	VISCARIA vulgaris Bernh. (Lychnis viscaria) P. Pink Muscipula E.5.ii; See also SILENE	May–June	——— 1½ ft
	YUCCA gloriosa L. S. White & green Yucca, or Indian bread BM t.1260; M 3.286; See also I.A	July–August	(1596) 4 ft
T	? ZEPHYRANTHES atamasco Herb. P. White Virginian Narcissus with a purplish flower (Asphodelus; Lily kind, bloush & white) BM 7.239; M 3.285	May–June	(1629) 6 in
T	ZINGIBER officinale Roscoe P. Red Ginger "which we heare has bin successfully planted"	June–August	1605 3 ft

Evelyn's Idea of the Garden: A Theory for All Seasons

JOHN DIXON HUNT

I

The importance of "Elysium Britannicum" must be clear to anyone who has struggled through the palimpsestial manuscript or, now, profited from reading the essays collected in this volume. Its value as a documentary conspectus of "gardenist"[1] ideas in the late seventeenth century probably needs little further argument, though a full realization of that scope will have to wait for its larger circulation in published form.[2] But Evelyn's conceptual interests are far less easy to register. Yet, of as much importance to anyone interested in landscape architecture as the evidence of his historical testimony is the theoretical value of his deliberations and memoranda; that, therefore, will be my topic here.

The centrality in John Evelyn's life and works of a preoccupation with the garden cannot be doubted. Though absorbed in a quite astonishing range of topics and projects during his eighty-five years,[3] he nonetheless committed himself tenaciously to the gardenist work. It was both business and recreation (among which "I reckon Gardening, Groves and Walks and other innocent Amenitys"[4]), both pragmatic and intellectual, physical as well as spiritual. There are many reasons for this dedication to gardens and gardening; Michael Hunter's paper in this volume, "John Evelyn in the 1650s,"

[1] I use this term of Horace Walpole's anachronistically, to refer to the whole range of Evelyn's practical, theoretical, and historical interests in the garden. See I. W. U. Chase, *Horace Walpole Gardenist,* Princeton, N.J., 1943, 184.

[2] I want to express my own gratitude to John Ingram, not only for the laborious work he undertook in transcribing Evelyn's manuscript, but also for his generosity in making the transcription available ahead of its publication to those of us involved with Dumbarton Oaks' seventeenth colloquium on landscape architecture.

[3] See Geoffrey Keynes, *John Evelyn: A Study in Bibliophily with a Bibliography of His Writings,* Oxford, 1968, both for some indication of the range of Evelyn's preoccupations and for clear evidence that writer's block cannot have been Evelyn's main problem with bringing "Elysium Britannicum" to a conclusion.

[4] *Memoires for my Grand-son,* Geoffrey Keynes, ed., London, 1926, 16. The garden as recreation was, perhaps, a theme especially suited to Evelyn during the interregnum, when he could otherwise not be "beneficiall to our countrey" (as quoted by Michael Hunter in this volume, "John Evelyn in the 1650s: A Virtuoso in Quest of a Role," 82, originally from George Evelyn to Richard Evelyn, April 3, 1637, in Evelyn Collection box of Evelyn period, loose letters).

has most usefully directed us to one of them. Evelyn, he argues, was a syncretic philsopher; it is, therefore, natural that he would have been attracted to a theme, the garden, privileged in its concentration of both natural and cultural elements and in its ambition to represent the whole world beyond its walls. To consider the garden was necessarily to synthesize a great number of prime human concerns. In Evelyn's explicit, and even more in his implied, claims for gardens, there lurks one of the more profound intuitions of the centrality of the garden in man's spiritual formation. The role of the garden parallels, if it does not coincide with, the Greek *paideia,* about which Joseph Levine writes: a totality of education, formation, and culture, for which the garden can be both site and symbol.[5] Hence, Evelyn's confidence, as stated in the "Elysium Britannicum," that "a gardiner becomes one of the most usefull members of Humane Societie" (p. 4).

What Evelyn's correspondent John Beale called "hortulan affaires"[6] were long associated with meditative and philosophical traditions, and they authorized Evelyn to elevate his writings on the garden, to yoke technological with philosophical and intellectual concerns and thus allow the gardener "seacret & powerfull influence . . . to operat upon humane spirits towards virtue and sanctitie."[7] In this respect, Michael Hunter was also right to remind us of the "highly literary" nature of "Elysium Britannicum,"[8] but this does not mean just fine periods and fancy phrases. It indicates the high status to which Evelyn wished to raise gardenist discourse; elevated style meant an elevated topic.

Yet, the opposite face of Evelyn's own syncretic inclinations, which found such a congenial territory in the garden's inclusiveness, was ambivalence and "fundamental uncertainty."[9] These are not themselves alien to garden experience, but they do tend to disable any intellectual attempt to determine an "idea of the garden." Evelyn's uncertainties may have arisen precisely because he and other gardenists were poised to pronounce some radical concepts; but whatever the reason, they must also be taken into consideration when pursuing this theme through the "Elysium Britannicum." They also have consequences for its incompletion.

His gardenist ideas can best be examined within three intellectual contexts that are more or less fully documented in Evelyn's day and will illuminate Evelyn's high ambitions, however flawed, for his gardenist work. These contexts are the dialogue between theory and, if not practice, then experimentation; the battle of ancients and moderns, on which Joseph Levine writes in this volume; and art and nature, which has always been a complex binary concept, and given our concerns in this volume, it is also the most important context of the three.

[5] Joseph Levine, this volume, "John Evelyn: Between the Ancients and the Moderns," 58. Evelyn's intuitions, in large measure, anticipate the vision of Rudolf Borchardt in *Der leidenschafliche Gärtner,* the first full text of which appeared in Borchardt's *Complete Works,* Stuttgart, 1968. There is an Italian translation, which is what I have read, *Il giardiniere Appassionato,* Milan, 1992. I am much indebted to Lucia Tongiorgi Tomasi for directing my attention to it.

[6] University of Sheffield, Hartlib MS 67\22\1A. See my essay on this theme, "Hortulan affaires," in Mark Greengrass, Michael Leslie, and Timothy Raylor, eds., *Samuel Hartlib and Universal Reformation: Studies in Intellectual Communication,* Cambridge, 1994.

[7] As cited by Hunter, "Evelyn in the 1650s," 104.

[8] Ibid., 102.

[9] Hunter's phrase, ibid., 99, referring to Evelyn's notes to his translation of Lucretius.

II

As a product of the scientific mentality we associate with the Royal Society, the "Elysium Britannicum" was necessarily dedicated to empirical enquiry. But Evelyn's own temperament seems to have been sufficiently at home with an attitude that authorized the accumulation of firsthand experience of gardens. His diary and correspondence, let alone the references and acknowledgments throughout the manuscript, show that he himself clearly lived by the advice that he gave to a young traveler in January 1657: "And I beseech you, forget not to informe yourselfe as diligently as may be, in things that belong to gardening."[10] That he missed no occasion on which to augment his fund of information is attested at every turn; he surely glances at himself in *Sculptura,* when he writes of Giacomo Favi that "this curious person neglected nothing, but went on collecting . . . There was nothing so small, and to appearance, trifling, which he did not cast his eyes upon."[11] He told John Beale, in 1679, that the "particulars" he wished to insert into the garden manuscript were "daily increasing," yet he also remarked that the "inexhaustible subject (I mean horticulture) [is] not yet fully digested in my mind."[12]

He glances here at the "paragone"—a word Evelyn himself employs in "Elysium Britannicum" (p. 290) to mean comparison but which also carried the sense of contest—between, on the one hand, the "enormous . . . heap"[13] of details that constituted much of his work for the "Elysium Britannicum" and, on the other, "the frame or Idea"[14] that would give them coherence. The slowness with which he constructed what we might call theoretical overviews, missing the wood for numbering of its trees, surely lies at the heart of his failure to complete the manuscript.

Evelyn claims that the "Elysium Britannicum" is the fruit of "solid and unsophisticated experiment" (p. 199), "unsophisticated" drawing its main force from a reference to the Greek sophists, who were notorious for privileging "rhetorical argument" over substance. There are innumerable times in the "Elysium Britannicum" when this predilection for experiment is made palpable, for instance, in the related senses of trying something out, relying on careful experience, as well as of concentrating on particulars.

He has a passion for lists: not simply for lists of plants, which one would expect from a practical guide to gardening (e.g., pp. 260, insert, and 267, and 278), but for lists that rhetorically relish the variety, the sheer abundance of examples: the minerals that may be used to create grottoes (pp. 135–36), an anatomy of Alexander Pope's Twickenham grotto *avant la lettre*; mountains that have figured in biblical experience (p. 147); and persons—"Patriarchs, Kings, and Heros"—whose statues might

[10] William Bray, ed., *The Diary of John Evelyn . . . to which are added a selection from his familiar letters,* revised by Henry B. Wheatley, 4 vols., London, 1879, hereafter cited as *Evelyn Letters,* I, 224–26, and E. S. de Beer, ed., *Diary of John Evelyn,* Oxford, 1955, III, 222, note.

[11] *Sculptura*, London, 1662, A5-b1v.

[12] As quoted in Arthur Ponsonby, *John Evelyn,* London, 1933, 269.

[13] *Acetaria; a Discourse of Sallets,* London, 1699, preface.

[14] Hunter, "Evelyn in the 1650s," 86, originally in letter from Evelyn to George Evelyn, October 15, 1658. In his address "To the Reader" of *Sylva,* Evelyn opposes "the Real Effects of the Experimental, Collecting, Examining, and Improving their scatter'd Phaenomena's" to the "Notional, and Formal way of delivering divers Systems and Bodies of Philosophy (falsely so call'd)": *Sylva; or a Discourse of Forest-Trees,* 3rd ed., London, 1679, A1v.

be placed in gardens (p. 154a). The visual equivalent of these rhetorical lists is his display of garden tools on pages 50 and 51.[15] Even as he generalizes, for example, about soils or plants, he often escapes into "sundry peculiarities in which they differ from one another" (p. 38, insertion).[16] The "Elysium" balances, sometimes awkwardly, sometimes agilely, between specific examples, or what were called "histories,"[17] and general ideas or those things that Evelyn says are "to be discovered by the mind only" (p. 256).[18]

The mind's control or overview of experimental evidence was equally vital to Evelyn's gardenist purposes, especially when we recall either the prejudices about the status of gardenist writings[19] or the conceptual and theoretical baggage with which the garden traveled in the seventeenth century. Among the most obvious of this cluster of associations, ideas, and even ideals, as the "Elysium" starts out by acknowledging, was the "memorie of that delicious place," Paradise, from which "our Forefathers" were exiled (p. 1).[20] That this is not a mere idle conceit has been well documented in John Prest's *The Garden of Eden*.[21] Viewing the hortulan world in all its detail and variety, through the lens of ideas or types, was another commonplace of the age: thus Evelyn notes, again in the opening pages of the manuscript, that when people "would frame a Type of Heaven, because there is nothing in Nature more worthy and illustrious they describe a Garden" (p. 2).

Beyond such controlling ideas and types lay the urgent need for the subject of horticulture to be defined, to establish for itself an idea of the hortulan world so as not to be prevailed over by its multitudinousness.[22] In this respect, the "Elysium Britannicum" is exactly like a contemporary cabi-

[15] These are illustrated in Theresa O'Malley's "Introduction to John Evelyn and the 'Elysium Britannicum,'" this volume, 14.

[16] For example, he may acknowledge "the ultimate design etc" (p. 38) as when he writes,

> The Earth does generally lye in beds, or couches stratum super stratum, in divers thicknesses; but for the most part, next to the surface, it is a foote thick, in some places deeper, more or lesse, which is ever the mould the most prolific, and naturaly endow'd for production of Plants as having bin temper'd and prepar'd by the activity, qualities, and operations of all those principles which we have before discoursed of; and so, from one degree to another, all the rest of the successive and subjacent beds. (p. 38)

Yet, at this point he cannot resist the urge to catalogue varieties: "(The usual sorts of mould are the pulla, alba, Topacea, rubrica, columbina . . .)" (p. 23).

[17] On the importance of case studies for English garden history, see Michel Baridon, "Ruins as Mental Construct," *Journal of Garden History* 5 (1985), 84–96.

[18] Here Evelyn is speaking of minute insects, in fact.

[19] See what even his old friend Thomas Henshaw wrote of the translation of Nicolas de Bonnefons' *The French Gardiner*—that it had taken Evelyn away from "studies of a higher and nobler nature" (as cited in Hunter, "Evelyn in the 1650s," 101, originally from a letter of Henshaw to Evelyn, February 28, 1658/59. 27).

[20] See also "as near as we can contrive [our Gardens] to the resemblance of that blessed abode [Paradise . . . of Gods own planting]": *Kalendarium Hortense,* 7th ed., London, 1683, 9.

[21] J. Prest, *The Garden of Eden: The Botanical Garden and the Re-Creation of Paradise,* New Haven, 1981.

[22] Here I echo a famous passage of Matthew Arnold in *Culture and Anarchy*, 1869, in which he urges his readers to study what he called "the intelligible law of things": p. 155 in the edition by J. Dover Wilson, Cambridge, 1960. John Aubrey's garden investigations offer a comparable case, where he and, indeed, we may often forget his underlying concern to track the "Italian way of gardening" through myriads of local examples and memoranda (Bodleian Library, Aubrey MS 2, fol. 53).

net of curiosities, so crammed with *naturalia* and *artificialia* that it sometimes defies coherence.[23] Its first chapter, indeed, is headed "A Garden derived, and defined, with its distinctions and sorts."

When John Beale first wrote to Samuel Hartlib, who passed the letter on to Evelyn, it was to express a similar concern for the "definition of a Garden."[24] The desire to raise the intellectual stakes of garden discourse by theory, as well as by practical experiment, was one way to persuade those who thought "this Arte [of gardening] an easy and insipid study" (p. 5). Elsewhere, Evelyn insists that he "pretend[s] not here to write to Cabbage-planters; but to the best refined of our Nation who delight in Gardens, and aspire to the perfections of the Arte (& for Institution)" (p. 10). His prospectus for the complete "Elysium Britannicum" sets out the range of materials that makes up the subject of gardening—"Scientia pluribus disciplinis, et variis eruditionibus ornata" (p. 5); such an agenda required a controlling "idea," a word he often uses.[25] When he observes of gilly-flowers that they are "impregnat with an Idea altogether celestiall and spiritual, which revives and cherishes them" (p. 12), I would take that as an analogy for his theoretical concerns.

His language may be literary, but it announces serious aims. He says that he wishes to "comprehend the nature of the Earth" (p. 4), "comprehend" meaning not only to understand but to take in the whole, to be comprehensive. He also writes of a "Royall & universall Plantation" (p. 54), "universall" also meaning, I think, comprehensive,[26] but extensive, complete, and perfect as well—an ideal garden that includes everything[27] or has universal application, a gardening work to end all gardening works: "These are forever" (p. 45). Such a large ambition presupposes some conceptual "frame or Idea."

Evelyn was not perhaps by temperament a theorizer, at least when we judge him by the theoretical delirium of the modern academy.[28] It is, indeed, with apparent relief at one point in the "Elysium" that he descends "now to the Particulars" from "Rules [that] may suffice for the Generall" (p. 281), and his *Sylva* opposes "particulars" to "hard words," "speculation," and "Rhapsodies."[29] Of course, the whole spirit of the new science encouraged this loyal member of the Royal Society in a hostility to "Fantasms and fruitless Speculations."[30] It was his constant business to denounce

[23] For discussions of the close connections and parallels between gardens and cabinets, see John Dixon Hunt, "'*Curiosities* to adorn *Cabinets* and *Gardens*,'" in Oliver Impey and Arthur MacGregor, eds., *The Origins of Museums: The Cabinet of Curiosities in Sixteenth- and Seventeenth-Century Europe,* Oxford, 1985, 193–203; Erik de Jong, "Nature and Art: The Leiden Hortus as 'musaeum,'" in L. Tjon Sie Fat and E. de Jong, eds., *The Authentic Garden,* Leiden, 1991, 37–60.

[24] University of Sheffield, Hartlib MS 67\22\1B.

[25] See his remarks on Spenser, in the "Elysium," 58; see also, among others, pp. 7 and 10. It is worth noting that the references to Spenser and Sidney are added by Evelyn to the lengthy description sent him by John Beale (for which see below, p. 286).

[26] "[T]o the end that there may be nothing defective to accomplish this Argument (& render it universal)" (p. 122).

[27] See his remark, discussed below, p. 279 that it is possible to create artificial echoes for gardens which, lacking real ones, are otherwise perfect, p. 168.

[28] But in this context we might do better to rely upon the classical and Johnsonian sense of theory as speculation.

[29] *Sylva,* 3rd ed., A2v.

[30] Ibid.

"spectres, Forms, Intentional Species, Vacuum, Occult Qualities, and other Inadaequate Notions."[31]

Yet, it seems to me that we lose a vital dimension of Evelyn's great hortulan enterprise when we neglect its necessary search for general principles, when we become hypnotized with the innumerable experiments and miss his own grapplings with theoretical and conceptual questions. He himself averred, in *Silva,* that "from a plentiful and well-furnish'd Magazine of true Experiments, they may in time advance to solemn and established Axioms, General Rules and Maximes; and a Structure may indeed lift up its head, such as may stand the shock of Time."[32] To see what "structure" of "general rules" struggled to emerge from his gardenist researches, I must turn to two other sets of binary concepts.

III

I have little to add to what has been written about Evelyn and the battle of ancients and moderns. His treatment of classical and modern authors always seems evenhanded; he does not set them against one another. When the esteemed elder Pliny falters, Evelyn's treatment of his lapse is good-mannered: "we cannot but wonder why Pliny should affirme, that [cypresse seedes] prosper not, if on the same day they be sowne, the raine falls on them: it is doubtlesse either a mistake, or some superstitious observation" (p. 70).

Yet, the central ambition of the "Elysium Britannicum"—to "refine upon what has bin sayd" (p. 199)—is an undertaking that is essentially modern. Building upon previous hortulan discourse—and the materials of Evelyn's very wide-ranging historical readings provide him, everywhere, with firm foundations—he wanted to establish his own distinctly up-to-date idea of the garden. In articulating a theory of gardening that would, nonetheless, acknowledge and accommodate ancient practices, he was alive to the essential paradox that such a theory had, of course, to be modern; namely, that it had to take its perspective from as recent a time as possible simply to avail itself of all available data and to conduct its enquiry in the new scientific spirit.[33] The "Artist Gardiner," he writes in the preface to *Acetaria,* takes many ages to be perfected.

However, gardening, by its very nature, occupied a special place in the ancient-modern paragone. Gardens were nothing if not alive, flourishing upon the ground, and (in short) modern. While it might be possible to write a convincing pindaric ode or to reproduce the classical orders of architecture, it was impossible to create a facsimile of an ancient garden, not least because of the absence of adequate models. Evelyn's Surrey neighbor and garden enthusiast Thomas Howard, earl of Arundel, had been a great collector of antiquities,[34] the sort of English virtuoso who would (in the words of an

[31] *Acetaria,* A3r. In his copy of the fourth edition of Evelyn's *Silva,* 1706, now at the Oak Spring Garden Library, Upperville, Va., Peter Collinson notes in a margin, "No credit to Monkish Stories," p. 219.

[32] "To the Reader," *Silva,* **3r.

[33] In this context, it is worth recalling that Clarence J. Glacken, *Traces on the Rhodian Shore: Nature and Culture in Western Thought from Ancient Times to the End of the Eighteenth Century,* Berkeley, 1967, stresses the modernity of Evelyn's forestry ideas which, he says, are "based on a philosophy of man's relation to his surroundings," p. 490.

[34] See "Elysium Britannicum," 154.

ironic Italian) have carted off the Colosseum had it been portable.[35] Yet, while amphitheaters or Elgin Marbles can be dismantled and transported, ancient gardens, even if they still existed, could not. So, when Sir William Temple said (and Alexander Pope echoed him in the 1710s)[36] that the garden of Alcinous in Homer's *Odyssey* provided all the necessary rules for a fine garden, they were acknowledging implicitly that ancient garden art could be recovered only by a double act of translation—from word into image and from past into present. Nor was translation considered a diminution or declension; rather, it enabled foreign work to discover fresh life and language.[37]

If the art of the garden were to flourish *anew* in late seventeenth-century England—an elysium britannicum—then it had to reinvent ancient forms that, as fresh inventions, would become, in their turn, modern. It was in that spirit that Evelyn redesigned the Albury garden for Arundel's grandson, as a memory theater of classical sites, even as it was at the same time a new and unique English landscape—"such a pausillipe is nowhere in England besides."[38]

An extra dimension of the ancient-modern paragone was the so-called progress of the arts.[39] This theme, alluded to obliquely at many points in the "Elysium Britannicum," would track the art of, say, poetry, from classical times through its supposed medieval hibernation, its rewakening in the Renaissance, and then its progress across Europe, until its final manifestation and apotheosis in England (if you were Swedish or French, then the finale came in Sweden or France; if you were Thomas Jefferson, then it would happen in America); and so it was with garden art. By virtue of his own translations (not just of garden items), and, we might add, his son's version of René Rapin's Latin poem on gardens, Evelyn was directly contributing to this transference, the cultural progress of gardenist ideas northward to England and into English.

This point of view is wholly explicit in William Wotton's *Reflections upon Ancient and Modern Learning,* to the second edition of which, in 1697, he adds a chapter, "Of ancient and modern agriculture and gardening."[40] Wotton is less cagey than Evelyn, and he cites the latter's *Sylva* as containing things that the "Ancients were strangers to," saying that it is a book that "out-does all that Theophrastus and Pliny have left us on that Subject."[41] The ancients fell "far short of the

[35] Edward Wright, *Some Observations Made in Travelling through France, Italy . . . ,* 2 vols., 1730, I, vii.

[36] See Pope's 1713 essay in *The Guardian,* reprinted in John Dixon Hunt and Peter Willis, eds., *The Genius of the Place: The English Landscape Garden, 1620–1820,* rev. ed., Cambridge, Mass., 1988, 206.

[37] Evelyn clearly implies that his translations are also interpretations. See Keynes, *Bibliography,* 166 and 224, as well as Edmund Waller's prefatory poem to Evelyn's translation, *An Essay on the First book of T. Lucretius Carus: De Rerum Natura,* 1656. I have explored the idea of garden translation more fully in "'Gard'ning can speak proper English,'" in Michael Leslie and Timothy Raylor, eds., *Culture and Cultivation in Early Modern England: Writing and the Land,* Leicester, 1992, 195–222.

[38] Quoted by Douglas Chambers during his discussion of this garden at the Dumbarton Oaks colloquium on "Elysium Britannicum." See "The Tomb in the Landscape: John Evelyn's Garden at Albury," *Journal of Garden History* 1 (1981), 37–54; see also, John Dixon Hunt, *Garden and Grove: The Italian Renaissance Garden in the English Imagination, 1600–1750,* London, 1986, 148–53.

[39] I have discussed this progress as it affects gardens in "Writing the English Garden: Horace Walpole and the Historiography of Landscape Architecture," *Connaissance et création au siècle des lumières: Mélanges Michel Baridon* (an issue of *Interfaces,* no. 4), Dijon, 1993, 163–80.

[40] W. Wotton, *Reflections upon Ancient and Modern Learning,* 2nd ed., London, 1697, chap. 22, 290–307.

[41] Ibid., 293.

Gardens and Villa's of the Princes and Great Men of the present Age";[42] there is far more variety in modern kitchen gardens, especially with their greenhouse culture.[43] Moderns excel, too, in the "great variety of plants remarkable for their beauty or smell" and "large gravel-walks, surrounding spacious grassplots, edged with beautiful borders," though he seems more dubious as to the diversifying of colors, "sickly or luxurious Beauties which are so commonly to be met with in our Gardens." Nonetheless, Wotton's general point is the clear, demonstrable superiority of modern over ancient gardening.[44]

Evelyn seems more evasive and ambivalent.[45] He will note how certain sundials achieved "a moderne Elegancy" (p. 158) of construction, how "This dyall we have much reformed from that of Bettinus & Schotti" (p. 194). In like spirit, he proposes supplanting pagan ornaments in gardens with Christian and modern philosophical imagery: the "obscene Priapus" and even the "lewd Strumpet," Flora, would thus give way to a whole roster of "sacred stories" and "reppresentations of (great &) vertuous Examples" (pp. 153–55). His botanical sections implicitly declare, too, a modern preeminence, in quantity and quality. But, beyond these few examples, he seems unwilling or unconcerned to champion contemporary achievements at the expense of the old. It is rare for him to come out and say, as in his address to the readers of *Sylva,* that he looks forward to a time when the deficiency of agriculture that Columella complained of "may attain its desired Remedy and Consummation in this [age] of Ours."[46] Yet, throughout the leaves of the "Elysium Britannicum," there is another strategy at work to affirm, more subtly, the supremacy of modern over ancient garden art; it works by deploying what is, I believe, a radical version of the art/nature paragone.

IV

In trying to come to terms with Evelyn's ideas here, we are hampered by a widespread predilection, since the late eighteenth century, for "natural" gardens and the corresponding assumption that Renaissance ones were somehow wholly artificial.[47] But it was perfectly clear to Evelyn that the garden was always the result of a collaboration between art and nature; between, if you will, the plenitude and random data of the natural world and man's control over it via technology, science, and design. Although recently writers have tried to make Evelyn a spokesman for natural gardening,[48] he provides, when carefully read, no hostages to that position. Succinctly put, Evelyn's double

[42] Ibid., 300.

[43] Ibid., 303. See also his remark that the ancients did not know how to bring the "Sun under Rules (if I may use so bold an Expression). . . . which yet, by their Wall-Plantations, our Gardeners do every Day," p. 305.

[44] Ibid., 304–5.

[45] However, in a letter to William Wotton of October 28, 1696, Evelyn writes that "the gardening and husbandry of the ancients . . . had certainly nothing approaching the elegancy of the present age": *Evelyn Letters,* IV, 12.

[46] *Sylva,* *3v. In the second edition of *The French Gardiner,* 1669, Evelyn mocks French gardenists "new come over, who think we are as much oblig'd to follow their mode of gardening as we do of their garments," The English Vineyard, fol. A6 recto.

[47] This predilection is ably diagnosed in William Chambers, *A Dissertation upon Oriental Gardening,* 2nd ed., London, 1772.

[48] See Peter H. Goodchild, "'No phantasticall utopia, but a reall place': John Evelyn, John Beale and Backbury Hill, Herefordshire," *Garden History* 19 (1991), 105–27; Timothy Mowl, "New Science, Old Order: The Gardens of the Great Rebellion," *Journal of Garden History* 13 (1993), 16–35.

achievement was to see once and for all that in gardening (1) there was no nature without art, nor art without nature, and (2) the adjudication of those collaborations was always culturally determined, that is to say, they differed according to the time and place of their implementation.

It is hard to know whether Evelyn himself was fully aware of the extraordinary nature of his achievement in this most problematical area. And it would take more space than is available here to demonstrate in detail how those two perceptions—they never achieve the status of formal propostions—underlie countless passages in the "Elysium Britannicum." But at the risk of being excessively schematic, they can be briefly described.

First and most obviously, Evelyn everywhere recognizes the paragone of art and nature: as he notes Sir Henry Wotton saying of the island of Rhodes filled with "as many Statues as living men," a garden too is a "poynt of fertility twixt Art & nature" (p. 155). The long poem of Strada's, quoted and translated in chapter thirteen of the "Elysium Britannicum" narrates one of those typical duels between a human artificer on the lute and the song of a nightingale; their mutual admiration and emulation are an emblem for Evelyn of the binary relationship between art and nature. This is a leitmotif of the manuscript. In strikingly modern-sounding jargon, he writes of how the "mediation of Art, supplie[s] in greate measure, what nature, or a [garden owner's] lesse propitious fate, has denied him" (p. 52); or, again, gardening is "that assisting Nature with the addition of Arte" (p. 53); or, "if Nature prove not so propitious, as to serve our Garden spontaneously with that, without which it will soone become a Wildernesse: Arte must supplie our needes" (p. 118a).

There is nothing extraordinary for the seventeenth century in these announcements of the joint participation of art and nature in garden making. What is arguably new, however, are Evelyn's reflections on how and, above all, why the *ratio* of art and nature shifts in different situations. This brings me to the second schematic point—that Evelyn always sees art and nature working in gardens toward representation. Within the garden, as *mutatis mutandis* in a painting or a dramatic performance, we see another world imitated, and when art reorganizes natural (and other) materials to that end, we are able to see them freshly and significantly. Sometimes, it will take more art to make some representations clear, sometimes less, even, on occasion, letting unmediated elements of the physical world represent themselves within the controlled environment of the garden.

Representation in gardens functions at both a local level and in larger ways. "Grottoes are invented to reppresent Dens and Caves" (p. 138), and mounts represent mountains.[49] By extension, the whole repertoire of garden forms contributes to representation, to presenting all over again the world outside. The features of gardens that Evelyn considers principal are "Groves, parterrs, Viridaria, hills, mounts, fields, walks, statues, Grotts, Fountains, Streams & frequent Enclosures" (pp. 77 and 91), and these all have a representational function. Hydraulic equipment, too, the "Elysium" explains, can "reppresent, Raine-bowes, Stormes, raine Thunder and other artificial Meteors [i.e., fireworks]" (p. 132), and its mechanisms can also re-create the "motion & chirpings of Birds, Satyres

[49] Evelyn writes that "Mounts are the . . . highest & most aspiring Relievos of Gardens, whither raysed by Art or Nature," p. 140. He continues some lines later that "in our conceit A mount raised with the perfect dimensions of the Greater Aegyptian Pyramid . . . would reppresent to our imagination one of the most sollemne and prodigious Monuments," p. 141. So much for his "naturalism" pure and simple!

1. Isaac de Caus, engraving of a fountain of Galatea and the cyclops (photo: from *New and rare Inventions of Water-Works . . .* London, 1659)

& other (vocal) Creatures, after a wonderfull manner" (p. 187); it can even make fresh air ("artificiall Ventiducts" being the prototype of air conditioning) (p. 144). And Evelyn also notes how alcoves imitate natural recesses, and inlay work represents "flowers, birds, Landskips . . . in their natural colours" (p. 143). By extension, we can also see garden wildernesses or labyrinths as gardenist imitations of the unmediated wild wood, and berceaux or cabinets as natural pathways or clearings in the forests.

Furthermore, sculpture augments the representational resources of gardens by showing action: "by this it is that we reppresent the figures of those (greate) Heros, & Genious's that have so well deserv'd of gardens" (p. 149). This admission of action into garden representations, what elsewhere in respect of hydraulic devices (Fig. 1) are called "Histories and Sceanes" (p. 138), contributes much to raising the status of gardening in the pantheon of fine arts, because the imitation of an action was, in the seventeenth century, the prime ambition of painting and literature.[50]

So far, so good and unexceptional, though we have largely lost touch with this notion of representation in gardens. But we may be better able to appreciate why Evelyn resents puerile

[50] Compare Beale's suggestion that Evelyn add a chapter on "Entertainments" to the "Elysium," because they are "intended, as it were scenically, to shew the riches, beauty, wonders, plenty, & delight of a Garden" (University of Sheffield, Hartlib MS 67\22\1A). In other words, entertainments in gardens are performances that enact or represent the best elements of gardens. For a contemporary discussion of action, see John Dryden's "Parallel of Poetry and Painting," prefaced to his translation of Du Fresnoy, *De arte graphica,* London, 1695.

imitations in gardens or those that have no evident model in the natural world. Armies of topiary figures are "lamely and wretchedly represented" (p. 97), and when he allows that corals could be "counterfeitted" in rockwork, the metaphor suggests some real qualms (p. 137). In fountains, the work should "be contrivd [*sic*] to resemble nature as much as possible" (p. 128), and on that score "artificial elevations" of water or *jets d'eau* (p. 123), for example, are less plausible.[51]

But a curious feature of some of these discussions is Evelyn's statements that (in this case he is writing of grottoes representing dens and caves) "they are also either Naturall or Artificial" (p. 138). On the one hand and straightforwardly, this implies that inventions and representations can apparently be either natural-looking or conspicuously artificial; alternatively and, I think, predominately, the remark claims that even actual dens and caves—i.e., what we colloquially term "natural" ones—are, in effect, also forms of representation, once they have been incorporated within the contrived space of a garden or park landscape.

The point to be drawn from this kind of remark—and there are many such—is not that Evelyn is Capability Brown or Uvedale Price before his time. It is undeniable that Evelyn seizes virtually every opportunity to argue for "naturall and less uniforme" effects (p. 138, here, on caves again). Natural "Groves and Wildernesses," for instance, are to be preferred over artificial ones (p. 90); so are natural falls of water (p. 128) and real rockwork (pp. 134 and 137). But he is equally content to assert that in each of those instances where "in the originall disposure of the plott, we find them not already planted by Nature" (p. 90), they are, nonetheless, to be invented, "contrivd to resemble nature as much as possible" (p. 90). Genuine echoes, for example, are often unobtainable in gardens, so he provides a recipe "to instruct you how to produce an Artificial Echo and by an innocent magick & without superstition, to raise up (& deprehend) that vocal (& fugitive) Nymph" (p. 168) (Fig. 2).

One further element of the same kind that is difficult to accommodate within our usual aesthetic discriminations of gardens as *either* artificial *or* natural is Evelyn's enthusiasm for painted, trompe l'oeil perspectives in French gardens (pp. 159–60) (Fig. 3); it seems to compare oddly to his advocacy elsewhere of natural effects. But perhaps the passage on the artificial echo helps here too, because it says that a garden, "but for this onely[,] wanted nothing of perfection" (p. 168). In other words, because a garden aims to be a perfect or universal world, it must have whatever is necessary from that world to complete its site—whether it be artificial echoes, imitation rockwork, or illusionary prospects. But why should gardens need to be such universal plantations, filled, if necessary, with things "Desembld & imitated" (p. 137)?

V

Evelyn's reiteration that art and nature are coterminous in gardens, endlessly aiding and abetting each other's efforts, recalls remarks by two mid-sixteenth-century Italian humanists. One of these, Jacopo Bonfadio, wrote that "nature incorporated with art is made the creator and conatural

[51] John Rea, too, in *Flora,* London, 1665, 1, similarily criticizes "ill done" effects.

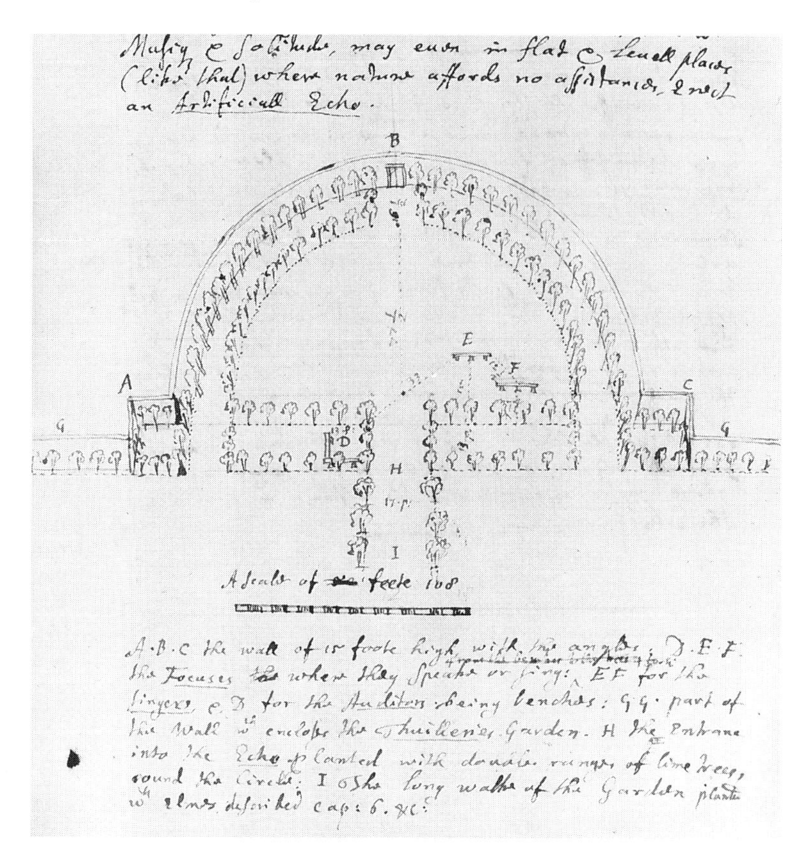

2. John Evelyn, An artificial echo, "Elysium Britannicum," 171. British Library, London (photo: John Ingram, reproduced with permission of the trustees of the will of Major Peter George Evelyn)

of art, and from both is made a third nature, which I would not know how to name."[52] We can see Evelyn's ideas on garden design as being closely in sympathy with this somewhat gnomic formulation.

Bonfadio's "terza natura" almost certainly alludes directly to a discussion in Cicero's *De natura deorum,* a work that Evelyn knew and cited in the "Elysium" manuscript (p. 45). In a passage on what today would probably be called the cultural landscape, Cicero writes of sowing corn, planting trees, fertilizing soil by irrigation, and managing rivers: "by means of our hands," he concludes, "we try to create as it were a second nature within the natural world."[53] Given the force of the Latin phrase, "alteram naturam," Cicero clearly posits the existence of a first nature.[54]

I have argued elsewhere that this triad of natures was a schema still available to gardenists and those concerned with landscape until well into the eighteenth century.[55] Gardens are third nature,

[52] Jacopo Bonfadio, *Lettere del cinquecento,* Turin, 1967, 501. For a comparable phrase, see Bartolomeo Taegio, *La Villa,* Milan, 1559, 155. For analysis of Bonfadio, see my "Paragone in Paradise: Translating the Garden," *Comparative Criticism* 18 (1996), 55–70.

[53] *De natura deorum,* II, 60, 151–52.

[54] Exactly what this first nature is does not really concern me here, except that the ambiguity inherent in its definition—both uncultured landscape or wilderness and landscape as noumenous or divine territory—exactly matches Shaftesbury's or Evelyn's relativist perception of human experience of unmediated territory. For some will readily see the divine in it; others will need to learn its mysteries.

[55] See my "Hortulan affaires" (as above, note 6).

3. Gabriel Perelle, engraving of the trompe l'oeil perspective in the garden of M. Fieubet, Paris (photo: Dumbarton Oaks)

inasmuch as they refine upon the second world of agriculture; Evelyn is constantly saying that gardening is "the most refin'd Part of Agriculture (the Philosophy of the Garden and Parterre only)."[56] Furthermore, second nature is what, since the Fall, men and women have had to carve out of the wild or first nature to make it habitable, useful, even beautiful. Gardens are the "third nature," because they are the culmination of this human reorganization of the environment; according to Bacon, gardens occupied a special place in this cultural scheme by coming to perfection after architecture, a point that Evelyn cites and elsewhere echoes.[57] In addition, given contemporary concerns with the progress of the arts, this perfection would be a British one.

So, when gardens seek to re-present the world outside through the materials and forms of their third nature, they are, in effect, copying in their own terms the other two natures.[58] The preface to

[56] Dedication to *Acetaria,* A5v.

[57] See "Elysium Britannicum," 3, referring of course to Bacon's essay "Of gardens." See also page 1—"it was somewhat long before they had arrived to any considerable perfection in this Arte (the first and noblest part of Agriculture)"—and page 2—"refined to their successive improvement." This became a commonplace, perhaps as a direct result of Bacon's remark. See William Wotton, for example, who discusses gardening after agriculture, because "Luxury always comes after Necessity": *Reflections,* 300.

[58] Thus, Evelyn's father-in-law observed that he preferred "those arbors in which all trees are assisted to the compleatest perfection of growth, fruite, beauty . . . ," as quoted by Douglas Chambers, "'Wild Pastorall Encounter': John Evelyn, John Beale and the Renegotiation of Pastoral in the Mid-Seventeenth Century," in *Culture and Cultivation* (as above, note 37), 174.

Acetaria refers to "that Great and Universal Plantation [i.e., the world], Epitomiz'd in our Gardens."[59] John Worlidge in *Systema Agriculturae* also observes that "Gardens, orchards, partirres, avenues . . . represent unto us epitomized, the form and idea of the more ample and spacious pleasant fields, groves, and other rustick objects."[60] Gardens are an epitome of that world, not only in the sense that botanical gardens tried to recover the plenitude of the lost Eden, but also in that they recall the attention of all gardenists to what the "Elysium" explains as "Now the Principle of all these Principles is nothing less then Nature herselfe" (p. 6).

Here we reach the most interesting aspect of Evelyn's theoretical endeavor: that the purpose of a garden's representation or epitome of "Nature herselfe" is to teach us about second and first natures, which is, of course, precisely why gardeners can be "most usefull members of Humane Societie" (p. 4). Some people will need to see nature mediated by art; others will have direct access to it.[61] The majority of humankind will, as it always does, hover betwixt and between: for these people, gardens were a sophisticated means of demonstrating both the mediation of art and the materials its representations interpreted. The degree of artificial interference in and, thus, comprehension of the physical world will differ according to society, region, and climate, even among individual gardeners. Each garden should be a fresh negotiation between the natural site and the arts of improvement and imitation available to its owner.

Some insight into this concept may be gained from Anthony Ashley Cooper, the third earl of Shaftesbury, in the years around the time of Evelyn's death.[62] Shaftesbury explained why the tailored forms of regular gardening needed to decrease gradually as we move away from the mansion, first into less strict geometry, then into various gradations of agricultural control and, finally, into the unmediated world of natural forms (Fig. 4). He argued that this declining scale of human control over the physical world, especially when viewed down the perspectival axes that were a feature of many contemporary layouts of country houses, was a lesson in understanding the inherent characters of all physical items. Being tutored within a garden by art's perfecting of natural forms, purging them of dross or accidents, educated the mind's appreciation of the unmediated forms in the larger landscape. Thus, *Sylva* praises "the great and masculine beauty which a wild Quincunx, as it were, of such trees would present to your eye," because the ability to recognize quincuncial order in the wild is a product of those hortulan tutorials.[63]

This concept is made quite palpable in contemporary bird's-eye views, what *Sylva* even offers as models for gardens, "Graphically plotted and design'd . . . by Mr Kniff, in near an hundred

[59] *Acetaria,* a4r.

[60] J. Worlidge, *Systema Agriculturae,* 1669, D1v. He is, in fact, writing of town gardens.

[61] See above, note 52, as well as the discussion of Beale and Casaubon in my essay, "Hortulan affaires." That essay together with that cited in note 36 and this one, constitute a three-pronged enquiry into English garden history between 1660 and 1730.

[62] Shaftesbury's unfinished *Second characters; or the Language of Forms* was edited by B. Rand, London, 1914; it and related texts, both published and manuscript, are discussed in David Leatherbarrow, "Character, Geometry and Perspective: The Third Earl of Shaftesbury's Principles of Garden Design," *Journal of Garden History* 4 (1984), 332–58.

[63] *Silva,* 4th ed., 297.

copper-plates" (Fig. 5).[64] These engravings provide an ideal or conceptual view—one that no person could ever have in days before hot-air balloons; sometimes it is ideal in the additional sense that the artist has been led to draw what the estate, as yet unfinished, would notionally look like. Such views show a progression from highly mediated gardens near the house, via less and less artificial orchards or groves, to agricultural land and, eventually, to wilderness; Evelyn himself followed this schema when he drew the family home of Wotton in 1653 (Fig. 6). It is a spectrum of human intervention from third to first nature that was also "epitomized" *within* the garden walls; here, a tripartite division often echoed the larger declension of artifice in its sequence of parterres de broderie near the house (pp. 76 and 277), a second, less organized segment, and finally an area that was frequently called a "wilderness" (Fig. 7).[65]

Much in Evelyn's work becomes clearer once we accept this conceptual framework. Painted perspectives, for example, provided gardens that naturally lacked them, with "views" out into other territories, thereby making more apparent the gradations of human meditation; at the same time, they drew attention to gardenist representation with a more conventional, "painter's" example.[66] Similarly, Evelyn's otherwise odd insistence on "Naturall or Artificial" grottoes is more readily understood (p. 75), when we see artifice as a temporary, enabling and educational device designed to return us to a proper understanding of natural ideas—so box hedges are "naturall & artificiall" (p. 77) and terraces provide "naturall & artificial Perspectives of the Gardens" (pp. 83–84). Variety—that crucial principle not only of garden art but also of seventeenth-century aesthetics and theology as well[67]—is also "both naturall and artificiall." Thus it is that natural effects, which are not the product of design, are still paradoxically representations: for they recall or represent themselves with perfect propriety and economy.

"Art, though it contend with Nature; yet might by no meanes justle it out" (p. 117), for the simple reason that gardening is all about understanding nature, not art; geometry is a tool for understanding the physical world, but not a prerequisite, as Sir Christopher Wren acknowledged when he

[64] Ibid., 305.

[65] There are many graphic illustrations of this tripartite division within gardens. For a verbal account, see Sir William Temple's account of Moor Park, in *The Genius of the Place*, 97–98.

[66] Compare Leonard Meager, who declares that the pleasure garden should be placed where it will yield most delight "in regard of its Prospect from your House": *The English Gardener*, 1670, 214; Moses Cook, *The manner of raising, ordering; and improving Forest and Fruit-Trees*, 1679, 137: "Do not . . . vail a pleasant Prospect (as too many doe) by making the walkes too narrow." The "Elysium Britannicum" urges that a short cradle walk could be "much protracted by Arte" (p. 163), and *Silva* that avenues not "terminate abruptly" (4th ed., 304 [printed as 204]); Evelyn's notes for *Silva* include André Mollet's remark that "the middle All[e]y should go out of the Garden Walk, out of sight into the Park" (as quoted in Chambers, "'Wild Pastorall Encounter,'" 174). In this respect, see also Henry Wotton's insistence upon "the Properties of a well chosen Prospect," because of the way it feeds the sight with "extent and varietie" (*The Elements of Architecture*, London, 1624, 4–5), a passage that Evelyn praises in "Elysium," 55. Evelyn himself, not surprisingly, owned a finely bound copy, designed for him by Abraham Bosse, of Jean Dubreuil, *La perspective pratique*, 3 vols., Paris, 1649–51, which passed through Christie's, London, in 1977. Dubreuil considers gardens in his first volume, published in 1642 and revised in 1651.

[67] H. V. S. Ogden, "The Principles of Variety and Contrast in Seventeenth-Century Aesthetics, and Milton's Poetry," *Journal of the History of Ideas* 10 (1949), 159–82.

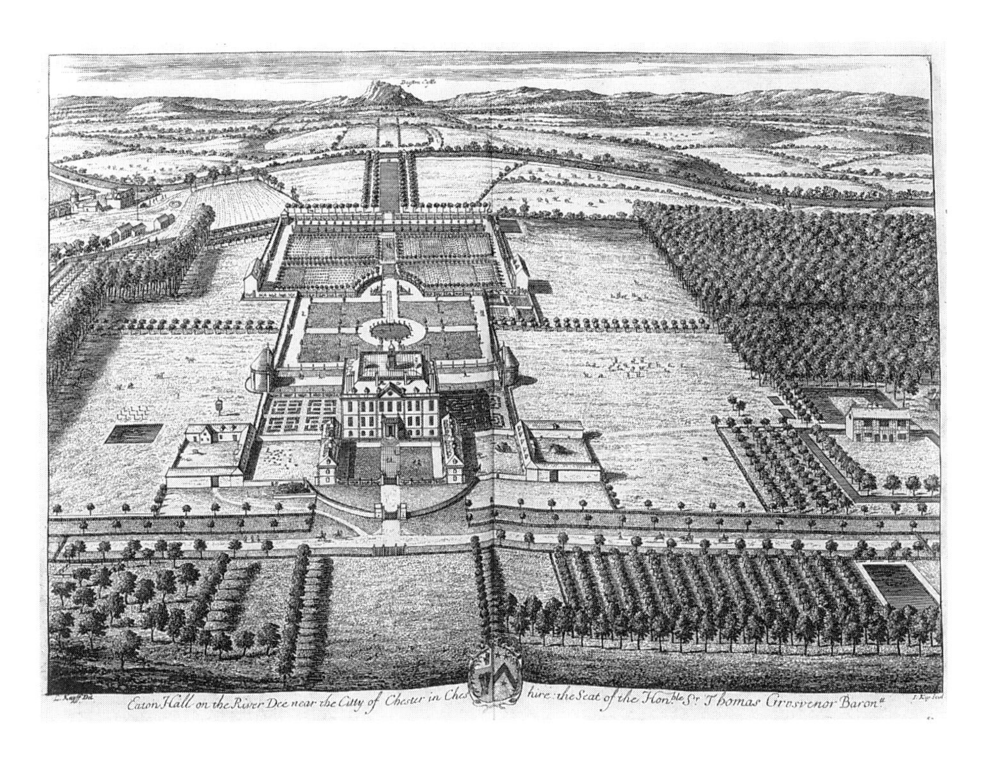

Eaton Hall on the River Dee near the City of Chester in Cheshire the Seat of the Hon.ble Sr Thomas Grosvenor Baron.t

4. Johannes Kip after Leonard Knyff, engraved view of Eaton Hall, Cheshire, from *Nouveau Théâtre de la Grande Bretagne,* I, London, 1715 (photo: Dumbarton Oaks)

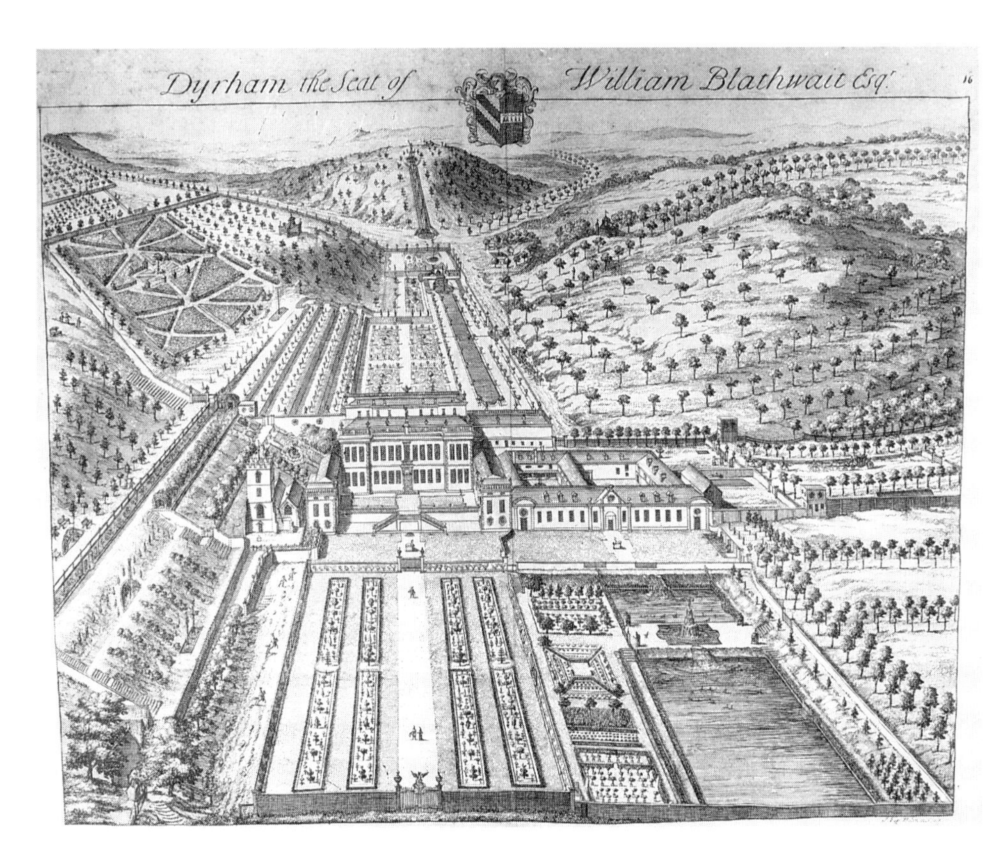

Dyrham the Seat of William Blathwait Esq.
16

5. Johannes Kip, engraved view of Dyrham Park, Gloucestershire, from *Nouveau Théâtre de la Grande Bretagne,* I, pt. 2, London, 1717 (photo: Dumbarton Oaks)

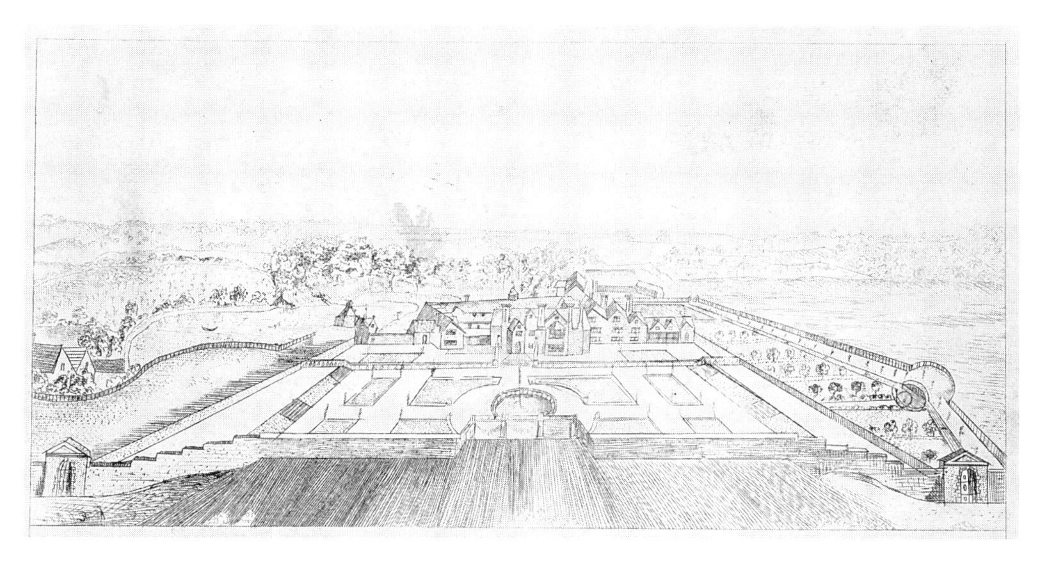

6. John Evelyn, drawing of the Evelyn family house at Wotton, Surrey, from the terrace above the gardens, 1653 (photo: British Museum)

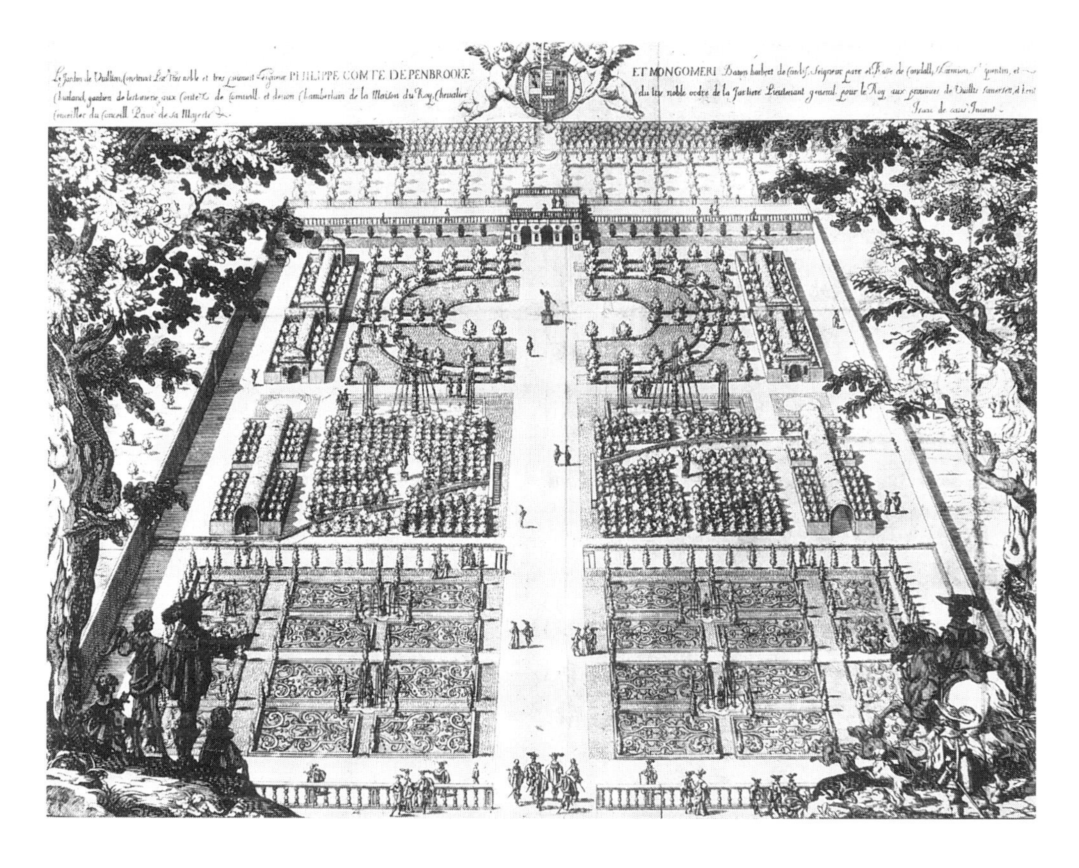

7. Isaac de Caus, engraved view of Wilton Gardens, 1640. Note that the usual tripartite order within the garden has been reversed, with the "wilderness" through which the river is allowed to run in its natural form coming between the two other modes of gardenist order (photo: private collection)

wrote of "natural or geometricall Beauty."[68] In this light we can better appreciate Evelyn's enthusiastic welcoming of John Beale's description of a site in the Backbury Hills of Herefordshire, which he wrote into folios 56–58 of the "Elysium Britannicum." But we can also understand why Evelyn added to the Beale passage he transcribed a final summary of the refashioning that art might be called upon to give to a natural scene: "to render it the uttmost accomplishments, it might have likewise the addition of Walls, Architecture, Porticos, Terraces, Statues, obelisks, Potts, Cascades, Fountains, Basons, pavilions, Avaries, Coronary gardens, Vineyards, Walks and other Artificial decorations" (p. 58).

I have discussed Beale's letter elsewhere,[69] and I only want to recall here his use of an accomplished natural site to explore the "definition of a Garden." Although Beale is scornful of "narrow mimicall way[s] of representation," he freely admits that a "vacancy" or missing element of a site may be filled up—with a "Hop-yard, where a busy Wood *gives the shape of a Wood*" (my italics); or "Mounts, Prospects, Precipices, & Caves . . . may bee soe representet to you," a point that is underlined by Evelyn's additions in the "Elysium" to his "source," Beale's letter, as well as by Beale's own recantation in a further letter, where he writes "you will not deeme mee so shallowe, as to dare seriously to compare our Herefordian Mountains with the Princelie & beautifull seates which doe surround the surcharging Metropolis"[70]

But physical interventions are not the only way to rethink a site; this can be accomplished also in the mind. Beale argues that the Backbury Hills "hath a perfect resemblance of an ancient flower garden." He sees its gardenist potential without the mediation of landscape architecture because—these are now Evelyn's words—"Nature has already bin (as we may truly say) so Artificiall" (p. 58); Evelyn continues by citing Edmund Spenser's lines on the Bower of Bliss as providing the essential "idea" (his word) of hortulan arrangements. So a "garden" is identified in the Backbury Hills by Beale and Evelyn because they see it through the lens of hortulan representations; however, Evelyn, who never went there, sees it only in his mind's eye. Furthermore, this ideal garden exemplifies the progress of the arts, because, as well as recalling ancient examples, it represents its own accomplished Britishness: Hartlib said (though erroneously)[71] that the site was inhabited by "the old Britains, the silures,"[72] and Evelyn noted that is in "our owne Country."[73]

Evelyn welcomed Beale's account of Backbury Hill into the "Elysium," because it could stand for the idea of the garden, toward which much else of his manuscript was moving. Not least of all, it was "no phantasticall *Utopia,* but a reall place," which offered experimentally what Beale's draft of

[68] From an "Appendix of architecture . . . " in C. Wren, *Parentalia*, London, 1750, 351. I am grateful to C. Allan Brown for drawing my attention to this passage.

[69] The letter is University of Sheffield, Hartlib MS 67\22; otherwise unidentified quotations in the following dicussion are from this letter, which is the topic of my essay, "Hortulan affaires," cited in note 6.

[70] Evelyn MS, British Library, London, letter 23.

[71] I am grateful to Michael Leslie for this information. See Leslie, "The Spiritual Husbandry of John Beale" in *Culture and Cultivation* (as above, note 37), 164.

[72] University of Sheffield, MS 67\22.

[73] Evelyn MS, British Library, London, letter 23.

a book on the pleasure garden explained theoretically: "in what points wee should disaffect the charges & cumber of Art, when the productions of Nature wil be more proper."[74]

VI

Theories often come to dominate the materials that they are meant to organize, though sometimes the influence works in the opposite direction. Evelyn's dedication to experiment was probably why his countless perceptions of the workings of art and nature in gardens were, in the end, never translated formally into propositions, let alone prescriptions. More crucially, the very thrust of his ideas was that each garden was *sui generis*, structured according to the site, the climate, and the intellectual-cum-spiritual needs of the owner. Evelyn's theory—"of incomporable use," as the "Elysium Britannicum" puts it—had to be "fit at all seasons" (p. 86), or, as in *Acetaria,* "the Hortulan Provision of the Golden Age fitted all Places, Times and Persons."[75] Its very thesis preempted the formulation of Evelyn's theory or idea in any but spare generality.

No gardener can afford to neglect either seasonal or climatic difference. Evelyn is no exception, and the leaves of his manuscript are studied with observations such as "yet is the Autumne a more proper Season for. . . ." (p. 63). His concern for variations in climate, regions, and seasons seems especially acute: "It will therefore be of high importance that our Gardner both observe & prepare for them [the fower Seasons] because the {due} knowledge of them will instruct him how {he is} to entertaine them" (p. 19). So, too, with the "variety of *climates*" (p. 6), and "what every region can, or cannot beare" (p. 13): this is especially crucial, of course, when what is in question is making the modern, British elysium preeminent above others, both ancient and modern. Here the challenge of a northern climate augments English achievements: as William Wotton put it, because it is more difficult to husband the earth in Great Britain than Sicily, so modern achievements may "justly come into Competition with any ancient Performances."[76]

Flexibility and adaptability on the part of the gardener, however, did not absolve Evelyn from the achievement of a "universal" garden (p. 3) or from groping toward some idea of such a garden. It seems obvious, however, that his constant dedication to seasonal, regional, and topographical difference, supported as it was by his experimental attitude, effectively prevented Evelyn from pursuing theory more energetically.[77] It did not, however, mean that he did not nourish this ambition of "building up a Body of real, and substantial Philosophy, which should never succomb to time, but with the ruines of Nature and the world it self."[78]

[74] These drafts of Beale's books (University of Sheffield, Hartlib MS 25\6\1A–4B) are usefully printed in *Culture and Cultivation,* 226–30; for the remark quoted, 229.

[75] *Acetaria,* 1706, 202.

[76] Wotton, *Reflections,* 296.

[77] See *Silva,* 4th ed., 83: "if some of the following Discourses seem less constant, or (upon ocassion) repugnant to one another, they are to be consider'd as relating only to the several Gusts [i.e., tastes] and Guises of Persons and Countries."

[78] *Silva,* 3rd ed., A2v. Compare Evelyn's letter to Sir Thomas Browne, where the society of "*Paradisi Cultores . . .* paradisean and hortulan saints" may happily "redeeme the tyme": G. Keynes, ed., *The Works of Sir Thomas Browne,* 4 vols., London, 1964, IV, 275.

His theoretical efforts, alert to many contextual differences, are in the final resort flexible enough to fit most occasions, or, as Evelyn put it himself, it enables a garden "of incomparable use, fit at all seasons" (p. 86). This achievement of what we might alternatively term the "ideal" garden depends upon both the due observance and skillful manipulation of climate and season: "to manage . . . [water] in all Seasons, where the presence & assistance of Art is called to interpose" (p. 118).

VII

I do not want to leave Evelyn and the "Elysium Britannicum" at that point. To be sure, the intrinsic interest of that flawed and unfinished work is undeniable; nor can its importance in the history of gardening practice and theory be gainsaid. But it has lessons for all seasons, indeed, for all climes and regions of landscape architecture. For, when its theoretical suggestions that this essay has extrapolated are deemed to be useful, when they serve as the basis for a viable theory of landscape architecture, then they must—qua theory—hold good for all seasons and all countries.

We, too, need every bit as much as Evelyn did in the seventeenth century an idea of the garden, so as not to be overwhelmed by the hundreds of opinions and options canvassed today (*tot homines, quot sententiae*). His shrewd sense of gardens as aiming to represent a given person's and culture's historical perception of his or her relationship with the physical world in its fullest complexity could also guide us today: guide us in our thinking about restoration and conservation of historical gardens—Can we really recover past mentality to such an extent that a facsimile of its gardens is worthwhile? Don't we want, as Evelyn surely did, modern gardens that address our concerns? What is the relationship of the thoroughly mediated garden and the designed landscape to the larger world of environmental purity? The "Elysium Britannicum" contains the seeds of a theory that would sustain coherent answers to these and other questions that we urgently need today. Evelyn's manuscript, taken in conjunction with his other gardenist writings, offers what he himself called a "Structure [of "general rules" that] may indeed lift up its head, such as stand the shock of Time."[79]

[79] "To the Reader," *Silva*, **3r.

Appendix
A Plan by John Evelyn for Henry Howard's Garden at Albury Park, Surrey

MICHAEL CHARLESWORTH

John Evelyn's plan for the garden of Henry Howard, later sixth duke of Norfolk, at Albury Park, Surrey, a photograph of which is published here for the first time (Fig. 1), forms part of an extra-illustrated copy of William Upcott's edition of *The Miscellaneous Writings of John Evelyn, Esq.*[1] The book was collected by Carl Pforzheimer before 1940 and is now part of the rare book library of the Harry Ransom Humanities Research Center of the University of Texas at Austin. Other extra-illustrated material includes manuscript letters from Evelyn containing passages that deal with gardening matters, and a sketch map of the Battle of Medway (1667).

The plan, measuring 18 × 29½ inches, is in ink and sepia wash over graphite. It is cropped at the sides and bottom. The various features visible in it are inscribed with fifty-five numbers, presumably to be referenced with a written key, which is, unfortunately, missing. In the bottom right corner are a scale of yards and a scale of perches ("pearches"). The compass rose shows the bottom of the plan to be oriented southwest. The plan also bears an inscription in ink: "This Designe of a Garden I made for the Duke of Norfolk at his house at Albury in Surrey since sold to Mr. Solicitor Finch." Further inscriptions in pencil read "J Evelyn" and "Evelyn."

Henry Howard became duke of Norfolk in 1677 and died in 1684. If the inscription had been written after his death, Evelyn would probably have designated him the "late Duke." The *Victoria County History of Surrey* (III, 73) states that Albury was conveyed to trustees for sale by Norfolk ca. 1680.[2] It is possible, therefore, that Norfolk sold Albury before his death, and the plan (or rather the

[1] William Upcott, ed., *The Miscellaneous Writings of John Evelyn, Esq. F.R.S.*, London, 1825; the plan is hinged into the volume at the dedication to the duke of Norfolk that prefaces Evelyn's translation of Roland Fréart's *An Idea of the Perfection of Painting*.

[2] E. S. de Beer, ed., *The Diary of John Evelyn,* 6 vols., Oxford, 1955, IV, 558 n.

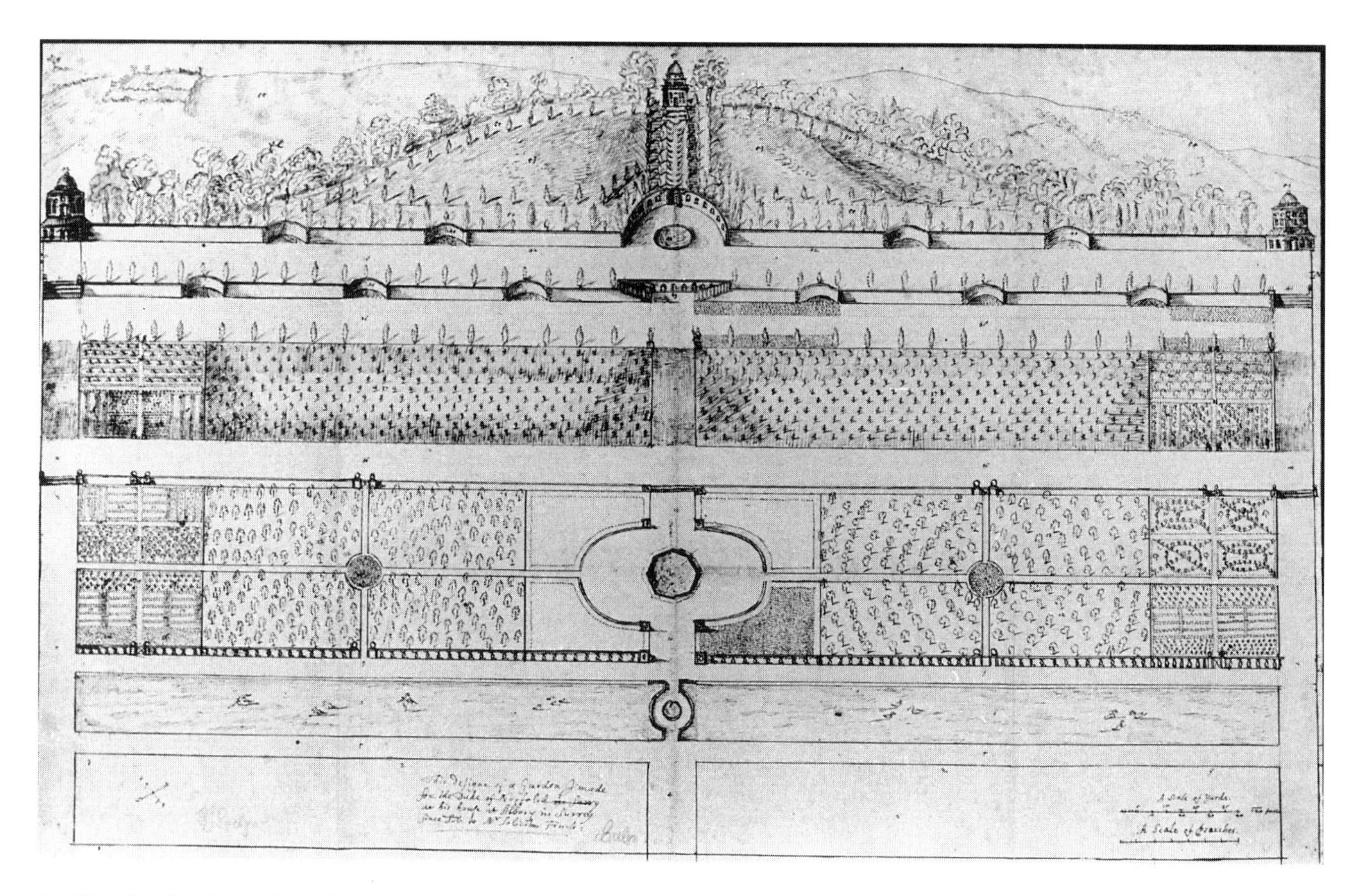

1. The plan for the garden of Henry Howard at Albury Park, Surrey (photo: from *The Miscellaneous Writings of John Evelyn, Esq.*, extra-illustrated copy, Harry Ransom Humanities Research Center, University of Texas at Austin)

inscription on it) dates from the interval between the sale and his death. On September 21, 1667, immediately after Evelyn had obtained from Henry Howard the gift of the Arundel Marbles for Oxford University, his diary records this entry: "This don, 21 I accompanied Mr. Howard to his Villa at Alburie, where I designed for him the plat for his Canale and Garden, with a Crypta thro' the hill etc."[3] Evelyn's drawing under consideration here is presumably a copy or later embellishment of the original "plat" or plan.

The plan shows, at the bottom, the canal, sixty feet wide, according to the antiquary John Aubrey,[4] spanned by a bridge with a hole in it for watching the surface of the water. In the first enclosures beyond the canal, different types of trees are distinguished; in the right hand enclosure they are planted concentrically around the grassy center circle, whereas on the left they are planted randomly. Between these enclosures lies an octagonal pool with fountain jet. Proceeding uphill beyond the first terrace the next two enclosures are planted with calligraphic squiggles that presumably signify vines in the "Vineyard of twelve Acres, of the same Length with the Canal, upon the Ascent of the Hill, which faceth the South," as recorded by Aubrey.[5] At either end of this and the

[3] Ibid., III, 496.

[4] John Aubrey, *The Natural History and Antiquities of the County of Surrey,* London, 1718, IV, 67.

[5] Ibid., IV, 67. The "vineyards" had been planted by September 23, 1670, when Evelyn visited: *Diary,* III, 561–62.

lowest level of enclosure are subdivided areas that suggest kitchen-gardening or (and this is perhaps more likely) varied types of fruit-growing.

The entrance to the second terrace is shown as being flanked by spear-carrying statues on square plinths. In front, the retaining wall of the third terrace is pierced by nine arches and to the east and west is bent by a total of six bays.[6] The cold bath was located below the third terrace, reached via the nine arches. Up flanking staircases, the viewer emerges on the third terrace. Along the southern edge of the terrace, tall pencil-like trees, suggestive of cypresses, are planted. However, later visitors have found yew growing there. To the east and west are shown four large bays, but by far the biggest bay opens opposite the stairs. It forms a semicircle concentric with the pond in front of it. In the center is the entrance to the famous "crypta" or "Pausilippe,"[7] a tunnel leading through the hill.

While the whole design is emphatically italianate,[8] the big bay suggests in particular the water theater of the Villa Aldobrandini at Frascati in Italy, another garden that Evelyn had visited in 1645. This similarity is made stronger by the cascade that is shown tumbling down to the center of the bay from the tower on the hillside above. It is flanked by steps that are in turn adjacent, on the east side, to a path around a grassy enclosure. The heavily emphasized central axis of the entire garden would have looked very striking rising up, when viewed from the vantage point of the bridge over the canal or from the house on the south side of the valley.

Nicely observed touches in the drawing are the details of the swans in the canal: to the left of center one is landing or stretching its wings, facing us, while further to the left another swan is running along the water, head characteristically low, in the act of taking off. Another nice observation is of the mixed woodland at the top of the hill at the back—done in sepia wash with a fine brush accentuated in places with pen and ink—that shows, apparently, deciduous trees in leaf, pines, a fir, and at least one dead (possibly stag-headed) tree.

One of the most striking features of the plan is the presence of three tall and imposing garden buildings. It may be that the two viewing pavilions at either end of the third terrace were never built, but John Aubrey describes a structure that stood outside the garden proper:

> In the Park here is a Spring called SHIRBURN Spring, which breaks out at the side of a Hill, over which is built a handsome banqueting House, which is surrounded (almost) with Trees, which yield a pleasant solemn Shade; Below this banqueting house is a Pond, which entertains you with the Reflection of the Trees above.
>
> The Water is very clear; it serves the House, and washeth away the Sand, as aforesaid, in making the Grot, Canal, etc. In the Wilderness adjacent to this Place are close Walks.[9]

[6] A similar arrangement, also featuring flanking stairways, existed at one of the terraces at St. Germain-en-Laye, in France, which Evelyn visited in 1644. See John Dixon Hunt, *Garden and Grove: The Italian Renaissance Garden in the English Imagination, 1600–1750,* London, 1986, 145–46; the section on Albury is on pp. 145–53.

[7] *Diary,* III, 561–62. The best discussion of the "Pausilippe" is by Douglas Chambers, "The Tomb in the Landscape; John Evelyn's Garden at Albury," *Journal of Garden History* 1 (1981), 37–54.

[8] On this issue, see especially Hunt, *Garden and Grove.* The garden is also discussed by David Jacques, "John Evelyn and the Idea of Paradise," *Landscape Design* 124 (1978), 36–38.

[9] Aubrey, *Natural History of Surrey,* IV, 69.

Aubrey may be describing a structure occupying the position of the imposing towerlike, domed, and apparently (to judge by crude shading on the left side) circular building at the head of the cascade in Evelyn's plan. Aubrey has already described how water from a spring was used to undermine and wash out the sandstone rock during the formation of the "crypta," and the "close walks" of the wilderness might be those shown to the east of the cascade on the plan.[10]

The most appreciative response to Albury came from the trenchant William Cobbett, writing 155 years after the garden's beginnings:

> They say that these gardens were laid out for one of the *Howards,* in the reign of Charles the Second, by Mr EVELYN, who wrote the *Sylva.* The mansion-house, which is by no means magnificent, stands on a little flat by the side of the parish church, having a steep, but not lofty, hill rising up on the south side of it. It looks right across the gardens, which lie on a slope of a hill which runs along at about a quarter of a mile distant from the front of the house. The gardens, of course, lie facing the south. Between the house and the gardens there is a very beautiful run of water, with a sort of little wild narrow sedgy meadow. The gardens are separated from this by a hedge, running along from east to west. From this hedge there go up the hill, at right angles, several other hedges, which divide the land here into distinct gardens, or orchards. Along at the top of these there goes a yew hedge, or, rather, a row of small yew trees, the trunks of which are bare for about eight or ten feet high, while the bottom branches come out on each side of the row about eight feet horizontally. This hedge, or row, is *a quarter of a mile long.* There is a nice hard sand-road under this species of umbrella; and, summer and winter, here is a most delightful walk! Behind this row of yews, there is a space, or garden (a quarter of a mile long you will observe) about thirty or forty feet wide as nearly as I can recollect. At the back of this garden, and facing the yew-tree row is a wall probably ten feet high, which forms the breastwork of a *terrace;* and it is this terrace which is the most beautiful thing I saw in the gardening way. It is a quarter of a mile long, and, I believe, between thirty and forty feet wide; of the finest green sward, and as level as a die.
>
> The wall, along at the back of this terrace, stands close against the hill, which you see with the trees and underwood upon it rising above the wall. So that here is the finest spot for fruit trees that can possibly be imagined. At both ends of this garden the trees in the park are lofty, and there are a pretty many of them. The hills on the south side of the mansion-house are covered in lofty trees, chiefly beeches and chestnut: so that, a warmer, more sheltered, spot than this, it seems impossible to imagine. Observe too, how judicious it was to plant the row of yew trees at the distance I have described from the wall which forms the breastwork of the terrace; that wall, as well as the wall at the back of the terrace, are covered with fruit trees, and the yew-tree row is just high enough to defend the former from winds, without injuring it by its shade. In the middle of the wall, at the back of the terrace, there is a recess, about thirty feet in front and twenty feet deep, and here is a *basin,* into which rises a spring coming out of the

[10] It should be pointed out, however, that Shirburn Spring rises a few hundred yards north of the terraces. Aubrey may instead have been describing a cluster of features—in effect a detached or outlying part of the garden—that was made around the water-source itself.

hill. The overflowings of this basin go under the terrace and down across the garden into the rivulet below. So that here is water at the top, across the middle, and along at the bottom of this garden. Take it altogether, this, certainly, is the prettiest garden that I ever beheld. There was taste and sound judgement at every step in the laying out of this place. Every where utility and convenience is combined with beauty. The terrace is by far the finest thing of the sort that I ever saw, and the whole thing altogether is a great compliment to the taste of the times in which it was formed.[11]

[11] William Cobbett, *Rural Rides* (1822), ed. George Woodcock, Harmondsworth, 1967, 98–100. By Cobbett's day Albury was owned by a "Mr. Drummond."

Biographies of the Authors

Douglas Chambers teaches in the English department at the University of Toronto and lectures about landscape and English garden history outside the university. His articles on early garden history have been published in *Garden History* and the *Journal of Garden History*. He is now writing a book on Restoration culture and literature and is editing the correspondence of John Evelyn. Chambers is also a gardener himself and has created in Ontario a *ferme ornée*—a type of eighteenth-century landscape garden that depends upon the treaty between agriculture and horticulture.

Michael Charlesworth edited *The English Garden: Literary Sources and Documents* (3 volumes, 1993) after receiving his Ph.D. in history and theory of art from the University of Kent at Canterbury in 1991. He has contributed chapters to *The Politics of the Picturesque* (1994), *Wood Notes Wild: Essays on the Poetry and Art of Ian Hamilton Finlay* (1995), and *Placing and Displacing Romanticism* (forthcoming from the Scolar Press). His essays on histories of photography, painting and drawing, and ancient and modern gardens have appeared in *Word & Image, Art History, Journal of Garden History,* and *Landscape Journal.* He is assistant professor of art history at the University of Texas at Austin, where he teaches nineteenth-century European painting and photography.

Alice T. Friedman is professor of art and co-director of the architecture program at Wellesley College. She is the author of *House and Household in Elizabethan England: Wollaton Hall and the Willoughby Family* (1988) and of numerous articles on English and American social and architectural history.

John Harvey is the author of numerous books on the history of architecture, garden history, and garden plants and their identification from old names in Latin and other languages. Among his works are *Gothic England, 1300–1550* (1947), *The Gothic World: A Survey of Architecture and Art, 1100–1600* (1950), *Cathedrals of England and Wales* (1974; revised edition 1988), *Mediaeval Craftsmen* (1975), and the biographical dictionary *English Mediaeval Architects to 1550* (1954; enlarged edition 1984; supplement 1987). His works on gardens and plants are *Early Gardening Catalogues* (1972), *Early Nurserymen* (1974), *Mediaeval Gardens* (1981), and *Restoring Period Gardens* (1988; revised edition 1993). Harvey was consultant architect to Winchester College from 1947 to 1986 and archivist to the college from 1949 to 1964. From 1982 to 1985 he was president of the Garden History Society.

John Dixon Hunt has been professor and chairman of the Department of Landscape Architecture in the Graduate School of Fine Arts, University of Pennsylvania since 1994. He was director of Studies in Landscape Architecture at Dumbarton Oaks from 1988 to 1991, after which he worked as academic advisor to Mrs. Paul Mellon at the Oak Spring Garden Library, Upperville, Virginia.

Michael Hunter is professor of history at Birkbeck College, University of London. He is the author of various books on late-seventeenth-century intellectual life, including *The Royal Society and Its Fellows, 1660–1700: The Morphology of a Scientific Institution* (1982; revised edition, 1994) and *Science and the Shape of Orthodoxy: Intellectual Change in Late Seventeenth-Century Britain* (1995). He is currently engaged in a major program of research on Robert Boyle. In this connection, he has published a guide (1992) to Boyle's extensive manuscripts, has edited a symposium volume entitled *Robert Boyle Reconsidered* (1994), and has produced a further volume, *Robert Boyle by Himself and His Friends* (1994).

John Ingram has advanced degrees in Russian and Slavic linguistics from Fordham and Brown Universities. He has worked in library special collections since 1976 and served as curator at Colonial Williamsburg's library from 1979 to 1994. He is currently chairman of the Department of Special Collections, George A. Smathers Libraries, University of Florida.

Mark Laird is a garden historian and preservation landscape architect. As a scholar and practitioner, he is involved in the reconstruction and restoration of historic planting. He is reviews editor for the *Journal of Garden History*.

Michael Leslie is professor of English at Rhodes College, Memphis, Tennessee, and dean of *British Studies At Oxford*. He was previously senior lecturer in English literature at the University of Sheffield, where he was also the director of the Hartlib Papers Project. He has published widely on Renaissance literature and the relationships between the verbal and visual arts, and on garden history. He has been an editor of both *Word & Image: A Journal of Verbal/Visual Enquiry* and the *Journal of Garden History*. He recently co-edited the volumes, *Culture and Cultivation in Early Modern England: Writing and the Land* (1992) and *Samuel Hartlib and Universal Reformation: Studies in Intellectual Communication* (1994) and the edition of the *Hartlib Papers* on two CD-ROMS (1995).

Joseph M. Levine, Distinguished Professor of History at Syracuse University, has written several books and many articles on the intellectual history of early modern Europe, most recently, *The Battle of the Books: History and Literature in Augustan England* (1991).

Therese O'Malley is associate dean at the Center for Advanced Study in the Visual Arts at the National Gallery of Art. In 1989 she received a doctoral degree from the University of Pennsylvania, where she wrote a dissertation on the planning of the National Mall in Washington, D.C., between 1791 and 1851. She has served on the Senior Fellows Committee at Dumbarton Oaks, the Board of Directors for the Society of Architectural Historians, and the editorial board of the *Journal of Garden History*. She publishes and lectures on the history of eighteenth- and nineteenth-century landscape architecture and garden design.

Joachim Wolschke-Bulmahn studied landscape architecture at the University of Hannover. During the 1980s, he also did research on the history of landscape architecture at Hannover. He received his Ph.D. from the University of Fine Arts, Berlin, Department of Architecture, in 1989. From September 1991 until June 1992, he was acting director of Studies in Landscape Architecture, Dumbarton Oaks, and from September 1992 until August 1996 was director of that program. In October 1996, he began a professorship in garden history at the University of Hannover. He has published widely on the history of landscape architecture and garden culture.

Index

Page references to illustrations are in italic.